A COMPILATION

OF THE

MESSAGES AND PAPERS

OF THE

PRESIDENTS

1789–1897

BY

JAMES D. RICHARDSON

A REPRESENTATIVE FROM THE STATE OF TENNESSE

VOLUME VI

PUBLISHED BY

AUTHORITY OF CONGRESS

1900

Prefatory Note

The Presidential papers during the period from March 4, 1861, to March 4, 1869, are contained in this volume. No other period of American history since the Revolution comprises so many events of surpassing importance. The Administrations of Presidents Lincoln and Johnson represent two distinct epochs. That of Abraham Lincoln was dedicated to the successful prosecution of the most stupendous war of modern times, while that of Andrew Johnson was dedicated to the reestablishment of peace and the restoration of the Union as it had existed prior to the war. Strange to say, it fell to the lot of the kind-hearted humanitarian, who loved peace and his fellow-man, to wage the bloody conflict of civil war, and the more aggressive, combative character directed the affairs of the Government while the land took upon itself the conditions of peace. Yet who can say that each was not best suited for his particular sphere of action? A greater lover of his kind has not filled the office of President since Thomas Jefferson, and no public servant ever left with the people a gentler memory than Abraham Lincoln. A more self-willed and determined Chief Executive has not held that office since Andrew Jackson, and no public servant ever left with the people a higher character for honesty, integrity, and sincerity of purpose and action than Andrew Johnson. The life of each of these two great men had been a series of obscure but heroic struggles; each had experienced a varied and checkered career; each reached the highest political station of earth. Their official state papers are of supreme interest, and comprise the utterances of President Lincoln while he in four years placed in the field nearly three millions of soldiers; what he said when victories were won or when his armies went down in defeat; what treasures of blood and money it cost to triumph; also, the utterances of President Johnson as he through his eventful term waged the fiercest political battle of our country's history in his efforts, along his own lines, for the restoration of peace and the reunion of the States.

Interesting papers relating to the death and funeral obsequies of President Lincoln have been inserted, as also the more important papers and proceedings connected with the impeachment of President Johnson.

Much time and labor have been expended in the compilation of this volume—more than on any one of the preceding—to the end that all papers of importance that could be found should be published; and I feel sure that no other collection of Presidential papers is so thorough and complete.

The perusal of these papers should enkindle within the heart of every citizen of the American Republic, whether he fought on the one side or the other in that unparalleled struggle, or whether he has come upon the scene since its closing, a greater love of country, a greater devotion to the cause of true liberty, and an undying resolve that all the blessings of a free government and the fullest liberty of the individual shall be perpetuated.

JAMES D. RICHARDSON.

NOVEMBER 25, 1897.

Abraham Lincoln

March 4, 1861, to April 15, 1865

From life by
T. B. Carpenter
1864

A. Lincoln

Abraham Lincoln

ABRAHAM LINCOLN was born in Hardin County, Ky., February 12, 1809. His earliest ancestor in America was Samuel Lincoln, of Norwich, England, who settled in Hingham, Mass., where he died, leaving a son, Mordecai, whose son of the same name removed to Monmouth, N. J.; and thence to Berks County, Pa., where he died in 1735. One of his sons, John, removed to Rockingham County, Va., and died there, leaving five sons, one of whom, named Abraham, emigrated to Kentucky about 1780. About 1784 he was killed by Indians, leaving three sons, Mordecai, Josiah, and Thomas, and two daughters. Their mother then located in Washington County, Ky., and there brought up her family. The youngest son, Thomas, learned the trade of a carpenter, and in 1806 married Nancy Hanks, a niece of the man with whom he learned his trade. They had three children, the second being Abraham, the future President of the United States. In 1816 Thomas Lincoln removed to Indiana, and settled on Little Pigeon Creek, not far distant from the Ohio River, where Abraham grew to manhood. He made the best use of his limited opportunities to acquire an education and at the same time prepare himself for business. At the age of 19 years he was intrusted with a cargo of farm products, which he took to New Orleans and sold. In 1830 his father again emigrated, and located in Macon County, Ill. Abraham by this time had attained the unusual stature of 6 feet 4 inches, and was of great muscular strength; joined with his father in building his cabin, clearing the field, and splitting the rails for fencing the farm. It was not long, however, before his father again changed his home, locating this time in Coles County, where he died in 1851 at the age of 73 years. Abraham left his father as soon as his farm was fenced and cleared and hired himself to a man named Denton Offutt, in Sangamon County, whom he assisted to build a flatboat; accompanied him to New Orleans on a trading voyage and returned with him to New Salem, Menard County, where Offutt opened a store for the sale of general merchandise. Mr. Lincoln remained with him for a time, during which he employed his leisure in constant reading and study. Learned the elements of English

3

grammar and made a beginning in the study of surveying and the principles of law. But the next year an Indian war began, and Lincoln volunteered in a company raised in Sangamon County and was immediately elected captain. His company was organized at Richland April 21, 1832; but his service in command of it was brief, for it was mustered out on May 27. Mr. Lincoln immediately reenlisted as a private and served for several weeks, being finally mustered out on June 16, 1832, by Lieutenant Robert Anderson, who afterwards commanded Fort Sumter at the beginning of the civil war. He returned to his home and made a brief but active canvass for the legislature, but was defeated. At this time he thought seriously of learning the blacksmith's trade, but an opportunity was offered him to buy a store, which he did, giving his notes for the purchase money. He was unfortunate in his selection of a partner, and the business soon went to wreck, leaving him burdened with a heavy debt, which he finally paid in full. He then applied himself earnestly to the study of the law. Was appointed postmaster of New Salem in 1833, and filled the office for three years. At the same time was appointed deputy county surveyor. In 1834 was elected to the legislature, and was reelected in 1836, 1838, and 1840, after which he declined further election. In his last two terms he was the candidate of his party for the speakership of the house of representatives. In 1837 removed to Springfield, where he entered into partnership with John T. Stuart and began the practice of the law. November 4, 1842, married Miss Mary Todd, daughter of Robert S. Todd, of Kentucky. In 1846 was elected to Congress over Rev. Peter Cartwright. Served only one term, and was not a candidate for reelection. While a member he advocated the abolition of slavery in the District of Columbia. Was an unsuccessful applicant for Commissioner of the General Land Office under President Taylor; was tendered the office of governor of Oregon Territory, which he declined. Was an able and influential exponent of the principles of the Whig party in Illinois, and did active campaign work. Was voted for by the Whig minority in the State legislature for United States Senator in 1855. As soon as the Republican party was fully organized throughout the country he became its leader in Illinois. In 1858 he was chosen by his party to oppose Stephen A. Douglas for the Senate, and challenged him to a joint debate. The challenge was accepted, and a most exciting debate followed, which attracted national attention. The legislature chosen was favorable to Mr. Douglas, and he was elected. In May, 1860, when the Republican convention met in Chicago, Mr. Lincoln was nominated for the Presidency, on the third ballot, over William H. Seward, who was his principal competitor. Was elected on November 6, receiving 180 electoral votes to 72 for John C. Breckinridge, 39 for John Bell, and 12 for Stephen A. Douglas. Was inaugurated March 4, 1861. On June 8, 1864, was unanimously renominated for the Presidency by the Republican convention at Baltimore, and at the election in November received

212 electoral votes to 21 for General McClellan. Was inaugurated for his second term March 4, 1865. Was shot by an assassin at Ford's Theater, in Washington, April 14, 1865, and died the next day. Was buried at Oak Ridge, near Springfield, Ill.

FIRST INAUGURAL ADDRESS.

Fellow-Citizens of the United States:

In compliance with a custom as old as the Government itself, I appear before you to address you briefly and to take in your presence the oath prescribed by the Constitution of the United States to be taken by the President "before he enters on the execution of his office."

I do not consider it necessary at present for me to discuss those matters of administration about which there is no special anxiety or excitement.

Apprehension seems to exist among the people of the Southern States that by the accession of a Republican Administration their property and their peace and personal security are to be endangered. There has never been any reasonable cause for such apprehension. Indeed, the most ample evidence to the contrary has all the while existed and been open to their inspection. It is found in nearly all the published speeches of him who now addresses you. I do but quote from one of those speeches when I declare that—

I have no purpose, directly or indirectly, to interfere with the institution of slavery in the States where it exists. I believe I have no lawful right to do so, and I have no inclination to do so.

Those who nominated and elected me did so with full knowledge that I had made this and many similar declarations and had never recanted them; and more than this, they placed in the platform for my acceptance, and as a law to themselves and to me, the clear and emphatic resolution which I now read:

Resolved, That the maintenance inviolate of the rights of the States, and especially the right of each State to order and control its own domestic institutions according to its own judgment exclusively, is essential to that balance of power on which the perfection and endurance of our political fabric depend; and we denounce the lawless invasion by armed force of the soil of any State or Territory, no matter under what pretext, as among the gravest of crimes.

I now reiterate these sentiments, and in doing so I only press upon the public attention the most conclusive evidence of which the case is susceptible that the property, peace, and security of no section are to be in any wise endangered by the now incoming Administration. I add, too, that all the protection which, consistently with the Constitution and the laws, can be given will be cheerfully given to all the States when lawfully demanded, for whatever cause—as cheerfully to one section as to another.

There is much controversy about the delivering up of fugitives from service or labor. The clause I now read is as plainly written in the Constitution as any other of its provisions:

No person held to service or labor in one State, under the laws thereof, escaping into another, shall in consequence of any law or regulation therein be discharged from such service or labor, but shall be delivered up on claim of the party to whom such service or labor may be due.

It is scarcely questioned that this provision was intended by those who made it for the reclaiming of what we call fugitive slaves; and the intention of the lawgiver is the law. All members of Congress swear their support to the whole Constitution—to this provision as much as to any other. To the proposition, then, that slaves whose cases come within the terms of this clause "shall be delivered up" their oaths are unanimous. Now, if they would make the effort in good temper, could they not with nearly equal unanimity frame and pass a law by means of which to keep good that unanimous oath?

There is some difference of opinion whether this clause should be enforced by national or by State authority, but surely that difference is not a very material one. If the slave is to be surrendered, it can be of but little consequence to him or to others by which authority it is done. And should anyone in any case be content that his oath shall go unkept on a merely unsubstantial controversy as to *how* it shall be kept?

Again: In any law upon this subject ought not all the safeguards of liberty known in civilized and humane jurisprudence to be introduced, so that a free man be not in any case surrendered as a slave? And might it not be well at the same time to provide by law for the enforcement of that clause in the Constitution which guarantees that "the citizens of each State shall be entitled to all privileges and immunities of citizens in the several States"?

I take the official oath to-day with no mental reservations and with no purpose to construe the Constitution or laws by any hypercritical rules; and while I do not choose now to specify particular acts of Congress as proper to be enforced, I do suggest that it will be much safer for all, both in official and private stations, to conform to and abide by all those acts which stand unrepealed than to violate any of them trusting to find impunity in having them held to be unconstitutional.

It is seventy-two years since the first inauguration of a President under our National Constitution. During that period fifteen different and greatly distinguished citizens have in succession administered the executive branch of the Government. They have conducted it through many perils, and generally with great success. Yet, with all this scope of precedent, I now enter upon the same task for the brief constitutional term

of four years under great and peculiar difficulty. A disruption of the Federal Union, heretofore only menaced, is now formidably attempted.

I hold that in contemplation of universal law and of the Constitution the Union of these States is perpetual. Perpetuity is implied, if not expressed, in the fundamental law of all national governments. It is safe to assert that no government proper ever had a provision in its organic law for its own termination. Continue to execute all the express provisions of our National Constitution, and the Union will endure forever, it being impossible to destroy it except by some action not provided for in the instrument itself.

Again: If the United States be not a government proper, but an association of States in the nature of contract merely, can it, as a contract, be peaceably unmade by less than all the parties who made it? One party to a contract may violate it—break it, so to speak—but does it not require all to lawfully rescind it?

Descending from these general principles, we find the proposition that in legal contemplation the Union is perpetual confirmed by the history of the Union itself. The Union is much older than the Constitution. It was formed, in fact, by the Articles of Association in 1774. It was matured and continued by the Declaration of Independence in 1776. It was further matured, and the faith of all the then thirteen States expressly plighted and engaged that it should be perpetual, by the Articles of Confederation in 1778. And finally, in 1787, one of the declared objects for ordaining and establishing the Constitution was "*to form a more perfect Union.*"

But if destruction of the Union by one or by a part only of the States be lawfully possible, the Union is *less* perfect than before the Constitution, having lost the vital element of perpetuity.

It follows from these views that no State upon its own mere motion can lawfully get out of the Union; that *resolves* and *ordinances* to that effect are legally void, and that acts of violence within any State or States against the authority of the United States are insurrectionary or revolutionary, according to circumstances.

I therefore consider that in view of the Constitution and the laws the Union is unbroken, and to the extent of my ability I shall take care, as the Constitution itself expressly enjoins upon me, that the laws of the Union be faithfully executed in all the States. Doing this I deem to be only a simple duty on my part, and I shall perform it so far as practicable unless my rightful masters, the American people, shall withhold the requisite means or in some authoritative manner direct the contrary. I trust this will not be regarded as a menace, but only as the declared purpose of the Union that it *will* constitutionally defend and maintain itself

In doing this there needs to be no bloodshed or violence, and there shall be none unless it be forced upon the national authority. The

power confided to me will be used to hold, occupy, and possess the property and places belonging to the Government and to collect the duties and imposts; but beyond what may be necessary for these objects, there will be no invasion, no using of force against or among the people anywhere. Where hostility to the United States in any interior locality shall be so great and universal as to prevent competent resident citizens from holding the Federal offices, there will be no attempt to force obnoxious strangers among the people for that object. While the strict legal right may exist in the Government to enforce the exercise of these offices, the attempt to do so would be so irritating and so nearly impracticable withal that I deem it better to forego for the time the uses of such offices.

The mails, unless repelled, will continue to be furnished in all parts of the Union. So far as possible the people everywhere shall have that sense of perfect security which is most favorable to calm thought and reflection. The course here indicated will be followed unless current events and experience shall show a modification or change to be proper, and in every case and exigency my best discretion will be exercised, according to circumstances actually existing and with a view and a hope of a peaceful solution of the national troubles and the restoration of fraternal sympathies and affections.

That there are persons in one section or another who seek to destroy the Union at all events and are glad of any pretext to do it I will neither affirm nor deny; but if there be such, I need address no word to them. To those, however, who really love the Union may I not speak?

Before entering upon so grave a matter as the destruction of our national fabric, with all its benefits, its memories, and its hopes, would it not be wise to ascertain precisely why we do it? Will you hazard so desperate a step while there is any possibility that any portion of the ills you fly from have no real existence? Will you, while the certain ills you fly to are greater than all the real ones you fly from, will you risk the commission of so fearful a mistake?

All profess to be content in the Union if all constitutional rights can be maintained. Is it true, then, that any right plainly written in the Constitution has been denied? I think not. Happily, the human mind is so constituted that no party can reach to the audacity of doing this. Think, if you can, of a single instance in which a plainly written provision of the Constitution has ever been denied. If by the mere force of numbers a majority should deprive a minority of any clearly written constitutional right, it might in a moral point of view justify revolution; certainly would if such right were a vital one. But such is not our case. All the vital rights of minorities and of individuals are so plainly assured to them by affirmations and negations, guaranties and prohibitions, in the Constitution that controversies never arise concerning them. But no organic law can ever be framed with a provision specifically applicable to every question which may occur in practical administration. No fore-

sight can anticipate nor any document of reasonable length contain express provisions for all possible questions. Shall fugitives from labor be surrendered by national or by State authority? The Constitution does not expressly say. *May* Congress prohibit slavery in the Territories? The Constitution does not expressly say. *Must* Congress protect slavery in the Territories? The Constitution does not expressly say.

From questions of this class spring all our constitutional controversies, and we divide upon them into majorities and minorities. If the minority will not acquiesce, the majority must, or the Government must cease. There is no other alternative, for continuing the Government is acquiescence on one side or the other. If a minority in such case will secede rather than acquiesce, they make a precedent which in turn will divide and ruin them, for a minority of their own will secede from them whenever a majority refuses to be controlled by such minority. For instance, why may not any portion of a new confederacy a year or two hence arbitrarily secede again, precisely as portions of the present Union now claim to secede from it? All who cherish disunion sentiments are now being educated to the exact temper of doing this.

Is there such perfect identity of interests among the States to compose a new union as to produce harmony only and prevent renewed secession?

Plainly the central idea of secession is the essence of anarchy. A majority held in restraint by constitutional checks and limitations, and always changing easily with deliberate changes of popular opinions and sentiments, is the only true sovereign of a free people. Whoever rejects it does of necessity fly to anarchy or to despotism. Unanimity is impossible. The rule of a minority, as a permanent arrangement, is wholly inadmissible; so that, rejecting the majority principle, anarchy or despotism in some form is all that is left.

I do not forget the position assumed by some that constitutional questions are to be decided by the Supreme Court, nor do I deny that such decisions must be binding in any case upon the parties to a suit as to the object of that suit, while they are also entitled to very high respect and consideration in all parallel cases by all other departments of the Government. And while it is obviously possible that such decision may be erroneous in any given case, still the evil effect following it, being limited to that particular case, with the chance that it may be overruled and never become a precedent for other cases, can better be borne than could the evils of a different practice. At the same time, the candid citizen must confess that if the policy of the Government upon vital questions affecting the whole people is to be irrevocably fixed by decisions of the Supreme Court, the instant they are made in ordinary litigation between parties in personal actions the people will have ceased to be their own rulers, having to that extent practically resigned their Government into the hands of that eminent tribunal. Nor is there in this view any assault upon the court or the judges. It is a duty from which they may not

shrink to decide cases properly brought before them, and it is no fault of theirs if others seek to turn their decisions to political purposes.

One section of our country believes slavery is *right* and ought to be extended, while the other believes it is *wrong* and ought not to be extended. This is the only substantial dispute. The fugitive-slave clause of the Constitution and the law for the suppression of the foreign slave trade are each as well enforced, perhaps, as any law can ever be in a community where the moral sense of the people imperfectly supports the law itself. The great body of the people abide by the dry legal obligation in both cases, and a few break over in each. This, I think, can not be perfectly cured, and it would be worse in both cases *after* the separation of the sections than before. The foreign slave trade, now imperfectly suppressed, would be ultimately revived without restriction in one section, while fugitive slaves, now only partially surrendered, would not be surrendered at all by the other.

Physically speaking, we can not separate. We can not remove our respective sections from each other nor build an impassable wall between them. A husband and wife may be divorced and go out of the presence and beyond the reach of each other, but the different parts of our country can not do this. They can not but remain face to face, and intercourse, either amicable or hostile, must continue between them. Is it possible, then, to make that intercourse more advantageous or more satisfactory *after* separation than *before*? Can aliens make treaties easier than friends can make laws? Can treaties be more faithfully enforced between aliens than laws can among friends? Suppose you go to war, you can not fight always; and when, after much loss on both sides and no gain on either, you cease fighting, the identical old questions, as to terms of intercourse, are again upon you.

This country, with its institutions, belongs to the people who inhabit it. Whenever they shall grow weary of the existing Government, they can exercise their *constitutional* right of amending it or their *revolutionary* right to dismember or overthrow it. I can not be ignorant of the fact that many worthy and patriotic citizens are desirous of having the National Constitution amended. While I make no recommendation of amendments, I fully recognize the rightful authority of the people over the whole subject, to be exercised in either of the modes prescribed in the instrument itself; and I should, under existing circumstances, favor rather than oppose a fair opportunity being afforded the people to act upon it. I will venture to add that to me the convention mode seems preferable, in that it allows amendments to originate with the people themselves, instead of only permitting them to take or reject propositions originated by others, not especially chosen for the purpose, and which might not be precisely such as they would wish to either accept or refuse. I understand a proposed amendment to the Constitution—which amendment, however, I have not seen—has passed Congress, to the effect

that the Federal Government shall never interfere with the domestic institutions of the States, including that of persons held to service. To avoid misconstruction of what I have said, I depart from my purpose not to speak of particular amendments so far as to say that, holding such a provision to now be implied constitutional law, I have no objection to its being made express and irrevocable.

The Chief Magistrate derives all his authority from the people, and they have conferred none upon him to fix terms for the separation of the States. The people themselves can do this also if they choose, but the Executive as such has nothing to do with it. His duty is to administer the present Government as it came to his hands and to transmit it unimpaired by him to his successor.

Why should there not be a patient confidence in the ultimate justice of the people? Is there any better or equal hope in the world? In our present differences, is either party without faith of being in the right? If the Almighty Ruler of Nations, with His eternal truth and justice, be on your side of the North, or on yours of the South, that truth and that justice will surely prevail by the judgment of this great tribunal of the American people.

By the frame of the Government under which we live this same people have wisely given their public servants but little power for mischief, and have with equal wisdom provided for the return of that little to their own hands at very short intervals. While the people retain their virtue and vigilance no Administration by any extreme of wickedness or folly can very seriously injure the Government in the short space of four years.

My countrymen, one and all, think calmly and *well* upon this whole subject. Nothing valuable can be lost by taking time. If there be an object to *hurry* any of you in hot haste to a step which you would never take *deliberately*, that object will be frustrated by taking time; but no good object can be frustrated by it. Such of you as are now dissatisfied still have the old Constitution unimpaired, and, on the sensitive point, the laws of your own framing under it; while the new Administration will have no immediate power, if it would, to change either. If it were admitted that you who are dissatisfied hold the right side in the dispute, there still is no single good reason for precipitate action. Intelligence, patriotism, Christianity, and a firm reliance on Him who has never yet forsaken this favored land are still competent to adjust in the best way all our present difficulty.

In *your* hands, my dissatisfied fellow-countrymen, and not in *mine*, is the momentous issue of civil war. The Government will not assail *you*. You can have no conflict without being yourselves the aggressors. *You* have no oath registered in heaven to destroy the Government, while *I* shall have the most solemn one to "preserve, protect, and defend it."

I am loath to close. We are not enemies, but friends. We must not be enemies.   Though passion may have strained it must not break our bonds of affection.   The mystic chords of memory, stretching from every battlefield and patriot grave to every living heart and hearthstone all over this broad land, will yet swell the chorus of the Union, when again touched, as surely they will be, by the better angels of our nature.

MARCH 4, 1861.

SPECIAL MESSAGES.

To the Senate: WASHINGTON, *March 16, 1861.*

The Senate has transmitted to me a copy of the message sent by my predecessor to that body on the 21st day of February last, proposing to take its advice on the subject of a proposition made by the British Government through its minister here to refer the matter in controversy between that Government and the Government of the United States to the arbitrament of the King of Sweden and Norway, the King of the Netherlands, or the Republic of the Swiss Confederation.

In that message my predecessor stated that he wished to submit to the Senate the precise questions following, namely:

Will the Senate approve a treaty referring to either of the sovereign powers above named the dispute now existing between the Governments of the United States and Great Britain concerning the boundary line between Vancouvers Island and the American continent?   In case the referee shall find himself unable to decide where the line is by the description of it in the treaty of 15th June, 1846, shall he be authorized to establish a line according to the treaty as nearly as possible?   Which of the three powers named by Great Britain as an arbiter shall be chosen by the United States?

I find no reason to disapprove of the course of my predecessor in this important matter, but, on the contrary, I not only shall receive the advice of the Senate therein cheerfully, but I respectfully ask the Senate for their advice on the three questions before recited.

ABRAHAM LINCOLN.

WASHINGTON, *March 26, 1861.*

To the Senate of the United States:

I have received a copy of a resolution of the Senate passed on the 25th instant, requesting me, if in my opinion not incompatible with the public interest, to communicate to the Senate the dispatches of Major Robert Anderson to the War Department during the time he has been in command of Fort Sumter.

On examining the correspondence thus called for I have, with the highest respect for the Senate, come to the conclusion that at the present moment the publication of it would be inexpedient.

ABRAHAM LINCOLN.

PROCLAMATIONS.

BY THE PRESIDENT OF THE UNITED STATES.

A PROCLAMATION.

Whereas the laws of the United States have been for some time past and now are opposed and the execution thereof obstructed in the States of South Carolina, Georgia, Alabama, Florida, Mississippi, Louisiana, and Texas by combinations too powerful to be suppressed by the ordinary course of judicial proceedings or by the powers vested in the marshals by law:

Now, therefore, I, Abraham Lincoln, President of the United States, in virtue of the power in me vested by the Constitution and the laws, have thought fit to call forth, and hereby do call forth, the militia of the several States of the Union to the aggregate number of 75,000, in order to suppress said combinations and to cause the laws to be duly executed.

The details for this object will be immediately communicated to the State authorities through the War Department.

I appeal to all loyal citizens to favor, facilitate, and aid this effort to maintain the honor, the integrity, and the existence of our National Union and the perpetuity of popular government and to redress wrongs already long enough endured.

I deem it proper to say that the first service assigned to the forces hereby called forth will probably be to repossess the forts, places, and property which have been seized from the Union; and in every event the utmost care will be observed, consistently with the objects aforesaid, to avoid any devastation, any destruction of or interference with property, or any disturbance of peaceful citizens in any part of the country.

And I hereby command the persons composing the combinations aforesaid to disperse and retire peaceably to their respective abodes within twenty days from this date.

Deeming that the present condition of public affairs presents an extraordinary occasion, I do hereby, in virtue of the power in me vested by the Constitution, convene both Houses of Congress. Senators and Representatives are therefore summoned to assemble at their respective chambers at 12 o'clock noon on Thursday, the 4th day of July next, then and there to consider and determine such measures as, in their wisdom, the public safety and interest may seem to demand.

In witness whereof I have hereunto set my hand and caused the seal of the United States to be affixed.

[SEAL.]   Done at the city of Washington, this 15th day of April, A. D. 1861, and of the Independence of the United States the eighty-fifth.

                                                    ABRAHAM LINCOLN.

By the President:

WILLIAM H. SEWARD, *Secretary of State.*

BY THE PRESIDENT OF THE UNITED STATES OF AMERICA.

A PROCLAMATION.

Whereas an insurrection against the Government of the United States has broken out in the States of South Carolina, Georgia, Alabama, Florida, Mississippi, Louisiana, and Texas, and the laws of the United States for the collection of the revenue can not be effectually executed therein conformably to that provision of the Constitution which requires duties to be uniform throughout the United States; and

Whereas a combination of persons engaged in such insurrection have threatened to grant pretended letters of marque to authorize the bearers thereof to commit assaults on the lives, vessels, and property of good citizens of the country lawfully engaged in commerce on the high seas and in waters of the United States; and

Whereas an Executive proclamation has been already issued requiring the persons engaged in these disorderly proceedings to desist therefrom, calling out a militia force for the purpose of repressing the same, and convening Congress in extraordinary session to deliberate and determine thereon:

Now, therefore, I, Abraham Lincoln, President of the United States, with a view to the same purposes before mentioned and to the protection of the public peace and the lives and property of quiet and orderly citizens pursuing their lawful occupations, until Congress shall have assembled and deliberated on the said unlawful proceedings or until the same shall have ceased, have further deemed it advisable to set on foot a blockade of the ports within the States aforesaid, in pursuance of the laws of the United States and of the law of nations in such case provided. For this purpose a competent force will be posted so as to prevent entrance and exit of vessels from the ports aforesaid. If, therefore, with a view to violate such blockade, a vessel shall approach or shall attempt to leave either of the said ports, she will be duly warned by the commander of one of the blockading vessels, who will indorse on her register the fact and date of such warning, and if the same vessel shall again attempt to enter or leave the blockaded port she will be captured and sent to the nearest convenient port for such proceedings against her and her cargo as prize as may be deemed advisable.

And I hereby proclaim and declare that if any person, under the pretended authority of the said States or under any other pretense, shall molest a vessel of the United States or the persons or cargo on board of her, such person will be held amenable to the laws of the United States for the prevention and punishment of piracy.

In witness whereof I have hereunto set my hand and caused the seal of the United States to be affixed.

[SEAL.]   Done at the city of Washington, this 19th day of April, A. D. 1861, and of the Independence of the United States the eighty-fifth.

                        ABRAHAM LINCOLN.

By the President:

WILLIAM H. SEWARD, *Secretary of State.*

BY THE PRESIDENT OF THE UNITED STATES OF AMERICA.

A PROCLAMATION.

Whereas, for the reasons assigned in my proclamation of the 19th instant, a blockade of the ports of the States of South Carolina, Georgia, Florida, Alabama, Louisiana, Mississippi, and Texas was ordered to be established; and

Whereas since that date public property of the United States has been seized, the collection of the revenue obstructed, and duly commissioned officers of the United States, while engaged in executing the orders of their superiors, have been arrested and held in custody as prisoners or have been impeded in the discharge of their official duties, without due legal process, by persons claiming to act under authorities of the States of Virginia and North Carolina, an efficient blockade of the ports of those States will also be established.

In witness whereof I have hereunto set my hand and caused the seal of the United States to be affixed.

[SEAL.]   Done at the city of Washington, this 27th day of April, A. D. 1861, and of the Independence of the United States the eighty-fifth.

                        ABRAHAM LINCOLN.

By the President:

WILLIAM H. SEWARD, *Secretary of State.*

BY THE PRESIDENT OF THE UNITED STATES.

A PROCLAMATION.

Whereas existing exigencies demand immediate and adequate measures for the protection of the National Constitution and the preservation of the National Union by the suppression of the insurrectionary combinations now existing in several States for opposing the laws of the Union and

obstructing the execution thereof, to which end a military force in addition to that called forth by my proclamation of the 15th day of April in the present year appears to be indispensably necessary:

Now, therefore, I, Abraham Lincoln, President of the United States and Commander in Chief of the Army and Navy thereof and of the militia of the several States when called into actual service, do hereby call into the service of the United States 42,034 volunteers to serve for the period of three years, unless sooner discharged, and to be mustered into service as infantry and cavalry. The proportions of each arm and the details of enrollment and organization will be made known through the Department of War.

And I also direct that the Regular Army of the United States be increased by the addition of eight regiments of infantry, one regiment of cavalry, and one regiment of artillery, making altogether a maximum aggregate increase of 22,714 officers and enlisted men, the details of which increase will also be made known through the Department of War.

And I further direct the enlistment for not less than one or more than three years of 18,000 seamen, in addition to the present force, for the naval service of the United States. The details of the enlistment and organization will be made known through the Department of the Navy.

The call for volunteers hereby made and the direction for the increase of the Regular Army and for the enlistment of seamen hereby given, together with the plan of organization adopted for the volunteer and for the regular forces hereby authorized, will be submitted to Congress as soon as assembled.

In the meantime I earnestly invoke the cooperation of all good citizens in the measures hereby adopted for the effectual suppression of unlawful violence, for the impartial enforcement of constitutional laws, and for the speediest possible restoration of peace and order, and with these of happiness and prosperity, throughout our country.

In testimony whereof I have hereunto set my hand and caused the seal of the United States to be affixed.

[SEAL.]   Done at the city of Washington, this 3d day of May, A. D. 1861, and of the Independence of the United States the eighty-fifth.

ABRAHAM LINCOLN.

By the President:

WILLIAM H. SEWARD, *Secretary of State.*

BY THE PRESIDENT OF THE UNITED STATES OF AMERICA.

A PROCLAMATION.

Whereas an insurrection exists in the State of Florida by which the lives, liberty, and property of loyal citizens of the United States are endangered; and

Whereas it is deemed proper that all needful measures should be taken

for the protection of such citizens and all officers of the United States in the discharge of their public duties in the State aforesaid:

Now, therefore, be it known that I, Abraham Lincoln, President of the United States, do hereby direct the commander of the forces of the United States on the Florida coast to permit no person to exercise any office or authority upon the islands of Key West, the Tortugas, and Santa Rosa which may be inconsistent with the laws and Constitution of the United States, authorizing him at the same time, if he shall find it necessary, to suspend there the writ of *habeas corpus* and to remove from the vicinity of the United States fortresses all dangerous or suspected persons.

In witness whereof I have hereunto set my hand and caused the seal of the United States to be affixed.

[SEAL.]   Done at the city of Washington, this 10th day of May, A. D. 1861, and of the Independence of the United States the eighty-fifth.

ABRAHAM LINCOLN.

By the President:

     WILLIAM H. SEWARD,
         Secretary of State.

EXECUTIVE ORDERS.

Lieutenant-General SCOTT.   WASHINGTON, *April 25, 1861.*

MY DEAR SIR: The Maryland legislature assembles to-morrow at Annapolis, and not improbably will take action to arm the people of that State against the United States. The question has been submitted to and considered by me whether it would not be justifiable, upon the ground of necessary defense, for you, as General in Chief of the United States Army, to arrest or disperse the members of that body. I think it would not be justifiable nor efficient for the desired object.

First. They have a clearly legal right to assemble, and we can not know in advance that their action will not be lawful and peaceful, and if we wait until they shall have acted their arrest or dispersion will not lessen the effect of their action.

Secondly. We can not permanently prevent their action. If we arrest them, we can not long hold them as prisoners, and when liberated they will immediately reassemble and take their action; and precisely the same if we simply disperse them—they will immediately reassemble in some other place.

I therefore conclude that it is only left to the Commanding General to watch and await their action, which, if it shall be to arm their people

against the United States, he is to adopt the most prompt and efficient means to counteract, even, if necessary, to the bombardment of their cities and, in the extremest necessity, the suspension of the writ of *habeas corpus*.

Your obedient servant,   ABRAHAM LINCOLN.

The COMMANDING GENERAL OF THE ARMY OF THE UNITED STATES:

You are engaged in suppressing an insurrection against the laws of the United States.   If at any point on or in the vicinity of any military line which is now or which shall be used between the city of Philadelphia and the city of Washington you find resistance which renders it necessary to suspend the writ of *habeas corpus* for the public safety, you personally, or through the officer in command at the point where resistance occurs, are authorized to suspend that writ.

Given under my hand and the seal of the United States, at the city [SEAL.] of Washington, this 27th day of April, 1861, and of the Independence of the United States the eighty-fifth.

ABRAHAM LINCOLN.

By the President of the United States:
WILLIAM H. SEWARD,
Secretary of State.

GENERAL ORDERS, No. 13.

WAR DEPARTMENT,
ADJUTANT-GENERAL'S OFFICE,
Washington, April 30, 1861.

The President directs that all officers of the Army, except those who have entered the service since the 1st instant, take and subscribe anew the oath of allegiance to the United States of America, as set forth in the tenth article of war.

Commanding officers will see to the prompt execution of this order, and report accordingly.

By order: L. THOMAS,
Adjutant-General.

To all who shall see these presents, greeting:

Know ye that, reposing special trust and confidence in the patriotism, valor, fidelity, and ability of Colonel Robert Anderson, United States Army, I have empowered him, and do hereby empower him, to receive into the Army of the United States as many regiments of volunteer troops from the State of Kentucky and from the western part of the State of Virginia as shall be willing to engage in the service of the United States

for the term of three years upon the terms and according to the plan proposed by the proclamation of May 3, 1861, and General Orders, No. 15, from the War Department, of May 4, 1861.

The troops whom he receives shall be on the same footing in every respect as those of the like kind called for in the proclamation above cited, except that the officers shall be commissioned by the United States. He is therefore carefully and diligently to discharge the duty hereby devolved upon him by doing and performing all manner of things thereunto belonging.

Given under my hand, at the city of Washington, this 7th day of May, A. D. 1861, and in the eighty-fifth year of the Independence of the United States.

ABRAHAM LINCOLN.

By the President:

SIMON CAMERON,
Secretary of War.

STATE DEPARTMENT, *June 20, 1861.*

The LIEUTENANT-GENERAL COMMANDING THE ARMIES OF THE UNITED STATES:

You or any officer you may designate will, in your discretion, suspend the writ of *habeas corpus* so far as may relate to Major Chase, lately of the Engineer Corps of the Army of the United States, now alleged to be guilty of treasonable practices against this Government.

ABRAHAM LINCOLN.

By the President:

WILLIAM H. SEWARD.

The COMMANDING GENERAL, ARMY OF THE UNITED STATES:

You are engaged in suppressing an insurrection against the laws of the United States. If at any point on or in the vicinity of any military line which is now or which shall be used between the city of New York and the city of Washington you find resistance which renders it necessary to suspend the writ of *habeas corpus* for the public safety, you personally, or through the officer in command at the point where resistance occurs, are authorized to suspend that writ.

Given under my hand and the seal of the United States, at the city [SEAL.] of Washington, this 2d day of July, A. D. 1861, and of the Independence of the United States the eighty-fifth.

ABRAHAM LINCOLN.

By the President:

WILLIAM H. SEWARD,
Secretary of State.

SPECIAL SESSION MESSAGE.

JULY 4, 1861.

Fellow-Citizens of the Senate and House of Representatives:

Having been convened on an extraordinary occasion, as authorized by the Constitution, your attention is not called to any ordinary subject of legislation.

At the beginning of the present Presidential term, four months ago, the functions of the Federal Government were found to be generally suspended within the several States of South Carolina, Georgia, Alabama, Mississippi, Louisiana, and Florida, excepting only those of the Post-Office Department.

Within these States all the forts, arsenals, dockyards, custom-houses, and the like, including the movable and stationary property in and about them, had been seized and were held in open hostility to this Government, excepting only Forts Pickens, Taylor, and Jefferson, on and near the Florida coast, and Fort Sumter, in Charleston Harbor, South Carolina. The forts thus seized had been put in improved condition, new ones had been built, and armed forces had been organized and were organizing, all avowedly with the same hostile purpose.

The forts remaining in the possession of the Federal Government in and near these States were either besieged or menaced by warlike preparations, and especially Fort Sumter was nearly surrounded by well-protected hostile batteries, with guns equal in quality to the best of its own and outnumbering the latter as perhaps ten to one. A disproportionate share of the Federal muskets and rifles had somehow found their way into these States, and had been seized to be used against the Government. Accumulations of the public revenue lying within them had been seized for the same object. The Navy was scattered in distant seas, leaving but a very small part of it within the immediate reach of the Government. Officers of the Federal Army and Navy had resigned in great numbers, and of those resigning a large proportion had taken up arms against the Government. Simultaneously and in connection with all this the purpose to sever the Federal Union was openly avowed. In accordance with this purpose, an ordinance had been adopted in each of these States declaring the States respectively to be separated from the National Union. A formula for instituting a combined government of these States had been promulgated, and this illegal organization, in the character of Confederate States, was already invoking recognition, aid, and intervention from foreign powers.

Finding this condition of things and believing it to be an imperative duty upon the incoming Executive to prevent, if possible, the consummation of such attempt to destroy the Federal Union, a choice of means to that end became indispensable. This choice was made, and was declared in the inaugural address. The policy chosen looked to the exhaustion of all peaceful measures before a resort to any stronger ones. It sought only to hold the public places and property not already wrested from the Government and to collect the revenue, relying for the rest on time, discussion, and the ballot box. It promised a continuance of the mails at Government expense to the very people who were resisting the Government, and it gave repeated pledges against any disturbance to any of the people or any of their rights. Of all that which a President might constitutionally and justifiably do in such a case, everything was forborne without which it was believed possible to keep the Government on foot.

On the 5th of March, the present incumbent's first full day in office, a letter of Major Anderson, commanding at Fort Sumter, written on the 28th of February and received at the War Department on the 4th of March, was by that Department placed in his hands. This letter expressed the professional opinion of the writer that reenforcements could not be thrown into that fort within the time for his relief rendered necessary by the limited supply of provisions, and with a view of holding possession of the same, with a force of less than 20,000 good and well-disciplined men. This opinion was concurred in by all the officers of his command, and their memoranda on the subject were made inclosures of Major Anderson's letter. The whole was immediately laid before Lieutenant-General Scott, who at once concurred with Major Anderson in opinion. On reflection, however, he took full time, consulting with other officers, both of the Army and the Navy, and at the end of four days came reluctantly, but decidedly, to the same conclusion as before. He also stated at the same time that no such sufficient force was then at the control of the Government or could be raised and brought to the ground within the time when the provisions in the fort would be exhausted. In a purely military point of view this reduced the duty of the Administration in the case to the mere matter of getting the garrison safely out of the fort.

It was believed, however, that to so abandon that position under the circumstances would be utterly ruinous; that the *necessity* under which it was to be done would not be fully understood; that by many it would be construed as a part of a *voluntary* policy; that at home it would discourage the friends of the Union, embolden its adversaries, and go far to insure to the latter a recognition abroad; that, in fact, it would be our national destruction consummated. This could not be allowed. Starvation was not yet upon the garrison, and ere it would be reached *Fort Pickens* might be reenforced. This last would be a clear indication of *policy*, and would better enable the country to accept the evacuation of Fort Sumter as a military *necessity*. An order was at once directed to be sent for the landing of the troops from the steamship *Brooklyn* into Fort Pickens. This order could not go by land, but must take the longer and slower route by sea. The first return news from the order was received just one week before the fall of Fort Sumter. The news itself was that the officer commanding the *Sabine*, to which vessel the troops had been transferred from the *Brooklyn*, acting upon some *quasi* armistice of the late Administration (and of the existence of which the present Administration, up to the time the order was dispatched, had only too vague and uncertain rumors to fix attention), had refused to land the troops. To now reenforce Fort Pickens before a crisis would be reached at Fort Sumter was impossible, rendered so by the near exhaustion of provisions in the latter-named fort. In precaution against such a conjuncture the Government had a few days before commenced preparing an expedition, as well adapted as might be, to relieve Fort Sumter, which expedition was intended to be ultimately used or not, according to circumstances. The strongest anticipated case for using it was now presented, and it was resolved to send it forward. As had been intended in this contingency, it was also resolved to notify the governor of South Carolina that he might expect an attempt would be made to provision the fort, and that if the attempt should not be resisted there would be no effort to throw in men, arms, or ammunition without further notice, or in case of an attack upon the fort. This notice was accordingly given, whereupon the fort was attacked and bombarded to its fall, without even awaiting the arrival of the provisioning expedition.

It is thus seen that the assault upon and reduction of Fort Sumter was in no sense a matter of self-defense on the part of the assailants. They well knew that the garrison in the fort could by no possibility commit aggression upon them. They knew—they were expressly notified— that the giving of bread to the few brave and hungry men of the garrison was all which would on that occasion be attempted, unless themselves, by resisting so much, should provoke more. They knew that this Government desired to keep the garrison in the fort, not to assail them, but merely to maintain visible possession, and thus to preserve the Union from actual and immediate dissolution, trusting, as hereinbefore stated, to time, discussion, and the ballot box for final adjustment; and they assailed and reduced the fort for precisely the reverse object—to drive out the visible authority of the Federal Union, and thus force it to immediate dissolution. That this was their object the Executive well understood; and having said to them in the inaugural address, "You can have no conflict without being yourselves the aggressors," he took pains not only to keep this declaration good, but also to keep the case so free from the power of ingenious sophistry as that the world should not be able to misunderstand it. By the affair at Fort Sumter, with its surrounding circumstances, that point was reached. Then and thereby the assailants of the Government began the conflict of arms, without a gun in sight or in expectancy to return their fire, save only the few in the fort, sent to that harbor years before for their own protection, and still ready to give that protection in whatever was lawful. In this act, discarding all else, they have forced upon the country the distinct issue, "Immediate dissolution or blood."

And this issue embraces more than the fate of these United States. It presents to the whole family of man the question whether a constitutional republic, or democracy—a government of the people by the same people—can or can not maintain its territorial integrity against its own domestic foes. It presents the question whether discontented individuals, too few in numbers to control administration according to organic law in any case, can always, upon the pretenses made in this case, or on any other pretenses, or arbitrarily without any pretense, break up their government, and thus practically put an end to free government upon the earth. It forces us to ask, Is there in all republics this inherent and fatal weakness? Must a government of necessity be too *strong* for the liberties of its own people, or too *weak* to maintain its own existence?

So viewing the issue, no choice was left but to call out the war power of the Government and so to resist force employed for its destruction by force for its preservation.

The call was made, and the response of the country was most gratifying, surpassing in unanimity and spirit the most sanguine expectation. Yet none of the States commonly called slave States, except Delaware, gave a regiment through regular State organization. A few regiments have been organized within some others of those States by individual enterprise and received into the Government service. Of course the seceded States, so called (and to which Texas had been joined about the time of the inauguration), gave no troops to the cause of the Union. The border States, so called, were not uniform in their action, some of them being almost *for* the Union, while in others, as Virginia, North Carolina, Tennessee, and Arkansas, the Union sentiment was nearly repressed and silenced. The course taken in Virginia was the most remarkable, perhaps the most important. A convention elected by the people of that State to consider this very question of disrupting the Federal Union was in session at the capital of Virginia when Fort Sumter fell. To this body the people had chosen a large majority of *professed* Union men. Almost immediately after the fall of Sumter many members of that majority went over to the original disunion minority, and with them adopted an ordinance for withdrawing the State from the Union. Whether this change was wrought by their great approval of the assault upon Sumter or their great resentment at the Government's resistance to that assault is not definitely known. Although they submitted the ordinance for ratification to a vote of the people, to be taken on a day then somewhat more than a month distant, the convention and the legislature (which was also in session at the same time and place), with leading men of the State not members of either, immediately commenced acting as if the State were already out of the Union. They pushed military preparations vigorously forward all over the State. They seized the United States armory at Harpers Ferry and the navy-yard at Gosport, near Norfolk. They received—perhaps invited—into their State large bodies of troops, with their warlike appointments, from the so-called seceded States. They formally entered into a treaty of temporary alliance and cooperation with the so-called "Confederate States," and sent members to their congress at Montgomery; and, finally, they permitted the insurrectionary government to be transferred to their capital at Richmond.

The people of Virginia have thus allowed this giant insurrection to make its nest within her borders, and this Government has no choice left but to deal with it *where* it finds it; and it has the less regret, as the loyal citizens have in due form claimed its protection. Those loyal citizens this Government is bound to recognize and protect, as being Virginia.

In the border States, so called—in fact, the Middle States—there are those who favor a policy which they call "armed neutrality;" that is, an arming of those States to prevent the Union forces passing one way or the disunion the other over their soil. This would be disunion completed. Figuratively speaking, it would be the building of an impassable wall along the line of separation, and yet not quite an impassable one, for, under the guise of neutrality, it would tie the hands of the Union men and freely pass supplies from among them to the insurrectionists, which it could not do as an open enemy. At a stroke it would take all the trouble off the hands of secession, except only what proceeds from the external blockade. It would do for the disunionists that which of all things they most desire—feed them well and give them disunion without a struggle of their own. It recognizes no fidelity to the Constitution, no obligation to maintain the Union; and while very many who have favored it are doubtless loyal citizens, it is, nevertheless, very injurious in effect.

Recurring to the action of the Government, it may be stated that at first a call was made for 75,000 militia, and rapidly following this a proclamation was issued for closing the ports of the insurrectionary districts by proceedings in the nature of blockade. So far all was believed to be strictly legal. At this point the insurrectionists announced their purpose to enter upon the practice of privateering.

Other calls were made for volunteers to serve three years unless sooner discharged, and also for large additions to the Regular Army and Navy. These measures, whether strictly legal or not, were ventured upon under what appeared to be a popular demand and a public necessity, trusting then, as now, that Congress would readily ratify them. It is believed that nothing has been done beyond the constitutional competency of Congress.

Soon after the first call for militia it was considered a duty to authorize the Commanding General in proper cases, according to his discretion, to suspend the privilege of the writ of *habeas corpus*, or, in other words, to arrest and detain without resort to the ordinary processes and forms of law such individuals as he might deem dangerous to the public safety. This authority has purposely been exercised but very sparingly. Nevertheless, the legality and propriety of what has been done under it are questioned, and the attention of the country has been called to the proposition that one who is sworn to "take care that the laws be faithfully executed" should not himself violate them. Of course some consideration was given to the questions of power and propriety before this matter was acted upon. The whole of the laws which were required to be faithfully executed were being resisted and failing of execution in nearly one-third of the States. Must they be allowed to finally fail of execution, even had it been perfectly clear that by the use of the means necessary to their execution some single law, made in such extreme tenderness of the citizen's liberty that practically it relieves more of the guilty than of the innocent, should to a very limited extent be violated? To state the question more directly, Are all the laws *but one* to go unexecuted, and the Government itself go to pieces lest that one be violated? Even in such a case, would not the official oath be broken if the Government should be overthrown when it was believed that disregarding the single law would tend to preserve it? But it was not believed that this question was presented. It was not believed that any law was violated. The provision of the Constitution that "the privilege of the writ of *habeas corpus* shall not be suspended unless when, in cases of rebellion or invasion, the public safety may require it" is equivalent to a provision—is a provision—that such privilege may be suspended when, in cases of rebellion or invasion, the public safety *does* require it. It was decided that we have a case of rebellion and that the public safety does require the qualified suspension of the privilege of the writ which was authorized to be made. Now it is insisted that Congress, and not the Executive, is vested with this power; but the Constitution itself is silent as to which or who is to exercise the power; and as the provision was plainly made for a dangerous emergency, it can not be believed the framers of the instrument intended that in every case the danger should run its course until Congress could be called together, the very assembling of which might be prevented, as was intended in this case, by the rebellion.

No more extended argument is now offered, as an opinion at some length will probably be presented by the Attorney-General. Whether there shall be any legislation upon the subject, and, if any, what, is submitted entirely to the better judgment of Congress.

The forbearance of this Government had been so extraordinary and so long continued as to lead some foreign nations to shape their action as if they supposed the early destruction of our National Union was probable. While this on discovery gave the Executive some concern, he is now happy to say that the sovereignty and rights of the United States are now everywhere practically respected by foreign powers, and a general sympathy with the country is manifested throughout the world.

The reports of the Secretaries of the Treasury, War, and the Navy will give the information in detail deemed necessary and convenient for your deliberation and action, while the Executive and all the Departments will stand ready to supply omissions or to communicate new facts considered important for you to know.

It is now recommended that you give the legal means for making this contest a short and a decisive one; that you place at the control of the Government for the work at least 400,000 men and $400,000,000. That number of men is about one-tenth of those of proper ages within the regions where apparently *all* are willing to engage, and the sum is less than a twenty-third part of the money value owned by the men who seem ready to devote the whole. A debt of $600,000,000 *now* is a less sum per head than was the debt of our Revolution when we came out of that struggle, and the money value in the country now bears even a greater proportion to what it was *then* than does the population. Surely each man has as strong a motive *now* to *preserve* our liberties as each had *then* to *establish* them.

A right result at this time will be worth more to the world than ten times the men and ten times the money. The evidence reaching us from the country leaves no doubt that the material for the work is abundant, and that it needs only the hand of legislation to give it legal sanction and the hand of the Executive to give it practical shape and efficiency. One of the greatest perplexities of the Government is to avoid receiving troops faster than it can provide for them. In a word, the people will save their Government if the Government itself will do its part only indifferently well.

It might seem at first thought to be of little difference whether the present movement at the South be called "secession" or "rebellion." The movers, however, well understand the difference. At the beginning they knew they could never raise their treason to any respectable magnitude by any name which implies *violation* of law. They knew their people possessed as much of moral sense, as much of devotion to law and order, and as much pride in and reverence for the history and Government of their common country as any other civilized and patriotic people. They knew they could make no advancement directly in the teeth of these strong and noble sentiments. Accordingly, they commenced by an insidious debauching of the public mind. They invented an ingenious sophism, which, if conceded, was followed by perfectly logical steps through all the incidents to the complete destruction of the Union. The sophism itself is that any State of the Union may *consistently* with the National Constitution, and therefore *lawfully* and *peacefully*, withdraw from the Union without the consent of the Union or of any other State. The little disguise that the supposed right is to be exercised only for just cause, themselves to be the sole judge of its justice, is too thin to merit any notice.

With rebellion thus sugar coated they have been drugging the public mind of their section for more than thirty years, and until at length they have brought many good men to a willingness to take up arms against the Government the day *after* some assemblage of men have enacted the farcical pretense of taking their State out of the Union who could have been brought to no such thing the day *before*.

This sophism derives much, perhaps the whole, of its currency from the assumption that there is some omnipotent and sacred supremacy pertaining to a *State*—to each State of our Federal Union. Our States have neither more nor less power than that reserved to them in the Union by the Constitution, no one of them ever having been a State *out* of the Union. The original ones passed into the Union even *before* they cast off their British colonial dependence, and the new ones each came into the Union directly from a condition of dependence, excepting Texas; and even Texas, in its temporary independence, was never designated a State. The new ones only took the designation of States on coming into the Union, while that name was first adopted for the old ones in and by the Declaration of Independence. Therein the "United Colonies" were declared to be "free and independent States;" but even then the object plainly was not to declare their independence of *one another* or of the *Union*, but directly the contrary, as their mutual pledge and their mutual action before, at the time, and afterwards abundantly show. The express plighting of faith by each and all of the original thirteen in the Articles of Confederation, two years later, that the Union shall be perpetual is most conclusive. Having never been States, either in substance or in name, *outside* of the Union, whence this magical omnipotence of "State rights," asserting a claim of power to lawfully destroy the Union itself? Much is said about the "sovereignty" of the States, but the word even is not in the National Constitution, nor, as is believed, in any of the State constitutions. What is a "sovereignty" in the political sense of the term? Would it be far wrong to define it "a political community without a political superior"? Tested by this, no one of our States, except Texas, ever was a sovereignty; and even Texas gave up the character on coming into the Union, by which act she acknowledged the Constitution of the United States and the laws and treaties of the United States made in pursuance of the Constitution to be for her the supreme law of the land. The States have their status in the Union, and they have no other legal status. If they break from this, they can only do so against law and by revolution. The Union, and not themselves separately, procured their independence and their liberty. By conquest or purchase the Union gave each of them whatever of independence and liberty it has. The Union is older than any of the States, and, in fact, it created them as States. Originally some dependent colonies made the Union, and in turn the Union threw off their old dependence for them and made them States, such as they are. Not one of them ever had a State constitution independent of the Union. Of course it is not forgotten that all the new States framed their constitutions before they entered the Union, nevertheless dependent upon and preparatory to coming into the Union.

Unquestionably the States have the powers and rights reserved to them in and by the National Constitution; but among these surely are not included all conceivable powers, however mischievous or destructive, but at most such only as were known in the world at the time as governmental powers; and certainly a power to destroy the Government itself had never been known as a governmental—as a merely administrative power. This relative matter of national power and State rights, as a principle, is no other than the principle of *generality* and *locality*. Whatever concerns the whole should be confided to the whole—to the General Government—while whatever concerns *only* the State should be left exclusively to the State. This is all there is of original principle about it. Whether the National Constitution in defining boundaries between the two has applied the principle with exact accuracy is not to be questioned. We are all bound by that defining without question.

What is now combated is the position that secession is *consistent* with the Constitution—is *lawful* and *peaceful*. It is not contended that there is any express law for it, and nothing should ever be implied as law which leads to unjust or absurd consequences. The nation purchased with money the countries out of which several of these States were formed. Is it just that they shall go off without leave and without refunding? The nation paid very large sums (in the aggregate, I believe, nearly a hundred millions) to relieve Florida of the aboriginal tribes. Is it just that she shall now be off without consent or without making any return? The nation is now in debt for money applied to the benefit of these so-called seceding States in common with the rest. Is it just either that creditors shall go unpaid or the remaining States pay the whole? A part of the present national debt was contracted to pay the old debts of Texas. Is it just that she shall leave and pay no part of this herself?

Again: If one State may secede, so may another; and when all shall have seceded none is left to pay the debts. Is this quite just to creditors? Did we notify them of this sage view of ours when we borrowed their money? If we now recognize this doctrine by allowing the seceders to go in peace, it is difficult to see what we can do if others choose to go or to extort terms upon which they will promise to remain.

The seceders insist that our Constitution admits of secession. They have assumed to make a national constitution of their own, in which of necessity they have either *discarded* or *retained* the right of secession, as they insist it exists in ours. If they have discarded it, they thereby admit that on principle it ought not to be in ours. If they have retained it, by their own construction of ours they show that to be consistent they must secede from one another whenever they shall find it the easiest way of settling their debts or effecting any other selfish or unjust object. The principle itself is one of disintegration, and upon which no government can possibly endure.

If all the States save one should assert the power to *drive* that one out of the Union, it is presumed the whole class of seceder politicians would at once deny the power and denounce the act as the greatest outrage upon State rights. But suppose that precisely the same act, instead of being called "driving the one out," should be called "the seceding of the others from that one," it would be exactly what the seceders claim to do, unless, indeed, they make the point that the one, because it is a minority, may rightfully do what the others, because they are a majority, may not rightfully do. These politicians are subtle and profound on the rights of minorities. They are not partial to that power which made the Constitution and speaks from the preamble, calling itself "we, the people."

It may well be questioned whether there is to-day a majority of the legally qualified voters of any State, except, perhaps, South Carolina, in favor of disunion. There is much reason to believe that the Union men are the majority in many, if not in every other one, of the so-called seceded States. The contrary has not been demonstrated in any one of them. It is ventured to affirm this even of Virginia and Tennessee; for the result of an election held in military camps, where the bayonets are all on one side of the question voted upon, can scarcely be considered as demonstrating popular sentiment. At such an election all that large class who are at once *for* the Union and *against* coercion would be coerced to vote against the Union.

It may be affirmed without extravagance that the free institutions we enjoy have developed the powers and improved the condition of our whole people beyond any example in the world. Of this we now have a striking and an impressive illustration. So large an army as the Government has now on foot was never before known without a soldier in it but who had taken his place there of his own free choice. But more than this, there are many single regiments whose members, one and another, possess full practical knowledge of all the arts, sciences, professions, and whatever else, whether useful or elegant, is known in the world; and there is scarcely one from which there could not be selected a President, a Cabinet, a Congress, and perhaps a court, abundantly competent to administer the Government itself. Nor do I say this is not true also in the army of our late friends, now adversaries in this contest; but if it is, so much better the reason why the Government which has conferred such benefits on both them and us should not be broken up. Whoever in any section proposes to abandon such a government would do well to consider in deference to what principle it is that he does it; what better he is likely to get in its stead; whether the substitute will give, or be intended to give, so much of good to the people. There are some foreshadowings on this subject. Our adversaries have adopted some declarations of independence in which, unlike the good old one penned by Jefferson, they omit the words "all men are created equal." Why? They have adopted a temporary national constitution, in the preamble of which, unlike our good old one signed by Washington, they omit "We, the people," and substitute "We, the deputies of the sovereign and independent States." Why? Why this deliberate pressing out of view the rights of men and the authority of the people?

This is essentially a people's contest. On the side of the Union it is a struggle for maintaining in the world that form and substance of government whose leading object is to elevate the condition of men; to lift artificial weights from all shoulders; to clear the paths of laudable pursuit for all; to afford all an unfettered start and a fair chance in the race of life. Yielding to partial and temporary departures, from necessity, this is the leading object of the Government for whose existence we contend.

I am most happy to believe that the plain people understand and appreciate this. It is worthy of note that while in this the Government's hour of trial large numbers of those in the Army and Navy who have been favored with the offices have resigned and proved false to the hand which had pampered them, not one common soldier or common sailor is known to have deserted his flag.

Great honor is due to those officers who remained true despite the example of their treacherous associates; but the greatest honor and most important fact of all is the unanimous firmness of the common soldiers and common sailors. To the last man, so far as known, they have successfully resisted the traitorous efforts of those whose commands but an hour before they obeyed as absolute law. This is the patriotic instinct of plain people. They understand without an argument that the destroying the Government which was made by Washington means no good to them.

Our popular Government has often been called an experiment. Two points in it our people have already settled—the successful *establishing* and the successful *administering* of it. One still remains—its successful *maintenance* against a formidable internal attempt to overthrow it. It is now for them to demonstrate to the world that those who can fairly carry an election can also suppress a rebellion; that ballots are the rightful and peaceful successors of bullets, and that when ballots have fairly and constitutionally decided there can be no successful appeal back to bullets; that there can be no successful appeal except to ballots themselves at succeeding elections. Such will be a great lesson of peace, teaching men that what they can not take by an election neither can they take it by a war; teaching all the folly of being the beginners of a war.

Lest there be some uneasiness in the minds of candid men as to what

is to be the course of the Government toward the Southern States *after* the rebellion shall have been suppressed, the Executive deems it proper to say it will be his purpose then, as ever, to be guided by the Constitution and the laws, and that he probably will have no different understanding of the powers and duties of the Federal Government relatively to the rights of the States and the people under the Constitution than that expressed in the inaugural address.

He desires to preserve the Government, that it may be administered for all as it was administered by the men who made it. Loyal citizens everywhere have the right to claim this of their government, and the government has no right to withhold or neglect it. It is not perceived that in giving it there is any coercion, any conquest, or any subjugation in any just sense of those terms.

The Constitution provides, and all the States have accepted the provision, that "the United States shall guarantee to every State in this Union a republican form of government." But if a State may lawfully go out of the Union, having done so it may also discard the republican form of government; so that to prevent its going out is an indispensable *means* to the *end* of maintaining the guaranty mentioned; and when an end is lawful and obligatory the indispensable means to it are also lawful and obligatory.

It was with the deepest regret that the Executive found the duty of employing the war power in defense of the Government forced upon him. He could but perform this duty or surrender the existence of the Government. No compromise by public servants could in this case be a cure; not that compromises are not often proper, but that no popular government can long survive a marked precedent that those who carry an election can only save the government from immediate destruction by giving up the main point upon which the people gave the election. The people themselves, and not their servants, can safely reverse their own deliberate decisions.

As a private citizen the Executive could not have consented that these institutions shall perish; much less could he in betrayal of so vast and so sacred a trust as these free people had confided to him. He felt that he had no moral right to shrink, nor even to count the chances of his own life, in what might follow. In full view of his great responsibility he has so far done what he has deemed his duty. You will now, according to your own judgment, perform yours. He sincerely hopes that your views and your action may so accord with his as to assure all faithful citizens who have been disturbed in their rights of a certain and speedy restoration to them under the Constitution and the laws.

And having thus chosen our course, without guile and with pure purpose, let us renew our trust in God and go forward without fear and with manly hearts.

ABRAHAM LINCOLN,

SPECIAL MESSAGES.

To the House of Representatives: WASHINGTON, *July 11, 1861.*

In answer to the resolution of the House of Representatives of the 9th instant, requesting a copy of correspondence upon the subject of the incorporation of the Dominican Republic with the Spanish Monarchy, I transmit a report from the Secretary of State, to whom the resolution was referred.

ABRAHAM LINCOLN.

WASHINGTON, *July, 1861.*

To the Senate and House of Representatives:

I transmit to Congress a copy of correspondence between the Secretary of State and Her Britannic Majesty's envoy extraordinary and minister plenipotentiary accredited to this Government, relative to an exhibition of the products of industry of all nations which is to take place at London in the course of next year. As citizens of the United States may justly pride themselves upon their proficiency in industrial arts, it is desirable that they should have proper facilities toward taking part in the exhibition. With this view I recommend such legislation by Congress at this session as may be necessary for that purpose.

ABRAHAM LINCOLN.

WASHINGTON, *July 19, 1861.*

To the Senate of the United States:

I transmit to the Senate, for its advice with a view to a formal execution of the instrument, the draft of a treaty informally agreed upon between the United States and the Delaware tribe of Indians, relative to certain lands of that tribe.

ABRAHAM LINCOLN.

WASHINGTON, *July 19, 1861.*

To the Senate and House of Representatives:

As the United States have, in common with Great Britain and France, a deep interest in the preservation and development of the fisheries adjacent to the northeastern coast and islands of this continent, it seems proper that we should concert with the Governments of those countries such measures as may be conducive to those important objects. With this view I transmit to Congress a copy of a correspondence between the Secretary of State and the British minister here, in which the latter proposes on behalf of his Government the appointment of a joint commission to inquire into the matter, in order that such ulterior measures may be adopted as may be

advisable for the objects proposed. Such legislation is recommended as may be necessary to enable the Executive to provide for a commissioner on behalf of the United States. ABRAHAM LINCOLN.

To the House of Representatives: WASHINGTON, *July 25, 1861.*

In answer to the resolution of the House of Representatives of the 22d instant, requesting a copy of the correspondence between this Government and foreign powers with reference to maritime rights, I transmit a report from the Secretary of State. ABRAHAM LINCOLN.

To the House of Representatives: WASHINGTON, *July 25, 1861.*

In answer to the resolution of the House of Representatives of the 15th instant, requesting a copy of the correspondence between this Government and foreign powers on the subject of the existing insurrection in the United States, I transmit a report from the Secretary of State.

ABRAHAM LINCOLN.

To the Senate: WASHINGTON, *July 27, 1861.*

In answer to the resolution of the Senate of the 25th instant, relative to the instructions to the ministers of the United States abroad in reference to the rebellion now existing in the southern portion of the Union, I transmit a report from the Secretary of State.

ABRAHAM LINCOLN.

To the House of Representatives: WASHINGTON, *July 27, 1861.*

In answer to the resolution of the House of Representatives of the 24th instant, asking the grounds, reasons, and evidence upon which the police commissioners of Baltimore were arrested and are now detained as prisoners at Fort McHenry, I have to state that it is judged to be incompatible with the public interest at this time to furnish the information called for by the resolution. ABRAHAM LINCOLN.

Hon. H. HAMLIN, EXECUTIVE OFFICE, *July 29, 1861.*
     President of the Senate.

SIR: I transmit herewith, to be laid before the Senate for its constitutional action thereon, articles of agreement and convention,* with accompanying papers. ABRAHAM LINCOLN.

* With confederated tribes of Arapahoe and Cheyenne Indians of the Upper Arkansas River.

To the Senate of the United States: JULY 30, 1861.

In answer to the resolution of the Senate of the 19th instant, request-ing information concerning the *quasi* armistice alluded to in my message of the 4th instant,* I transmit a report from the Secretary of the Navy.

ABRAHAM LINCOLN.

To the Senate of the United States: JULY 30, 1861.

In answer to the resolution of the Senate of the 23d instant, requesting information concerning the imprisonment of Lieutenant John J. Worden [John L. Worden], of the United States Navy, I transmit a report from the Secretary of the Navy.   ABRAHAM LINCOLN.

WASHINGTON, *August 1, 1861.*

To the Senate of the United States:

I submit herewith, for consideration with a view to ratification, a postal treaty between the United States of America and the United Mexican States, concluded by their respective plenipotentiaries on the 31st ultimo.

ABRAHAM LINCOLN.

WASHINGTON, *August 2, 1861.*

To the House of Representatives:

In answer to the resolution of the House of Representatives of yester-day, requesting information regarding the imprisonment of loyal citizens of the United States by the forces now in rebellion against this Govern-ment, I transmit a report from the Secretary of State and the copy of a telegraphic dispatch by which it was accompanied.

ABRAHAM LINCOLN.

AUGUST 2, 1861.

To the Senate of the United States:

The resolution of your honorable body which is herewith returned has been submitted to the Secretary of the Navy, who has made the report upon it which I have the honor to inclose herewith.

I have the honor to add that the same rule stated by the Secretary of the Navy is found in section 5 of the Army Regulations published in 1861. It certainly is competent for Congress to change this rule by law, but it is respectfully suggested that a rule of so long standing and of so extensive application should not be hastily changed, nor by any authority less than the full lawmaking power.

ABRAHAM LINCOLN.

* See p. 22.

NAVY DEPARTMENT, *August 2, 1861.*

The PRESIDENT OF THE UNITED STATES.

SIR: I have the honor to acknowledge the receipt of the resolution of the Senate of the 31st ultimo, in relation to the recent nominations of lieutenants of marines, which nominations were directed to "be returned to the President and he be informed that the Senate adhere to the opinion expressed in the resolution passed by them on the 19th of July instant, and that the Senate are of opinion that rank and position in the Army, Navy, or Marine Corps should not be decided by lot, but that, all other things being equal, preference should be given to age."

If I understand correctly the resolution of the Senate, it is an expression of opinion on the part of that body against the Army Regulations, which are made applicable to the Marine Corps—regulations that have been in existence almost from the commencement of the Government.

In the published edition of Army Regulations when Mr. Calhoun was Secretary of War, section 1, article 3, it is expressly stated that the questions respecting the rank of officers arising from the sameness of dates in commissions of the same grade shall be decided, first, by a reference to the relative rank of the parties in the regular forces (including the United States Marine Corps) at the time the present appointments or promotions were made; second, by reference to former rank therein taken away by derangement or disbandment; third, by reference to former rank therein given up by resignation; fourth, by lottery.

And in the last edition of Army Regulations, before me, published in 1857, it is specified in article 2, section 5, that "when commissions are of the same date the rank is to be decided between officers of the same regiment or corps by the order of appointment; between officers of different regiments or corps, first, by rank in actual service when appointed; second, by former rank and service in the Army or Marine Corps; third, by lottery among such as have not been in the military service of the United States."

The rule here laid down governed in the appointment of the lieutenants of marines who have been nominated the present session to the Senate. Their order of rank was determined by lottery, agreeably to the published Army Regulations, and applied by those regulations specifically to the Marine Corps.

The gentlemen thus appointed in conformity to regulations have been mustered into service and done duty under fire. One of the number has fallen in the rank and place assigned him according to those regulations, and to set them aside and make a new order in conflict with the regulations will, I apprehend, be deemed, if not *ex post facto*, almost invidious.

In this matter the Department has no feeling, but it is desirable that it should be distinctly settled whether hereafter the Army Regulations are to govern in the question of rank in the Marine Corps or whether they are to be set aside by resolution of the Senate.

I have the honor to return the papers and subscribe myself, very respectfully, your obedient servant,

GIDEON WELLES.

EXECUTIVE MANSION, *August 5, 1861.*

To the Senate of the United States:

In answer to the resolution of your honorable body of date July 31, 1861, requesting the President to inform the Senate whether the Hon. James H. Lane, a member of that body from Kansas, has been appointed a brigadier-general in the Army of the United States, and, if so, whether he has accepted such appointment, I have the honor to transmit herewith certain papers, numbered 1, 2, 3, 4, 5, 6, and 7, which taken together explain themselves, and which contain all the information I possess upon the questions propounded.

It was my intention, as shown by my letter of June 20, 1861, to appoint Hon. James H. Lane, of Kansas, a brigadier-general of United States Volunteers, in anticipation of the act of Congress since passed for raising such volunteers; and I have no further knowledge upon the subject except as derived from the papers herewith inclosed.

ABRAHAM LINCOLN.

PROCLAMATIONS.

BY THE PRESIDENT OF THE UNITED STATES OF AMERICA.

A PROCLAMATION.

Whereas a joint committee of both Houses of Congress has waited on the President of the United States and requested him to "recommend a day of public humiliation, prayer, and fasting to be observed by the people of the United States with religious solemnities and the offering of fervent supplications to Almighty God for the safety and welfare of these States, His blessings on their arms, and a speedy restoration of peace;" and

Whereas it is fit and becoming in all people at all times to acknowledge and revere the supreme government of God, to bow in humble submission to His chastisements, to confess and deplore their sins and transgressions in the full conviction that the fear of the Lord is the beginning of wisdom, and to pray with all fervency and contrition for the pardon of their past offenses and for a blessing upon their present and prospective action; and

Whereas when our own beloved country, once, by the blessing of God, united, prosperous, and happy, is now afflicted with faction and civil war, it is peculiarly fit for us to recognize the hand of God in this terrible visitation, and in sorrowful remembrance of our own faults and crimes as a nation and as individuals to humble ourselves before Him and to pray for His mercy—to pray that we may be spared further punishment, though most justly deserved; that our arms may be blessed and made effectual for the reestablishment of law, order, and peace throughout the wide extent of our country; and that the inestimable boon of civil and religious liberty, earned under His guidance and blessing by the labors and sufferings of our fathers, may be restored in all its original excellence:

Therefore I, Abraham Lincoln, President of the United States, do appoint the last Thursday in September next as a day of humiliation, prayer, and fasting for all the people of the nation. And I do earnestly recommend to all the people, and especially to all ministers and teachers of religion of all denominations and to all heads of families, to observe and keep that day according to their several creeds and modes of worship in all humility and with all religious solemnity, to the end that the united prayer of the nation may ascend to the Throne of Grace and bring down plentiful blessings upon our country.

In testimony whereof I have hereunto set my hand and caused the seal of the United States to be affixed, this 12th day of August, [SEAL.] A. D. 1861, and of the Independence of the United States of America the eighty-sixth.

ABRAHAM LINCOLN.

By the President:

WILLIAM H. SEWARD, *Secretary of State.*

BY THE PRESIDENT OF THE UNITED STATES OF AMERICA.

A PROCLAMATION.

Whereas on the 15th day of April, 1861, the President of the United States, in view of an insurrection against the laws, Constitution, and Government of the United States which had broken out within the States of South Carolina, Georgia, Alabama, Florida, Mississippi, Louisiana, and Texas, and in pursuance of the provisions of the act entitled "An act to provide for calling forth the militia to execute the laws of the Union, suppress insurrections, and repel invasions, and to repeal the act now in force for that purpose," approved February 28, 1795, did call forth the militia to suppress said insurrection and to cause the laws of the Union to be duly executed, and the insurgents have failed to disperse by the time directed by the President; and

Whereas such insurrection has since broken out, and yet exists, within the States of Virginia, North Carolina, Tennessee, and Arkansas; and

Whereas the insurgents in all the said States claim to act under the authority thereof, and such claim is not disclaimed or repudiated by the persons exercising the functions of government in such State or States or in the part or parts thereof in which such combinations exist, nor has such insurrection been suppressed by said States:

Now, therefore, I, Abraham Lincoln, President of the United States, in pursuance of an act of Congress approved July 13, 1861, do hereby declare that the inhabitants of the said States of Georgia, South Carolina, Virginia, North Carolina, Tennessee, Alabama, Louisiana, Texas, Arkansas, Mississippi, and Florida (except the inhabitants of that part of the State of Virginia lying west of the Alleghany Mountains and of such other parts of that State and the other States hereinbefore named as may maintain a loyal adhesion to the Union and the Constitution or may be from time to time occupied and controlled by forces of the United States engaged in the dispersion of said insurgents) are in a state of insurrection against the United States, and that all commercial intercourse between the same and the inhabitants thereof, with the exceptions aforesaid, and the citizens of other States and other parts of the United States is unlawful, and will remain unlawful until such insurrection shall cease or has been suppressed; that all goods and chattels, wares and merchandise, coming from any of said States, with the exceptions aforesaid, into other parts of the United States without the special license and permission of the President, through the Secretary of the Treasury, or proceeding to any of said States, with the exceptions aforesaid, by land or water, together with the vessel or vehicle conveying the same or conveying persons to or from said States, with said exceptions, will be forfeited to the United States; and that from and after fifteen days from the issuing of this proclamation all ships and vessels belonging in whole or in part to any citizen or inhabitant of any of said States, with said exceptions, found at sea or in any port of the United States will be forfeited to the United States; and I hereby enjoin upon all district attorneys, marshals, and officers of the revenue and of the military and naval forces of the United States to be vigilant in the execution of said act and in the enforcement of the penalties and forfeitures imposed or declared by it, leaving any party who may think himself aggrieved thereby to his application to the Secretary of the Treasury for the remission of any penalty or forfeiture, which the said Secretary is authorized by law to grant if in his judgment the special circumstances of any case shall require such remission.

In witness whereof I have hereunto set my hand and caused the seal of the United States to be affixed.

[SEAL.]   Done at the city of Washington, this 16th day of August, A. D. 1861, and of the Independence of the United States the eighty-sixth.

ABRAHAM LINCOLN.

By the President:

WILLIAM H. SEWARD,
Secretary of State.

EXECUTIVE ORDERS.

JULY 31, 1861.

The marshal of the United States in the vicinity of forts where political prisoners are held will supply decent lodging and subsistence for such prisoners, unless they shall prefer to provide in those respects for themselves, in which cases they will be allowed to do so by the commanding officers in charge.

Approved, and the Secretary of State will transmit the order to marshals, the Lieutenant-General, and Secretary of the Interior.

ABRAHAM LINCOLN.

AUGUST 7, 1861.

By the fifty-seventh article of the act of Congress entitled "An act for establishing rules and articles for the government of the armies of the United States," approved April 10, 1806, holding correspondence with or giving intelligence to the enemy, either directly or indirectly, is made punishable by death, or such other punishment as shall be ordered by the sentence of a court-martial. Public safety requires strict enforcement of this article.

It is therefore ordered, That all correspondence and communication, verbally or by writing, printing, or telegraphing, respecting operations of the Army or military movements on land or water, or respecting the troops, camps, arsenals, intrenchments, or military affairs within the several military districts, by which intelligence shall be, directly or indirectly, given to the enemy, without the authority and sanction of the major-general in command, be, and the same are, absolutely prohibited, and from and after the date of this order persons violating the same will be proceeded against under the fifty-seventh article of war.

SIMON CAMERON.

Approved:

A. LINCOLN.

GENERAL ORDER.

EXECUTIVE OF THE UNITED STATES, *October 4, 1861*.

Flag-officers of the United States Navy authorized to wear a square flag at the mizzenmast head will take rank with major-generals of the United States Army.

ABRAHAM LINCOLN.

WASHINGTON, *October 14, 1861*.

Lieutenant-General WINFIELD SCOTT:

The military line of the United States for the suppression of the insurrection may be extended so far as Bangor, in Maine. You and any officer acting under your authority are hereby authorized to suspend the writ of *habeas corpus* in any place between that place and the city of Washington.

ABRAHAM LINCOLN.

By the President:

WILLIAM H. SEWARD,
Secretary of State.

GENERAL ORDERS, No. 94.

WAR DEPARTMENT,
ADJUTANT-GENERAL'S OFFICE,
Washington, November 1, 1861.

The following order from the President of the United States, announcing the retirement from active command of the honored veteran Lieutenant-General Winfield Scott, will be read by the Army with profound regret:

EXECUTIVE MANSION,
Washington, November 1, 1861.

On the 1st day of November, A. D. 1861, upon his own application to the President of the United States, Brevet Lieutenant-General Winfield Scott is ordered to be placed, and hereby is placed, upon the list of retired officers of the Army of the United States, without reduction in his current pay, subsistence, or allowances.

The American people will hear with sadness and deep emotion that General Scott has withdrawn from the active control of the Army, while the President and a unanimous Cabinet express their own and the nation's sympathy in his personal affliction and their profound sense of the important public services rendered by him to his country during his long and brilliant career, among which will ever be gratefully distinguished his faithful devotion to the Constitution, the Union, and the flag when assailed by parricidal rebellion.

ABRAHAM LINCOLN.

The President is pleased to direct that Major-General George B. McClellan assume the command of the Army of the United States. The headquarters of the Army will be established in the city of Washington. All communications intended for the Commanding General will hereafter be addressed direct to the Adjutant-General. The duplicate returns, orders, and other papers heretofore sent to the Assistant Adjutant-General, Headquarters of the Army, will be discontinued.

By order of the Secretary of War:

L. THOMAS,
Adjutant-General.

EXECUTIVE MANSION,
Washington, November 5, 1861.

The governor of the State of Missouri, acting under the direction of the convention of that State, proposes to the Government of the United States that he will raise a military force, to serve within the State as State militia during the war there, to cooperate with the troops in the service of the United States in repelling the invasion of the State and suppressing rebellion therein; the said State militia to be embodied and to be held in the camp and in the field, drilled, disciplined, and governed according to the Army Regulations and subject to the Articles of War; the said State militia not to be ordered out of the State except for the immediate defense of the State of Missouri, but to cooperate with the troops in the service of the United States in military operations within the State or necessary to its defense, and when officers of the State militia act with officers in the service of the United States of the same grade the officers of the United States service shall command the combined force; the State militia to be armed, equipped, clothed, subsisted, transported, and paid by the United States during such time as they shall be actually engaged as an embodied military force in service in accordance with Regulations of the United States Army or general orders as issued from time to time.

In order that the Treasury of the United States may not be burdened with the pay of unnecessary officers, the governor proposes that, although the State law requires him to appoint upon the general staff an adjutant-general, a commissary-general, an inspector-general, a quartermaster-general, a paymaster-general, and a surgeon-general, each with the rank of colonel of cavalry, yet he proposes that the Government of the United States pay only the adjutant-general, the quartermaster-general, and inspector-general, their services being necessary in the relations which would exist between the State militia and the United States. The governor further proposes that, while he is allowed by the State law to appoint aids-de-camp to the governor at his discretion, with the rank of colonel, three only shall be reported to the United States for payment. He also proposes that the State militia shall be commanded by a single major-general and by such number of brigadier-generals as shall allow one for a brigade of not less than four regiments, and that no greater number of staff officers shall be appointed for regimental, brigade, and division duties than as provided for in the act of Congress of the 22d July, 1861; and that, whatever be the rank of such officers as fixed by the law of the State, the compensation that they shall receive from the United States shall only be that which belongs to the rank given by said act of Congress to officers in the United States service performing the same duties.

The field officers of a regiment in the State militia are one colonel, one lieutenant-colonel, and one major, and the company officers are a captain, a first lieutenant, and a second lieutenant.

The governor proposes that, as the money to be disbursed is the money of the United States, such staff officers in the service of the United States as may be necessary to act as disbursing officers for the State militia shall be assigned by the War Department for that duty; or, if such can not be spared from their present duty, he will appoint such persons disbursing officers for the State militia as the President of the United States may designate. Such regulations as may be required, in the judgment of the President, to insure regularity of returns and to protect the United States from any fraudulent practices shall be observed and obeyed by all in office in the State militia.

The above propositions are accepted on the part of the United States, and the Secretary of War is directed to make the necessary orders upon the Ordnance, Quartermaster's, Commissary, Pay, and Medical departments to carry this agreement into effect. He will cause the necessary staff officers in the United States service to be detailed for duty in connection with the Missouri State militia, and will order them to make the necessary provision in their respective offices for fulfilling this agreement. All requisitions upon the different officers of the United States under this agreement to be made in substance in the same mode for the Missouri State militia as similar requisitions are made for troops in the service of the United States; and the Secretary of War will cause any additional regulations that may be necessary to insure regularity and economy in carrying this agreement into effect to be adopted and communicated to the governor of Missouri for the government of the Missouri State militia.

[Indorsement.]

NOVEMBER 6, 1861.

This plan approved, with the modification that the governor stipulates that when he commissions a major-general of militia it shall be the same person at the time in command of the United States Department of the West; and in case the United States shall change such commander of the department, he (the governor) will revoke the State commission given to the person relieved and give one to the person substituted to the United States command of said department.

A. LINCOLN.

GENERAL ORDERS, NO. 96.

WAR DEPARTMENT,
ADJUTANT-GENERAL'S OFFICE,
Washington, November 7, 1861.

Authority to raise a force of State militia, to serve during the war, is granted, by direction of the President, to the governor of Missouri. This force is to cooperate with the troops in the service of the United States in repelling the invasion of the State of Missouri and in suppressing rebellion therein. It is to be held, in camp and in the field, drilled, disciplined, and governed according to the Regulations of the United States Army and subject to the Articles of War; but it is not to be ordered out of the State of Missouri except for the immediate defense of the said State.

The State forces thus authorized will be, during such time as they shall be actually engaged as an embodied military force in active service, armed, equipped, clothed, subsisted, transported, and paid by the United States in accordance with the Regulations of the United States Army and such orders as may from time to time be issued from the War Department, and in no other manner; and they shall be considered as disbanded from the service of the United States whenever the President may so direct.

In connection with this force the governor is authorized to appoint the following officers, who will be recognized and paid by the United States, to wit: One major-general, to command the whole of the State forces brought into service, who shall be the same person appointed by the President to command the United States Military Department of the West, and shall retain his commission as major-general of the State forces only during his command of the said department; one adjutant-general, one inspector-general, and one quartermaster-general, each with the rank and pay of a colonel of cavalry; three aids-de-camp to the governor, each with the rank and pay of a colonel of infantry; brigadier-generals at the rate of one to a brigade of not less than four regiments; and division, brigade, and regimental staff officers not to exceed in numbers those provided for in the organization prescribed by the act approved July 22, 1861, "for the employment of volunteers," nor to be more highly compensated by the United States, whatever their nominal rank in the State service, than officers performing the same duties under that act.

The field officers of a regiment to be one colonel, one lieutenant-colonel, and one major, and the officers of a company to be one captain, one first and one second lieutenant.

When officers of the said State forces shall act in conjunction with officers of the United States Army of the same grade, the latter shall command the combined force.

All disbursements of money made to these troops or in consequence of their employment by the United States shall be made by disbursing officers of the United States Army, assigned by the War Department, or specially appointed by the President for that purpose, who will make their requisitions upon the different supply departments in the same manner for the Missouri State forces as similar requisitions are made for other volunteer troops in the service of the United States.

The Secretary of War will cause any additional regulations that may be necessary for the purpose of promoting economy, insuring regularity of returns, and protecting the United States from fraudulent practices to be adopted and published for the government of the said State forces, and the same will be obeyed and observed by all in office under the authority of the State of Missouri.

By order:

JULIUS P. GARESCHÉ,
Assistant Adjutant-General.

GENERAL ORDERS, NO. 100.

HEADQUARTERS OF THE ARMY,
ADJUTANT-GENERAL'S OFFICE,
Washington, November 16, 1861.

Complaint has been made to the President of the United States that certain persons within the State of Virginia, in places occupied by the forces of the United States, claim to be incumbents of civil offices—State, county, and municipal—by alleged authority from the Commonwealth of Virginia, in disregard and violation of the "declaration of the people of Virginia represented in convention at the city of Wheeling, Thursday, June 13, 1861," and of the ordinances of said convention, and of the acts of the general assembly held by authority of said convention.

It is therefore ordered, by direction of the President, that if any person shall hereafter attempt within the State of Virginia, under the alleged authority of said Commonwealth, to exercise any official powers of a civil nature within the limits of any of the commands of the occupying forces of the United States, unless in pursuance of the declaration and ordinances of the convention assembled at Wheeling on the 13th day of June, 1861, and the acts of the general assembly held by authority of said convention, such attempt shall be treated as an act of hostility against the United States, and such person shall be taken into military custody.

Commanding officers are directed to enforce this order within their respective commands.

*   *   *   *   *   *   *

By command of Major-General McClellan:

L. THOMAS, *Adjutant-General.*

EXECUTIVE MANSION, *Washington, November 27, 1861.*

The municipal authorities of Washington and Georgetown, in this District, having appointed to-morrow, the 28th instant, as a day of thanksgiving, the several Departments will on that occasion be closed, in order that the officers of the Government may partake in the ceremonies.

ABRAHAM LINCOLN.

FIRST ANNUAL MESSAGE.

WASHINGTON, *December 3, 1861.*

Fellow-Citizens of the Senate and House of Representatives:

In the midst of unprecedented political troubles we have cause of great gratitude to God for unusual good health and most abundant harvests.

You will not be surprised to learn that in the peculiar exigencies of the times our intercourse with foreign nations has been attended with profound solicitude, chiefly turning upon our own domestic affairs.

A disloyal portion of the American people have during the whole year been engaged in an attempt to divide and destroy the Union. A nation which endures factious domestic division is exposed to disrespect abroad, and one party, if not both, is sure sooner or later to invoke foreign intervention.

Nations thus tempted to interfere are not always able to resist the counsels of seeming expediency and ungenerous ambition, although measures adopted under such influences seldom fail to be unfortunate and injurious to those adopting them.

The disloyal citizens of the United States who have offered the ruin of our country in return for the aid and comfort which they have invoked abroad have received less patronage and encouragement than they probably expected. If it were just to suppose, as the insurgents have seemed to assume, that foreign nations in this case, discarding all moral, social, and treaty obligations, would act solely and selfishly for the most speedy restoration of commerce, including especially the acquisition of cotton, those nations appear as yet not to have seen their way to their object more directly or clearly through the destruction than through the preservation of the Union. If we could dare to believe that foreign nations are actuated by no higher principle than this, I am quite sure a sound argument could be made to show them that they can reach their aim more readily and easily by aiding to crush this rebellion than by giving encouragement to it.

The principal lever relied on by the insurgents for exciting foreign nations to hostility against us, as already intimated, is the embarrassment of commerce. Those nations, however, not improbably saw from the first that it was the Union which made as well our foreign as our domestic commerce. They can scarcely have failed to perceive that the effort for disunion produces the existing difficulty, and that one strong nation promises more durable peace and a more extensive, valuable, and reliable commerce than can the same nation broken into hostile fragments.

It is not my purpose to review our discussions with foreign states, because, whatever might be their wishes or dispositions, the integrity of our country and the stability of our Government mainly depend not upon them, but on the loyalty, virtue, patriotism, and intelligence of the American people. The correspondence itself, with the usual reservations, is herewith submitted.

I venture to hope it will appear that we have practiced prudence and liberality toward foreign powers, averting causes of irritation and with firmness maintaining our own rights and honor.

Since, however, it is apparent that here, as in every other state, foreign dangers necessarily attend domestic difficulties, I recommend that adequate and ample measures be adopted for maintaining the public defenses on every side. While under this general recommendation provision for defending our seacoast line readily occurs to the mind, I also in the same connection ask the attention of Congress to our great lakes and rivers. It is believed that some fortifications and depots of arms and munitions, with harbor and navigation improvements, all at well-selected points upon these, would be of great importance to the national defense and preservation. I ask attention to the views of the Secretary of War, expressed in his report, upon the same general subject.

I deem it of importance that the loyal regions of east Tennessee and western North Carolina should be connected with Kentucky and other faithful parts of the Union by railroad. I therefore recommend, as a military measure, that Congress provide for the construction of such road as speedily as possible. Kentucky no doubt will cooperate, and through her legislature make the most judicious selection of a line. The northern terminus must connect with some existing railroad, and whether the route shall be from Lexington or Nicholasville to the Cumberland Gap, or from Lebanon to the Tennessee line, in the direction of Knoxville, or on some still different line, can easily be determined. Kentucky and the General Government cooperating, the work can be completed in a very short time, and when done it will be not only of vast present usefulness, but also a valuable permanent improvement, worth its cost in all the future.

Some treaties, designed chiefly for the interests of commerce, and having no grave political importance, have been negotiated, and will be submitted to the Senate for their consideration.

Although we have failed to induce some of the commercial powers to adopt a desirable melioration of the rigor of maritime war, we have removed all obstructions from the way of this humane reform except such as are merely of temporary and accidental occurrence.

I invite your attention to the correspondence between Her Britannic Majesty's minister accredited to this Government and the Secretary of State relative to the detention of the British ship *Perthshire* in June last by the United States steamer *Massachusetts* for a supposed breach of the blockade. As this detention was occasioned by an obvious misapprehension of the facts, and as justice requires that we should commit no belligerent act not founded in strict right as sanctioned by public law, I recommend that an appropriation be made to satisfy the reasonable demand of the owners of the vessel for her detention.

I repeat the recommendation of my predecessor in his annual message to Congress in December last in regard to the disposition of the surplus which will probably remain after satisfying the claims of American citizens against China, pursuant to the awards of the commissioners under the act of the 3d of March, 1859. If, however, it should not be deemed advisable to carry that recommendation into effect, I would suggest that authority be given for investing the principal, over the proceeds of the surplus referred to, in good securities, with a view to the satisfaction of such other just claims of our citizens against China as are not unlikely to arise hereafter in the course of our extensive trade with that Empire.

By the act of the 5th of August last Congress authorized the President to instruct the commanders of suitable vessels to defend themselves against and to capture pirates. This authority has been exercised in a single instance only. For the more effectual protection of our extensive and valuable commerce in the Eastern seas especially, it seems to me that it would also be advisable to authorize the commanders of sailing vessels to recapture any prizes which pirates may make of United States vessels and their cargoes, and the consular courts now established by law in Eastern countries to adjudicate the cases in the event that this should not be objected to by the local authorities.

If any good reason exists why we should persevere longer in withholding our recognition of the independence and sovereignty of Hayti and Liberia, I am unable to discern it. Unwilling, however, to inaugurate a novel policy in regard to them without the approbation of Congress, I submit for your consideration the expediency of an appropriation for maintaining a chargé d'affaires near each of those new States. It does not admit of doubt that important commercial advantages might be secured by favorable treaties with them.

The operations of the Treasury during the period which has elapsed since your adjournment have been conducted with signal success. The patriotism of the people has placed at the disposal of the Government the large means demanded by the public exigencies. Much of the national loan has been taken by citizens of the industrial classes, whose confidence in their country's faith and zeal for their country's deliverance from present peril have induced them to contribute to the support of the Government the whole of their limited acquisitions. This fact imposes peculiar obligations to economy in disbursement and energy in action.

The revenue from all sources, including loans, for the financial year ending on the 30th of June, 1861, was $86,835,900.27, and the expenditures for the same period, including payments on account of the public debt, were $84,578,834.47, leaving a balance in the Treasury on the 1st of July of $2,257,065.80. For the first quarter of the financial year ending on the 30th of September, 1861, the receipts from all sources, including the balance of the 1st of July, were $102,532,509.27, and the expenses $98,239,733.09, leaving a balance on the 1st of October, 1861, of $4,292,776.18.

Estimates for the remaining three quarters of the year and for the financial year 1863, together with his views of ways and means for meeting the demands contemplated by them, will be submitted to Congress by the Secretary of the Treasury. It is gratifying to know that the expenditures made necessary by the rebellion are not beyond the resources of the loyal people, and to believe that the same patriotism which has thus far sustained the Government will continue to sustain it till peace and union shall again bless the land.

I respectfully refer to the report of the Secretary of War for information respecting the numerical strength of the Army and for recommendations having in view an increase of its efficiency and the well-being of the various branches of the service intrusted to his care. It is gratifying to know that the patriotism of the people has proved equal to the occasion, and that the number of troops tendered greatly exceeds the force which Congress authorized me to call into the field.

I refer with pleasure to those portions of his report which make allusion to the creditable degree of discipline already attained by our troops and to the excellent sanitary condition of the entire Army.

The recommendation of the Secretary for an organization of the militia upon a uniform basis is a subject of vital importance to the future safety of the country, and is commended to the serious attention of Congress.

The large addition to the Regular Army, in connection with the defection that has so considerably diminished the number of its officers, gives peculiar importance to his recommendation for increasing the corps of cadets to the greatest capacity of the Military Academy.

By mere omission, I presume, Congress has failed to provide chaplains for hospitals occupied by volunteers. This subject was brought to my notice, and I was induced to draw up the form of a letter, one copy of which, properly addressed, has been delivered to each of the persons, and at the dates respectively named and stated in a schedule, containing also the form of the letter marked A, and herewith transmitted.

These gentlemen, I understand, entered upon the duties designated at the times respectively stated in the schedule, and have labored faithfully therein ever since. I therefore recommend that they be compensated at the same rate as chaplains in the Army. I further suggest that general provision be made for chaplains to serve at hospitals, as well as with regiments.

The report of the Secretary of the Navy presents in detail the operations of that branch of the service, the activity and energy which have characterized its administration, and the results of measures to increase its efficiency and power. Such have been the additions, by construction and purchase, that it may almost be said a navy has been created and brought into service since our difficulties commenced.

Besides blockading our extensive coast, squadrons larger than ever before assembled under our flag have been put afloat and performed deeds which have increased our naval renown.

I would invite special attention to the recommendation of the Secretary for a more perfect organization of the Navy by introducing additional grades in the service.

The present organization is defective and unsatisfactory, and the suggestions submitted by the Department will, it is believed, if adopted, obviate the difficulties alluded to, promote harmony, and increase the efficiency of the Navy.

There are three vacancies on the bench of the Supreme Court—two by the decease of Justices Daniel and McLean and one by the resignation of Justice Campbell. I have so far forborne making nominations to fill these vacancies for reasons which I will now state. Two of the outgoing judges resided within the States now overrun by revolt, so that if successors were appointed in the same localities they could not now serve upon their circuits; and many of the most competent men there probably would not take the personal hazard of accepting to serve, even here, upon the Supreme bench. I have been unwilling to throw all the appointments northward, thus disabling myself from doing justice to the South on the return of peace; although I may remark that to transfer to the North one which has heretofore been in the South would not, with reference to territory and population, be unjust.

During the long and brilliant judicial career of Judge McLean his circuit grew into an empire—altogether too large for any one judge to give the courts therein more than a nominal attendance—rising in population from 1,470,018 in 1830 to 6,151,405 in 1860.

Besides this, the country generally has outgrown our present judicial system. If uniformity was at all intended, the system requires that all the States shall be accommodated with circuit courts, attended by Supreme judges, while, in fact, Wisconsin, Minnesota, Iowa, Kansas, Florida, Texas, California, and Oregon have never had any such courts. Nor can this well be remedied without a change in the system, because the adding of judges to the Supreme Court, enough for the accommodation of all parts of the country with circuit courts, would create a court altogether too numerous for a judicial body of any sort. And the evil, if it be one, will increase as new States come into the Union. Circuit courts are useful or they are not useful. If useful, no State should be denied them; if not useful, no State should have them. Let them be provided for all or abolished as to all.

Three modifications occur to me, either of which, I think, would be an improvement upon our present system. Let the Supreme Court be of convenient number in every event; then, first, let the whole country be divided into circuits of convenient size, the Supreme judges to serve in a number of them corresponding to their own number, and independent circuit judges be provided for all the rest; or, secondly, let the Supreme judges be relieved from circuit duties and circuit judges provided for all the circuits; or, thirdly, dispense with circuit courts altogether, leaving the judicial functions wholly to the district courts and an independent Supreme Court.

I respectfully recommend to the consideration of Congress the present condition of the statute laws, with the hope that Congress will be able to find an easy remedy for many of the inconveniences and evils which constantly embarrass those engaged in the practical administration of them. Since the organization of the Government Congress has enacted some 5,000 acts and joint resolutions, which fill more than 6,000 closely printed pages and are scattered through many volumes. Many of these acts have been drawn in haste and without sufficient caution, so that their provisions are often obscure in themselves or in conflict with each other, or at least so doubtful as to render it very difficult for even the best-informed persons to ascertain precisely what the statute law really is.

It seems to me very important that the statute laws should be made as plain and intelligible as possible, and be reduced to as small a compass as may consist with the fullness and precision of the will of the Legislature and the perspicuity of its language. This well done would, I think, greatly facilitate the labors of those whose duty it is to assist in the administration of the laws, and would be a lasting benefit to the people, by placing before them in a more accessible and intelligible form the laws which so deeply concern their interests and their duties.

I am informed by some whose opinions I respect that all the acts of Congress now in force and of a permanent and general nature might be revised and rewritten so as to be embraced in one volume (or at most two volumes) of ordinary and convenient size; and I respectfully recommend to Congress to consider of the subject, and if my suggestion be approved to devise such plan as to their wisdom shall seem most proper for the attainment of the end proposed.

One of the unavoidable consequences of the present insurrection is the entire suppression in many places of all the ordinary means of administering civil justice by the officers and in the forms of existing law. This is the case, in whole or in part, in all the insurgent States; and as our armies advance upon and take possession of parts of those States the practical evil becomes more apparent. There are no courts nor officers to whom the citizens of other States may apply for the enforcement of their lawful claims against citizens of the insurgent States, and there is a vast amount of debt constituting such claims. Some have estimated it as high as $200,000,000, due in large part from insurgents in open rebellion to loyal citizens who are even now making great sacrifices in the discharge of their patriotic duty to support the Government.

Under these circumstances I have been urgently solicited to establish by military power courts to administer summary justice in such cases. I have thus far declined to do it, not because I had any doubt that the end proposed—the collection of the debts—was just and right in itself, but because I have been unwilling to go beyond the pressure of necessity in the unusual exercise of power. But the powers of Congress, I suppose, are equal to the anomalous occasion, and therefore I refer the whole matter to Congress, with the hope that a plan may be devised for the administration of justice in all such parts of the insurgent States and Territories as may be under the control of this Government, whether by a voluntary return to allegiance and order or by the power of our arms; this, however, not to be a permanent institution, but a temporary substitute, and to cease as soon as the ordinary courts can be reestablished in peace.

It is important that some more convenient means should be provided, if possible, for the adjustment of claims against the Government, especially in view of their increased number by reason of the war. It is as much the duty of Government to render prompt justice against itself in favor of citizens as it is to administer the same between private individuals. The investigation and adjudication of claims in their nature belong to the judicial department. Besides, it is apparent that the attention of Congress will be more than usually engaged for some time to come with great national questions. It was intended by the organization of the Court of Claims mainly to remove this branch of business from the halls of Congress; but while the court has proved to be an effective and valuable means of investigation, it in great degree fails to effect the object of its creation for want of power to make its judgments final.

Fully aware of the delicacy, not to say the danger, of the subject, I commend to your careful consideration whether this power of making judgments final may not properly be given to the court, reserving the right of appeal on questions of law to the Supreme Court, with such other provisions as experience may have shown to be necessary.

I ask attention to the report of the Postmaster-General, the following being a summary statement of the condition of the Department:

The revenue from all sources during the fiscal year ending June 30, 1861, including the annual permanent appropriation of $700,000 for the transportation of "free mail matter," was $9,049,296.40, being about 2 per cent less than the revenue for 1860.

The expenditures were $13,606,759.11, showing a decrease of more than 8 per cent as compared with those of the previous year and leaving an excess of expenditure over the revenue for the last fiscal year of $4,557,462.71.

The gross revenue for the year ending June 30, 1863, is estimated at an increase of 4 per cent on that of 1861, making $8,683,000, to which should be added the earnings of the Department in carrying free matter, viz, $700,000, making $9,383,000.

The total expenditures for 1863 are estimated at $12,528,000, leaving an estimated deficiency of $3,145,000 to be supplied from the Treasury in addition to the permanent appropriation.

The present insurrection shows, I think, that the extension of this District across the Potomac River at the time of establishing the capital here was eminently wise, and consequently that the relinquishment of that portion of it which lies within the State of Virginia was unwise and dangerous. I submit for your consideration the expediency of regaining that part of the District and the restoration of the original boundaries thereof through negotiations with the State of Virginia.

The report of the Secretary of the Interior, with the accompanying documents, exhibits the condition of the several branches of the public business pertaining to that Department. The depressing influences of the insurrection have been specially felt in the operations of the Patent and General Land Offices. The cash receipts from the sales of public lands during the past year have exceeded the expenses of our land system only about $200,000. The sales have been entirely suspended in the Southern States, while the interruptions to the business of the country and the diversion of large numbers of men from labor to military service have obstructed settlements in the new States and Territories of the Northwest.

The receipts of the Patent Office have declined in nine months about $100,000, rendering a large reduction of the force employed necessary to make it self-sustaining.

The demands upon the Pension Office will be largely increased by the insurrection. Numerous applications for pensions, based upon the casualties of the existing war, have already been made. There is reason to believe that many who are now upon the pension rolls and in receipt of the bounty of the Government are in the ranks of the insurgent army or giving them aid and comfort. The Secretary of the Interior has directed a suspension of the payment of the pensions of such persons upon proof of their disloyalty. I recommend that Congress authorize that officer to cause the names of such persons to be stricken from the pension rolls.

The relations of the Government with the Indian tribes have been greatly disturbed by the insurrection, especially in the southern superintendency and in that of New Mexico. The Indian country south of Kansas is in the possession of insurgents from Texas and Arkansas. The agents of the United States appointed since the 4th of March for this superintendency have been unable to reach their posts, while the most of those who were in office before that time have espoused the insurrectionary cause, and assume to exercise the powers of agents by virtue of commissions from the insurrectionists. It has been stated in the public press that a portion of those Indians have been organized as a military force and are attached to the army of the insurgents. Although the Government has no official information upon this subject, letters have been written to the Commissioner of Indian Affairs by several prominent chiefs giving assurance of their loyalty to the United States and expressing a wish for the presence of Federal troops to protect them. It is believed that upon the repossession of the country by the Federal forces the Indians will readily cease all hostile demonstrations and resume their former relations to the Government.

Agriculture, confessedly the largest interest of the nation, has not a department nor a bureau, but a clerkship only, assigned to it in the Government. · While it is fortunate that this great interest is so independent in its nature as to not have demanded and extorted more from the Government, I respectfully ask Congress to consider whether something more can not be given voluntarily with general advantage.

Annual reports exhibiting the condition of our agriculture, commerce, and manufactures would present a fund of information of great practical value to the country. While I make no suggestion as to details, I venture the opinion that an agricultural and statistical bureau might profitably be organized.

The execution of the laws for the suppression of the African slave trade has been confided to the Department of the Interior. It is a subject of gratulation that the efforts which have been made for the suppression of this inhuman traffic have been recently attended with unusual success. Five vessels being fitted out for the slave trade have been seized and condemned. Two mates of vessels engaged in the trade and one person in equipping a vessel as a slaver have been convicted and subjected to the penalty of fine and imprisonment, and one captain, taken with a cargo of Africans on board his vessel, has been convicted of the highest grade of offense under our laws, the punishment of which is death.

The Territories of Colorado, Dakota, and Nevada, created by the last Congress, have been organized, and civil administration has been inaugurated therein under auspices especially gratifying when it is considered that the leaven of treason was found existing in some of these new countries when the Federal officers arrived there.

The abundant natural resources of these Territories, with the security and protection afforded by organized government, will doubtless invite to them a large immigration when peace shall restore the business of the country to its accustomed channels. I submit the resolutions of the legislature of Colorado, which evidence the patriotic spirit of the people of the Territory. So far the authority of the United States has been upheld in all the Territories, as it is hoped it will be in the future. I commend their interests and defense to the enlightened and generous care of Congress.

I recommend to the favorable consideration of Congress the interests of the District of Columbia. The insurrection has been the cause of much suffering and sacrifice to its inhabitants, and as they have no representative in Congress that body should not overlook their just claims upon the Government.

At your late session a joint resolution was adopted authorizing the President to take measures for facilitating a proper representation of the industrial interests of the United States at the exhibition of the industry of all nations to be holden at London in the year 1862. I regret to say I have been unable to give personal attention to this subject—a subject at once so interesting in itself and so extensively and intimately connected with the material prosperity of the world. Through the Secretaries of

State and of the Interior a plan or system has been devised and partly matured, and which will be laid before you.

Under and by virtue of the act of Congress entitled "An act to confiscate property used for insurrectionary purposes," approved August 6, 1861, the legal claims of certain persons to the labor and service of certain other persons have become forfeited, and numbers of the latter thus liberated are already dependent on the United States and must be provided for in some way. Besides this, it is not impossible that some of the States will pass similar enactments for their own benefit respectively, and by operation of which persons of the same class will be thrown upon them for disposal. In such case I recommend that Congress provide for accepting such persons from such States, according to some mode of valuation, in lieu, *pro tanto*, of direct taxes, or upon some other plan to be agreed on with such States respectively; that such persons, on such acceptance by the General Government, be at once deemed free, and that in any event steps be taken for colonizing both classes (or the one first mentioned if the other shall not be brought into existence) at some place or places in a climate congenial to them. It might be well to consider, too, whether the free colored people already in the United States could not, so far as individuals may desire, be included in such colonization.

To carry out the plan of colonization may involve the acquiring of territory, and also the appropriation of money beyond that to be expended in the territorial acquisition. Having practiced the acquisition of territory for nearly sixty years, the question of constitutional power to do so is no longer an open one with us. The power was questioned at first by Mr. Jefferson, who, however, in the purchase of Louisiana, yielded his scruples on the plea of great expediency. If it be said that the only legitimate object of acquiring territory is to furnish homes for white men, this measure effects that object, for the emigration of colored men leaves additional room for white men remaining or coming here. Mr. Jefferson, however, placed the importance of procuring Louisiana more on political and commercial grounds than on providing room for population.

On this whole proposition, including the appropriation of money with the acquisition of territory, does not the expediency amount to absolute necessity—that without which the Government itself can not be perpetuated?

The war continues. In considering the policy to be adopted for suppressing the insurrection I have been anxious and careful that the inevitable conflict for this purpose shall not degenerate into a violent and remorseless revolutionary struggle. I have therefore in every case thought it proper to keep the integrity of the Union prominent as the primary object of the contest on our part, leaving all questions which are not of vital military importance to the more deliberate action of the Legislature.

In the exercise of my best discretion I have adhered to the blockade of the ports held by the insurgents, instead of putting in force by proclamation the law of Congress enacted at the late session for closing those ports.

So also, obeying the dictates of prudence, as well as the obligations of law, instead of transcending I have adhered to the act of Congress to confiscate property used for insurrectionary purposes. If a new law upon the same subject shall be proposed, its propriety will be duly considered. The Union must be preserved, and hence all indispensable means must be employed. We should not be in haste to determine that radical and extreme measures, which may reach the loyal as well as the disloyal, are indispensable.

The inaugural address at the beginning of the Administration and the message to Congress at the late special session were both mainly devoted to the domestic controversy out of which the insurrection and consequent war have sprung. Nothing now occurs to add or subtract to or from the principles or general purposes stated and expressed in those documents.

The last ray of hope for preserving the Union peaceably expired at the assault upon Fort Sumter, and a general review of what has occurred since may not be unprofitable. What was painfully uncertain then is much better defined and more distinct now, and the progress of events is plainly in the right direction. The insurgents confidently claimed a strong support from north of Mason and Dixon's line, and the friends of the Union were not free from apprehension on the point. This, however, was soon settled definitely, and on the right side. South of the line noble little Delaware led off right from the first. Maryland was made to *seem* against the Union. Our soldiers were assaulted, bridges were burned, and railroads torn up within her limits, and we were many days at one time without the ability to bring a single regiment over her soil to the capital. Now her bridges and railroads are repaired and open to the Government; she already gives seven regiments to the cause of the Union, and none to the enemy; and her people, at a regular election, have sustained the Union by a larger majority and a larger aggregate vote than they ever before gave to any candidate or any question. Kentucky, too, for some time in doubt, is now decidedly and, I think, unchangeably ranged on the side of the Union. Missouri is comparatively quiet, and, I believe, can not again be overrun by the insurrectionists. These three States of Maryland, Kentucky, and Missouri, neither of which would promise a single soldier at first, have now an aggregate of not less than 40,000 in the field for the Union, while of their citizens certainly not more than a third of that number, and they of doubtful whereabouts and doubtful existence, are in arms against us. After a somewhat bloody struggle of months, winter closes on the Union people of western Virginia, leaving them masters of their own country.

An insurgent force of about 1,500, for months dominating the narrow peninsular region constituting the counties of Accomac and Northampton, and known as Eastern Shore of Virginia, together with some contiguous parts of Maryland, have laid down their arms, and the people there have renewed their allegiance to and accepted the protection of the old flag. This leaves no armed insurrectionist north of the Potomac or east of the Chesapeake.

Also we have obtained a footing at each of the isolated points on the southern coast of Hatteras, Port Royal, Tybee Island (near Savannah), and Ship Island; and we likewise have some general accounts of popular movements in behalf of the Union in North Carolina and Tennessee.

These things demonstrate that the cause of the Union is advancing steadily and certainly southward.

Since your last adjournment Lieutenant-General Scott has retired from the head of the Army. During his long life the nation has not been unmindful of his merit; yet on calling to mind how faithfully, ably, and brilliantly he has served the country, from a time far back in our history, when few of the now living had been born, and thenceforward continually, I can not but think we are still his debtors. I submit, therefore, for your consideration what further mark of recognition is due to him, and to ourselves as a grateful people.

With the retirement of General Scott came the Executive duty of appointing in his stead a General in Chief of the Army. It is a fortunate circumstance that neither in council nor country was there, so far as I know, any difference of opinion as to the proper person to be selected. The retiring chief repeatedly expressed his judgment in favor of General McClellan for the position, and in this the nation seemed to give a unanimous concurrence. The designation of General McClellan is therefore in considerable degree the selection of the country as well as of the Executive, and hence there is better reason to hope there will be given him the confidence and cordial support thus by fair implication promised, and without which he can not with so full efficiency serve the country.

It has been said that one bad general is better than two good ones, and the saying is true if taken to mean no more than that an army is better directed by a single mind, though inferior, than by two superior ones at variance and cross-purposes with each other.

And the same is true in all joint operations wherein those engaged *can* have none but a common end in view and *can* differ only as to the choice of means. In a storm at sea no one on board *can* wish the ship to sink, and yet not unfrequently all go down together because too many will direct and no single mind can be allowed to control.

It continues to develop that the insurrection is largely, if not exclusively, a war upon the first principle of popular government—the rights of the people. Conclusive evidence of this is found in the most grave and maturely considered public documents, as well as in the general tone of the insurgents. In those documents we find the abridgment of the existing right of suffrage and the denial to the people of all right to participate in the selection of public officers except the legislative boldly advocated, with labored arguments to prove that large control of the people in government is the source of all political evil. Monarchy itself is sometimes hinted at as a possible refuge from the power of the people.

In my present position I could scarcely be justified were I to omit raising a warning voice against this approach of returning despotism.

It is not needed nor fitting here that a general argument should be made in favor of popular institutions, but there is one point, with its connections, not so hackneyed as most others, to which I ask a brief attention. It is the effort to place *capital* on an equal footing with, if not above, *labor* in the structure of government. It is assumed that labor is available only in connection with capital; that nobody labors unless somebody else, owning capital, somehow by the use of it induces him to labor. This assumed, it is next considered whether it is best that capital shall *hire* laborers, and thus induce them to work by their own consent, or *buy* them and drive them to it without their consent. Having proceeded so far, it is naturally concluded that all laborers are either *hired* laborers or what we call slaves. And further, it is assumed that whoever is once a hired laborer is fixed in that condition for life.

Now there is no such relation between capital and labor as assumed, nor is there any such thing as a free man being fixed for life in the condition of a hired laborer. Both these assumptions are false, and all inferences from them are groundless.

Labor is prior to and independent of capital. Capital is only the fruit of labor, and could never have existed if labor had not first existed. Labor is the superior of capital, and deserves much the higher consideration. Capital has its rights, which are as worthy of protection as any other rights. Nor is it denied that there is, and probably always will be, a relation between labor and capital producing mutual benefits. The error is in assuming that the whole labor of community exists within that relation. A few men own capital, and that few avoid labor themselves, and with their capital hire or buy another few to labor for them. A large majority belong to neither class—neither work for others nor have others working for them. In most of the Southern States a majority of the whole people of all colors are neither slaves nor masters, while in the Northern a large majority are neither hirers nor hired. Men, with their families—wives, sons, and daughters—work for themselves on their farms, in their houses, and in their shops, taking the whole product to themselves, and asking no favors of capital on the one hand nor of hired laborers or slaves on the other. It is not forgotten that a considerable number of persons mingle their own labor with capital; that is, they labor with their own hands and also buy or hire others to labor for them; but this is only a mixed and not a distinct class. No principle stated is disturbed by the existence of this mixed class.

Again, as has already been said, there is not of necessity any such thing as the free hired laborer being fixed to that condition for life. Many independent men everywhere in these States a few years back in their lives were hired laborers. The prudent, penniless beginner in the world labors for wages awhile, saves a surplus with which to buy tools or land for himself, then labors on his own account another while, and at length hires another new beginner to help him. This is the just and generous and prosperous system which opens the way to all, gives hope to all, and consequent energy and progress and improvement of condition to all. No men living are more worthy to be trusted than those who toil up from poverty; none less inclined to take or touch aught which they have not honestly earned. Let them beware of surrendering a political power which they already possess, and which if surrendered will surely be used to close the door of advancement against such as they and to fix new disabilities and burdens upon them till all of liberty shall be lost.

From the first taking of our national census to the last are seventy years, and we find our population at the end of the period eight times as great as it was at the beginning. The increase of those other things which men deem desirable has been even greater. We thus have at one view what the popular principle, applied to Government through the machinery of the States and the Union, has produced in a given time, and also what if firmly maintained it promises for the future. There are already among us those who if the Union be preserved will live to see it contain 250,000,000. The struggle *of* to-day is not altogether *for* to-day; it is for a vast future also. With a reliance on Providence all the more firm and earnest, let us proceed in the great task which events have devolved upon us.

ABRAHAM LINCOLN.

SPECIAL MESSAGES.

WASHINGTON, *December 4, 1861.*

To the House of Representatives:

I transmit herewith a report from the Secretary of State, in reply to the resolution of the House of Representatives of the 31st July last, upon the subject of increasing and extending trade and commerce of the United States with foreign countries.

ABRAHAM LINCOLN.

WASHINGTON, *December 4, 1861.*

To the House of Representatives:

I transmit herewith a report from the Secretary of State, in reply to the resolution of the House of Representatives of the 13th July last, in relation to the correspondence between this Government and foreign nations respecting the rights of blockade, privateering, and the recognition of the so-called Confederate States.

ABRAHAM LINCOLN.

WASHINGTON, *December 5, 1861.*

To the Senate of the United States:

I transmit to the Senate, for its consideration with a view to ratification, a treaty between the United States of America and His Majesty the King of Hanover, concerning the abolition of the Stade or Brunshausen dues, signed at Berlin on the 6th November, 1861.

ABRAHAM LINCOLN.

WASHINGTON, *December 9, 1861.*

To the House of Representatives:

I transmit herewith a report from the Secretary of State, in reply to the resolution of the House of the 4th instant, relative to the intervention of certain European powers in the affairs of Mexico.

ABRAHAM LINCOLN.

EXECUTIVE MANSION,
Washington, December 14, 1861.

To the Senate of the United States:

In compliance with the resolution of your honorable body "that the President be requested to furnish to the Senate copies of the charges, testimony, and finding of the recent court of inquiry in the case of Colonel Dixon S. Miles, of the United States Army," I have the honor to transmit herewith the copies desired, which have been procured from the War Department.

ABRAHAM LINCOLN.

WASHINGTON, *December 16, 1861.*

To the Senate of the United States:

I submit to the Senate, for consideration with a view to ratification, the amendments introduced by the Constituent National Assembly of Bolivia in its decree of ratification into the treaty of peace, friendship, commerce, and navigation concluded with that Republic on the 13th of May, 1858, an official translation of which decree accompanies this message, with the original treaty. As the time within which the exchange of ratifications should be effected is limited, I recommend, in view of the delay which must necessarily occur and the difficulty of reaching the seat of Government of that Republic, that the time within which such exchange shall take place be extended in the following terms: "Within such period as may be mutually convenient to both Governments."

ABRAHAM LINCOLN.

WASHINGTON, *December 17, 1861.*

To the Senate and House of Representatives:

I transmit to the Senate and House of Representatives copies of the correspondence between the Secretary of State, Secretary of War, and the governor of the State of Maine on the subject of the fortification of the seacoast and Lakes.

ABRAHAM LINCOLN.

WASHINGTON, *December 17, 1861.*

To the Senate of the United States:

I transmit to the Senate, for its advice, a copy of a draft for a convention with the Republic of Mexico, proposed to the Government of that Republic by Mr. Corwin, the minister of the United States accredited to that Government, together with the correspondence relating to it.

As the subject is of momentous interest to the two Governments at this juncture, the early consideration of it by the Senate is very desirable.

ABRAHAM LINCOLN.

WASHINGTON, *December 20, 1861.*

To the Senate and House of Representatives:

I transmit to Congress a letter from the secretary of the executive committee of the commission appointed to represent the interests of those American citizens who may desire to become exhibitors at the industrial exhibition to be held in London in 1862, and a memorial of that commission, with a report of the executive committee thereof and copies of circulars announcing the decisions of Her Majesty's commissioners in London, giving directions to be observed in regard to articles intended for exhibition, and also of circular forms of application, demands for space, approvals, etc., according to the rules prescribed by the British commissioners.

As these papers fully set forth the requirements necessary to enable those citizens of the United States who may wish to become exhibitors to avail themselves of the privileges of the exhibition, I commend them to your early consideration, especially in view of the near approach of the time when the exhibition will begin.

ABRAHAM LINCOLN.

WASHINGTON, *December 23, 1861.*

To the House of Representatives:

In compliance with the resolution of the House of Representatives of the 13th July last, requesting information respecting the Asiatic cooly trade, I transmit a report from the Secretary of State, with the documents which accompanied it.

ABRAHAM LINCOLN.

WASHINGTON, *December 30, 1861.*

To the Senate and House of Representatives:

I transmit to Congress a correspondence which has taken place between the Secretary of State and authorities of Great Britain and France on the subject of the recent removal of certain citizens* of the United States from the British mail steamer *Trent* by order of Captain Wilkes, in command of the United States war steamer *San Jacinto.*

ABRAHAM LINCOLN.

WASHINGTON, *January 2, 1862.*

To the Senate and House of Representatives:

I transmit to Congress a copy of a letter to the Secretary of State from James R. Partridge, secretary to the executive committee to the industrial exhibition to be held in London in the course of the present year, and a copy of the correspondence to which it refers, relative to a vessel for the purpose of taking such articles as persons in this country may wish to exhibit on that occasion. As it appears that no naval vessel can be spared for the purpose, I recommend that authority be given to charter a suitable merchant vessel, in order that facilities similar to those afforded by the Government for the exhibition of 1851 may also be extended to those citizens of the United States who may desire to contribute to the exhibition of this year.

ABRAHAM LINCOLN.

WASHINGTON, D. C., *January 3, 1862.*

To the Senate of the United States:

I transmit to the Senate, for its constitutional action thereon, a treaty concluded on the 15th November, 1861, between William W. Ross, agent on the part of the United States, and the chiefs and headmen of the tribe of Pottawatomie Indians, with accompanying communications from the Secretary of the Interior and Commissioner of Indian Affairs, the latter of which proposes certain modifications of said treaty, which are also referred for the consideration of the Senate.

ABRAHAM LINCOLN.

WASHINGTON, *January 10, 1862.*

To the Senate and House of Representatives:

I transmit to Congress a translation of an instruction to the minister of His Majesty the Emperor of Austria accredited to this Government, and a copy of a note to that minister from the Secretary of State, relative to the questions involved in the taking from the British steamer

* James M. Mason and John Slidell, Confederate envoys to England and France, respectively, and two others.

Trent of certain citizens of the United States by order of Captain Wilkes, of the United States Navy. This correspondence may be considered as a sequel to that previously communicated to Congress relating to the same subject.

ABRAHAM LINCOLN.

WASHINGTON, *January 17, 1862.*

To the Senate and House of Representatives:

I transmit to Congress a translation of an instruction to the minister of His Majesty the King of Prussia accredited to this Government, and a copy of a note to that minister from the Secretary of State, relating to the capture and detention of certain citizens of the United States, passengers on board the British steamer *Trent,* by order of Captain Wilkes, of the United States Navy.

ABRAHAM LINCOLN.

WASHINGTON, D. C., *January 17, 1862.*

To the Senate of the United States:

I transmit herewith, for the consideration of the Senate, a petition of certain members of the Pottawatomie tribe of Indians, complaining of the treaty made by W. W. Ross on the 15th November last with that tribe, which treaty was laid before the Senate for its constitutional action in my communication to that body dated the 6th [3d] instant.

A letter of the 16th instant from the Secretary of the Interior, inclosing a report of the Commissioner of Indian Affairs dated the 15th instant, in relation to the subject, is also herewith transmitted.

ABRAHAM LINCOLN.

WASHINGTON, D. C., *January, 1862.*

To the Senate of the United States:

I transmit herewith, for the constitutional action of the Senate, articles of agreement and convention concluded at Niobrara, Nebraska Territory, on the 14th day of November, 1860, between J. Shaw Gregory, agent on the part of the United States, and the chiefs and headmen of the Poncas tribe of Indians, being supplementary to the treaty with said tribe made on the 12th day of March, 1858.

I also transmit a letter, dated the 4th instant, from the Secretary of the Interior, inclosing a copy of a report of the Commissioner of Indian Affairs of the 20th September, 1861, in relation to the subject.

ABRAHAM LINCOLN.

WASHINGTON, *January 24, 1862.*

To the Senate and House of Representatives:

I submit to Congress the accompanying copy of a correspondence between the Secretary of State, the Spanish minister, and the Secretary of the Navy, concerning the case of the bark *Providencia*, a Spanish vessel seized on her voyage from Havana to New York by a steamer of the United States Blockading Squadron and subsequently released. I recommend the appropriation of the amount of the award of the referee.

ABRAHAM LINCOLN.

WASHINGTON, *January 24, 1862.*

To the Senate of the United States:

I lay before the Senate a dispatch which has just been received from Mr. Corwin, our minister to Mexico. It communicates important information concerning the war which is waged against Mexico by the combined powers of Spain, France, and Great Britain.

Mr. Corwin asks instructions by which to regulate his proceedings so as to save our national interests in the case of an adjustment of the difficulties between the belligerents. I have heretofore submitted to the Senate a request for its advice upon the question pending by treaty for making a loan to Mexico, which Mr. Corwin thinks will in any case be expedient. It seems to be my duty now to solicit an early action of the Senate upon the subject, to the end that I may cause such instructions to be given to Mr. Corwin as will enable him to act in the manner which, while it will most carefully guard the interests of our country, will at the same time be most beneficial to Mexico.

ABRAHAM LINCOLN.

WASHINGTON, *January 28, 1862.*

To the Senate of the United States:

I submit to the Senate, for its consideration with a view to ratification, a treaty of extradition concluded by Mr. Corwin with the Mexican Government on the 11th of December last.

I also submit a postal convention concluded by that gentleman at the same time, and a copy of his dispatch of the 24th of the same month explanatory of the provisions of both these instruments, and the reasons for the nonratification by Mexico of the postal convention concluded in this city on the 31st of July last and approved by the Senate on the 6th of August.

A copy of a letter from the Postmaster-General to the Secretary of State in relation to Mr. Corwin's postal convention is also herewith communicated. The advice of the Senate as to the expediency of accepting that convention as a substitute for the one of the 31st of July last is requested.

ABRAHAM LINCOLN.

WASHINGTON, *January 31, 1862.*

To the Senate and House of Representatives:

As a sequel to the correspondence on the subject previously communicated, I transmit to Congress extracts from a dispatch of the 20th ultimo from Mr. Adams, United States minister at London, to the Secretary of State, and a copy of an instruction from Earl Russell to Lord Lyons of the 10th instant, relative to the removal of certain citizens of the United States from the British mail steamer *Trent* by order of the commander of the United States war steamer *San Jacinto.*

                                        ABRAHAM LINCOLN.

                              WASHINGTON CITY, *February 4, 1862.*
To the Senate of the United States:

The third section of the "Act further to promote the efficiency of the Navy," approved December 21, 1861, provides—

That the President of the United States, by and with the advice and consent of the Senate, shall have the authority to detail from the retired list of the Navy for the command of squadrons and single ships such officers as he may believe that the good of the service requires to be thus placed in command; and such officers may, if upon the recommendation of the President of the United States they shall receive a vote of thanks of Congress for their services and gallantry in action against an enemy, be restored to the active list, and not otherwise.

In conformity with this law, Captain Samuel F. Du Pont, of the Navy was nominated to the Senate for continuance as the flag-officer in command of the squadron which recently rendered such important service to the Union in the expedition to the coast of South Carolina.

Believing that no occasion could arise which would more fully correspond with the intention of the law or be more pregnant with happy influence as an example, I cordially recommend that Captain Samuel F. Du Pont receive a vote of thanks of Congress for his services and gallantry displayed in the capture of Forts Walker and Beauregard, commanding the entrance of Port Royal Harbor, on the 7th of November, 1861.

                                        ABRAHAM LINCOLN.

                                 WASHINGTON, *February 7, 1862.*
To the Senate of the United States:

In answer to the resolution of the Senate of the 5th instant, requesting a communication of any recent correspondence relating to the presentation of American citizens to the Court of France, I transmit a copy of a dispatch of the 14th ultimo from the United States minister at Paris to the Secretary of State and of an instruction of Mr. Seward to Mr. Dayton of the 3d instant.

                                        ABRAHAM LINCOLN.

                                WASHINGTON, *February 12, 1862.*
To the Senate and House of Representatives:

I transmit to Congress a copy of a special treaty between the United States and His Majesty the King of Hanover for the abolition of the Stade dues, which was signed at Berlin on the 6th of November last.   In this treaty, already approved by the Senate and ratified on the part of the United States, it is stipulated that the sums specified in Articles III and IV to be paid to the Hanoverian Government shall be paid at Berlin on the day of the exchange of ratifications. I therefore recommend that seasonable provision be made to enable the Executive to carry this stipulation into effect.

ABRAHAM LINCOLN.

WASHINGTON CITY, *February 15, 1862.*

To the Senate and House of Representatives of the United States:

The third section of the "Act further to promote the efficiency of the Navy," approved December 21, 1861, provides—

That the President of the United States, by and with the advice and consent of the Senate, shall have the authority to detail from the retired list of the Navy for the command of squadrons and single ships such officers as he may believe that the good of the service requires to be thus placed in command; and such officers may, if upon the recommendation of the President of the United States they shall receive a vote of thanks of Congress for their services and gallantry in action against an enemy, be restored to the active list, and not otherwise.

In conformity with this law, Captain Louis M. Goldsborough, of the Navy, was nominated to the Senate for continuance as the flag-officer in command of the North Atlantic Blockading Squadron, which recently rendered such important service to the Union in the expedition to the coast of North Carolina.

Believing that no occasion could arise which would more fully correspond with the intention of the law or be more pregnant with happy influence as an example, I cordially recommend that Captain Louis M. Goldsborough receive a vote of thanks of Congress for his services and gallantry displayed in the combined attack of the forces commanded by him and Brigadier-General Burnside in the capture of Roanoke Island and the destruction of rebel gunboats on the 7th, 8th, and 10th of February, 1862.

ABRAHAM LINCOLN.

WASHINGTON, *February 21, 1862.*

To the Senate and House of Representatives:

The President of the United States was last evening plunged into affliction by the death of a beloved child. The heads of the Departments, in consideration of this distressing event, have thought it would be agreeable to Congress and to the American people that the official and private buildings occupied by them should not be illuminated in the evening of the 22d instant.

WILLIAM H. SEWARD.　CALEB B. SMITH.
S. P. CHASE.　M. BLAIR.
EDWIN M. STANTON.　EDWARD BATES.
GIDEON WELLES.

WASHINGTON, *February 25, 1862.*

To the Senate and House of Representatives:

I transmit to Congress a copy of an instruction from Prince Gortchakoff to Mr. De Stoeckl, the minister of His Imperial Majesty the Emperor of Russia accredited to this Government, and of a note of the Secretary of State to the latter, relative to the adjustment of the question between the United States and Great Britain growing out of the removal of certain of our citizens from the British mail steamer *Trent* by order of the commander of the United States war steamer *San Jacinto.*

ABRAHAM LINCOLN.

WASHINGTON, *February 26, 1862.*

To the Senate and House of Representatives:

In transmitting to Congress the accompanying copy of two letters, bearing date the 14th of February, 1861, from His Majesty the Major King of Siam to the President of the United States, and of the President's answer thereto, I submit for their consideration the question as to the proper place of deposit of the gifts received with the royal letters referred to.

ABRAHAM LINCOLN.

WASHINGTON, *February 27, 1862.*

To the Senate of the United States:

Lieutenant-General Scott has advised me that while he would cheerfully accept a commission as additional minister to Mexico, with a view to promote the interests of the United States and of peace, yet his infirmities are such that he could not be able to reach the capital of that country by any existing mode of travel, and he therefore deems it his duty to decline the important mission I had proposed for him. For this reason I withdraw the nomination in this respect heretofore submitted to the Senate. It is hardly necessary to add that the nomination was made without any knowledge of it on his part.

ABRAHAM LINCOLN.

WASHINGTON, *March 3, 1862.*

To the Senate and House of Representatives:

I transmit to Congress a copy of a dispatch to the Secretary of State from the minister resident of the United States at Lisbon, concerning recent measures which have been adopted by the Government of Portugal intended to encourage the growth and to enlarge the area of the culture of cotton in its African possessions.

ABRAHAM LINCOLN.

WASHINGTON, *March 3, 1862.*

To the Senate and House of Representatives:

I transmit to Congress a translation of an instruction to the minister of His Majesty the King of Italy accredited to this Government, and a copy of a note to that minister from the Secretary of State, relating to the settlement of the question arising out of the capture and detention of certain citizens of the United States, passengers on board the British steamer *Trent*, by order of Captain Wilkes, of the United States Navy.

ABRAHAM LINCOLN.

WASHINGTON, *March 3, 1862.*

To the Senate of the United States:

I transmit to the Senate a translation of a note addressed to the Secretary of State on the 1st instant by General P. A. Herran, envoy extraordinary and minister plenipotentiary of the Granadian Confederation, with a translation of the communication accompanying that note from the special commissioner of that Republic, together with a copy of a letter from the special commissioner of the United States of the 26th ultimo, under the convention of the 10th September, 1857, setting forth the impracticability of disposing of the cases submitted to the joint commission now in session under the convention within the period prescribed therein.

I recommend, therefore, that the Senate consent to the extension of time for —— days from and after the expiration of the time limited by the convention.

ABRAHAM LINCOLN.

WASHINGTON, *March 3, 1862.*

To the House of Representatives of the United States:

I transmit herewith a communication* of the Secretary of War, inclosing a report of the Adjutant-General, in answer to a resolution of the House of Representatives of the 22d of January, 1862.

ABRAHAM LINCOLN.

WASHINGTON, *March 5, 1862.*

To the Senate of the United States:

I submit to the Senate, for its consideration, a copy of a message addressed to that body by my immediate predecessor on the 12th February, 1861, relating to the award made by the joint commission under the convention between the United States and Paraguay of the 4th February, 1859, together with the original "journal of the proceedings" of the commission and a printed copy of the "statements and arguments—and for

---

* Relating to assignment of officers of the Army to duty.

the Republic," and request the advice of the Senate as to the final acquiescence in or rejection of the award of the commissioner by the Government of the United States. As the "journal" is an original document, pertaining to the archives of the Department of State, it is proper, when the Senate shall have arrived at a conclusion on the subject, that the volume be returned to the custody of the Secretary of State.

ABRAHAM LINCOLN.

MARCH 6, 1862.

Fellow-Citizens of the Senate and House of Representatives:

I recommend the adoption of a joint resolution by your honorable bodies, which shall be substantially as follows:

Resolved, That the United States ought to cooperate with any State which may adopt gradual abolishment of slavery, giving to such State pecuniary aid, to be used by such State, in its discretion, to compensate for the inconveniences, public and private, produced by such change of system.

If the proposition contained in the resolution does not meet the approval of Congress and the country, there is the end; but if it does command such approval, I deem it of importance that the States and people immediately interested should be at once distinctly notified of the fact, so that they may begin to consider whether to accept or reject it. The Federal Government would find its highest interest in such a measure, as one of the most efficient means of self-preservation. The leaders of the existing insurrection entertain the hope that this Government will ultimately be forced to acknowledge the independence of some part of the disaffected region, and that all the slave States north of such part will then say, "The Union for which we have struggled being already gone, we now choose to go with the Southern section." To deprive them of this hope substantially ends the rebellion, and the initiation of emancipation completely deprives them of it as to all the States initiating it. The point is not that *all* the States tolerating slavery would very soon, if at all, initiate emancipation; but that while the offer is equally made to all, the more northern shall by such initiation make it certain to the more southern that in no event will the former ever join the latter in their proposed confederacy. I say "initiation" because, in my judgment, gradual and not sudden emancipation is better for all. In the mere financial or pecuniary view any member of Congress with the census tables and Treasury reports before him can readily see for himself how very soon the current expenditures of this war would purchase, at fair valuation, all the slaves in any named State. Such a proposition on the part of the General Government sets up no claim of a right by Federal authority to interfere with slavery within State limits, referring, as it does, the absolute control of the subject in each case to the State and its people immediately interested. It is proposed as a matter of perfectly free choice with them.

In the annual message last December I thought fit to say "the Union must be preserved, and hence all indispensable means must be employed.'' I said this not hastily, but deliberately. War has been made and continues to be an indispensable means to this end. A practical reacknowledgment of the national authority would render the war unnecessary, and it would at once cease. If, however, resistance continues, the war must also continue; and it is impossible to foresee all the incidents which may attend and all the ruin which may follow it. Such as may seem indispensable or may obviously promise great efficiency toward ending the struggle must and will come.

The proposition now made (though an offer only), I hope it may be esteemed no offense to ask whether the pecuniary consideration tendered would not be of more value to the States and private persons concerned than are the institution and property in it in the present aspect of affairs.

While it is true that the adoption of the proposed resolution would be merely initiatory, and not within itself a practical measure, it is recommended in the hope that it would soon lead to important practical results. In full view of my great responsibility to my God and to my country, I earnestly beg the attention of Congress and the people to the subject.

ABRAHAM LINCOLN.

WASHINGTON, D. C., *March 7, 1862.*
To the Senate of the United States:

I transmit herewith, for the constitutional action of the Senate thereon, a treaty concluded at Paola, Kans., on the 18th day of August, between Seth Clover, commissioner on the part of the United States, and the delegates of the united tribes of Kaskaskia and Peoria, Piankeshaw, and Wea Indians.

I also transmit a communication of the Secretary of the Interior of the 6th instant and accompanying papers from the Acting Commissioner of Indian Affairs, in relation to the subject.

ABRAHAM LINCOLN.

WASHINGTON, *March 12, 1862.*
To the Senate of the United States:

In compliance with the resolution of the Senate of the 11th instant, requesting ''a copy of any correspondence on the records or files of the Department of State in regard to railway systems in Europe,'' I transmit a report from the Secretary of State and the papers by which it was accompanied.

ABRAHAM LINCOLN.

WASHINGTON, *March 14, 1862.*
To the Senate of the United States:

With reference to my recent message on the subject of claims of citizens of the United States on the Government of Paraguay, I transmit a copy of three memorials of the claimants and of their closing arguments in the case, together with extracts from a dispatch from Mr. Bowlin, the late commissioner of the United States to that country. These extracts show that President Lopez offered and expected to pay a large sum of money as a compromise of the claims.

ABRAHAM LINCOLN.

WASHINGTON, *March 14, 1862.*

To the Senate and House of Representatives:

I submit to Congress the accompanying copy of a correspondence between the Secretary of State, the Danish chargé d'affaires, and the Secretary of the Navy, concerning the case of the bark *Jorgen Lorentzen*, a Danish vessel seized on her voyage from Rio Janeiro to Havana by the United States ship *Morning Light* and subsequently released. I recommend the appropriation of the amount of the award of the referees.

ABRAHAM LINCOLN.

WASHINGTON CITY, *March 20, 1862.*

To the Senate and House of Representatives:

The third section of the "Act further to promote the efficiency of the Navy," approved December 21, 1861, provides—

That the President of the United States, by and with the advice and consent of the Senate, shall have the authority to detail from the retired list of the Navy for the command of squadrons and single ships such officers as he may believe that the good of the service requires to be thus placed in command; and such officers may, if upon the recommendation of the President of the United States they shall receive a vote of thanks of Congress for their services and gallantry in action against an enemy, be restored to the active list, and not otherwise.

In conformity with this law, Captain Samuel F. Du Pont, of the Navy, was nominated to the Senate for continuance as the flag-officer in command of the squadron which recently rendered such important service to the Union in the expedition to the coasts of South Carolina, Georgia, and Florida.

Believing that no occasion could arise which would more fully correspond with the intention of the law or be more pregnant with happy influence as an example, I cordially recommend that Captain Samuel F. Du Pont receive a vote of thanks of Congress for his service and gallantry displayed in the capture since the 21st December, 1861, of various points on the coasts of Georgia and Florida, particularly Brunswick, Cumberland Island and Sound, Amelia Island, the towns of St. Marys, St. Augustine, and Jacksonville and Fernandina.

ABRAHAM LINCOLN.

WASHINGTON, *March 26, 1862.*

To the Senate and House of Representatives:

I transmit a copy of a communication* of the 21st of December last addressed to the Secretary of State by the governor of the Territory of Nevada, and commend to the particular attention of Congress those parts of it which show that further legislation is desirable for the public welfare in that quarter. ABRAHAM LINCOLN.

WASHINGTON, *March 31, 1862.*

To the Senate of the United States:

I transmit to the Senate, for its consideration with a view to ratification, a treaty of commerce and navigation between the United States and the Ottoman Empire, signed at Constantinople on the 25th of last month. Extracts from a dispatch of the same date, upon the subject of the treaty, from Mr. Morris, the United States minister at Constantinople, to the Secretary of State, are also herewith communicated.

It will be noticed that the exchange of ratifications is to take place within three months from the date of the instrument. This renders it desirable that the Senate should decide in regard to it as soon as this may be convenient, for if that decision be favorable the ratifications of this Government must reach Constantinople prior to the expiration of the three months adverted to. ABRAHAM LINCOLN.

WASHINGTON, *April 5, 1862.*

To the House of Representatives:

In compliance with the resolution of the House of Representatives of yesterday, requesting any information which may have been received at the Department of State showing the system of revenue and finance now existing in any foreign country, I transmit a copy of a recent dispatch from Mr. Pike, the United States minister at The Hague. This is understood to be the only information on the subject of the resolution recently received which has not been made public. ABRAHAM LINCOLN.

WASHINGTON, *April 10, 1862.*

To the Senate of the United States:

I transmit to the Senate, for its consideration with a view to ratification, a treaty between the United States and Her Britannic Majesty for the suppression of the slave trade. A copy of the correspondence between the Secretary of State and Lord Lyons on the subject of the treaty is also herewith transmitted. ABRAHAM LINCOLN.

*Containing a narrative of incidents pertaining to the government of the Territory of Nevada.

WASHINGTON, *April 14, 1862.*

To the House of Representatives:

In compliance with the resolution of the House of Representatives of the 3d ultimo, requesting information in regard to the present condition of Mexico, I transmit a report from the Secretary of State and the documents by which it was accompanied.

ABRAHAM LINCOLN.

WASHINGTON, *April 15, 1862.*

To the Senate of the United States:

On the 26th of June, 1860, the Senate approved of the treaty of friendship and commerce between the United States and Nicaragua, signed on the 16th of March, 1859, with certain amendments.

On the next day, namely, June 27, 1860, the Senate adopted a resolution extending the period for the exchange of the ratifications of the treaty for six months from that date; that is, until the 27th of December, 1860.

Although the amendments of the Senate were immediately transmitted to our minister in Nicaragua for submission to the Government of that Republic, he failed, notwithstanding earnest efforts, to induce that Government to call an extra session of Congress to take into consideration the amendments of the Senate of the United States within the supplementary time named in the resolution of June 27, 1860, for the exchange of ratifications.

It was not until the 25th of March, 1861, nearly three months after the expiration of the six months extended by the Senate resolution, that the Congress of Nicaragua acted favorably upon the amendments of the Senate of the United States.

A translation of the decree of the Nicaraguan Government approving the treaty as amended, with an additional amendment, is herewith inclosed.

It will be perceived that while the ratification of Nicaragua recites literally the second amendment of the Senate and accepts it with an additional clause, it does not in explicit terms accept the first amendment of the Senate, striking out the last clause of the sixteenth article.

That amendment is of so much importance that the adoption or rejection of it by the Government of Nicaragua should not be left to construction or inference.

The final amendment of that Government properly extended the time of exchanging ratifications for an additional twelve months. That time has expired. For obvious reasons connected with our internal affairs, the subject has not sooner been submitted to the Senate, but the treaty is now laid before that body, with this brief historical sketch and the decree of the Nicaraguan Government, for such further advice as may be deemed necessary and proper in regard to the acceptance or rejection of the amendments of Nicaragua.

ABRAHAM LINCOLN.

WASHINGTON, *April 15, 1862.*

To the Senate of the United States:

In consequence of the delay attending the approval by the Senate of the extradition treaty with Mexico signed on the 11th December last, it is impossible to effect the exchange of ratifications of that and the postal convention of the same date within the period assigned by those instruments.

I recommend, therefore, the passage of a resolution at the earliest practicable moment extending the time specified in the eighth article of the extradition treaty and in the twelfth article of the postal convention for the exchange of ratifications for sixty days from and after the 11th June next, the date of the expiration of the period named for that purpose in both instruments.

ABRAHAM LINCOLN.

WASHINGTON, D. C., *April 15, 1862.*

To the Senate of the United States:

I transmit herewith, for the consideration and such constitutional action as the Senate may deem proper to take, a treaty negotiated on the 6th March, 1861, between late Agent Vanderslice, on the part of the United States, and certain delegates of the Sac and Fox of the Missouri and the Iowa tribes of Indians; also certain petitions of said tribes, praying that the treaty may be ratified with an amendment as set forth in said petitions. A letter of the Secretary of the Interior, with a report of the Commissioner of Indian Affairs and letter of the present agent of the Indians, accompany the treaty and petitions.

ABRAHAM LINCOLN.

APRIL 16, 1862.

Fellow-Citizens of the Senate and House of Representatives:

The act entitled "An act for the release of certain persons held to service or labor in the District of Columbia" has this day been approved and signed.

I have never doubted the constitutional authority of Congress to abolish slavery in this District, and I have ever desired to see the national capital freed from the institution in some satisfactory way. Hence there has never been in my mind any question upon the subject except the one of expediency, arising in view of all the circumstances. If there be matters within and about this act which might have taken a course or shape more satisfactory to my judgment, I do not attempt to specify them. I am gratified that the two principles of compensation and colonization are both recognized and practically applied in the act.

In the matter of compensation, it is provided that claims may be presented within ninety days from the passage of the act, "but not thereafter;" and there is no saving for minors, femes covert, insane or absent persons. I presume this is an omission by mere oversight, and I recommend that it be supplied by an amendatory or supplemental act.

ABRAHAM LINCOLN.

WASHINGTON, *April 18, 1862.*

To the Senate and House of Representatives:

I transmit to Congress a copy of a correspondence between the Secretary of State and Benjamin E. Brewster, of Philadelphia, relative to the arrest in that city of Simon Cameron, late Secretary of War, at the suit of Pierce Butler, for trespass *vi et armis*, assault and battery, and false imprisonment.

ABRAHAM LINCOLN.

EXECUTIVE MANSION,
Washington, April 24, 1862.

To the Senate of the United States:

In obedience to your resolution of the 17th instant, I herewith communicate the testimony and judgment of the recent naval court of inquiry in the case of Lieutenant Charles E. Fleming, of the United States Navy; also the testimony and finding of the naval retiring board in the case of the said Lieutenant Fleming.

I have the honor to state that the judgment and finding aforesaid have not been approved by me.

ABRAHAM LINCOLN.

WASHINGTON, *April 26, 1862.*

To the House of Representatives:

In compliance with the resolution of the House of Representatives of the 24th of February last, requesting information in regard to insurgent privateers in foreign ports, I transmit a report from the Secretary of State and the documents by which it was accompanied.

ABRAHAM LINCOLN.

EXECUTIVE MANSION,
Washington, May 1, 1862.

To the Senate of the United States:

In answer to the resolution of the Senate in relation to Brigadier-General Stone, I have the honor to state that he was arrested and imprisoned under my general authority, and upon evidence which, whether he be guilty or innocent, required, as appears to me, such proceedings to be had against him for the public safety. I deem it incompatible with the public interest, as also, perhaps, unjust to General Stone, to make a more particular statement of the evidence.

He has not been tried because in the state of military operations at the time of his arrest and since the officers to constitute a court-martial and for witnesses could not be withdrawn from duty without serious injury to the service. He will be allowed a trial without any unnecessary delay, the charges and specifications will be furnished him in due season, and every facility for his defense will be afforded him by the War Department.

ABRAHAM LINCOLN.

EXECUTIVE MANSION,
Washington, May 1, 1862.

To the Senate of the United States:

In accordance with the suggestion of the Secretary of the Treasury contained in the accompanying letter, I have the honor to transmit the inclosed petition and report thereon of the Third Auditor for the consideration of Congress.

ABRAHAM LINCOLN.

WASHINGTON, D. C., *May 14, 1862.*

To the Senate and House of Representatives:

The third section of the "Act further to promote the efficiency of the Navy," approved 21st of December, 1861, provides—

That the President of the United States, by and with the advice and consent of the Senate, shall have the authority to detail from the retired list of the Navy for the command of squadrons and single ships such officers as he may believe that the good of the service requires to be thus placed in command; and such officers may, if upon the recommendation of the President of the United States they shall receive a vote of thanks of Congress for their services and gallantry in action against an enemy, be restored to the active list, and not otherwise.

In conformity with this law, Captain David G. Farragut was nominated to the Senate for continuance as the flag-officer in command of the squadron which recently rendered such important service to the Union by his successful operations on the Lower Mississippi and capture of New Orleans.

Believing that no occasion could arise which would more fully correspond with the intention of the law or be more pregnant with happy influence as an example, I cordially recommend that Captain D. G. Farragut receive a vote of thanks of Congress for his services and gallantry displayed in the capture since 21st December, 1861, of Forts Jackson and St. Philip, city of New Orleans, and the destruction of various rebel gunboats, rams, etc.

ABRAHAM LINCOLN.

WASHINGTON, D. C., *May 14, 1862.*

To the Senate and House of Representatives:

I submit herewith a list of naval officers who commanded vessels engaged in the recent brilliant operations of the squadron commanded by Flag-Officer Farragut, which led to the capture of Forts Jackson and St. Philip, city of New Orleans, and the destruction of rebel gunboats, rams, etc., in April, 1862. For their services and gallantry on those occasions I cordially recommend that they should by name receive a vote of thanks of Congress.

LIST.

Captain Theodorus Bailey.
Captain Henry W. Morris.
Captain Thomas T. Craven.
Commander Henry H. Bell.
Commander Samuel Phillips Lee.
Commander Samuel Swartwout.
Commander Melancton Smith.
Commander Charles Stewart Boggs.
Commander John De Camp.
Commander James Alden.
Commander David D. Porter.
Commander Richard Wainwright.
Commander William B. Renshaw.
Lieutenant Commanding Abram D. Harrell.
Lieutenant Commanding Edward Donaldson.
Lieutenant Commanding George H. Preble.
Lieutenant Commanding Edward T. Nichols.
Lieutenant Commanding Jonathan M. Wainwright.
Lieutenant Commanding John Guest.
Lieutenant Commanding Charles H. B. Caldwell.
Lieutenant Commanding Napoleon B. Harrison.
Lieutenant Commanding Albert N. Smith.
Lieutenant Commanding Pierce Crosby.
Lieutenant Commanding George M. Ransom.
Lieutenant Commanding Watson Smith.
Lieutenant Commanding John H. Russell.
Lieutenant Commanding Walter W. Queen.
Lieutenant Commanding K. Randolph Breese.
Acting Lieutenant Commanding Selim E. Woodworth.
Acting Lieutenant Commanding Charles H. Baldwin.

ABRAHAM LINCOLN.

EXECUTIVE OFFICE, *May, 1862.*

To the Senate of the United States:

I transmit herewith, for the constitutional action of the Senate, a treaty negotiated on the 13th of March, 1862, between H. W. Farnsworth, a commissioner on the part of the United States, and the authorized representatives of the Kansas tribe of Indians.

A communication from the Secretary of the Interior, together with a letter of the Commissioner of Indian Affairs, suggesting certain amendments to the treaty and inclosing papers relating thereto, are also transmitted.

ABRAHAM LINCOLN.

WASHINGTON, *May 21, 1862.*

To the Senate:

In answer to the resolution of the Senate of the 14th instant, requesting information in regard to arrests in the State of Kentucky, I transmit a report from the Secretary of War, to whom the resolution was referred.

ABRAHAM LINCOLN.

WASHINGTON, *May 22, 1862.*

To the House of Representatives:

In compliance with the resolution of the House of Representatives of the 20th instant, requesting information in regard to the indemnity obtained by the consul-general of the United States at Alexandria, Egypt, for the maltreatment of Faris-El-Hakim, an agent in the employ of the American missionaries in that country, I transmit a report from the Secretary of State and the documents by which it was accompanied.

ABRAHAM LINCOLN.

WASHINGTON, *May 23, 1862.*

To the House of Representatives:

I transmit a report from the Secretary of State, in answer to the resolution of the House of Representatives of the 22d instant, calling for further correspondence relative to Mexican affairs.

ABRAHAM LINCOLN.

[The same message was sent to the Senate, in answer to a resolution of that body.]

WASHINGTON, *May 26, 1862.*

To the Senate and House of Representatives:

The insurrection which is yet existing in the United States and aims at the overthrow of the Federal Constitution and the Union was clandestinely prepared during the winter of 1860 and 1861, and assumed an open organization in the form of a treasonable provisional government at Montgomery, in Alabama, on the 18th day of February, 1861. On the 12th day of April, 1861, the insurgents committed the flagrant act of civil war by the bombardment and capture of Fort Sumter, which cut off the hope of immediate conciliation. Immediately afterwards all the roads and avenues to this city were obstructed, and the capital was put into the condition of a siege. The mails in every direction were stopped, and the lines of telegraph cut off by the insurgents, and military and naval forces which had been called out by the Government for the defense of Washington were prevented from reaching the city by organized and combined treasonable resistance in the State of Maryland. There was no adequate and effective organization for the public defense.   Congress had indefinitely adjourned.   There was no time to convene them. It became necessary for me to choose whether, using only the existing means, agencies, and processes which Congress had provided, I should let the Government fall at once into ruin or whether, availing myself of the broader powers conferred by the Constitution in cases of insurrection, I would make an effort to save it, with all its blessings, for the present age and for posterity.

I thereupon summoned my constitutional advisers, the heads of all the Departments, to meet on Sunday, the 20th day of April, 1861, at the office of the Navy Department, and then and there, with their unanimous concurrence, I directed that an armed revenue cutter should proceed to sea to afford protection to the commercial marine, and especially the California treasure ships then on their way to this coast.   I also directed the commandant of the navy-yard at Boston to purchase or charter and arm as quickly as possible five steamships for purposes of public defense.   I directed the commandant of the navy-yard at Philadelphia to purchase or charter and arm an equal number for the same purpose.   I directed the commandant at New York to purchase or charter and arm an equal number.   I directed Commander Gillis to purchase or charter and arm and put to sea two other vessels.   Similar directions were given to Commodore Du Pont, with a view to the opening of passages by water to and from the capital.   I directed the several officers to take the advice and obtain the aid and efficient services in the matter of His Excellency Edwin D. Morgan, the governor of New York, or in his absence George D. Morgan, William M. Evarts, R. M. Blatchford, and Moses H. Grinnell, who were by my directions especially empowered by the Secretary of the Navy to act for his Department in that crisis in matters pertaining to the forwarding of troops and supplies for the public defense.

On the same occasion I directed that Governor Morgan and Alexander Cummings, of the city of New York, should be authorized by the Secretary of War, Simon Cameron, to make all necessary arrangements for the transportation of troops and munitions of war, in aid and assistance of the officers of the Army of the United States, until communication by mails and telegraph should be completely reestablished between the cities of Washington and New York.   No security was required to be given by them, and either of them was authorized to act in case of inability to consult with the other.

On the same occasion I authorized and directed the Secretary of the Treasury to advance, without requiring security, $2,000,000 of public money to John A. Dix, George Opdyke, and Richard M. Blatchford, of New York, to be used by them in meeting such requisitions as should be directly consequent upon the military and naval measures necessary for the defense and support of the Government, requiring them only to act without compensation and to report their transactions when duly called upon.

The several Departments of the Government at that time contained so large a number of disloyal persons that it would have been impossible to provide safely through official agents only for the performance of the duties thus confided to citizens favorably known for their ability, loyalty, and patriotism.

The several orders issued upon these occurrences were transmitted by private messengers, who pursued a circuitous way to the seaboard cities, inland across the States of Pennsylvania and Ohio and the northern lakes. I believe that by these and other similar measures taken in that crisis, some of which were without any authority of law, the Government was saved from overthrow. I am not aware that a dollar of the public funds thus confided without authority of law to unofficial persons was either lost or wasted, although apprehensions of such misdirection occurred to me as objections to those extraordinary proceedings, and were necessarily overruled.

I recall these transactions now because my attention has been directed to a resolution which was passed by the House of Representatives on the 30th day of last month, which is in these words:

Resolved, That Simon Cameron, late Secretary of War, by investing Alexander Cummings with the control of large sums of the public money and authority to purchase military supplies without restriction, without requiring from him any guaranty for the faithful performance of his duties, when the services of competent public officers were available, and by involving the Government in a vast number of contracts with persons not legitimately engaged in the business pertaining to the subject-matter of such contracts, especially in the purchase of arms for future delivery, has adopted a policy highly injurious to the public service, and deserves the censure of the House.

Congress will see that I should be wanting equally in candor and in justice if I should leave the censure expressed in this resolution to rest exclusively or chiefly upon Mr. Cameron. The same sentiment is unanimously entertained by the heads of Departments who participated in the proceedings which the House of Representatives has censured. It is due to Mr. Cameron to say that although he fully approved the proceedings they were not moved nor suggested by himself, and that not only the President, but all the other heads of Departments, were at least equally responsible with him for whatever error, wrong, or fault was committed in the premises.

ABRAHAM LINCOLN.

WASHINGTON, *May 30, 1862.*

To the Senate of the United States:

I transmit to the Senate, for its consideration with a view to ratification, a treaty of amity, commerce, consular privileges, and extradition between the United States and the Republic of Salvador, signed in this city on the 29th instant. It is believed that though this instrument contains no stipulation which may not be found in some subsisting treaty between the United States and foreign powers, it will prove to be mutually advantageous.   Several of the Republics of this hemisphere, among which is Salvador, are alarmed at a supposed sentiment tending to reactionary movements against republican institutions on this continent.   It seems, therefore, to be proper that we should show to any of them who may apply for that purpose that, compatibly with our cardinal policy and with an enlightened view of our own interests, we are willing to encourage them by strengthening our ties of good will and good neighborhood with them.

                              ABRAHAM LINCOLN.

                              WASHINGTON, *June 4, 1862.*
To the Senate of the United States:

In compliance with the resolution of the Senate of the 29th ultimo, adopted in executive session, requesting information in regard to the claims of citizens of the United States on Paraguay and the correspondence relating thereto, I transmit a report from the Secretary of State and the documents by which it was accompanied.

                              ABRAHAM LINCOLN.

                              WASHINGTON, *June 4, 1862.*
To the House of Representatives:

I transmit herewith a report of the Secretary of War, in answer to the resolution of the House of Representatives of the 2d of June, in relation to the authority and action of the Hon. Edward Stanly, military governor of North Carolina.

                              ABRAHAM LINCOLN.

                              WASHINGTON, *June 10, 1862.*
To the Senate and House of Representatives:

I transmit to Congress a copy of a treaty for the suppression of the African slave trade, between the United States and Her Britannic Majesty, signed in this city on the 7th of April last, and the ratifications of which were exchanged at London on the 20th ultimo.

A copy of the correspondence which preceded the conclusion of the instrument between the Secretary of State and Lord Lyons, Her Britannic Majesty's envoy extraordinary and minister plenipotentiary, is also herewith transmitted.

It is desirable that such legislation as may be necessary to carry the treaty into effect should be enacted as soon as may comport with the convenience of Congress.

                              ABRAHAM LINCOLN.

EXECUTIVE MANSION,
Washington, June 12, 1862.

To the Honorable House of Representatives:

In obedience to the resolution of your honorable body of the 9th instant, requesting certain information in regard to the circuit court of the United States for the State of California, and the judge of said court, I have the honor to transmit a letter of the Attorney-General, with copies of two other letters and of an indorsement of my own upon one of them; all which, taken together, contain all the information within my power to give upon the subject. ABRAHAM LINCOLN.

EXECUTIVE MANSION,
Washington, June 13, 1862.

Fellow-Citizens of the Senate and House of Representatives:

I herewith transmit a memorial addressed and presented to me in behalf of the State of New York in favor of enlarging the locks of the Erie and Oswego Canal. While I have not given nor have leisure to give the subject a careful examination, its great importance is obvious and unquestionable. The large amount of valuable statistical information which is collated and presented in the memorial will greatly facilitate the mature consideration of the subject, which I respectfully ask for it at your hands. ABRAHAM LINCOLN.

EXECUTIVE MANSION,
Washington City, June 17, 1862.

The SPEAKER OF THE HOUSE OF REPRESENTATIVES:

The resolution of the House of Representatives of the 9th instant, asking whether any legislation is necessary in order to give effect to the provisions of the act of April 16, 1862, providing for the reorganization of the Medical Department of the Army, was referred to the Secretary of War, whose report thereon is herewith communicated. ABRAHAM LINCOLN.

WASHINGTON, *June 23, 1862.*

To the Senate of the United States:

On the 7th day of December, 1861, I submitted to the Senate the project of a treaty between the United States and Mexico which had been proposed to me by Mr. Corwin, our minister to Mexico, and respectfully requested the advice of the Senate thereupon.

On the 25th day of February last a resolution was adopted by the Senate to the effect "that it is not advisable to negotiate a treaty that will require the United States to assume any portion of the principal or interest of the debt of Mexico, or that will require the concurrence of European powers.''

This resolution having been duly communicated to me, ..otice thereof was immediately given by the Secretary of State to Mr. Corwin, and he was informed that he was to consider his instructions upon the subject referred to modified by this resolution and would govern his course accordingly. That dispatch failed to reach Mr. Corwin, by reason of the disturbed condition of Mexico, until a very recent date, Mr. Corwin being without instructions, or thus practically left without instructions, to negotiate further with Mexico.

In view of the very important events occurring there, he has thought that the interests of the United States would be promoted by the conclusion of two treaties which should provide for a loan to that Republic. He has therefore signed such treaties, and they having been duly ratified by the Government of Mexico he has transmitted them to me for my consideration. The action of the Senate is of course conclusive against an acceptance of the treaties on my part. I have, nevertheless, thought it just to our excellent minister in Mexico and respectful to the Government of that Republic to lay the treaties before the Senate, together with the correspondence which has occurred in relation to them. In performing this duty I have only to add that the importance of the subject thus submitted to the Senate can not be overestimated, and I shall cheerfully receive and consider with the highest respect any further advice the Senate may think proper to give upon the subject.

ABRAHAM LINCOLN.

EXECUTIVE MANSION,
Washington, June 26, 1862.

To the Senate of the United States:

The accompanying treaty, made and concluded at the city of Washington on the 24th day of June, 1862, between the United States and the united bands of the Ottawa Indians of Blanchards Fork and of Roche de Boeuf, in Kansas, is transmitted for the consideration and constitutional action of the Senate, agreeably to recommendation of inclosed letter from the Secretary of the Interior of this date.

ABRAHAM LINCOLN.

WASHINGTON, *July 1, 1862.*

To the Senate and House of Representatives:

I most cordially recommend that Captain Andrew H. Foote, of the United States Navy, receive a vote of thanks of Congress for his eminent services in organizing the flotilla on the Western waters, and for his gallantry at Fort Henry, Fort Donelson, Island No. 10, and at various other places, whilst in command of the naval forces, embracing a period of nearly ten months.

ABRAHAM LINCOLN.

WASHINGTON, D. C., *July 5, 1862.*

To the Senate of the United States:

I transmit herewith, for the constitutional action of the Senate thereon, a treaty negotiated in this city on the 3d instant with the Sac and Fox Indians of the Mississippi.

Letters from the Secretary of the Interior and Commissioner of Indian Affairs accompany the treaty.

ABRAHAM LINCOLN.

WASHINGTON, *July 9, 1862.*

To the Senate of the United States:

I transmit to the Senate, for consideration with a view to ratification, a postal convention with Costa Rica, concluded at San Jose on the 9th June last.

ABRAHAM LINCOLN.

WASHINGTON, D. C., *July 11, 1862.*

To the Senate of the United States:

I transmit to the Senate, for its constitutional action thereon, a treaty negotiated at the Kickapoo Agency on the 28th of June, 1862, between Charles B. Keith, commissioner on the part of the United States, and the chiefs, headmen, and delegates of the Kickapoo Indians of Kansas.

A letter of the Commissioner of Indian Affairs of the 10th instant is also transmitted, suggesting amendments to the treaty for the consideration of the Senate.

ABRAHAM LINCOLN.

WASHINGTON, D. C., *July 11, 1862.*

To the Senate and House of Representatives:

I recommend that the thanks of Congress be given to the following officers of the United States Navy:

Captain James L. Lardner, for meritorious conduct at the battle of Port Royal and distinguished services on the coast of the United States against the enemy.

Captain Charles Henry Davis, for distinguished services in conflict with the enemy at Fort Pillow, at Memphis, and for successful operations at other points in the waters of the Mississippi River.

Commander John A. Dahlgren, for distinguished services in the line of his profession, improvements in ordnance, and zealous and efficient labors in the ordnance branch of the service.

Commander Stephen C. Rowan, for distinguished services in the waters of North Carolina, and particularly in the capture of Newbern, being in chief command of the naval forces.

Commander David D. Porter, for distinguished services in the conception and preparation of the means used for the capture of the forts below New Orleans, and for highly meritorious conduct in the management of the mortar flotilla during the bombardment of Forts Jackson and St. Philip.

Captain Silas H. Stringham, now on the retired list, for distinguished services in the capture of Forts Hatteras and Clark.

ABRAHAM LINCOLN.

WASHINGTON, *July 12, 1862.*

To the House of Representatives:

I transmit a report of the Secretary of State upon the subject of the resolution of the House of Representatives of the 9th ultimo, requesting information in regard to the relations between the United States and foreign powers.

ABRAHAM LINCOLN.

WASHINGTON, D. C., *July 14, 1862.*

Fellow-Citizens of the Senate and House of Representatives:

Herewith is a draft of a bill to compensate any State which may abolish slavery within its limits, the passage of which substantially as presented I respectfully and earnestly recommend.

ABRAHAM LINCOLN.

Be it enacted by the Senate and House of Representatives of the United States of America in Congress assembled, That whenever the President of the United States shall be satisfied that any State shall have lawfully abolished slavery within and throughout such State, either immediately or gradually, it shall be the duty of the President, assisted by the Secretary of the Treasury, to prepare and deliver to such State an amount of 6 per cent interest-bearing bonds of the United States equal to the aggregate value at $—— per head of all the slaves within such State as reported by the census of the year 1860; the whole amount for any one State to be delivered at once if the abolishment be immediate, or in equal annual installments if it be gradual, interest to begin running on each bond at the time of its delivery, and not before.

And be it further enacted, That if any State, having so received any such bonds, shall at any time afterwards by law reintroduce or tolerate slavery within its limits contrary to the act of abolishment upon which such bonds shall have been received, said bonds so received by said State shall at once be null and void, in whosesoever hands they may be, and such State shall refund to the United States all interest which may have been paid on such bonds.

EXECUTIVE MANSION,
Washington, July 15, 1862.

Hon. SOLOMON FOOT,
President pro tempore of the Senate.

SIR: Please inform the Senate that I shall be obliged if they will postpone the adjournment at least one day beyond the time which I understand to be now fixed for it.

Your obedient servant,

ABRAHAM LINCOLN.

[The same message was addressed to Hon. Galusha A. Grow, Speaker of the House of Representatives.]

JULY 17, 1862.

Fellow-Citizens of the Senate and House of Representatives:

Considering the bill for "An act to suppress insurrection, to punish treason and rebellion, to seize and confiscate the property of rebels, and for other purposes," and the joint resolution explanatory of said act as being substantially one, I have approved and signed both.

Before I was informed of the passage of the resolution I had prepared the draft of a message stating objections to the bill becoming a law, a copy of which draft is herewith transmitted.

ABRAHAM LINCOLN.

Fellow-Citizens of the House of Representatives:

I herewith return to your honorable body, in which it originated, the bill for an act entitled "An act to suppress treason and rebellion, to seize and confiscate the property of rebels, and for other purposes," together with my objections to its becoming a law.

There is much in the bill to which I perceive no objection. It is wholly prospective, and touches neither person nor property of any loyal citizen, in which particulars it is just and proper. The first and second sections provide for the conviction and punishment of persons who shall be guilty of treason and persons who shall "incite, set on foot, assist, or engage in any rebellion or insurrection against the authority of the United States or the laws thereof, or shall give aid and comfort thereto, or shall engage in or give aid and comfort to any such existing rebellion or insurrection." By fair construction persons within these sections are not to be punished without regular trials in duly constituted courts, under the forms and all the substantial provisions of law and of the Constitution applicable to their several cases. To this I perceive no objection, especially as such persons would be within the general pardoning power and also the special provision for pardon and amnesty contained in this act.

It is also provided that the slaves of persons convicted under these sections shall be free. I think there is an unfortunate form of expression rather than a substantial objection in this. It is startling to say that Congress can free a slave within a State, and yet if it were said the ownership of the slave had first been transferred to the nation and that Congress had then liberated him the difficulty would at once vanish. And this is the real case. The traitor against the General Government forfeits his slave at least as justly as he does any other property, and he forfeits both to the Government against which he offends. The Government, so far as there can be ownership, thus owns the forfeited slaves, and the question for Congress in regard to them is, "Shall they be made free or be sold to new masters?" I perceive no objection to Congress deciding in advance that they shall be free. To the high honor of Kentucky, as I am informed, she has been the owner of some slaves by escheat and has sold none, but liberated all. I hope the same is true of some other States. Indeed I do not believe it would be physically possible for the General Government to return persons so circumstanced to actual slavery. I believe there would be physical resistance to it which could neither be turned aside by argument nor driven away by force. In this view I have no objection to this feature of the bill. Another matter involved in these two sections, and running through other parts of the act, will be noticed hereafter.

I perceive no objection to the third and fourth sections.

So far as I wish to notice the fifth and sixth sections, they may be considered together. That the enforcement of these sections would do no injustice to the persons embraced within them is clear. That those who make a causeless war should be compelled to pay the cost of it is too obviously just to be called in question. To give governmental protection to the property of persons who have abandoned it and gone on a crusade to overthrow that same government is absurd if considered in the mere light of justice. The severest justice may not always be the best policy. The principle of seizing and appropriating the property of the persons embraced within these sections is certainly not very objectionable, but a justly discriminating application of it would be very difficult, and to a great extent impossible. And would it not be wise to place a power of remission somewhere, so that these persons may know they have something to lose by persisting and something to save by desisting? I am not sure whether such power of remission is or is not within section 13.

Without any special act of Congress, I think our military commanders, when, in military phrase, "they are within the enemy's country," should in an orderly manner seize and use whatever of real or personal property may be necessary or convenient for their commands, at the same time preserving in some way the evidence of what they do.

What I have said in regard to slaves while commenting on the first and second sections is applicable to the ninth, with the difference that no provision is made in the whole act for determining whether a particular individual slave does or does not fall within the classes defined in that section. He is to be free upon certain conditions, but whether those conditions do or do not pertain to him no mode of ascertaining is provided. This could be easily supplied.

To the tenth section I make no objection. The oath therein required seems to be proper, and the remainder of the section is substantially identical with a law already existing.

The eleventh section simply assumes to confer discretionary powers upon the Executive. Without the law I have no hesitation to go as far in the direction indicated as I may at any time deem expedient. And I am ready to say now, I think it is proper for our military commanders to employ as laborers as many persons of African descent as can be used to advantage.

The twelfth and thirteenth sections are somewhat better than objectionable, and the fourteenth is entirely proper if all other parts of the act shall stand.

That to which I chiefly object pervades most parts of the act, but more distinctly appears in the first, second, seventh, and eighth sections. It is the sum of those provisions which results in the divesting of title forever. For the causes of treason and the ingredients of treason not amounting to the full crime it declares forfeiture extending beyond the lives of the guilty parties, whereas the Constitution of the United States declares that "no attainder of treason shall work corruption of blood, or forfeiture except during the life of the person attainted." True, there seems to be no formal attainder in this case; still, I think the greater punishment can not be constitutionally inflicted in a different form for the same offense. With great respect I am constrained to say I think this feature of the act is unconstitutional. It would not be difficult to modify it.

I may remark that this provision of the Constitution, put in language borrowed from Great Britain, applies only in this country to real or landed estate.

Again, this act, by proceedings *in rem*, forfeits property for the ingredients of treason without a conviction of the supposed criminal or a personal hearing given him in any proceeding. That we may not touch property lying within our reach because we can not give personal notice to an owner who is absent endeavoring to destroy the Government is certainly not very satisfactory. Still, the owner may not be thus engaged; and I think a reasonable time should be provided for such parties to appear and have personal hearings. Similar provisions are not uncommon in connection with proceedings *in rem*.

For the reasons stated, I return the bill to the House, in which it originated.

JULY 17, 1862.

Fellow-Citizens of the Senate and House of Representatives:

I have inadvertently omitted so long to inform you that in March last Mr. Cornelius Vanderbilt, of New York, gratuitously presented to the United States the ocean steamer *Vanderbilt*, by many esteemed the finest merchant ship in the world. She has ever since been and still is doing valuable service to the Government. For the patriotic act in making this magnificent and valuable present to the country, I recommend that some suitable acknowledgment be made.

ABRAHAM LINCOLN.

VETO MESSAGES.

JUNE 23, 1862.

To the Senate of the United States:

The bill which has passed the House of Representatives and the Senate entitled "An act to repeal that part of an act of Congress which prohibits the circulation of bank notes of a less denomination than $5 in the District of Columbia" has received my attentive consideration, and I now return it to the Senate, in which it originated, with the following objections:

1. The bill proposes to repeal the existing legislation prohibiting the circulation of bank notes of a less denomination than $5 within the District of Columbia without permitting the issuing of such bills by banks not now legally authorized to issue them. In my judgment it will be found impracticable in the present condition of the currency to make such a discrimination. The banks have generally suspended specie payments, and a legal sanction given to the circulation of the irredeemable notes of one class of them will almost certainly be so extended in practical operation as to include those of all classes, whether authorized or unauthorized. If this view be correct, the currency of the District,

should this act become a law will certainly and greatly deteriorate, to the serious injury of honest trade and honest labor.

2. This bill seems to contemplate no end which can not be otherwise more certainly and beneficially attained. During the existing war it is peculiarly the duty of the National Government to secure to the people a sound circulating medium. This duty has been under existing circumstances satisfactorily performed, in part at least, by authorizing the issue of United States notes, receivable for all Government dues except customs, and made a legal tender for all debts, public and private, except interest on public debt. The object of the bill submitted to me, namely, that of providing a small-note currency during the present suspension, can be fully accomplished by authorizing the issue, as part of any new emission of United States notes made necessary by the circumstances of the country, of notes of a similar character but of less denomination than $5. Such an issue would answer all the beneficial purposes of the bill, would save a considerable amount to the Treasury in interest, would greatly facilitate payments to soldiers and other creditors of small sums, and would furnish to the people a currency as safe as their own Government.

Entertaining these objections to the bill, I feel myself constrained to withhold from it my approval and return it for the further consideration and action of Congress.

ABRAHAM LINCOLN.

EXECUTIVE MANSION, *July 2, 1862.*
To the Senate of the United States:

I herewith return to your honorable body, in which it originated, an act entitled ''An act to provide for additional medical officers of the volunteer service,'' without my approval.

My reason for so doing is that I have approved an act of the same title passed by Congress after the passage of the one first mentioned for the express purpose of correcting errors in and superseding the same, as I am informed.

ABRAHAM LINCOLN.

PROCLAMATIONS.

BY THE PRESIDENT OF THE UNITED STATES OF AMERICA.

A PROCLAMATION.

It is recommended to the people of the United States that they assemble in their customary places of meeting for public solemnities on the 22d day of February instant and celebrate the anniversary of the birth of the Father of his Country by causing to be read to them his immortal Farewell Address.

Given under my hand and the seal of the United States, at Washington, the 19th day of February, A. D. 1862, and of the Independence of the United States of America the eighty-sixth.

[SEAL.]

ABRAHAM LINCOLN.

By the President:

WILLIAM H. SEWARD,
Secretary of State.

BY THE PRESIDENT OF THE UNITED STATES OF AMERICA.

A PROCLAMATION.

It has pleased Almighty God to vouchsafe signal victories to the land and naval forces engaged in suppressing an internal rebellion, and at the same time to avert from our country the dangers of foreign intervention and invasion.

It is therefore recommended to the people of the United States that at their next weekly assemblages in their accustomed places of public worship which shall occur after notice of this proclamation shall have been received they especially acknowledge and render thanks to our Heavenly Father for these inestimable blessings, that they then and there implore spiritual consolation in behalf of all who have been brought into affliction by the casualties and calamities of sedition and civil war, and that they reverently invoke the divine guidance for our national counsels, to the end that they may speedily result in the restoration of peace, harmony, and unity throughout our borders and hasten the establishment of fraternal relations among all the countries of the earth.

In witness whereof I have hereunto set my hand and caused the seal of the United States to be affixed.

[SEAL.]

Done at the city of Washington, this 10th day of April, A. D. 1862, and of the Independence of the United States the eighty-sixth.

ABRAHAM LINCOLN.

By the President:

WILLIAM H. SEWARD,
Secretary of State.

BY THE PRESIDENT OF THE UNITED STATES OF AMERICA.

A PROCLAMATION.

Whereas by my proclamation of the 19th of April, 1861, it was declared that the ports of certain States, including those of Beaufort, in the State of North Carolina; Port Royal, in the State of South Carolina;

and New Orleans, in the State of Louisiana, were, for reasons therein set forth, intended to be placed under blockade; and

Whereas the said ports of Beaufort, Port Royal, and New Orleans have since been blockaded; but as the blockade of the same ports may now be safely relaxed with advantage to the interests of commerce:

Now, therefore, be it known that I, Abraham Lincoln, President of the United States, pursuant to the authority in me vested by the fifth section of the act of Congress approved on the 13th of July last, entitled "An act further to provide for the collection of duties on imports, and for other purposes," do hereby declare that the blockade of the said ports of Beaufort, Port Royal, and New Orleans shall so far cease and determine, from and after the 1st day of June next, that commercial intercourse with those ports, except as to persons, things, and information contraband of war, may from that time be carried on subject to the laws of the United States and to the limitations and in pursuance of the regulations which are prescribed by the Secretary of the Treasury in his order of this date, which is appended to this proclamation.

In witness whereof I have hereunto set my hand and caused the seal of the United States to be affixed.

[SEAL.]   Done at the city of Washington, this 12th day of May, A. D. 1862, and of the Independence of the United States the eighty-sixth.

ABRAHAM LINCOLN.

By the President:

WILLIAM H. SEWARD,
        Secretary of State.

REGULATIONS RELATING TO TRADE WITH PORTS OPENED BY PROCLAMATION.

TREASURY DEPARTMENT, *May 12, 1862.*

1. To vessels clearing from foreign ports and destined to ports opened by the proclamation of the President of the United States of this date, namely, Beaufort, in North Carolina; Port Royal, in South Carolina, and New Orleans, in Louisiana, licenses will be granted by consuls of the United States upon satisfactory evidence that the vessels so licensed will convey no persons, property, or information contraband of war either to or from the said ports, which licenses shall be exhibited to the collector of the port to which said vessels may be respectively bound immediately on arrival, and, if required, to any officer in charge of the blockade; and on leaving either of said ports every vessel will be required to have a clearance from the collector of the customs, according to law, showing no violation of the conditions of the license. Any violation of said conditions will involve the forfeiture and condemnation of the vessel and cargo and the exclusion of all parties concerned from any further privilege of entering the United States during the war for any purpose whatever.

2. To vessels of the United States clearing coastwise for the ports aforesaid licenses can only be obtained from the Treasury Department.

3. In all other respects the existing blockade remains in full force and effect as hitherto established and maintained, nor is it relaxed by the proclamation except in regard to the ports to which the relaxation is by that instrument expressly applied.

S. P. CHASE, *Secretary of the Treasury.*

By the President of the United States of America.

A PROCLAMATION.

Whereas there appears in the public prints what purports to be a proclamation of Major-General Hunter, in the words and figures following, to wit·

HEADQUARTERS DEPARTMENT OF THE SOUTH,
Hilton Head, S. C., May 9, 1862.

General Orders, No. 11.—The three States of Georgia, Florida, and South Carolina, comprising the Military Department of the South, having deliberately declared themselves no longer under the protection of the United States of America, and having taken up arms against the said United States, it becomes a military necessity to declare them under martial law. This was accordingly done on the 25th day of April, 1862. Slavery and martial law in a free country are altogether incompatible; the persons in these three States—Georgia, Florida, and South Carolina—heretofore held as slaves are therefore declared forever free.

DAVID HUNTER,
Major-General Commanding.

Official:

ED. W. SMITH,
Acting Assistant Adjutant-General.

And whereas the same is producing some excitement and misunderstanding:

Therefore I, Abraham Lincoln, President of the United States, proclaim and declare that the Government of the United States had no knowledge, information, or belief of an intention on the part of General Hunter to issue such a proclamation, nor has it yet any authentic information that the document is genuine; and, further, that neither General Hunter nor any other commander or person has been authorized by the Government of the United States to make proclamations declaring the slaves of any State free, and that the supposed proclamation now in question, whether genuine or false, is altogether void so far as respects such declaration.

I further make known that whether it be competent for me, as Commander in Chief of the Army and Navy, to declare the slaves of any State or States free, and whether at any time, in any case, it shall have become a necessity indispensable to the maintenance of the Government to exercise such supposed power, are questions which, under my responsibility, I reserve to myself, and which I can not feel justified in leaving to the decision of commanders in the field. These are totally different questions from those of police regulations in armies and camps.

On the 6th day of March last, by a special message, I recommended to Congress the adoption of a joint resolution to be substantially as follows:

Resolved, That the United States ought to cooperate with any State which may adopt a gradual abolishment of slavery, giving to such State pecuniary aid, to be used by such State, in its discretion, to compensate for the inconveniences, public and private, produced by such change of system.

The resolution, in the language above quoted, was adopted by large majorities in both branches of Congress, and now stands an authentic, definite, and solemn proposal of the nation to the States and people most immediately interested in the subject-matter. To the people of those States I now earnestly appeal—I do not argue; I beseech you to make the arguments for yourselves; you can not, if you would, be blind to the signs of the times. I beg of you a calm and enlarged consideration of them, ranging, if it may be, far above personal and partisan politics. This proposal makes common cause for a common object, casting no reproaches upon any. It acts not the Pharisee. The change it contemplates would come gently as the dews of heaven, not rending or wrecking anything. Will you not embrace it? So much good has not been done by one effort in all past time as, in the providence of God, it is now your high privilege to do. May the vast future not have to lament that you have neglected it.

In witness whereof I have hereunto set my hand and caused the seal of the United States to be affixed.

[SEAL.]   Done at the city of Washington, this 19th day of May, A. D. 1862, and of the Independence of the United States the eighty-sixth.

ABRAHAM LINCOLN.

By the President:

WILLIAM H. SEWARD, *Secretary of State.*

BY THE PRESIDENT OF THE UNITED STATES OF AMERICA.

A PROCLAMATION.

Whereas in and by the second section of an act of Congress passed on the 7th day of June, A. D. 1862, entitled ''An act for the collection of direct taxes in insurrectionary districts within the United States, and for other purposes,'' it is made the duty of the President to declare, on or before the 1st day of July then next following, by his proclamation, in what States and parts of States insurrection exists:

Now, therefore, be it known that I, Abraham Lincoln, President of the United States of America, do hereby declare and proclaim that the States of South Carolina, Florida, Georgia, Alabama, Louisiana, Texas, Mississippi, Arkansas, Tennessee, North Carolina, and the State of Virginia except the following counties—Hancock, Brooke, Ohio, Marshall, Wetzel, Marion, Monongalia, Preston, Taylor, Pleasants, Tyler, Ritchie, Doddridge, Harrison, Wood, Jackson, Wirt, Roane, Calhoun, Gilmer, Barbour, Tucker, Lewis, Braxton, Upshur, Randolph, Mason, Putnam, Kanawha, Clay, Nicholas, Cabell, Wayne, Boone, Logan, Wyoming, Webster, Fayette, and Raleigh—are now in insurrection and rebellion, and by reason thereof the civil authority of the United States is obstructed so that the provisions of the ''Act to provide increased revenue from imports, to pay the interest on the public debt, and for other purposes," approved August 5, 1861, can not be peaceably executed; and that the taxes legally chargeable upon real estate under the act last aforesaid lying within the States and parts of States as aforesaid, together with a penalty of 50 *per centum* of said taxes, shall be a lien upon the tracts or lots of the same, severally charged, till paid.

In witness whereof I have hereunto set my hand and caused the seal of the United States to be affixed.

[SEAL.]   Done at the city of Washington, this 1st day of July, A. D. 1862, and of the Independence of the United States of America the eighty-sixth.   ABRAHAM LINCOLN.

By the President:

     F. W. SEWARD,
       Acting Secretary of State.

BY THE PRESIDENT OF THE UNITED STATES OF AMERICA.

A PROCLAMATION.

In pursuance of the sixth section of the act of Congress entitled "An act to suppress insurrection and to punish treason and rebellion, to seize and confiscate property of rebels, and for other purposes," approved July 17, 1862, and which act and the joint resolution explanatory thereof are herewith published, I, Abraham Lincoln, President of the United States, do hereby proclaim to and warn all persons within the contemplation of said sixth section to cease participating in, aiding, countenancing, or abetting the existing rebellion or any rebellion against the Government of the United States and to return to their proper allegiance to the United States on pain of the forfeitures and seizures as within and by said sixth section provided.

In testimony whereof I have hereunto set my hand and caused the seal of the United States to be affixed.

[SEAL.]   Done at the city of Washington, this 25th day of July, A. D. 1862, and of the Independence of the United States the eighty-seventh.   ABRAHAM LINCOLN.

By the President:

     WILLIAM H. SEWARD,
       Secretary of State.

[From Statutes at Large (Little, Brown & Co.), Vol. XII, p. 589.]

AN ACT to suppress insurrection, to punish treason and rebellion, to seize and confiscate the property of rebels, and for other purposes.

Be it enacted by the Senate and House of Representatives of the United States of America in Congress assembled, That every person who shall hereafter commit the crime of treason against the United States, and shall be adjudged guilty thereof, shall suffer death, and all his slaves, if any, shall be declared and made free; or, at the discretion of the court, he shall be imprisoned for not less than five years and fined not less than $10,000, and all his slaves, if any, shall be declared and made free; said fine shall be levied and collected on any or all of the property, real and personal, excluding slaves, of which the said person so convicted was the owner at the time of committing the said crime, any sale or conveyance to the contrary notwithstanding.

SEC. 2. *And be it further enacted*, That if any person shall hereafter incite, set on foot, assist, or engage in any rebellion or insurrection against the authority of the United States or the laws thereof, or shall give aid or comfort thereto, or shall engage in or give aid and comfort to any such existing rebellion or insurrection, and be convicted thereof, such person shall be punished by imprisonment for a period not exceeding ten years, or by a fine not exceeding $10,000, and by the liberation of all his slaves, if any he have; or by both of said punishments, at the discretion of the court.

SEC. 3. *And be it further enacted*, That every person guilty of either of the offenses described in this act shall be forever incapable and disqualified to hold any office under the United States.

SEC. 4. *And be it further enacted*, That this act shall not be construed in any way to affect or alter the prosecution, conviction, or punishment of any person or persons guilty of treason against the United States before the passage of this act, unless such person is convicted under this act.

SEC. 5. *And be it further enacted*, That to insure the speedy termination of the present rebellion it shall be the duty of the President of the United States to cause the seizure of all the estate and property, money, stocks, credits, and effects of the persons hereinafter named in this section, and to apply and use the same and the proceeds thereof for the support of the Army of the United States; that is to say:

First. Of any person hereafter acting as an officer of the army or navy of the rebels in arms against the Government of the United States.

Secondly. Of any person hereafter acting as president, vice-president, member of congress, judge of any court, cabinet officer, foreign minister, commissioner, or consul of the so-called Confederate States of America.

Thirdly. Of any person acting as governor of a State, member of a convention or legislature, or judge of any court of any of the so-called Confederate States of America.

Fourthly. Of any person who, having held an office of honor, trust, or profit in the United States, shall hereafter hold an office in the so-called Confederate States of America.

Fifthly. Of any person hereafter holding any office or agency under the government of the so-called Confederate States of America, or under any of the several States of the said Confederacy, or the laws thereof, whether such office or agency be national, State, or municipal in its name or character: *Provided*, That the persons thirdly, fourthly, and fifthly above described shall have accepted their appointment or election since the date of the pretended ordinance of secession of the State, or shall have taken an oath of allegiance to or to support the constitution of the so-called Confederate States.

Sixthly. Of any person who, owning property in any loyal State or Territory of the United States, or in the District of Columbia, shall hereafter assist and give aid and comfort to such rebellion; and all sales, transfers, or conveyances of any such property shall be null and void; and it shall be a sufficient bar to any suit brought by such person for the possession or the use of such property, or any of it, to allege and prove that he is one of the persons described in this section.

SEC. 6. *And be it further enacted*, That if any person within any State or Territory of the United States, other than those named as aforesaid, after the passage of this act, being engaged in armed rebellion against the Government of the United States, or aiding or abetting such rebellion, shall not, within sixty days after public warning and proclamation duly given and made by the President of the United States, cease to aid, countenance, and abet such rebellion, and return to his allegiance to the United States, all the estate and property, moneys, stocks, and credits of such person shall be liable to seizure as aforesaid, and it shall be the duty of the President to seize and use them as aforesaid, or the proceeds thereof. And all sales, transfers, or conveyances of any such property after the expiration of the said sixty days from the date of such warning and proclamation shall be null and void; and it shall be a sufficient bar to any suit brought by such person for the possession or the use of such property, or any of it, to allege and prove that he is one of the persons described in this section.

SEC. 7. *And be it further enacted*, That to secure the condemnation and sale of any of such property, after the same shall have been seized, so that it may be made available for the purpose aforesaid, proceedings *in rem* shall be instituted in the name of the United States in any district court thereof, or in any Territorial court, or in the United States district court for the District of Columbia, within which the property above described, or any part thereof, may be found, or into which the same, if movable, may first be brought, which proceedings shall conform as nearly as may be to proceedings in admiralty or revenue cases; and if said property, whether real or personal, shall be found to have belonged to a person engaged in rebellion, or who has given aid or comfort thereto, the same shall be condemned as enemies' property and become the property of the United States, and may be disposed of as the court shall decree and the proceeds thereof paid into the Treasury of the United States for the purposes aforesaid.

SEC. 8. *And be it further enacted*, That the several courts aforesaid shall have power to make such orders, establish such forms of decree and sale, and direct such deeds and conveyances to be executed and delivered by the marshals thereof where real estate shall be the subject of sale as shall fitly and efficiently effect the purposes of this act, and vest in the purchasers of such property good and valid titles thereto. And the said courts shall have power to allow such fees and charges of their officers as shall be reasonable and proper in the premises.

SEC. 9. *And be it further enacted*, That all slaves of persons who shall hereafter be engaged in rebellion against the Government of the United States, or who shall in any way give aid or comfort thereto, escaping from such persons and taking refuge within the lines of the army, and all slaves captured from such persons or deserted by them and coming under the control of the Government of the United States, and all slaves of such persons found on [or] being within any place occupied by rebel forces and afterwards occupied by the forces of the United States, shall be deemed captives of war, and shall be forever free of their servitude, and not again held as slaves.

SEC. 10. *And be it further enacted*, That no slave escaping into any State, Territory, or the District of Columbia from any other State shall be delivered up or in any way impeded or hindered of his liberty except for crime or some offense against the laws, unless the person claiming said fugitive shall first make oath that the person to whom the labor or service of such fugitive is alleged to be due is his lawful owner and has not borne arms against the United States in the present rebellion nor in any way given aid and comfort thereto; and no person engaged in the military or naval service of the United States shall, under any pretense whatever, assume to decide on the validity of the claim of any person to the service or labor of any other person, or surrender up any such person to the claimant, on pain of being dismissed from the service.

SEC. 11. *And be it further enacted*, That the President of the United States is authorized to employ as many persons of African descent as he may deem necessary and proper for the suppression of this rebellion, and for this purpose he may organize and use them in such manner as he may judge best for the public welfare.

Sɛc. 12. *And be it further enacted,* That the President of the United States is hereby authorized to make provision for the transportation, colonization, and settlement, in some tropical country beyond the limits of the United States, of such persons of the African race, made free by the provisions of this act, as may be willing to emigrate, having first obtained the consent of the Government of said country to their protection and settlement within the same, with all the rights and privileges of freemen.

Sɛc. 13. *And be it further enacted,* That the President is hereby authorized, at any time hereafter, by proclamation, to extend to persons who may have participated in the existing rebellion in any State or part thereof pardon and amnesty, with such exceptions and at such time and on such conditions as he may deem expedient for the public welfare.

Sɛc. 14. *And be it further enacted,* That the courts of the United States shall have full power to institute proceedings, make orders and decrees, issue process, and do all other things necessary to carry this act into effect.

Approved, July 17, 1862.

[From Statutes at Large (Little, Brown & Co.), Vol. XII, p. 627.]

JOINT RESOLUTION explanatory of "An act to suppress insurrection, to punish treason and rebellion, to seize and confiscate the property of rebels, and for other purposes."

Resolved by the Senate and House of Representatives of the United States of America in Congress assembled, That the provisions of the third clause of the fifth section of "An act to suppress insurrection, to punish treason and rebellion, to seize and confiscate the property of rebels, and for other purposes" shall be so construed as not to apply to any act or acts done prior to the passage thereof, nor to include any member of a State legislature or judge of any State court who has not in accepting or entering upon his office taken an oath to support the constitution of the so-called "Confederate States of America;" nor shall any punishment or proceedings under said act be so construed as to work a forfeiture of the real estate of the offender beyond his natural life.

Approved, July 17, 1862.

By the President of the United States of America.

A PROCLAMATION.

I, Abraham Lincoln, President of the United States of America and Commander in Chief of the Army and Navy thereof, do hereby proclaim and declare that hereafter, as heretofore, the war will be prosecuted for the object of practically restoring the constitutional relation between the United States and each of the States and the people thereof in which States that relation is or may be suspended or disturbed.

That it is my purpose, upon the next meeting of Congress, to again recommend the adoption of a practical measure tendering pecuniary aid to the free acceptance or rejection of all slave States, so called, the people whereof may not then be in rebellion against the United States, and which States may then have voluntarily adopted, or thereafter may voluntarily adopt, immediate or gradual abolishment of slavery within their respective limits; and that the effort to colonize persons of African descent with their consent upon this continent or elsewhere, with the previously obtained consent of the governments existing there, will be continued.

That on the 1st day of January, A. D. 1863, all persons held as slaves within any State or designated part of a State the people whereof shall then be in rebellion against the United States shall be then, thenceforward, and forever free; and the executive government of the United States, including the military and naval authority thereof, will recognize and maintain the freedom of such persons and will do no act or acts to repress such persons, or any of them, in any efforts they may make for their actual freedom.

That the Executive will on the 1st day of January aforesaid, by proclamation, designate the States and parts of States, if any, in which the people thereof, respectively, shall then be in rebellion against the United States; and the fact that any State or the people thereof shall on that day be in good faith represented in the Congress of the United States by members chosen thereto at elections wherein a majority of the qualified voters of such State shall have participated shall, in the absence of strong countervailing testimony, be deemed conclusive evidence that such State and the people thereof are not then in rebellion against the United States.

That attention is hereby called to an act of Congress entitled "An act to make an additional article of war," approved March 13, 1862, and which act is in the words and figure following:

Be it enacted by the Senate and House of Representatives of the United States of America in Congress assembled, That hereafter the following shall be promulgated as an additional article of war for the government of the Army of the United States, and shall be obeyed and observed as such:

ART. —. All officers or persons in the military or naval service of the United States are prohibited from employing any of the forces under their respective commands for the purpose of returning fugitives from service or labor who may have escaped from any persons to whom such service or labor is claimed to be due, and any officer who shall be found guilty by a court-martial of violating this article shall be dismissed from the service.

SEC. 2. *And be it further enacted*, That this act shall take effect from and after its passage.

Also to the ninth and tenth sections of an act entitled "An act to suppress insurrection, to punish treason and rebellion, to seize and confiscate the property of rebels, and for other purposes," approved July 17, 1862, and which sections are in the words and figures following:

SEC. 9. *And be it further enacted*, That all slaves of persons who shall hereafter be engaged in rebellion against the Government of the United States, or who shall in any way give aid or comfort thereto, escaping from such persons and taking refuge within the lines of the army, and all slaves captured from such persons or deserted by them and coming under the control of the Government of the United States, and all slaves of such persons found on [or] being within any place occupied by rebel forces and afterwards occupied by the forces of the United States, shall be deemed captives of war and shall be forever free of their servitude and not again held as slaves.

SEC. 10. *And be it further enacted*, That no slave escaping into any State, Territory, or the District of Columbia from any other State shall be delivered up or in any way impeded or hindered of his liberty except for crime or some offense against the laws, unless the person claiming said fugitive shall first make oath that the person to whom the labor or service of such fugitive is alleged to be due is his lawful owner and has not borne arms against the United States in the present rebellion nor in any way given aid and comfort thereto; and no person engaged in the military or naval service of the United States shall, under any pretense whatever, assume to decide on the validity of the claim of any person to the service or labor of any other person or surrender up any such person to the claimant on pain of being dismissed from the service.

And I do hereby enjoin upon and order all persons engaged in the military and naval service of the United States to observe, obey, and enforce within their respective spheres of service the act and sections above recited.

And the Executive will in due time recommend that all citizens of the United States who shall have remained loyal thereto throughout the rebellion shall, upon the restoration of the constitutional relation between the United States and their respective States and people, if that relation shall have been suspended or disturbed, be compensated for all losses by acts of the United States, including the loss of slaves.

In witness whereof I have hereunto set my hand and caused the seal of the United States to be affixed.

.[SEAL.]   Done at the city of Washington, this 22d day of September, A. D. 1862, and of the Independence of the United States the eighty-seventh.   ABRAHAM LINCOLN.

By the President:

WILLIAM H. SEWARD, *Secretary of State.*

BY THE PRESIDENT OF THE UNITED STATES OF AMERICA.

A PROCLAMATION.

Whereas it has become necessary to call into service not only volunteers, but also portions of the militia of the States by draft in order to suppress the insurrection existing in the United States, and disloyal persons are not adequately restrained by the ordinary processes of law from hindering this measure and from giving aid and comfort in various ways to the insurrection:

Now, therefore, be it ordered, first, that during the existing insurrection, and as a necessary measure for suppressing the same, all rebels and insurgents, their aiders and abettors, within the United States, and all persons discouraging volunteer enlistments, resisting militia drafts, or guilty of any disloyal practice affording aid and comfort to rebels against the authority of the United States, shall be subject to martial law and liable to trial and punishment by courts-martial or military commissions; second, that the writ of *habeas corpus* is suspended in respect to all persons arrested, or who are now or hereafter during the rebellion shall be imprisoned in any fort, camp, arsenal, military prison, or other place of confinement by any military authority or by the sentence of any court-martial or military commission.

In witness whereof I have hereunto set my hand and caused the seal of the United States to be affixed.

[SEAL.]   Done at the city of Washington, this 24th day of September, A. D. 1862, and of the Independence of the United States the eighty-seventh.

ABRAHAM LINCOLN.

By the President:

WILLIAM H. SEWARD,
Secretary of State.

EXECUTIVE ORDERS.

Major-General H. W. HALLECK,
Commanding in the Department of Missouri.

GENERAL: As an insurrection exists in the United States and is in arms in the State of Missouri, you are hereby authorized and empowered to suspend the writ of *habeas corpus* within the limits of the military division under your command and to exercise martial law as you find it necessary, in your discretion, to secure the public safety and the authority of the United States.

In witness whereof I have hereunto set my hand and caused the seal of the United States to be affixed, at Washington, this 2d day of December, A. D. 1861.

[SEAL.]

ABRAHAM LINCOLN.

By the President:

WILLIAM H. SEWARD,
Secretary of State.

GENERAL ORDERS, No. 111.

HEADQUARTERS OF THE ARMY,
ADJUTANT-GENERAL'S OFFICE,
Washington, December 30, 1861.

*   *   *   *   *   *   *

JOINT RESOLUTION expressive of the recognition by Congress of the gallant and patriotic services of the late Brigadier-General Nathaniel Lyon and the officers and soldiers under his command at the battle of Springfield, Mo.

Resolved by the Senate and House of Representatives of the United States of America in Congress assembled, 1. That Congress deems it just and proper to enter upon its records a recognition of the eminent and patriotic services of the late Brigadier-General Nathaniel Lyon. The country to whose service he devoted his life will guard and preserve his fame as a part of its own glory.

2. That the thanks of Congress are hereby given to the brave officers and soldiers who, under the command of the late General Lyon, sustained the honor of the flag and achieved victory against overwhelming numbers at the battle of Springfield, in Missouri; and that, in order to commemorate an event so honorable to the country and to themselves, it is ordered that each regiment engaged shall be authorized to bear upon its colors the word "Springfield," embroidered in letters of gold. And the President of the United States is hereby requested to cause these resolutions to be read at the head of every regiment in the Army of the United States.

The President of the United States directs that the foregoing joint resolution be read at the head of every regiment in the Army of the United States.

By command of Major-General McClellan:

L. THOMAS,
Adjutant-General.

WAR DEPARTMENT, *January 22, 1862.*

The President, Commander in Chief of the Army and Navy, has received information of a brilliant victory by the United States forces over a large body of armed traitors and rebels at Mill Springs, in the State of Kentucky. He returns thanks to the gallant officers and soldiers who won that victory, and when the official reports shall be received the military and personal valor displayed in battle will be acknowledged and rewarded in a fitting manner.

The courage that encountered and vanquished the greatly superior numbers of the rebel force, pursued and attacked them in their intrenchments, and paused not until the enemy was completely routed merits and receives commendation.

The purpose of this war is to attack, pursue, and destroy a rebellious enemy and to deliver the country from danger menaced by traitors. Alacrity, daring, courageous spirit, and patriotic zeal on all occasions and under every circumstance are expected from the Army of the United States. In the prompt and spirited movements and daring battle of Mill Springs the nation will realize its hopes, and the people of the United States will rejoice to honor every soldier and officer who proves his courage by charging with the bayonet and storming intrenchments or in the blaze of the enemy's fire.

By order of the President:

EDWIN M. STANTON,
Secretary of War.

PRESIDENT'S GENERAL WAR ORDER NO. 1.

EXECUTIVE MANSION,
Washington, January 27, 1862.

Ordered, That the 22d day of February, 1862, be the day for a general movement of the land and naval forces of the United States against the insurgent forces; that especially the army at and about Fortress Monroe, the Army of the Potomac, the Army of Western Virginia, the army near Munfordville, Ky., the army and flotilla at Cairo, and a naval force in the Gulf of Mexico be ready to move on that day.

That all other forces, both land and naval, with their respective commanders, obey existing orders for the time and be ready to obey additional orders when duly given.

That the heads of Departments, and especially the Secretaries of War and of the Navy, with all their subordinates, and the General in Chief, with all other commanders and subordinates of land and naval forces, will severally be held to their strict and full responsibilities for prompt execution of this order.   ABRAHAM LINCOLN.

PRESIDENT'S SPECIAL WAR ORDER NO. 1.

EXECUTIVE MANSION,
Washington, January 31, 1862.

Ordered, That all the disposable force of the Army of the Potomac, after providing safely for the defense of Washington, be formed into an expedition for the immediate object of seizing and occupying a point upon the railroad southwestward of what is known as Manassas Junction; all details to be in the discretion of the General in Chief, and the expedition to move before or on the 22d day of February next.

A. LINCOLN.

WAR DEPARTMENT,
Washington City, February 11, 1862.

Ordered, That D. C. McCallum be, and he is hereby, appointed military director and superintendent of railroads in the United States, with authority to enter upon, take possession of, hold, and use all railroads, engines, cars, locomotives, equipments, appendages, and appurtenances that may be required for the transport of troops, arms, ammunition, and military supplies of the United States, and to do and perform all acts and things that may be necessary or proper to be done for the safe and speedy transport aforesaid.

By order of the President, Commander in Chief of the Army and Navy of the United States: EDWIN M. STANTON,
Secretary of War.

WAR DEPARTMENT, *February 13, 1862.*

Ordered, 1. That all applications to go south across the military lines of the United States be made to Major-General John A. Dix, commanding at Baltimore, who will grant or refuse the same at his discretion.

2. That all prisoners of war and other persons imprisoned by authority of any department of the Government who shall be released on parole or exchange shall report themselves immediately on their arrival at Baltimore to Major-General Dix and be subject to his direction while remaining in that city. Any failure to observe this order will be taken as a forfeiture of the parole or exchange.

The regulation heretofore existing which required passes across the military lines of the United States to be signed by the Secretary of State and countersigned by the General Commanding is rescinded.

By order of the President:

EDWIN M. STANTON,
Secretary of War.

EXECUTIVE ORDER No. 1, RELATING TO POLITICAL PRISONERS.

WAR DEPARTMENT,
Washington, February 14, 1862.

The breaking out of a formidable insurrection based on a conflict of political ideas, being an event without precedent in the United States, was necessarily attended by great confusion and perplexity of the public mind. Disloyalty before unsuspected suddenly became bold, and treason astonished the world by bringing at once into the field military forces superior in number to the standing Army of the United States.

Every department of the Government was paralyzed by treason. Defection appeared in the Senate, in the House of Representatives, in the Cabinet, in the Federal courts; ministers and consuls returned from foreign countries to enter the insurrectionary councils or land or naval forces; commanding and other officers of the Army and in the Navy betrayed our councils or deserted their posts for commands in the insurgent forces. Treason was flagrant in the revenue and in the post-office service, as well as in the Territorial governments and in the Indian reserves.

Not only governors, judges, legislators, and ministerial officers in the States, but even whole States rushed one after another with apparent unanimity into rebellion. The capital was besieged and its connection with all the States cut off.

Even in the portions of the country which were most loyal political combinations and secret societies were formed furthering the work of disunion, while, from motives of disloyalty or cupidity or from excited passions or perverted sympathies, individuals were found furnishing men, money, and materials of war and supplies to the insurgents' military and naval forces. Armies, ships, fortifications, navy-yards, arsenals, military posts, and garrisons one after another were betrayed or abandoned to the insurgents.

Congress had not anticipated, and so had not provided for, the emergency. The municipal authorities were powerless and inactive. The judicial machinery seemed as if it had been designed, not to sustain the Government, but to embarrass and betray it.

Foreign intervention, openly invited and industriously instigated by the abettors of the insurrection, became imminent, and has only been prevented by the practice of strict and impartial justice, with the most perfect moderation, in our intercourse with nations.

The public mind was alarmed and apprehensive, though fortunately not distracted or disheartened. It seemed to be doubtful whether the Federal Government, which one year before had been thought a model worthy of universal acceptance, had indeed the ability to defend and maintain itself.

Some reverses, which, perhaps, were unavoidable, suffered by newly levied and inefficient forces, discouraged the loyal and gave new hopes to the insurgents. Voluntary enlistments seemed about to cease and desertions commenced. Parties speculated upon the question whether conscription had not become necessary to fill up the armies of the United States.

In this emergency the President felt it his duty to employ with energy the extraordinary powers which the Constitution confides to him in cases of insurrection. He called into the field such military and naval forces, unauthorized by the existing laws, as seemed necessary. He directed measures to prevent the use of the post-office for treasonable correspondence. He subjected passengers to and from foreign countries to new passport regulations, and he instituted a blockade, suspended the writ of *habeas corpus* in various places, and caused persons who were represented to him as being or about to engage in disloyal and treasonable practices to be arrested by special civil as well as military agencies and detained in military custody when necessary to prevent them and deter others from such practices. Examinations of such cases were instituted, and some of the persons so arrested have been discharged from time to time under circumstances or upon conditions compatible, as was thought, with the public safety.

Meantime a favorable change of public opinion has occurred. The line between loyalty and disloyalty is plainly defined. The whole structure of the Government is firm and stable. Apprehension of public danger and facilities for treasonable practices have diminished with the passions which prompted heedless persons to adopt them. The insurrection is believed to have culminated and to be declining.

The President, in view of these facts, and anxious to favor a return to the normal course of the Administration as far as regard for the public welfare will allow, directs that all political prisoners or state prisoners now held in military custody be released on their subscribing to a parole engaging them to render no aid or comfort to the enemies in hostility to the United States.

The Secretary of War will, however, in his discretion, except from the effect of this order any persons detained as spies in the service of the insurgents, or others whose release at the present moment may be deemed incompatible with the public safety.

To all persons who shall be so released and who shall keep their parole the President grants an amnesty for any past offenses of treason or disloyalty which they may have committed.

Extraordinary arrests will hereafter be made under the direction of the military authorities alone.

By order of the President:

EDWIN M. STANTON,
Secretary of War.

THE PRESIDENT'S THANKS TO THE FORCES THAT CAPTURED FORT HENRY AND ROANOKE ISLAND.

WASHINGTON CITY, D. C., *February 15, 1862.*

The President, Commander in Chief of the Army and Navy, returns thanks to Brigadier-General Burnside and Flag-Officer Goldsborough, and to Brigadier-General Grant and Flag-Officer Foote, and the land and naval forces under their respective commands, for their gallant achievements in the capture of Fort Henry and at Roanoke Island. While it will be no ordinary pleasure for him to acknowledge and reward in a becoming manner the valor of the living, he also recognizes his duty to pay fitting honor to the memory of the gallant dead. The charge at Roanoke Island, like the bayonet charge at Mill Springs, proves that the close grapple and sharp steel of loyal and patriotic soldiers must always put rebels and traitors to flight.

The late achievements of the Navy show that the flag of the Union, once borne in proud glory around the world by naval heroes, will soon again float over every rebel city and stronghold, and that it shall forever be honored and respected as the emblem of liberty and union in every land and upon every sea.

By order of the President:

EDWIN M. STANTON,
Secretary of War.

GIDEON WELLES,
Secretary of the Navy.

WAR DEPARTMENT,
Washington City, D. C., February 17, 1862.

Brigadier-General F. W. LANDER:

The President directs me to say that he has observed with pleasure the activity and enterprise manifested by yourself and the officers and soldiers of your command. You have shown how much may be done in the worst weather and worst roads by a spirited officer at the head of a small force of brave men, unwilling to waste life in camp when the enemies of their country are within reach. Your brilliant success is a happy presage of what may be expected when the Army of the Potomac shall be led to the field by their gallant general.

EDWIN M. STANTON,
Secretary of War.

GENERAL ORDERS, No. 16.

HEADQUARTERS OF THE ARMY,
ADJUTANT-GENERAL'S OFFICE,
Washington, February 18, 1862.

I. The following concurrent resolutions of the two Houses of the Congress of the United States are published for the information of the Army:

Resolved, That the two Houses will assemble in the Chamber of the House of Representatives on Saturday, the 22d day of February instant, at 12 o'clock meridian, and that in the presence of the two Houses of Congress thus assembled the Farewell Address of George Washington to the people of the United States shall be read; and that the President of the Senate and the Speaker of the House of Representatives be requested to invite the President of the United States, the heads of the several Departments, the judges of the Supreme Court, the representatives from all foreign governments near this Government, and such officers of the Army and Navy and distinguished citizens as may then be at the seat of Government to be present on that occasion.

Resolved, That the President of the United States, Commander in Chief of the Army and Navy, be requested to direct that orders be issued for the reading to the Army and Navy of the United States of the Farewell Address of George Washington, or such parts thereof as he may select, on the 22d day of February instant.

II. In compliance with the foregoing resolutions, the President of the United States, Commander in Chief of the Army and Navy, orders that the following extracts from the Farewell Address of George Washington be read to the troops at every military post and at the head of the several regiments and corps of the Army:

Interwoven as is the love of liberty with every ligament of your hearts, no recommendation of mine is necessary to fortify or confirm the attachment.

The unity of government which constitutes you one people is also now dear to you. It is justly so, for it is a main pillar in the edifice of your real independence, the support of your tranquillity at home, your peace abroad, of your safety, of your prosperity, of that very liberty which you so highly prize. But as it is easy to foresee that from different causes and from different quarters much pains will be taken, many artifices employed, to weaken in your minds the conviction of this truth, as this is the point in your political fortress against which the batteries of internal and external enemies will be most constantly and actively (though often covertly and insidiously) directed, it is of infinite moment that you should properly estimate the immense value of your national union to your collective and individual happiness; that you should cherish a cordial, habitual, and immovable attachment to it; accustoming yourselves to think and speak of it as of the palladium of your political safety and prosperity; watching for its preservation with jealous anxiety; discountenancing whatever may suggest even a suspicion that it can in any event be abandoned, and indignantly frowning upon the first dawning of every attempt to alienate any portion of our country from the rest or to enfeeble the sacred ties which now link together the various parts.

For this you have every inducement of sympathy and interest. Citizens by birth or choice of a common country, that country has a right to concentrate your affections. The name of American, which belongs to you in your national capacity, must always exalt the just pride of patriotism more than any appellation derived from local discriminations. With slight shades of difference, you have the same religion, manners, habits, and political principles. You have in a common cause fought and triumphed together. The independence and liberty you possess are the work of joint councils and joint efforts, of common dangers, sufferings, and successes.

  *   *   *   *   *   *   *

While, then, every part of our country thus feels an immediate and particular interest in union, all the parts combined can not fail to find in the united mass of means and efforts greater strength, greater resource, proportionably greater security from external danger, a less frequent interruption of their peace by foreign nations, and, what is of inestimable value, they must derive from union an exemption from those broils and wars between themselves which so frequently afflict neighboring countries not tied together by the same governments, which their own rivalships alone would be sufficient to produce, but which opposite foreign alliances, attachments, and intrigues would stimulate and imbitter. Hence, likewise, they will avoid the necessity of those overgrown military establishments which, under any form of government, are inauspicious to liberty, and which are to be regarded as particularly hostile to republican liberty. In this sense it is that your union ought to be considered as a main prop of your liberty, and that the love of the one ought to endear to you the preservation of the other.

  *   *   *   *   *   *   *

To the efficacy and permanency of your union a government for the whole is indispensable. No alliances, however strict, between the parts can be an adequate substitute. They must inevitably experience the infractions and interruptions which all alliances in all times have experienced. Sensible of this momentous truth, you have improved upon your first essay by the adoption of a Constitution of Government better calculated than your former for an intimate union and for the efficacious management of your common concerns. This Government, the offspring of our own choice, uninfluenced and unawed, adopted upon full investigation and mature deliberation, completely free in its principles, in the distribution of its powers, uniting security with energy, and containing within itself a provision for its own amendment, has a just claim to your confidence and your support. Respect for its authority, compliance with its laws, acquiescence in its measures, are duties enjoined by the fundamental maxims of true liberty. The basis of our political systems is the right of the people to make and to alter their constitutions of government. But the constitution which at any time exists till changed by an explicit and authentic act of the whole people is sacredly obligatory upon all. The very idea of the power and the right of the people to establish government presupposes the duty of every individual to obey the established government.

All obstructions to the execution of the laws, all combinations and associations, under whatever plausible character, with the real design to direct, control, counteract, or awe the regular deliberation and action of the constituted authorities, are destructive of this fundamental principle and of fatal tendency. They serve to organize faction; to give it an artificial and extraordinary force; to put in the place of the delegated will of the nation the will of a party, often a small but artful and enterprising minority of the community, and, according to the alternate triumphs of different parties, to make the public administration the mirror of the ill-concerted and incongruous projects of faction rather than the organ of consistent and wholesome plans, digested by common counsels and modified by mutual interests.

  *   *   *   *   *   *   *

Of all the dispositions and habits which lead to political prosperity, religion and morality are indispensable supports. In vain would that man claim the tribute of patriotism who should labor to subvert these great pillars of human happiness—these firmest props of the duties of men and citizens. The mere politician, equally with the pious man, ought to respect and to cherish them. A volume could not trace all their connections with private and public felicity. Let it simply be asked, Where is the security for property, for reputation, for life, if the sense of religious obligation *desert* the oaths which are the instruments of investigation in courts of justice? And let us with caution indulge the supposition that morality can be maintained without religion. Whatever may be conceded to the influence of refined education on minds of peculiar structure, reason and experience both forbid us to expect that national morality can prevail in exclusion of religious principle.

It is substantially true that virtue or morality is a necessary spring of popular government. The rule indeed extends with more or less force to every species of free government. Who that is a sincere friend to it can look with indifference upon attempts to shake the foundation of the fabric? Promote, then, as an object of primary importance, institutions for the general diffusion of knowledge. In proportion as the structure of a government gives force to public opinion, it is essential that public opinion should be enlightened.

*   *   *   *   *   *

Observe good faith and justice toward all nations. Cultivate peace and harmony with all. Religion and morality enjoin this conduct. And can it be that good policy does not equally enjoin it? It will be worthy of a free, enlightened, and at no distant period a great nation to give to mankind the magnanimous and too novel example of a people always guided by an exalted justice and benevolence. Who can doubt that in the course of time and things the fruits of such a plan would richly repay any temporary advantages which might be lost by a steady adherence to it? Can it be that Providence has not connected the permanent felicity of a nation with its virtue? The experiment, at least, is recommended by every sentiment which ennobles human nature. Alas! is it rendered impossible by its vices?

*   *   *   *   *   *   *

Harmony, liberal intercourse with all nations, are recommended by policy, humanity, and interest. But even our commercial policy should hold an equal and impartial hand, neither seeking nor granting exclusive favors or preferences; consulting the natural course of things; diffusing and diversifying by gentle means the streams of commerce, but forcing nothing; establishing with powers so disposed, in order to give trade a stable course, to define the rights of our merchants, and to enable the Government to support them, conventional rules of intercourse, the best that present circumstances and mutual opinion will permit, but temporary and liable to be from time to time abandoned or varied as experience and circumstances shall dictate; constantly keeping in view that it is folly in one nation to look for disinterested favors from another; that it must pay with a portion of its independence for whatever it may accept under that character; that by such acceptance it may place itself in the condition of having given equivalents for nominal favors, and yet of being reproached with ingratitude for not giving more. There can be no greater error than to expect or calculate upon real favors from nation to nation. It is an illusion which experience must cure, which a just pride ought to discard.

In offering to you, my countrymen, these counsels of an old and affectionate friend I dare not hope they will make the strong and lasting impression I could wish—that they will control the usual current of the passions or prevent our nation from running the course which has hitherto marked the destiny of nations. But if I may even flatter myself that they may be productive of some partial benefit, some occasional good—that they may now and then recur to moderate the fury of party spirit, to warn against the mischiefs of foreign intrigue, to guard against the impostures of pretended patriotism—this hope will be a full recompense for the solicitude for your welfare by which they have been dictated.

*   *   *   *   *   *   *

Though in reviewing the incidents of my Administration I am unconscious of intentional error, I am nevertheless too sensible of my defects not to think it probable that I may have committed many errors.   Whatever they may be, I fervently beseech the Almighty to avert or mitigate the evils to which they may tend.   I shall also carry with me the hope that my country will never cease to view them with indulgence, and that, after forty-five years of my life dedicated to its service with an upright zeal, the faults of incompetent abilities will be consigned to oblivion, as myself must soon be to the mansions of rest.

Relying on its kindness in this as in other things, and actuated by that fervent love toward it which is so natural to a man who views in it the native soil of himself and his progenitors for several generations, I anticipate with pleasing expectation that retreat in which I promise myself to realize without alloy the sweet enjoyment of partaking in the midst of my fellow-citizens the benign influence of good laws under a free government—the ever-favorite object of my heart, and the happy reward, as I trust, of our mutual cares, labors, and dangers.

By command of Major-General McClellan:

L. THOMAS,
Adjutant-General.

WAR DEPARTMENT,
Washington City, D. C., February 18, 1862.

Ordered by the President, Commander in Chief of the Army and Navy of the United States, That on the 22d day of February, in the Hall of the House of Representatives, immediately after the Farewell Address of George Washington shall have been read, the rebel flags lately captured by the United States forces shall be presented to Congress by the Adjutant-General, to be disposed of as Congress may direct.

By order of the President:

EDWIN M. STANTON,
Secretary of War.

WAR DEPARTMENT,
Washington City, February 25, 1862.

Ordered, first. On and after the 26th day of February instant the President, by virtue of the act of Congress, takes military possession of all the telegraph lines in the United States.

Second. All telegraphic communications in regard to military operations not expressly authorized by the War Department, the General Commanding, or the generals commanding armies in the field, in the several departments, are absolutely forbidden.

Third. All newspapers publishing military news, however obtained and by whatever medium received, not authorized by the official authority mentioned in the preceding paragraph will be excluded thereafter from receiving information by telegraph or from transmitting their papers by railroad.

Fourth. Edward S. Sanford is made military supervisor of telegraphic messages throughout the United States. Anson Stager is made military superintendent of all telegraph lines and offices in the United States.

Fifth. This possession and control of the telegraph lines is not intended to interfere in any respect with the ordinary affairs of the companies or with private business.

By order of the President:

EDWIN M. STANTON,
Secretary of War.

WAR DEPARTMENT,
Washington, February 27, 1862.

It is ordered, first. That a special commission of two persons, one of military rank and the other in civil life, be appointed to examine the cases of the state prisoners remaining in the military custody of the United States, and to determine whether, in view of the public safety and the existing rebellion, they should be discharged or remain in military custody or be remitted to the civil tribunals for trial.

Second. That Major-General John A. Dix, commanding in Baltimore, and the Hon. Edwards Pierrepont, of New York, be, and they are hereby, appointed commissioners for the purposes above mentioned, and they are authorized to examine, hear, and determine the cases aforesaid, *ex parte* and in a summary manner, at such times and places as in their discretion they may appoint, and make full report to the War Department.

By order of the President:

EDWIN M. STANTON,
Secretary of War.

BY THE PRESIDENT OF THE UNITED STATES.

WASHINGTON, *February 28, 1862.*

Considering that the existing circumstances of the country allow a partial restoration of commercial intercourse between the inhabitants of those parts of the United States heretofore declared to be in insurrection and the citizens of the loyal States of the Union, and exercising the authority and discretion confided to me by the act of Congress approved July 13, 1861, entitled "An act further to provide for the collection of duties on imports, and for other purposes," I hereby license and permit such commercial intercourse in all cases within the rules and regulations which have been or may be prescribed by the Secretary of the Treasury for the conducting and carrying on of the same on the inland waters and ways of the United States.

ABRAHAM LINCOLN.

PRESIDENT'S GENERAL WAR ORDER NO. 2.

EXECUTIVE MANSION,
Washington, March 8, 1862.

Ordered, 1. That the major-general commanding the Army of the Potomac proceed forthwith to organize that part of the said army destined to enter upon active operations (including the reserve, but excluding the troops to be left in the fortifications about Washington) into four army corps, to be commanded according to seniority of rank, as follows:

First Corps to consist of four divisions, and to be commanded by Major-General I. McDowell.

Second Corps to consist of three divisions, and to be commanded by Brigadier-General E. V. Sumner.

Third Corps to consist of three divisions, and to be commanded by Brigadier-General S. P. Heintzelman.

Fourth Corps to consist of three divisions, and to be commanded by Brigadier-General E. D. Keyes.

2. That the divisions now commanded by the officers above assigned to the commands of army corps shall be embraced in and form part of their respective corps.

3. The forces left for the defense of Washington will be placed in command of Brigadier-General James S. Wadsworth, who shall also be military governor of the District of Columbia.

4. That this order be executed with such promptness and dispatch as not to delay the commencement of the operations already directed to be undertaken by the Army of the Potomac.

5. A fifth army corps, to be commanded by Major-General N. P. Banks, will be formed from his own and General Shields's (late General Lander's) divisions.

ABRAHAM LINCOLN.

PRESIDENT'S GENERAL WAR ORDER NO. 3.

EXECUTIVE MANSION,
Washington, March 8, 1862.

Ordered, That no change of the base of operations of the Army of the Potomac shall be made without leaving in and about Washington such a force as in the opinion of the General in Chief and the commanders of all the army corps shall leave said city entirely secure.

That no more than two army corps (about 50,000 troops) of said Army of the Potomac shall be moved *en route* for a new base of operations until the navigation of the Potomac from Washington to the Chesapeake Bay shall be freed from enemy's batteries and other obstructions, or until the President shall hereafter give express permission.

That any movements as aforesaid *en route* for a new base of operations which may be ordered by the General in Chief, and which may be intended to move upon the Chesapeake Bay, shall begin to move upon the bay as early as the 18th day of March instant, and the General in Chief shall be responsible that it so move as early as that day.

Ordered, That the Army and Navy cooperate in an immediate effort to capture the enemy's batteries upon the Potomac between Washington and the Chesapeake Bay.

A. LINCOLN.

PRESIDENT'S SPECIAL WAR ORDER No. 3.

EXECUTIVE MANSION,
Washington, March 11, 1862.

Major-General McClellan having personally taken the field at the head of the Army of the Potomac, until otherwise ordered he is relieved from the command of the other military departments, he retaining command of the Department of the Potomac.

Ordered further, That the departments now under the respective commands of Generals Halleck and Hunter, together with so much of that under General Buell as lies west of a north and south line indefinitely drawn through Knoxville, Tenn., be consolidated and designated the Department of the Mississippi, and that until otherwise ordered Major-General Halleck have command of said department.

Ordered also, That the country west of the Department of the Potomac and east of the Department of the Mississippi be a military department, to be called the Mountain Department, and that the same be commanded by Major-General Frémont.

That all the commanders of departments, after the receipt of this order by them, respectively report severally and directly to the Secretary of War, and that prompt, full, and frequent reports will be expected of all and each of them.

ABRAHAM LINCOLN.

WAR DEPARTMENT, *March 13, 1862.*

Major-General GEORGE B. McCLELLAN:

The President, having considered the plan of operations agreed upon by yourself and the commanders of army corps, makes no objection to the same, but gives the following directions as to its execution:

1. Leave such force at Manassas Junction as shall make it entirely certain that the enemy shall not repossess himself of that position and line of communication.

2. Leave Washington entirely secure.

3. Move the remainder of the force down the Potomac, choosing a new base at Fortress Monroe, or anywhere between here and there, or, at all events, move such remainder of the army at once in pursuit of the enemy by some route.

EDWIN M. STANTON, *Secretary of War.*

[From the Daily National Intelligencer, March 28, 1862.]

NAVY DEPARTMENT, *March 15, 1862.*

Lieutenant JOHN L. WORDEN, United States Navy,
Commanding United States Steamer Monitor, Washington.

SIR: The naval action which took place on the 10th instant between the *Monitor* and *Merrimac* at Hampton Roads, when your vessel, with two guns, engaged a powerful armored steamer of at least eight guns, and after a few hours' conflict repelled her formidable antagonist, has excited general admiration and received the applause of the whole country.

The President directs me, while earnestly and deeply sympathizing with you in the injuries which you have sustained, but which it is believed are but temporary, to thank you and your command for the heroism you have displayed and the great service you have rendered.

The action of the 10th and the performance, power, and capabilities of the *Monitor* must effect a radical change in naval warfare.

Flag-Officer Goldsborough, in your absence, will be furnished by the Department with a copy of this letter of thanks and instructed to cause it to be read to the officers and crew of the *Monitor.*

I am, very respectfully, your obedient servant,

GIDEON WELLES.

WAR DEPARTMENT,
Washington, D. C., April 5, 1862.

Major-General JOHN A. DIX:

Ordered, That Major-General John A. Dix, commanding at Baltimore, be, and he is, authorized and empowered at his discretion—

First. To assume and exercise control over the police of the city of Baltimore; to supersede and remove the civil police or any part thereof and establish a military police in said city.

Second. To arrest and imprison disloyal persons, declare martial law, and suspend the writ of *habeas corpus* in the city of Baltimore or any part of his command, and to exercise and perform all military power, function, and authority that he may deem proper for the safety of his command or to secure obedience and respect to the authority and Government of the United States.

By order of the President:

EDWIN M. STANTON,
Secretary of War.

[From the Daily National Intelligencer, May 17, 1862.]

The skillful and gallant movements of Major-General John E. Wool and the forces under his command, which resulted in the surrender of Norfolk and the evacuation of strong batteries erected by the rebels on Sewells

Point and Craney Island and the destruction of the rebel ironclad steamer *Merrimac*, are regarded by the President as among the most important successes of the present war. He therefore orders that his thanks as Commander in Chief of the Army and Navy be communicated by the War Department to Major-General John E. Wool and the officers and soldiers of his command for their gallantry and good conduct in the brilliant operations mentioned.

By order of the President, made at the city of Norfolk on the 11th day of May, 1862:

EDWIN M. STANTON,
Secretary of War.

WAR DEPARTMENT, *May 25, 1862.*

Ordered: By virtue of the authority vested by act of Congress, the President takes military possession of all the railroads in the United States from and after this date until further order, and directs that the respective railroad companies, their officers and servants, shall hold themselves in readiness for the transportation of such troops and munitions of war as may be ordered by the military authorities, to the exclusion of all other business.

By order of the Secretary of War:

M. C. MEIGS,
Quartermaster-General.

WAR DEPARTMENT,
Washington, D. C., May 28, 1862.

Colonel HAUPT.

SIR: You are hereby appointed chief of construction and transportation in the Department of the Rappahannock, with the rank of colonel, and attached to the staff of Major-General McDowell.

You are authorized to do whatever you may deem expedient to open for use in the shortest possible time all military railroads now or hereafter required in said department; to use the same for transportation under such rules and regulations as you may prescribe; to appoint such assistants and employees as you may deem necessary, define their duties and fix their compensation; to make requisitions upon any of the military authorities, with the approval of the Commanding General, for such temporary or permanent details of men as may be required for the construction or protection of lines of communication; to use such Government steamers and transports as you may deem necessary; to pass free of charge in such steamers and transports and on other military roads all persons whose services may be required in construction or transportation; to purchase all such machinery, rolling stock, and supplies as the proper use and operation of the said railroads may require, and certify the same to the Quartermaster-General, who shall make payment therefor. You are also authorized to form a permanent corps of artificers, organized, officered, and equipped in such manner as you may prescribe; to supply said corps with rations, transportation, tools, and implements by requisitions upon the proper departments; to employ civilians as foremen and assistants, under such rules and rates of compensation as you may deem expedient; to make such additions to ordinary rations when actually at work as you may deem necessary.

You are also authorized to take possession of and use all railroads, engines, cars, buildings, machinery, and appurtenances within the geographical limits of the Department of the Rappahannock, and all authority heretofore given to other parties which may in any way conflict with the instructions herein contained are and will be without force and effect in the said Department of the Rappahannock from and after this date.

By order of the President, Commander in Chief of the Army and Navy of the United States:

EDWIN M. STANTON,
Secretary of War.

WAR DEPARTMENT,
Washington City, D. C., May 30, 1862.

All regiments of militia or of three-months' volunteers who have offered their services under the recent call of the War Department, and who have so far perfected their organization as to be able to report for orders at St. Louis, at Columbus, or at Washington City by the 10th of June, will be mustered into the service of the United States for three months from that date, the pay of each volunteer or militiaman commencing from the date of his enlistment.

Under the call for three-years' volunteers 50,000 men will be accepted as raised and reported by the respective State governors.

By order of the President:

EDWIN M. STANTON,
Secretary of War.

NEW YORK, *June 30, 1862.*

To the Governors of the several States:

The capture of New Orleans, Norfolk, and Corinth by the national forces has enabled the insurgents to concentrate a large force at and about Richmond, which place we must take with the least possible delay; in fact, there will soon be no formidable insurgent force except at Richmond. With so large an army there, the enemy can threaten us on the Potomac and elsewhere. Until we have reestablished the national authority, all these places must be held, and we must keep a respectable force in front of Washington. But this, from the diminished strength of our Army by sickness and casualties, renders an addition to it necessary in order to close the struggle which has been prosecuted for the last three months with energy and success. Rather than hazard the misapprehension of our military condition and of groundless alarm by a call for troops by proclamation, I have deemed it best to address you in this form. To accomplish the object stated we require without delay 150,000 men, including those recently called for by the Secretary of War. Thus reenforced our gallant Army will be enabled to realize the hopes and expectations of the Government and the people.

ABRAHAM LINCOLN.

JUNE 28, 1862.

The PRESIDENT:

The undersigned, governors of States of the Union, impressed with the belief that the citizens of the States which they respectively represent are of one accord in the hearty desire that the recent successes of the Federal arms may be followed up by measures which must insure the speedy restoration of the Union, and believing that, in view of the present state of the important military movements now in progress and the reduced condition of our effective forces in the field, resulting from the usual and unavoidable casualties in the service, the time has arrived for prompt and vigorous measures to be adopted by the people in support of the great interests committed to your charge, respectfully request, if it meets with your entire approval, that you at once call upon the several States for such number of men as may be required to fill up all military organizations now in the field, and add to the armies heretofore organized such additional number of men as may, in your judgment, be necessary to garrison and hold all the numerous cities and military positions that have been captured by our armies, and to speedily crush the rebellion that still exists in several of the Southern States, thus practically restoring to the civilized world our great and good Government. All believe that the decisive moment is near at hand, and to that end the people of the United States are desirous to aid promptly in furnishing all reenforcements that you may deem needful to sustain our Government.

> ISRAEL WASHBURN, Jr., Governor of Maine; H. S. BERRY, Governor of New Hampshire; FREDERICK HOLBROOK, Governor of Vermont; WILLIAM A. BUCKINGHAM, Governor of Connecticut; E. D. MORGAN, Governor of New York; CHARLES S. OLDEN, Governor of New Jersey; A. G. CURTIN, Governor of Pennsylvania; A. W. BRADFORD, Governor of Maryland; F. H. PEIRPOINT, Governor of Virginia; AUSTIN BLAIR, Governor of Michigan; J. B. TEMPLE, President Military Board of Kentucky; ANDREW JOHNSON, Governor of Tennessee; H. R. GAMBLE, Governor of Missouri; O. P. MORTON, Governor of Indiana; DAVID TODD, Governor of Ohio; ALEXANDER RAMSEY, Governor of Minnesota; RICHARD YATES, Governor of Illinois; EDWARD SALOMON, Governor of Wisconsin.

EXECUTIVE MANSION,

Washington, July 1, 1862.

GENTLEMEN: Fully concurring in the wisdom of the views expressed to me in so patriotic a manner by you in the communication of the 28th day of June, I have decided to call into the service an additional force of 300,000 men. I suggest and recommend that the troops should be chiefly of infantry. The quota of your State would be ———. I trust that they may be enrolled without delay, so as to bring this unnecessary and injurious civil war to a speedy and satisfactory conclusion. An order fixing the quotas of the respective States will be issued by the War Department to-morrow.

ABRAHAM LINCOLN.

EXECUTIVE MANSION,
Washington, July 11, 1862.

Ordered, That Major-General Henry W. Halleck be assigned to command the whole land forces of the United States as General in Chief, and that he repair to this capital as soon as he can with safety to the positions and operations within the department under his charge.

A. LINCOLN.

Whereas, in the judgment of the President, the public safety does require that the railroad line called and known as the Southwest Branch of the Pacific Railroad in the State of Missouri be repaired, extended, and completed from Rolla to Lebanon, in the direction to Springfield, in the said State, the same being necessary to the successful and economical conduct of the war and to the maintenance of the authority of the Government in the Southwest:

Therefore, under and in virtue of the act of Congress entitled "An act to authorize the President of the United States in certain cases to take possession of railroad and telegraph lines, and for other purposes," approved January 31, 1862, it is—

Ordered, That the portion of the said railroad line which reaches from Rolla to Lebanon be repaired, extended, and completed, so as to be made available for the military uses of the Government, as speedily as may be. And inasmuch as, upon the part of the said line from Rolla to the stream called Little Piney a considerable portion of the necessary work has already been done by the railroad company, and the road to this extent may be completed at comparatively small cost, it is ordered that the said line from Rolla to and across Little Piney be first completed, and as soon as possible.

The Secretary of War is charged with the execution of this order. And to facilitate the speedy execution of the work, he is directed, at his discretion, to take possession and control of the whole or such part of the said railroad line, and the whole or such part of the rolling stock, offices, shops, buildings, and all their appendages and appurtenances, as he may judge necessary or convenient for the early completion of the road from Rolla to Lebanon.

Done at the city of Washington, July 11, 1862.

ABRAHAM LINCOLN.

GENERAL ORDERS, No. 82.

WAR DEPARTMENT,
ADJUTANT-GENERAL'S OFFICE,
Washington, July 21, 1862.

The following order has been received from the President of the United States:

Representations have been made to the President by the ministers of various foreign powers in amity with the United States that subjects of such powers have during the present insurrection been obliged or required by military authorities to take an oath of general or qualified allegiance to this Government. It is the duty of all aliens residing in the United States to submit to and obey the laws and respect the authority of the Government. For any proceeding or conduct inconsistent with this obligation and subversive of that authority they may rightfully be subjected to military restraints when this may be necessary. But they can not be required to take an oath of allegiance to this Government, because it conflicts with the duty they owe to their own sovereigns. All such obligations heretofore taken are therefore remitted and annulled. Military commanders will abstain from imposing similar obligations in future, and will in lieu thereof adopt such other restraints of the character indicated as they shall find necessary, convenient, and effectual for the public safety. It is further directed that whenever any order shall be made affecting the personal liberty of an alien reports of the same and of the causes thereof shall be made to the War Department for the consideration of the Department of State.

By order of the Secretary of War:

L. THOMAS,
Adjutant-General.

WAR DEPARTMENT, *July 22, 1862.*

1. *Ordered*, That military commanders within the States of Virginia, South Carolina, Georgia, Florida, Alabama, Mississippi, Louisiana, Texas, and Arkansas in an orderly manner seize and use any property, real or personal, which may be necessary or convenient for their several commands as supplies or for other military purposes; and that while property may be destroyed for proper military objects, none shall be destroyed in wantonness or malice.

2. That military and naval commanders shall employ as laborers within and from said States so many persons of African descent as can be advantageously used for military or naval purposes, giving them reasonable wages for their labor.

3. That as to both property and persons of African descent accounts shall be kept sufficiently accurate and in detail to show quantities and amounts and from whom both property and such persons shall have

come, as a basis upon which compensation can be made in proper cases; and the several Departments of this Government shall attend to and perform their appropriate parts toward the execution of these orders.

By order of the President:

EDWIN M. STANTON,
Secretary of War.

GENERAL ORDERS, No. 89.

WAR DEPARTMENT,
ADJUTANT-GENERAL'S OFFICE,
Washington, July 25, 1862.

I. The following order of the President of the United States communicates information of the death of ex-President Martin Van Buren:

WASHINGTON, *July 25, 1862.*

The President with deep regret announces to the people of the United States the decease, at Kinderhook, N. Y., on the 24th instant, of his honored predecessor Martin Van Buren.

This event will occasion mourning in the nation for the loss of a citizen and a public servant whose memory will be gratefully cherished. Although it has occurred at a time when his country is afflicted with division and civil war, the grief of his patriotic friends will measurably be assuaged by the consciousness that while suffering with disease and seeing his end approaching his prayers were for the restoration of the authority of the Government of which he had been the head and for peace and good will among his fellow-citizens.

As a mark of respect for his memory, it is ordered that the Executive Mansion and the several Executive Departments, except those of War and the Navy, be immediately placed in mourning and all business be suspended during to-morrow.

It is further ordered that the War and Navy Departments cause suitable military and naval honors to be paid on this occasion to the memory of the illustrious dead.

ABRAHAM LINCOLN.

II. On the day after the receipt of this order the troops will be paraded at 10 o'clock a. m. and the order read to them. The national flag will be displayed at half-staff. At dawn of day thirteen guns will be fired, and afterwards at intervals of thirty minutes between rising and setting sun a single gun, and at the close of the day a national salute of thirty-four guns. The officers of the Army will wear crape on the left arm and on their swords and the colors of the several regiments will be put in mourning for the period of six months.

By order of the Secretary of War:

L. THOMAS,
Adjutant-General.

GENERAL ORDER.

NAVY DEPARTMENT, *July 25, 1862.*

The death of ex-President Martin Van Buren is announced in the following order of the President of the United States:

[For order see preceding page.]

In pursuance of the foregoing order, it is hereby directed that thirty minute guns, commencing at noon, be fired on the day after the receipt of this general order at the navy-yards, naval stations, and on board the vessels of the Navy in commission; that their flags be displayed at half-mast for one week, and that crape be worn on the left arm by all officers of the Navy for a period of six months.

GIDEON WELLES, *Secretary of the Navy.*

WAR DEPARTMENT,
Washington City, D. C., July 31, 1862.

The absence of officers and privates from their duty under various pre-texts while receiving pay, at great expense and burden to the Government, makes it necessary that efficient measures be taken to enforce their return to duty or that their places be supplied by those who will not take pay while rendering no service. This evil, moreover, tends greatly to discourage the patriotic impulses of those who would contribute to support the families of faithful soldiers.

It is therefore ordered by the President—

I. That on Monday, the 11th day of August, all leaves of absence and furloughs, by whomsoever given, unless by the War Department, are revoked and absolutely annulled, and all officers capable of service are required forthwith to join their respective commands and all privates capable of service to join their regiments, under penalty of a dismissal from the service, or such penalty as a court-martial may award, unless the absence be occasioned by lawful cause.

II. The only excuses allowed for the absence of officers or privates after the 11th day of August are:

First. The order or leave of the War Department.

Second. Disability from wounds received in service.

Third. Disability from disease that renders the party unfit for military duty. But any officer or private whose health permits him to visit watering places or places of amusement, or to make social visits or walk about the town, city, or neighborhood in which he may be, will be considered fit for military duty and as evading duty by absence from his command or ranks.

III. On Monday, the 18th day of August, at 10 o'clock a. m., each regiment and corps shall be mustered. The absentees will be marked, three lists of the same made out, and within forty-eight hours after the muster one copy shall be sent to the Adjutant-General of the Army, one to the commander of the corps, the third to be retained; and all officers and privates fit for duty absent at that time will be regarded as absent without cause, their pay will be stopped, and they dismissed from the service or treated as deserters unless restored; and no officer shall be restored to his rank unless by the judgment of a court of inquiry, to be approved by the President, he shall establish that his absence was with good cause.

IV. Commanders of corps, divisions, brigades, regiments, and detached posts are strictly enjoined to enforce the muster and return aforesaid. Any officer failing in his duty herein will be deemed guilty of gross neglect of duty and be dismissed from the service.

V. A commissioner shall be appointed by the Secretary of War to superintend the execution of this order in the respective States.

The United States marshals in the respective districts, the mayor and chief of police of any town or city, the sheriff of the respective counties in each State, all postmasters and justices of the peace, are authorized to act as special provost-marshals to arrest any officer or private soldier fit for duty who may be found absent from his command without just cause and convey him to the nearest military post or depot. The transportation, reasonable expenses of this duty, and $5 will be paid for each officer or private so arrested and delivered.

By order of the President:

E. M. STANTON, *Secretary of War.*

WAR DEPARTMENT,
Washington City, D. C., August 4, 1862.

Ordered, I. That a draft of 300,000 militia be immediately called into the service of the United States, to serve for nine months unless sooner discharged. The Secretary of War will assign the quotas to the States and establish regulations for the draft.

II. That if any State shall not by the 15th of August furnish its quota of the additional 300,000 volunteers authorized by law the deficiency of volunteers in that State will also be made up by special draft from the militia. The Secretary of War will establish regulations for this purpose.

III. Regulations will be prepared by the War Department and presented to the President with the object of securing the promotion of officers of the Army and Volunteers for meritorious and distinguished services and of preventing the nomination or appointment in the military service of incompetent or unworthy officers. The regulations will also provide for ridding the service of such incompetent persons as now hold commissions in it.

By order of the President:

EDWIN M. STANTON, *Secretary of War.*

War Department,
Washington, D. C., August 8, 1862.

By direction of the President of the United States, it is hereby ordered that until further order no citizen liable to be drafted into the militia shall be allowed to go to a foreign country. And all marshals, deputy marshals, and military officers of the United States are directed, and all police authorities, especially at the ports of the United States on the seaboard and on the frontier, are requested, to see that this order is faithfully carried into effect. And they are hereby authorized and directed to arrest and detain any person or persons about to depart from the United States in violation of this order, and report to Major L. C. Turner, judge-advocate at Washington City, for further instructions respecting the person or persons so arrested or detained.

II. Any person liable to draft who shall absent himself from his county or State before such draft is made will be arrested by any provost-marshal or other United States or State officer, wherever he may be found within the jurisdiction of the United States, and be conveyed to the nearest military post or depot and placed on military duty for the term of the draft; and the expenses of his own arrest and conveyance to such post or depot, and also the sum of $5, as a reward to the officer who shall make such arrest, shall be deducted from his pay.

III. The writ of *habeas corpus* is hereby suspended in respect to all persons so arrested and detained, and in respect to all persons arrested for disloyal practices.

EDWIN M. STANTON,
Secretary of War.

War Department,
Washington City, D. C., August 14, 1862.

Order Respecting Volunteers and Militia.

Ordered, first. That after the 15th of this month bounty and advanced pay shall not be paid to volunteers for any new regiments, but only to volunteers for regiments now in the field and volunteers to fill up new regiments now organizing, but not yet full.

Second. Volunteers to fill up new regiments now organizing will be received and paid the bounty and advanced pay until the 22d day of this month, and if not completed by that time the incomplete regiments will be consolidated and superfluous officers mustered out.

Third. Volunteers to fill up the old regiments will be received and paid the bounty and advanced pay until the 1st day of September.

Fourth. The draft for 300,000 militia called for by the President will be made on Wednesday, the 3d day of September, between the hours of 9 a. m. and 5 p. m., and continue from day to day between the same hours until completed.

Fifth. If the old regiments should not be filled up by volunteers before the 1st day of September, a special draft will be ordered for the deficiency.

Sixth. The exigencies of the service require that officers now in the field should remain with their commands, and no officer now in the field in the regular or volunteer service will under any circumstances be detailed to accept a new command.

By order of the President:

EDWIN M. STANTON,
Secretary of War.

SPECIAL ORDERS, No. 218.

HEADQUARTERS OF THE ARMY,
ADJUTANT-GENERAL'S OFFICE,
Washington, September 2, 1862.

*   *   *   *   *   *   *

By direction of the President, all the clerks and employees of the civil Departments and all the employees on the public buildings in Washington will be immediately organized into companies, under the direction of Brigadier-General Wadsworth, and will be armed and supplied with ammunition, for the defense of the capital.

By command of Major-General Halleck:

E. D. TOWNSEND,
Assistant Adjutant-General.

EXECUTIVE ORDER ESTABLISHING A PROVISIONAL COURT IN LOUISIANA.

EXECUTIVE MANSION,
Washington City, October 20, 1862.

The insurrection which has for some time prevailed in several of the States of this Union, including Louisiana, having temporarily subverted and swept away the civil institutions of that State, including the judiciary and the judicial authorities of the Union, so that it has become necessary to hold the State in military occupation, and it being indispensably necessary that there shall be some judicial tribunal existing there capable of administering justice, I have therefore thought it proper to appoint, and I do hereby constitute, a provisional court, which shall be a court of record, for the State of Louisiana; and I do hereby appoint Charles A. Peabody, of New York, to be a provisional judge to hold said court, with authority to hear, try, and determine all causes, civil and criminal, including causes in law, equity, revenue, and admiralty, and particularly all such powers and jurisdiction as belong to the district and circuit courts of the United States, conforming his proceedings so far as possible to the course of proceedings and practice which has been customary in the courts of the United States and Louisiana, his judgment to be final and conclusive. And I do hereby authorize and empower the said judge to make and establish such rules and regulations as may be necessary for the exercise of his jurisdiction, and empower the said judge to appoint a prosecuting attorney, marshal, and clerk of the said court, who shall perform the functions of attorney, marshal, and clerk according to such proceedings and practice as before mentioned and such rules and regulations as may be made and established by said judge. These appointments are to continue during the pleasure of the President, not extending beyond the military occupation of the city of New Orleans or the restoration of the civil authority in that city and in the State of Louisiana. These officers shall be paid, out of the contingent fund of the War Department, compensation as follows: The judge at the rate of $3,500 per annum; the prosecuting attorney, including the fees, at the rate of $3,000 per annum; the marshal, including the fees, at the rate of $3,000 per annum; and the clerk, including the fees, at the rate of $2,500 per annum; such compensations to be certified by the Secretary of War. A copy of this order, certified by the Secretary of War and delivered to such judge, shall be deemed and held to be a sufficient commission.

ABRAHAM LINCOLN,
President of the United States.

EXECUTIVE MANSION,
Washington, October 29, 1862.

Two associate justices of the Supreme Court of the United States having been appointed since the last adjournment of said court, and consequently no allotment of the members of said court to the several circuits having been made by them, according to the fifth section of the act of Congress entitled "An act to amend the judicial system of the United States," approved April 29, 1802, I, Abraham Lincoln, President of the United States, in virtue of said section, do make an allotment of the justices of said court to the circuits now existing by law, as follows:

For the first circuit: Nathan Clifford, associate justice.
For the second circuit: Samuel Nelson, associate justice.
For the third circuit: Robert C. Grier, associate justice.
For the fourth circuit: Roger B. Taney, Chief Justice.
For the fifth circuit: James M. Wayne, associate justice.
For the sixth circuit: John Catron, associate justice.
For the seventh circuit: Noah H. Swayne, associate justice.
For the eighth circuit: David Davis, associate justice.
For the ninth circuit: Samuel F. Miller, associate justice.

ABRAHAM LINCOLN.

EXECUTIVE MANSION,
Washington, November 5, 1862.

By direction of the President, it is ordered that Major-General Mc-Clellan be relieved from the command of the Army of the Potomac, and that Major-General Burnside take the command of that army; also that Major-General Hunter take command of the corps in said army which is now commanded by General Burnside; that Major-General Fitz John Porter be relieved from the command of the corps he now commands in said army, and that Major-General Hooker take command of said corps.

The General in Chief is authorized, in [his] discretion, to issue an order substantially as the above forthwith, or so soon as he may deem proper.

A. LINCOLN.

EXECUTIVE MANSION, *November 7, 1862.*

Ordered, That Brigadier-General Ellet report to Rear-Admiral Porter for instructions, and act under his direction until otherwise ordered by the War Department.

ABRAHAM LINCOLN.

EXECUTIVE MANSION,
Washington, November 12, 1862.

Ordered, first. That clearances issued by the Treasury Department for vessels or merchandise bound for the port of Norfolk for the military necessities of the department, certified by the military commandant at Fort Monroe, shall be allowed to enter said port.

Second. That vessels and domestic produce from Norfolk, permitted by the military commandant at Fort Monroe for the military purposes of his command, shall on his permit be allowed to pass from said port to their destination in any port not blockaded by the United States.

A. LINCOLN.

[From the Daily National Intelligencer, November 25, 1862.]

EXECUTIVE MANSION, *November 13, 1862.*

Ordered by the President of the United States, That the Attorney-General be charged with the superintendence and direction of all proceedings to be had under the act of Congress of the 17th of July, 1862, entitled "An act to suppress insurrection, to punish treason and rebellion, to seize and confiscate the property of rebels, and for other purposes," in so far as may concern the seizure, prosecution, and condemnation of the estate, property, and effects of rebels and traitors, as mentioned and provided for in the fifth, sixth, and seventh sections of the said act of Congress. And the Attorney-General is authorized and required to give to the attorneys and marshals of the United States such instructions and directions as he may find needful and convenient touching all such seizures, prosecutions, and condemnations, and, moreover, to authorize all such attorneys and marshals, whenever there may be reasonable ground to fear any forcible resistance to them in the discharge of their respective duties in this behalf, to call upon any military officer in command of the forces of the United States to give to them such aid, protection, and support as may be necessary to enable them safely and efficiently to discharge their respective duties; and all such commanding officers are required promptly to obey such call, and to render the necessary service as far as may be in their power consistently with their other duties.

ABRAHAM LINCOLN.

By the President:
> EDWARD BATES,
>> *Attorney-General.*

GENERAL ORDER RESPECTING THE OBSERVANCE OF THE SABBATH DAY IN THE ARMY AND NAVY.

EXECUTIVE MANSION,
Washington, November 15, 1862.

The President, Commander in Chief of the Army and Navy, desires and enjoins the orderly observance of the Sabbath by the officers and men in the military and naval service. The importance for man and beast of the prescribed weekly rest, the sacred rights of Christian soldiers and sailors, a becoming deference to the best sentiment of a Christian people, and a due regard for the divine will demand that Sunday labor in the Army and Navy be reduced to the measure of strict necessity.

The discipline and character of the national forces should not suffer nor the cause they defend be imperiled by the profanation of the day or name of the Most High. "At this time of public distress," adopting the words of Washington in 1776, "men may find enough to do in the service of God and their country without abandoning themselves to vice and immorality." The first general order issued by the Father of his Country after the Declaration of Independence indicates the spirit in which our institutions were founded and should ever be defended:

The General hopes and trusts that every officer and man will endeavor to live and act as becomes a Christian soldier defending the dearest rights and liberties of his country.

ABRAHAM LINCOLN.

EXECUTIVE MANSION,
Washington City, November 21, 1862.

Ordered, That no arms, ammunition, or munitions of war be cleared or allowed to be exported from the United States until further order; that any clearances for arms, ammunition, or munitions of war issued heretofore by the Treasury Department be vacated if the articles have not passed without the United States, and the articles stopped; that the Secretary of War hold possession of the arms, etc., recently seized by his order at Rouses Point, bound for Canada.

ABRAHAM LINCOLN.

SECOND ANNUAL MESSAGE.

DECEMBER 1, 1862.

Fellow-Citizens of the Senate and House of Representatives:

Since your last annual assembling another year of health and bountiful harvests has passed, and while it has not pleased the Almighty to bless us with a return of peace, we can but press on, guided by the best light He gives us, trusting that in His own good time and wise way all will yet be well.

The correspondence touching foreign affairs which has taken place during the last year is herewith submitted, in virtual compliance with a request to that effect made by the House of Representatives near the close of the last session of Congress.

If the condition of our relations with other nations is less gratifying than it has usually been at former periods, it is certainly more satisfactory than a nation so unhappily distracted as we are might reasonably have apprehended. In the month of June last there were some grounds to expect that the maritime powers which at the beginning of our domestic difficulties so unwisely and unnecessarily, as we think, recognized the insurgents as a belligerent would soon recede from that position, which has proved only less injurious to themselves than to our own country. But the temporary reverses which afterwards befell the national arms, and which were exaggerated by our own disloyal citizens abroad, have hitherto delayed that act of simple justice.

The civil war, which has so radically changed for the moment the occupations and habits of the American people, has necessarily disturbed the social condition and affected very deeply the prosperity of the nations with which we have carried on a commerce that has been steadily increasing throughout a period of half a century. It has at the same time excited political ambitions and apprehensions which have produced a profound agitation throughout the civilized world. In this unusual agitation we have forborne from taking part in any controversy between foreign states and between parties or factions in such states. We have attempted no propagandism and acknowledged no revolution. But we have left to every nation the exclusive conduct and management of its own affairs. Our struggle has been, of course, contemplated by foreign nations with reference less to its own merits than to its supposed and often exaggerated effects and consequences resulting to those nations themselves. Nevertheless, complaint on the part of this Government, even if it were just, would certainly be unwise.

The treaty with Great Britain for the suppression of the slave trade has been put into operation with a good prospect of complete success. It is an occasion of special pleasure to acknowledge that the execution of it on the part of Her Majesty's Government has been marked with a jealous respect for the authority of the United States and the rights of their moral and loyal citizens.

The convention with Hanover for the abolition of the Stade dues has been carried into full effect under the act of Congress for that purpose.

A blockade of 3,000 miles of seacoast could not be established and vigorously enforced in a season of great commercial activity like the present without committing occasional mistakes and inflicting unintentional injuries upon foreign nations and their subjects.

A civil war occurring in a country where foreigners reside and carry on trade under treaty stipulations is necessarily fruitful of complaints of the violation of neutral rights. All such collisions tend to excite misapprehensions, and possibly to produce mutual reclamations between nations which have a common interest in preserving peace and friendship. In clear cases of these kinds I· have so far as possible heard and redressed complaints which have been presented by friendly powers. There is still, however, a large and an augmenting number of doubtful cases upon which the Government is unable to agree with the governments whose protection is demanded by the claimants. There are, moreover, many cases in which the United States or their citizens suffer wrongs from the naval or military authorities of foreign nations which the governments of those states are not at once prepared to redress. I have proposed to some of the foreign states thus interested mutual conventions to examine and adjust such complaints. This proposition has been made especially to Great Britain, to France, to Spain, and to Prussia. In each case it has been kindly received, but has not yet been formally adopted.

I deem it my duty to recommend an appropriation in behalf of the owners of the Norwegian bark *Admiral P. Tordenskiold*, which vessel was in May, 1861, prevented by the commander of the blockading force off Charleston from leaving that port with cargo, notwithstanding a similar privilege had shortly before been granted to an English vessel. I have directed the Secretary of State to cause the papers in the case to be communicated to the proper committees.

Applications have been made to me by many free Americans of African descent to favor their emigration, with a view to such colonization as was contemplated in recent acts of Congress. Other parties, at home and abroad—some from interested motives, others upon patriotic considerations, and still others influenced by philanthropic sentiments—have suggested similar measures, while, on the other hand, several of the Spanish American Republics have protested against the sending of such colonies to their respective territories. Under these circumstances I have declined to move any such colony to any state without first obtaining the consent of its government, with an agreement on its part to receive and protect such emigrants in all the rights of freemen; and I have at the same time offered to the several States situated within the Tropics, or having colonies there, to negotiate with them, subject to the advice and consent of the Senate, to favor the voluntary emigration of persons of that class to their respective territories, upon conditions which shall be equal, just, and humane. Liberia and Hayti are as yet the only countries to which colonists of African descent from here could go with certainty of being received and adopted as citizens; and I regret to say such persons contemplating colonization do not seem so willing to migrate to those countries as to some others, nor so willing as I think their interest demands. I believe, however, opinion among them in this respect is improving, and that ere long there will be an augmented and considerable migration to both these countries from the United States.

The new commercial treaty between the United States and the Sultan of Turkey has been carried into execution.

A commercial and consular treaty has been negotiated, subject to the Senate's consent, with Liberia, and a similar negotiation is now pending with the Republic of Hayti. A considerable improvement of the national commerce is expected to result from these measures.

Our relations with Great Britain, France, Spain, Portugal, Russia, Prussia, Denmark, Sweden, Austria, the Netherlands, Italy, Rome, and the other European States remain undisturbed. Very favorable relations also continue to be maintained with Turkey, Morocco, China, and Japan.

During the last year there has not only been no change of our previous relations with the independent States of our own continent, but more friendly sentiments than have heretofore existed are believed to be entertained by these neighbors, whose safety and progress are so intimately connected with our own. This statement especially applies to Mexico, Nicaragua, Costa Rica, Honduras, Peru, and Chile.

The commission under the convention with the Republic of New Granada closed its session without having audited and passed upon all the claims which were submitted to it. A proposition is pending to revive the convention, that it may be able to do more complete justice. The joint commission between the United States and the Republic of Costa Rica has completed its labors and submitted its report.

I have favored the project for connecting the United States with Europe by an Atlantic telegraph, and a similar project to extend the telegraph from San Francisco to connect by a Pacific telegraph with the line which is being extended across the Russian Empire.

The Territories of the United States, with unimportant exceptions, have remained undisturbed by the civil war; and they are exhibiting such evidence of prosperity as justifies an expectation that some of them will soon be in a condition to be organized as States and be constitutionally admitted into the Federal Union.

The immense mineral resources of some of those Territories ought to be developed as rapidly as possible. Every step in that direction would have a tendency to improve the revenues of the Government and diminish the burdens of the people. It is worthy of your serious consideration whether some extraordinary measures to promote that end can not be adopted. The means which suggests itself as most likely to be effective is a scientific exploration of the mineral regions in those Territories with a view to the publication of its results at home and in foreign countries— results which can not fail to be auspicious.

The condition of the finances will claim your most diligent consideration. The vast expenditures incident to the military and naval operations required for the suppression of the rebellion have hitherto been met with a promptitude and certainty unusual in similar circumstances, and the public credit has been fully maintained. The continuance of the war, however, and the increased disbursements made necessary by the augmented forces now in the field demand your best reflections as to the best modes of providing the necessary revenue without injury to business and with the least possible burdens upon labor.

The suspension of specie payments by the banks soon after the commencement of your last session made large issues of United States notes unavoidable. In no other way could the payment of the troops and the satisfaction of other just demands be so economically or so well provided for. The judicious legislation of Congress, securing the receivability of these notes for loans and internal duties and making them a legal tender for other debts, has made them an universal currency, and has satisfied, partially at least, and for the time, the long-felt want of an uniform circulating medium, saving thereby to the people immense sums in discounts and exchanges.

A return to specie payments, however, at the earliest period compatible with due regard to all interests concerned should ever be kept in view. Fluctuations in the value of currency are always injurious, and to reduce these fluctuations to the lowest possible point will always be a leading purpose in wise legislation. Convertibility, prompt and certain convertibility, into coin is generally acknowledged to be the best and surest safeguard against them; and it is extremely doubtful whether a circulation of United States notes payable in coin and sufficiently large for the wants of the people can be permanently, usefully, and safely maintained.

Is there, then, any other mode in which the necessary provision for the public wants can be made and the great advantages of a safe and uniform currency secured?

I know of none which promises so certain results and is at the same time so unobjectionable as the organization of banking associations, under a general act of Congress, well guarded in its provisions. To such associations the Government might furnish circulating notes, on the security of United States bonds deposited in the Treasury. These notes, prepared under the supervision of proper officers, being uniform in appearance and security and convertible always into coin, would at once protect labor against the evils of a vicious currency and facilitate commerce by cheap and safe exchanges.

A moderate reservation from the interest on the bonds would compensate the United States for the preparation and distribution of the notes and a general supervision of the system, and would lighten the burden of that part of the public debt employed as securities. The public credit, moreover, would be greatly improved and the negotiation of new loans greatly facilitated by the steady market demand for Government bonds which the adoption of the proposed system would create.

It is an additional recommendation of the measure, of considerable weight, in my judgment, that it would reconcile as far as possible all existing interests by the opportunity offered to existing institutions to reorganize under the act, substituting only the secured uniform national circulation for the local and various circulation, secured and unsecured, now issued by them.

The receipts into the Treasury from all sources, including loans and balance from the preceding year, for the fiscal year ending on the 30th June, 1862, were $583,885,247.06, of which sum $49,056,397.62 were derived from customs; $1,795,331.73 from the direct tax; from public lands, $152,203.77; from miscellaneous sources, $931,787.64; from loans in all forms, $529,692,460.50. The remainder, $2,257,065.80, was the balance from last year.

The disbursements during the same period were: For Congressional, executive, and judicial purposes, $5,939,009.29; for foreign intercourse, $1,339,710.35; for miscellaneous expenses, including the mints, loans, Post-Office deficiencies, collection of revenue, and other like charges, $14,129,771.50; for expenses under the Interior Department, $3,102,-985.52; under the War Department, $394,368,407.36; under the Navy Department, $42,674,569.69; for interest on public debt, $13,190,324.45; and for payment of public debt, including reimbursement of temporary loan and redemptions, $96,096,922.09; making an aggregate of $570,-841,700.25, and leaving a balance in the Treasury on the 1st day of July, 1862, of $13,043,546.81.

It should be observed that the sum of $96,096,922.09, expended for reimbursements and redemption of public debt, being included also in the loans made, may be properly deducted both from receipts and expenditures, leaving the actual receipts for the year $487,788,324.97, and the expenditures $474,744,778.16.

Other information on the subject of the finances will be found in the report of the Secretary of the Treasury, to whose statements and views I invite your most candid and considerate attention.

The reports of the Secretaries of War and of the Navy are herewith transmitted. These reports, though lengthy, are scarcely more than brief abstracts of the very numerous and extensive transactions and operations conducted through those Departments. Nor could I give a summary of them here upon any principle which would admit of its being much shorter than the reports themselves. I therefore content myself with laying the reports before you and asking your attention to them.

It gives me pleasure to report a decided improvement in the financial condition of the Post-Office Department as compared with several preceding years. The receipts for the fiscal year 1861 amounted to $8,349,296.40, which embraced the revenue from all the States of the Union for three quarters of that year. Notwithstanding the cessation of revenue from the so-called seceded States during the last fiscal year, the increase of the correspondence of the loyal States has been sufficient to produce a revenue during the same year of $8,299,820.90, being only $50,000 less than was derived from all the States of the Union during the previous year. The expenditures show a still more favorable result. The amount expended in 1861 was $13,606,759.11. For the last year the amount has been reduced to $11,125,364.13, showing a decrease of about $2,481,000 in the expenditures as compared with the preceding year, and about $3,750,000 as compared with the fiscal year 1860. The deficiency in the Department for the previous year was $4,551,966.98. For the last fiscal year it was reduced to $2,112,814.57. These favorable results are in part owing to the cessation of mail service in the insurrectionary States and in part to a careful review of all expenditures in that Department in the interest of economy. The efficiency of the postal service, it is believed, has also been much improved. The Postmaster-General has also opened a correspondence through the Department of State with foreign governments proposing a convention of postal representatives for the purpose of simplifying the rates of foreign postage and to expedite the foreign mails. This proposition, equally important to our adopted citizens and to the commercial interests of this country, has been favorably entertained and agreed to by all the governments from whom replies have been received.

I ask the attention of Congress to the suggestions of the Postmaster-General in his report respecting the further legislation required, in his opinion, for the benefit of the postal service.

The Secretary of the Interior reports as follows in regard to the public lands:

The public lands have ceased to be a source of revenue. From the 1st July, 1861, to the 30th September, 1862, the entire cash receipts from the sale of lands were $137,476.26—a sum much less than the expenses of our land system during the same period. The homestead law, which will take effect on the 1st of January next, offers such inducements to settlers that sales for cash can not be expected to an extent sufficient to meet the expenses of the General Land Office and the cost of surveying and bringing the land into market.

The discrepancy between the sum here stated as arising from the sales of the public lands and the sum derived from the same source as reported from the Treasury Department arises, as I understand, from the fact that the periods of time, though apparently, were not really coincident at the beginning point, the Treasury report including a considerable sum now which had previously been reported from the Interior, sufficiently large to greatly overreach the sum derived from the three months now reported upon by the Interior and not by the Treasury.

The Indian tribes upon our frontiers have during the past year manifested a spirit of insubordination, and at several points have engaged in open hostilities against the white settlements in their vicinity. The tribes occupying the Indian country south of Kansas renounced their allegiance to the United States and entered into treaties with the insurgents. Those who remained loyal to the United States were driven from the country. The chief of the Cherokees has visited this city for the purpose of restoring the former relations of the tribe with the United States. He alleges that they were constrained by superior force to enter into treaties with the insurgents, and that the United States neglected to furnish the protection which their treaty stipulations required.

In the month of August last the Sioux Indians in Minnesota attacked the settlements in their vicinity with extreme ferocity, killing indiscriminately men, women, and children. This attack was wholly unexpected, and therefore no means of defense had been provided. It is estimated that not less than 800 persons were killed by the Indians, and a large amount of property was destroyed. How this outbreak was induced is not definitely known, and suspicions, which may be unjust, need not to be stated. Information was received by the Indian Bureau from different sources about the time hostilities were commenced that a simultaneous attack was to be made upon the white settlements by all the tribes between the Mississippi River and the Rocky Mountains. The State of Minnesota has suffered great injury from this Indian war. A large portion of her territory has been depopulated, and a severe loss has been sustained by the destruction of property. The people of that State manifest much anxiety for the removal of the tribes beyond the limits of the State as a guaranty against future hostilities. The Commissioner of Indian Affairs will furnish full details. I submit for your especial consideration whether our Indian system shall not be remodeled. Many wise and good men have impressed me with the belief that this can be profitably done.

I submit a statement of the proceedings of commissioners, which shows the progress that has been made in the enterprise of constructing the

Pacific Railroad. And this suggests the earliest completion of this road, and also the favorable action of Congress upon the projects now pending before them for enlarging the capacities of the great canals in New York and Illinois, as being of vital and rapidly increasing importance to the whole nation, and especially to the vast interior region hereinafter to be noticed at some greater length. I purpose having prepared and laid before you at an early day some interesting and valuable statistical information upon this subject. The military and commercial importance of enlarging the Illinois and Michigan Canal and improving the Illinois River is presented in the report of Colonel Webster to the Secretary of War, and now transmitted to Congress. I respectfully ask attention to it.

To carry out the provisions of the act of Congress of the 15th of May last, I have caused the Department of Agriculture of the United States to be organized.

The Commissioner informs me that within the period of a few months this Department has established an extensive system of correspondence and exchanges, both at home and abroad, which promises to effect highly beneficial results in the development of a correct knowledge of recent improvements in agriculture, in the introduction of new products, and in the collection of the agricultural statistics of the different States.

Also, that it will soon be prepared to distribute largely seeds, cereals, plants, and cuttings, and has already published and liberally diffused much valuable information in anticipation of a more elaborate report, which will in due time be furnished, embracing some valuable tests in chemical science now in progress in the laboratory.

The creation of this Department was for the more immediate benefit of a large class of our most valuable citizens, and I trust that the liberal basis upon which it has been organized will not only meet your approbation, but that it will realize at no distant day all the fondest anticipations of its most sanguine friends and become the fruitful source of advantage to all our people.

On the 22d day of September last a proclamation was issued by the Executive, a copy of which is herewith submitted.

In accordance with the purpose expressed in the second paragraph of that paper, I now respectfully recall your attention to what may be called "compensated emancipation."

A nation may be said to consist of its territory, its people, and its laws. The territory is the only part which is of certain durability. "One generation passeth away and another generation cometh, but the earth abideth forever." It is of the first importance to duly consider and estimate this ever-enduring part. That portion of the earth's surface which is owned and inhabited by the people of the United States is well adapted to be the home of one national family, and it is not well adapted for two or more. Its vast extent and its variety of climate and productions are of advantage in this age for one people, whatever they might have been in former ages. Steam, telegraphs, and intelligence have brought these to be an advantageous combination for one united people.

In the inaugural address I briefly pointed out the total inadequacy of disunion as a remedy for the differences between the people of the two sections. I did so in language which I can not improve, and which, therefore, I beg to repeat:

One section of our country believes slavery is *right* and ought to be extended, while the other believes it is *wrong* and ought not to be extended. This is the only substantial dispute. The fugitive-slave clause of the Constitution and the law for the suppression of the foreign slave trade are each as well enforced, perhaps, as any law can ever be in a community where the moral sense of the people imperfectly supports the law itself. The great body of the people abide by the dry legal obligation in both cases, and a few break over in each. This I think, can not be perfectly cured, and it would be worse in both cases *after* the separation of the sections than before. The foreign slave trade, now imperfectly suppressed, would be ultimately revived without restriction in one section, while fugitive slaves, now only partially surrendered, would not be surrendered at all by the other.

Physically speaking, we can not separate. We can not remove our respective sections from each other nor build an impassable wall between them. A husband and wife may be divorced and go out of the presence and beyond the reach of each other, but the different parts of our country can not do this. They can not but remain face to face, and intercourse, either amicable or hostile, must continue between them. Is it possible, then, to make that intercourse more advantageous or more satisfactory *after* separation than *before*? Can aliens make treaties easier than friends can make laws? Can treaties be more faithfully enforced between aliens than laws can among friends? Suppose you go to war, you can not fight always; and when, after much loss on both sides and no gain on either, you cease fighting, the identical old questions, as to terms of intercourse, are again upon you.

There is no line, straight or crooked, suitable for a national boundary upon which to divide. Trace through, from east to west, upon the line between the free and slave country, and we shall find a little more than one-third of its length are rivers, easy to be crossed, and populated, or soon to be populated, thickly upon both sides; while nearly all its remaining length are merely surveyors' lines, over which people may walk back and forth without any consciousness of their presence. No part of this line can be made any more difficult to pass by writing it down on paper or parchment as a national boundary. The fact of separation, if it comes, gives up on the part of the seceding section the fugitive-slave clause, along with all other constitutional obligations upon the section seceded from, while I should expect no treaty stipulation would ever be made to take its place.

But there is another difficulty. The great interior region bounded east by the Alleghanies, north by the British dominions, west by the Rocky Mountains, and south by the line along which the culture of corn and cotton meets, and which includes part of Virginia, part of Tennessee, all of Kentucky, Ohio, Indiana, Michigan, Wisconsin, Illinois, Missouri, Kansas, Iowa, Minnesota, and the Territories of Dakota, Nebraska, and part of Colorado, already has above 10,000,000 people, and will have

50,000,000 within fifty years if not prevented by any political folly or mistake. It contains more than one-third of the country owned by the United States—certainly more than 1,000,000 square miles. Once half as populous as Massachusetts already is, it would have more than 75,000,000 people. A glance at the map shows that, territorially speaking, it is the great body of the Republic. The other parts are but marginal borders to it, the magnificent region sloping west from the Rocky Mountains to the Pacific being the deepest and also the richest in undeveloped resources. In the production of provisions, grains, grasses, and all which proceed from them this great interior region is naturally one of the most important in the world. Ascertain from the statistics the small proportion of the region which has as yet been brought into cultivation, and also the large and rapidly increasing amount of its products, and we shall be overwhelmed with the magnitude of the prospect presented. And yet this region has no seacoast—touches no ocean anywhere. As part of one nation, its people now find, and may forever find, their way to Europe by New York, to South America and Africa by New Orleans, and to Asia by San Francisco; but separate our common country into two nations, as designed by the present rebellion, and every man of this great interior region is thereby cut off from some one or more of these outlets, not perhaps by a physical barrier, but by embarrassing and onerous trade regulations.

And this is true, *wherever* a dividing or boundary line may be fixed. Place it between the now free and slave country, or place it south of Kentucky or north of Ohio, and still the truth remains that none south of it can trade to any port or place north of it, and none north of it can trade to any port or place south of it, except upon terms dictated by a government foreign to them. These outlets, east, west, and south, are indispensable to the well-being of the people inhabiting and to inhabit this vast interior region. *Which* of the three may be the best is no proper question. All are better than either, and all of right belong to that people and to their successors forever. True to themselves, they will not ask *where* a line of separation shall be, but will vow rather that there shall be no such line. Nor are the marginal regions less interested in these communications to and through them to the great outside world. They, too, and each of them, must have access to this Egypt of the West without paying toll at the crossing of any national boundary.

Our national strife springs not from our permanent part; not from the land we inhabit; not from our national homestead. There is no possible severing of this but would multiply and not mitigate evils among us. In all its adaptations and aptitudes it demands union and abhors separation. In fact, it would ere long force reunion, however much of blood and treasure the separation might have cost.

Our strife pertains to ourselves—to the passing generations of men—and it can without convulsion be hushed forever with the passing of one generation.

In this view I recommend the adoption of the following resolution and articles amendatory to the Constitution of the United States:

Resolved by the Senate and House of Representatives of the United States of America in Congress assembled (two-thirds of both Houses concurring), That the following articles be proposed to the legislatures (or conventions) of the several States as amendments to the Constitution of the United States, all or any of which articles, when ratified by three-fourths of the said legislatures (or conventions), to be valid as part or parts of the said Constitution, viz:

ART. —. Every State wherein slavery now exists which shall abolish the same therein at any time or times before the 1st day of January, A. D. 1900, shall receive compensation from the United States as follows, to wit:

The President of the United States shall deliver to every such State bonds of the United States bearing interest at the rate of —— per cent per annum to an amount equal to the aggregate sum of ——— for each slave shown to have been therein by the Eighth Census of the United States, said bonds to be delivered to such State by installments or in one parcel at the completion of the abolishment, accordingly as the same shall have been gradual or at one time within such State; and interest shall begin to run upon any such bond only from the proper time of its delivery as aforesaid. Any State having received bonds as aforesaid and afterwards reintroducing or tolerating slavery therein shall refund to the United States the bonds so received, or the value thereof, and all interest paid thereon.

ART. —. All slaves who shall have enjoyed actual freedom by the chances of the war at any time before the end of the rebellion shall be forever free; but all owners of such who shall not have been disloyal shall be compensated for them at the same rates as is provided for States adopting abolishment of slavery, but in such way that no slave shall be twice accounted for.

ART. —. Congress may appropriate money and otherwise provide for colonizing free colored persons with their own consent at any place or places without the United States.

I beg indulgence to discuss these proposed articles at some length. Without slavery the rebellion could never have existed; without slavery it could not continue.

Among the friends of the Union there is great diversity of sentiment and of policy in regard to slavery and the African race amongst us. Some would perpetuate slavery; some would abolish it suddenly and without compensation; some would abolish it gradually and with compensation; some would remove the freed people from us, and some would retain them with us; and there are yet other minor diversities. Because of these diversities we waste much strength in struggles among ourselves. By mutual concession we should harmonize and act together. This would be compromise, but it would be compromise among the friends and not with the enemies of the Union. These articles are intended to embody a plan of such mutual concessions. If the plan shall be adopted, it is assumed that emancipation will follow, at least in several of the States.

As to the first article, the main points are, first, the emancipation; secondly, the length of time for consummating it (thirty-seven years); and, thirdly, the compensation.

The emancipation will be unsatisfactory to the advocates of perpetual slavery, but the length of time should greatly mitigate their dissatisfaction. The time spares both races from the evils of sudden derangement—in fact, from the necessity of any derangement—while most of those whose habitual course of thought will be disturbed by the measure will have passed away before its consummation. They will never see it. Another class will hail the prospect of emancipation, but will deprecate the length of time. They will feel that it gives too little to the now living slaves. But it really gives them much. It saves them from the vagrant destitution which must largely attend immediate emancipation in localities where their numbers are very great, and it gives the inspiring assurance that their posterity shall be free forever. The plan leaves to each State choosing to act under it to abolish slavery now or at the end of the century, or at any intermediate time, or by degrees extending over the whole or any part of the period, and it obliges no two States to proceed alike. It also provides for compensation, and generally the mode of making it. This, it would seem, must further mitigate the dissatisfaction of those who favor perpetual slavery, and especially of those who are to receive the compensation. Doubtless some of those who are to pay and not to receive will object. Yet the measure is both just and economical. In a certain sense the liberation of slaves is the destruction of property—property acquired by descent or by purchase, the same as any other property. It is no less true for having been often said that the people of the South are not more responsible for the original introduction of this property than are the people of the North; and when it is remembered how unhesitatingly we all use cotton and sugar and share the profits of dealing in them, it may not be quite safe to say that the South has been more responsible than the North for its continuance. If, then, for a common object this property is to be sacrificed, is it not just that it be done at a common charge?

And if with less money, or money more easily paid, we can preserve the benefits of the Union by this means than we can by the war alone, is it not also economical to do it? Let us consider it, then. Let us ascertain the sum we have expended in the war since compensated emancipation was proposed last March, and consider whether if that measure had been promptly accepted by even some of the slave States the same sum would not have done more to close the war than has been otherwise done. If so, the measure would save money, and in that view would be a prudent and economical measure. Certainly it is not so easy to pay *something* as it is to pay *nothing*, but it is easier to pay a *large* sum than it is to pay a *larger* one. And it is easier to pay any sum *when* we are able than it is to pay it *before* we are able. The war requires large sums, and requires them at once. The aggregate sum necessary for compensated emancipation of course would be large. But it would require no ready cash, nor the bonds even any faster than the emancipation progresses. This might not, and probably would not, close before the end of the thirty-seven years. At that time we shall probably have a hundred millions of people to share the burden, instead of thirty-one millions as now. And not only so, but the increase of our population may be expected to continue for a long time after that period as rapidly as before, because our territory will not have become full. I do not state this inconsiderately. At the same ratio of increase which we have maintained, on an average, from our first national census, in 1790, until that of 1860, we should in 1900 have a population of 103,208,415. And why may we not continue that ratio far beyond that period? Our abundant room, our broad national homestead, is our ample resource. Were our territory as limited as are the British Isles, very certainly our population could not expand as stated. Instead of receiving the foreign born as now, we should be compelled to send part of the native born away. But such is not our condition. We have 2,963,000 square miles. Europe has 3,800,000, with a population averaging 73⅓ persons to the square mile. Why may not our country at some time average as many? Is it less fertile? Has it more waste surface by mountains, rivers, lakes, deserts, or other causes? Is it inferior to Europe in any natural advantage? If, then, we are at some time to be as populous as Europe, how soon? As to when this *may* be, we can judge by the past and the present; as to when it *will* be, if ever, depends much on whether we maintain the Union. Several of our States are already above the average of Europe—73⅓ to the square mile. Massachusetts has 157; Rhode Island, 133; Connecticut, 99; New York and New Jersey, each 80. Also two other great States, Pennsylvania and Ohio, are not far below, the former having 63 and the latter 59. The States already above the European average, except New York, have increased in as rapid a ratio since passing that point as ever before, while no one of them is equal to some other parts of our country in natural capacity for sustaining a dense population.

Taking the nation in the aggregate, and we find its population and ratio of increase for the several decennial periods to be as follows:

Year.	Population.	Ratio of increase.
		Per cent.
1790	3,929,827	....
1800	5,305,937	35.02
1810	7,239,814	36.45
1820	9,638,131	33.13
1830	12,866,020	33.49
1840	17,069,453	32.67
1850	23,191,876	35.87
1860	31,443,790	35.58

This shows an average decennial increase of 34.60 per cent in population through the seventy years from our first to our last census yet taken. It is seen that the ratio of increase at no one of these seven periods is either 2 per cent below or 2 per cent above the average, thus showing how inflexible, and consequently how reliable, the law of increase in our case is. Assuming that it will continue, it gives the following results:

Year.	Population.
1870	42,323,341
1880	56,967,216
1890	76,677,872
1900	103,208,415
1910	138,918,526
1920	186,984,335
1930	251,680,914

These figures show that our country *may* be as populous as Europe now is at some point between 1920 and 1930—say about 1925—our territory, at 73⅓ persons to the square mile, being of capacity to contain 217,186,000.

And we *will* reach this, too, if we do not ourselves relinquish the chance by the folly and evils of disunion or by long and exhausting war springing from the only great element of national discord among us. While it can not be foreseen exactly how much one huge example of secession, breeding lesser ones indefinitely, would retard population, civilization, and prosperity, no one can doubt that the extent of it would be very great and injurious.

The proposed emancipation would shorten the war, perpetuate peace, insure this increase of population, and proportionately the wealth of the country. With these we should pay all the emancipation would cost, together with our other debt, easier than we should pay our other debt without it. If we had allowed our old national debt to run at 6 per cent per annum, simple interest, from the end of our revolutionary struggle until to-day, without paying anything on either principal or interest, each man of us would owe less upon that debt now than each man owed upon it then; and this because our increase of men through the whole period has been greater than 6 per cent—has run faster than the interest upon the debt. Thus time alone relieves a debtor nation, so long as its population increases faster than unpaid interest accumulates on its debt.

This fact would be no excuse for delaying payment of what is justly due, but it shows the great importance of time in this connection—the great advantage of a policy by which we shall not have to pay until we number 100,000,000 what by a different policy we would have to pay now, when we number but 31,000,000. In a word, it shows that a dollar will be much harder to pay for the war than will be a dollar for emancipation on the proposed plan. And then the latter will cost no blood, no precious life. It will be a saving of both.

As to the second article, I think it would be impracticable to return to bondage the class of persons therein contemplated. Some of them, doubtless, in the property sense belong to loyal owners, and hence provision is made in this article for compensating such.

The third article relates to the future of the freed people. It does not oblige, but merely authorizes Congress to aid in colonizing such as may consent. This ought not to be regarded as objectionable on the one hand or on the other, insomuch as it comes to nothing unless by the mutual consent of the people to be deported and the American voters, through their representatives in Congress.

I can not make it better known than it already is that I strongly favor colonization; and yet I wish to say there is an objection urged against free colored persons remaining in the country which is largely imaginary, if not sometimes malicious.

It is insisted that their presence would injure and displace white labor and white laborers. If there ever could be a proper time for mere catch arguments, that time surely is not now. In times like the present men should utter nothing for which they would not willingly be responsible through time and in eternity. Is it true, then, that colored people can displace any more white labor by being free than by remaining slaves? If they stay in their old places, they jostle no white laborers; if they leave their old places, they leave them open to white laborers. Logically, there is neither more nor less of it. Emancipation, even without deportation, would probably enhance the wages of white labor, and very surely would not reduce them. Thus the customary amount of labor would still have to be performed—the freed people would surely not do more than their old proportion of it, and very probably for a time would do less, leaving an increased part to white laborers, bringing their labor into greater demand, and consequently enhancing the wages of it. With deportation, even to a limited extent, enhanced wages to white labor is mathematically certain. Labor is like any other commodity in the market—increase the demand for it and you increase the price of it. Reduce the supply of black labor by colonizing the black laborer out of the country, and by precisely so much you increase the demand for and wages of white labor.

But it is dreaded that the freed people will swarm forth and cover the whole land. Are they not already in the land? Will liberation make them any more numerous? Equally distributed among the whites of the whole country, and there would be but one colored to seven whites. Could the one in any way greatly disturb the seven? There are many communities now having more than one free colored person to seven whites and this without any apparent consciousness of evil from it. The District of Columbia and the States of Maryland and Delaware are all in this condition. The District has more than one free colored to six whites, and yet in its frequent petitions to Congress I believe it has never presented the presence of free colored persons as one of its grievances. But why should emancipation South send the free people North? People of any color seldom run unless there be something to run from. *Heretofore* colored people to some extent have fled North from bondage, and *now*, perhaps, from both bondage and destitution. But if gradual emancipation and deportation be adopted, they will have neither to flee from. Their old masters will give them wages at least until new laborers can be procured, and the freedmen in turn will gladly give their labor for the wages till new homes can be found for them in congenial climes and with people of their own blood and race. This proposition can be trusted on the mutual interests involved. And in any event, can not the North decide for itself whether to receive them?

Again, as practice proves more than theory in any case, has there been any irruption of colored people northward because of the abolishment of slavery in this District last spring?

What I have said of the proportion of free colored persons to the whites in the District is from the census of 1860, having no reference to persons called contrabands nor to those made free by the act of Congress abolishing slavery here.

The plan consisting of these articles is recommended, not but that a restoration of the national authority would be accepted without its adoption.

Nor will the war nor proceedings under the proclamation of September 22, 1862, be stayed because of the *recommendation* of this plan. Its timely *adoption*, I doubt not, would bring restoration, and thereby stay both.

And notwithstanding this plan, the recommendation that Congress provide by law for compensating any State which may adopt emancipation before this plan shall have been acted upon is hereby earnestly renewed. Such would be only an advance part of the plan, and the same arguments apply to both.

This plan is recommended as a means, not in exclusion of, but additional to, all others for restoring and preserving the national authority throughout the Union. The subject is presented exclusively in its economical aspect. The plan would, I am confident, secure peace more speedily and maintain it more permanently than can be done by force alone, while all it would cost, considering amounts and manner of payment and times of payment, would be easier paid than will be the additional cost of the war if we rely solely upon force. It is much, very much, that it would cost no blood at all.

The plan is proposed as permanent constitutional law. It can not become such without the concurrence of, first, two-thirds of Congress, and afterwards three-fourths of the States. The requisite three-fourths of the States will necessarily include seven of the slave States. Their concurrence, if obtained, will give assurance of their severally adopting emancipation at no very distant day upon the new constitutional terms. This assurance would end the struggle now and save the Union forever.

I do not forget the gravity which should characterize a paper addressed to the Congress of the nation by the Chief Magistrate of the nation, nor do I forget that some of you are my seniors, nor that many of you have more experience than I in the conduct of public affairs. Yet I trust that in view of the great responsibility resting upon me you will perceive no want of respect to yourselves in any undue earnestness I may seem to display.

Is it doubted, then, that the plan I propose, if adopted, would shorten the war, and thus lessen its expenditure of money and of blood? Is it doubted that it would restore the national authority and national prosperity and perpetuate both indefinitely? Is it doubted that we here— Congress and Executive—can secure its adoption? Will not the good people respond to a united and earnest appeal from us? Can we, can they, by any other means so certainly or so speedily assure these vital objects? We can succeed only by concert. It is not "Can *any* of us *imagine* better?" but "Can we *all* do better?" Object whatsoever is possible, still the question recurs, "Can we do better?" The dogmas of the quiet past are inadequate to the stormy present. The occasion is piled high with difficulty, and we must rise with the occasion. As our case is new, so we must think anew and act anew. We must disenthrall ourselves, and then we shall save our country.

Fellow-citizens, *we* can not escape history. We of this Congress and this Administration will be remembered in spite of ourselves. No personal significance or insignificance can spare one or another of us. The fiery trial through which we pass will light us down in honor or dishonor to the latest generation. We *say* we are for the Union. The world will not forget that we say this. We know how to save the Union. The world knows we do know how to save it. We, even *we here*, hold the power and bear the responsibility. In *giving* freedom to the *slave* we *assure* freedom to the *free*—honorable alike in what we give and what we preserve. We shall nobly save or meanly lose the last best hope of earth. Other means may succeed; this could not fail. The way is plain, peaceful, generous, just—a way which if followed the world will forever applaud and God must forever bless.

ABRAHAM LINCOLN.

SPECIAL MESSAGES.

WASHINGTON, *December 3, 1862.*

To the Senate and House of Representatives:

On the 3d of November, 1861, a collision took place off the coast of Cuba between the United States war steamer *San Jacinto* and the French brig *Jules et Marie*, resulting in serious damage to the latter. The obligation of this Government to make amends therefor could not be questioned if the injury resulted from any fault on the part of the *San Jacinto*.

With a view to ascertain this, the subject was referred to a commission of the United States and French naval officers at New York, with a naval officer of Italy as an arbiter. The conclusion arrived at was that the collision was occasioned by the failure of the *San Jacinto* seasonably to reverse her engine. It then became necessary to ascertain the amount of indemnification due to the injured party. The United States consul-general at Havana was consequently instructed to confer with the consul of France on this point, and they have determined that the sum of $9,500 is an equitable allowance under the circumstances.

I recommend an appropriation of this sum for the benefit of the owners of the *Jules et Marie*.

A copy of the letter of Mr. Shufeldt, the consul-general of the United States at Havana, to the Secretary of State on the subject is herewith transmitted.

ABRAHAM LINCOLN.

WASHINGTON, D. C., *December 8, 1862.*

To the Senate and House of Representatives:

In conformity to the law of July 16, 1862, I most cordially recommend that Commander John L. Worden, United States Navy, receive a vote of thanks of Congress for the eminent skill and gallantry exhibited by him in the late remarkable battle between the United States ironclad steamer *Monitor*, under his command, and the rebel ironclad steamer *Merrimac*, in March last.

The thanks of Congress for his services on the occasion referred to were tendered by a resolution approved July 11, 1862, but the recommendation is now specially made in order to comply with the requirements of the ninth section of the act of July 16, 1862, which is in the following words, viz:

That any line officer of the Navy or Marine Corps may be advanced one grade if upon recommendation of the President by name he receives the thanks of Congress for highly distinguished conduct in conflict with the enemy or for extraordinary heroism in the line of his profession.

ABRAHAM LINCOLN.

WASHINGTON, D. C., *December 9, 1862.*

To the Senate of the United States:

In compliance with the resolution of the Senate of the United States of the 13th of March last, requesting a copy of the correspondence relative to the attempted seizure of Mr. Fauchet by the commander of the *Africa* within the waters of the United States, I transmit a report from the Secretary of State and the documents by which it was accompanied.

ABRAHAM LINCOLN.

WASHINGTON, D. C., *December 10, 1862.*

To the Senate and House of Representatives:

In conformity to the law of July 16, 1862, I most cordially recommend that Lieutenant-Commander George U. Morris, United States Navy, receive a vote of thanks of Congress for the determined valor and heroism displayed in his defense of the United States ship of war *Cumberland*, temporarily under his command, in the naval engagement at Hampton Roads on the 8th March, 1862, with the rebel ironclad steam frigate *Merrimac.*

ABRAHAM LINCOLN.

WASHINGTON, *December 10, 1862.*

To the House of Representatives:

In answer to the resolution of the House of Representatives of the 17th of July last, requesting the communication of correspondence relating to the arrest of a part of the crew of the brig *Sumter* at Tangier, Morocco, I herewith transmit a report from the Secretary of State.

ABRAHAM LINCOLN.

To the Senate of the United States:

In compliance with your resolution of December 5, 1862, requesting the President "to furnish the Senate with all information in his possession touching the late Indian barbarities in the State of Minnesota, and also the evidence in his possession upon which some of the principal actors and headmen were tried and condemned to death," I have the honor to state that on receipt of said resolution I transmitted the same to the Secretary of the Interior, accompanied by a note a copy of which is herewith inclosed, marked A, and in response to which I received through that Department a letter of the Commissioner of Indian Affairs, a copy of which is herewith inclosed, marked B.

I further state that on the 8th day of November last I received a long telegraphic dispatch from Major-General Pope, at St. Paul, Minn., simply announcing the names of the persons sentenced to be hanged. I immediately telegraphed to have transcripts of the records in all the cases forwarded to me, which transcripts, however, did not reach me until two or three days before the present meeting of Congress. Meantime I received, through telegraphic dispatches and otherwise, appeals in behalf of the condemned, appeals for their execution, and expressions of opinion as to proper policy in regard to them and to the Indians generally in that vicinity, none of which, as I understand, falls within the scope of your inquiry. After the arrival of the transcripts of records, but before I had sufficient opportunity to examine them, I received a joint letter from one of the Senators and two of the Representatives from Minnesota, which contains some statements of fact not found in the records of the trials, and for which reason I herewith transmit a copy, marked C. I also, for the same reason, inclose a printed memorial of the citizens of St. Paul addressed to me and forwarded with the letter aforesaid.

Anxious to not act with so much clemency as to encourage another outbreak on the one hand, nor with so much severity as to be real cruelty on the other, I caused a careful examination of the records of trials to be made, in view of first ordering the execution of such as had been proved guilty of violating females. Contrary to my expectations, only two of this class were found. I then directed a further examination, and a classification of all who were proven to have participated in *massacres*, as distinguished from participation in *battles*. This class numbered forty, and included the two convicted of female violation. One of the number is strongly recommended by the commission which tried them for commutation to ten years' imprisonment. I have ordered the other thirty-nine to be executed on Friday, the 19th instant. The order was dispatched from here on Monday, the 8th instant, by a messenger to General Sibley, and a copy of which order is herewith transmitted, marked D.

An abstract of the evidence as to the forty is herewith inclosed, marked E.

To avoid the immense amount of copying, I lay before the Senate the original transcripts of the records of trials as received by me.

This is as full and complete a response to the resolution as it is in my power to make.

ABRAHAM LINCOLN.

DECEMBER 11, 1862.

WASHINGTON, *December 11, 1862.*

To the Senate of the United States:

I transmit to the Senate, for its consideration with a view to ratification, a treaty between the United States and the Republic of Liberia, signed at London by the plenipotentiaries of the parties on the 21st of October last.

ABRAHAM LINCOLN.

DECEMBER 12, 1862.

Fellow-Citizens of the Senate and House of Representatives:

I have in my possession three valuable swords, formerly the property of General David E. Twiggs, which I now place at the disposal of Congress. They are forwarded to me from New Orleans by Major-General Benjamin F. Butler. If they or any of them shall be by Congress disposed of in reward or compliment of military service, I think General Butler is entitled to the first consideration. A copy of the General's letter to me accompanying the swords is herewith transmitted.

ABRAHAM LINCOLN.

WASHINGTON, D. C., *December 13, 1862.*

To the Senate of the United States:

In the list of nominations transmitted to the Senate under date of the 1st instant Captain William M. Glendy, United States Navy, was included therein for promotion to the grade of commodore.

Since submitting this nomination it appears that this officer was ineligible for the advancement to which he had been nominated in consequence of his age, being 62 on the 23d of May, 1862, and under the law of 21st December, 1861, should, had this fact been known to the Navy Department, have been transferred to the retired list on the day when he completed sixty-two years.

The nomination of Captain Glendy is accordingly withdrawn.

It is due to this officer to state that at the period of the passage of the law of December, 1861, he was and still is absent on duty on a foreign station, and the certificate of his age required by the Navy Department was only received a few days since.

ABRAHAM LINCOLN.

WASHINGTON, *December 18, 1862.*

To the Senate and House of Representatives:

I transmit a copy of a dispatch to the Secretary of State from Mr. Adams, United States minister at London, and of the correspondence to which it refers between that gentleman and Mr. Panizzi, the principal librarian of the British Museum, relative to certain valuable publications presented to the Library of Congress.

ABRAHAM LINCOLN.

WASHINGTON, *December 22, 1862.*

To the Senate of the United States:

In compliance with the resolution of the Senate of the 15th instant, requesting a copy of the report of the Hon. Reverdy Johnson,* I transmit a communication from the Secretary of State and the documents by which it was accompanied.

ABRAHAM LINCOLN.

WASHINGTON, *December 24, 1862.*

To the Senate and House of Representatives:

I transmit, for the consideration of Congress, a report from the Secretary of State on the subject of consular pupils.

ABRAHAM LINCOLN.

*United States commissioner at New Orleans.

WASHINGTON, *January 2, 1863.*

To the Senate and House of Representatives:

I submit to Congress the expediency of extending to other Departments of the Government the authority conferred on the President by the eighth section of the act of the 8th of May, 1792, to appoint a person to temporarily discharge the duties of Secretary of State, Secretary of the Treasury, and Secretary of War in case of the death, absence from the seat of Government, or sickness of either of those officers.

ABRAHAM LINCOLN.

WASHINGTON, *January 3, 1863.*

To the Senate of the United States:

I transmit to the Senate, for consideration with a view to ratification, a convention for the mutual adjustment of claims between the United States and Ecuador, signed by the respective plenipotentiaries of the two Governments in Guayaquil on the 25th November ultimo.

ABRAHAM LINCOLN.

WASHINGTON, *January 5, 1863.*

To the House of Representatives:

In compliance with the resolution of the House of Representatives of the 22d ultimo, in relation to the alleged interference of our minister to Mexico in favor of the French, I transmit a report from the Secretary of State and the papers with which it is accompanied.

ABRAHAM LINCOLN.

WASHINGTON, *January 9, 1863.*

To the Senate and House of Representatives:

I transmit for the consideration of Congress, and with a view to the adoption of such measures in relation to the subject of it as may be deemed expedient, a copy of a note of the 8th instant addressed to the Secretary of State by the minister resident of the Hanseatic Republics accredited to this Government, concerning an international agricultural exhibition to be held next summer in the city of Hamburg.

ABRAHAM LINCOLN.

WASHINGTON, *January 14, 1863.*

To the House of Representatives:

The Secretary of State has submitted to me a resolution of the House of Representatives of the 5th instant, which has been delivered to him, and which is in the following words:

Resolved, That the Secretary of State be requested to communicate to this House, if not in his judgment incompatible with the public interest, why our minister in

New Granada has not presented his credentials to the actual Government of that country; also the reasons for which Señor Murillo is not recognized by the United States as the diplomatic representative of the Mosquera Government of that country; also what negotiations have been had, if any, with General Herran, as the representative of Ospina's Government in New Granada, since it went into existence.

On the 12th day of December, 1846, a treaty of amity, peace, and concord was concluded between the United States of America and the Republic of New Granada, which is still in force. On the 7th day of December, 1847, General Pedro Alcántara Herran, who had been duly accredited, was received here as the envoy extraordinary and minister plenipotentiary of that Republic. On the 30th day of August, 1849, Señor Don Rafael Rivas was received by this Government as chargé d'affaires of the same Republic. On the 5th day of December, 1851, a consular convention was concluded between that Republic and the United States, which treaty was signed on behalf of the Republic of Granada by the same Señor Rivas. This treaty is still in force. On the 27th of April, 1852, Señor Don Victoriano de Diego Paredes was received as chargé d'affaires of the Republic of New Granada. On the 20th of June, 1855, General Pedro Alcántara Herran was again received as envoy extraordinary and minister plenipotentiary, duly accredited by the Republic of New Granada, and he has ever since remained, under the same credentials, as the representative of that Republic near the Government of the United States. On the 10th of September, 1857, a claims convention was concluded between the United States and the Republic of Granada. This convention is still in force, and has in part been executed. In May, 1858, the constitution of the Republic was remodeled, and the nation assumed the political title of "The Granadian Confederacy." This fact was formally announced to this Government, but without any change in their representative here. Previously to the 4th day of March, 1861, a revolutionary war against the Republic of New Granada, which had thus been recognized and treated with by the United States, broke out in New Granada, assuming to set up a new government under the name of "The United States of Colombia." This war has had various vicissitudes, sometimes favorable, sometimes adverse, to the revolutionary movements. The revolutionary organization has hitherto been simply a military provisionary power, and no definitive constitution of government has yet been established in New Granada in place of that organized by the constitution of 1858. The minister of the United States to the Granadian Confederacy, who was appointed on the 29th day of May, 1861, was directed, in view of the occupation of the capital by the revolutionary party and of the uncertainty of the civil war, not to present his credentials to either the Government of the Granadian Confederacy or to the provisional military Government, but to conduct his affairs informally, as is customary in such cases, and to report the progress of events and await the instructions of this Government. The advices which have been received from him have not hitherto been sufficiently conclusive to determine me to recognize the revolutionary Government. General Herran being here, with full authority from the Government of New Granada, which had been so long recognized by the United States, I have not received any representative from the revolutionary Government, which has not yet been recognized, because such a proceeding would in itself be an act of recognition.

Official communications have been had on various incidental and occasional questions with General Herran as the minister plenipotentiary and envoy extraordinary of the Granadian Confederacy, but in no other character. No definitive measure or proceeding has resulted from these communications, and a communication of them at present would not, in my judgment, be compatible with the public interest.

ABRAHAM LINCOLN.

To the Senate and House of Representatives: JANUARY 17, 1863.

I have signed the joint resolution to provide for the immediate payment of the Army and Navy of the United States, passed by the House of Representatives on the 14th and by the Senate on the 15th instant.

The joint resolution is a simple authority, amounting, however, under existing circumstances, to a direction, to the Secretary of the Treasury to make an additional issue of $100,000,000 in United States notes, if so much money is needed, for the payment of the Army and Navy.

My approval is given in order that every possible facility may be afforded for the prompt discharge of all arrears of pay due to our soldiers and our sailors.

While giving this approval, however, I think it my duty to express my sincere regret that it has been found necessary to authorize so large an additional issue of United States notes, when this circulation and that of the suspended banks together have become already so redundant as to increase prices beyond real values, thereby augmenting the cost of living to the injury of labor, and the cost of supplies to the injury of the whole country.

It seems very plain that continued issues of United States notes without any check to the issues of suspended banks and without adequate provision for the raising of money by loans and for funding the issues so as to keep them within due limits must soon produce disastrous consequences; and this matter appears to me so important that I feel bound to avail myself of this occasion to ask the special attention of Congress to it.

That Congress has power to regulate the currency of the country can hardly admit of doubt, and that a judicious measure to prevent the deterioration of this currency, by a seasonable taxation of bank circulation or otherwise, is needed seems equally clear. Independently of this general consideration, it would be unjust to the people at large to exempt banks enjoying the special privilege of circulation from their just proportion of the public burdens.

In order to raise money by way of loans most easily and cheaply, it is clearly necessary to give every possible support to the public credit. To that end a uniform currency, in which taxes, subscriptions to loans, and all other ordinary public dues, as well as all private dues, may be paid, is almost, if not quite, indispensable. Such a currency can be furnished by banking associations, organized under a general act of Congress, as suggested in my message at the beginning of the present session. The securing of this circulation by the pledge of United States bonds, as therein suggested, would still further facilitate loans by increasing the present and causing a future demand for such bonds.

In view of the actual financial embarrassments of the Government and of the greater embarrassments sure to come if the necessary means of relief be not afforded, I feel that I should not perform my duty by a simple announcement of my approval of the joint resolution, which proposes relief only by increasing circulation, without expressing my earnest desire that measures such in substance as those I have just referred to may receive the early sanction of Congress.

By such measures, in my opinion, will payment be most certainly secured, not only to the Army and Navy, but to all honest creditors of the Government, and satisfactory provision made for future demands on the Treasury.

ABRAHAM LINCOLN.

WASHINGTON, *January 20, 1863.*

To the Senate of the United States:

I transmit herewith a report from the Secretary of State, in answer to the resolution of the Senate relative to the correspondence between this Government and the Mexican minister in relation to the exportation of articles contraband of war for the use of the French army in Mexico.

ABRAHAM LINCOLN.

EXECUTIVE MANSION,
Washington, January 21, 1863.

Gentlemen of the Senate and House of Representatives:

I submit herewith, for your consideration, the joint resolutions of the corporate authorities of the city of Washington adopted September 27, 1862, and a memorial of the same under date of October 28, 1862, both relating to and urging the construction of certain railroads concentrating upon the city of Washington.

In presenting this memorial and the joint resolutions to you I am not prepared to say more than that the subject is one of great practical importance and that I hope it will receive the attention of Congress.

ABRAHAM LINCOLN.

WASHINGTON, *January 23, 1863.*

To the Senate and House of Representatives:

I transmit, for the consideration of Congress, a report from the Secretary of State, transmitting the regulations, decrees, and orders for the government of the United States consular courts in Turkey.

ABRAHAM LINCOLN.

WASHINGTON, *January 26, 1863.*

To the Senate of the United States:

In compliance with the resolution of the Senate of the 13th instant, requesting a copy of certain correspondence respecting the capture of British vessels sailing from one British port to another having on board contraband of war intended for the use of the insurgents, I have the honor to transmit a report from the Secretary of State and the documents by which it was accompanied.

ABRAHAM LINCOLN.

WASHINGTON CITY, *January 28, 1863.*

To the Senate and House of Representatives:

In conformity to the law of July 16, 1862, I most cordially recommend that Commander David D. Porter, United States Navy, acting rear-admiral, commanding the Mississippi Squadron, receive a vote of thanks of Congress for the bravery and skill displayed in the attack on the post of Arkansas, which surrendered to the combined military and naval forces on the 10th instant.

ABRAHAM LINCOLN.

WASHINGTON, *February 4, 1863.*

To the House of Representatives:

In compliance with the resolution of the House of Representatives of the 5th December last, requesting information upon the present condition of Mexico, I transmit a report from the Secretary of State and the papers by which it was accompanied.

ABRAHAM LINCOLN.

WASHINGTON, D. C., *February 4, 1863.*

To the Senate of the United States:

In pursuance of the joint resolution of Congress approved 3d February, 1863, tendering its thanks to Commander John L. Worden, United States Navy, I nominate that officer to be a captain in the Navy on the active list from the 3d February, 1863.

It may be proper to state that the number of captains authorized by the second section of the act of 16th July, 1862, is now full, but presuming that the meaning of the ninth section of the same act is that the officer receiving the vote of thanks shall immediately be advanced one grade I have made the nomination.

ABRAHAM LINCOLN.

WASHINGTON, *February 5, 1863.*
To the Senate of the United States:

I submit to the Senate, for consideration with a view to ratification, a "convention between the United States of America and the Republic of Peru for the settlement of the pending claims of the citizens of either country against the other," signed at Lima on the 12th January ultimo, with the following amendment:

Article 1, strike out the words "the claims of the American citizens Dr. Charles Easton, Edmund Sartori, and the owners of the whale ship *William Lee* against the Government of Peru, and the Peruvian citizen Stephen Montano against the Government of the United States," and insert: *all claims of citizens of the United States against the Government of Peru and of citizens of Peru against the Government of the United States which have not been embraced in conventional or diplomatic agreement between the two Governments or their plenipotentiaries, and statements of which soliciting the interposition of either Government may previously to the exchange of the ratifications of this convention have been filed in the Department of State at Washington or the department for foreign affairs at Lima, etc.*

This amendment is considered desirable, as there are believed to be other claims proper for the consideration of the commission which are not among those specified in the original article, and because it is at least questionable whether either Government would be justified in incurring the expense of a commission for the sole purpose of disposing of the claims mentioned in that article.

ABRAHAM LINCOLN.

WASHINGTON, *February 5, 1863.*
To the Senate of the United States:

I submit to the Senate, for consideration with a view to ratification, a "convention between the United States of America and the Republic of Peru, providing for the reference to the King of Belgium of the claims arising out of the capture and confiscation of the ships *Lizzie Thompson* and *Georgiana*," signed at Lima on the 20th December, 1862.

ABRAHAM LINCOLN.

WASHINGTON, *February 6, 1863.*
To the Senate of the United States:

In compliance with the resolution of the Senate of the United States of yesterday, requesting information in regard to the death of General Ward, a citizen of the United States in the military service of the Chinese Government, I transmit a copy of a dispatch of the 27th of October last, and of its accompaniment, from the minister of the United States in China.

ABRAHAM LINCOLN.

WASHINGTON, *February 6, 1863.*

To the Senate of the United States:

I transmit herewith a report* from the Secretary of State, with accompanying documents, in answer to the resolution of the Senate of the 30th ultimo.

ABRAHAM LINCOLN.

WASHINGTON, *February 10, 1863.*

To the Senate of the United States:

In answer to the resolution of the Senate of yesterday, requesting information touching the visit of Mr. Mercier to Richmond in April last, I transmit a report from the Secretary of State, to whom the resolution was referred.

ABRAHAM LINCOLN.

WASHINGTON, D. C., *February 12, 1863.*

To the Senate of the United States:

On the 4th of September, 1862, Commander George Henry Preble, United States Navy, then senior officer in command of the naval force off the harbor of Mobile, was guilty of inexcusable neglect in permitting the armed steamer *Oreto* in open daylight to run the blockade. For his omission to perform his whole duty on that occasion and the injury thereby inflicted on the service and the country, his name was stricken from the list of naval officers and he was dismissed the service.

Since his dismissal earnest application has been made for his restoration to his former position by Senators and naval officers, on the ground that his fault was an error of judgment, and that the example in his case has already had its effect in preventing a repetition of similar neglect.

I therefore, on this application and representation, and in consideration of his previous fair record, do hereby nominate George Henry Preble to be a commander in the Navy from the 16th July, 1862, to take rank on the active list next after Commander Edward Donaldson, and to fill a vacancy occasioned by the death of Commander J. M. Wainwright.

ABRAHAM LINCOLN.

WASHINGTON, D. C., *February 12, 1863.*

To the Senate of the United States:

On the 24th August, 1861, Commander Roger Perry, United States Navy, was dismissed from the service under a misapprehension in regard to his loyalty to the Government, from the circumstance that several oaths were transmitted to him and the Navy Department failed to receive any recognition of them. After his dismissal, and upon his assurance that the oath failed to reach him and his readiness to execute it, he was

*Relating to the building of ships of war for the Japanese Government.

recommissioned to his original position on the 4th September following. On the same day, 4th September, he was ordered to command the sloop of war *Vandalia;* on the 22d this order was revoked and he was ordered to duty in the Mississippi Squadron, and on the 23d January, 1862, was detached sick, and has since remained unemployed. The advisory board under the act of 16th July, 1862, did not recommend him for further promotion.

This last commission, having been issued during the recess of the Senate, expired at the end of the succeeding session, 17th July, 1862, from which date, not having been nominated to the Senate, he ceased to be a commander in the Navy.

To correct the omission to nominate this officer to the Senate at its last session, I now nominate Commander Roger Perry to be a commander in the Navy from the 14th September, 1855, to take his relative position on the list of commanders not recommended for further promotion.

ABRAHAM LINCOLN.

WASHINGTON, *February 12, 1863.*
To the Senate of the United States:

In answer to the resolution of the Senate of the 10th instant, requesting information on the subjects of mediation, arbitration, or other measures looking to the termination of the existing civil war, I transmit a report from the Secretary of State and the documents by which it was accompanied.

ABRAHAM LINCOLN.

WASHINGTON, *February 13, 1863.*
To the Senate of the United States:

I transmit to the Senate, in answer to their resolution of the 12th instant, the accompanying report * from the Secretary of State.

ABRAHAM LINCOLN.

WASHINGTON, *February 13, 1863.*
Hon. GALUSHA A. GROW,
    Speaker of the House of Representatives.

SIR: I herewith communicate to the House of Representatives, in answer to their resolution of the 18th of December last, a report from the Secretary of the Interior, containing all the information in the possession of the Department respecting the causes of the recent outbreaks of the Indian tribes in the Northwest which has not heretofore been transmitted to Congress.

ABRAHAM LINCOLN.

*Relating to the use of negroes by the French army in Mexico.

EXECUTIVE OFFICE, *February 17, 1863.*

To the Senate of the United States:

I transmit herewith, for the constitutional action of the Senate thereon, a treaty made and concluded on the 3d day of February, 1863, between W. W. Ross, commissioner on the part of the United States, and the chiefs and headmen of the Pottawatomie Nation of Indians of Kansas, which, it appears from the accompanying letter from the Secretary of the Interior of the 17th instant, is intended to be amendatory of the treaty concluded with said Indians on the 15th November, 1862.

ABRAHAM LINCOLN.

WASHINGTON, *February 18, 1863.*

To the Senate of the United States:

I transmit to the Senate, for consideration with a view to its ratification, an additional article to the treaty between the United States and Great Britain of the 7th of April, 1862, for the suppression of the African slave trade, which was concluded and signed at Washington on the 17th instant by the Secretary of State and Her Britannic Majesty's minister accredited to this Government.

ABRAHAM LINCOLN.

WASHINGTON, D. C., *February 19, 1863.*

To the Senate of the United States:

Congress on my recommendation passed a resolution, approved 7th February, 1863, tendering its thanks to Commodore Charles Henry Davis for "distinguished service in conflict with the enemy at Fort Pillow, at Memphis, and for successful operations at other points in the waters of the Mississippi River."

I therefore, in conformity with the seventh section of the act approved 16th July, 1862, nominate Commodore Charles Henry Davis to be a rear-admiral in the Navy on the active list from the 7th February, 1863.

Captain John A. Dahlgren having in said resolution of the 7th February in like manner received the thanks of Congress "for distinguished service in the line of his profession, improvements in ordnance, and zealous and efficient labors in the ordnance branch of the service," I therefore, in conformity with the seventh section of the act of 16th July, 1862, nominate Captain John A. Dahlgren to be a rear-admiral in the Navy on the active list from the 7th February, 1863.

The ninth section of the act of July, 1862, authorizes "any line officer of the Navy or Marine Corps to be advanced one grade if upon recommendation of the President by name he receives the thanks of Congress for highly distinguished conduct in conflict with the enemy or for extraordinary heroism in the line of his profession," and Captain Stephen C. Rowan and Commander David D. Porter having each on my recommendation received the thanks of Congress for distinguished service, by resolution or the 7th February, 1863, I do therefore nominate Captain Stephen C. Rowan to be a commodore in the Navy on the active list from the 7th February, 1863. Commander David D. Porter to be a captain in the Navy on the active list from the 7th February, 1863.

If this nomination should be confirmed, there will be vacancies in the several grades to which these officers are nominated for promotion.

ABRAHAM LINCOLN.

WAR DEPARTMENT,
Washington City, February 25, 1863.
The PRESIDENT OF THE UNITED STATES SENATE.

SIR: In answer to the Senate resolution of the 21st instant, I have the honor to inclose herewith a letter of the 24th instant from the Secretary of War, by which it appears that there are 438 assistant quartermasters, 387 commissaries of subsistence, and 343 additional paymasters now in the volunteer service, including those before the Senate for confirmation.

I am, sir, very respectfully, your obedient servant,

ABRAHAM LINCOLN.

WASHINGTON, D. C., *February 25, 1863.*
To the Senate of the United States:

I nominate Passed Midshipmen Samuel Pearce and Nathaniel T. West, now on the retired list, to be ensigns in the Navy on the retired list.

These nominations are made in conformity with the fourth section of the act to amend an act entitled "An act to promote the efficiency of the Navy," approved 16th January, 1857, and are induced by the following considerations:

The pay of a passed midshipman on the retired list as fixed by the "Act for the better organization of the military establishment," approved 3d August, 1861, amounted, including rations, to $788 per annum. By the "Act to establish and equalize the grade of line officers of the United States Navy," approved 16th July, 1862, the grade or rank of passed midshipman, which was the next below that of master, was discontinued and that of ensign was established, being now the next grade below that of master and the only grade in the line list between those of master and midshipman. The same act fixes the pay of officers on the retired list, omitting the grade of passed midshipman, and prohibits the allowance of rations to retired officers. The effect of this was to reduce the pay of a passed midshipman on the retired list from $788 to $350 per annum, or less than half of previous rate.

This was no doubt an unintended result of the law, operating exclusively on the two passed midshipmen then on the retired list, and their promotion or transfer to the equivalent grade of ensign would not completely indemnify them, the pay of an ensign on the retired list being only $500 per annum. It is the only relief, however, which is deemed within the intention of the existing laws, and it is the more willingly recommended in this case, as there is nothing in the character of the officers to be relieved which would make it objectionable. These are the only cases of the kind. ABRAHAM LINCOLN.

WASHINGTON, *February 28, 1863.*

To the Senate of the United States:

In compliance with the resolution of the Senate of the 26th instant, requesting a copy of any correspondence which may have taken place between me and workingmen in England, I transmit the papers mentioned in the subjoined list. ABRAHAM LINCOLN.

WASHINGTON, *February 28, 1863.*

To the Senate and House of Representatives:

I transmit, for the consideration of Congress, a dispatch to the Secretary of State from the United States consul at Liverpool, and the address to which it refers, of the distressed operatives of Blackburn, in England, to the New York relief committee and to the inhabitants of the United States generally. ABRAHAM LINCOLN.

WASHINGTON, *March 2, 1863.*

To the Senate and House of Representatives:

I transmit to Congress a copy of a preamble and joint resolution of the legislative assembly of the Territory of New Mexico, accepting the benefits of the act of Congress approved the 2d of July last, entitled "An act donating public lands to the several States and Territories which may provide colleges for the benefit of agriculture and the mechanic arts." ABRAHAM LINCOLN.

PROCLAMATION.

BY THE PRESIDENT OF THE UNITED STATES OF AMERICA.

A PROCLAMATION.

Whereas on the 22d day of September, A. D. 1862, a proclamation was issued by the President of the United States, containing, among other things, the following, to wit:

That on the 1st day of January, A. D. 1863, all persons held as slaves within any State or designated part of a State the people whereof shall then be in rebellion against the United States shall be then, thenceforward, and forever free; and the executive government of the United States, including the military and naval authority thereof, will recognize and maintain the freedom of such persons and will do no act or acts to repress such persons, or any of them, in any efforts they may make for their actual freedom.

That the Executive will on the 1st day of January aforesaid, by proclamation, designate the States and parts of States, if any, in which the people thereof, respectively, shall then be in rebellion against the United States; and the fact that any State or the people thereof shall on that day be in good faith represented in the Congress of the United States by members chosen thereto at elections wherein a majority of the qualified voters of such States shall have participated shall, in the absence of strong countervailing testimony, be deemed conclusive evidence that such State and the people thereof are not then in rebellion against the United States.

Now, therefore, I, Abraham Lincoln, President of the United States, by virtue of the power in me vested as Commander in Chief of the Army and Navy of the United States in time of actual armed rebellion against the authority and Government of the United States, and as a fit and necessary war measure for suppressing said rebellion, do, on this 1st day of January, A. D. 1863, and in accordance with my purpose so to do, publicly proclaimed for the full period of one hundred days from the day first above mentioned, order and designate as the States and parts of States wherein the people thereof, respectively, are this day in rebellion against the United States the following, to wit:

Arkansas, Texas, Louisiana (except the parishes of St. Bernard, Plaquemines, Jefferson, St. John, St. Charles, St. James, Ascension, Assumption, Terrebonne, Lafourche, St. Mary, St. Martin, and Orleans, including the city of New Orleans), Mississippi, Alabama, Florida, Georgia, South Carolina, North Carolina, and Virginia (except the forty-eight counties designated as West Virginia, and also the counties of Berkeley, Accomac, Northampton, Elizabeth City, York, Princess Anne, and Norfolk, including the cities of Norfolk and Portsmouth), and which excepted parts are for the present left precisely as if this proclamation were not issued.

And by virtue of the power and for the purpose aforesaid, I do order and declare that all persons held as slaves within said designated States and parts of States are and henceforward shall be free, and that the executive government of the United States, including the military and naval authorities thereof, will recognize and maintain the freedom of said persons.

And I hereby enjoin upon the people so declared to be free to abstain from all violence, unless in necessary self-defense; and I recommend to them that in all cases when allowed they labor faithfully for reasonable wages.

And I further declare and make known that such persons of suitable condition will be received into the armed service of the United States to garrison forts, positions, stations, and other places and to man vessels of all sorts in said service.

The Proclamation of Emancipation.

And upon this act, sincerely believed to be an act of justice, warranted by the Constitution upon military necessity, I invoke the considerate judgment of mankind and the gracious favor of Almighty God.

In witness whereof I have hereunto set my hand and caused the seal of the United States to be affixed.

[SEAL.]   Done at the city of Washington, this 1st day of January, A. D. 1863, and of the Independence of the United States of America the eighty-seventh.

ABRAHAM LINCOLN.

By the President:

WILLIAM H. SEWARD, *Secretary of State.*

EXECUTIVE ORDERS.

EXECUTIVE MANSION,
Washington, December 22, 1862.

To the Army of the Potomac:

I have just read your commanding general's preliminary report of the battle of Fredericksburg. Although you were not successful, the attempt was not an error nor the failure other than an accident. The courage with which you in an open field maintained the contest against an intrenched foe and the consummate skill and success with which you crossed and recrossed the river in face of the enemy show that you possess all the qualities of a great army, which will yet give victory to the cause of the country and of popular government. Condoling with the mourners for the dead and sympathizing with the severely wounded, I congratulate you that the number of both is comparatively so small.

I tender to you, officers and soldiers, the thanks of the nation.

ABRAHAM LINCOLN.

EXECUTIVE MANSION,
Washington, January 4, 1863.

Hon. GIDEON WELLES,
Secretary of the Navy.

DEAR SIR: As many persons who come well recommended for loyalty and service to the Union cause, and who are refugees from rebel oppression in the State of Virginia, make application to me for authority and permission to remove their families and property to protection within the Union lines by means of our armed gunboats on the Potomac River and Chesapeake Bay, you are hereby requested to hear and consider all such applications and to grant such assistance to this class of persons as in your judgment their merits may render proper and as may in each case be consistent with the perfect and complete efficiency of the naval service and with military expediency.

ABRAHAM LINCOLN.

EXECUTIVE MANSION, *January 8, 1863.*

Ordered by the President:

Whereas on the 13th day of November, 1862, it was ordered that the Attorney-General be charged with the superintendence and direction of all proceedings to be had under the act of Congress of the 17th of July, entitled "An act to suppress insurrection, to punish treason and rebellion, and to seize and confiscate the property of rebels, and for other purposes," in so far as may concern the seizure, prosecution, and condemnation of the estate, property, and effects of rebels and traitors, as mentioned and provided for in the fifth, sixth, and seventh sections of the said act of Congress; and

Whereas since that time it has been ascertained that divers prosecutions have been instituted in the courts of the United States for the condemnation of property of rebels and traitors under the act of Congress of August 6, 1861, entitled "An act to confiscate property used for insurrectionary purposes," which equally require the superintending care of the Government: Therefore

It is now further ordered by the President, That the Attorney-General be charged with superintendence and direction of all proceedings to be had under the said last-mentioned act (the act of 1861) as fully in all respects as under the first-mentioned act (the act of 1862).

ABRAHAM LINCOLN.

By the President:
    EDW. BATES,
        Attorney-General.

Whereas by the twelfth section of an act of Congress entitled "An act to aid in the construction of a railroad and telegraph line from the Missouri River to the Pacific Ocean, and to secure to the Government the use of the same for postal, military, and other purposes," approved July 1, 1862, it is made the duty of the President of the United States to determine the uniform width of the track of the entire line of the said railroad and the branches of the same; and

Whereas application has been made to me by the Leavenworth, Pawnee and Western Railroad Company, a company authorized by the act of Congress above mentioned to construct a branch of said railroad, to fix the gauge thereof:

Now, therefore, I, Abraham Lincoln, President of the United States of America, do determine that the uniform width of the track of said railroad and all its branches which are provided for in the aforesaid act of Congress shall be 5 feet, and that this order be filed in the office of the Secretary of the Interior for the information and guidance of all concerned.

Done at the city of Washington, this 21st day of January, A. D. 1863.

ABRAHAM LINCOLN.

PROCLAMATION.

BY THE PRESIDENT OF THE UNITED STATES OF AMERICA.

A PROCLAMATION.

Whereas objects of interest to the United States require that the Senate should be convened at 12 o'clock on the 4th of March next to receive and act upon such communications as may be made to it on the part of the Executive:

Now, therefore, I, Abraham Lincoln, President of the United States, have considered it to be my duty to issue this my proclamation, declaring that an extraordinary occasion requires the Senate of the United States to convene for the transaction of business at the Capitol, in the city of Washington, on the 4th day of March next, at 12 o'clock at noon on that day, of which all who shall at that time be entitled to act as members of that body are hereby required to take notice.

Given under my hand and the seal of the United States, at Washington, the 28th day of February, A. D. 1863, and of the Independence of the United States of America the eighty-seventh.

[SEAL.]

ABRAHAM LINCOLN.

By the President:
WILLIAM H. SEWARD,
Secretary of State.

SPECIAL MESSAGES.

WASHINGTON, *March 5, 1863.*

To the Senate of the United States:

For the reasons stated by the Secretary of War, I present the nomination of the persons named in the accompanying communication for confirmation of the rank which they held at the time they fell in the service of their country.

ABRAHAM LINCOLN.

WAR DEPARTMENT,
Washington, March 5, 1863.

The PRESIDENT OF THE UNITED STATES.

SIR: The following-named persons having fallen in battle after having received appointments to the grades for which they are herein nominated, I have the honor to propose that their names be submitted to the Senate for confirmation of their rank, as a token of this Government's approbation of their distinguished merit. This has been the practice of the Department in similar cases, brevet nominations and confirmations having been made after the decease of gallant officers.

To be major-generals.

Brigadier-General Philip Kearny, of the United States Volunteers, July 14, 1862. (Killed in the battle of Chantilly.)

Brigadier-General Israel B. Richardson, of the United States Volunteers, July 4, 1862. (Died of wounds received at the battle of Antietam.)

Brigadier-General Jesse L. Reno, of the United States Volunteers, July 18, 1862. (Killed in the battle of South Mountain.)

To be brigadier-general.

Captain William R. Terrill, of the Fifth United States Artillery, September 9, 1862. (Killed in the battle of Perryville.)

I am, sir, with great respect, your obedient servant,

EDWIN M. STANTON,
Secretary of War.

WASHINGTON, *March 5, 1863.*

To the Senate of the United States:

For the reasons stated by the Secretary of War, I present the nomination of the persons named in the accompanying communication for confirmation of the rank of major-general, in which capacity they were acting at the time they fell in battle.

ABRAHAM LINCOLN.

WAR DEPARTMENT,
Washington, March 5, 1863.

The PRESIDENT OF THE UNITED STATES.

SIR: The following-named persons having fallen in battle while performing the duty and exercising command as major-generals, a rank which they had earned in the service of their country, I have the honor to propose that their names be submitted to the Senate for confirmation, as a token of the Government's appreciation of their distinguished merit. This is in accordance with the practice in similar cases, brevet nominations and confirmations having been made after the decease of gallant officers.

To be major-generals of volunteers.

Brigadier-General Joseph K. F. Mansfield, of the United States Army, July 18, 1862. (Died of wounds received in the battle of Antietam, Md.)

Brigadier-General Isaac I. Stevens, of the United States Volunteers, July 18, 1862. (Killed in the battle of Chantilly, Va.)

I am, sir, with great respect, your obedient servant,

EDWIN M. STANTON,
Secretary of War.

EXECUTIVE MANSION, *March 12, 1863.*

To the Senate of the United States:

I herewith transmit to the Senate, for its consideration and ratification, a treaty with the chiefs and headmen of the Chippewas of the Mississippi and the Pillagers and Lake Winnibigoshish bands of Chippewa Indians.

ABRAHAM LINCOLN.

PROCLAMATIONS.

[From Final Report of the Provost-Marshal-General (March 17, 1866), p. 218.]

BY THE PRESIDENT OF THE UNITED STATES.

A PROCLAMATION.

EXECUTIVE MANSION, *March 10, 1863.*

In pursuance of the twenty-sixth section of the act of Congress entitled "An act for enrolling and calling out the national forces, and for other purposes," approved on the 3d day of March, 1863, I, Abraham Lincoln, President and Commander in Chief of the Army and Navy of the United States, do hereby order and command that all soldiers enlisted or drafted in the service of the United States now absent from their regiments without leave shall forthwith return to their respective regiments.

And I do hereby declare and proclaim that all soldiers now absent from their respective regiments without leave who shall, on or before the 1st day of April, 1863, report themselves at any rendezvous designated by the general orders of the War Department No. 58, hereto annexed, may be restored to their respective regiments without punishment, except the forfeiture of pay and allowances during their absence; and all who do not return within the time above specified shall be arrested as deserters and punished as the law provides; and

Whereas evil-disposed and disloyal persons at sundry places have enticed and procured soldiers to desert and absent themselves from their regiments, thereby weakening the strength of the armies and prolonging the war, giving aid and comfort to the enemy, and cruelly exposing the gallant and faithful soldiers remaining in the ranks to increased hardships and danger:

I do therefore call upon all patriotic and faithful citizens to oppose and resist the aforementioned dangerous and treasonable crimes, and to aid in restoring to their regiments all soldiers absent without leave, and to assist in the execution of the act of Congress "for enrolling and calling out the national forces, and for other purposes," and to support the proper authorities in the prosecution and punishment of offenders against said act and in suppressing the insurrection and rebellion.

In testimony whereof I have hereunto set my hand.

Done at the city of Washington, this 10th day of March, A. D. 1863, and of the Independence of the United States the eighty-seventh.

ABRAHAM LINCOLN.

By the President:
EDWIN M. STANTON,
Secretary of War.

GENERAL ORDERS, No. 58.

> WAR DEPARTMENT,
> ADJUTANT-GENERAL'S OFFICE,
> *Washington, March 10, 1863.*

I. The following is the twenty-sixth section of the act "for enrolling and calling out the national forces, and for other purposes," approved March 3, 1863:

"SEC. 26. *And be it further enacted*, That immediately after the passage of this act the President shall issue his proclamation declaring that all soldiers now absent from their regiments without leave may return, within a time specified, to such place or places as he may indicate in his proclamation, and be restored to their respective regiments without punishment, except the forfeiture of their pay and allowances during their absence; and all deserters who shall not return within the time so specified by the President shall, upon being arrested, be punished as the law provides."

II. The following places* are designated as rendezvous to which soldiers absent without leave may report themselves to the officers named on or before the 1st day of April next under the proclamation of the President of this date.

III. Commanding officers at the above-named places of rendezvous, or, in the absence of commanding officers, superintendents of recruiting service, recruiting officers, and mustering and disbursing officers, will take charge of all soldiers presenting themselves as above directed and cause their names to be enrolled, and copy of said roll will, on or before the 10th day of April, be sent to the Adjutant-General of the Army.

The soldiers so reporting themselves will be sent without delay to their several regiments, a list of those sent being furnished to the commanding officer of the regiment and a duplicate to the Adjutant-General of the Army. The commanding officer of the regiment will immediately report to the Adjutant-General of the Army the receipt of any soldiers so sent to him.

By order of the Secretary of War:

> L. THOMAS,
> *Adjutant-General.*

BY THE PRESIDENT OF THE UNITED STATES OF AMERICA.

A PROCLAMATION.

Whereas the Senate of the United States, devoutly recognizing the supreme authority and just government of Almighty God in all the affairs of men and of nations, has by a resolution requested the President to designate and set apart a day for national prayer and humiliation; and

Whereas it is the duty of nations as well as of men to own their dependence upon the overruling power of God, to confess their sins and transgressions in humble sorrow, yet with assured hope that genuine repentance will lead to mercy and pardon, and to recognize the sublime truth, announced in the Holy Scriptures and proven by all history, that those nations only are blessed whose God is the Lord;

And, insomuch as we know that by His divine law nations, like individuals, are subjected to punishments and chastisements in this world, may we not justly fear that the awful calamity of civil war which now desolates the land may be but a punishment inflicted upon us for our

* Omitted.

presumptuous sins, to the needful end of our national reformation as a whole people? We have been the recipients of the choicest bounties of Heaven; we have been preserved these many years in peace and prosperity; we have grown in numbers, wealth, and power as no other nation has ever grown. But we have forgotten God. We have forgotten the gracious hand which preserved us in peace and multiplied and enriched and strengthened us, and we have vainly imagined, in the deceitfulness of our hearts, that all these blessings were produced by some superior wisdom and virtue of our own. Intoxicated with unbroken success, we have become too self-sufficient to feel the necessity of redeeming and preserving grace, too proud to pray to the God that made us.

It behooves us, then, to humble ourselves before the offended Power, to confess our national sins, and to pray for clemency and forgiveness.

Now, therefore, in compliance with the request, and fully concurring in the views of the Senate, I do by this my proclamation designate and set apart Thursday, the 30th day of April, 1863, as a day of national humiliation, fasting, and prayer. And I do hereby request all the people to abstain on that day from their ordinary secular pursuits, and to unite at their several places of public worship and their respective homes in keeping the day holy to the Lord and devoted to the humble discharge of the religious duties proper to that solemn occasion.

All this being done in sincerity and truth, let us then rest humbly in the hope authorized by the divine teachings that the united cry of the nation will be heard on high and answered with blessings no less than the pardon of our national sins and the restoration of our now divided and suffering country to its former happy condition of unity and peace.

In witness whereof I have hereunto set my hand and caused the seal of the United States to be affixed.

[SEAL.] Done at the city of Washington, this 30th day of March, A. D. 1863, and of the Independence of the United States the eighty-seventh. ABRAHAM LINCOLN.

By the President:

WILLIAM H. SEWARD, *Secretary of State.*

BY THE PRESIDENT OF THE UNITED STATES OF AMERICA.

A PROCLAMATION.

Whereas, in pursuance of the act of Congress approved July 13, 1861, I did, by proclamation dated August 16, 1861, declare that the inhabitants of the States of Georgia, South Carolina, Virginia, North Carolina, Tennessee, Alabama, Louisiana, Texas, Arkansas, Mississippi, and Florida (except the inhabitants of that part of Virginia lying west of the Alleghany Mountains and of such other parts of that State and the other States hereinbefore named as might maintain a legal adhesion to the

Union and the Constitution or might be from time to time occupied and controlled by forces of the United States engaged in the dispersion of said insurgents) were in a state of insurrection against the United States, and that all commercial intercourse between the same and the inhabitants thereof, with the exceptions aforesaid, and the citizens of other States and other parts of the United States was unlawful and would remain unlawful until such insurrection should cease or be suppressed, and that all goods and chattels, wares and merchandise, coming from any of said States, with the exceptions aforesaid, into other parts of the United States without the license and permission of the President, through the Secretary of the Treasury, or proceeding to any of said States, with the exceptions aforesaid, by land or water, together with the vessel or vehicle conveying the same to or from said States, with the exceptions aforesaid, would be forfeited to the United States; and

Whereas experience has shown that the exceptions made in and by said proclamation embarrass the due enforcement of said act of July 13, 1861, and the proper regulation of the commercial intercourse authorized by said act with the loyal citizens of said States:

Now, therefore, I, Abraham Lincoln, President of the United States, do hereby revoke the said exceptions, and declare that the inhabitants of the States of Georgia, South Carolina, North Carolina, Tennessee, Alabama, Louisiana, Texas, Arkansas, Mississippi, Florida, and Virginia (except the forty-eight counties of Virginia designated as West Virginia, and except also the ports of New Orleans, Key West, Port Royal, and Beaufort, in North Carolina) are in a state of insurrection against the United States, and that all commercial intercourse not licensed and conducted as provided in said act between the said States and the inhabitants thereof, with the exceptions aforesaid, and the citizens of other States and other parts of the United States is unlawful and will remain unlawful until such insurrection shall cease or has been suppressed and notice thereof has been duly given by proclamation; and all cotton, tobacco, and other products, and all other goods and chattels, wares and merchandise, coming from any of said States, with the exceptions aforesaid, into other parts of the United States, or proceeding to any of said States, with the exceptions aforesaid, without the license and permission of the President, through the Secretary of the Treasury, will, together with the vessel or vehicle conveying the same, be forfeited to the United States.

In witness whereof I have hereunto set my hand and caused the seal of the United States to be affixed.

[SEAL.]   Done at the city of Washington, this 2d day of April, A. D. 1863, and of the Independence of the United States of America the eighty-seventh.

ABRAHAM LINCOLN.

By the President:

WILLIAM H. SEWARD, *Secretary of State.*

ABRAHAM LINCOLN, PRESIDENT OF THE UNITED STATES OF AMERICA.

To all to whom these presents shall come, greeting:

Know ye that, whereas a paper bearing date the 31st day of December last, purporting to be an agreement between the United States and one Bernard Kock for immigration of persons of African extraction to a dependency of the Republic of Hayti, was signed by me on behalf of the party of the first part; but whereas the said instrument was and has since remained incomplete in consequence of the seal of the United States not having been thereunto affixed; and whereas I have been moved by considerations by me deemed sufficient to withhold my authority for affixing the said seal:

Now, therefore, be it known that I, Abraham Lincoln, President of the United States, do hereby authorize the Secretary of State to cancel my signature to the instrument aforesaid.

Done at Washington, this 16th day of April, A. D. 1863.

[SEAL.]   ABRAHAM LINCOLN.

By the President:

WILLIAM H. SEWARD,
Secretary of State.

BY THE PRESIDENT OF THE UNITED STATES OF AMERICA.

A PROCLAMATION.

Whereas by the act of Congress approved the 31st day of December last the State of West Virginia was declared to be one of the United States of America, and was admitted into the Union on an equal footing with the original States in all respects whatever, upon the condition that certain changes should be duly made in the proposed constitution for that State; and

Whereas proof of a compliance with that condition, as required by the second section of the act aforesaid has been submitted to me:

Now, therefore, be it known that I, Abraham Lincoln, President of the United States, do hereby, in pursuance of the act of Congress aforesaid, declare and proclaim that the said act shall take effect and be in force from and after sixty days from the date hereof.

In witness whereof I have hereunto set my hand and caused the seal of the United States to be affixed.

[SEAL.]   Done at the city of Washington, this 20th day of April, A. D. 1863, and of the Independence of the United States the eighty-seventh.

ABRAHAM LINCOLN.

By the President:

WILLIAM H. SEWARD,
Secretary of State.

By the President of the United States of America.

A PROCLAMATION.

Whereas the Congress of the United States at its last session enacted a law entitled "An act for enrolling and calling out the national forces and for other purposes," which was approved on the 3d day of March last; and

Whereas it is recited in the said act that there now exists in the United States an insurrection and rebellion against the authority thereof, and it is, under the Constitution of the United States, the duty of the Government to suppress insurrection and rebellion, to guarantee to each State a republican form of government, and to preserve the public tranquillity; and

Whereas for these high purposes a military force is indispensable, to raise and support which all persons ought willingly to contribute; and

Whereas no service can be more praiseworthy and honorable than that which is rendered for the maintenance of the Constitution and Union and the consequent preservation of free government; and

Whereas, for the reasons thus recited, it was enacted by the said statute that all able-bodied male citizens of the United States and persons of foreign birth who shall have declared on oath their intention to become citizens under and in pursuance of the laws thereof, between the ages of 20 and 45 years (with certain exceptions not necessary to be here mentioned), are declared to constitute the national forces, and shall be liable to perform military duty in the service of the United States when called out by the President for that purpose; and

Whereas it is claimed by and in behalf of persons of foreign birth within the ages specified in said act who have heretofore declared on oath their intentions to become citizens under and in pursuance of the laws of the United States, and who have not exercised the right of suffrage or any other political franchise under the laws of the United States or of any of the States thereof, that they are not absolutely concluded by their aforesaid declaration of intention from renouncing their purpose to become citizens, and that, on the contrary, such persons, under treaties or the law of nations, retain a right to renounce that purpose and to forego the privileges of citizenship and residence within the United States under the obligations imposed by the aforesaid act of Congress:

Now, therefore, to avoid all misapprehensions concerning the liability of persons concerned to perform the service required by such enactment, and to give it full effect, I do hereby order and proclaim that no plea of alienage will be received or allowed to exempt from the obligations imposed by the aforesaid act of Congress any person of foreign birth who shall have declared on oath his intention to become a citizen of the United States under the laws thereof, and who shall be found within the United States at any time during the continuance of the present insurrection and rebellion or after the expiration of the period of sixty-five days from the date of this proclamation, nor shall any such plea of alienage be allowed in favor of any such person who has so as aforesaid declared his intention to become a citizen of the United States and shall have exercised at any time the right of suffrage or any other political franchise within the United States under the laws thereof or under the laws of any of the several States.

In witness whereof I have hereunto set my hand and caused the seal of the United States to be affixed.

[SEAL.]   Done at the city of Washington, this 8th day of May, A. D. 1863, and of the Independence of the United States the eighty-seventh.

ABRAHAM LINCOLN.

By the President:

WILLIAM H. SEWARD, *Secretary of State.*

BY THE PRESIDENT OF THE UNITED STATES OF AMERICA.

A PROCLAMATION.

Whereas the armed insurrectionary combinations now existing in several of the States are threatening to make inroads into the States of Maryland, West Virginia, Pennsylvania, and Ohio, requiring immediately an additional military force for the service of the United States:

Now, therefore, I, Abraham Lincoln, President of the United States and Commander in Chief of the Army and Navy thereof and of the militia of the several States when called into actual service, do hereby call into the service of the United States 100,000 militia from the States following, namely: From the State of Maryland, 10,000; from the State of Pennsylvania, 50,000; from the State of Ohio, 30,000; from the State of West Virginia, 10,000—to be mustered into the service of the United States forthwith and to serve for the period of six months from the date of such muster into said service, unless sooner discharged; to be mustered in as infantry, artillery, and cavalry, in proportions which will be made known through the War Department, which Department will also designate the several places of rendezvous. These militia to be organized according to the rules and regulations of the volunteer service and such orders as may hereafter be issued. The States aforesaid will be respectively credited under the enrollment act for the militia services rendered under this proclamation.

In testimony whereof I have hereunto set my hand and caused the seal of the United States to be affixed.

[SEAL.]   Done at the city of Washington, this 15th day of June, A. D. 1863, and of the Independence of the United States the eighty-seventh.

ABRAHAM LINCOLN.

By the President:

WILLIAM H. SEWARD, *Secretary of State.*

By the President of the United States of America.

A PROCLAMATION.

It has pleased Almighty God to hearken to the supplications and prayers of an afflicted people and to vouchsafe to the Army and the Navy of the United States victories on land and on the sea so signal and so effective as to furnish reasonable grounds for augmented confidence that the Union of these States will be maintained, their Constitution preserved, and their peace and prosperity permanently restored. But these victories have been accorded not without sacrifices of life, limb, health, and liberty, incurred by brave, loyal, and patriotic citizens. Domestic affliction in every part of the country follows in the train of these fearful bereavements. It is meet and right to recognize and confess the presence of the Almighty Father and the power of His hand equally in these triumphs and in these sorrows:

Now, therefore, be it known that I do set apart Thursday, the 6th day of August next, to be observed as a day for national thanksgiving, praise, and prayer, and I invite the people of the United States to assemble on that occasion in their customary places of worship and in the forms approved by their own consciences render the homage due to the Divine Majesty for the wonderful things He has done in the nation's behalf and invoke the influence of His Holy Spirit to subdue the anger which has produced and so long sustained a needless and cruel rebellion, to change the hearts of the insurgents, to guide the counsels of the Government with wisdom adequate to so great a national emergency, and to visit with tender care and consolation throughout the length and breadth of our land all those who, through the vicissitudes of marches, voyages, battles, and sieges, have been brought to suffer in mind, body, or estate, and finally to lead the whole nation through the paths of repentance and submission to the divine will back to the perfect enjoyment of union and fraternal peace.

In witness whereof I have hereunto set my hand and caused the seal of the United States to be affixed.

[SEAL.]   Done at the city of Washington, this 15th day of July, A. D. 1863, and of the Independence of the United States of America the eighty-eighth.

ABRAHAM LINCOLN.

By the President:

WILLIAM H. SEWARD, *Secretary of State.*

By the President of the United States of America.

A PROCLAMATION.

Whereas the Constitution of the United States has ordained that the privilege of the writ of *habeas corpus* shall not be suspended unless when, in cases of rebellion or invasion, the public safety may require it; and

Whereas a rebellion was existing on the 3d day of March, 1863, which rebellion is still existing; and

Whereas by a statute which was approved on that day it was enacted by the Senate and House of Representatives of the United States in Congress assembled that during the present insurrection the President of the United States, whenever in his judgment the public safety may require, is authorized to suspend the privilege of the writ of *habeas corpus* in any case throughout the United States or any part thereof; and

Whereas, in the judgment of the President, the public safety does require that the privilege of the said writ shall now be suspended throughout the United States in the cases where, by the authority of the President of the United States, military, naval, and civil officers of the United States, or any of them, hold persons under their command or in their custody, either as prisoners of war, spies, or aiders or abettors of the enemy, or officers, soldiers, or seamen enrolled or drafted or mustered or enlisted in or belonging to the land or naval forces of the United States, or as deserters therefrom, or otherwise amenable to military law or the rules and articles of war or the rules or regulations prescribed for the military or naval services by authority of the President of the United States, or for resisting a draft, or for any other offense against the military or naval service:

Now, therefore, I, Abraham Lincoln, President of the United States, do hereby proclaim and make known to all whom it may concern that the privilege of the writ of *habeas corpus* is suspended throughout the United States in the several cases before mentioned, and that this suspension will continue throughout the duration of the said rebellion or until this proclamation shall, by a subsequent one to be issued by the President of the United States, be modified or revoked. And I do hereby require all magistrates, attorneys, and other civil officers within the United States and all officers and others in the military and naval services of the United States to take distinct notice of this suspension and to give it full effect, and all citizens of the United States to conduct and govern themselves accordingly and in conformity with the Constitution of the United States and the laws of Congress in such case made and provided.

In testimony whereof I have hereunto set my hand and caused the seal of the United States to be affixed this 15th day of September, [SEAL.] A. D. 1863, and of the Independence of the United States of America the eighty-eighth.

ABRAHAM LINCOLN.

By the President:

WILLIAM H. SEWARD, *Secretary of State.*

BY THE PRESIDENT OF THE UNITED STATES OF AMERICA.

A PROCLAMATION.

Whereas in my proclamation of the 27th of April, 1861, the ports of the States of Virginia and North Carolina were, for reasons therein set forth, placed under blockade; and

Whereas the port of Alexandria, Va., has since been blockaded, but as the blockade of said port may now be safely relaxed with advantage to the interests of commerce:

Now, therefore, be it known that I, Abraham Lincoln, President of the United States, pursuant to the authority in me vested by the fifth section of the act of Congress approved on the 13th of July, 1861, entitled "An act further to provide for the collection of duties on imports and for other purposes," do hereby declare that the blockade of the said port of Alexandria shall so far cease and determine from and after this date that commercial intercourse with said port, except as to persons, things, and information contraband of war, may from this date be carried on, subject to the laws of the United States and to the limitations and in pursuance of the regulations which are prescribed by the Secretary of the Treasury in his order which is appended to my proclamation of the 12th of May, 1862.

In witness whereof I have hereunto set my hand and caused the seal of the United States to be affixed.

[SEAL.]   Done at the city of Washington, this 24th day of September, A. D. 1863, and of the Independence of the United States the eighty-eighth.

                                   ABRAHAM LINCOLN.
By the President:

WILLIAM H. SEWARD, *Secretary of State.*

BY THE PRESIDENT OF THE UNITED STATES OF AMERICA.

A PROCLAMATION.

The year that is drawing toward its close has been filled with the blessings of fruitful fields and healthful skies. To these bounties, which are so constantly enjoyed that we are prone to forget the source from which they come, others have been added which are of so extraordinary a nature that they can not fail to penetrate and soften even the heart which is habitually insensible to the ever-watchful providence of Almighty God.

In the midst of a civil war of unequaled magnitude and severity, which has sometimes seemed to foreign states to invite and to provoke their aggression, peace has been preserved with all nations, order has been maintained, the laws have been respected and obeyed, and harmony has prevailed everywhere, except in the theater of military conflict, while that theater has been greatly contracted by the advancing armies and navies of the Union.

Needful diversions of wealth and of strength from the fields of peaceful industry to the national defense have not arrested the plow, the shuttle, or the ship; the ax has enlarged the borders of our settlements, and the mines, as well of iron and coal as of the precious metals, have yielded even more abundantly than heretofore. Population has steadily increased notwithstanding the waste that has been made in the camp, the siege, and the battlefield, and the country, rejoicing in the consciousness of augmented strength and vigor, is permitted to expect continuance of years with large increase of freedom.

No human counsel hath devised nor hath any mortal hand worked out these great things. They are the gracious gifts of the Most High God, who, while dealing with us in anger for our sins, hath nevertheless remembered mercy.

It has seemed to me fit and proper that they should be solemnly, reverently, and gratefully acknowledged, as with one heart and one voice, by the whole American people. I do therefore invite my fellow-citizens in every part of the United States, and also those who are at sea and those who are sojourning in foreign lands, to set apart and observe the last Thursday of November next as a day of thanksgiving and praise to our beneficent Father who dwelleth in the heavens. And I recommend to them that while offering up the ascriptions justly due to Him for such singular deliverances and blessings they do also, with humble penitence for our national perverseness and disobedience, commend to His tender care all those who have become widows, orphans, mourners, or sufferers in the lamentable civil strife in which we are unavoidably engaged, and fervently implore the interposition of the Almighty hand to heal the wounds of the nation and to restore it, as soon as may be consistent with the divine purposes, to the full enjoyment of peace, harmony, tranquillity, and union.

In testimony whereof I have hereunto set my hand and caused the seal of the United States to be affixed.

[SEAL.] Done at the city of Washington, this 3d day of October, A. D. 1863, and of the Independence of the United States the eighty-eighth.

ABRAHAM LINCOLN.

By the President:

WILLIAM H. SEWARD, *Secretary of State.*

BY THE PRESIDENT OF THE UNITED STATES OF AMERICA.

A PROCLAMATION.

Whereas the term of service of a part of the volunteer forces of the United States will expire during the coming year; and

Whereas, in addition to the men raised by the present draft, it is deemed expedient to call out 300,000 volunteers to serve for three years or the war, not, however, exceeding three years:

Now, therefore, I, Abraham Lincoln, President of the United States and Commander in Chief of the Army and Navy thereof and of the militia of the several States when called into actual service, do issue this my proclamation, calling upon the governors of the different States to raise and have enlisted into the United States service for the various companies and regiments in the field from their respective States their quotas of 300,000 men.

I further proclaim that all volunteers thus called out and duly enlisted shall receive advance pay, premium, and bounty, as heretofore communicated to the governors of States by the War Department through the Provost-Marshal-General's Office by special letters.

I further proclaim that all volunteers received under this call, as well as all others not heretofore credited, shall be duly credited on and deducted from the quotas established for the next draft.

I further proclaim that if any State shall fail to raise the quota assigned to it by the War Department under this call, then a draft for the deficiency in said quota shall be made on said State, or on the districts of said State, for their due proportion of said quota; and the said draft shall commence on the 5th day of January, 1864.

And I further proclaim that nothing in this proclamation shall interfere with existing orders, or those which may be issued, for the present draft in the States where it is now in progress or where it has not yet commenced.

The quotas of the States and districts will be assigned by the War Department, through the Provost-Marshal-General's Office, due regard being had for the men heretofore furnished, whether by volunteering or drafting, and the recruiting will be conducted in accordance with such instructions as have been or may be issued by that Department.

In issuing this proclamation I address myself not only to the governors of the several States, but also to the good and loyal people thereof, invoking them to lend their willing, cheerful, and effective aid to the measures thus adopted, with a view to reenforce our victorious armies now in the field and bring our needful military operations to a prosperous end, thus closing forever the fountains of sedition and civil war.

In witness whereof I have hereunto set my hand and caused the seal of the United States to be affixed.

[SEAL.]   Done at the city of Washington, this 17th day of October, A. D. 1863, and of the Independence of the United States the eighty-eighth.

ABRAHAM LINCOLN.

By the President:

WILLIAM H. SEWARD, *Secretary of State*.

EXECUTIVE ORDERS.

EXECUTIVE MANSION,
Washington, March 31, 1863.

Whereas by the act of Congress approved July 13, 1861, entitled "An act to provide for the collection of duties on imports, and for other purposes," all commercial intercourse between the inhabitants of such States as should by proclamation be declared in insurrection against the United

States and the citizens of the rest of the United States was prohibited so long as such condition of hostility should continue, except as the same shall be licensed and permitted by the President to be conducted and carried on only in pursuance of rules and regulations prescribed by the Secretary of the Treasury; and

Whereas it appears that a partial restoration of such intercourse between the inhabitants of sundry places and sections heretofore declared in insurrection in pursuance of said act and the citizens of the rest of the United States will favorably affect the public interests:

Now, therefore, I, Abraham Lincoln, President of the United States, exercising the authority and discretion confided to me by the said act of Congress, do hereby license and permit such commercial intercourse between the citizens of loyal States and the inhabitants of such insurrectionary States in the cases and under the restrictions described and expressed in the regulations prescribed by the Secretary of the Treasury bearing even date with these presents, or in such other regulations as he may hereafter, with my approval, prescribe.

ABRAHAM LINCOLN.

EXECUTIVE MANSION,
Washington, June 22, 1863.

Whereas the act of Congress approved the 3d day of March, A. D. 1863, entitled "An act to provide circuit courts for the districts of California and Oregon, and for other purposes," authorized the appointment of one additional associate justice of the Supreme Court of the United States, and provided that the districts of California and Oregon should constitute the tenth circuit and that the other circuits should remain as then constituted by law; and

Whereas Stephen J. Field was appointed the said additional associate justice of the Supreme Court since the last adjournment of said court, and consequently he was not allotted to the said circuit according to the fifth section of the act of Congress entitled "An act to amend the judicial system of the United States," approved the 29th day of April, 1802:

Now I, Abraham Lincoln, President of the United States, under the authority of said section, do allot the said associate justice, Stephen J. Field, to the said tenth circuit.

ABRAHAM LINCOLN.

Attest:

TITIAN J. COFFEY,
Attorney-General ad interim.

WAR DEPARTMENT,
Washington, July 4, 1863—10 a. m.

The President announces to the country that news from the Army of the Potomac up to 10 o'clock p. m. of the 3d is such as to cover that army with the highest honor, to promise a great success to the cause of the Union, and to claim the condolence of all for the many gallant fallen; and that for this he especially desires that on this day He whose will, not ours, should ever be done be everywhere remembered and ever reverenced with profoundest gratitude.

ABRAHAM LINCOLN.

GENERAL ORDERS, No. 211.

WAR DEPARTMENT,
ADJUTANT-GENERAL'S OFFICE,
Washington, July 9, 1863.

ORDER ABOLISHING MILITARY GOVERNORSHIP OF ARKANSAS.

Ordered, That the appointment of John S. Phelps as military governor of the State of Arkansas and of Amos F. Eno as secretary be revoked, and the office of military governor in said State is abolished, and that all authority, appointments, and power heretofore granted to and exercised by them, or either of them, as military governor or secretary, or by any person or persons appointed by or acting under them, is hereby revoked and annulled.

By order of the President:

E. D. TOWNSEND,
Assistant Adjutant-General.

EXECUTIVE MANSION,
Washington, July 25, 1863.

Hon. SECRETARY OF THE NAVY.

SIR: Certain matters have come to my notice, and considered by me, which induce me to believe that it will conduce to the public interest for you to add to the general instructions given to our naval commanders in relation to contraband trade propositions substantially as follows, to wit:

First. You will avoid the reality, and as far as possible the appearance, of using any neutral port to watch neutral vessels, and then to dart out and seize them on their departure.

NOTE.—Complaint is made that this has been practiced at the port of St. Thomas, which practice, if it exists, is disapproved and must cease.

Second. You will not in any case detain the crew of a captured neutral vessel or any other subject of a neutral power on board such vessel, as prisoners of war or otherwise, except the small number necessary as witnesses in the prize court.

NOTE.—The practice here forbidden is also charged to exist, which, if true, is disapproved and must cease.

My dear sir, it is not intended to be insinuated that you have been remiss in the performance of the arduous and responsible duties of your Department, which, I take pleasure in affirming, has in your hands been conducted with admirable success. Yet, while your subordinates are almost of necessity brought into angry collision with the subjects of foreign states, the representatives of those states and yourself do not come into immediate contact for the purpose of keeping the peace, in spite of such collisions. At that point there is an ultimate and heavy responsibility upon me.

What I propose is in strict accordance with international law, and is therefore unobjectionable; whilst, if it does no other good, it will contribute to sustain a considerable portion of the present British ministry in their places, who, if displaced, are sure to be replaced by others more unfavorable to us.

Your obedient servant,   ABRAHAM LINCOLN.

EXECUTIVE MANSION,
Washington, July 30, 1863.

It is the duty of every government to give protection to its citizens, of whatever class, color, or condition, and especially to those who are duly organized as soldiers in the public service. The law of nations and the usages and customs of war, as carried on by civilized powers, permit no distinction as to color in the treatment of prisoners of war as public enemies. To sell or enslave any captured person on account of his color, and for no offense against the laws of war, is a relapse into barbarism and a crime against the civilization of the age.

The Government of the United States will give the same protection to all its soldiers, and if the enemy shall sell or enslave anyone because of his color the offense shall be punished by retaliation upon the enemy's prisoners in our possession.

It is therefore ordered, That for every soldier of the United States killed in violation of the laws of war a rebel soldier shall be executed, and for every one enslaved by the enemy or sold into slavery a rebel soldier shall be placed at hard labor on the public works and continued at such labor until the other shall be released and receive the treatment due to a prisoner of war.

ABRAHAM LINCOLN.

EXECUTIVE MANSION,
Washington City, August 25, 1863.

Ordered, first. That clearances issued by the Treasury Department for vessels or merchandise bound for the port of New Orleans for the military necessities of the department, certified by Brigadier-General Shepley, the military governor of Louisiana, shall be allowed to enter said port.

Second. That vessels and domestic produce from New Orleans permitted by the military governor of Louisiana at New Orleans for the military purpose of his department shall on his permit be allowed to pass from said port to its destination to any port not blockaded by the United States.

A. LINCOLN.

WAR DEPARTMENT,
Washington City, August 31, 1863.

Ordered, That the Executive order of November 21, 1862, prohibiting the exportation of arms, ammunition, or munitions of war from the United States, be, and the same hereby is, modified so far as to permit the exportation of imported arms, ammunition, and munitions of war to the ports whence they were shipped for the United States.

By order of the President:

[EDWIN M. STANTON.]

EXECUTIVE MANSION,
Washington, September 4, 1863.

Ordered, That the Executive order dated November 21, 1862, prohibiting the exportation from the United States of arms, ammunition, or munitions of war, under which the commandants of departments were, by order of the Secretary of War dated May 13, 1863, directed to prohibit the purchase and sale for exportation from the United States of all horses and mules within their respective commands, and to take and appropriate to the use of the United States any horses, mules, and live stock designed for exportation, be so far modified that any arms heretofore imported into the United States may be reexported to the place of original shipment, and that any live stock raised in any State or Territory bounded by the Pacific Ocean may be exported from any port of such State or Territory.

ABRAHAM LINCOLN.

WAR DEPARTMENT,
Washington City, September 24, 1863.

Ordered by the President of the United States, That Major-General Hooker be, and he is hereby, authorized to take military possession of all railroads, with their cars, locomotives, plants, and equipments, that may be necessary for the execution of the military operation committed to his charge; and all officers, agents, and employees of said roads are directed to render their aid and assistance therein and to respect and obey his commands, pursuant to the act of Congress in such case made and provided.

EDWIN M. STANTON, *Secretary of War.*

EXECUTIVE MANSION,
Washington, November 10, 1863.

In consideration of the peculiar circumstances and pursuant to the comity deemed to be due to friendly powers, any tobacco in the United

States belonging to the government either of France, Austria, or any other state with which this country is at peace, and which tobacco was purchased and paid for by such government prior to the 4th day of March, 1861, may be exported from any port of the United States under the supervision and upon the responsibility of naval officers of such governments and in conformity to such regulations as may be presented by the Secretary of State of the United States, and not otherwise.

ABRAHAM LINCOLN.

THIRD ANNUAL MESSAGE.

DECEMBER 8, 1863.

Fellow-Citizens of the Senate and House of Representatives:

Another year of health and of sufficiently abundant harvests has passed. For these, and especially for the improved condition of our national affairs, our renewed and profoundest gratitude to God is due.

We remain in peace and friendship with foreign powers.

The efforts of disloyal citizens of the United States to involve us in foreign wars to aid an inexcusable insurrection have been unavailing. Her Britannic Majesty's Government, as was justly expected, have exercised their authority to prevent the departure of new hostile expeditions from British ports. The Emperor of France has by a like proceeding promptly vindicated the neutrality which he proclaimed at the beginning of the contest. Questions of great intricacy and importance have arisen out of the blockade and other belligerent operations between the Government and several of the maritime powers, but they have been discussed and, as far as was possible, accommodated in a spirit of frankness, justice, and mutual good will. It is especially gratifying that our prize courts, by the impartiality of their adjudications, have commanded the respect and confidence of maritime powers.

The supplemental treaty between the United States and Great Britain for the suppression of the African slave trade, made on the 17th day of February last, has been duly ratified and carried into execution. It is believed that so far as American ports and American citizens are concerned that inhuman and odious traffic has been brought to an end.

I shall submit for the consideration of the Senate a convention for the adjustment of possessory claims in Washington Territory arising out of the treaty of the 15th June, 1846, between the United States and Great Britain, and which have been the source of some disquiet among the citizens of that now rapidly improving part of the country.

A novel and important question, involving the extent of the maritime jurisdiction of Spain in the waters which surround the island of Cuba, has been debated without reaching an agreement, and it is proposed in an amicable spirit to refer it to the arbitrament of a friendly power. A convention for that purpose will be submitted to the Senate.

I have thought it proper, subject to the approval of the Senate, to concur with the interested commercial powers in an arrangement for the liquidation of the Scheldt dues, upon the principles which have been heretofore adopted in regard to the imposts upon navigation in the waters of Denmark.

The long-pending controversy between this Government and that of Chile touching the seizure at Sitana, in Peru, by Chilean officers, of a large amount in treasure belonging to citizens of the United States has been brought to a close by the award of His Majesty the King of the Belgians, to whose arbitration the question was referred by the parties. The subject was thoroughly and patiently examined by that justly respected magistrate, and although the sum awarded to the claimants may not have been as large as they expected there is no reason to distrust the wisdom of His Majesty's decision. That decision was promptly complied with by Chile when intelligence in regard to it reached that country.

The joint commission under the act of the last session for carrying into effect the convention with Peru on the subject of claims has been organized at Lima, and is engaged in the business intrusted to it.

Difficulties concerning interoceanic transit through Nicaragua are in course of amicable adjustment.

In conformity with principles set forth in my last annual message, I have received a representative from the United States of Colombia, and have accredited a minister to that Republic.

Incidents occurring in the progress of our civil war have forced upon my attention the uncertain state of international questions touching the rights of foreigners in this country and of United States citizens abroad. In regard to some governments these rights are at least partially defined by treaties. In no instance, however, is it expressly stipulated that in the event of civil war a foreigner residing in this country within the lines of the insurgents is to be exempted from the rule which classes him as a belligerent, in whose behalf the Government of his country can not expect any privileges or immunities distinct from that character. I regret to say, however, that such claims have been put forward, and in some instances in behalf of foreigners who have lived in the United States the greater part of their lives.

There is reason to believe that many persons born in foreign countries who have declared their intention to become citizens, or who have been fully naturalized, have evaded the military duty required of them by denying the fact and thereby throwing upon the Government the burden of proof. It has been found difficult or impracticable to obtain this proof, from the want of guides to the proper sources of information. These might be supplied by requiring clerks of courts where declarations of intention may be made or naturalizations effected to send periodically lists of the names of the persons naturalized or declaring their intention to become citizens to the Secretary of the Interior, in whose Department those names might be arranged and printed for general information.

There is also reason to believe that foreigners frequently become citizens of the United States for the sole purpose of evading duties imposed by the laws of their native countries, to which on becoming naturalized here they at once repair, and though never returning to the United States they still claim the interposition of this Government as citizens. Many altercations and great prejudices have heretofore arisen out of this abuse. It is therefore submitted to your serious consideration. It might be advisable to fix a limit beyond which no citizen of the United States residing abroad may claim the interposition of his Government.

The right of suffrage has often been assumed and exercised by aliens under pretenses of naturalization, which they have disavowed when drafted into the military service. I submit the expediency of such an amendment of the law as will make the fact of voting an estoppel against any plea of exemption from military service or other civil obligation on the ground of alienage.

In common with other Western powers, our relations with Japan have been brought into serious jeopardy through the perverse opposition of the hereditary aristocracy of the Empire to the enlightened and liberal policy of the Tycoon, designed to bring the country into the society of nations. It is hoped, although not with entire confidence, that these difficulties may be peacefully overcome. I ask your attention to the claim of the minister residing there for the damages he sustained in the destruction by fire of the residence of the legation at Yedo.

Satisfactory arrangements have been made with the Emperor of Russia, which, it is believed, will result in effecting a continuous line of telegraph through that Empire from our Pacific coast.

I recommend to your favorable consideration the subject of an international telegraph across the Atlantic Ocean, and also of a telegraph between this capital and the national forts along the Atlantic seaboard and the Gulf of Mexico. Such communications, established with any reasonable outlay, would be economical as well as effective aids to the diplomatic, military, and naval service.

The consular system of the United States, under the enactments of the last Congress, begins to be self-sustaining, and there is reason to hope that it may become entirely so with the increase of trade which will ensue whenever peace is restored. Our ministers abroad have been faithful in defending American rights. In protecting commercial interests our consuls have necessarily had to encounter increased labors and responsibilities growing out of the war. These they have for the most part met and discharged with zeal and efficiency. This acknowledgment justly includes those consuls who, residing in Morocco, Egypt, Turkey,

Japan, China, and other Oriental countries, are charged with complex functions and extraordinary powers.

The condition of the several organized Territories is generally satisfactory, although Indian disturbances in New Mexico have not been entirely suppressed. The mineral resources of Colorado, Nevada, Idaho, New Mexico, and Arizona are proving far richer than has been heretofore understood. I lay before you a communication on this subject from the governor of New Mexico. I again submit to your consideration the expediency of establishing a system for the encouragement of immigration. Although this source of national wealth and strength is again flowing with greater freedom than for several years before the insurrection occurred, there is still a great deficiency of laborers in every field of industry, especially in agriculture and in our mines, as well of iron and coal as of the precious metals. While the demand for labor is much increased here, tens of thousands of persons, destitute of remunerative occupation, are thronging our foreign consulates and offering to emigrate to the United States if essential, but very cheap, assistance can be afforded them. It is easy to see that under the sharp discipline of civil war the nation is beginning a new life. This noble effort demands the aid and ought to receive the attention and support of the Government.

Injuries unforeseen by the Government and unintended may in some cases have been inflicted on the subjects or citizens of foreign countries, both at sea and on land, by persons in the service of the United States. As this Government expects redress from other powers when similar injuries are inflicted by persons in their service upon citizens of the United States, we must be prepared to do justice to foreigners. If the existing judicial tribunals are inadequate to this purpose, a special court may be authorized, with power to hear and decide such claims of the character referred to as may have arisen under treaties and the public law. Conventions for adjusting the claims by joint commission have been proposed to some governments, but no definitive answer to the proposition has yet been received from any.

In the course of the session I shall probably have occasion to request you to provide indemnification to claimants where decrees of restitution have been rendered and damages awarded by admiralty courts, and in other cases where this Government may be acknowledged to be liable in principle and where the amount of that liability has been ascertained by an informal arbitration.

The proper officers of the Treasury have deemed themselves required by the law of the United States upon the subject to demand a tax upon the incomes of foreign consuls in this country. While such a demand may not in strictness be in derogation of public law, or perhaps of any existing treaty between the United States and a foreign country, the expediency of so far modifying the act as to exempt from tax the income of such consuls as are not citizens of the United States, derived from the emoluments of their office or from property not situated in the United States, is submitted to your serious consideration. I make this suggestion upon the ground that a comity which ought to be reciprocated exempts our consuls in all other countries from taxation to the extent thus indicated. The United States, I think, ought not to be exceptionally illiberal to international trade and commerce.

The operations of the Treasury during the last year have been successfully conducted. The enactment by Congress of a national banking law has proved a valuable support of the public credit, and the general legislation in relation to loans has fully answered the expectations of its favorers. Some amendments may be required to perfect existing laws, but no change in their principles or general scope is believed to be needed.

Since these measures have been in operation all demands on the Treasury, including the pay of the Army and Navy, have been promptly met and fully satisfied. No considerable body of troops, it is believed, were ever more amply provided and more liberally and punctually paid, and it may be added that by no people were the burdens incident to a great war ever more cheerfully borne.

The receipts during the year from all sources, including loans and balance in the Treasury at its commencement, were $901,125,674.86, and the aggregate disbursements $895,796,630.65, leaving a balance on the 1st of July, 1863, of $5,329,044.21. Of the receipts there were derived from customs $69,059,642.40, from internal revenue $37,640,787.95, from direct tax $1,485,103.61, from lands $167,617.17, from miscellaneous sources $3,046,615.35, and from loans $776,682,361.57, making the aggregate $901,125,674.86. Of the disbursements there were for the civil service $23,253,922.08, for pensions and Indians $4,216,520.79, for interest on public debt $24,729,846.51, for the War Department $599,298,600.83, for the Navy Department $63,211,105.27, for payment of funded and temporary debt $181,086,635.07, making the aggregate $895,796,630.65 and leaving the balance of $5,329,044.21. But the payment of funded and temporary debt, having been made from moneys borrowed during the year, must be regarded as merely nominal payments and the moneys borrowed to make them as merely nominal receipts, and their amount, $181,086,635.07, should therefore be deducted both from receipts and disbursements. This being done there remains as actual receipts $720,039,039.79 and the actual disbursements $714,709,995.58, leaving the balance as already stated.

The actual receipts and disbursements for the first quarter and the estimated receipts and disbursements for the remaining three quarters of the current fiscal year (1864) will be shown in detail by the report of the Secretary of the Treasury, to which I invite your attention. It is sufficient to say here that it is not believed that actual results will exhibit a state of the finances less favorable to the country than the estimates of that officer heretofore submitted, while it is confidently expected that at the close of the year both disbursements and debt will be found very considerably less than has been anticipated.

The report of the Secretary of War is a document of great interest. It consists of—

1. The military operations of the year, detailed in the report of the General in Chief.

2. The organization of colored persons into the war service.

3. The exchange of prisoners, fully set forth in the letter of General Hitchcock.

4. The operations under the act for enrolling and calling out the national forces, detailed in the report of the Provost-Marshal-General.

5. The organization of the invalid corps, and

6. The operation of the several departments of the Quartermaster-General, Commissary-General, Paymaster-General, Chief of Engineers, Chief of Ordnance, and Surgeon-General.

It has appeared impossible to make a valuable summary of this report, except such as would be too extended for this place, and hence I content myself by asking your careful attention to the report itself.

The duties devolving on the naval branch of the service during the year and throughout the whole of this unhappy contest have been discharged with fidelity and eminent success. The extensive blockade has been constantly increasing in efficiency as the Navy has expanded, yet on so long a line it has so far been impossible to entirely suppress illicit trade. From returns received at the Navy Department it appears that more than 1,000 vessels have been captured since the blockade was instituted, and that the value of prizes already sent in for adjudication amounts to over $13,000,000.

The naval force of the United States consists at this time of 588 vessels completed and in the course of completion, and of these 75 are ironclad or armored steamers. The events of the war give an increased interest and importance to the Navy which will probably extend beyond the war itself.

The armored vessels in our Navy completed and in service, or which are under contract and approaching completion, are believed to exceed in number those of any other power; but while these may be relied upon for harbor defense and coast service, others of greater strength and capacity will be necessary for cruising purposes and to maintain our rightful position on the ocean.

The change that has taken place in naval vessels and naval warfare since the introduction of steam as a motive power for ships of war demands either a corresponding change in some of our existing navy-yards or the establishment of new ones for the construction and necessary repair of modern naval vessels. No inconsiderable embarrassment, delay, and public injury have been experienced from the want of such governmental establishments. The necessity of such a navy-yard, so furnished, at some suitable place upon the Atlantic seaboard has on repeated occasions been brought to the attention of Congress by the Navy Department, and is again presented in the report of the Secretary which accompanies this communication. I think it my duty to invite your special attention to this subject, and also to that of establishing a yard and depot for naval purposes upon one of the Western rivers. A naval force has been created on those interior waters, and under many disadvantages, within little more than two years, exceeding in numbers the whole naval force of the country at the commencement of the present Administration. Satisfactory and important as have been the performances of the heroic men of the Navy at this interesting period, they are scarcely more wonderful than the success of our mechanics and artisans in the production of war vessels, which has created a new form of naval power.

Our country has advantages superior to any other nation in our resources of iron and timber, with inexhaustible quantities of fuel in the immediate vicinity of both, and all available and in close proximity to navigable waters. Without the advantage of public works, the resources of the nation have been developed and its power displayed in the construction of a Navy of such magnitude, which has at the very period of its creation rendered signal service to the Union.

The increase of the number of seamen in the public service from 7,500 men in the spring of 1861 to about 34,000 at the present time has been accomplished without special legislation or extraordinary bounties to promote that increase. It has been found, however, that the operation of the draft, with the high bounties paid for army recruits, is beginning to affect injuriously the naval service, and will, if not corrected, be likely to impair its efficiency by detaching seamen from their proper vocation and inducing them to enter the Army. I therefore respectfully suggest that Congress might aid both the army and naval services by a definite provision on this subject which would at the same time be equitable to the communities more especially interested.

I commend to your consideration the suggestions of the Secretary of the Navy in regard to the policy of fostering and training seamen and also the education of officers and engineers for the naval service. The Naval Academy is rendering signal service in preparing midshipmen for the highly responsible duties which in after life they will be required to perform. In order that the country should not be deprived of the proper quota of educated officers, for which legal provision has been made at the naval school, the vacancies caused by the neglect or omission to make nominations from the States in insurrection have been filled by the Secretary of the Navy. The school is now more full and complete than at any former period, and in every respect entitled to the favorable consideration of Congress.

During the past fiscal year the financial condition of the Post-Office Department has been one of increasing prosperity, and I am gratified in being able to state that the actual postal revenue has nearly equaled the entire expenditures, the latter amounting to $11,314,206.84 and the former to $11,163,789.59, leaving a deficiency of but $150,417.25.   In 1860, the year immediately preceding the rebellion, the deficiency amounted to $5,656,705.49, the postal receipts of that year being $2,645,722.19 less than those of 1863.   The decrease since 1860 in the annual amount of transportation has been only about 25 per cent, but the annual expenditure on account of the same has been reduced 35 per cent.   It is manifest, therefore, that the Post-Office Department may become self-sustaining in a few years, even with the restoration of the whole service.

The international conference of postal delegates from the principal countries of Europe and America, which was called at the suggestion of the Postmaster-General, met at Paris on the 11th of May last and concluded its deliberations on the 8th of June.   The principles established by the conference as best adapted to facilitate postal intercourse between nations and as the basis of future postal conventions inaugurate a general system of uniform international charges at reduced rates of postage, and can not fail to produce beneficial results.

I refer you to the report of the Secretary of the Interior, which is herewith laid before you, for useful and varied information in relation to the public lands, Indian affairs, patents, pensions, and other matters of public concern pertaining to his Department.

The quantity of land disposed of during the last and the first quarter of the present fiscal years was 3,841,549 acres, of which 161,911 acres were sold for cash, 1,456,514 acres were taken up under the homestead law, and the residue disposed of under laws granting lands for military bounties, for railroad and other purposes.   It also appears that the sale of the public lands is largely on the increase.

It has long been a cherished opinion of some of our wisest statesmen that the people of the United States had a higher and more enduring interest in the early settlement and substantial cultivation of the public lands than in the amount of direct revenue to be derived from the sale of them. This opinion has had a controlling influence in shaping legislation upon the subject of our national domain.   I may cite as evidence of this the liberal measures adopted in reference to actual settlers; the grant to the States of the overflowed lands within their limits, in order to their being reclaimed and rendered fit for cultivation; the grants to railway companies of alternate sections of land upon the contemplated lines of their roads, which when completed will so largely multiply the facilities for reaching our distant possessions.   This policy has received its most signal and beneficent illustration in the recent enactment granting homesteads to actual settlers.   Since the 1st day of January last the before-mentioned quantity of 1,456,514 acres of land have been taken up under its provisions.   This fact and the amount of sales furnish gratifying evidence of increasing settlement upon the public lands, notwithstanding the great struggle in which the energies of the nation have been engaged, and which has required so large a withdrawal of our citizens from their accustomed pursuits. I cordially concur in the recommendation of the Secretary of the Interior suggesting a modification of the act in favor of those engaged in the military and naval service of the United States. I doubt not that Congress will cheerfully adopt such measures as will, without essentially changing the general features of the system, secure to the greatest practicable extent its benefits to those who have left their homes in the defense of the country in this arduous crisis.

I invite your attention to the views of the Secretary as to the propriety of raising by appropriate legislation a revenue from the mineral lands of the United States.

The measures provided at your last session for the removal of certain Indian tribes have been carried into effect. Sundry treaties have been negotiated, which will in due time be submitted for the constitutional action of the Senate. They contain stipulations for extinguishing the possessory rights of the Indians to large and valuable tracts of lands. It is hoped that the effect of these treaties will result in the establishment of permanent friendly relations with such of these tribes as have been brought into frequent and bloody collision with our outlying settlements and emigrants. Sound policy and our imperative duty to these wards of the Government demand our anxious and constant attention to their material well-being, to their progress in the arts of civilization, and, above all, to that moral training which under the blessing of Divine Providence will confer upon them the elevated and sanctifying influences, the hopes and consolations, of the Christian faith.

I suggested in my last annual message the propriety of remodeling our Indian system. Subsequent events have satisfied me of its necessity. The details set forth in the report of the Secretary evince the urgent need for immediate legislative action.

I commend the benevolent institutions established or patronized by the Government in this District to your generous and fostering care.

The attention of Congress during the last session was engaged to some extent with a proposition for enlarging the water communication between the Mississippi River and the northeastern seaboard, which proposition, however, failed for the time. Since then, upon a call of the greatest respectability, a convention has been held at Chicago upon the same subject, a summary of whose views is contained in a memorial addressed to the President and Congress, and which I now have the honor to lay before you. That this interest is one which ere long will force its own way I do not entertain a doubt, while it is submitted entirely to your wisdom as to what can be done now. Augmented interest is given to this subject by the actual commencement of work upon the Pacific Railroad, under auspices so favorable to rapid progress and completion. The enlarged navigation becomes a palpable need to the great road.

I transmit the second annual report of the Commissioner of the Department of Agriculture, asking your attention to the developments in that vital interest of the nation.

When Congress assembled a year ago, the war had already lasted nearly twenty months, and there had been many conflicts on both land and sea, with varying results; the rebellion had been pressed back into reduced limits; yet the tone of public feeling and opinion, at home and abroad, was not satisfactory. With other signs, the popular elections then just past indicated uneasiness among ourselves, while, amid much that was cold and menacing, the kindest words coming from Europe were uttered in accents of pity that we were too blind to surrender a hopeless cause. Our commerce was suffering greatly by a few armed vessels built upon and furnished from foreign shores, and we were threatened with such additions from the same quarter as would sweep our trade from the sea and raise our blockade. We had failed to elicit from European Governments anything hopeful upon this subject. The preliminary emancipation proclamation, issued in September, was running its assigned period to the beginning of the new year. A month later the final proclamation came, including the announcement that colored men of suitable condition would be received into the war service. The policy of emancipation and of employing black soldiers gave to the future a new aspect, about which hope and fear and doubt contended in uncertain conflict. According to our political system, as a matter of civil administration, the General Government had no lawful power to effect emancipation in any State, and for a long time it had been hoped that the rebellion could be suppressed without resorting to it as a military measure. It was all the while deemed possible that the necessity for it might come, and that if it should the crisis of the contest would then be presented. It came, and, as was anticipated, it was followed by dark and doubtful days. Eleven months having now passed, we are permitted to take another review. The rebel borders are pressed still farther back, and by the complete opening of the Mississippi the country dominated by the rebellion is divided into distinct parts, with no practical communication between them. Tennessee and Arkansas have been substantially cleared of insurgent control, and influential citizens in each, owners of slaves and advocates of slavery at the beginning of the rebellion, now declare openly for emancipation in their respective States. Of those States not included in the emancipation proclamation, Maryland and Missouri, neither of which three years ago would tolerate any restraint upon the extension of slavery into new Territories, only dispute now as to the best mode of removing it within their own limits.

Of those who were slaves at the beginning of the rebellion full 100,000 are now in the United States military service, about one-half of which number actually bear arms in the ranks, thus giving the double advantage of taking so much labor from the insurgent cause and supplying the places which otherwise must be filled with so many white men. So far as tested, it is difficult to say they are not as good soldiers as any. No servile insurrection or tendency to violence or cruelty has marked the measures of emancipation and arming the blacks. These measures have been much discussed in foreign countries, and, contemporary with such discussion, the tone of public sentiment there is much improved. At home the same measures have been fully discussed, supported, criticised, and denounced, and the annual elections following are highly encouraging to those whose official duty it is to bear the country through this great trial. Thus we have the new reckoning. The crisis which threatened to divide the friends of the Union is past.

Looking now to the present and future, and with reference to a resumption of the national authority within the States wherein that authority has been suspended, I have thought fit to issue a proclamation, a copy of which is herewith transmitted.* On examination of this proclamation it will appear, as is believed, that nothing will be attempted beyond what is amply justified by the Constitution. True, the form of an oath is given, but no man is coerced to take it. The man is only promised a pardon in case he voluntarily takes the oath. The Constitution authorizes the Executive to grant or withhold the pardon at his own absolute discretion, and this includes the power to grant on terms, as is fully established by judicial and other authorities.

It is also proffered that if in any of the States named a State government shall be in the mode prescribed set up, such government shall be recognized and guaranteed by the United States, and that under it the State shall, on the constitutional conditions, be protected against invasion and domestic violence. The constitutional obligation of the United States to guarantee to every State in the Union a republican form of government and to protect the State in the cases stated is explicit and full. But why tender the benefits of this provision only to a State government set up in this particular way? This section of the Constitution contemplates a case wherein the element within a State favorable to republican government in the Union may be too feeble for an opposite and hostile element external to or even within the State, and such are precisely the cases with which we are now dealing.

An attempt to guarantee and protect a revived State government, constructed in whole or in preponderating part from the very element against whose hostility and violence it is to be protected, is simply absurd. There must be a test by which to separate the opposing elements, so as to build only from the sound; and that test is a sufficiently liberal one which accepts as sound whoever will make a sworn recantation of his former unsoundness.

But if it be proper to require as a test of admission to the political body an oath of allegiance to the Constitution of the United States and to the

---

*See proclamation dated December 8, 1863, pp. 213–215.

Union under it, why also to the laws and proclamations in regard to slavery? Those laws and proclamations were enacted and put forth for the purpose of aiding in the suppression of the rebellion. To give them their fullest effect there had to be a pledge for their maintenance. In my judgment, they have aided and will further aid the cause for which they were intended. To now abandon them would be not only to relinquish a lever of power, but would also be a cruel and an astounding breach of faith. I may add at this point that while I remain in my present position I shall not attempt to retract or modify the emancipation proclamation, nor shall I return to slavery any person who is free by the terms of that proclamation or by any of the acts of Congress. For these and other reasons it is thought best that support of these measures shall be included in the oath, and it is believed the Executive may lawfully claim it in return for pardon and restoration of forfeited rights, which he has clear constitutional power to withhold altogether or grant upon the terms which he shall deem wisest for the public interest. It should be observed also that this part of the oath is subject to the modifying and abrogating power of legislation and supreme judicial decision.

The proposed acquiescence of the National Executive in any reasonable temporary State arrangement for the freed people is made with the view of possibly modifying the confusion and destitution which must at best attend all classes by a total revolution of labor throughout whole States. It is hoped that the already deeply afflicted people in those States may be somewhat more ready to give up the cause of their affliction if to this extent this vital matter be left to themselves, while no power of the National Executive to prevent an abuse is abridged by the proposition.

The suggestion in the proclamation as to maintaining the political framework of the States on what is called reconstruction is made in the hope that it may do good without danger of harm. It will save labor and avoid great confusion.

But why any proclamation now upon this subject? This question is beset with the conflicting views that the step might be delayed too long or be taken too soon. In some States the elements for resumption seem ready for action, but remain inactive apparently for want of a rallying point—a plan of action. Why shall A adopt the plan of B rather than B that of A? And if A and B should agree, how can they know but that the General Government here will reject their plan? By the proclamation a plan is presented which may be accepted by them as a rallying point, and which they are assured in advance will not be rejected here. This may bring them to act sooner than they otherwise would.

The objections to a premature presentation of a plan by the National Executive consist in the danger of committals on points which could be more safely left to further developments. Care has been taken to so shape the document as to avoid embarrassments from this source. Saying that on certain terms certain classes will be pardoned with rights restored, it is not said that other classes or other terms will never be included. Saying that reconstruction will be accepted if presented in a specified way, it is not said it will never be accepted in any other way.

The movements by State action for emancipation in several of the States not included in the emancipation proclamation are matters of profound gratulation. And while I do not repeat in detail what I have heretofore so earnestly urged upon this subject, my general views and feelings remain unchanged; and I trust that Congress will omit no fair opportunity of aiding these important steps to a great consummation.

In the midst of other cares, however important, we must not lose sight of the fact that the war power is still our main reliance. To that power alone can we look yet for a time to give confidence to the people in the contested regions that the insurgent power will not again overrun them. Until that confidence shall be established little can be done anywhere for what is called reconstruction. Hence our chiefest care must still be directed to the Army and Navy, who have thus far borne their harder part so nobly and well; and it may be esteemed fortunate that in giving the greatest efficiency to these indispensable arms we do also honorably recognize the gallant men, from commander to sentinel, who compose them, and to whom more than to others the world must stand indebted for the home of freedom disenthralled, regenerated, enlarged, and perpetuated.

ABRAHAM LINCOLN.

SPECIAL MESSAGES.

WASHINGTON, D. C., *December 8, 1863.*

To the Senate and House of Representatives:

In conformity to the law of July 16, 1862, I most cordially recommend that Captain John Rodgers, United States Navy, receive a vote of thanks from Congress for the eminent skill and gallantry exhibited by him in the engagement with the rebel armed ironclad steamer *Fingal*, alias *Atlanta*, whilst in command of the United States ironclad steamer *Weehawken*, which led to her capture on the 17th June, 1863, and also for the zeal, bravery, and general good conduct shown by this officer on many occasions.

This recommendation is specially made in order to comply with the requirements of the ninth section of the aforesaid act, which is in the following words, viz:

That any line officer of the Navy or Marine Corps may be advanced one grade if upon recommendation of the President by name he receives the thanks of Congress for highly distinguished conduct in conflict with the enemy or for extraordinary heroism in the line of his profession.

ABRAHAM LINCOLN.

WASHINGTON, D. C., *December 8, 1863.*

To the Senate of the United States:

Congress, on my recommendation, passed a resolution, approved 7th February, 1863, tendering its thanks to Commander D. D. Porter "for the bravery and skill displayed in the attack on the post of Arkansas on the 10th January, 1863," and in consideration of those services, together with his efficient labors and vigilance subsequently displayed in thwarting the efforts of the rebels to obstruct the Mississippi and its tributaries and the important part rendered by the squadron under his command, which led to the surrender of Vicksburg.

I do therefore, in conformity to the seventh section of the act approved 16th July, 1862, nominate Commander D. D. Porter to be a rear-admiral in the Navy on the active list from the 4th July, 1863, to fill an existing vacancy.

ABRAHAM LINCOLN.

WASHINGTON, *December 10, 1863.*

To the Senate and House of Representatives:

I transmit herewith a report, dated the 9th instant, with the accompanying papers, received from the Secretary of State in compliance with the requirements of the sixteenth and eighteenth sections of the act entitled "An act to regulate the diplomatic and consular systems of the United States," approved August 18, 1856.   ABRAHAM LINCOLN.

EXECUTIVE MANSION,
Washington, December, 1863.

To the Senate of the United States:

I lay before the Senate, for its constitutional action thereon, a treaty concluded at Le Roy, Kans., on the 29th day of August, 1863, between William P. Dole, Commissioner of Indian Affairs, and William G. Coffin, superintendent of Indian affairs of the southern superintendency, commissioners on the part of the United States, and the chiefs and headmen of the Great and Little Osage tribe of Indians of the State of Kansas.

A communication from the Secretary of the Interior, dated the 12th instant, accompanies the treaty.   ABRAHAM LINCOLN.

EXECUTIVE MANSION,
Washington, December, 1863.

To the Senate of the United States:

I lay before the Senate, for its constitutional action thereon, a treaty concluded on the 7th day of October, 1863, at Conejos, Colorado Territory, between John Evans, governor and *ex officio* superintendent of Indian affairs of said Territory; Michael Steck, superintendent of Indian affairs for the Territory of New Mexico; Simeon Whitely and Lafayette Head,

Indian agents, commissioners on the part of the United States, and the chiefs and warriors of the Tabeguache band of Utah Indians.

I also transmit a report of the Secretary of the Interior of the 12th instant, submitting the treaty; an extract from the last annual report of Governor Evans, of Colorado Territory, relating to its negotiation, and a map upon which is delineated the boundaries of the country ceded by the Indians and that retained for their own use.

ABRAHAM LINCOLN.

EXECUTIVE MANSION,
Washington, December, 1863.

To the Senate of the United States:

I lay before the Senate, for its constitutional action thereon, a treaty concluded at the city of Washington on the 6th day of April, 1863, between John P. Usher, commissioner on the part of the United States, and the chiefs and headmen of the Comanche, Kiowa, and Apache tribes of Indians, duly authorized thereto.

A letter of the Secretary of the Interior of the 12th instant accompanies the treaty.

ABRAHAM LINCOLN.

EXECUTIVE MANSION,
Washington, December, 1863.

To the Senate of the United States:

I lay before the Senate, for its constitutional action thereon, a treaty concluded at the Sac and Fox Agency, in Kansas, on the 2d day of September, 1863, between William P. Dole, Commissioner of Indian Affairs, commissioner on the part of the United States, and the New York Indians, represented by duly authorized members of the bands of said tribe.

A letter of the Secretary of the Interior of the 12th instant accompanies the treaty.

ABRAHAM LINCOLN.

EXECUTIVE MANSION,
Washington, December, 1863.

To the Senate of the United States:

I lay before the Senate, for its constitutional action thereon, a treaty concluded at the Sac and Fox Agency, in Kansas, on the 3d day of September, 1863, between William P. Dole, Commissioner of Indian Affairs, and William G. Coffin, superintendent of Indian affairs for the southern superintendency, on the part of the United States, and the Creek Nation of Indians, represented by its chiefs.

A letter from the Secretary of the Interior, dated the 12th instant, accompanies the treaty.

ABRAHAM LINCOLN.

EXECUTIVE MANSION,
Washington, December, 1863.

To the Senate of the United States:

I lay before the Senate, for its constitutional action thereon, a treaty concluded at the Sac and Fox Agency, in Kansas, on the 4th day of September, 1863, between William P. Dole, Commissioner of Indian Affairs, and Henry W. Martin, agent for the Sacs and Foxes, commissioners on the part of the United States, and the united tribes of Sac and Fox Indians of the Mississippi.

A letter from the Secretary of the Interior, dated the 12th instant, accompanies the treaty.

ABRAHAM LINCOLN.

WASHINGTON, *December 15, 1863.*

To the Senate of the United States:

In answer to the resolution of the Senate of the 11th of March last, requesting certain information touching persons in the service of this Government, I transmit a report from the Secretary of State, to whom the resolution was referred.

ABRAHAM LINCOLN.

WASHINGTON, *December 17, 1863.*

To the Senate of the United States:

I transmit to the Senate, for consideration with a view to its ratification, a convention between the United States and Her Britannic Majesty for the final adjustment of the claims of the Hudsons Bay and Pugets Sound Agricultural Companies, signed in this city on the 1st day of July last (1863).

ABRAHAM LINCOLN.

DECEMBER 17, 1863.

To the Senate and House of Representatives of the United States:

Herewith I lay before you a letter addressed to myself by a committee of gentlemen representing the freedmen's aid societies in Boston, New York, Philadelphia, and Cincinnati. The subject of the letter, as indicated above, is one of great magnitude and importance, and one which these gentlemen, of known ability and high character, seem to have considered with great attention and care. Not having the time to form a mature judgment of my own as to whether the plan they suggest is the best, I submit the whole subject to Congress, deeming that their attention thereto is almost imperatively demanded.

ABRAHAM LINCOLN.

WASHINGTON, *December 22, 1863.*

To the Senate of the United States:

I transmit to the Senate, for its consideration with a view to ratification, two conventions between the United States and His Belgian Majesty, signed at Brussels on the 20th May and the 20th of July last, respectively, and both relating to the extinguishment of the Scheldt dues, etc. A copy of so much of the correspondence between the Secretary of State and Mr. Sanford, the minister resident of the United States at Brussels, on the subject of the conventions as is necessary to a full understanding of it is also herewith transmitted.

ABRAHAM LINCOLN.

WASHINGTON, *December 23, 1863.*

To the Senate and House of Representatives:

I transmit to Congress a copy of the report to the Secretary of State of the commissioners on the part of the United States under the convention with Peru of the 12th of January last, on the subject of claims. It will be noticed that two claims of Peruvian citizens on this Government have been allowed. An appropriation for the discharge of the obligations of the United States in these cases is requested.

ABRAHAM LINCOLN.

JANUARY 5, 1864.

Gentlemen of the Senate and House of Representatives:

By a joint resolution of your honorable bodies approved December 23, 1863, the paying of bounties to veteran volunteers, as now practiced by the War Department, is, to the extent of $300 in each case, prohibited after this 5th day of the present month. I transmit for your consideration a communication from the Secretary of War, accompanied by one from the Provost-Marshal-General to him, both relating to the subject above mentioned. I earnestly recommend that the law be so modified as to allow bounties to be paid as they now are, at least until the ensuing 1st day of February.

I am not without anxiety lest I appear to be importunate in thus recalling your attention to a subject upon which you have so recently acted, and nothing but a deep conviction that the public interest demands it could induce me to incur the hazard of being misunderstood on this point. The Executive approval was given by me to the resolution mentioned, and it is now by a closer attention and a fuller knowledge of facts that I feel constrained to recommend a reconsideration of the subject.

ABRAHAM LINCOLN.

WASHINGTON, *January 7, 1864.*

To the Senate and House of Representatives:

I transmit to Congress a copy of the decree of the court of the United States for the southern district of New York, awarding the sum of $17,150.66 for the illegal capture of the British schooner *Glen,* and request that an appropriation of that amount may be made as an indemnification to the parties interested.

ABRAHAM LINCOLN.

EXECUTIVE MANSION,
Washington, January, 1864.

To the Senate of the United States:

I herewith lay before the Senate, for its constitutional action thereon, the following-described treaties, viz:

A treaty made at Fort Bridger, Utah Territory, on the 2d day of July, 1863, between the United States and the chiefs, principal men, and warriors of the eastern bands of the Shoshonee Nation of Indians.

A treaty made at Box Elder, Utah Territory, on the 30th day of July, 1863, between the United States and the chiefs and warriors of the northwestern bands of the Shoshonee Nation of Indians.

A treaty made at Ruby Valley, Nevada Territory, on the 1st day of October, 1863, between the United States and the chiefs, principal men, and warriors of the Shoshonee Nation of Indians.

A treaty made at Tuilla Valley, Utah Territory, on the 12th day of October, 1863, between the United States and the chiefs, principal men, and warriors of the Goship bands of Shoshonee Indians.

A treaty made at Soda Springs, in Idaho Territory, on the 14th day of October, 1863, between the United States and the chiefs of the mixed bands of Bannacks and Shoshonees, occupying the valley of the Shoshonee River.

A letter of the Secretary of the Interior of the 5th instant, a copy of a report of the 30th ultimo, from the Commissioner of Indian Affairs, a copy of a communication from Governor Doty, superintendent of Indian Affairs, Utah Territory, dated November 10, 1863, relating to the Indians parties to the several treaties herein named, and a map, furnished by that gentleman, are herewith transmitted.

ABRAHAM LINCOLN,

EXECUTIVE MANSION,
Washington, January, 1864.

To the Senate of the United States:

I herewith lay before the Senate, for its constitutional action thereon, a treaty made at the Old Crossing of Red Lake River, in the State of Minnesota, on the 2d day of October, 1863, between Alexander Ramsey and Ashley C. Morrill, commissioners on the part of the United States, and the chiefs, headmen, and warriors of the Red Lake and Pembina bands of Chippewa Indians.

A letter of the Secretary of the Interior of the 8th instant, together with a communication from the Commissioner of Indian Affairs of the 5th instant and copies of Mr. Ramsey's report and journal, relating to the treaty, and a map showing the territory ceded, are herewith transmitted.

ABRAHAM LINCOLN.

EXECUTIVE MANSION, *January 12, 1864.*

To the Senate of the United States:

In accordance with the request of the Senate conveyed in their resolution of the 16th of December, 1863, desiring any information in my possession relative to the alleged exceptional treatment of Kansas troops when captured by those in rebellion, I have the honor to transmit a communication from the Secretary of War, accompanied by reports from the General in Chief of the Army and the Commissary-General of Prisoners relative to the subject-matter of the resolution.

ABRAHAM LINCOLN.

JANUARY 20, 1864.

Gentlemen of the Senate and House of Representatives:

In accordance with a letter addressed by the Secretary of State, with my approval, to the Hon. Joseph A. Wright, of Indiana, that patriotic and distinguished gentleman repaired to Europe and attended the International Agricultural Exhibition, held at Hamburg last year, and has since his return made a report to me, which, it is believed, can not fail to be of general interest, and especially so to the agricultural community. I transmit for your consideration copies of the letters and report. While it appears by the letter that no reimbursement of expenses or compensation was promised him, I submit whether reasonable allowance should not be made him for them.

ABRAHAM LINCOLN.

WASHINGTON, *January 21, 1864.*

To the Senate of the United States:

In compliance with the resolution of the Senate of yesterday, respecting the recent destruction by fire of the Church of the Compañía at Santiago, Chile, and the efforts of citizens of the United States to rescue the victims of the conflagration, I transmit a report from the Secretary of State, with the papers accompanying it.

ABRAHAM LINCOLN.

WASHINGTON, *January 23, 1864.*

To the Senate of the United States:

I transmit to the Senate a copy of a dispatch of the 12th of April last, addressed by Anson Burlingame, esq., the minister of the United States to China, to the Secretary of State, relative to a modification of the twenty-first article of a treaty between the United States and China of the 18th of June, 1858, a printed copy of which is also herewith transmitted.

These papers are submitted to the consideration of the Senate with a view to their advice and consent being given to the modification of the said twenty-first article, as explained in the said dispatch and its accompaniments.

ABRAHAM LINCOLN.

WASHINGTON, *January 29, 1864.*

To the Senate of the United States:

I transmit herewith a report from the Secretary of State, in answer to the resolution of the Senate respecting the correspondence with the authorities of Great Britain in relation to the proposed pursuit of hostile bands of the Sioux Indians into the Hudson Bay territories.

ABRAHAM LINCOLN.

To the Senate: WASHINGTON, *February 4, 1864.*

In compliance with the resolution of the Senate of the 26th ultimo, requesting "a copy of all the correspondence between the authorities of the United States and the rebel authorities on the exchange of prisoners, and the different propositions connected with that subject," I transmit herewith a report from the Secretary of War and the papers with which it is accompanied.   ABRAHAM LINCOLN.

WASHINGTON, *February 5, 1864.*

To the Senate of the United States:

In answer to the resolution of the Senate of yesterday on the subject of a reciprocity treaty with the Sandwich Islands, I transmit a report from the Secretary of State, to whom the resolution was referred.

ABRAHAM LINCOLN.

WASHINGTON, *February 16, 1864.*

To the Senate and House of Representatives:

I transmit to Congress a report from the Secretary of State, with the accompanying papers, relative to the claim on this Government of the owners of the French ship *La Manche,* and recommend an appropriation for the satisfaction of the claim, pursuant to the award of the arbitrators.

ABRAHAM LINCOLN.

WASHINGTON, *February 16, 1864.*

To the House of Representatives of the United States:

In answer to the resolution of the House of Representatives of the 8th instant, requesting information touching the arrest of the United States consul-general to the British North American Provinces, and certain official communications respecting Canadian commerce, I transmit a report from the Secretary of State and the documents by which it was accompanied.

ABRAHAM LINCOLN.

WASHINGTON, *February 22, 1864.*

To the Senate and House of Representatives:

I transmit to Congress the copy of a correspondence which has recently taken place between Her Britannic Majesty's minister accredited to this Government and the Secretary of State, in order that the expediency of sanctioning the acceptance by the master of the American schooner *Highlander* of a present of a watch which the lords of the committee of Her Majesty's privy council for trade propose to present to him in recognition of services rendered by him to the crew of the British vessel *Pearl* may be taken into consideration.   ABRAHAM LINCOLN.

EXECUTIVE MANSION, *February, 1864.*

To the Senate of the United States:

I communicate to the Senate herewith, for its constitutional action thereon, the articles of agreement and convention made and concluded at the city of Washington on the 25th day of the present month by and between William P. Dole, as commissioner on the part of the United States, and the duly authorized delegates of the Swan Creek and Black River Chippewas and the Munsees or Christian Indians in Kansas.

ABRAHAM LINCOLN.

WASHINGTON, *February 29, 1864.*

To the House of Representatives:

In answer to the resolution of the House of Representatives of the 26th instant, I transmit herewith a report from the Secretary of War, relative to the reenlistment of veteran volunteers.

ABRAHAM LINCOLN.

EXECUTIVE MANSION,
Washington, February 29, 1864.

To the Senate of the United States:

I nominate Ulysses S. Grant, now a major-general in the military service, to be lieutenant-general in the Army of the United States.

ABRAHAM LINCOLN.

EXECUTIVE MANSION, *March, 1864.*

To the Senate of the United States:

I transmit herewith a report* of the Secretary of the Interior of the 11th instant, containing the information requested in Senate resolution of the 29th ultimo.   ABRAHAM LINCOLN.

*Relating to the amount of money received for the sale of the Wea trust lands in Kansas, etc.

EXECUTIVE MANSION, *March 9, 1864.*

To the Senate of the United States:

In compliance with a resolution of the Senate of the 1st instant, respecting the points of commencement of the Union Pacific Railroad, on the one hundredth degree of west longitude, and of the branch road, from the western boundary of Iowa to the said one hundredth degree of longitude, I transmit the accompanying report from the Secretary of the Interior, containing the information called for.

I deem it proper to add that on the 17th day of November last an Executive order was made upon this subject and delivered to the vice-president of the Union Pacific Railroad Company, which fixed the point on the western boundary of the State of Iowa from which the company should construct their branch road to the one hundredth degree of west longitude, and declared it to be within the limits of the township in Iowa opposite the town of Omaha, in Nebraska. Since then the company has represented to me that upon actual surveys made it has determined upon the precise point of departure of their said branch road from the Missouri River, and located the same as described in the accompanying report of the Secretary of the Interior, which point is within the limits designated in the order of November last; and inasmuch as that order is not of record in any of the Executive Departments, and the company having desired a more definite one, I have made the order of which a copy is herewith, and caused the same to be filed in the Department of the Interior.

ABRAHAM LINCOLN.

EXECUTIVE OFFICE, *March 12, 1864.*

To the Senate of the United States:

In obedience to the resolution of the Senate of the 28th of January last, I communicate herewith a report, with accompanying papers, from the Secretary of the Interior, showing what portion of the appropriations for the colonization of persons of African descent has been expended and the several steps which have been taken for the execution of the acts of Congress on that subject.

ABRAHAM LINCOLN.

WASHINGTON, *March 14, 1864.*

To the Senate and House of Representatives:

I transmit to Congress a copy of a treaty between the United States and Great Britain for the final settlement of the claims of the Hudsons Bay and Pugets Sound Agricultural Companies, concluded on the 1st of July last, the ratifications of which were exchanged in this city on the 5th instant, and recommend an appropriation to carry into effect the first, second, and third articles thereof.

ABRAHAM LINCOLN.

WASHINGTON, *March 14, 1864.*

To the Senate and House of Representatives:

On the 25th day of November, 1862, a convention for the mutual adjustment of claims pending between the United States and Ecuador was signed at Quito by the plenipotentiaries of the contracting parties. A copy is herewith inclosed.

This convention, already ratified by this Government, has been sent to Quito for the customary exchange of ratifications, which it is not doubted will be promptly effected. As the stipulations of the instrument require that the commissioners who are to be appointed pursuant to its provisions shall meet at Guayaquil within ninety days after such exchange, it is desirable that the legislation necessary to give effect to the convention on the part of the United States should anticipate the usual course of proceeding.

I therefore invite the early attention of Congress to the subject.

ABRAHAM LINCOLN.

EXECUTIVE OFFICE,
Washington, March 22, 1864.

To the Senate of the United States:

I herewith lay before the Senate, for its constitutional action thereon, a treaty made and concluded in Washington City on the 18th instant by and between William P. Dole, Commissioner of Indian Affairs, and the Shawnee Indians, represented by their duly authorized delegates.

A report of the Secretary of the Interior and a communication of the Commissioner of Indian Affairs accompany the treaty.

ABRAHAM LINCOLN.

WASHINGTON, *March 24, 1864.*

To the Senate of the United States:

In reply to the resolution of the Senate of the 15th instant, in relation to the establishment of monarchical governments in Central and South America, I transmit a report from the Secretary of State, to whom the subject was referred.

ABRAHAM LINCOLN.

MARCH 29, 1864.

To the Senate and House of Representatives:

Mr. Charles B. Stuart, consulting engineer, appointed such by me upon invitation of the governor of New York, according to a law of that State, has made a report upon the proposed improvements to pass gunboats from tide water to the northern and northwestern lakes, which report is herewith respectfully submitted for your consideration.

ABRAHAM LINCOLN.

EXECUTIVE OFFICE,
Washington, April 4, 1864.

To the Senate of the United States:

I herewith lay before the Senate, for its constitutional action thereon, a treaty concluded June 9, 1863, between C. H. Hale, superintendent of Indian affairs, Charles Hutchins and S. D. Howe, Indian agents, on the part of the United States, and the chiefs, headmen, and delegates of the Nez Percé tribe of Indians in Washington Territory.

A report of the Secretary of the Interior of the 1st instant, with a letter from the Commissioner of Indian Affairs of the 2d ultimo, proposing amendments to the treaty, together with a report of Superintendent Hale on the subject and a synopsis of the proceedings of the council held with the Nez Percé Indians, are herewith transmitted for the consideration of the Senate.

ABRAHAM LINCOLN.

WASHINGTON, *April 7, 1864.*

To the House of Representatives:

I transmit herewith a report from the Secretary of War, in answer to the resolution of the House of Representatives of the 4th instant, in relation to Major N. H. McLean.

ABRAHAM LINCOLN.

WASHINGTON CITY, *April 15, 1864.*

To the Senate of the United States:

I herewith lay before the Senate, for its constitutional action thereon, a supplemental treaty negotiated on the 12th of April, 1864, with the Red Lake and Pembina bands of Chippewa Indians.

A report of the Secretary of the Interior of this date and a communication from the Acting Commissioner of Indian Affairs accompany the treaty.

ABRAHAM LINCOLN.

WASHINGTON, *April 23, 1864.*

To the Senate of the United States:

I transmit herewith a report from the Secretary of War, in answer to the resolutions passed by the Senate in executive session on the 14th and 18th of April, 1864.

ABRAHAM LINCOLN.

WAR DEPARTMENT,
Washington City, April 22, 1864.

The PRESIDENT OF THE UNITED STATES.

SIR: In answer to the Senate resolutions of April 14 and April 18, I have the honor to state that the nominations of Colonel Hiram Burnham, Colonel Edward M.

McCook, Colonel Lewis A. Grant, and Colonel Edward Hatch are not either of them made to fill any vacancy in the proper sense of that term. They are not made to fill a command vacated by any other general, but are independent nominations, and if confirmed the officers will be assigned to such command as the General Commanding may deem proper. But in consequence of the resignations of Generals Miller, Boyle, and Beatty and the death of General Champlin, their confirmations will be within the number of brigadiers allowed by law.

Your obedient servant, EDWIN M. STANTON,
Secretary of War.

WASHINGTON, *April 23, 1864.*

To the Senate and House of Representatives:

I transmit to Congress a copy of a note of the 19th instant from Lord Lyons to the Secretary of State, on the subject of two British naval officers who recently received medical treatment at the naval hospital at Norfolk. The expediency of authorizing Surgeon Solomon Sharp to accept the piece of plate to which the note refers, as an acknowledgment of his services, is submitted to your consideration.

ABRAHAM LINCOLN.

APRIL 28, 1864.

To the House of Representatives:

In obedience to the resolution of your honorable body a copy of which is herewith returned, I have the honor to make the following brief statement, which is believed to contain the information sought.

Prior to and at the meeting of the present Congress Robert C. Schenck, of Ohio, and Frank P. Blair, jr., of Missouri, members elect thereto, by and with the consent of the Senate held commissions from the Executive as major-generals in the Volunteer Army. General Schenck tendered the resignation of his said commission and took his seat in the House of Representatives at the assembling thereof upon the distinct verbal understanding with the Secretary of War and the Executive that he might at any time during the session, at his own pleasure, withdraw said resignation and return to the field. General Blair was, by temporary assignment of General Sherman, in command of a corps through the battles in front of Chattanooga and in the march to the relief of Knoxville, which occurred in the latter days of November and early days of December last, and of course was not present at the assembling of Congress. When he subsequently arrived here, he sought and was allowed by the Secretary of War and the Executive the same conditions and promise as allowed and made to General Schenck. General Schenck has not applied to withdraw his resignation, but when General Grant was made lieutenant-general, producing some change of commanders, General Blair sought to be assigned to the command of a corps. This was made known to Generals Grant and Sherman and assented to by them, and the particular corps for him designated. This was all arranged and understood, as now remembered, so much as a month ago, but the formal withdrawal of General Blair's resignation and making the order assigning him to the command of a corps were not consummated at the War Department until last week, perhaps on the 23d of April instant. As a summary of the whole, it may be stated that General Blair holds no military commission or appointment other than as herein stated, and that it is believed he is now acting as a major-general upon the assumed validity of the commission herein stated, in connection with the facts herein stated, and not otherwise. There are some letters, notes, telegrams, orders, entries, and perhaps other documents in connection with this subject, which it is believed would throw no additional light upon it, but which will be cheerfully furnished if desired.

ABRAHAM LINCOLN.

APRIL 28, 1864.

To the Honorable the Senate and House of Representatives:

I have the honor to transmit herewith an address to the President of the United States, and through him to both Houses of Congress, on the condition and wants of the people of east Tennessee, and asking their attention to the necessity of some action on the part of the Government for their relief, and which address is presented by a committee of an organization called "The East Tennessee Relief Association."

Deeply commiserating the condition of these most loyal and suffering people, I am unprepared to make any specific recommendation for their relief. The military is doing and will continue to do the best for them within its power. Their address represents that the construction of direct railroad communication between Knoxville and Cincinnati by way of central Kentucky would be of great consequence in the present emergency. It may be remembered that in the annual message of December, 1861, such railroad construction was recommended. I now add that, with the hearty concurrence of Congress, I would yet be pleased to construct a road, both for the relief of these people and for its continuing military importance.

ABRAHAM LINCOLN.

WASHINGTON, *April 29, 1864.*

To the Senate of the United States:

In compliance with the resolution of the Senate of the 27th instant, requesting information in regard to the condition of affairs in the Territory of Nevada, I transmit a copy of a letter of the 25th of last month addressed to the Secretary of State by James W. Nye, the governor of that Territory.

ABRAHAM LINCOLN.

To the Honorable the House of Representatives:

MAY 2, 1864.

In compliance with the request contained in your resolution of the 29th ultimo, a copy of which resolution is herewith returned, I have the honor to transmit the following:

EXECUTIVE MANSION,
Washington, November 2, 1863.

Hon. MONTGOMERY BLAIR.

MY DEAR SIR: Some days ago I understood you to say that your brother, General Frank Blair, desired to be guided by my wishes as to whether he will occupy his seat in Congress or remain in the field. My wish, then, is compounded of what I believe will be best for the country and best for him, and it is that he will come here, put his military commission in my hands, take his seat, go into caucus with our friends, abide the nominations, help elect the nominees, and thus aid to organize a House of Representatives which will really support the Government in the war. If the result shall be the election of himself as Speaker, let him serve in that position; if not, let him retake his commission and return to the Army. For the country, this will heal a dangerous schism. For him, it will relieve from a dangerous position. By a misunderstanding, as I think, he is in danger of being permanently separated from those with whom only he can ever have a real sympathy—the sincere opponents of slavery. It will be a mistake if he shall allow the provocations offered him by insincere timeservers to drive him from the house of his own building. He is young yet. He has abundant talents, quite enough to occupy all his time without devoting any to temper. He is rising in military skill and usefulness. His recent appointment to the command of a corps by one so competent to judge as General Sherman proves this. In that line he can serve both the country and himself more profitably than he could as a Member of Congress upon the floor. The foregoing is what I would say if Frank Blair were my brother instead of yours.

Yours, truly,

A. LINCOLN.

HEADQUARTERS MIDDLE DEPARTMENT, EIGHTH ARMY CORPS,
Baltimore, Md., November 13, 1863.

Hon. E. M. STANTON,
    Secretary of War.

SIR: Inclosed I forward to the President my resignation, to take effect on the 5th of December.

I respectfully request, however, that I may be relieved from my command at an earlier day, say by the 20th instant, or as soon thereafter as some officer can be ordered to succeed me. While I desire to derange the plans or hurry the action of the Department as little as possible, it will be a great convenience to me to secure some little time before the session of Congress for a necessary journey and for some preparations for myself and family in view of my approaching change of residence and occupation. I could also spend two or three days very profitably, I think, to the service of my successor after his arrival here.

I have the honor to be, very respectfully, your obedient servant,

ROBT. C. SCHENCK, *Major-General.*

HEADQUARTERS MIDDLE DEPARTMENT, EIGHTH ARMY CORPS,
Baltimore, Md., November 13, 1863.

The PRESIDENT OF THE UNITED STATES.

SIR: Having concluded to accept the place of Member of Congress in the House of Representatives, to which I was elected in October, 1862, I hereby tender the resignation of my commission as a major-general of United States Volunteers, to take effect on the 5th day of December next.

I shall leave the military service with much reluctance and a sacrifice of personal feelings and desires, and only consent to do so in the hope that in another capacity I may be able to do some effective service in the cause of my country and Government in this time of peculiar trial.

I have the honor to be, very respectfully, your obedient servant,

ROBT. C. SCHENCK,
Major-General.

[Indorsement on the foregoing letter.]

The resignation of General Schenck is accepted, and he is authorized to turn over his command to Brigadier-General Lockwood at any time.

EDWIN M. STANTON,
Secretary of War.

ADJUTANT-GENERAL'S OFFICE,
Washington, November 21, 1863.

Major-General ROBERT C. SCHENCK,
United States Volunteers, Commanding Middle Department, Baltimore, Md.

SIR: Your resignation has been accepted by the President of the United States, to take effect the 5th day of December, 1863.

I am, sir, very respectfully, your obedient servant,

E. D. TOWNSEND,
Assistant Adjutant-General.

WASHINGTON, *January 1, 1864.*

The PRESIDENT OF THE UNITED STATES,
Washington City, D. C.:

I hereby tender my resignation as a major-general of the United States Volunteers.

Respectfully,

FRANK P. BLAIR,
Major-General, United States Volunteers.

JANUARY 12, 1864.

Accepted, by order of the President.

EDWIN M. STANTON,
Secretary of War.

ADJUTANT-GENERAL'S OFFICE,
Washington, January 12, 1864.

Major-General FRANCIS P. BLAIR,
U. S. Volunteers.

(Care of Hon. M. Blair, Washington, D. C.)

SIR: Your resignation has been accepted by the President of the United States, to take effect this day.

I am, sir, very respectfully, your obedient servant,

JAS. A. HARDIE,
Assistant Adjutant-General.

[Telegram.]

EXECUTIVE MANSION,
Washington, D. C., March 15, 1864.

Lieutenant-General GRANT,
Nashville, Tenn.:

General McPherson having been assigned to the command of a department, could not General Frank Blair, without difficulty or detriment to the service, be assigned to command the corps he commanded a while last autumn?

A. LINCOLN.

[Telegram.]

NASHVILLE, TENN., *March 16, 1864—10 a. m.*

His Excellency the PRESIDENT:

General Logan commands the corps referred to in your dispatch. I will see General Sherman in a few days and consult him about the transfer, and answer.

U. S. GRANT,
Lieutenant-General.

[Telegram.]

NASHVILLE, TENN., *March 17, 1864.*

His Excellency A. LINCOLN,
President of the United States:

General Sherman is here. He consents to the transfer of General Logan to the Seventeenth Corps and the appointment of General F. P. Blair to the Fifteenth Corps.

U. S. GRANT,
Lieutenant-General.

[Telegram.]

HUNTSVILLE, ALA., *March 26, 1864.*

His Excellency A. LINCOLN,
President of the United States:

I understand by the papers that it is contemplated to make a change of commanders of the Fifteenth and Seventeenth Army Corps, so as to transfer me to the Seventeenth. I hope this will not be done. I fully understand the organization of the Fifteenth Corps now, of which I have labored to complete the organization this winter. Earnestly hope that the change may not be made.

JOHN A. LOGAN,
Major-General.

[Telegram.]

OFFICE UNITED STATES MILITARY TELEGRAPH,
War Department.

The following telegram received at Washington 9 a. m. March 31, 1864, from Culpeper Court-House, 11.30 p. m., dated March 30, 1864:

"Major-General W. T. SHERMAN,
"*Nashville:*

"General F. P. Blair will be assigned to the Seventeenth (17th) Corps, and not the Fifteenth (15th). Assign General Joseph Hooker, subject to the approval of the President, to any other corps command you may have, and break up the anomaly of one general commanding two (2) corps.

"U. S. GRANT,
"*Lieutenant-General, Commanding.*"

From a long dispatch of April 2, 1864, from General Sherman to General Grant, presenting his plan for disposing the forces under his command, the following extracts, being the only parts pertinent to the subject now under consideration, are taken:

After a full consultation with all my army commanders, I have settled down to the following conclusions, to which I would like to have the President's consent before I make the orders:

*   *   *   *   *   *   *

Third. General McPherson. * * * His [three] corps to be commanded by Major-Generals Logan, Blair, and Dodge. * * *

OFFICE UNITED STATES MILITARY TELEGRAPH,
War Department.

The following telegram received at Washington 3 p. m. April 10, 1864, from Culpeper Court-House, Va., 10 p. m., dated April 9, 1864:

"Major-General H. W. HALLECK,
"*Chief of Staff:*

"Will you please ascertain if General F. P. Blair is to be sent to General Sherman. If not, an army-corps commander will have to be named for the Fifteenth Corps.

"U. S. GRANT, *Lieutenant-General.*"

The PRESIDENT: WASHINGTON, *April 20, 1864.*

You will do me a great favor by giving the order assigning me to the command of the Seventeenth Army Corps immediately, as I desire to leave Washington the next Saturday to join the command. I also request the assignment of Captain Andrew J. Alexander, of Third Regiment United States Cavalry, as adjutant-general of the Seventeenth Corps, with the rank of lieutenant-colonel. The present adjutant, or rather the former adjutant, Colonel Clark, has, I understand, been retained by General McPherson as adjutant-general of the department, and the place of adjutant-general of the corps is necessarily vacant.

I also request the appointment of George A. Maguire, formerly captain Thirty-first Missouri Volunteer Infantry, as major and aid-de-camp, and Lieutenant Logan Tompkins, Twenty-first Missouri Volunteer Infantry, as captain and aid-de-camp on my staff.

Respectfully,

FRANK P. BLAIR.

[Indorsements.]

Honorable SECRETARY OF WAR: APRIL 21, 1864.

Please have General Halleck make the proper order in this case.

A. LINCOLN.

Referred to General Halleck, chief of staff.

EDWIN M. STANTON, *Secretary of War.*

EXECUTIVE MANSION,
Honorable SECRETARY OF WAR. *Washington, April 23, 1864.*

MY DEAR SIR: According to our understanding with Major-General Frank P. Blair at the time he took his seat in Congress last winter, he now asks to withdraw his resignation as major-general, then tendered, and be sent to the field. Let this be done. Let the order sending him be such as shown me to-day by the Adjutant-General, only dropping from it the names of Maguire and Tompkins.

Yours, truly, A. LINCOLN.

[Indorsement.]

APRIL 23, 1864.
Referred to the Adjutant-General.

EDWIN M. STANTON, *Secretary of War.*

Hon. E. M. STANTON, WASHINGTON CITY, D. C., *April 23, 1864.*
Secretary of War:

I respectfully request to withdraw my resignation as major-general of the United States Volunteers, tendered on the 12th day of January, 1864.

Respectfully,

FRANK P. BLAIR.

GENERAL ORDERS, No. 178.

WAR DEPARTMENT,
ADJUTANT-GENERAL'S OFFICE,
Washington, April 23, 1864.

I. Major-General F. P. Blair, jr., is assigned to the command of the Seventeenth Army Corps.

II. Captain Andrew J. Alexander, Third Regiment United States Cavalry, is assigned as assistant adjutant-general of the Seventeenth Army Corps, with the rank of lieutenant-colonel, under the tenth section of the act approved July 17, 1862.

By order of the President of the United States:

E. D. TOWNSEND,
Assistant Adjutant-General.

The foregoing constitutes all sought by the resolution so far as is remembered or has been found upon diligent search.

ABRAHAM LINCOLN.

MAY 7, 1864.

To the Senate of the United States:

In compliance with the request contained in a resolution of the Senate dated April 30, 1864, I herewith transmit to your honorable body a copy of the opinion by the Attorney-General on the rights of colored persons in the Army or volunteer service of the United States, together with the accompanying papers.

ABRAHAM LINCOLN.

WASHINGTON, *May 12, 1864.*

To the Senate of the United States:

In answer to the resolution of the Senate of the 9th instant, requesting a copy of correspondence relative to a controversy between the Republics of Chile and Bolivia, I transmit a report from the Secretary of State, to whom the resolution was referred.

ABRAHAM LINCOLN.

EXECUTIVE MANSION,
Washington, May 14, 1864.

To the Senate of the United States:

I transmit herewith a report of the Secretary of the Interior of the 14th instant, and accompanying papers, in answer to a resolution of the Senate of the 14th ultimo, in the following words, viz:

Resolved, That the President of the United States be requested to communicate to the Senate the reasons, if any exist, why the refugee Indians in the State of Kansas are not returned to their homes.

ABRAHAM LINCOLN

EXECUTIVE MANSION,
Washington, May 17, 1864.

To the Senate of the United States:

I herewith lay before the Senate, for its constitutional action thereon, a treaty concluded on the 7th instant in this city between William P. Dole, Commissioner of Indian Affairs, and Clark W. Thompson, superintendent of Indian affairs, northern superintendency, on the part of the United States, and the chief Hole-in-the-day and Mis-qua-dace for and on behalf of the Chippewas of the Mississippi, and the Pillager and Lake Winnibigoshish bands of Chippewa Indians in Minnesota.

A communication from the Secretary of the Interior of the 17th instant, with a statement and copies of reports of the Commissioner of Indian Affairs of the 12th and 17th instant, accompany the treaty.

ABRAHAM LINCOLN.

WASHINGTON, D. C., *May 24, 1864.*

To the Senate of the United States:

I recommend Lieutenant-Commander Francis A. Roe for advancement in his grade five numbers, to take rank next after Lieutenant-Commander John H. Upshur, for distinguished conduct in battle in command of the United States steamer *Sassacus* in her attack on and attempt to run down the rebel ironclad ram *Albemarle* on the 5th of May, 1864.

I also recommend that First Assistant Engineer James M. Hobby be advanced thirty numbers in his grade for distinguished conduct in battle and extraordinary heroism, as mentioned in the report of Lieutenant-Commander Francis A. Roe, commanding the United States steamer *Sassacus* in her action with the rebel ram *Albemarle* on the 5th May, 1864.

ABRAHAM LINCOLN.

WASHINGTON, *May 24, 1864.*

To the House of Representatives:

In answer to the resolution of the House of Representatives of yesterday on the subject of the joint resolution of the 4th of last month relative to Mexico, I transmit a report from the Secretary of State, to whom the resolution was referred.

ABRAHAM LINCOLN.

WASHINGTON, *May 28, 1864.*

To the Senate of the United States:

In reply to a resolution of the Senate of the 25th instant, relating to Mexican affairs, I transmit a partial report from the Secretary of State of this date, with the papers therein mentioned.

ABRAHAM LINCOLN.

WASHINGTON, *May 31, 1864.*

To the Senate of the United States:

I transmit to the Senate, in answer to their resolution of the 28th instant, a report* from the Secretary of State, with accompanying documents.

ABRAHAM LINCOLN.

WASHINGTON, D. C., *June 8, 1864.*

To the Senate and House of Representatives:

I have the honor to submit, for the consideration of Congress, a letter and inclosure † from the Secretary of War, with my concurrence in the recommendation therein made.

ABRAHAM LINCOLN.

WASHINGTON, *June 13, 1864.*

To the Senate of the United States:

In compliance with the resolution of the Senate of the 4th of March, 1864, I transmit herewith a report from the Secretary of War in the case of William Yokum, with accompanying papers.

ABRAHAM LINCOLN.

WASHINGTON, *June 13, 1864.*

To the Senate of the United States:

I transmit herewith, for consideration with a view to ratification, a convention between the United States of America and the United Colombian States, signed by the plenipotentiaries of the contracting powers on the 10th February last, providing for a revival of the joint commission on claims under the convention of 10th September, 1857, with New Granada.

ABRAHAM LINCOLN.

WASHINGTON, *June 18, 1864.*

To the Senate of the United States:

In further answer to the Senate's resolution of the 28th ultimo, requesting to be informed whether the President "has, and when, authorized a person alleged to have committed a crime against Spain or any of its dependencies to be delivered up to officers of that Government, and whether such delivery was had, and, if so, under what authority of law or of treaty it was done," I transmit a copy of a dispatch of the 10th instant to the Secretary of State from the acting consul of the United States at Havana.

ABRAHAM LINCOLN.

---

* Relating to the delivery of a person charged with crime against Spain to the officers of that Government.

† Report from the Provost-Marshal-General, showing the result of the draft to fill a deficiency in the quotas of certain States, and recommending a repeal of the clause in the enrollment act commonly known as the three-hundred-dollar clause.

EXECUTIVE MANSION, *June 21, 1864.*

To the Senate of the United States:

I herewith communicate to the Senate, for its constitutional action thereon, the articles of agreement and convention made and concluded at the city of Washington on the 15th instant between the United States and the Delaware Indians of Kansas, referred to in the accompanying communication of the present date from the Secretary of the Interior.

ABRAHAM LINCOLN.

EXECUTIVE MANSION, *Washington, June 24, 1864.*

To the Senate of the United States:

I herewith lay before the Senate, for its constitutional action thereon, a treaty made and concluded at the city of Washington on the 11th day of June, 1864, by and between William P. Dole, Commissioner of Indian Affairs, and Hiram W. Farnsworth, United States Indian agent, commissioners on the part of the United States, and the chiefs and headmen of the Kansas tribe of Indians.

A communication of the Secretary of the Interior of the 18th instant, with a copy of report of Commissioner of Indian Affairs of the 13th instant, accompany the treaty.

ABRAHAM LINCOLN.

WASHINGTON, *June 28, 1864.*

To the Senate of the United States:

In answer to the resolution of the Senate of the 24th instant, requesting information in regard to the alleged enlistment in foreign countries of recruits for the military and naval service of the United States, I transmit reports from the Secretaries of State, of War, and of the Navy, respectively.

ABRAHAM LINCOLN.

WASHINGTON, *June 28, 1864.*

To the Senate of the United States:

In compliance with the resolution of the Senate of the 16th of last month, requesting information in regard to the maltreatment of passengers and seamen on board ships plying between New York and Aspinwall, I transmit a report from the Secretary of State, to whom the resolution was referred.

ABRAHAM LINCOLN.

WASHINGTON, *July 2, 1864.*

To the Senate of the United States:

In answer to the resolution of the Senate of the 6th ultimo, requesting information upon the subject of the African slave trade, I transmit a report from the Secretary of State and the papers by which it was accompanied.

ABRAHAM LINCOLN.

PROCLAMATIONS.

BY THE PRESIDENT OF THE UNITED STATES OF AMERICA.

A PROCLAMATION.

Whereas in and by the Constitution of the United States it is provided that the President "shall have power to grant reprieves and pardons for offenses against the United States, except in cases of impeachment;" and

Whereas a rebellion now exists whereby the loyal State governments of several States have for a long time been subverted, and many persons have committed and are now guilty of treason against the United States; and

Whereas, with reference to said rebellion and treason, laws have been enacted by Congress declaring forfeitures and confiscation of property and liberation of slaves, all upon terms and conditions therein stated, and also declaring that the President was thereby authorized at any time thereafter, by proclamation, to extend to persons who may have participated in the existing rebellion in any State or part thereof pardon and amnesty, with such exceptions and at such times and on such conditions as he may deem expedient for the public welfare; and

Whereas the Congressional declaration for limited and conditional pardon accords with well-established judicial exposition of the pardoning power; and

Whereas, with reference to said rebellion, the President of the United States has issued several proclamations with provisions in regard to the liberation of slaves; and

Whereas it is now desired by some persons heretofore engaged in said rebellion to resume their allegiance to the United States and to reinaugurate loyal State governments within and for their respective States:

Therefore, I, Abraham Lincoln, President of the United States, do proclaim, declare, and make known to all persons who have, directly or by implication, participated in the existing rebellion, except as hereinafter excepted, that a full pardon is hereby granted to them and each of them, with restoration of all rights of property, except as to slaves and in property cases where rights of third parties shall have intervened, and upon the condition that every such person shall take and subscribe an oath and thenceforward keep and maintain said oath inviolate, and which oath shall be registered for permanent preservation and shall be of the tenor and effect following, to wit:

I, —— ——, do solemnly swear, in presence of Almighty God, that I will henceforth faithfully support, protect, and defend the Constitution of the United States and the Union of the States thereunder; and that I will in like manner abide by and faithfully support all acts of Congress passed during the existing rebellion with reference to slaves, so long and so far as not repealed, modified, or held void by Congress or by decision of the Supreme Court; and that I will in like manner abide by and faithfully support all proclamations of the President made during the existing rebellion having reference to slaves, so long and so far as not modified or declared void by decision of the Supreme Court. So help me God.

The persons excepted from the benefits of the foregoing provisions are all who are or shall have been civil or diplomatic officers or agents of the so-called Confederate Government; all who have left judicial stations under the United States to aid the rebellion; all who are or shall have been military or naval officers of said so-called Confederate Government above the rank of colonel in the army or of lieutenant in the navy; all who left seats in the United States Congress to aid the rebellion; all who resigned commissions in the Army or Navy of the United States and afterwards aided the rebellion; and all who have engaged in any way in treating colored persons, or white persons in charge of such, otherwise than lawfully as prisoners of war, and which persons may have been found in the United States service as soldiers, seamen, or in any other capacity.

And I do further proclaim, declare, and make known that whenever, in any of the States of Arkansas, Texas, Louisiana, Mississippi, Tennessee, Alabama, Georgia, Florida, South Carolina, and North Carolina, a number of persons, not less than one-tenth in number of the votes cast in such State at the Presidential election of the year A. D. 1860, each having taken the oath aforesaid, and not having since violated it, and being a qualified voter by the election law of the State existing immediately before the so-called act of secession, and excluding all others, shall reestablish a State government which shall be republican and in nowise contravening said oath, such shall be recognized as the true government of the State, and the State shall receive thereunder the benefits of the constitutional provision which declares that "the United States shall guarantee to every State in this Union a republican form of government and shall protect each of them against invasion, and, on application of the legislature, or the executive (when the legislature can not be convened), against domestic violence."

And I do further proclaim, declare, and make known that any provision which may be adopted by such State government in relation to the freed people of such State which shall recognize and declare their permanent freedom, provide for their education, and which may yet be consistent as a temporary arrangement with their present condition as a laboring, landless, and homeless class, will not be objected to by the National Executive.

And it is suggested as not improper that in constructing a loyal State government in any State the name of the State, the boundary, the subdivisions, the constitution, and the general code of laws as before the rebellion be maintained, subject only to the modifications made necessary by the conditions hereinbefore stated, and such others, if any, not contravening said conditions and which may be deemed expedient by those framing the new State government.

To avoid misunderstanding, it may be proper to say that this proclamation, so far as it relates to State governments, has no reference to States wherein loyal State governments have all the while been maintained. And for the same reason it may be proper to further say that whether members sent to Congress from any State shall be admitted to seats constitutionally rests exclusively with the respective Houses, and not to any extent with the Executive. And, still further, that this proclamation is intended to present the people of the States wherein the national authority has been suspended and loyal State governments have been subverted a mode in and by which the national authority and loyal State governments may be reestablished within said States or in any of them; and while the mode presented is the best the Executive can suggest, with his present impressions, it must not be understood that no other possible mode would be acceptable.

Given under my hand at the city of Washington, the 8th day of December, A. D. 1863, and of the Independence of the United States of America the eighty-eighth.

[SEAL.]

ABRAHAM LINCOLN.

By the President:

WILLIAM H. SEWARD, *Secretary of State.*

BY THE PRESIDENT OF THE UNITED STATES OF AMERICA.

A PROCLAMATION.

Whereas by an act of the Congress of the United States of the 24th of May, 1828, entitled "An act in addition to an act entitled 'An act concerning discriminating duties of tonnage and impost' and to equalize the duties on Prussian vessels and their cargoes," it is provided that upon satisfactory evidence being given to the President of the United States by the government of any foreign nation that no discriminating duties of tonnage or impost are imposed or levied in the ports of the said nation upon vessels wholly belonging to citizens of the United States or upon the produce, manufactures, or merchandise imported in the same from the United States or from any foreign country, the President is thereby authorized to issue his proclamation declaring that the foreign discriminating duties of tonnage and impost within the United States are and shall be suspended and discontinued so far as respects the vessels of the said foreign nation and the produce, manufactures, or merchandise imported into the United States in the same from the said foreign nation or from any other foreign country, the said suspension to take effect from the time of such notification being given to the President of the United States and to continue so long as the reciprocal exemption of vessels belonging to citizens of the United States and their cargoes, as aforesaid, shall be continued, and no longer; and

Whereas satisfactory evidence has lately been received by me through an official communication of Señor Don Luis Molina, envoy extraordinary and minister plenipotentiary of the Republic of Nicaragua, under date of the 28th of November, 1863, that no other or higher duties of tonnage and impost have been imposed or levied since the 2d day of August, 1838, in the ports of Nicaragua upon vessels wholly belonging to citizens of the United States and upon the produce, manufactures, or merchandise imported in the same from the United States and from any foreign country whatever than are levied on Nicaraguan ships and their cargoes in the same ports under like circumstances:

Now, therefore, I, Abraham Lincoln, President of the United States of America, do hereby declare and proclaim that so much of the several acts imposing discriminating duties of tonnage and impost within the United States are and shall be suspended and discontinued so far as respects the vessels of Nicaragua and the produce, manufactures, and merchandise imported into the United States in the same from the dominions of Nicaragua and from any other foreign country whatever, the said suspension to take effect from the day above mentioned and to continue thenceforward so long as the reciprocal exemption of the vessels of the United States and the produce, manufactures, and merchandise imported into the dominions of Nicaragua in the same, as aforesaid, shall be continued on the part of the Government of Nicaragua.

Given under my hand at the city of Washington, the 16th day of December, A. D. 1863, and the eighty-eighth of the Independence of the United States.

[SEAL.]

ABRAHAM LINCOLN.

By the President:

WILLIAM H. SEWARD,
Secretary of State.

BY THE PRESIDENT OF THE UNITED STATES OF AMERICA.

A PROCLAMATION.

Whereas by my proclamation of the 19th of April, 1861, the ports of the States of South Carolina, Georgia, Alabama, Florida, Mississippi, Louisiana, and Texas were, for reasons therein set forth, placed under blockade; and

Whereas the port of Brownsville, in the district of Brazos Santiago, in the State of Texas, has since been blockaded, but as the blockade of said port may now be safely relaxed with advantage to the interests of commerce:

Now, therefore, be it known that I, Abraham Lincoln, President of the United States, pursuant to the authority in me vested by the fifth section of the act of Congress approved on the 13th of July, 1861, entitled "An act further to provide for the collection of duties on imports and for other purposes,'' do hereby declare that the blockade of the said port of Brownsville shall so far cease and determine from and after this date that commercial intercourse with said port, except as to persons, things, and information hereinafter specified, may from this date be carried on subject to the laws of the United States, to the regulations prescribed by the Secretary of the Treasury, and, until the rebellion shall have been suppressed, to such orders as may be promulgated by the general commanding the department or by an officer duly authorized by him and commanding at said port. This proclamation does not authorize or allow the shipment or conveyance of persons in or intending to enter the service of the insurgents, or of things or information intended for their use or for their aid or comfort, nor, except upon the permission of the Secretary of War or of some officer duly authorized by him, of the following prohibited articles, namely: Cannon, mortars, firearms, pistols, bombs, grenades, powder, saltpeter, sulphur, balls, bullets, pikes, swords, boarding caps (always excepting the quantity of the said articles which may be necessary for the defense of the ship and those who compose the crew), saddles, bridles, cartridge-bag material, percussion and other caps, clothing adapted for uniforms, sailcloth of all kinds, hemp and cordage, intoxicating drinks other than beer and light native wines.

To vessels clearing from foreign ports and destined to the port of Brownsville, opened by this proclamation, licenses will be granted by consuls of the United States upon satisfactory evidence that the vessel so licensed will convey no persons, property, or information excepted or prohibited above either to or from the said port, which licenses shall be exhibited to the collector of said port immediately on arrival, and, if required, to any officer in charge of the blockade; and on leaving said port every vessel will be required to have a clearance from the collector of the customs, according to law, showing no violation of the conditions of the license. Any violations of said conditions will involve the forfeiture and condemnation of the vessel and cargo and the exclusion of all parties concerned from any further privilege of entering the United States during the war for any purpose whatever.

In all respects except as herein specified the existing blockade remains in full force and effect as hitherto established and maintained, nor is it relaxed by this proclamation except in regard to the port to which relaxation is or has been expressly applied.

In witness whereof I have hereunto set my hand and caused the seal of the United States to be affixed.

[SEAL.]   Done at the city of Washington, this 18th day of February, A. D. 1864, and of the Independence of the United States the eighty-eighth.

ABRAHAM LINCOLN.

By the President:
WILLIAM H. SEWARD, *Secretary of State.*

By the President of the United States of America.

A PROCLAMATION.

Whereas it has become necessary to define the cases in which insurgent enemies are entitled to the benefits of the proclamation of the President of the United States which was made on the 8th day of December, 1863, and the manner in which they shall proceed to avail themselves of those benefits; and

Whereas the objects of that proclamation were to suppress the insurrection and to restore the authority of the United States; and

Whereas the amnesty therein proposed by the President was offered with reference to these objects alone:

Now, therefore, I, Abraham Lincoln, President of the United States, do hereby proclaim and declare that the said proclamation does not apply to the cases of persons who at the time when they seek to obtain the benefits thereof by taking the oath thereby prescribed are in military, naval, or civil confinement or custody, or under bonds, or on parole of the civil, military, or naval authorities or agents of the United States as prisoners of war, or persons detained for offenses of any kind, either before or after conviction, and that, on the contrary, it does apply only to those persons who, being yet at large and free from any arrest, confinement, or duress, shall voluntarily come forward and take the said oath with the purpose of restoring peace and establishing the national authority. Prisoners excluded from the amnesty offered in the said proclamation may apply to the President for clemency, like all other offenders, and their applications will receive due consideration.

I do further declare and proclaim that the oath prescribed in the aforesaid proclamation of the 8th of December, 1863, may be taken and subscribed before any commissioned officer, civil, military, or naval, in the service of the United States or any civil or military officer of a State or Territory not in insurrection who by the laws thereof may be qualified for administering oaths. All officers who receive such oaths are hereby authorized to give certificates thereon to the persons respectively by whom they are made, and such officers are hereby required to transmit the original records of such oaths at as early a day as may be convenient to the Department of State, where they will be deposited and remain in the archives of the Government. The Secretary of State will keep a register thereof, and will on application, in proper cases, issue certificates of such records in the customary form of official certificates.

In testimony whereof I have hereunto set my hand and caused the seal of the United States to be affixed.

[SEAL.] Done at the city of Washington, the 26th day of March, A. D. 1864, and of the Independence of the United States the eighty-eighth.

ABRAHAM LINCOLN.

By the President:

WILLIAM H. SEWARD, *Secretary of State.*

ABRAHAM LINCOLN, PRESIDENT OF THE UNITED STATES OF AMERICA.

To all whom it may concern:

An exequatur bearing date the 3d day of May, 1850, having been issued to Charles Hunt, a citizen of the United States, recognizing him as consul of Belgium for St. Louis, Mo., and declaring him free to exercise and enjoy such functions, powers, and privileges as are allowed to the consuls of the most favored nations in the United States, and the said Hunt having sought to screen himself from his military duty to his country in consequence of thus being invested with the consular functions of a foreign power in the United States, it is deemed advisable that the said Charles Hunt should no longer be permitted to continue in the exercise of said functions, powers, and privileges:

These are, therefore, to declare that I no longer recognize the said Charles Hunt as consul of Belgium for St. Louis, Mo., and will not permit him to exercise or enjoy any of the functions, powers, or privileges allowed to consuls of that nation, and that I do hereby wholly revoke and annul the said exequatur heretofore given and do declare the same to be absolutely null and void from this day forward.

In testimony whereof I have caused these letters to be made patent and the seal of the United States of America to be hereunto affixed.

[SEAL.]   Given under my hand, at Washington, this 19th day of May, A. D. 1864, and of the Independence of the United States of America the eighty-eighth.

ABRAHAM LINCOLN.

By the President:
    WILLIAM H. SEWARD,
        Secretary of State.

BY THE PRESIDENT OF THE UNITED STATES OF AMERICA.

A PROCLAMATION.

Whereas by a proclamation which was issued on the 15th day of April, 1861, the President of the United States announced and declared that the laws of the United States had been for some time past, and then were, opposed and the execution thereof obstructed in certain States therein mentioned by combinations too powerful to be suppressed by the ordinary course of judicial proceedings or by the powers vested in the marshals by law; and

Whereas immediately after the issuing of the said proclamation the land and naval forces of the United States were put into activity to suppress the said insurrection and rebellion; and

Whereas the Congress of the United States by an act approved on the 3d day of March, 1863, did enact that during the said rebellion the

President of the United States, whenever in his judgment the public safety may require it, is authorized to suspend the privilege of the writ of *habeas corpus* in any case throughout the United States or in any part thereof; and

Whereas the said insurrection and rebellion still continue, endangering the existence of the Constitution and Government of the United States; and

Whereas the military forces of the United States are now actively engaged in suppressing the said insurrection and rebellion in various parts of the States where the said rebellion has been successful in obstructing the laws and public authorities, especially in the States of Virginia and Georgia; and

Whereas on the 15th day of September last the President of the United States duly issued his proclamation, wherein he declared that the privilege of the writ of *habeas corpus* should be suspended throughout the United States in the cases where, by the authority of the President of the United States, military, naval, and civil officers of the United States, or any of them, hold persons under their command or in their custody, either as prisoners of war, spies, or aiders or abettors of the enemy, or officers, soldiers, or seamen enrolled or drafted or mustered or enlisted in or belonging to the land or naval forces of the United States, or as deserters therefrom, or otherwise amenable to military law or the rules and articles of war or the rules or regulations prescribed for the military or naval services by authority of the President of the United States, or for resisting a draft, or for any other offense against the military or naval service; and

Whereas many citizens of the State of Kentucky have joined the forces of the insurgents, and such insurgents have on several occasions entered the said State of Kentucky in large force, and, not without aid and comfort furnished by disaffected and disloyal citizens of the United States residing therein, have not only greatly disturbed the public peace, but have overborne the civil authorities and made flagrant civil war, destroying property and life in various parts of that State; and

Whereas it has been made known to the President of the United States by the officers commanding the national armies that combinations have been formed in the said State of Kentucky with a purpose of inciting rebel forces to renew the said operations of civil war within the said State and thereby to embarrass the United States armies now operating in the said States of Virginia and Georgia and even to endanger their safety:

Now, therefore, I, Abraham Lincoln, President of the United States, by virtue of the authority vested in me by the Constitution and laws, do hereby declare that in my judgment the public safety especially requires that the suspension of the privilege of the writ of *habeas corpus*, so proclaimed in the said proclamation of the 15th of September, 1863, be made effectual and be duly enforced in and throughout the said State of Kentucky, and that martial law be for the present established therein. I do therefore hereby require of the military officers in the said State that the privileges of the writ of *habeas corpus* be effectually suspended within the said State, according to the aforesaid proclamation, and that martial law be established therein, to take effect from the date of this proclamation, the said suspension and establishment of martial law to continue until this proclamation shall be revoked or modified, but not beyond the period when the said rebellion shall have been suppressed or come to an end. And I do hereby require and command as well all military officers as all civil officers and authorities existing or found within the said State of Kentucky to take notice of this proclamation and to give full effect to the same.

The martial law herein proclaimed and the things in that respect herein ordered will not be deemed or taken to interfere with the holding of lawful elections, or with the proceedings of the constitutional legislature of Kentucky, or with the administration of justice in the courts of law existing therein between citizens of the United States in suits or proceedings which do not affect the military operations or the constituted authorities of the Government of the United States.

In testimony whereof I have hereunto set my hand and caused the seal of the United States to be affixed.

[SEAL.] Done at the city of Washington, this 5th day of July, A. D. 1864, and of the Independence of the United States the eighty-ninth.

ABRAHAM LINCOLN.

By the President:
WILLIAM H. SEWARD,
Secretary of State.

BY THE PRESIDENT OF THE UNITED STATES.

A PROCLAMATION.

Whereas the Senate and House of Representatives at their last session adopted a concurrent resolution, which was approved on the 2d day of July instant and which was in the words following, namely:

That the President of the United States be requested to appoint a day for humiliation and prayer by the people of the United States; that he request his constitutional advisers at the head of the Executive Departments to unite with him as Chief Magistrate of the nation, at the city of Washington, and the members of Congress, and all magistrates, all civil, military, and naval officers, all soldiers, sailors, and marines, with all loyal and law-abiding people, to convene at their usual places of worship, or wherever they may be, to confess and to repent of their manifold sins; to implore the compassion and forgiveness of the Almighty, that, if consistent with His will, the existing rebellion may be speedily suppressed and the supremacy of the Constitution and laws of the United States may be established throughout all the States; to implore

Him, as the Supreme Ruler of the World, not to destroy us as a people, nor suffer us to be destroyed by the hostility or connivance of other nations or by obstinate adhesion to our own counsels, which may be in conflict with His eternal purposes, and to implore Him to enlighten the mind of the nation to know and do His will, humbly believing that it is in accordance with His will that our place should be maintained as a united people among the family of nations; to implore Him to grant to our armed defenders and the masses of the people that courage, power of resistance, and endurance necessary to secure that result; to implore Him in His infinite goodness to soften the hearts, enlighten the minds, and quicken the consciences of those in rebellion, that they may lay down their arms and speedily return to their allegiance to the United States, that they may not be utterly destroyed, that the effusion of blood may be stayed, and that unity and fraternity may be restored and peace established throughout all our borders:

Now, therefore, I, Abraham Lincoln, President of the United States, cordially concurring with the Congress of the United States in the penitential and pious sentiments expressed in the aforesaid resolution and heartily approving of the devotional design and purpose thereof, do hereby appoint the first Thursday of August next to be observed by the people of the United States as a day of national humiliation and prayer.

I do hereby further invite and request the heads of the Executive Departments of this Government, together with all legislators, all judges and magistrates, and all other persons exercising authority in the land, whether civil, military, or naval, and all soldiers, seamen, and marines in the national service, and all the other loyal and law-abiding people of the United States, to assemble in their preferred places of public worship on that day, and there and then to render to the almighty and merciful Ruler of the Universe such homages and such confessions and to offer to Him such supplications as the Congress of the United States have in their aforesaid resolution so solemnly, so earnestly, and so reverently recommended.

In testimony whereof I have hereunto set my hand and caused the seal of the United States to be affixed.

[SEAL.]   Done at the city of Washington, this 7th day of July, A. D. 1864, and of the Independence of the United States the eighty-ninth.

ABRAHAM LINCOLN.

By the President:

WILLIAM H. SEWARD,
Secretary of State.

BY THE PRESIDENT OF THE UNITED STATES.

A PROCLAMATION.

Whereas at the late session Congress passed a bill "to guarantee to certain States whose governments have been usurped or overthrown a republican form of government," a copy of which is hereunto annexed; and

Whereas the said bill was presented to the President of the United

States for his approval less than one hour before the *sine die* adjournment of said session, and was not signed by him; and

Whereas the said bill contains, among other things, a plan for restoring the States in rebellion to their proper practical relation in the Union, which plan expresses the sense of Congress upon that subject, and which plan it is now thought fit to lay before the people for their consideration:

Now, therefore, I, Abraham Lincoln, President of the United States, do proclaim, declare, and make known that while I am (as I was in December last, when, by proclamation, I propounded a plan for restoration) unprepared by a formal approval of this bill to be inflexibly committed to any single plan of restoration, and while I am also unprepared to declare that the free State constitutions and governments already adopted and installed in Arkansas and Louisiana shall be set aside and held for naught, thereby repelling and discouraging the loyal citizens who have set up the same as to further effort, or to declare a constitutional competency in Congress to abolish slavery in States, but am at the same time sincerely hoping and expecting that a constitutional amendment abolishing slavery throughout the nation may be adopted, nevertheless I am fully satisfied with the system for restoration contained in the bill as one very proper plan for the loyal people of any State choosing to adopt it, and that I am and at all times shall be prepared to give the Executive aid and assistance to any such people so soon as the military resistance to the United States shall have been suppressed in any such State and the people thereof shall have sufficiently returned to their obedience to the Constitution and the laws of the United States, in which cases military governors will be appointed with directions to proceed according to the bill.

In testimony whereof I have hereunto set my hand and caused the seal of the United States to be affixed.

[SEAL.]   Done at the city of Washington, this 8th day of July, A. D. 1864, and of the Independence of the United States the eighty-ninth.

ABRAHAM LINCOLN.

By the President:

WILLIAM H. SEWARD,
Secretary of State.

[H. R. 244, Thirty-eighth Congress, first session.]

AN ACT to guarantee to certain States whose governments have been usurped or overthrown a republican form of government.

Be it enacted by the Senate and House of Representatives of the United States of America in Congress assembled, That in the States declared in rebellion against the United States the President shall, by and with the advice and consent of the Senate, appoint for each a provisional governor, whose pay and emoluments shall not exceed that of a brigadier-general of volunteers, who shall be charged with the civil administration of such State until a State government therein shall be recognized as hereinafter provided.

SEC. 2. *And be it further enacted,* That so soon as the military resistance to the United States shall have been suppressed in any such State and the people thereof shall have sufficiently returned to their obedience to the Constitution and the laws of the United States the provisional governor shall direct the marshal of the United States, as speedily as may be, to name a sufficient number of deputies, and to enroll all white male citizens of the United States resident in the State in their respective counties, and to request each one to take the oath to support the Constitution of the United States, and in his enrollment to designate those who take and those who refuse to take that oath, which rolls shall be forthwith returned to the provisional governor; and if the persons taking that oath shall amount to a majority of the persons enrolled in the State, he shall, by proclamation, invite the loyal people of the State to elect delegates to a convention charged to declare the will of the people of the State relative to the reestablishment of a State government, subject to and in conformity with the Constitution of the United States.

SEC. 3. *And be it further enacted,* That the convention shall consist of as many members as both houses of the last constitutional State legislature, apportioned by the provisional governor among the counties, parishes, or districts of the State, in proportion to the white population returned as electors by the marshal in compliance with the provisions of this act. The provisional governor shall, by proclamation, declare the number of delegates to be elected by each county, parish, or election district; name a day of election not less than thirty days thereafter; designate the places of voting in each county, parish, or district, conforming as nearly as may be convenient to the places used in the State elections next preceding the rebellion; appoint one or more commissioners to hold the election at each place of voting, and provide an adequate force to keep the peace during the election.

SEC. 4. *And be it further enacted,* That the delegates shall be elected by the loyal white male citizens of the United States of the age of 21 years, and resident at the time in the county, parish, or district in which they shall offer to vote, and enrolled as aforesaid, or absent in the military service of the United States, and who shall take and subscribe the oath of allegiance to the United States in the form contained in the act of Congress of July 2, 1862; and all such citizens of the United States who are in the military service of the United States shall vote at the headquarters of their respective commands, under such regulations as may be prescribed by the provisional governor for the taking and return of their votes; but no person who has held or exercised any office, civil or military, State or Confederate, under the rebel usurpation, or who has voluntarily borne arms against the United States, shall vote or be eligible to be elected as delegate at such election.

SEC. 5. *And be it further enacted,* That the said commissioners, or either of them, shall hold the election in conformity with this act, and, so far as may be consistent therewith, shall proceed in the manner used in the State prior to the rebellion. The oath of allegiance shall be taken and subscribed on the poll book by every voter in the form above prescribed, but every person known by or proved to the commissioners to have held or exercised any office, civil or military, State or Confederate, under the rebel usurpation, or to have voluntarily borne arms against the United States, shall be excluded though he offer to take the oath; and in case any person who shall have borne arms against the United States shall offer to vote, he shall be deemed to have borne arms voluntarily unless he shall prove the contrary by the testimony of a qualified voter. The poll book, showing the name and oath of each voter, shall be returned to the provisional governor by the commissioners of election, or the one acting, and the provisional governor shall canvass such returns and declare the person having the highest number of votes elected.

SEC. 6. *And be it further enacted,* That the provisional governor shall, by proclamation, convene the delegates elected as aforesaid at the capital of the State on a day not more than three months after the election, giving at least thirty days' notice of such day. In case the said capital shall in his judgment be unfit, he shall in his proclamation appoint another place. He shall preside over the deliberations of the convention and administer to each delegate, before taking his seat in the convention, the oath of allegiance to the United States in the form above prescribed.

SEC. 7. *And be it further enacted*, That the convention shall declare on behalf of the people of the State their submission to the Constitution and laws of the United States, and shall adopt the following provisions, hereby prescribed by the United States in the execution of the constitutional duty to guarantee a republican form of government to every State, and incorporate them in the constitution of the State; that is to say:

First. No person who has held or exercised any office, civil or military (except offices merely ministerial and military offices below the grade of colonel), State or Confederate, under the usurping power, shall vote for or be a member of the legislature or governor.

Second. Involuntary servitude is forever prohibited, and the freedom of all persons is guaranteed in said State.

Third. No debt, State or Confederate, created by or under the sanction of the usurping power shall be recognized or paid by the State.

SEC. 8. *And be it further enacted*, That when the convention shall have adopted those provisions it shall proceed to reestablish a republican form of government and ordain a constitution containing those provisions, which, when adopted, the convention shall by ordinance provide for submitting to the people of the State entitled to vote under this law, at an election to be held in the manner prescribed by the act for the election of delegates, but at a time and place named by the convention, at which election the said electors, and none others, shall vote directly for or against such constitution and form of State government. And the returns of said election shall be made to the provisional governor, who shall canvass the same in the presence of the electors, and if a majority of the votes cast shall be for the constitution and form of government, he shall certify the same, with a copy thereof, to the President of the United States, who, after obtaining the assent of Congress, shall, by proclamation, recognize the government so established, and none other, as the constitutional government of the State; and from the date of such recognition, and not before, Senators and Representatives and electors for President and Vice-President may be elected in such State, according to the laws of the State and of the United States.

SEC. 9. *And be it further enacted*, That if the convention shall refuse to reestablish the State government on the conditions aforesaid the provisional governor shall declare it dissolved; but it shall be the duty of the President, whenever he shall have reason to believe that a sufficient number of the people of the State entitled to vote under this act, in number not less than a majority of those enrolled as aforesaid, are willing to reestablish a State government on the conditions aforesaid, to direct the provisional governor to order another election of delegates to a convention for the purpose and in the manner prescribed in this act, and to proceed in all respects as hereinbefore provided, either to dissolve the convention or to certify the State government reestablished by it to the President.

SEC. 10. *And be it further enacted*, That until the United States shall have recognized a republican form of State government the provisional governor in each of said States shall see that this act and the laws of the United States and the laws of the State in force when the State government was overthrown by the rebellion are faithfully executed within the State; but no law or usage whereby any person was heretofore held in involuntary servitude shall be recognized or enforced by any court or officer in such State; and the laws for the trial and punishment of white persons shall extend to all persons, and jurors shall have the qualifications of voters under this law for delegates to the convention. The President shall appoint such officer provided for by the laws of the State when its government was overthrown as he may find necessary to the civil administration of the State, all which officers shall be entitled to receive the fees and emoluments provided by the State laws for such officers.

SEC. 11. *And be it further enacted*, That until the recognition of a State government as aforesaid the provisional governor shall, under such regulations as he may prescribe, cause to be assessed, levied, and collected, for the year 1864 and every year thereafter, the taxes provided by the laws of such State to be levied during the fiscal year preceding the overthrow of the State government thereof, in the manner prescribed by the laws of the State, as nearly as may be; and the officers appointed as aforesaid are vested with all powers of levying and collecting such taxes, by distress or sale, as were vested in any officers or tribunal of the State government aforesaid for those purposes. The proceeds of such taxes shall be accounted for to the provisional governor and be by him applied to the expenses of the administration of the laws in such State, subject to the direction of the President, and the surplus shall be deposited in the Treasury of the United States to the credit of such State, to be paid to the State upon an appropriation therefor to be made when a republican form of government shall be recognized therein by the United States.

SEC. 12. *And be it further enacted*, That all persons held to involuntary servitude or labor in the States aforesaid are hereby emancipated and discharged therefrom, and they and their posterity shall be forever free. And if any such persons or their posterity shall be restrained of liberty under pretense of any claim to such service or labor, the courts of the United States shall, on *habeas corpus*, discharge them.

SEC. 13. *And be it further enacted*, That if any person declared free by this act, or any law of the United States or any proclamation of the President, be restrained of liberty with intent to be held in or reduced to involuntary servitude or labor, the person convicted before a court of competent jurisdiction of such act shall be punished by fine of not less than $1,500 and be imprisoned not less than five nor more than twenty years.

SEC. 14. *And be it further enacted*, That every person who shall hereafter hold or exercise any office, civil or military (except offices merely ministerial and military offices below the grade of colonel), in the rebel service, State or Confederate, is hereby declared not to be a citizen of the United States.

BY THE PRESIDENT OF THE UNITED STATES OF AMERICA.

A PROCLAMATION.

Whereas by the act approved July 4, 1864, entitled "An act further to regulate and provide for the enrolling and calling out the national forces and for other purposes," it is provided that the President of the United States may, "at his discretion, at any time hereafter, call for any number of men, as volunteers for the respective terms of one, two, and three years for military service," and "that in case the quota or any part thereof of any town, township, ward of a city, precinct, or election district, or of a county not so subdivided, shall not be filled within the space of fifty days after such call, then the President shall immediately order a draft for one year to fill such quota or any part thereof which may be unfilled;" and

Whereas the new enrollment heretofore ordered is so far completed as that the aforementioned act of Congress may now be put in operation for recruiting and keeping up the strength of the armies in the field, for garrisons, and such military operations as may be required for the purpose of suppressing the rebellion and restoring the authority of the United States Government in the insurgent States:

Now, therefore, I, Abraham Lincoln, President of the United States, do issue this my call for 500,000 volunteers for the military service: *Provided, nevertheless,* That this call shall be reduced by all credits which may be established under section 8 of the aforesaid act on account of persons who have entered the naval service during the present rebellion and by credits for men furnished to the military service in excess of calls heretofore made. Volunteers will be accepted under this call for one, two, or three years, as they may elect, and will be entitled to the bounty provided by the law for the period of service for which they enlist.

And I hereby proclaim, order, and direct that immediately after the 5th day of September, 1864, being fifty days from the date of this call, a draft for troops to serve for one year shall be had in every town, township, ward of a city, precinct, or election district, or county not so subdivided, to fill the quota which shall be assigned to it under this call or any part thereof which may be unfilled by volunteers on the said 5th day of September, 1864.

In testimony whereof I have hereunto set my hand and caused the seal of the United States to be affixed.

[SEAL.]   Done at the city of Washington, this 18th day of July, A. D. 1864, and of the Independence of the United States the eighty-ninth.

ABRAHAM LINCOLN.

By the President:

WILLIAM H. SEWARD,
    Secretary of State.

BY THE PRESIDENT OF THE UNITED STATES OF AMERICA.

A PROCLAMATION.

Whereas the act of Congress of the 28th of September, 1850, entitled "An act to create additional collection districts in the State of California, and to change the existing districts therein, and to modify the existing collection districts in the United States," extends to merchandise warehoused under bond the privilege of being exported to the British North American Provinces adjoining the United States in the manner prescribed in the act of Congress of the 3d of March, 1845, which designates certain frontier ports through which merchandise may be exported, and further provides "that such other ports, situated on the frontiers of the United States adjoining the British North American Provinces, as may hereafter be found expedient may have extended to them the like privileges on the recommendation of the Secretary of the Treasury and proclamation duly made by the President of the United States specially designating the ports to which the aforesaid privileges are to be extended:"

Now, therefore, I, Abraham Lincoln, President of the United States of America, in accordance with the recommendation of the Secretary of the Treasury, do hereby declare and proclaim that the port of Newport, in the State of Vermont, is and shall be entitled to all the privileges in regard to the exportation of merchandise in bond to the British North American Provinces adjoining the United States which are extended to the ports enumerated in the seventh section of the act of Congress of the 3d of March, 1845, aforesaid, from and after the date of this proclamation.

In witness whereof I have hereunto set my hand and caused the seal of the United States to be affixed.

[SEAL.]　　　Done at the city of Washington, this 18th day of August, A. D. 1864, and of the Independence of the United States of America the eighty-ninth.

ABRAHAM LINCOLN.

By the President:

WILLIAM H. SEWARD,
　　Secretary of State.

BY THE PRESIDENT OF THE UNITED STATES OF AMERICA.

A PROCLAMATION.

It has pleased Almighty God to prolong our national life another year, defending us with His guardian care against unfriendly designs from abroad and vouchsafing to us in His mercy many and signal victories over the enemy, who is of our own household. It has also pleased our Heavenly Father to favor as well our citizens in their homes as our soldiers in their camps and our sailors on the rivers and seas with unusual health. He has largely augmented our free population by emancipation and by immigration, while He has opened to us new sources of wealth and has crowned the labor of our workingmen in every department of industry with abundant rewards. Moreover, He has been pleased to animate and inspire our minds and hearts with fortitude, courage, and resolution sufficient for the great trial of civil war into which we have been brought by our adherence as a nation to the cause of freedom and humanity, and to afford to us reasonable hopes of an ultimate and happy deliverance from all our dangers and afflictions:

Now, therefore, I, Abraham Lincoln, President of the United States, do hereby appoint and set apart the last Thursday in November next as a day which I desire to be observed by all my fellow-citizens, wherever they may then be, as a day of thanksgiving and praise to Almighty God, the beneficent Creator and Ruler of the Universe. And I do further recommend to my fellow-citizens aforesaid that on that occasion they do reverently humble themselves in the dust and from thence offer up penitent and fervent prayers and supplications to the Great Disposer of Events for a return of the inestimable blessings of peace, union, and harmony throughout the land which it has pleased Him to assign as a dwelling place for ourselves and for our posterity throughout all generations.

In testimony whereof I have hereunto set my hand and caused the seal of the United States to be affixed.

[SEAL.] Done at the city of Washington, this 20th day of October, A. D. 1864, and of the Independence of the United States the eighty-ninth.

ABRAHAM LINCOLN.

By the President:

WILLIAM H. SEWARD,
Secretary of State.

BY THE PRESIDENT OF THE UNITED STATES OF AMERICA.

A PROCLAMATION.

Whereas the Congress of the United States passed an act, which was approved on the 21st day of March last, entitled "An act to enable the people of Nevada to form a constitution and State government and for the admission of such State into the Union on an equal footing with the original States;" and

Whereas the said constitution and State government have been formed, pursuant to the conditions prescribed by the fifth section of the act of Congress aforesaid, and the certificate required by the said act and also a copy of the constitution and ordinances have been submitted to the President of the United States:

Now, therefore, be it known that I, Abraham Lincoln, President of the United States, in accordance with the duty imposed upon me by the act of Congress aforesaid, do hereby declare and proclaim that the said State of Nevada is admitted into the Union on an equal footing with the original States.

In witness whereof I have hereunto set my hand and caused the seal of the United States to be affixed.

[SEAL.] Done at the city of Washington, this 31st day of October, A. D. 1864, and of the Independence of the United States the eighty-ninth.

ABRAHAM LINCOLN.

By the President:

WILLIAM H. SEWARD,
Secretary of State.

By the President of the United States of America.

A PROCLAMATION.

Whereas by my proclamation of the 19th of April, 1861, it was declared that the ports of certain States, including those of Norfolk, in the State of Virginia, Fernandina and Pensacola, in the State of Florida, were, for reasons therein set forth, intended to be placed under blockade; and

Whereas the said ports were subsequently blockaded accordingly, but having for some time past been in the military possession of the United States, it is deemed advisable that they should be opened to domestic and foreign commerce:

Now, therefore, be it known that I, Abraham Lincoln, President of the United States, pursuant to the authority in me vested by the fifth section of the act of Congress approved on the 13th of July, 1861, entitled "An act further to provide for the collection of duties on imports, and for other purposes," do hereby declare that the blockade of the said ports of Norfolk, Fernandina, and Pensacola shall so far cease and determine, from and after the 1st day of December next, that commercial intercourse with those ports, except as to persons, things, and information contraband of war, may from that time be carried on, subject to the laws of the United States, to the limitations and in pursuance of the regulations which may be prescribed by the Secretary of the Treasury, and to such military and naval regulations as are now in force or may hereafter be found necessary.

In witness whereof I have hereunto set my hand and caused the seal of the United States to be affixed.

[SEAL.]   Done at the city of Washington, this 19th day of November, A. D. 1864, and of the Independence of the United States the eighty-ninth.

ABRAHAM LINCOLN.

By the President:

WILLIAM H. SEWARD,
    Secretary of State.

EXECUTIVE ORDERS.

EXECUTIVE MANSION,
Washington, D. C., December 7, 1863.

Reliable information being received that the insurgent force is retreating from east Tennessee under circumstances rendering it probable that the Union forces can not hereafter be dislodged from that important position, and esteeming this to be of high national consequence, I recommend that all loyal people do, on receipt of this information, assemble at their places of worship and render special homage and gratitude to Almighty God for this great advancement of the national cause.

A. LINCOLN.

GENERAL ORDERS, No. 398.

WAR DEPARTMENT,
ADJUTANT-GENERAL'S OFFICE,
Washington, December 21, 1863.

The following joint resolution by the Senate and House of Representatives of the United States is published to the Army:

JOINT RESOLUTION of thanks to Major-General Ulysses S. Grant and the officers and soldiers who have fought under his command during this rebellion, and providing that the President of the United States shall cause a medal to be struck, to be presented to Major-General Grant in the name of the people of the United States of America.

Be it resolved by the Senate and House of Representatives of the United States of America in Congress assembled, That the thanks of Congress be, and they hereby are, presented to Major-General Ulysses S. Grant, and through him to the officers and soldiers who have fought under his command during this rebellion, for their gallantry and good conduct in the battles in which they have been engaged; and that the President of the United States be requested to cause a gold medal to be struck, with suitable emblems, devices, and inscriptions, to be presented to Major-General Grant.

SEC. 2. *And be it further resolved,* That when the said medal shall have been struck the President shall cause a copy of this joint resolution to be engrossed on parchment, and shall transmit the same, together with the said medal, to Major-General Grant, to be presented to him in the name of the people of the United States of America.

SEC. 3. *And be it further resolved,* That a sufficient sum of money to carry this resolution into effect is hereby appropriated out of any money in the Treasury not otherwise appropriated.

SCHUYLER COLFAX,
Speaker of the House of Representatives.

H. HAMLIN,
Vice-President of the United States and President of the Senate.

Approved, December 17, 1863.

ABRAHAM LINCOLN.

By order of the Secretary of War:

E. D. TOWNSEND,
Assistant Adjutant-General.

EXECUTIVE MANSION, *January 9, 1864.*

Information having been received that Caleb B. Smith, late Secretary of the Interior, has departed this life at his residence in Indiana, it is ordered that the executive buildings at the seat of the Government be draped in mourning for the period of fourteen days in honor of his memory as a prudent and loyal counselor and a faithful and effective coadjutor of the Administration in a time of public difficulty and peril.

The Secretary of State will communicate a copy of this order to the family of the deceased, together with proper expressions of the profound sympathy of the President and the heads of Departments in their irreparable bereavement.

ABRAHAM LINCOLN.

WAR DEPARTMENT,
Washington City, January 12, 1864.

It is hereby ordered, That all orders and records relating to the Missouri troops, designated, respectively, as Missouri State Militia (M. S. M.) and as Enrolled Missouri Militia (E. M. M.), and which are or have been on file in the offices of the adjutant-generals or their assistants at the different headquarters located in the State of Missouri, shall be open to the inspection of the general assembly of Missouri or of persons commissioned by it, and that copies of such records be furnished them when called for.

By order of the President:

EDWIN M. STANTON,
Secretary of War.

EXECUTIVE MANSION, *February 1, 1864.*

Ordered, That a draft for 500,000 men, to serve for three years or during the war, be made on the 10th day of March next for the military service of the United States, crediting and deducting therefrom so many as may have been enlisted or drafted into the service prior to the 1st day of March and not heretofore credited.

ABRAHAM LINCOLN.

EXECUTIVE MANSION, *February 1, 1864.*

Hon. EDWIN M. STANTON,
Secretary of War.

SIR: You are directed to have a transport (either a steam or sailing vessel, as may be deemed proper by the Quartermaster-General) sent to the colored colony established by the United States at the island of Vache, on the coast of San Domingo, to bring back to this country such of the colonists there as desire to return. You will have the transport furnished with suitable supplies for that purpose, and detail an officer of the Quartermaster's Department, who, under special instructions to be given, shall have charge of the business. The colonists will be brought to Washington, unless otherwise hereafter directed, and be employed and provided for at the camps for colored persons around that city. Those only will be brought from the island who desire to return, and their effects will be brought with them.

ABRAHAM LINCOLN.

GENERAL ORDERS, No. 76.

WAR DEPARTMENT,
ADJUTANT-GENERAL'S OFFICE,
Washington, February 26, 1864.

SENTENCE OF DESERTERS.

The President directs that the sentences of all deserters who have been condemned by court-martial to death, and that have not been otherwise acted upon by him, be mitigated to imprisonment during the war at the Dry Tortugas, Florida, where they will be sent under suitable guards by orders from army commanders.

The commanding generals, who have power to act on proceedings of courts-martial in such cases, are authorized in special cases to restore to duty deserters under sentence, when in their judgment the service will be thereby benefited.

Copies of all orders issued under the foregoing instructions will be immediately forwarded to the Adjutant-General and to the Judge-Advocate-General.

By order of the Secretary of War:

E. D. TOWNSEND,
Assistant Adjutant-General.

EXECUTIVE MANSION,
Washington, March 7, 1864.

Whereas by an Executive order of the 10th of November last permission was given to export certain tobacco belonging to the French Government from insurgent territory, which tobacco was supposed to have been purchased and paid for prior to the 4th day of March, 1861; but whereas it was subsequently ascertained that a part at least of the said tobacco had been purchased subsequently to that date, which fact made it necessary to suspend the carrying into effect of the said order; but whereas, pursuant to mutual explanations, a satisfactory understanding upon the subject has now been reached, it is directed that the order aforesaid may be carried into effect, it being understood that the quantity of French tobacco so to be exported shall not exceed 7,000 hogsheads, and that it is the same tobacco respecting the exportation of which application was originally made by the French Government.

ABRAHAM LINCOLN.

In pursuance of the provisions of section 14 of the act of Congress entitled "An act to aid in the construction of a railroad and telegraph line from the Missouri River to the Pacific Ocean, and to secure to the Government the use of the same for postal, military, and other purposes," approved July 1, 1862, authorizing and directing the President of the United States to fix the point on the western boundary of the State of Iowa from which the Union Pacific Railroad Company is by said section authorized and required to construct a single line of railroad and telegraph upon the most direct and practicable route, subject to the approval of the President of the United States, so as to form a connection with the lines of said company at some point on the one hundredth meridian of longitude in said section named, I, Abraham Lincoln, President of the United States, do, upon the application of the said company, designate and establish such first above-named point on the western boundary of the State of Iowa east of and opposite to the east line of section 10, in township 15 north, of range 13 east, of the sixth principal meridian, in the Territory of Nebraska.

Done at the city of Washington, this 7th day of March, A. D. 1864.

ABRAHAM LINCOLN.

EXECUTIVE MANSION,
Washington, D. C., March 10, 1864.

Under the authority of an act of Congress to revive the grade of lieutenant-general in the United States Army, approved February 29, 1864, Lieutenant-General Ulysses S. Grant, United States Army, is assigned to the command of the armies of the United States.

ABRAHAM LINCOLN.

GENERAL ORDERS, No. 98.

WAR DEPARTMENT,
ADJUTANT-GENERAL'S OFFICE,
Washington, March 12, 1864.

The President of the United States orders as follows:

I. Major-General H. W. Halleck is, at his own request, relieved from duty as General in Chief of the Army, and Lieutenant-General U. S. Grant is assigned to the command of the armies of the United States. The headquarters of the Army will be in Washington and also with Lieutenant-General Grant in the field.

II. Major-General H. W. Halleck is assigned to duty in Washington as chief of staff of the Army, under the direction of the Secretary of War and the Lieutenant-General Commanding. His orders will be obeyed and respected accordingly.

III. Major-General W. T. Sherman is assigned to the command of the Military Division of the Mississippi, composed of the departments of the Ohio, the Cumberland, the Tennessee and the Arkansas.

IV. Major-General J. B. McPherson is assigned to the command of the Department and Army of the Tennessee.

V. In relieving Major-General Halleck from duty as General in Chief, the President desires to express his approbation and thanks for the able and zealous manner in which the arduous and responsible duties of that position have been performed.

By order of the Secretary of War:

E. D. TOWNSEND,
Assistant Adjutant-General.

EXECUTIVE MANSION,
Washington, March 14, 1864.

In order to supply the force required to be drafted for the Navy and to provide an adequate reserve force for all contingencies, in addition to the 500,000 men called for February 1, 1864, a call is hereby made and a draft ordered for 200,000 men for the military service (Army, Navy, and Marine Corps) of the United States.

The proportional quotas for the different wards, towns, townships, precincts, or election districts, or counties, will be made known through the Provost-Marshal-General's Bureau, and account will be taken of the credits and deficiencies on former quotas.

The 15th day of April, 1864, is designated as the time up to which the numbers required from each ward of a city, town, etc., may be raised by voluntary enlistment, and drafts will be made in each ward of a city, town, etc., which shall not have filled the quota assigned to it within the time designated for the number required to fill said quotas. The drafts will be commenced as soon after the 15th of April as practicable.

The Government bounties as now paid continue until April 1, 1864, at which time the additional bounties cease. On and after that date $100 bounty only will be paid, as provided by the act approved July 22, 1861.

ABRAHAM LINCOLN.

EXECUTIVE MANSION, *April 2, 1864.*

Ordered, That the Executive order of September 4, 1863, in relation to the exportation of live stock from the United States, be so extended as to prohibit the exportation of all classes of salted provisions from any part of the United States to any foreign port, except that meats cured, salted, or packed in any State or Territory bordering on the Pacific Ocean may be exported from any port of such State or Territory.

ABRAHAM LINCOLN.

The PRESIDENT OF THE UNITED STATES:

I. The governors of Ohio, Indiana, Illinois, Iowa, and Wisconsin offer to the President infantry troops for the approaching campaign as follows:

Ohio	30,000
Indiana	20,000
Illinois	20,000
Iowa	10,000
Wisconsin	5,000

II. The term of service to be one hundred days, reckoning from the date of muster into the service of the United States, unless sooner discharged.

III. The troops to be mustered into the service of the United States by regiments, when the regiments are filled up, according to regulations, to the minimum strength, the regiments to be organized according to the regulations of the War Department. The whole number to be furnished within twenty days from date of notice of the acceptance of this proposition.

IV. The troops to be clothed, armed, equipped, subsisted, transported, and paid as other United States infantry volunteers, and to serve in fortifications, or wherever their services may be required, within or without their respective States.

V. No bounty to be paid the troops, nor the service charged or credited on any draft.

VI. The draft for three years' service to go on in any State or district where the quota is not filled up; but if any officer or soldier in this special service should be drafted he shall be credited for the service rendered.

JOHN BROUGH,
Governor of Ohio.

O. P. MORTON,
Governor of Indiana.

RICHARD YATES,
Governor of Illinois.

WM. M. STONE,
Governor of Iowa.

JAMES T. LEWIS,
Governor of Wisconsin.

APRIL 23, 1864.

The foregoing proposition of the governors is accepted, and the Secretary of War is directed to carry it into execution.

A. LINCOLN.

EXECUTIVE MANSION,
Washington, May 9, 1864.

To the Friends of the Union and Liberty:

Enough is known of the army operations within the last five days to claim our especial gratitude to God, while what remains undone demands our most sincere prayers to and reliance upon Him, without whom all human efforts are in vain. I recommend that all patriots, at their homes, in their places of public worship, and wherever they may be, unite in common thanksgiving and prayer to Almighty God.

ABRAHAM LINCOLN.

Executive Mansion,
Washington, *May 18, 1864.*

Major-General John A. Dix,
Commanding at New York:

Whereas there has been wickedly and traitorously printed and published this morning in the New York World and New York Journal of Commerce, newspapers printed and published in the city of New York, a false and spurious proclamation purporting to be signed by the President and to be countersigned by the Secretary of State, which publication is of a treasonable nature, designed to give aid and comfort to the enemies of the United States and to the rebels now at war against the Government and their aiders and abettors, you are therefore hereby commanded forthwith to arrest and imprison in any fort or military prison in your command the editors, proprietors, and publishers of the aforesaid newspapers, and all such persons as, after public notice has been given of the falsehood of said publication, print and publish the same with intent to give aid and comfort to the enemy; and you will hold the persons so arrested in close custody until they can be brought to trial before a military commission for their offense. You will also take possession by military force of the printing establishments of the New York World and Journal of Commerce, and hold the same until further orders, and prohibit any further publication therefrom.   A. LINCOLN.

Executive Mansion, *Washington, D. C.*

The President of the United States directs that the four persons whose names follow, to wit, Hon. Clement C. Clay, Hon. Jacob Thompson, Professor James P. Holcombe, George N. Sanders, shall have safe conduct to the city of Washington in company with the Hon. Horace Greeley, and shall be exempt from arrest or annoyance of any kind from any officer of the United States during their journey to the said city of Washington.

By order of the President: JOHN HAY,
Major and Assistant Adjutant-General.

Executive Mansion,
Washington, *July 18, 1864.*

To whom it may concern:

Any proposition which embraces the restoration of peace, the integrity of the whole Union, and the abandonment of slavery, and which comes by and with an authority that can control the armies now at war against the United States, will be received and considered by the executive government of the United States, and will be met by liberal terms on other substantial and collateral points; and the bearer or bearers thereof shall have safe conduct both ways.   ABRAHAM LINCOLN.

EXECUTIVE MANSION, *Washington, August 31, 1864.*

Any person or persons engaged in bringing out cotton, in strict conformity with authority given by W. P. Fessenden, Secretary of the United States Treasury, must not be hindered by the War, Navy, or any other Department of the Government or any person engaged under any of said Departments.

ABRAHAM LINCOLN.

EXECUTIVE MANSION, *September 3, 1864.*

The national thanks are tendered by the President to Major-General William T. Sherman and the gallant officers and soldiers of his command before Atlanta for the distinguished ability, courage, and perseverance displayed in the campaign in Georgia, which, under divine favor, has resulted in the capture of the city of Atlanta. The marches, battles, sieges, and other military operations that have signalized this campaign must render it famous in the annals of war, and have entitled those who have participated therein to the applause and thanks of the nation.

ABRAHAM LINCOLN.

EXECUTIVE MANSION,
Washington City, September 3, 1864.

Ordered, first. That on Monday, the 5th day of September, commencing at the hour of 12 o'clock noon, there shall be given a salute of 100 guns at the arsenal and navy-yard at Washington, and on Tuesday, the 6th of September, or on the day after the receipt of this order, at each arsenal and navy-yard in the United States, for the recent brilliant achievements of the fleet and land forces of the United States in the harbor of Mobile and in the reduction of Fort Powell, Fort Gaines, and Fort Morgan. The Secretary of War and Secretary of the Navy will issue the necessary directions in their respective Departments for the execution of this order.

Second. That on Wednesday, the 7th day of September, commencing at the hour of 12 o'clock noon, there shall be fired a salute of 100 guns at the arsenal at Washington, and at New York, Boston, Philadelphia, Baltimore, Pittsburg, Newport, Ky., and St. Louis, and at New Orleans, Mobile, Pensacola, Hilton Head, and New Berne the day after the receipt of this order, for the brilliant achievements of the army under command of Major-General Sherman in the State of Georgia and the capture of Atlanta. The Secretary of War will issue directions for the execution of this order.

ABRAHAM LINCOLN.

EXECUTIVE MANSION, *Washington, September 3, 1864.*

The signal success that Divine Providence has recently vouchsafed to the operations of the United States fleet and army in the harbor of

Mobile, and the reduction of Fort Powell, Fort Gaines, and Fort Morgan, and the glorious achievements of the army under Major-General Sherman in the State of Georgia, resulting in the capture of the city of Atlanta, call for devout acknowledgment to the Supreme Being, in whose hands are the destinies of nations. It is therefore requested that on next Sunday, in all places of public worship in the United States, thanksgiving be offered to Him for His mercy in preserving our national existence against the insurgent rebels who so long have been waging a cruel war against the Government of the United States for its overthrow; and also that prayer be made for the divine protection to our brave soldiers and their leaders in the field, who have so often and so gallantly periled their lives in battling with the enemy, and for blessing and comfort from the Father of Mercies to the sick, wounded, and prisoners, and to the orphans and widows of those who have fallen in the service of their country; and that He will continue to uphold the Government of the United States against all the efforts of public enemies and secret foes.

ABRAHAM LINCOLN.

EXECUTIVE MANSION, *September 3, 1864.*

The national thanks are tendered by the President to Admiral Farragut and Major-General Canby for the skill and harmony with which the recent operations in Mobile Harbor and against Fort Powell, Fort Gaines, and Fort Morgan were planned and carried into execution; also to Admiral Farragut and Major-General Granger, under whose immediate command they were conducted, and to the gallant commanders on sea and land, and to the sailors and soldiers engaged in the operations, for their energy and courage, which, under the blessing of Providence, have been crowned with brilliant success and have won for them the applause and thanks of the nation.

ABRAHAM LINCOLN.

EXECUTIVE MANSION,
Washington City, September 10, 1864.

The term of one hundred days for which the National Guard of Ohio volunteered having expired, the President directs an official acknowledgment to be made of their patriotic and valuable services during the recent campaigns. The term of service of their enlistment was short, but distinguished by memorable events. In the Valley of the Shenandoah, on the Peninsula, in the operations on the James River, around Petersburg and Richmond, in the battle of Monocacy, and in the intrenchments of Washington, and in other important service, the National Guard of Ohio performed with alacrity the duty of patriotic volunteers, for which they are entitled to and are hereby tendered, through the governor of their State, the national thanks.

The Secretary of War is directed to transmit a copy of this order to the governor of Ohio and to cause a certificate of their honorable service to be delivered to the officers and soldiers of the Ohio National Guard who recently served in the military force of the United States as volunteers for one hundred days.

ABRAHAM LINCOLN.

EXECUTIVE MANSION, *September 24, 1864.*

I. Congress having authorized the purchase for the United States of the product of States declared in insurrection, and the Secretary of the Treasury having designated New Orleans, Memphis, Nashville, Pensacola, Port Royal, Beaufort, N. C., and Norfolk as places of purchase, and with my approval appointed agents and made regulations under which said products may be purchased: Therefore,

II. All persons, except such as may be in the civil, military, or naval service of the Government, having in their possession any products of States declared in insurrection which said agents are authorized to purchase, and all persons owning or controlling such products therein, are authorized to convey such products to either of the places which have been hereby or may hereafter be designated as places of purchase, and such products so destined shall not be liable to detention, seizure, or forfeiture while *in transitu* or in store awaiting transportation.

III. Any person having the certificate of a purchasing agent, as prescribed by Treasury Regulations, VIII, is authorized to pass, with the necessary means of transportation, to the points named in said certificate, and to return therefrom with the products required for the fulfillment of the stipulations set forth in said certificate.

IV. Any person having sold and delivered to a purchasing agent any products of an insurrectionary State in accordance with the regulations in relation thereto, and having in his possession a certificate setting forth the fact of such purchase and sale, the character and quantity of products, and the aggregate amount paid therefor, as prescribed by Regulation IX, shall be permitted by the military authority commanding at the place of sale to purchase from any authorized dealer at such place, or any other place in a loyal State, merchandise and other articles not contraband of war nor prohibited by the order of the War Department, nor coin, bullion, or foreign exchange, to an amount not exceeding in value one-third of the aggregate value of the products sold by him, as certified by the agent purchasing; and the merchandise and other articles so purchased may be transported by the same route and to the same place from and by which the products sold and delivered reached the purchasing agent, as set forth in the certificate; and such merchandise and other articles shall have safe conduct, and shall not be subject to detention, seizure, or forfeiture while being transported to the places and by the route set forth in the said certificate.

V. Generals commanding military districts and commandants of military posts and detachments, and officers commanding fleets, flotillas, and gunboats, will give safe conduct to persons and products, merchandise, and other articles duly authorized as aforesaid, and not contraband of war or prohibited by order of the War Department, or the orders of such generals commanding, or other duly authorized military or naval officer, made in pursuance thereof; and all persons hindering or preventing such safe conduct of persons or property will be deemed guilty of a military offense and punished accordingly.

VI. Any person transporting or attempting to transport any merchandise or other articles, except in pursuance of regulations of the Secretary of the Treasury dated July 29, 1864, or in pursuance of this order, or transporting or attempting to transport any merchandise or other articles contraband of war or forbidden by any order of the War Department, will be deemed guilty of a military offense and punished accordingly; and all products of insurrectionary States found *in transitu* to any other person or place than a purchasing agent and a designated place of purchase shall be seized and forfeited to the United States, except such as may be moving to a loyal State under duly authorized permits of a proper officer of the Treasury Department, as prescribed by Regulation XXXVIII, concerning "commercial intercourse," dated July 29, 1864, or such as may have been found abandoned or have been captured and are moving in pursuance of the act of March 12, 1863.

VII. No military or naval officer of the United States, or person in the military or naval service, nor any civil officer, except such as are appointed for that purpose, shall engage in trade or traffic in the products of insurrectionary States, or furnish transportation therefor, under pain of being deemed guilty of unlawful trading with the enemy and punished accordingly.

VIII. The Secretary of War will make such general orders or regulations as will insure the proper observance and execution of this order, and the Secretary of the Navy will give instructions to officers commanding fleets, flotillas, and gunboats in conformity therewith.

ABRAHAM LINCOLN.

EXECUTIVE MANSION,
Washington, October 1, 1864.

SPECIAL EXECUTIVE ORDER RETURNING THANKS TO THE VOLUNTEERS FOR ONE HUNDRED DAYS FROM THE STATES OF INDIANA, ILLINOIS, IOWA, AND WISCONSIN.

The term of one hundred days for which volunteers from the States of Indiana, Illinois, Iowa, and Wisconsin volunteered, under the call of their respective governors, in the months of May and June, to aid in the campaign of General Sherman, having expired, the President directs an official acknowledgment to be made of their patriotic service. It was their good fortune to render efficient service in the brilliant operations in the Southwest and to contribute to the victories of the national arms over the rebel forces in Georgia under command of Johnston and Hood. On all occasions and in every service to which they were assigned their duty as patriotic volunteers was performed with alacrity and courage, for which they are entitled to and are hereby tendered the national thanks through the governors of their respective States.

The Secretary of War is directed to transmit a copy of this order to the governors of Indiana, Illinois, Iowa, and Wisconsin and to cause a certificate of their honorable service to be delivered to the officers and soldiers of the States above named who recently served in the military force of the United States as volunteers for one hundred days.

A. LINCOLN.

EXECUTIVE MANSION,
Washington, October 12, 1864.

The Japanese Government having caused the construction at New York of a vessel of war called the *Fusigama*, and application having been made for the clearance of the same, in order that it may proceed to Japan, it is ordered, in view of the state of affairs in that country and of its relation with the United States, that a compliance with the application be for the present suspended.

ABRAHAM LINCOLN.

GENERAL ORDERS, No. 282.

WAR DEPARTMENT,
ADJUTANT-GENERAL'S OFFICE,
Washington, November 14, 1864.

Ordered by the President, I. That the resignation of George B. McClellan as major-general in the United States Army, dated November 8 and received by the Adjutant-General on the 10th instant, be accepted as of the 8th of November.

II. That for the personal gallantry, military skill, and just confidence in the courage and patriotism of his troops displayed by Philip H. Sheridan on the 19th day of October at Cedar Run, whereby, under the blessing of Providence, his routed army was reorganized, a great national disaster averted, and a brilliant victory achieved over the rebels for the third time in pitched battle within thirty days, Philip H. Sheridan is appointed major-general in the United States Army, to rank as such from the 8th day of November, 1864.

By order of the President of the United States:

E. D. TOWNSEND, *Assistant Adjutant-General.*

EXECUTIVE MANSION,
Washington, December 3, 1864.

A war steamer, called the *Funayma Solace*, having been built in this country for the Japanese Government and at the instance of that Government, it is deemed to comport with the public interest, in view of the unsettled condition of the relations of the United States with that Empire, that the steamer should not be allowed to proceed to Japan. If, however, the Secretary of the Navy should ascertain that the steamer is adapted to our service, he is authorized to purchase her, but the purchase money will be held in trust toward satisfying any valid claims which may be presented by the Japanese on account of the construction of the steamer and the failure to deliver the same, as above set forth.

ABRAHAM LINCOLN.

FOURTH ANNUAL MESSAGE.

DECEMBER 6, 1864.

Fellow-Citizens of the Senate and House of Representatives:

Again the blessings of health and abundant harvests claim our profoundest gratitude to Almighty God.

The condition of our foreign affairs is reasonably satisfactory.

Mexico continues to be a theater of civil war. While our political relations with that country have undergone no change, we have at the same time strictly maintained neutrality between the belligerents.

At the request of the States of Costa Rica and Nicaragua, a competent engineer has been authorized to make a survey of the river San Juan and the port of San Juan. It is a source of much satisfaction that the difficulties which for a moment excited some political apprehensions and caused a closing of the interoceanic transit route have been amicably adjusted, and that there is a good prospect that the route will soon be reopened with an increase of capacity and adaptation. We could not exaggerate either the commercial or the political importance of that great improvement.

It would be doing injustice to an important South American State not to acknowledge the directness, frankness, and cordiality with which the United States of Colombia have entered into intimate relations with this Government. A claims convention has been constituted to complete the unfinished work of the one which closed its session in 1861.

The new liberal constitution of Venezuela having gone into effect with the universal acquiescence of the people, the Government under it has been recognized and diplomatic intercourse with it has opened in a cordial

and friendly spirit.   The long-deferred Aves Island claim has been satisfactorily paid and discharged.

Mutual payments have been made of the claims awarded by the late
joint commission for the settlement of claims between the United States
and Peru.   An earnest and cordial friendship continues to exist between
the two countries, and such efforts as were in my power have been used
to remove misunderstanding and avert a threatened war between Peru
and Spain.

Our relations are of the most friendly nature with Chile, the Argentine Republic, Bolivia, Costa Rica, Paraguay, San Salvador, and Hayti.

During the past year no differences of any kind have arisen with any
of those Republics, and, on the other hand, their sympathies with the
United States are constantly expressed with cordiality and earnestness.

The claim arising from the seizure of the cargo of the brig *Macedonian*
in 1821 has been paid in full by the Government of Chile.

Civil war continues in the Spanish part of San Domingo, apparently
without prospect of an early close.

Official correspondence has been freely opened with Liberia, and it
gives us a pleasing view of social and political progress in that Republic.   It may be expected to derive new vigor from American influence,
improved by the rapid disappearance of slavery in the United States.

I solicit your authority to furnish to the Republic a gunboat at moderate cost, to be reimbursed to the United States by installments.   Such
a vessel is needed for the safety of that State against the native African
races, and in Liberian hands it would be more effective in arresting the
African slave trade than a squadron in our own hands.   The possession
of the least organized naval force would stimulate a generous ambition in
the Republic, and the confidence which we should manifest by furnishing
it would win forbearance and favor toward the colony from all civilized
nations.

The proposed overland telegraph between America and Europe, by the
way of Behring's Straits and Asiatic Russia, which was sanctioned by
Congress at the last session, has been undertaken, under very favorable
circumstances, by an association of American citizens, with the cordial
good will and support as well of this Government as of those of Great
Britain and Russia.   Assurances have been received from most of the
South American States of their high appreciation of the enterprise and
their readiness to cooperate in constructing lines tributary to that world-
encircling communication.   I learn with much satisfaction that the noble
design of a telegraphic communication between the eastern coast of
America and Great Britain has been renewed, with full expectation
of its early accomplishment.

Thus it is hoped that with the return of domestic peace the country
will be able to resume with energy and advantage its former high career
of commerce and civilization.

Our very popular and estimable representative in Egypt died in April last. An unpleasant altercation which arose between the temporary incumbent of the office and the Government of the Pasha resulted in a suspension of intercourse. The evil was promptly corrected on the arrival of the successor in the consulate, and our relations with Egypt, as well as our relations with the Barbary Powers, are entirely satisfactory.

The rebellion which has so long been flagrant in China has at last been suppressed, with the cooperating good offices of this Government and of the other Western commercial States. The judicial consular establishment there has become very difficult and onerous, and it will need legislative revision to adapt it to the extension of our commerce and to the more intimate intercourse which has been instituted with the Government and people of that vast Empire. China seems to be accepting with hearty good will the conventional laws which regulate commercial and social intercourse among the Western nations.

Owing to the peculiar situation of Japan and the anomalous form of its Government, the action of that Empire in performing treaty stipulations is inconstant and capricious. Nevertheless, good progress has been effected by the Western powers, moving with enlightened concert. Our own pecuniary claims have been allowed or put in course of settlement, and the inland sea has been reopened to commerce. There is reason also to believe that these proceedings have increased rather than diminished the friendship of Japan toward the United States.

The ports of Norfolk, Fernandina, and Pensacola have been opened by proclamation. It is hoped that foreign merchants will now consider whether it is not safer and more profitable to themselves, as well as just to the United States, to resort to these and other open ports than it is to pursue, through many hazards and at vast cost, a contraband trade with other ports which are closed, if not by actual military occupation, at least by a lawful and effective blockade.

For myself, I have no doubt of the power and duty of the Executive, under the law of nations, to exclude enemies of the human race from an asylum in the United States. If Congress should think that proceedings in such cases lack the authority of law, or ought to be further regulated by it, I recommend that provision be made for effectually preventing foreign slave traders from acquiring domicile and facilities for their criminal occupation in our country.

It is possible that if it were a new and open question the maritime powers, with the lights they now enjoy, would not concede the privileges of a naval belligerent to the insurgents of the United States, destitute, as they are, and always have been, equally of ships of war and of ports and harbors. Disloyal emissaries have been neither less assiduous nor more successful during the last year than they were before that time in their efforts, under favor of that privilege, to embroil our country in foreign wars. The desire and determination of the governments of the maritime states to defeat that design are believed to be as sincere as and can not be more earnest than our own. Nevertheless, unforeseen political difficulties have arisen, especially in Brazilian and British ports and on the northern boundary of the United States, which have required, and are likely to continue to require, the practice of constant vigilance and a just and conciliatory spirit on the part of the United States, as well as of the nations concerned and their governments.

Commissioners have been appointed under the treaty with Great Britain on the adjustment of the claims of the Hudsons Bay and Pugets Sound Agricultural Companies, in Oregon, and are now proceeding to the execution of the trust assigned to them.

In view of the insecurity of life and property in the region adjacent to the Canadian border, by reason of recent assaults and depredations committed by inimical and desperate persons who are harbored there, it has been thought proper to give notice that after the expiration of six months, the period conditionally stipulated in the existing arrangement with Great Britain, the United States must hold themselves at liberty to increase their naval armament upon the Lakes if they shall find that proceeding necessary. The condition of the border will necessarily come into consideration in connection with the question of continuing or modifying the rights of transit from Canada through the United States, as well as the regulation of imposts, which were temporarily established by the reciprocity treaty of the 5th June, 1854.

I desire, however, to be understood while making this statement that the colonial authorities of Canada are not deemed to be intentionally unjust or unfriendly toward the United States, but, on the contrary, there is every reason to expect that, with the approval of the Imperial Government, they will take the necessary measures to prevent new incursions across the border.

The act passed at the last session for the encouragement of immigration has so far as was possible been put into operation. It seems to need amendment which will enable the officers of the Government to prevent the practice of frauds against the immigrants while on their way and on their arrival in the ports, so as to secure them here a free choice of avocations and places of settlement. A liberal disposition toward this great national policy is manifested by most of the European States, and ought to be reciprocated on our part by giving the immigrants effective national protection. I regard our immigrants as one of the principal replenishing streams which are appointed by Providence to repair the ravages of internal war and its wastes of national strength and health. All that is necessary is to secure the flow of that stream in its present fullness, and to that end the Government must in every way make it manifest that it neither needs nor designs to impose involuntary military service upon those who come from other lands to cast their lot in our country.

The financial affairs of the Government have been successfully administered during the last year. The legislation of the last session of Congress has beneficially affected the revenues, although sufficient time has not yet elapsed to experience the full effect of several of the provisions of the acts of Congress imposing increased taxation.

The receipts during the year from all sources, upon the basis of warrants signed by the Secretary of the Treasury, including loans and the balance in the Treasury on the 1st day of July, 1863, were $1,394,796,007.62, and the aggregate disbursements, upon the same basis, were $1,298,056,-101.89, leaving a balance in the Treasury, as shown by warrants, of $96,739,905.73.

Deduct from these amounts the amount of the principal of the public debt redeemed and the amount of issues in substitution therefor, and the actual cash operations of the Treasury were: Receipts, $884,076,646.57; disbursements, $865,234,087.86; which leaves a cash balance in the Treasury of $18,842,558.71.

Of the receipts there were derived from customs $102,316,152.99, from lands $588,333.29, from direct taxes $475,648.96, from internal revenue $109,741,134.10, from miscellaneous sources $47,511,448.10, and from loans applied to actual expenditures, including former balance, $623,-443,929.13.

There were disbursed for the civil service $27,505,599.46, for pensions and Indians $7,517,930.97, for the War Department $690,791,842.97, for the Navy Department $85,733,292.77, for interest on the public debt $53,685,421.69, making an aggregate of $865,234,087.86 and leaving a balance in the Treasury of $18,842,558.71, as before stated.

For the actual receipts and disbursements for the first quarter and the estimated receipts and disbursements for the three remaining quarters of the current fiscal year, and the general operations of the Treasury in detail, I refer you to the report of the Secretary of the Treasury. I concur with him in the opinion that the proportion of moneys required to meet the expenses consequent upon the war derived from taxation should be still further increased; and I earnestly invite your attention to this subject, to the end that there may be such additional legislation as shall be required to meet the just expectations of the Secretary.

The public debt on the 1st day of July last, as appears by the books of the Treasury, amounted to $1,740,690,489.49. Probably, should the war continue for another year, that amount may be increased by not far from five hundred millions. Held, as it is, for the most part by our own people, it has become a substantial branch of national, though private, property. For obvious reasons the more nearly this property can be distributed among all the people the better. To favor such general distribution, greater inducements to become owners might, perhaps, with good effect and without injury be presented to persons of limited means. With this view I suggest whether it might not be both competent and expedient for Congress to provide that a limited amount of some future issue of public securities might be held by any *bona fide* purchaser exempt from taxation and from seizure for debt, under such restrictions and limitations as might be necessary to guard against abuse of so important a privilege. This would enable every prudent person to set aside a small annuity against a possible day of want.

Privileges like these would render the possession of such securities to the amount limited most desirable to every person of small means who might be able to save enough for the purpose. The great advantage of citizens being creditors as well as debtors with relation to the public debt is obvious. Men readily perceive that they can not be much oppressed by a debt which they owe to themselves.

The public debt on the 1st day of July last, although somewhat exceeding the estimate of the Secretary of the Treasury made to Congress at the commencement of the last session, falls short of the estimate of that officer made in the preceding December as to its probable amount at the beginning of this year by the sum of $3,995,097.31. This fact exhibits a satisfactory condition and conduct of the operations of the Treasury.

The national banking system is proving to be acceptable to capitalists and to the people. On the 25th day of November 584 national banks had been organized, a considerable number of which were conversions from State banks. Changes from State systems to the national system are rapidly taking place, and it is hoped that very soon there will be in the United States no banks of issue not authorized by Congress and no bank-note circulation not secured by the Government. That the Government and the people will derive great benefit from this change in the banking systems of the country can hardly be questioned. The national system will create a reliable and permanent influence in support of the national credit and protect the people against losses in the use of paper money. Whether or not any further legislation is advisable for the suppression of State-bank issues it will be for Congress to determine. It seems quite clear that the Treasury can not be satisfactorily conducted unless the Government can exercise a restraining power over the bank-note circulation of the country.

The report of the Secretary of War and the accompanying documents will detail the campaigns of the armies in the field since the date of the last annual message, and also the operations of the several administrative bureaus of the War Department during the last year. It will also specify the measures deemed essential for the national defense and to keep up and supply the requisite military force.

The report of the Secretary of the Navy presents a comprehensive and satisfactory exhibit of the affairs of that Department and of the naval service. It is a subject of congratulation and laudable pride to our countrymen that a Navy of such vast proportions has been organized in so brief a period and conducted with so much efficiency and success.

The general exhibit of the Navy, including vessels under construction on the 1st of December, 1864, shows a total of 671 vessels, carrying 4,610 guns, and of 510,396 tons, being an actual increase during the year, over and above all losses by shipwreck or in battle, of 83 vessels, 167 guns, and 42,427 tons.

The total number of men at this time in the naval service, including officers, is about 51,000.

There have been captured by the Navy during the year 324 vessels, and the whole number of naval captures since hostilities commenced is 1,379, of which 267 are steamers.

The gross proceeds arising from the sale of condemned prize property thus far reported amount to $14,396,250.51. A large amount of such proceeds is still under adjudication and yet to be reported.

The total expenditure of the Navy Department of every description, including the cost of the immense squadrons that have been called into existence from the 4th of March, 1861, to the 1st of November, 1864, is $238,647,262.35.

Your favorable consideration is invited to the various recommendations of the Secretary of the Navy, especially in regard to a navy-yard and suitable establishment for the construction and repair of iron vessels and the machinery and armature for our ships, to which reference was made in my last annual message.

Your attention is also invited to the views expressed in the report in relation to the legislation of Congress at its last session in respect to prize on our inland waters.

I cordially concur in the recommendation of the Secretary as to the propriety of creating the new rank of vice-admiral in our naval service.

Your attention is invited to the report of the Postmaster-General for a detailed account of the operations and financial condition of the Post-Office Department.

The postal revenues for the year ending June 30, 1864, amounted to $12,438,253.78 and the expenditures to $12,644,786.20, the excess of expenditures over receipts being $206,652.42.

The views presented by the Postmaster-General on the subject of special grants by the Government in aid of the establishment of new lines of ocean mail steamships and the policy he recommends for the development of increased commercial intercourse with adjacent and neighboring countries should receive the careful consideration of Congress.

It is of noteworthy interest that the steady expansion of population, improvement, and governmental institutions over the new and unoccupied portions of our country have scarcely been checked, much less impeded or destroyed, by our great civil war, which at first glance would seem to have absorbed almost the entire energies of the nation.

The organization and admission of the State of Nevada has been completed in conformity with law, and thus our excellent system is firmly established in the mountains, which once seemed a barren and uninhabitable waste between the Atlantic States and those which have grown up on the coast of the Pacific Ocean.

The Territories of the Union are generally in a condition of prosperity and rapid growth. Idaho and Montana, by reason of their great distance and the interruption of communication with them by Indian hostilities, have been only partially organized; but it is understood that these difficulties are about to disappear, which will permit their governments, like those of the others, to go into speedy and full operation.

As intimately connected with and promotive of this material growth of the nation, I ask the attention of Congress to the valuable information and important recommendations relating to the public lands, Indian affairs, the Pacific Railroad, and mineral discoveries contained in the report of the Secretary of the Interior which is herewith transmitted, and which report also embraces the subjects of patents, pensions, and other topics of public interest pertaining to his Department.

The quantity of public land disposed of during the five quarters ending on the 30th of September last was 4,221,342 acres, of which 1,538,614 acres were entered under the homestead law. The remainder was located with military land warrants, agricultural scrip certified to States for railroads, and sold for cash. The cash received from sales and location fees was $1,019,446.

The income from sales during the fiscal year ending June 30, 1864, was $678,007.21, against $136,077.95 received during the preceding year. The aggregate number of acres surveyed during the year has been equal to the quantity disposed of, and there is open to settlement about 133,000,000 acres of surveyed land.

The great enterprise of connecting the Atlantic with the Pacific States by railways and telegraph lines has been entered upon with a vigor that gives assurance of success, notwithstanding the embarrassments arising from the prevailing high prices of materials and labor. The route of the main line of the road has been definitely located for 100 miles westward from the initial point at Omaha City, Nebr., and a preliminary location of the Pacific Railroad of California has been made from Sacramento eastward to the great bend of the Truckee River in Nevada.

Numerous discoveries of gold, silver, and cinnabar mines have been added to the many heretofore known, and the country occupied by the Sierra Nevada and Rocky mountains and the subordinate ranges now teems with enterprising labor, which is richly remunerative. It is believed that the product of the mines of precious metals in that region has during the year reached, if not exceeded, one hundred millions in value.

It was recommended in my last annual message that our Indian system be remodeled. Congress at its last session, acting upon the recommendation, did provide for reorganizing the system in California, and it is believed that under the present organization the management of the Indians there will be attended with reasonable success. Much yet remains to be done to provide for the proper government of the Indians in other parts of the country, to render it secure for the advancing settler, and to provide for the welfare of the Indian. The Secretary reiterates his recommendations, and to them the attention of Congress is invited.

The liberal provisions made by Congress for paying pensions to invalid soldiers and sailors of the Republic and to the widows, orphans, and dependent mothers of those who have fallen in battle or died of disease contracted or of wounds received in the service of their country have been diligently administered. There have been added to the pension rolls during the year ending the 30th day of June last the names of 16,770 invalid soldiers and of 271 disabled seamen, making the present number of army invalid pensioners 22,767 and of navy invalid pensioners 712.

Of widows, orphans, and mothers 22,198 have been placed on the army pension rolls and 248 on the navy rolls. The present number of army pensioners of this class is 25,433 and of navy pensioners 793. At the beginning of the year the number of Revolutionary pensioners was 1,430. Only 12 of them were soldiers, of whom 7 have since died. The remainder are those who under the law receive pensions because of relationship to Revolutionary soldiers. During the year ending the 30th of June, 1864, $4,504,616.92 have been paid to pensioners of all classes.

I cheerfully commend to your continued patronage the benevolent institutions of the District of Columbia which have hitherto been established or fostered by Congress, and respectfully refer for information concerning them and in relation to the Washington Aqueduct, the Capitol, and other matters of local interest to the report of the Secretary.

The Agricultural Department, under the supervision of its present energetic and faithful head, is rapidly commending itself to the great and vital interest it was created to advance It is peculiarly the people's Department, in which they feel more directly concerned than in any other. I commend it to the continued attention and fostering care of Congress.

The war continues. Since the last annual message all the important lines and positions then occupied by our forces have been maintained and our arms have steadily advanced, thus liberating the regions left in rear, so that Missouri, Kentucky, Tennessee, and parts of other States have again produced reasonably fair crops.

The most remarkable feature in the military operations of the year is General Sherman's attempted march of 300 miles directly through the insurgent region. It tends to show a great increase of our relative strength that our General in Chief should feel able to confront and hold in check every active force of the enemy, and yet to detach a well-appointed large army to move on such an expedition. The result not yet being known, conjecture in regard to it is not here indulged.

Important movements have also occurred during the year to the effect of molding society for durability in the Union. Although short of complete success, it is much in the right direction that 12,000 citizens in each of the States of Arkansas and Louisiana have organized loyal State governments, with free constitutions, and are earnestly struggling to maintain and administer them. The movements in the same direction, more extensive though less definite, in Missouri, Kentucky, and Tennessee should not be overlooked. But Maryland presents the example of complete success. Maryland is secure to liberty and union for all the future. The genius of rebellion will no more claim Maryland. Like another foul spirit being driven out, it may seek to tear her, but it will woo her no more.

At the last session of Congress a proposed amendment of the Constitution abolishing slavery throughout the United States passed the Senate, but failed for lack of the requisite two-thirds vote in the House of Representatives. Although the present is the same Congress and nearly the same members, and without questioning the wisdom or patriotism of those who stood in opposition, I venture to recommend the reconsideration and passage of the measure at the present session. Of course the abstract question is not changed; but an intervening election shows almost certainly that the next Congress will pass the measure if this does not. Hence there is only a question of *time* as to when the proposed amendment will go to the States for their action. And as it is to so go at all events, may we not agree that the sooner the better? It is not claimed that the election has imposed a duty on members to change their views or their votes any further than, as an additional element to be considered, their judgment may be affected by it. It is the voice of the people now for the first time heard upon the question. In a great national crisis like ours unanimity of action among those seeking a common end is very desirable— almost indispensable. And yet no approach to such unanimity is attainable unless some deference shall be paid to the will of the majority simply because it is the will of the majority. In this case the common end is the maintenance of the Union, and among the means to secure that end such will, through the election, is most clearly declared in favor of such constitutional amendment.

The most reliable indication of public purpose in this country is derived through our popular elections. Judging by the recent canvass and its result, the purpose of the people within the loyal States to maintain the integrity of the Union was never more firm nor more nearly unanimous than now. The extraordinary calmness and good order with which the millions of voters met and mingled at the polls give strong assurance of this. Not only all those who supported the Union ticket, so called, but a great majority of the opposing party also may be fairly claimed to entertain and to be actuated by the same purpose. It is an unanswerable argument to this effect that no candidate for any office whatever, high or low, has ventured to seek votes on the avowal that he was for giving up the Union. There have been much impugning of motives and much heated controversy as to the proper means and best mode of advancing the Union cause, but on the distinct issue of Union or no Union the politicians have shown their instinctive knowledge that there is no diversity among the people. In affording the people the fair opportunity of showing one to another and to the world this firmness and unanimity of purpose, the election has been of vast value to the national cause.

The election has exhibited another fact not less valuable to be known— the fact that we do not approach exhaustion in the most important branch of national resources, that of living men. While it is melancholy to reflect that the war has filled so many graves and carried mourning to so many hearts, it is some relief to know that, compared with the surviving, the fallen have been so few. While corps and divisions and brigades and regiments have formed and fought and dwindled and gone out of existence, a great majority of the men who composed them are still living. The same is true of the naval service. The election returns prove this. So many voters could not else be found. The States regularly holding elections, both now and four years ago, to wit, California, Connecticut, Delaware, Illinois, Indiana, Iowa, Kentucky, Maine, Maryland, Massachusetts, Michigan, Minnesota, Missouri, New Hampshire, New Jersey, New York, Ohio, Oregon, Pennsylvania, Rhode Island, Vermont, West Virginia, and Wisconsin, cast 3,982,011 votes now, against 3,870,222 cast then, showing an aggregate now of 3,982,011. To this is to be added 33,762 cast now in the new States of Kansas and Nevada, which States did not vote in 1860, thus swelling the aggregate to 4,015,773 and the net increase during the three years and a half of war to 145,551. A table is appended showing particulars. To this again should be added the number of all soldiers in the field from Massachusetts, Rhode Island, New Jersey, Delaware, Indiana, Illinois, and California, who by the laws of those States could not vote away from their homes, and which number can not be less than 90,000. Nor yet is this all. The number in organized Territories is triple now what it was four years ago, while thousands, white and black, join us as the national arms press back the insurgent lines. So much is shown, affirmatively and negatively, by the election. It is not material to inquire *how* the increase has been produced or to show that it would have been *greater* but for the war, which is probably true. The important fact remains demonstrated that we have *more* men *now* than we had when the war *began;* that we are not exhausted nor in process of exhaustion; that we are *gaining* strength and may if need be maintain the contest indefinitely. This as to men. Material resources are now more complete and abundant than ever.

The national resources, then, are unexhausted, and, as we believe, inexhaustible. The public purpose to reestablish and maintain the national authority is unchanged, and, as we believe, unchangeable. The manner of continuing the effort remains to choose. On careful consideration of all the evidence accessible it seems to me that no attempt at negotiation with the insurgent leader could result in any good. He would accept nothing short of severance of the Union, precisely what we will not and can not give. His declarations to this effect are explicit and oft repeated. He does not attempt to deceive us. He affords us no excuse to deceive ourselves. He can not voluntarily reaccept the Union; we can not voluntarily yield it. Between him and us the issue is distinct, simple, and inflexible. It is an issue which can only be tried by war and decided by victory. If we yield, we are beaten; if the Southern people fail him, he is beaten. Either way it would be the victory and defeat following war. What is true, however, of him who heads the insurgent cause is not necessarily true of those who follow. Although he can not reaccept the Union, they can. Some of them, we know, already desire peace and reunion. The number of such may increase. They can at any moment have peace simply by laying down their arms and submitting to the national authority under the Constitution. After so much the Government could not, if it would, maintain war against them. The loyal people would not sustain or allow it. If questions should remain, we would adjust them by the peaceful means of legislation, conference, courts, and votes, operating only in constitutional and lawful channels. Some certain, and other possible, questions are and would be beyond the Executive power to adjust; as, for instance, the admission of members into Congress and whatever might require the appropriation of money. The Executive power itself would be greatly diminished by the cessation of actual war. Pardons and remissions of forfeitures, however, would still be within Executive control. In what spirit and temper this control would be exercised can be fairly judged of by the past.

A year ago general pardon and amnesty, upon specified terms, were offered to all except certain designated classes, and it was at the same time made known that the excepted classes were still within contemplation of special clemency. During the year many availed themselves of the general provision, and many more would, only that the signs of bad faith in some led to such precautionary measures as rendered the practical process less easy and certain. During the same time also special pardons have been granted to individuals of the excepted classes, and no voluntary application has been denied. Thus practically the door has been for a full year open to all except such as were not in condition to make free choice; that is, such as were in custody or under constraint. It is still so open to all. But the time may come, probably will come, when public duty shall demand that it be closed and that in lieu more rigorous measures than heretofore shall be adopted.

In presenting the abandonment of armed resistance to the national authority on the part of the insurgents as the only indispensable condition to ending the war on the part of the Government, I retract nothing heretofore said as to slavery. I repeat the declaration made a year ago, that "while I remain in my present position I shall not attempt to retract or modify the emancipation proclamation, nor shall I return to slavery any person who is free by the terms of that proclamation or by any of the acts of Congress." If the people should, by whatever mode or means, make it an Executive duty to reenslave such persons, another, and not I, must be their instrument to perform it.

In stating a single condition of peace I mean simply to say that the war will cease on the part of the Government whenever it shall have ceased on the part of those who began it.

ABRAHAM LINCOLN.

Table showing the aggregate votes in the States named at the Presidential elections respectively, in 1860 and 1864.

State.	1860.	1864.
California	118,840	*110,000
Connecticut	77,246	86,616
Delaware	16,039	16,924
Illinois	339,693	348,235
Indiana	272,143	280,645
Iowa	128,331	143,331
Kentucky	146,216	*91,300
Maine	97,918	115,141
Maryland	92,502	72,703
Massachusetts	169,533	175,487
Michigan	154,747	162,413
Minnesota	34,799	42,534
Missouri	165,538	*90,000
New Hampshire	65,953	69,111
New Jersey	121,125	128,680
New York	675,156	730,664
Ohio	442,441	470,745
Oregon	14,410	†14,410
Pennsylvania	476,442	572,697
Rhode Island	19,931	22,187
Vermont	42,844	55,811
West Virginia	46,195	33,874
Wisconsin	152,180	148,513
	3,870,222	3,982,011
Kansas	....	17,234
Nevada	....	16,528
		33,762
		3,982,011
Total	....	4,015,773
		3,870,222
Net increase	....	145,551

*Nearly.   †Estimated.

SPECIAL MESSAGES.

WASHINGTON CITY, *December 5, 1864.*

To the Senate and House of Representatives:

In conformity to the law of July 16, 1862, I most cordially recommend that Captain John A. Winslow, United States Navy, receive a vote of thanks from Congress for the skill and gallantry exhibited by him in the brilliant action, while in command of the United States steamer *Kearsarge*, which led to the total destruction of the piratical craft *Alabama* on the 19th of June, 1864—a vessel superior in tonnage, superior in number of guns, and superior in number of crew.

This recommendation is specially made in order to comply with the requirements of the ninth section of the aforesaid act, which is in the following words, namely:

That any line officer of the Navy or Marine Corps may be advanced one grade if upon recommendation of the President by name he receives the thanks of Congress for highly distinguished conduct in conflict with the enemy or for extraordinary heroism in the line of his profession.

ABRAHAM LINCOLN.

WASHINGTON CITY, *December 5, 1864.*

To the Senate and House of Representatives:

In conformity to the law of July 16, 1862, I most cordially recommend that Lieutenant William B. Cushing, United States Navy, receive a vote of thanks from Congress for his important, gallant, and perilous achievement in destroying the rebel ironclad steamer *Albemarle* on the night of the 27th of October, 1864, at Plymouth, N. C.

The destruction of so formidable a vessel, which had resisted the continued attacks of a number of our vessels on former occasions, is an important event touching our future naval and military operations, and would reflect honor on any officer, and redounds to the credit of this young officer and the few brave comrades who assisted in this successful and daring undertaking.

This recommendation is specially made in order to comply with the requirements of the ninth section of the aforesaid act, which is in the following words, namely:

That any line officer of the Navy or Marine Corps may be advanced one grade if upon recommendation of the President by name he receives the thanks of Congress for highly distinguished conduct in conflict with the enemy or for extraordinary heroism in the line of his profession.

ABRAHAM LINCOLN.

WASHINGTON CITY, *December 5, 1864.*

To the Senate of the United States:

By virtue of the authority contained in the sixth section of the act of 21st April, 1864, which enacts "that any officer in the naval service, by and with the advice and consent of the Senate, may be advanced not exceeding thirty numbers in his own grade for distinguished conduct in battle or extraordinary heroism," I recommend Commander William H. Macomb, United States Navy, for advancement in his grade ten numbers, to take rank next after Commander William Ronckendorff, for distinguished conduct in the capture of the town of Plymouth, N. C., with its batteries, ordnance stores, etc., on the 31st October, 1864, by a portion of the naval division under his command. The affair was executed in a most creditable manner. ABRAHAM LINCOLN.

WASHINGTON CITY, *December 5, 1864.*

To the Senate of the United States:

By virtue of the authority contained in the sixth section of the act of 21st April, 1864, which enacts "that any officer in the naval service, by and with the advice and consent of the Senate, may be advanced not exceeding thirty numbers in his own grade for distinguished conduct in battle or extraordinary heroism," I recommend Lieutenant-Commander James S. Thornton, United States Navy, the executive officer of the United States steamer *Kearsarge*, for advancement in his grade ten numbers, to take rank next after Lieutenant-Commander William D. Whiting, for his good conduct and faithful discharge of his duties in the brilliant action with the rebel steamer *Alabama*, which led to the destruction of that vessel on the 19th June, 1864. ABRAHAM LINCOLN.

WASHINGTON, *December 7, 1864.*

To the Senate of the United States:

In answer to the Senate's resolution of yesterday, requesting information in regard to aid furnished to the rebellion by British subjects, I transmit a report from the Secretary of State and the documents by which it was accompanied. ABRAHAM LINCOLN.

WASHINGTON, *December 13, 1864.*

To the Senate of the United States:

I transmit to the Senate, for consideration with a view to ratification, "a treaty of friendship, commerce, and navigation between the United States of America and the Republic of Honduras," signed by their respective plenipotentiaries at Comayagua on the 4th of July (1864) last. ABRAHAM LINCOLN.

WASHINGTON, *December 13, 1864.*

To the Senate of the United States:

I transmit to the Senate, for consideration with a view to ratification, "a treaty of amity, commerce, and navigation, and for the extradition of fugitive criminals, between the United States of America and the Republic of Hayti, signed by their respective plenipotentiaries at Port au Prince on the 3d of November" last.

ABRAHAM LINCOLN.

WASHINGTON, *January 7, 1865.*

To the Senate and House of Representatives:

I transmit to Congress a copy of two treaties between the United States and Belgium, for the extinguishment of the Scheldt dues, etc., concluded on the 20th of May, 1863, and 20th of July, 1863, respectively, the ratifications of which were exchanged at Brussels on the 24th of June last; and I recommend an appropriation to carry into effect the provisions thereof relative to the payment of the proportion of the United States toward the capitalization of the said dues.

ABRAHAM LINCOLN.

EXECUTIVE MANSION,
Washington, January 9, 1865.

Hon. SCHUYLER COLFAX,
Speaker House of Representatives.

SIR: I transmit herewith the letter of the Secretary of War, with accompanying report of the Adjutant-General, in reply to the resolution of the House of Representatives dated December 7, 1864, requesting me "to communicate to the House the report made by Colonel Thomas M. Key of an interview between himself and General Howell Cobb on the 14th day of June, 1862, on the bank of the Chickahominy, on the subject of the exchange of prisoners of war."

I am, sir, very respectfully, your obedient servant,

ABRAHAM LINCOLN.

WASHINGTON, *January 9, 1865.*

To the Senate of the United States:

In compliance with the resolution of the Senate of the 15th ultimo, requesting information concerning an arrangement limiting the naval armament on the Lakes, I transmit a report of this date from the Secretary of State, to whom the resolution was referred.

ABRAHAM LINCOLN.

EXECUTIVE MANSION,
Washington, January 17, 1865.

To the Senate of the United States:

I herewith lay before the Senate, for its constitutional action thereon, a treaty concluded at the Isabella Indian Reservation, in the State of Michigan, on the 18th day of October, 1864, between H. J. Alvord, special commissioner, and D. C. Leach, United States Indian agent, acting as commissioner on the part of the United States, and the chiefs and headmen of the Chippewas of Saginaw, Swan Creek, and Black River, in the State of Michigan, parties to the treaty of August 2, 1855, with amendments.

A letter of the Secretary of the Interior of the 12th instant and a copy of a communication of the Commissioner of Indian Affairs of the 22d ultimo, with inclosure, accompany the treaty.

ABRAHAM LINCOLN.

WASHINGTON, D. C., *January 31, 1865.*

Hon. H. HAMLIN,
 President of the Senate:

I transmit herewith a communication from the Secretary of War, covering papers bearing on the arrest and imprisonment of Colonel Richard T. Jacobs, lieutenant-governor of the State of Kentucky, and Colonel Frank Wolford, one of the Presidential electors of that State, requested by resolution of the Senate dated December 20, 1864.

ABRAHAM LINCOLN.

WASHINGTON, *February 4, 1865.*

To the Senate of the United States:

In compliance with the resolution of the Senate of the 13th ultimo, requesting information upon the present condition of Mexico and the case of the French war transport steamer *Rhine*, I transmit a report from the Secretary of State and the papers by which it was accompanied.

ABRAHAM LINCOLN.

WASHINGTON, *February 8, 1865.*

To the Senate and House of Representatives:

I transmit to Congress a copy of a note of the 4th instant addressed by J. Hume Burnley, esq., Her Britannic Majesty's chargé d'affaires, to the Secretary of State, relative to a sword which it is proposed to present to Captain Henry S. Stellwagen, commanding the United States frigate *Constitution*, as a mark of gratitude for his services to the British brigantine *Mersey*. The expediency of sanctioning the acceptance of the gift is submitted to your consideration.

ABRAHAM LINCOLN.

EXECUTIVE MANSION, *February 8, 1865.*

To the Honorable the Senate and House of Representatives:

The joint resolution entitled ''Joint resolution declaring certain States not entitled to representation in the electoral college'' has been signed by the Executive in deference to the view of Congress implied in its passage and presentation to him. In his own view, however, the two Houses of Congress, convened under the twelfth article of the Constitution, have complete power to exclude from counting all electoral votes deemed by them to be illegal, and it is not competent for the Executive to defeat or obstruct that power by a veto, as would be the case if his action were at all essential in the matter. He disclaims all right of the Executive to interfere in any way in the matter of canvassing or counting electoral votes, and he also disclaims that by signing said resolution he has expressed any opinion on the recitals of the preamble or any judgment of his own upon the subject of the resolution.   ABRAHAM LINCOLN.

WASHINGTON, *February 10, 1865.*

To the Senate of the United States:

In answer to the resolution of the Senate of the 8th instant, requesting information concerning recent conversations or communications with insurgents under Executive sanction, I transmit a report from the Secretary of State, to whom the resolution was referred.

ABRAHAM LINCOLN.

EXECUTIVE MANSION, *February 10, 1865.*

To the Honorable the House of Representatives:

In response to your resolution of the 8th instant, requesting information in relation to a conference recently held in Hampton Roads, I have the honor to state that on the day of the date I gave Francis P. Blair, sr., a card, written on as follows, to wit:

DECEMBER 28, 1864.

Allow the bearer, F. P. Blair, sr., to pass our lines, go South, and return.

A. LINCOLN.

That at the time I was informed that Mr. Blair sought the card as a means of getting to Richmond, Va., but he was given no authority to speak or act for the Government, nor was I informed of anything he would say or do on his own account or otherwise. Afterwards Mr. Blair told me that he had been to Richmond and had seen Mr. Jefferson Davis; and he (Mr. B.) at the same time left with me a manuscript letter, as follows, to wit:

F. P. BLAIR, Esq.   RICHMOND, VA., *January 12, 1865.*

SIR: I have deemed it proper, and probably desirable to you, to give you in this form the substance of remarks made by me, to be repeated by you to President Lincoln, etc., etc.

I have no disposition to find obstacles in forms, and am willing, now as heretofore, to enter into negotiations for the restoration of peace, and am ready to send a commission whenever I have reason to suppose it will be received, or to receive a commission if the United States Government shall choose to send one. That notwithstanding the rejection of our former offers, I would, if you could promise that a commissioner, minister, or other agent would be received, appoint one immediately, and renew the effort to enter into conference with a view to secure peace to the two countries.

Yours, etc., JEFFERSON DAVIS.

Afterwards, and with the view that it should be shown to Mr. Davis, I wrote and delivered to Mr. Blair a letter, as follows, to wit:

WASHINGTON, *January 18, 1865.*
F. P. BLAIR, Esq.

SIR: Your having shown me Mr. Davis's letter to you of the 12th instant, you may say to him that I have constantly been, am now, and shall continue ready to receive any agent whom he or any other influential person now resisting the national authority may informally send to me with the view of securing peace to the people of our one common country.

Yours, etc., A. LINCOLN.

Afterwards Mr. Blair dictated for and authorized me to make an entry on the back of my retained copy of the letter last above recited, which entry is as follows:

JANUARY 28, 1865.

To-day Mr. Blair tells me that on the 21st instant he delivered to Mr. Davis the original of which the within is a copy, and left it with him; that at the time of delivering it Mr. Davis read it over twice in Mr. Blair's presence, at the close of which he (Mr. Blair) remarked that the part about "our one common country" related to the part of Mr. Davis's letter about "the two countries," to which Mr. Davis replied that he so understood it. A. LINCOLN.

Afterwards the Secretary of War placed in my hands the following telegram, indorsed by him, as appears:

OFFICE UNITED STATES MILITARY TELEGRAPH,
War Department.

The following telegram received at Washington January 29, 1865, from headquarters Army of James, 6.30 p. m., January 29, 1865:

"Hon. EDWIN M. STANTON,
"*Secretary of War:*

"The following dispatch just received from Major-General Parke, who refers it to me for my action. I refer it to you in Lieutenant-General Grant's absence.

"E. O. C. ORD, *Major-General, Commanding.*"

'HEADQUARTERS ARMY OF POTOMAC,
'*January 29, 1865—4 p. m.*
'Major-General E. O. C. ORD,
'*Headquarters Army of James:*

'The following dispatch is forwarded to you for your action. Since I have no knowledge of General Grant's having had any understanding of this kind, I refer the matter to you as the ranking officer present in the two armies.

'JNO. G. PARKE, *Major-General, Commanding.*'

'FROM HEADQUARTERS NINTH ARMY CORPS, *29th.*

'Major-General JNO. G. PARKE,

'*Headquarters Army of Potomac:*

'Alexander H. Stephens, R. M. T. Hunter, and J. A. Campbell desire to cross my lines, in accordance with an understanding claimed to exist with Lieutenant-General Grant, on their way to Washington as peace commissioners. Shall they be admitted? They desire an early answer, to come through immediately. Would like to reach City Point to-night if they can. If they can not do this, they would like to come through at 10 a. m. to-morrow morning.

'O. B. WILCOX,

'*Major-General, Commanding Ninth Corps.*'

"JANUARY 29—8.30 p. m.

"Respectfully referred to the President for such instructions as he may be pleased to give.

"EDWIN M. STANTON,

"*Secretary of War.*"

It appears that about the time of placing the foregoing telegram in my hands the Secretary of War dispatched General Ord as follows, to wit:

WAR DEPARTMENT,

Washington City, January 29, 1865—10 p. m.

Major-General ORD.   (Sent at 2 a. m. 30th.)

SIR: This Department has no knowledge of any understanding by General Grant to allow any person to come within his lines as commissioner of any sort. You will therefore allow no one to come into your lines under such character or profession until you receive the President's instructions, to whom your telegram will be submitted for his directions.

EDWIN M. STANTON,

Secretary of War.

Afterwards, by my direction, the Secretary of War telegraphed General Ord as follows, to wit:

WAR DEPARTMENT,

Washington, D. C., January 30, 1865—10.30 a. m.

Major-General E. O. C. ORD,

Headquarters Army of the James.

SIR: By direction of the President, you are instructed to inform the three gentlemen, Messrs. Stephens, Hunter, and Campbell, that a messenger will be dispatched to them at or near where they now are without unnecessary delay.

EDWIN M. STANTON,

Secretary of War.

Afterwards I prepared and put into the hands of Major Thomas T. Eckert the following instructions and message:

EXECUTIVE MANSION,

Washington, January 30, 1865.

Major T. T. ECKERT.

SIR: You will proceed with the documents placed in your hands, and on reaching General Ord will deliver him the letter addressed to him by the Secretary of War; then, by General Ord's assistance, procure an interview with Messrs. Stephens, Hunter, and Campbell, or any of them. Deliver to him or them the paper on which your own letter is written. Note on the copy which you retain the time of delivery and to whom delivered. Receive their answer in writing, waiting a reasonable time for it, and which, if it contain their decision to come through without further condition, will be your warrant to ask General Ord to pass them through, as directed in the letter of the Secretary of War to him. If by their answer they decline to come, or propose other terms, do not have them pass through. And this being your whole duty, return and report to me.

A. LINCOLN.

CITY POINT, VA., *February 1, 1865.*

Messrs. ALEXANDER H. STEPHENS, J. A. CAMPBELL, and R. M. T. HUNTER.

GENTLEMEN: I am instructed by the President of the United States to place this paper in your hands, with the information that if you pass through the United States military lines it will be understood that you do so for the purpose of an informal conference on the basis of the letter a copy of which is on the reverse side of this sheet, and that if you choose to pass on such understanding, and so notify me in writing, I will procure the commanding general to pass you through the lines and to Fortress Monroe under such military precautions as he may deem prudent, and at which place you will be met in due time by some person or persons for the purpose of such informal conference; and, further, that you shall have protection, safe conduct, and safe return in all events.

THOMAS T. ECKERT,
Major and Aid-de-Camp.

WASHINGTON, *January 18, 1865.*

F. P. BLAIR, Esq.

SIR: Your having shown me Mr. Davis's letter to you of the 12th instant, you may say to him that I have constantly been, am now, and shall continue ready to receive any agent whom he or any other influential person now resisting the national authority may informally send to me with the view of securing peace to the people of our one common country.

Yours, etc.,

A. LINCOLN.

Afterwards, but before Major Eckert had departed, the following dispatch was received from General Grant:

OFFICE UNITED STATES MILITARY TELEGRAPH,
War Department.

The following telegram received at Washington January 31, 1865, from City Point, Va., 10.30 a. m., January 30, 1865:

"His Excellency ABRAHAM LINCOLN,
"*President of the United States:*

"The following communication was received here last evening:

'PETERSBURG, VA., *January 30, 1865.*

'Lieutenant-General U. S. GRANT,
'*Commanding Armies United States.*

'SIR: We desire to pass your lines under safe conduct, and to proceed to Washington to hold a conference with President Lincoln upon the subject of the existing war, and with a view of ascertaining upon what terms it may be terminated, in pursuance of the course indicated by him in his letter to Mr. Blair of January 18, 1865, of which we presume you have a copy; and if not, we wish to see you in person, if convenient, and to confer with you upon the subject.

'Very respectfully, yours,

'ALEXANDER H. STEPHENS.
'J. A. CAMPBELL.
'R. M. T. HUNTER.'

"I have sent directions to receive these gentlemen, and expect to have them at my quarters this evening, awaiting your instructions.

> "U. S. GRANT,
> "*Lieutenant-General, Commanding Armies United States.*"

This, it will be perceived, transferred General Ord's agency in the matter to General Grant. I resolved, however, to send Major Eckert forward with his message, and accordingly telegraphed General Grant as follows, to wit:

> EXECUTIVE MANSION,
> *Washington, January 31, 1865.*
> (Sent at 1.30 p. m.)

Lieutenant-General GRANT,
　　　City Point, Va.:

A messenger is coming to you on the business contained in your dispatch. Detain the gentlemen in comfortable quarters until he arrives, and then act upon the message he brings as far as applicable, it having been made up to pass through General Ord's hands, and when the gentlemen were supposed to be beyond our lines.

> A. LINCOLN.

When Major Eckert departed, he bore with him a letter of the Secretary of War to General Grant, as follows, to wit:

> WAR DEPARTMENT,
> *Washington, D. C., January 30, 1865.*

Lieutenant-General GRANT,
　　　Commanding, etc.

GENERAL: The President desires that you will please procure for the bearer, Major Thomas T. Eckert, an interview with Messrs. Stephens, Hunter, and Campbell, and if on his return to you he requests it pass them through our lines to Fortress Monroe by such route and under such military precautions as you may deem prudent, giving them protection and comfortable quarters while there, and that you let none of this have any effect upon your movements or plans.

By order of the President:

> EDWIN M. STANTON,
> *Secretary of War.*

Supposing the proper point to be then reached, I dispatched the Secretary of State with the following instructions, Major Eckert, however, going ahead of him:

> EXECUTIVE MANSION,
> *Washington, January 31, 1865.*

Hon. WILLIAM H. SEWARD,
　　　Secretary of State:

You will proceed to Fortress Monroe, Va., there to meet and informally confer with Messrs. Stephens, Hunter, and Campbell on the basis of my letter to F. P. Blair, esq., of January 18, 1865, a copy of which you have.

You will make known to them that three things are indispensable, to wit:

1. The restoration of the national authority throughout all the States.

2. No receding by the Executive of the United States on the slavery question from the position assumed thereon in the ate annual message to Congress and in preceding documents.

3. No cessation of hostilities short of an end of the war and the disbanding of all forces hostile to the Government.

You will inform them that all propositions of theirs not inconsistent with the above will be considered and passed upon in a spirit of sincere liberality. You will hear all they may choose to say and report it to me.

You will not assume to definitely consummate anything.

Yours, etc.,
ABRAHAM LINCOLN.

On the day of its date the following telegram was sent to General Grant:

WAR DEPARTMENT,
Washington, D. C., February 1, 1865.
(Sent at 9.30 a. m.)

Lieutenant-General GRANT,
City Point, Va.:

Let nothing which is transpiring change, hinder, or delay your military movements or plans.
A. LINCOLN.

Afterwards the following dispatch was received from General Grant:

OFFICE UNITED STATES MILITARY TELEGRAPH,
War Department.

The following telegram received at Washington 2.30 p. m. February 1, 1865, from City Point, Va., February 1, 12.30 p. m., 1865:

"His Excellency A. LINCOLN,
"*President United States:*

"Your dispatch received. There will be no armistice in consequence of the presence of Mr. Stephens and others within our lines. The troops are kept in readiness to move at the shortest notice if occasion should justify it.

"U. S. GRANT, *Lieutenant-General.*"

To notify Major Eckert that the Secretary of State would be at Fortress Monroe, and to put them in communication, the following dispatch was sent:

WAR DEPARTMENT,
Washington, D. C., February 1, 1865.

Major T. T. ECKERT,
Care of General Grant, City Point, Va.:

Call at Fortress Monroe and put yourself under direction of Mr. S., whom you will find there.
A. LINCOLN.

On the morning of the 2d instant the following telegrams were received by me respectively from the Secretary of State and Major Eckert:

FORT MONROE, VA., *February 1, 1865—11.30 p. m.*

The PRESIDENT OF THE UNITED STATES:

Arrived at 10 this evening. Richmond party not here. I remain here.

WILLIAM H. SEWARD.

CITY POINT, VA., *February 1, 1865—10 p. m.*

His Excellency A. LINCOLN,
President of the United States:

I have the honor to report the delivery of your communication and my letter at 4.15 this afternoon, to which I received a reply at 6 p. m., but not satisfactory.

At 8 p. m. the following note, addressed to General Grant, was received:

"Lieutenant-General GRANT.   "CITY POINT, VA., *February 1, 1865*.

"SIR: We desire to go to Washington City to confer informally with the President personally in reference to the matters mentioned in his letter to Mr. Blair of the 18th January ultimo, without any personal compromise on any question in the letter. We have the permission to do so from the authorities in Richmond.

"Very respectfully, yours,

"ALEX. H. STEPHENS.
"R. M. T. HUNTER.
"J. A. CAMPBELL."

At 9.30 p. m. I notified them that they could not proceed further unless they complied with the terms expressed in my letter. The point of meeting designated in the above note would not, in my opinion, be insisted upon. Think Fort Monroe would be acceptable. Having complied with my instructions, I will return to Washington to-morrow unless otherwise ordered.

THOS. T. ECKERT, *Major, etc.*

On reading this dispatch of Major Eckert I was about to recall him and the Secretary of State, when the following telegram of General Grant to the Secretary of War was shown me:

OFFICE UNITED STATES MILITARY TELEGRAPH,
War Department.

The following telegram received at Washington 4.35 a. m. February 2, 1865, from City Point, Va., February 1, 10.30 p. m., 1865:

"Hon. EDWIN M. STANTON,
        "*Secretary of War:*

"Now that the interview between Major Eckert, under his written instructions, and Mr. Stephens and party has ended, I will state confidentially, but not officially to become a matter of record, that I am convinced upon conversation with Messrs. Stephens and Hunter that their intentions are good and their desire sincere to restore peace and union. I have not felt myself at liberty to express even views of my own or to account for my reticency. This has placed me in an awkward position, which I could have avoided by not seeing them in the first instance. I fear now their going back without any expression from anyone in authority will have a bad influence. At the same time, I recognize the difficulties in the way of receiving these informal commissioners at this time, and do not know what to recommend. I am sorry, however, that Mr. Lincoln can not have an interview with the two named in this dispatch, if not all three now within our lines. Their letter to me was all that the President's instructions contemplated to secure their safe conduct if they had used the same language to Major Eckert.

"U. S. GRANT, *Lieutenant-General.*"

This dispatch of General Grant changed my purpose, and accordingly I telegraphed him and the Secretary of State, respectively, as follows:

WAR DEPARTMENT,
Washington, D. C., February 2, 1865.
(Sent at 9 a. m.)

Lieutenant-General GRANT,
        City Point, Va.:

Say to the gentlemen I will meet them personally at Fortress Monroe as soon as I can get there.

A. LINCOLN.

WAR DEPARTMENT,
Washington, D. C., February 2, 1865.
(Sent at 9 a. m.)

Hon. WILLIAM H. SEWARD,
Fortress Monroe, Va.:

Induced by a dispatch from General Grant, I join you at Fort Monroe as soon as I can come.

A. LINCOLN.

Before starting, the following dispatch was shown me. I proceeded, nevertheless.

OFFICE UNITED STATES MILITARY TELEGRAPH,
War Department.

The following telegram received at Washington February 2, 1865, from City Point, Va., 9 a. m., February 2, 1865:

"Hon. WILLIAM H. SEWARD,
"*Secretary of State, Fort Monroe:*

"The gentlemen here have accepted the proposed terms, and will leave for Fort Monroe at 9.30 a. m.

"U. S. GRANT,
"*Lieutenant-General.*"

(Copy to Hon. Edwin M. Stanton, Secretary of War, Washington.)

On the night of the 2d I reached Hampton Roads, found the Secretary of State and Major Eckert on a steamer anchored offshore, and learned of them that the Richmond gentlemen were on another steamer also anchored offshore, in the Roads, and that the Secretary of State had not yet seen or communicated with them. I ascertained that Major Eckert had literally complied with his instructions, and I saw for the first time the answer of the Richmond gentlemen to him, which in his dispatch to me of the 1st he characterizes as "not satisfactory." That answer is as follows, to wit:

CITY POINT, VA., *February 1, 1865.*

THOMAS T. ECKERT,
Major and Aid-de-Camp.

MAJOR: Your note, delivered by yourself this day, has been considered. In reply we have to say that we were furnished with a copy of the letter of President Lincoln to Francis P. Blair, esq., of the 18th of January ultimo, another copy of which is appended to your note.

Our instructions are contained in a letter of which the following is a copy:

"RICHMOND, *January 28, 1865.*

"In conformity with the letter of Mr. Lincoln, of which the foregoing is a copy, you are to proceed to Washington City for informal conference with him upon the issues involved in the existing war, and for the purpose of securing peace to the two countries.

'With great respect, your obedient servant,

"JEFFERSON DAVIS."

The substantial object to be obtained by the informal conference is to ascertain upon what terms the existing war can be terminated honorably.

Our instructions contemplate a personal interview between President Lincoln and ourselves at Washington City, but with this explanation we are ready to meet any person or persons that President Lincoln may appoint at such place as he may designate.

Our earnest desire is that a just and honorable peace may be agreed upon, and we are prepared to receive or to submit propositions which may possibly lead to the attainment of that end.

Very respectfully, yours,

ALEXANDER H. STEPHENS.
R. M. T. HUNTER.
JOHN A. CAMPBELL.

A note of these gentlemen, subsequently addressed to General Grant, has already been given in Major Eckert's dispatch of the 1st instant.

I also here saw, for the first time, the following note addressed by the Richmond gentlemen to Major Eckert:

THOMAS T. ECKERT,   CITY POINT, VA., *February 2, 1865.*
    Major and Aid-de-Camp.

MAJOR: In reply to your verbal statement that your instructions did not allow you to alter the conditions upon which a passport could be given to us, we say that we are willing to proceed to Fortress Monroe and there to have an informal conference with any person or persons that President Lincoln may appoint on the basis of his letter to Francis P. Blair of the 18th of January ultimo, or upon any other terms or conditions that he may hereafter propose not inconsistent with the essential principles of self-government and popular rights, upon which our institutions are founded.

It is our earnest wish to ascertain, after a free interchange of ideas and information, upon what principles and terms, if any, a just and honorable peace can be established without the further effusion of blood, and to contribute our utmost efforts to accomplish such a result.

We think it better to add that in accepting your passport we are not to be understood as committing ourselves to anything but to carry to this informal conference the views and feelings above expressed.

Very respectfully, yours, etc.,

ALEXANDER H. STEPHENS.
J. A. CAMPBELL.
R. M. T. HUNTER.

NOTE.—The above communication was delivered to me at Fort Monroe at 4.30 p. m. February 2 by Lieutenant-Colonel Babcock, of General Grant's staff.

THOMAS T. ECKERT,
Major and Aid-de-Camp.

On the morning of the 3d the three gentlemen, Messrs. Stephens, Hunter, and Campbell, came aboard of our steamer and had an interview with the Secretary of State and myself of several hours' duration. No question of preliminaries to the meeting was then and there made or mentioned; no other person was present; no papers were exchanged or produced; and it was in advance agreed that the conversation was to be informal and verbal merely. On our part the whole substance of the instructions to the Secretary of State hereinbefore recited was stated and insisted upon, and nothing was said inconsistent therewith; while by the other party it was not said that in any event or on any condition they *ever* would consent to reunion, and yet they equally omitted to declare that they *never* would so consent. They seemed to desire a postponement of that question and the adoption of some other course first, which, as some of them seemed to argue, might or might not lead to reunion, but which course we thought would amount to an indefinite postponement. The conference ended without result.

The foregoing, containing, as is believed, all the information sought, is respectfully submitted. ABRAHAM LINCOLN.

WASHINGTON, *February 13, 1865.*

To the Senate and House of Representatives:

I transmit to Congress a copy of a dispatch of the 12th ultimo, addressed to the Secretary of State by the minister resident of the United States at Stockholm, relating to an international exhibition to be held at Bergen, in Norway, during the coming summer. The expediency of any legislation upon the subject is submitted for your consideration.

ABRAHAM LINCOLN.

WASHINGTON, *February 13, 1865.*

To the Senate and House of Representatives:

I transmit to Congress a copy of a note of the 2d instant, addressed to the Secretary of State by the Commander J. C. de Figaniere a Moraô, envoy extraordinary and minister plenipotentiary of His Most Faithful Majesty the King of Portugal, calling attention to a proposed international exhibition at the city of Oporto, to be opened in August next, and inviting contributions thereto of the products of American manufactures and industry. The expediency of any legislation on the subject is submitted for your consideration. ABRAHAM LINCOLN.

WASHINGTON, *February 25, 1865.*

To the Senate of the United States:

In compliance with the resolution of the Senate of the 23d instant, I transmit herewith a report from the Secretary of War, with the accompanying General Orders, No. 23,* issued by Major-General Banks at New Orleans, February 3, 1864. ABRAHAM LINCOLN.

EXECUTIVE MANSION,
Washington, February 27, 1865.

To the Senate of the United States:

I herewith lay before the Senate, for its constitutional action thereon, a treaty made and concluded with the Klamath and Modoc tribes of Indians of Oregon, at Fort Klamath, on the 5th day of October, 1864.

A letter of the Secretary of the Interior of this date, a copy of the

---

* On the subject of compensated plantation labor, public or private.

report of the Commissioner of Indian Affairs of the 24th instant, and a communication of the superintendent of Indian affairs in Oregon accompany the treaty.

ABRAHAM LINCOLN.

EXECUTIVE MANSION,
Washington, D. C., February 28, 1865.

Hon. H. HAMLIN,
    President United States Senate.

SIR: In reply to the resolution of the Senate dated February 14, 1865, I transmit herewith a communication from the Secretary of War, forwarding a copy of the report of the court of inquiry "in respect to the explosion of the mine in front of Petersburg."

I am, sir, very respectfully, your obedient servant,

ABRAHAM LINCOLN.

WASHINGTON, D. C., *March 2, 1865.*

Hon. SCHUYLER COLFAX,
    Speaker of the House of Representatives:

I transmit herewith the report of the Secretary of War, which, with my permission, has been delayed until the present time to enable the Lieutenant-General to furnish his report.

A. LINCOLN.

[The same message was addressed to the President of the Senate.]

WASHINGTON, *March 3, 1865.*

To the Senate and House of Representatives:

I herewith transmit to Congress a report, dated 1st instant, with the accompanying papers, received from the Secretary of State in compliance with the requirements of the eighteenth section of the act entitled "An act to regulate the diplomatic and consular systems of the United States," approved August 18, 1856.

ABRAHAM LINCOLN.

VETO MESSAGE.*

EXECUTIVE MANSION, *January 5, 1865.*

To the House of Representatives of the United States:

I herewith return to your honorable body, in which it originated, a "Joint resolution to correct certain clerical errors in the internal-revenue act," without my approval.

My reason for so doing is that I am informed that this joint resolution

---

* Pocket veto.

was prepared during the last moments of the last session of Congress for the purpose of correcting certain errors of reference in the internal-revenue act which were discovered on an examination of an official copy procured from the State Department a few hours only before the adjournment. It passed the House and went to the Senate, where a vote was taken upon it, but by some accident it was not presented to the President of the Senate for his signature.

Since the adjournment of the last session of Congress other errors of a kind similar to those which this resolution was designed to correct have been discovered in the law, and it is now thought most expedient to include all the necessary corrections in one act or resolution.

The attention of the proper committee of the House has, I am informed, been already directed to the preparation of a bill for this purpose.

ABRAHAM LINCOLN.

PROCLAMATIONS.

By the President of the United States.

A PROCLAMATION.

Whereas by the act approved July 4, 1864, entitled "An act further to regulate and provide for the enrolling and calling out the national forces, and for other purposes," it is provided that the President of the United States may, "at his discretion, at any time hereafter, call for any number of men, as volunteers for the respective terms of one, two, and three years for military service," and "that in case the quota or any part thereof of any town, township, ward of a city, precinct, or election district, or of any county not so subdivided, shall not be filled within the space of fifty days after such call, then the President shall immediately order a draft for one year to fill such quota or any part thereof which may be unfilled;" and

Whereas by the credits allowed in accordance with the act of Congress on the call for 500,000 men, made July 18, 1864, the number of men to be obtained under that call was reduced to 280,000; and

Whereas the operations of the enemy in certain States have rendered it impracticable to procure from them their full quotas of troops under said call; and

Whereas from the foregoing causes but 240,000 men have been put into the Army, Navy, and Marine Corps under the said call of July 18, 1864, leaving a deficiency on that call of two hundred and sixty thousand (260,000):

Now, therefore, I, Abraham Lincoln, President of the United States of

America, in order to supply the aforesaid deficiency and to provide for casualties in the military and naval service of the United States, do issue this my call for three hundred thousand (300,000) volunteers to serve for one, two, or three years. The quotas of the States, districts, and subdistricts under this call will be assigned by the War Department through the bureau of the Provost-Marshal-General of the United States, and "in case the quota or any part thereof of any town, township, ward of a city, precinct, or election district, or of any county not so subdivided, shall not be filled" before the 15th day of February, 1865, then a draft shall be made to fill such quota or any part thereof under this call which may be unfilled on said 15th day of February, 1865.

In testimony whereof I have hereunto set my hand and caused the seal of the United States to be affixed.

[SEAL.]   Done at the city of Washington, this 19th day of December, A. D. 1864, and of the Independence of the United States the eighty-ninth.

ABRAHAM LINCOLN.

By the President:
        WILLIAM H. SEWARD,
                Secretary of State.

BY THE PRESIDENT OF THE UNITED STATES OF AMERICA.

A PROCLAMATION.

Whereas the act of Congress of the 28th of September, 1850, entitled "An act to create additional collection districts in the State of California, and to change the existing districts therein, and to modify the existing collection districts in the United States," extends to merchandise warehoused under bond the privilege of being exported to the British North American Provinces adjoining the United States in the manner prescribed in the act of Congress of the 3d of March, 1845, which designates certain frontier ports through which merchandise may be exported, and further provides "that such other ports situated on the frontiers of the United States adjoining the British North American Provinces as may hereafter be found expedient may have extended to them the like privileges on the recommendation of the Secretary of the Treasury and proclamation duly made by the President of the United States specially designating the ports to which the aforesaid privileges are to be extended:"

Now, therefore, I, Abraham Lincoln, President of the United States of America, in accordance with the recommendation of the Secretary of the Treasury, do hereby declare and proclaim that the port of St. Albans, in the State of Vermont, is and shall be entitled to all the privileges in regard to the exportation of merchandise in bond to the British North American Provinces adjoining the United States which are extended to the ports enumerated in the seventh section of the act of Congress of the 3d of March, 1845, aforesaid, from and after the date of this proclamation.

In witness whereof I have hereunto set my hand and caused the seal of the United States to be affixed.

[SEAL.]   Done at the city of Washington, this 10th day of January, A. D. 1865, and of the Independence of the United States of America the eighty-ninth.

ABRAHAM LINCOLN.

By the President:
WILLIAM H. SEWARD,
Secretary of State.

BY THE PRESIDENT OF THE UNITED STATES OF AMERICA.

A PROCLAMATION.

Whereas objects of interest to the United States require that the Senate should be convened at 12 o'clock on the 4th of March next to receive and act upon such communications as may be made to it on the part of the Executive:

Now, therefore, I, Abraham Lincoln, President of the United States, have considered it to be my duty to issue this my proclamation, declaring that an extraordinary occasion requires the Senate of the United States to convene for the transaction of business at the Capitol, in the city of Washington, on the 4th day of March next, at 12 o'clock at noon on that day, of which all who shall at that time be entitled to act as members of that body are hereby required to take notice.

Given under my hand and the seal of the United States at Washington, the 17th day of February, A. D. 1865, and of the Independence of the United States of America the eighty-ninth.

[SEAL.]

ABRAHAM LINCOLN.

By the President:
WILLIAM H. SEWARD,
Secretary of State.

EXECUTIVE ORDERS.

EXECUTIVE MANSION, *December 10, 1864.*

Ordered, first. That Major-General William F. Smith and the Hon. Henry Stanbery be, and they are hereby, appointed special commissioners to investigate and report, for the information of the President, upon the civil and military administration in the military division bordering upon and west of the Mississippi, under such instructions as shall be issued by authority of the President and the War Department.

Second. Said commissioners shall have power to examine witnesses upon oath, and to take such proofs, orally or in writing, upon the subject-matters of investigation as they may deem expedient, and return the same together with their report.

Third. All officers and persons in the military, naval, and revenue services, or in any branch of the public service under the authority of the United States Government, are required, upon subpœna issued by direction of the said commissioners, to appear before them at such time and place as may be designated in said subpœna and to give testimony on oath touching such matters as may be inquired of by the commissioners, and to produce such books, papers, writings, and documents as they may be notified or required to produce by the commissioners, and as may be in their possession.

Fourth. Said special commissioners shall also investigate and report upon any other matters that may hereafter be directed by the Secretary of War, and shall with all convenient dispatch make report to him in writing of their investigation, and shall also from time to time make special reports to the Secretary of War upon such matters as they may deem of importance to the public interests.

Fifth. The Secretary of War shall assign to the said commissioners such aid and assistance as may be required for the performance of their duties, and make such just and reasonable allowances and compensation for the said commissioners and for the persons employed by them as he may deem proper.

ABRAHAM LINCOLN.

DEPARTMENT OF STATE,
Washington, December 17, 1864.

The President directs that, except immigrant passengers directly entering an American port by sea, henceforth no traveler shall be allowed to enter the United States from a foreign country without a passport. If a citizen, the passport must be from this Department or from some United States minister or consul abroad; and if an alien, from the competent authority of his own country, the passport to be countersigned by a diplomatic agent or consul of the United States. This regulation is intended to apply especially to persons proposing to come to the United States from the neighboring British Provinces. Its observance will be strictly enforced by all officers, civil, military, and naval, in the service of the United States, and the State and municipal authorities are requested to aid in its execution. It is expected, however, that no immigrant passenger coming in manner aforesaid will be obstructed, or any other persons who may set out on their way hither before intelligence of this regulation could reasonably be expected to reach the country from which they may have started.

WILLIAM H. SEWARD.

WASHINGTON, D. C., *December 31, 1864.*

By the authority conferred upon the President of the United States by the second section of the act of Congress approved July 2, 1864, entitled "An act to amend an act to aid in the construction of a railroad and telegraph line from the Missouri River to the Pacific Ocean," etc., I, Abraham Lincoln, President of the United States, do hereby designate the Merchants' National Bank, Boston; the Chicago and Rock Island Railroad Company's office, Chicago; the First National Bank at Philadelphia; the First National Bank at Baltimore; the First National Bank at Cincinnati, and the Third National Bank at St. Louis, in addition to the general office of the Union Pacific Railroad Company in the city of New York, as the places at which the said Union Pacific Railroad Company shall cause books to be kept open to receive subscriptions to the capital stock of said company. ABRAHAM LINCOLN.

EXECUTIVE MANSION, *Washington City, January 20, 1865.*

Ordered, That no clearances for the exportation of hay from the United States be granted until further orders, unless the same shall have been placed on shipboard before the publication hereof.

ABRAHAM LINCOLN.

EXECUTIVE MANSION, *Washington City, February 6, 1865.*

Whereas complaints are made in some localities respecting the assignments of quotas and credits allowed for the pending call of troops to fill up the armies:

Now, in order to determine all controversies in respect thereto and to avoid any delay in filling up the armies, it is ordered that the Attorney-General, Brigadier-General Richard Delafield, and Colonel C. W. Foster be, and they are hereby, constituted a board to examine into the proper quotas and credits of the respective States and districts under the call of December 19, 1864, with directions, if any errors be found therein, to make such corrections as the law and facts may require and report their determination to the Provost-Marshal-General. The determination of said board to be final and conclusive, and the draft to be made in conformity therewith.

2. The Provost-Marshal-General is ordered to make the draft in the respective districts as speedily as the same can be done after the 15th of this month. ABRAHAM LINCOLN.

WASHINGTON, *February 13, 1865.*

To the Military Officers Commanding in West Tennessee:

While I can not order as within requested, allow me to say that it is my wish for you to relieve the people from all burdens, harassments, and oppressions so far as is possible consistently with your military necessities;

that the object of the war being to restore and maintain the blessings of peace and good government, I desire you to help, and not hinder, every advance in that direction.

Of your military necessities you must judge and execute, but please do so in the spirit and with the purpose above indicated.

ABRAHAM LINCOLN.

[From the Daily National Intelligencer, February 22, 1865.]

DEPARTMENT OF STATE,
Washington, February 21, 1865.

The Department buildings will be illuminated on the night of Washington's birthday, in honor of the recent triumphs of the Union.

By order of the President:

WILLIAM H. SEWARD.

SECOND INAUGURAL ADDRESS.

FELLOW-COUNTRYMEN: At this second appearing to take the oath of the Presidential office there is less occasion for an extended address than there was at the first. Then a statement somewhat in detail of a course to be pursued seemed fitting and proper. Now, at the expiration of four years, during which public declarations have been constantly called forth on every point and phase of the great contest which still absorbs the attention and engrosses the energies of the nation, little that is new could be presented. The progress of our arms, upon which all else chiefly depends, is as well known to the public as to myself, and it is, I trust, reasonably satisfactory and encouraging to all. With high hope for the future, no prediction in regard to it is ventured.

On the occasion corresponding to this four years ago all thoughts were anxiously directed to an impending civil war. All dreaded it, all sought to avert it. While the inaugural address was being delivered from this place, devoted altogether to *saving* the Union without war, insurgent agents were in the city seeking to *destroy* it without war—seeking to dissolve the Union and divide effects by negotiation. Both parties deprecated war, but one of them would *make* war rather than let the nation survive, and the other would *accept* war rather than let it perish, and the war came.

One-eighth of the whole population were colored slaves, not distributed generally over the Union, but localized in the southern part of it. These slaves constituted a peculiar and powerful interest. All knew that this interest was somehow the cause of the war. To strengthen, perpetuate, and extend this interest was the object for which the insurgents would rend the Union even by war, while the Government claimed no right to do more than to restrict the territorial enlargement of it. Neither party expected for the war the magnitude or the duration which it has already attained. Neither anticipated that the *cause* of the conflict might cease with or even before the conflict itself should cease. Each looked for an easier triumph, and a result less fundamental and astounding. Both read the same Bible and pray to the same God, and each invokes His aid against the other. It may seem strange that any men should dare to ask a just God's assistance in wringing their bread from the sweat of other men's faces, but let us judge not, that we be not judged. The prayers of both could not be answered. That of neither has been answered fully. The Almighty has His own purposes. "Woe unto the world because of offenses; for it must needs be that offenses come, but woe to that man by whom the offense cometh." If we shall suppose that American slavery is one of those offenses which, in the providence of God, must needs come, but which, having continued through His appointed time, He now wills to remove, and that He gives to both North and South this terrible war as the woe due to those by whom the offense came, shall we discern therein any departure from those divine attributes which the believers in a living God always ascribe to Him? Fondly do we hope, fervently do we pray, that this mighty scourge of war may speedily pass away. Yet, if God wills that it continue until all the wealth piled by the bondsman's two hundred and fifty years of unrequited toil shall be sunk, and until every drop of blood drawn with the lash shall be paid by another drawn with the sword, as was said three thousand years ago, so still it must be said "the judgments of the Lord are true and righteous altogether."

With malice toward none, with charity for all, with firmness in the right as God gives us to see the right, let us strive on to finish the work we are in, to bind up the nation's wounds, to care for him who shall have borne the battle and for his widow and his orphan, to do all which may achieve and cherish a just and lasting peace among ourselves and with all nations.

MARCH 4, 1865.

SPECIAL MESSAGES.

WASHINGTON, D. C., *March 8, 1865.*

To the Senate of the United States:

The fourth section of the law of 16th January, 1857, provides that reserved officers may be promoted on the reserved list, by and with the advice and consent of the Senate, and under this authority various officers of the Navy have been promoted one grade from time to time.

I therefore nominate Commander John J. Young, now on the reserved list, to be a captain in the Navy on the reserved list from the 12th August, 1854, the date when he was entitled to his regular promotion had he not been overslaughed. It is due to this officer to state that he was passed over in consequence of physical disability, this disability having occurred in the discharge of his duties; and prior to his misfortune he bore the reputation of an efficient and correct officer, and subsequently has evinced a willingness to perform whatever duties were assigned him.

ABRAHAM LINCOLN.

WASHINGTON, *March 8, 1865.*

To the Senate of the United States:

In answer to the Senate's resolution of the 6th instant, requesting the return of a certain joint resolution,* I transmit a report from the Secretary of State.

ABRAHAM LINCOLN.

PROCLAMATIONS.

BY THE PRESIDENT OF THE UNITED STATES OF AMERICA.

A PROCLAMATION.

Whereas the twenty-first section of the act of Congress approved on the 3d instant, entitled "An act to amend the several acts heretofore passed to provide for the enrolling and calling out the national forces and for other purposes," requires "that, in addition to the other lawful penalties of the crime of desertion from the military or naval service, all persons who have deserted the military or naval service of the United States who shall not return to said service or report themselves to a provost-marshal within sixty days after the proclamation hereinafter mentioned shall be deemed and taken to have voluntarily relinquished and forfeited their rights of citizenship and their rights to become citizens, and such deserters shall be forever incapable of holding any office of trust or profit under the United States or of exercising any rights of citizens thereof; and all persons who shall hereafter desert the military or naval service, and all persons who, being duly enrolled, shall depart the jurisdiction of the district in which he is enrolled or go beyond the limits of the United States with intent to avoid any draft into the military or naval service duly ordered, shall be liable to the penalties of this section. And the President is hereby authorized and required, forthwith on the passage of this act, to issue his proclamation setting forth the provisions of this section, in which proclamation the President is requested to notify all

---

*Entitled "Joint resolution in relation to certain railroads."

deserters returning within sixty days as aforesaid that they shall be pardoned on condition of returning to their regiments and companies or to such other organizations as they may be assigned to until they shall have served for a period of time equal to their original term of enlistment:"

Now, therefore, be it known that I, Abraham Lincoln, President of the United States, do issue this my proclamation, as required by said act, ordering and requiring all deserters to return to their proper posts; and I do hereby notify them that all deserters who shall, within sixty days from the date of this proclamation, viz, on or before the 10th day of May, 1865, return to service or report themselves to a provost-marshal shall be pardoned, on condition that they return to their regiments and companies or to such other organizations as they may be assigned to and serve the remainder of their original terms of enlistment and in addition thereto a period equal to the time lost by desertion.

In testimony whereof I have hereunto set my hand and caused the seal of the United States to be affixed.

[SEAL.] Done at the city of Washington, this 11th day of March, A. D. 1865, and of the Independence of the United States the eighty-ninth.

ABRAHAM LINCOLN.

By the President:

WILLIAM H. SEWARD,
Secretary of State.

BY THE PRESIDENT OF THE UNITED STATES OF AMERICA.

A PROCLAMATION.

Whereas reliable information has been received that hostile Indians within the limits of the United States have been furnished with arms and munitions of war by persons dwelling in conterminous foreign territory, and are thereby enabled to prosecute their savage warfare upon the exposed and sparse settlements of the frontier:

Now, therefore, be it known that I, Abraham Lincoln, President of the United States of America, do hereby proclaim and direct that all persons detected in that nefarious traffic shall be arrested and tried by court-martial at the nearest military post, and if convicted shall receive the punishment due to their deserts.

In witness whereof I have hereunto set my hand and caused the seal of the United States to be affixed.

[SEAL.] Done at the city of Washington, this 17th day of March, A. D. 1865, and of the Independence of the United States the eighty-ninth.

ABRAHAM LINCOLN.

By the President:

WILLIAM H. SEWARD,
Secretary of State.

By the President of the United States of America.

A PROCLAMATION.

Whereas by my proclamations of the 19th and 27th days of April, A. D. 1861, the ports of the United States in the States of Virginia, North Carolina, South Carolina, Georgia, Florida, Alabama, Mississippi, Louisiana, and Texas were declared to be subject to blockade; but

Whereas the said blockade has, in consequence of actual military occupation by this Government, since been conditionally set aside or relaxed in respect to the ports of Norfolk and Alexandria, in the State of Virginia; Beaufort, in the State of North Carolina; Port Royal, in the State of South Carolina; Pensacola and Fernandina, in the State of Florida; and New Orleans, in the State of Louisiana; and

Whereas by the fourth section of the act of Congre   pproved on the 13th of July, 1861, entitled "An act further to provide or the collection of duties on imports, and for other purposes," the President, for the reasons therein set forth, is authorized to close certain ports of entry:

Now, therefore, be it known that I, Abraham Lincoln, President of the United States, do hereby proclaim that the ports of Richmond, Tappahannock, Cherrystone, Yorktown, and Petersburg, in Virginia; of Camden (Elizabeth City), Edenton, Plymouth, Washington, Newbern, Ocracoke, and Wilmington, in North Carolina; of Charleston, Georgetown, and Beaufort, in South Carolina; of Savannah, St. Marys, and Brunswick (Darien), in Georgia; of Mobile, in Alabama; of Pearl River (Shieldsboro), Natchez, and Vicksburg, in Mississippi; of St. Augustine, Key West, St. Marks (Port Leon), St. Johns (Jacksonville), and Apalachicola, in Florida; of Teche (Franklin), in Louisiana; of Galveston, La Salle, Brazos de Santiago (Point Isabel), and Brownsville, in Texas, are hereby closed, and all right of importation, warehousing, and other privileges shall, in respect to the ports aforesaid, cease until they shall have again been opened by order of the President; and if while said ports are so closed any ship or vessel from beyond the United States or having on board any articles subject to duties shall attempt to enter any such port, the same, together with its tackle, apparel, furniture, and cargo, shall be forfeited to the United States.

In witness whereof I have hereunto set my hand and caused the seal of the United States to be affixed.

[SEAL.]   Done at the city of Washington, this 11th day of April, A. D. 1865, and of the Independence of the United States of America the eighty-ninth.

ABRAHAM LINCOLN.

By the President:

WILLIAM H. SEWARD,
Secretary of State.

By the President of the United States of America.

A PROCLAMATION.

Whereas by my proclamation of this date the port of Key West, in the State of Florida, was inadvertently included among those which are not open to commerce:

Now, therefore, be it known that I, Abraham Lincoln, President of the United States, do hereby declare and make known that the said port of Key West is and shall remain open to foreign and domestic commerce upon the same conditions by which that commerce has there hitherto been governed.

In testimony whereof I have hereunto set my hand and caused the seal of the United States to be affixed.

[SEAL.]   Done at the city of Washington, this 11th day of April, A. D. 1865, and of the Independence of the United States of America the eighty-ninth.   ABRAHAM LINCOLN.

By the President:

WILLIAM H. SEWARD, *Secretary of State.*

By the President of the United States of America.

A PROCLAMATION.

Whereas for some time past vessels of war of the United States have been refused in certain foreign ports privileges and immunities to which they were entitled by treaty, public law, or the comity of nations, at the same time that vessels of war of the country wherein the said privileges and immunities have been withheld have enjoyed them fully and uninterruptedly in ports of the United States, which condition of things has not always been forcibly resisted by the United States, although, on the other hand, they have not at any time failed to protest against and declare their dissatisfaction with the same. In the view of the United States, no condition any longer exists which can be claimed to justify the denial to them by any one of such nations of customary naval rights as has heretofore been so unnecessarily persisted in.

Now, therefore, I, Abraham Lincoln, President of the United States, do hereby make known that if after a reasonable time shall have elapsed for intelligence of this proclamation to have reached any foreign country in whose ports the said privileges and immunities shall have been refused as aforesaid they shall continue to be so refused, then and thenceforth the same privileges and immunities shall be refused to the vessels of war of that country in the ports of the United States; and this refusal shall continue until war vessels of the United States shall have been placed upon an entire equality in the foreign ports aforesaid with similar vessels of other countries. The United States, whatever claim or pretense may have existed heretofore, are now, at least, entitled to claim and concede an entire and friendly equality of rights and hospitalities with all maritime nations.

In witness whereof I have hereunto set my hand and caused the seal of the United States to be affixed.

[SEAL.]   Done at the city of Washington, this 11th day of April, A. D. 1865, and of the Independence of the United States of America the eighty-ninth.

         ABRAHAM LINCOLN.

By the President:

     WILLIAM H. SEWARD,

        Secretary of State.

EXECUTIVE ORDERS.

DEPARTMENT OF STATE,
Washington, March 8, 1865.

Whereas, pursuant to the order of the President of the United States, directions were issued from this Department, under date of the 17th of December, 1864, requiring passports from all travelers entering the United States, except immigrant passengers directly entering an American port from a foreign country; but whereas information has recently been received which affords reasonable grounds to expect that Her Britannic Majesty's Government and the executive and legislative branches of the government of Canada have taken and will continue to take such steps as may be looked for from a friendly neighbor and will be effectual toward preventing hostile incursions from Canadian territory into the United States, the President directs that from and after this date the order above referred to requiring passports shall be modified, and so much thereof as relates to persons entering this country from Canada shall be rescinded, saving and reserving the order in all other respects in full force.

        WILLIAM H. SEWARD.

DEPARTMENT OF STATE,
Washington, March 14, 1865.

The President directs that all persons who now are or hereafter shall be found within the United States who have been engaged in holding intercourse or trade with the insurgents by sea, if they are citizens of the United States or domiciled aliens, shall be arrested and held as prisoners of war until the war shall close, subject, nevertheless, to prosecution, trial, and conviction for any offense committed by them as spies or otherwise against the laws of war. The President further directs that all nonresident foreigners who now are or hereafter shall be found in the

United States, and who have been or shall have been engaged in violating the blockade of the insurgent ports, shall leave the United States within twelve days from the publication of this order, or from their subsequent arrival in the United States, if on the Atlantic side, and forty days if on the Pacific side, of the country; and such persons shall not return to the United States during the continuance of the war. Provost-marshals and marshals of the United States will arrest and commit to military custody all such offenders as shall disregard this order, whether they have passports or not, and they will be detained in such custody until the end of the war, or until discharged by subsequent orders of the President.

W. H. SEWARD,
Secretary of State.

GENERAL ORDERS, No. 50.

WAR DEPARTMENT,
ADJUTANT-GENERAL'S OFFICE,
Washington, March 27, 1865.

Ordered, first. That at the hour of noon on the 14th day of April, 1865, Brevet Major-General Anderson will raise and plant upon the ruins of Fort Sumter, in Charleston Harbor, the same United States flag which floated over the battlements of that fort during the rebel assault, and which was lowered and saluted by him and the small force of his command when the works were evacuated on the 14th day of April, 1861.

Second. That the flag, when raised, be saluted by one hundred guns from Fort Sumter and by a national salute from every fort and rebel battery that fired upon Fort Sumter.

Third. That suitable ceremonies be had upon the occasion, under the direction of Major-General William T. Sherman, whose military operations compelled the rebels to evacuate Charleston, or, in his absence, under the charge of Major-General Q. A. Gillmore, commanding the department. Among the ceremonies will be the delivery of a public address by the Rev. Henry Ward Beecher.

Fourth. That the naval forces at Charleston and their commander on that station be invited to participate in the ceremonies of the occasion.

By order of the President of the United States:

EDWIN M. STANTON,
Secretary of War.

To all whom these presents may concern:

Whereas for some time past evil-disposed persons have crossed the borders of the United States or entered their ports by sea from countries where they are tolerated, and have committed capital felonies against the property and life of American citizens, as well in the cities as in the rural districts of the country:

Now, therefore, in the name and by the authority of the President of the United States, I do hereby make known that a reward of $1,000 will be paid at this Department for the capture of each of such offenders, upon his conviction by a civil or military tribunal, to whomsoever shall arrest and deliver such offenders into the custody of the civil or military authorities of the United States. And the like reward will be paid upon the same terms for the capture of any such persons so entering the United States whose offenses shall be committed subsequently to the publication of this notice.

A reward of $500 will be paid upon conviction for the arrest of any person who shall have aided and abetted offenders of the class before named within the territory of the United States.

Given under my hand and the seal of the Department of State, at Washington, this 4th day of April, A. D. 1865.

[SEAL.]   WILLIAM H. SEWARD,
                                                        Secretary of State.

DEATH OF PRESIDENT LINCOLN.

ANNOUNCEMENT TO THE VICE-PRESIDENT.

[From the original, Department of State.]

WASHINGTON CITY, D. C.,
April 15, 1865.

ANDREW JOHNSON,
    Vice-President of the United States.

SIR: Abraham Lincoln, President of the United States, was shot by an assassin last evening at Ford's Theater, in this city, and died at the hour of twenty-two minutes after 7 o'clock.

About the same time at which the President was shot an assassin entered the sick chamber of the Hon. William H. Seward, Secretary of State, and stabbed him in several places—in the throat, neck, and face—severely if not mortally wounding him. Other members of the Secretary's family were dangerously wounded by the assassin while making his escape. By the death of President Lincoln the office of President has devolved, under the Constitution, upon you. The emergency of the Government demands that you should immediately qualify, according to the requirements of the Constitution, and enter upon the duties of President of the United States. If you will please make known your pleasure, such arrangements as you deem proper will be made.

Your obedient servants,

HUGH McCULLOCH,	W. DENNISON,
Secretary of the Treasury.	*Postmaster-General.*
EDWIN M. STANTON,	J. P. USHER,
Secretary of War.	*Secretary of the Interior.*
GIDEON WELLES,	JAMES SPEED,
Secretary of Navy.	*Attorney-General.*

[From the Daily National Intelligencer, April 17, 1865.]

The Vice-President responded that it would be agreeable to him to qualify himself for the high office to which he had been so unexpectedly called, under such melancholy circumstances, at his rooms at the Kirkwood Hotel; and at 11 o'clock a.m. [15th] the oath of office was administered to him by Chief Justice Chase, of the Supreme Court of the United States, in the presence of nearly all the Cabinet officers; the Hon. Solomon Foot, United States Senator from Vermont; the Hon. Alexander Ramsey, United States Senator from Minnesota; the Hon. Richard Yates, United States Senator from Illinois; the Hon. John. P. Hale, late Senator from New Hampshire; General Farnsworth, of the House of Representatives, from Illinois; F. P. Blair, sr.; Hon. Montgomery Blair, late Postmaster-General, and some others.

[For Inaugural Address of President Johnson, see pp. 305–306.]

ANNOUNCEMENT TO REPRESENTATIVES OF THE UNITED STATES ABROAD.

[From official records, Department of State.]

CIRCULAR.

DEPARTMENT OF STATE,
Washington, April 17, 1865.

SIR: The melancholy duty devolves upon me officially to apprise you of the assassination of the President at Ford's Theater, in this city, in the evening of the 14th instant. He died the next morning from the effects of the wound.

About the same time an attempt was made to assassinate the Secretary of State in his own house, where he was in bed suffering from the effects of the late accident. The attempt failed, but Mr. Seward was severely cut, on the face especially, it is supposed with a bowie knife. Mr. F. W. Seward was felled by a blow or blows on the head, and for some time afterwards was apparently unconscious. Both the Secretary and Assistant Secretary are better, especially the former.

Andrew Johnson has formally entered upon the duties of President.

I have been authorized temporarily to act as Secretary of State.

I am, sir, your obedient servant,

W. HUNTER, *Acting Secretary.*

ANNOUNCEMENT TO REPRESENTATIVES OF FOREIGN GOVERNMENTS IN THE UNITED STATES.

[From official records, Department of State.]

DEPARTMENT OF STATE,
Washington, April 15, 1865.

SIR: It is my great misfortune to be obliged to inform you of events not less afflicting to the people of the United States than distressing to my own feelings and the feelings of all those connected with the Government.

The President of the United States was shot with a pistol last night, while attending a theater in this city, and expired this morning from the effects of the wound. At about the same time an attempt was made to assassinate the Secretary of State, which, though it fortunately failed, left him severely, but it is hoped not dangerously, wounded with a knife or dagger. Mr. F. W. Seward was also struck on the head with a heavy weapon, and is in a critical condition from the effect of the blows.

Pursuant to the provision of the Constitution of the United States, Andrew Johnson, the Vice-President, has formally assumed the functions of President. I have by him been authorized to perform the duties of Secretary of State until otherwise ordered.

I avail myself of the occasion to offer to you the assurance of my distinguished consideration.

W. HUNTER, *Acting Secretary.*

ANNOUNCEMENT TO THE ARMY.

[From official records, War Department.]

GENERAL ORDERS, NO. 66.

WAR DEPARTMENT,
ADJUTANT-GENERAL'S OFFICE,
Washington, April 16, 1865.

The following order of the Secretary of War announces to the armies of the United States the untimely and lamentable death of the illustrious Abraham Lincoln, late President of the United States:

WAR DEPARTMENT, *Washington City, April 16, 1865.*

The distressing duty has devolved upon the Secretary of War to announce to the armies of the United States that at twenty-two minutes after 7 o'clock on the morning of Saturday, the 15th day of April, 1865, Abraham Lincoln, President of the United States, died of a mortal wound inflicted upon him by an assassin.

The armies of the United States will share with their fellow-citizens the feelings of grief and horror inspired by this most atrocious murder of their great and beloved President and Commander in Chief, and with profound sorrow will mourn his death as a national calamity.

The headquarters of every department, post, station, fort, and arsenal will be draped in mourning for thirty days, and appropriate funeral honors will be paid by every army, and in every department, and at every military post, and at the Military Academy at West Point, to the memory of the late illustrious Chief Magistrate of the nation and Commander in Chief of its armies.

Lieutenant-General Grant will give the necessary instructions for carrying this order into effect.

EDWIN M. STANTON,
Secretary of War.

On the day after the receipt of this order at the headquarters of each military division, department, army, post, station, fort, and arsenal and at the Military Academy at West Point the troops and cadets will be paraded at 10 o'clock a. m. and the order read to them, after which all labors and operations for the day will cease and be suspended as far as practicable in a state of war.

The national flag will be displayed at half-staff.

At dawn of day thirteen guns will be fired, and afterwards at intervals of thirty minutes between the rising and setting sun a single gun, and at the close of the day a national salute of thirty-six guns.

The officers of the armies of the United States will wear the badge of mourning on the left arm and on their swords and the colors of their commands and regiments will be put in mourning for the period of six months.

By command of Lieutenant-General Grant:

W. A. NICHOLS, *Assistant Adjutant-General.*

ANNOUNCEMENT TO THE NAVY.

[From General Orders and Circulars, Navy Department, 1863 to 1887.]

GENERAL ORDER No. 51.

NAVY DEPARTMENT, *Washington, April 15, 1865.*

The Department announces with profound sorrow to the officers and men of the Navy and Marine Corps the death of Abraham Lincoln, late President of the United States. Stricken down by the hand of an assassin on the evening of the 14th instant, when surrounded by his family and friends, he lingered a few hours after receiving the fatal wound, and died at 7 o'clock 22 minutes this morning.

A grateful people had given their willing confidence to the patriot and statesman under whose wise and successful administration the nation was just emerging from the civil strife which for four years has afflicted the land when this terrible calamity fell upon the country. To him our gratitude was justly due, for to him, under God, more than to any other person, are we indebted for the successful vindication of the integrity of the Union and the maintenance of the power of the Republic.

The officers of the Navy and of the Marine Corps will, as a manifestation of their respect for the exalted character, eminent position, and inestimable public services of the late President, and as an indication of their sense of the calamity which the country has sustained, wear the usual badge of mourning for six months.

The Department further directs that upon the day following the receipt of this order the commandants of squadrons, navy-yards, and stations will cause the ensign of every vessel in their several commands to be hoisted at half-mast, and a gun to be fired every half hour, beginning at sunrise and ending at sunset. The flags of the several navy-yards and marine barracks will also be hoisted at half-mast.

GIDEON WELLES,
Secretary of the Navy.

ANNOUNCEMENT TO THE REVENUE MARINE.

[From the Daily National Intelligencer, April 18, 1865.]

GENERAL ORDER.

TREASURY DEPARTMENT, *April 17, 1865.*

The Secretary of the Treasury with profound sorrow announces to the Revenue Marine the death of Abraham Lincoln, late President of the United States. He died in this city on the morning of the 15th instant, at twenty-two minutes past 7 o'clock.

The officers of the Revenue Marine will, as a manifestation of their respect for the exalted character and eminent public services of the illustrious dead and of their sense of the calamity the country has sustained by this afflicting dispensation of Providence, wear crape on the left arm and upon the hilt of the sword for six months.

It is further directed that funeral honors be paid on board all revenue vessels in commission by firing thirty-six minute guns, commencing at meridian, on the day after the receipt of this order, and by wearing their flags at half-mast.

HUGH McCULLOCH,
Secretary of the Treasury.

ACTION OF SENATORS AND REPRESENTATIVES IN WASHINGTON.

[From Appendix to Memorial Address on the Life and Character of Abraham Lincoln.]

The members of the Thirty-ninth Congress then in Washington met in the Senate reception room, at the Capitol, on the 17th of April, 1865, at noon. Hon. Lafayette S. Foster, of Connecticut, President *pro tempore* of the Senate, was called to the chair, and the Hon. Schuyler Colfax, of Indiana, Speaker of the House in the Thirty-eighth Congress, was chosen secretary.

Senator Foot, of Vermont, who was visibly affected, stated that the object of the meeting was to make arrangements relative to the funeral of the deceased President of the United States.

On motion of Senator Sumner, of Massachusetts, a committee of five members from each House was ordered to report at 4 p. m. what action would be fitting for the meeting to take.

The chairman appointed Senators Sumner, of Massachusetts; Harris, of New York; Johnson, of Maryland; Ramsey, of Minnesota, and Conness, of California, and Representatives Washburne, of Illinois; Smith, of Kentucky; Schenck, of Ohio; Pike, of Maine, and Coffroth, of Pennsylvania; and on motion of Mr. Schenck the chairman and secretary of the meeting were added to the committee, and then the meeting adjourned until 4 p. m.

The meeting reassembled at 4 p. m., pursuant to adjournment.

Mr. Sumner, from the committee heretofore appointed, reported that they had selected as pallbearers on the part of the Senate Mr. Foster, of Connecticut; Mr. Morgan, of New York; Mr. Johnson, of Maryland; Mr. Yates, of Illinois; Mr. Wade, of Ohio, and Mr. Conness, of California; on the part of the House, Mr. Dawes, of Massachusetts; Mr. Coffroth, of Pennsylvania; Mr. Smith, of Kentucky; Mr. Colfax, of Indiana; Mr. Worthington, of Nevada, and Mr. Washburne, of Illinois.

They also recommended the appointment of one member of Congress from each State and Territory to act as a Congressional committee to accompany the remains of the late President to Illinois, and presented the following names as such committee, the chairman of the meeting to have the authority of appointing hereafter for the States and Territories not represented to-day from which members may be present at the Capitol by the day of the funeral.

Maine, Mr. Pike; New Hampshire, Mr. E. H. Rollins; Vermont, Mr. Foot; Massachusetts, Mr. Sumner; Rhode Island, Mr. Anthony; Connecticut, Mr. Dixon; New York, Mr. Harris; Pennsylvania, Mr. Cowan; Ohio, Mr. Schenck; Kentucky, Mr. Smith; Indiana, Mr. Julian; Illinois, the delegation; Michigan, Mr. Chandler; Iowa, Mr. Harlan; California, Mr. Shannon; Minnesota, Mr. Ramsey; Oregon, Mr. Williams; Kansas, Mr. S. Clarke; West Virginia, Mr. Whaley; Nevada, Mr. Nye; Nebraska, Mr. Hitchcock; Colorado, Mr. Bradford; Dakota, Mr. Todd; Idaho, Mr. Wallace.

The committee also recommended the adoption of the following resolution:

Resolved, That the Sergeants-at-Arms of the Senate and House, with their necessary assistants, be requested to attend the committee accompanying the remains of the late President, and to make all the necessary arrangements.

All of which was concurred in unanimously.

Mr. Sumner, from the same committee, also reported the following, which was unanimously agreed to:

The members of the Senate and House of Representatives now assembled in Washington, humbly confessing their dependence upon Almighty God, who rules all that is done for human good, make haste at this informal meeting to express the emotions with which they have been filled by the appalling tragedy which has deprived the nation of its head and covered the land with mourning; and in further declaration of their sentiments unanimously resolve:

1. That in testimony of their veneration and affection for the illustrious dead, who has been permitted, under Providence, to do so much for his country and for liberty, they will unite in the funeral services and by an appropriate committee will accompany his remains to their place of burial in the State from which he was taken for the national service.

2. That in the life of Abraham Lincoln, who by the benignant favor of republican institutions rose from humble beginnings to the heights of power and fame, they recognize an example of purity, simplicity, and virtue which should be a lesson to mankind, while in his death they recognize a martyr whose memory will become more precious as men learn to prize those principles of constitutional order and those rights—civil, political, and human—for which he was made a sacrifice.

3. That they invite the President of the United States, by solemn proclamation, to recommend to the people of the United States to assemble on a day to be appointed by him, publicly to testify their grief and to dwell on the good which has been done on earth by him whom we now mourn.

4. That a copy of these resolutions be communicated to the President of the United States, and also that a copy be communicated to the afflicted widow of the late President as an expression of sympathy in her great bereavement.

The meeting then adjourned.

ORDERS OF THE HEADS OF THE EXECUTIVE DEPARTMENTS.

[From official records, Department of State.]

DEPARTMENT OF STATE,
Washington, April 17, 1865.

It is hereby ordered that, in honor to the memory of our late illustrious Chief Magistrate, all officers and others subject to the orders of the Secretary of State wear crape upon the left arm for the period of six months.

W. HUNTER,
Acting Secretary.

[From official records, Treasury Department.]

TREASURY DEPARTMENT,
Washington, April 17, 1865.

It is hereby ordered that, in honor to the memory of our late illustrious Chief Magistrate, all officers and others subject to the orders of the Secretary of the Treasury wear crape upon the left arm for the period of six months.

H. McCULLOCH,
Secretary of the Treasury.

[From official records, War Department.]

GENERAL ORDERS, No. 69.

WAR DEPARTMENT,
ADJUTANT-GENERAL'S OFFICE,
Washington, April 17, 1865.

By direction of the President of the United States the War Department will be closed on Wednesday next, the day of the funeral of the late President of the United States.

Labor on that day will be suspended at all military posts and on all public works under the direction of the War Department. The flags at all military posts, stations, forts, and buildings will be kept at half-staff during the day, and at 12 o'clock m. twenty-one minute guns will be fired from all forts and at all military posts and at the Military Academy.

By order of the Secretary of War:

W. A. NICHOLS,
Assistant Adjutant-General.

[From General Orders and Circulars, Navy Department, 1863 to 1887.]

SPECIAL ORDER.

APRIL 17, 1865.

By order of the President of the United States the Navy Department will be closed on Wednesday next, the day of the funeral solemnities of the late President of the United States. Labor will also be suspended on that day at each of the navy-yards and naval stations and upon all the vessels of the United States. The flags of all vessels and at all the navy yards and stations and marine barracks will be kept at half-mast during the day, and at 12 o'clock m. twenty-one minute guns will be fired by the senior officer of each squadron and the commandants of the navy yards and stations.

GIDEON WELLES,
Secretary of the Navy.

[From the Daily National Intelligencer, April 18, 1865.]

POST-OFFICE DEPARTMENT,
Washington, April 17, 1865.

To Deputy Postmasters:

Business in all the post-offices of the United States will be suspended and the offices closed from 11 a. m. to 3 p. m. on Wednesday, the 19th instant, during the funeral solemnities of Abraham Lincoln, late President of the United States.

W. DENNISON,
Postmaster-General.

[From official records, Post-Office Department.]

SPECIAL ORDER.

POST-OFFICE DEPARTMENT,
Washington, April 18, 1865.

It is hereby ordered that, in honor of the memory of Abraham Lincoln, our lamented Chief Magistrate, the officers and employees of this Department wear crape upon the left arm for the period of six months.

W. DENNISON,
Postmaster-General.

[From official records, Department of the Interior.]

DEPARTMENT OF THE INTERIOR,
Washington, April 18, 1865.

It is hereby ordered that, in honor of the memory of the late Chief Magistrate of the nation, the officers and employees of this Department wear crape upon the left arm for the period of six months.

J. P. USHER,
Secretary.

FUNERAL ANNOUNCEMENT TO THE PUBLIC.

[From the Daily National Intelligencer, April 17, 1865.]

DEPARTMENT OF STATE,
Washington, April 17, 1865.

To the People of the United States:

The undersigned is directed to announce that the funeral ceremonies of the late lamented Chief Magistrate will take place at the Executive Mansion, in this city, at 12 o'clock m. on Wednesday, the 19th instant.

The various religious denominations throughout the country are invited to meet in their respective places of worship at that hour for the purpose of solemnizing the occasion with appropriate ceremonies.

W. HUNTER,
Acting Secretary of State.

OFFICIAL ARRANGEMENTS FOR THE FUNERAL.

[From official records, War Department.]

WAR DEPARTMENT,
ADJUTANT-GENERAL'S OFFICE,
Washington, April 17, 1865.

The following order of arrangement is directed:

ORDER OF THE PROCESSION.

FUNERAL ESCORT.
(In column of march.)

One regiment of cavalry.
Two batteries of artillery.
Battalion of marines.
Two regiments of infantry.
Commander of escort and staff.
Dismounted officers of Marine Corps, Navy, and Army, in the order named.
Mounted officers of Marine Corps, Navy, and Army, in the order named.
(All military officers to be in uniform, with side arms.)

CIVIC PROCESSION.

Marshal.
Clergy in attendance.
The Surgeon-General of the United States Army and physicians to the deceased.
Hearse.

Pallbearers.

On the part of the Senate: Mr. Foster, of Connecticut; Mr. Morgan, of New York; Mr. Johnson, of Maryland; Mr. Yates, of Illinois; Mr. Wade, of Ohio; Mr. Conness, of California.

On the part of the House: Mr. Dawes, of Massachusetts; Mr. Coffroth, of Pennsylvania; Mr. Smith, of Kentucky; Mr. Colfax, of Indiana; Mr. Worthington, of Nevada; Mr. Washburne, of Illinois.

Army: Lieutenant-General U. S. Grant; Major-General H. W. Halleck; Brevet Brigadier-General W. A. Nichols.

Navy: Vice-Admiral D. G. Farragut; Rear-Admiral W. B. Shubrick; Colonel Jacob Zelin, Marine Corps.

Civilians: O. H. Browning, George Ashman, Thomas Corwin, Simon Cameron.

Family.
Relatives.
The delegations of the States of Illinois and Kentucky, as mourners.
The President.
The Cabinet ministers.
The diplomatic corps.

Ex-Presidents.

The Chief Justice and Associate Justices of the Supreme Court.

The Senate of the United States.

Preceded by their officers.

Members of the House of Representatives of the United States.

Governors of the several States and Territories.

Legislatures of the several States and Territories.

The Federal judiciary and the judiciary of the several States and Territories.

The Assistant Secretaries of State, Treasury, War, Navy, Interior, and the Assistant Postmasters-General, and the Assistant Attorney-General.

Officers of the Smithsonian Institution.

The members and officers of the Sanitary and Christian Commissions.

Corporate authorities of Washington, Georgetown, and other cities.

Delegations of the several States.

The reverend the clergy of the various denominations.

The clerks and employees of the several Departments and bureaus, preceded by the heads of such bureaus and their respective chief clerks.

Such societies as may wish to join the procession.

Citizens and strangers.

The troops designated to form the escort will assemble in the Avenue, north of the President's house, and form line precisely at 11 o'clock a. m. on Wednesday, the 19th instant, with the left resting on Fifteenth street. The procession will move precisely at 2 o'clock p. m., on the conclusion of the religious services at the Executive Mansion (appointed to commence at 12 o'clock m.), when minute guns will be fired by detachments of artillery stationed near St. John's Church, the City Hall, and at the Capitol. At the same hour the bells of the several churches in Washington, Georgetown, and Alexandria will be tolled.

At sunrise on Wednesday, the 19th instant, a Federal salute will be fired from the military stations in the vicinity of Washington, minute guns between the hours of 12 and 3 o'clock, and a national salute at the setting of the sun.

The usual badge of mourning will be worn on the left arm and on the hilt of the sword.

By order of the Secretary of War:

W. A. NICHOLS,
Assistant Adjutant-General.

The funeral ceremonies took place in the East Room of the Executive Mansion at noon on the 19th of April, and the remains were then escorted to the Capitol, where they lay in state in the Rotunda.

On the morning of April 21 the remains were taken from the Capitol and placed in a funeral car, in which they were taken to Springfield, Ill. Halting at the principal cities along the route, that appropriate honors might be paid to the deceased, the funeral cortege arrived on the 3d of May at Springfield, Ill., and the next day the remains were deposited in Oak Ridge Cemetery, near that city.

GUARD OF HONOR.

[From official records, War Department.]

GENERAL ORDERS, No. 72.

WAR DEPARTMENT,
ADJUTANT-GENERAL'S OFFICE,
Washington, April 20, 1865.

The following general officers and guard of honor will accompany the remains of the late President from the city of Washington to Springfield, the capital of the State of Illinois, and continue with them until they are consigned to their final resting place:

Brevet Brigadier-General E. D. Townsend, Assistant Adjutant-General, to represent the Secretary of War.

Brevet Brigadier-General Charles Thomas, Assistant Quartermaster-General.*

Brigadier-General A. B. Eaton, Commissary-General of Subsistence.

Brevet Major-General J. G. Barnard, Lieutenant-Colonel of Engineers.

Brigadier-General G. D. Ramsay, Ordnance Department.

Brigadier-General A. P. Howe, Chief of Artillery.

Brevet Brigadier-General D. C. McCallum, Superintendent Military Railroads.

Major-General D. Hunter, United States Volunteers.

Brigadier-General J. C. Caldwell, United States Volunteers.

Twenty-five picked men, under a captain.

By order of the Secretary of War:

E. D. TOWNSEND,
Assistant Adjutant-General.

[From official records, Navy Department.]

SPECIAL ORDER.

APRIL 20, 1865.

The following officers of the Navy and Marine Corps will accompany the remains of the late President from the city of Washington to Springfield, the capital of the State of Illinois, and continue with them until they are consigned to their final resting place:

Rear-Admiral Charles Henry Davis, Chief Bureau Navigation.

Captain William Rogers Taylor, United States Navy.

Major Thomas Y. Field, United States Marine Corps.

GIDEON WELLES,
Secretary of the Navy.

* Brevet Brigadier-General James A. Ekin, Quartermaster's Department, United States Army, substituted.

ACTION OF CONGRESS.

[From Appendix to Memorial Address on the Life and Character of Abraham Lincoln.]

President Johnson, in his annual message to Congress at the commencement of the session of 1865–66, thus announced the death of his predecessor:

To express gratitude to God in the name of the people for the preservation of the United States is my first duty in addressing you. Our thoughts next revert to the death of the late President by an act of parricidal treason. The grief of the nation is still fresh. It finds some solace in the consideration that he lived to enjoy the highest proof of its confidence by entering on the renewed term of the Chief Magistracy to which he had been elected; that he brought the civil war substantially to a close; that his loss was deplored in all parts of the Union, and that foreign nations have rendered justice to his memory.

Hon. E. B. Washburne, of Illinois, immediately after the President's message had been read in the House of Representatives, offered the following joint resolution, which was unanimously adopted:

Resolved, That a committee of one member from each State represented in this House be appointed on the part of this House, to join such committee as may be appointed on the part of the Senate, to consider and report by what token of respect and affection it may be proper for the Congress of the United States to express the deep sensibility of the nation to the event of the decease of their late President, Abraham Lincoln, and that so much of the message of the President as refers to that melancholy event be referred to said committee.

On motion of Hon. Solomon Foot, the Senate unanimously concurred in the passage of the resolution, and the following joint committee was appointed, thirteen on the part of the Senate and one for every State represented (twenty-four) on the part of the House of Representatives:

Senate: Hon. Solomon Foot, Vermont; Hon. Richard Yates, Illinois; Hon. Benjamin F. Wade, Ohio; Hon. William Pitt Fessenden, Maine; Hon. Henry Wilson, Massachusetts; Hon. James R. Doolittle, Wisconsin; Hon. James H. Lane, Kansas; Hon. Ira Harris, New York; Hon. James W. Nesmith, Oregon; Hon. Henry S. Lane, Indiana; Hon. Waitman T. Willey, West Virginia; Hon. Charles R. Buckalew, Pennsylvania; Hon. John B. Henderson, Missouri.

House of Representatives: Hon. Elihu B. Washburne, Illinois; Hon. James G. Blaine, Maine; Hon. James W. Patterson, New Hampshire; Hon. Justin S. Morrill, Vermont; Hon. Nathaniel P. Banks, Massachusetts; Hon. Thomas A. Jenckes, Rhode Island; Hon. Henry C. Deming, Connecticut; Hon. John A. Griswold, New York; Hon. Edwin R. V. Wright, New Jersey; Hon. Thaddeus Stevens, Pennsylvania; Hon. John A. Nicholson, Delaware; Hon. Francis Thomas, Maryland; Hon. Robert C. Schenck, Ohio; Hon. George S. Shanklin, Kentucky; Hon. Godlove S. Orth, Indiana; Hon. Joseph W. McClurg, Missouri; Hon. Fernando C. Beaman, Michigan; Hon. John A. Kasson, Iowa; Hon. Ithamar C. Sloan, Wisconsin; Hon. William Higby, California; Hon. William Windom,

Minnesota; Hon. J. H. D. Henderson, Oregon; Hon. Sidney Clarke, Kansas; Hon. Kellian V. Whaley, West Virginia.

The joint committee made the following report, which was concurred in by both Houses *nem. con.:*

Whereas the melancholy event of the violent and tragic death of Abraham Lincoln, late President of the United States, having occurred during the recess of Congress, and the two Houses sharing in the general grief and desiring to manifest their sensibility upon the occasion of the public bereavement: Therefore,

Be it resolved by the Senate (the House of Representatives concurring), That the two Houses of Congress will assemble in the Hall of the House of Representatives on Monday, the 12th day of February next, that being his anniversary birthday, at the hour of 12 m., and that, in the presence of the two Houses there assembled, an address upon the life and character of Abraham Lincoln, late President of the United States, be pronounced by Hon. Edwin M. Stanton,* and that the President of the Senate *pro tempore* and the Speaker of the House of Representatives be requested to invite the President of the United States, the heads of the several Departments, the judges of the Supreme Court, the representatives of the foreign governments near this Government, and such officers of the Army and Navy as have received the thanks of Congress who may then be at the seat of Government to be present on the occasion.

And be it further resolved, That the President of the United States be requested to transmit a copy of these resolutions to Mrs. Lincoln, and to assure her of the profound sympathy of the two Houses of Congress for her deep personal affliction and of their sincere condolence for the late national bereavement.

[For proclamations of President Johnson recommending, in consequence of the assassination of Abraham Lincoln, late President of the United States, a day for special humiliation and prayer, see pp. 306–307, and for Executive order in connection therewith see p. 339. For Executive order closing the Executive Office and the Departments on the day of the funeral of the late President, at Springfield, Ill., see p. 335. For Executive order closing the public offices April 14, 1866, in commemoration of the assassination of the late President, see p. 440.]

* Mr. Stanton having declined, Hon. George Bancroft, of New York, in response to an invitation from the joint committee, consented to deliver the address.

Andrew Johnson

April 15, 1865, to March 4, 1869

Andrew Johnson

Andrew Johnson

ANDREW JOHNSON was born in Raleigh, N. C., December 29, 1808. His parents were very poor. When he was 4 years old his father died of injuries received in rescuing a person from drowning. At the age of 10 years Andrew was apprenticed to a tailor. His early education was almost entirely neglected, and, notwithstanding his natural craving to learn, he never spent a day in school. Was taught the alphabet by a fellow-workman, borrowed a book, and learned to read. In 1824 removed to Laurens Court-House, S. C., where he worked as a journeyman tailor. In May, 1826, returned to Raleigh, and in September, with his mother and stepfather, set out for Greeneville, Tenn., in a two-wheeled cart drawn by a blind pony. Here he married Eliza McCardle, a woman of refinement, who taught him to write, and read to him while he was at work during the day. It was not until he had been in Congress that he learned to write with ease. From Greeneville went to the West, but returned after the lapse of a year. In 1828 was elected alderman; was reelected in 1829 and 1830, and in 1830 was advanced to the mayoralty, which office he held for three years. In 1831 was appointed by the county court a trustee of Rhea Academy, and about this time participated in the debates of a society at Greeneville College. In 1834 advocated the adoption of a new State constitution, by which the influence of the large landholders was abridged. In 1835 represented Greene and Washington counties in the legislature. Was defeated for the legislature in 1837, but in 1839 was reelected. In 1836 supported Hugh L. White for the Presidency, and in the political altercations between John Bell and James K. Polk, which distracted Tennessee at the time, supported the former. Mr. Johnson was the only ardent follower of Bell that failed to go over to the Whig party. Was an elector for the State at large on the Van Buren ticket in 1840, and made a State reputation by the force of his oratory. In 1841 was elected to the State senate from Greene and Hawkins counties, and while in that body was one of the "immortal thirteen" Democrats who, having it in their power to prevent the election of a Whig Senator, did so by refusing to meet the house in joint convention; also proposed that the basis of representation should rest upon white votes, without regard to the ownership of slaves. Was elected to Congress in 1843 over John A. Asken, a United States Bank Democrat, who was supported by the Whigs. His first speech was in support of the resolution to restore to General Jackson the fine imposed upon him at New Orleans; also supported the annexation of Texas. In 1845 was reelected, and supported Polk's Administration. Was regularly reelected to Congress until 1853. During this period opposed all expenditures for internal improvements that were not general; resisted and defeated the proposed contingent tax of 10 per cent on tea and coffee; made his celebrated defense of the veto power; urged the adoption of the homestead law, which was obnoxious to the extreme Southern element of his party; supported the compromise measures of 1850 as a matter of expediency, but opposed compromises in general as a sacrifice of principle. Was elected governor of Tennessee in 1853 over Gustavus A. Henry, the "Eagle Orator" of the State. In his message to the legislature he dwelt upon the homestead law and other measures for the benefit of the working classes, and earned the title of the "Mechanic Governor." Opposed the Know-nothing movement with characteristic vehemence. Was reelected governor in 1855, defeating Meredith P. Gentry, the Whig-American candidate, after a most remarkable canvass. The Kansas-Nebraska bill received his earnest support. In 1857 was elected to the United States Senate, where he urged the passage of the homestead bill, and on May 20, 1858, made his greatest speech on this subject. Opposed the grant of aid for the construction of a Pacific railroad. Was prominent in debate, and frequently clashed with Southern supporters of the Administration. His pronounced Unionism estranged him from the extremists on the Southern side, while his acceptance of slavery as an institution guaranteed by the Constitution caused him to hold aloof from the Republicans on the other. At the Democratic convention at Charleston, S. C., in 1860 was a candidate for the Presidential nomination, but received only the vote of Tennessee, and when the convention reassembled in Baltimore withdrew his name. In the canvass that followed supported John C. Breckinridge. At the session of Congress beginning in December, 1860, took decided and unequivocal grounds in opposition to secession, and on December 13 introduced a joint resolution proposing to amend the Constitution so as to elect the President and Vice-President by district votes, Senators by a direct popular vote, and to limit the terms of Federal judges to twelve years, the judges to be equally divided between slaveholding and non-slaveholding States. In his speech on this resolution, December 18 and 19, declared his unyielding opposition to secession and announced his intention to stand by and act under the Constitution. Retained his seat in the Senate until appointed by President Lincoln military governor of Tennessee, March 4, 1862. March 12 reached Nashville, and organized a provisional government for the State; March 18 issued a proclamation in which he appealed to the people to return to their allegiance, to uphold the law, and to accept "a full and complete amnesty for all past acts and declarations;" April 5 removed the mayor and other officials of Nashville for refusing to take the oath of allegiance to the United States, and appointed others; urged the holding of Union meetings throughout the State, and frequently attended them in person; completed the railroad from Nashville to the Tennessee River; raised twenty-five regiments for service in the State; December 8, 1862, issued a proclamation ordering Congressional elections, and on the 15th levied an assessment upon the richer Southern sympathizers "in behalf of the many helpless widows, wives, and children in the city of Nashville who have been reduced to poverty and wretchedness in consequence of their husbands, sons, and fathers having been forced into the armies of this unholy and nefarious rebellion." Was nominated for Vice-President of the United States at the national Republican convention at Baltimore June 8, 1864, and was elected on November 8. In his letter of acceptance of the nomination Mr. Johnson virtually disclaimed any departure from his principles as a Democrat, but placed his acceptance upon the ground of "the higher duty of first preserving the Government." On the night of the 14th of April, 1865, President Lincoln was shot by an assassin and died the next morning. At 11 o'clock a. m. April 15 Mr. Johnson was sworn in as President, at his rooms in the Kirkwood House, Washington, by Chief Justice Chase, in the presence of nearly all the Cabinet officers and others. April 29, 1865, issued a proclamation for the removal of trade restrictions in most of the insurrectionary States, which, being in contravention of an act of Congress, was subsequently modified. May 9 issued an Executive order restoring Virginia to the Union. May 22 proclaimed all ports, except four in Texas, opened to foreign commerce on July 1, 1865. May 29 issued a general amnesty proclamation, after which the fundamental and irreconcilable differences between President Johnson and the party that had elevated him to power became more apparent. He exercised the veto power to a very great extent, but it was generally nullified by the two-thirds votes of both Houses. From May 29 to July 13, 1865, proclaimed provisional governors for North Carolina, Mississippi, Georgia, Texas, Alabama, South Carolina, and Florida, whose duties were to reorganize the State governments. The State governments were reorganized, but the Republicans claimed that the laws passed were so stringent in reference to the negroes that it was a worse form of slavery than the old. The thirteenth amendment to the Constitution became a law December 18, 1865, with Mr. Johnson's concurrence. The first breach between the President and the party in power was the veto of the Freedmen's Bureau bill, in February, 1866, which was designed to protect the negroes. March 27 vetoed the civil-rights bill, but it was passed over his veto. In a message of June 22, 1866, opposed the joint resolution proposing the fourteenth amendment to the Constitution. In June, 1866, the Republicans in Congress brought forward their plan of reconstruction, called the "Congressional plan," in contradistinction to that of the President. The chief features of the Congressional plan were to give the negroes the right to vote, to protect them in this right, and to prevent Confederate leaders from voting. January 5, 1867, vetoed the act giving negroes the right of suffrage in the District of Columbia, but it was passed over his veto. An attempt was made to impeach the President, but it failed. In January, 1867, a bill was passed to deprive the President of the power to proclaim general amnesty, which he disregarded. Measures were adopted looking to the meeting of the Fortieth and all subsequent Congresses immediately after the adjournment of the preceding. The President was deprived of the command of the Army by a rider to the army appropriation bill, which provided that his orders should only be given through the General, who was not to be removed without the previous consent of the Senate. The bill admitting Nebraska, providing that no law should ever be passed in that State denying the right of suffrage to any person because of his color or race, was vetoed by the President, but passed over his veto. March 2, 1867, vetoed the act to provide for the more efficient government of the rebel States, but it was passed over his veto. It embodied the Congressional plan of reconstruction, and divided the Southern States into five military districts, each under an officer of the Army not under the rank of brigadier-general, who was to exercise all the functions of government until the citizens had "formed a constitution of government in conformity with the Constitution of the United States in all respects." On the same day vetoed the tenure-of-office act, which was also passed over his veto. It provided that civil officers should remain in office until the confirmation of their successors; that the members of the Cabinet should be removed only with the consent of the Senate, and that when Congress was not in session the President could suspend but not remove any official, and in case the Senate at the next session should not ratify the suspension the suspended official should be reinducted into his office. August 5, 1867, requested Edwin M. Stanton to resign his office as Secretary of War. Mr. Stanton refused, was suspended, and General Grant was appointed Secretary of War *ad interim*. When Congress met, the Senate refused to ratify the suspension. General Grant then resigned, and Mr. Stanton resumed the duties of his office. The President removed him and appointed Lorenzo Thomas, Adjutant-General of the Army, Secretary of War *ad interim*. The Senate declared this act illegal, and Mr. Stanton refused to comply, and notified the Speaker of the House. On February 24, 1868, the House of Representatives resolved to impeach the President, and on March 2 and 3 articles of impeachment were agreed upon by the House of Representatives, and on the 4th were presented to the Senate. The trial began on March 30. May 16 the test vote was had;

thirty-five Senators voted for conviction and nineteen for acquittal. A change of one vote would have carried conviction. A verdict of acquittal was entered, and the Senate sitting as a court of impeachment adjourned *sine die*. After the expiration of his term the ex-President returned to Tennessee. Was a candidate for the United States Senate, but was defeated. In 1872 was an unsuccessful candidate for Congressman from the State at large. In January, 1875, was elected to the United States Senate, and took his seat at the extra session of that year. Shortly after the session began made a speech which was a skillful but bitter attack upon President Grant. While visiting his daughter near Elizabethton, in Carter County, Tenn., was stricken with paralysis July 30, 1875, and died the following day. He was buried at Greeneville, Tenn.

INAUGURAL ADDRESS.

[From the Sunday Morning Chronicle, Washington, April 16, 1865, and The Sun, Baltimore, April 17, 1865.]

GENTLEMEN: I must be permitted to say that I have been almost overwhelmed by the announcement of the sad event which has so recently occurred. I feel incompetent to perform duties so important and responsible as those which have been so unexpectedly thrown upon me. As to an indication of any policy which may be pursued by me in the administration of the Government, I have to say that that must be left for development as the Administration progresses. The message or declaration must be made by the acts as they transpire. The only assurance that I can now give of the future is reference to the past. The course which I have taken in the past in connection with this rebellion must be regarded as a guaranty of the future. My past public life, which has been long and laborious, has been founded, as I in good conscience believe, upon a great principle of right, which lies at the basis of all things. The best energies of my life have been spent in endeavoring to establish and perpetuate the principles of free government, and I believe that the Government in passing through its present perils will settle down upon principles consonant with popular rights more permanent and enduring than heretofore. I must be permitted to say, if I understand the feelings of my own heart, that I have long labored to ameliorate and elevate the condition of the great mass of the American people. Toil and an honest advocacy of the great principles of free government have been my lot. Duties have been mine; consequences are God's. This has been the foundation of my political creed, and I feel that in the end the Government will triumph and that these great principles will be permanently established.

In conclusion, gentlemen, let me say that I want your encouragement and countenance. I shall ask and rely upon you and others in carrying the Government through its present perils. I feel in making this request that it will be heartily responded to by you and all other patriots and lovers of the rights and interests of a free people.

APRIL 15, 1865.

PROCLAMATIONS.

BY THE PRESIDENT OF THE UNITED STATES OF AMERICA.

A PROCLAMATION.

Whereas, by my direction, the Acting Secretary of State, in a notice to the public of the 17th, requested the various religious denominations to assemble on the 19th instant, on the occasion of the obsequies of Abraham Lincoln, late President of the United States, and to observe the same with appropriate ceremonies; but

Whereas our country has become one great house of mourning, where the head of the family has been taken away, and believing that a special period should be assigned for again humbling ourselves before Almighty God, in order that the bereavement may be sanctified to the nation:

Now, therefore, in order to mitigate that grief on earth which can only be assuaged by communion with the Father in heaven, and in compliance with the wishes of Senators and Representatives in Congress, communicated to me by resolutions adopted at the National Capitol, I, Andrew Johnson, President of the United States, do hereby appoint Thursday, the 25th day of May next, to be observed, wherever in the United States the flag of the country may be respected, as a day of humiliation and mourning, and I recommend my fellow-citizens then to assemble in their respective places of worship, there to unite in solemn service to Almighty God in memory of the good man who has been removed, so that all shall be occupied at the same time in contemplation of his virtues and in sorrow for his sudden and violent end.

In witness whereof I have hereunto set my hand and caused the seal of the United States to be affixed.

[SEAL.] Done at the city of Washington, the 25th day of April, A. D. 1865, and of the Independence of the United States of America the eighty-ninth.

ANDREW JOHNSON.

By the President:

W. HUNTER,
Acting Secretary of State.

BY THE PRESIDENT OF THE UNITED STATES OF AMERICA.

A PROCLAMATION.

Whereas by my proclamation of the 25th instant Thursday, the 25th day of next month, was recommended as a day for special humiliation and prayer in consequence of the assassination of Abraham Lincoln, late President of the United States; but

Whereas my attention has since been called to the fact that the day aforesaid is sacred to large numbers of Christians as one of rejoicing for the ascension of the Savior:

Now, therefore, be it known that I, Andrew Johnson, President of the United States, do hereby suggest that the religious services recommended as aforesaid should be postponed until Thursday, the 1st day of June next.

In testimony whereof I have hereunto set my hand and caused the seal of the United States to be affixed.

[SEAL.]   Done at the city of Washington, this 29th day of April, A. D. 1865, and of the Independence of the United States of America the eighty-ninth.

ANDREW JOHNSON.

By the President:
W. HUNTER,
Acting Secretary of State.

BY THE PRESIDENT OF THE UNITED STATES OF AMERICA.

A PROCLAMATION.

Whereas it appears from evidence in the Bureau of Military Justice that the atrocious murder of the late President, Abraham Lincoln, and the attempted assassination of the Hon. William H. Seward, Secretary of State, were incited, concerted, and procured by and between Jefferson Davis, late of Richmond, Va., and Jacob Thompson, Clement C. Clay, Beverley Tucker, George N. Sanders, William C. Cleary, and other rebels and traitors against the Government of the United States harbored in Canada:

Now, therefore, to the end that justice may be done, I, Andrew Johnson, President of the United States, do offer and promise for the arrest of said persons, or either of them, within the limits of the United States, so that they can be brought to trial, the following rewards:

One hundred thousand dollars for the arrest of Jefferson Davis.

Twenty-five thousand dollars for the arrest of Clement C. Clay.

Twenty-five thousand dollars for the arrest of Jacob Thompson, late of Mississippi.

Twenty-five thousand dollars for the arrest of George N. Sanders.

Twenty-five thousand dollars for the arrest of Beverley Tucker.

Ten thousand dollars for the arrest of William C. Cleary, late clerk of Clement C. Clay.

The Provost-Marshal-General of the United States is directed to cause a description of said persons, with notice of the above rewards, to be published.

In testimony whereof I have hereunto set my hand and caused the seal of the United States to be affixed.

[SEAL.]   Done at the city of Washington, this 2d day of May, A. D. 1865, and of the Independence of the United States of America the eighty-ninth.

ANDREW JOHNSON.

By the President:

W. HUNTER,
    Acting Secretary of State.

BY THE PRESIDENT OF THE UNITED STATES OF AMERICA.

A PROCLAMATION.

Whereas the President of the United States, by his proclamation of the 19th day of April, 1861, did declare certain States therein mentioned in insurrection against the Government of the United States; and

Whereas armed resistance to the authority of this Government in the said insurrectionary States may be regarded as virtually at an end, and the persons by whom that resistance, as well as the operations of insurgent cruisers, was directed are fugitives or captives; and

Whereas it is understood that some of those cruisers are still infesting the high seas and others are preparing to capture, burn, and destroy vessels of the United States:

Now, therefore, be it known that I, Andrew Johnson, President of the United States, hereby enjoin all naval, military, and civil officers of the United States diligently to endeavor, by all lawful means, to arrest the said cruisers and to bring them into a port of the United States, in order that they may be prevented from committing further depredations on commerce and that the persons on board of them may no longer enjoy impunity for their crimes.

And I do further proclaim and declare that if, after a reasonable time shall have elapsed for this proclamation to become known in the ports of nations claiming to have been neutrals, the said insurgent cruisers and the persons on board of them shall continue to receive hospitality in the said ports, this Government will deem itself justified in refusing hospitality to the public vessels of such nations in ports of the United States and in adopting such other measures as may be deemed advisable toward vindicating the national sovereignty.

In witness whereof I have hereunto set my hand and caused the seal of the United States to be affixed.

[SEAL.]   Done at the city of Washington, this 10th day of May, A. D. 1865, and of the Independence of the United States of America the eighty-ninth.

ANDREW JOHNSON.

By the President:

W. HUNTER,
Acting Secretary of State.

BY THE PRESIDENT OF THE UNITED STATES OF AMERICA.

A PROCLAMATION.

Whereas by the proclamation of the President of the 11th day of April last certain ports of the United States therein specified, which had previously been subject to blockade, were, for objects of public safety, declared, in conformity with previous special legislation of Congress, to be closed against foreign commerce during the national will, to be thereafter expressed and made known by the President; and

Whereas events and circumstances have since occurred which, in my judgment, render it expedient to remove that restriction, except as to the ports of Galveston, La Salle, Brazos de Santiago (Point Isabel), and Brownsville, in the State of Texas:

Now, therefore, be it known that I, Andrew Johnson, President of the United States, do hereby declare that the ports aforesaid, not excepted as above, shall be open to foreign commerce from and after the 1st day of July next; that commercial intercourse with the said ports may from that time be carried on, subject to the laws of the United States and in pursuance of such regulations as may be prescribed by the Secretary of the Treasury. If, however, any vessel from a foreign port shall enter any of the before-named excepted ports in the State of Texas, she will continue to be held liable to the penalties prescribed by the act of Congress approved on the 13th day of July, 1861, and the persons on board of her to such penalties as may be incurred, pursuant to the laws of war, for trading or attempting to trade with an enemy.

And I, Andrew Johnson, President of the United States, do hereby declare and make known that the United States of America do henceforth disallow to all persons trading or attempting to trade in any ports of the United States in violation of the laws thereof all pretense of belligerent rights and privileges; and I give notice that from the date of this proclamation all such offenders will be held and dealt with as pirates.

It is also ordered that all restrictions upon trade heretofore imposed in the territory of the United States east of the Mississippi River, save those relating to contraband of war, to the reservation of the rights of the United States to property purchased in the territory of an enemy, and to the 25 per cent upon purchases of cotton be removed. All provisions of the internal-revenue law will be carried into effect under the proper officers.

In witness whereof I have hereunto set my hand and caused the seal of the United States to be affixed.

[SEAL].   Done at the city of Washington, this 22d day of May, A. D. 1865, and of the Independence of the United States of America the eighty-ninth.

ANDREW JOHNSON.

By the President:

W. HUNTER,
Acting Secretary of State.

BY THE PRESIDENT OF THE UNITED STATES OF AMERICA.

A PROCLAMATION.

Whereas the President of the United States, on the 8th day of December, A. D. 1863, and on the 26th day of March, A. D. 1864, did, with the object to suppress the existing rebellion, to induce all persons to return to their loyalty, and to restore the authority of the United States, issue proclamations offering amnesty and pardon to certain persons who had, directly or by implication, participated in the said rebellion; and

Whereas many persons who had so engaged in said rebellion have, since the issuance of said proclamations, failed or neglected to take the benefits offered thereby; and

Whereas many persons who have been justly deprived of all claim to amnesty and pardon thereunder by reason of their participation, directly or by implication, in said rebellion and continued hostility to the Government of the United States since the date of said proclamations now desire to apply for and obtain amnesty and pardon.

To the end, therefore, that the authority of the Government of the United States may be restored and that peace, order, and freedom may be established, I, Andrew Johnson, President of the United States, do proclaim and declare that I hereby grant to all persons who have, directly or indirectly, participated in the existing rebellion, except as hereinafter excepted, amnesty and pardon, with restoration of all rights of property, except as to slaves and except in cases where legal proceedings under the laws of the United States providing for the confiscation of property of persons engaged in rebellion have been instituted; but upon the condition, nevertheless, that every such person shall take and subscribe the following oath (or affirmation) and thenceforward keep and maintain said oath inviolate, and which oath shall be registered for permanent preservation and shall be of the tenor and effect following, to wit:

I, —— ——, do solemnly swear (or affirm), in presence of Almighty God, that I will henceforth faithfully support, protect, and defend the Constitution of the United

States and the Union of the States thereunder, and that I will in like manner abide by and faithfully support all laws and proclamations which have been made during the existing rebellion with reference to the emancipation of slaves. So help me God.

The following classes of persons are excepted from the benefits of this proclamation:

First. All who are or shall have been pretended civil or diplomatic officers or otherwise domestic or foreign agents of the pretended Confederate government.

Second. All who left judicial stations under the United States to aid the rebellion.

Third. All who shall have been military or naval officers of said pretended Confederate government above the rank of colonel in the army or lieutenant in the navy.

Fourth. All who left seats in the Congress of the United States to aid the rebellion.

Fifth. All who resigned or tendered resignations of their commissions in the Army or Navy of the United States to evade duty in resisting the rebellion.

Sixth. All who have engaged in any way in treating otherwise than lawfully as prisoners of war persons found in the United States service as officers, soldiers, seamen, or in other capacities.

Seventh. All persons who have been or are absentees from the United States for the purpose of aiding the rebellion.

Eighth. All military and naval officers in the rebel service who were educated by the Government in the Military Academy at West Point or the United States Naval Academy.

Ninth. All persons who held the pretended offices of governors of States in insurrection against the United States.

Tenth. All persons who left their homes within the jurisdiction and protection of the United States and passed beyond the Federal military lines into the pretended Confederate States for the purpose of aiding the rebellion.

Eleventh. All persons who have been engaged in the destruction of the commerce of the United States upon the high seas and all persons who have made raids into the United States from Canada or been engaged in destroying the commerce of the United States upon the lakes and rivers that separate the British Provinces from the United States.

Twelfth. All persons who, at the time when they seek to obtain the benefits hereof by taking the oath herein prescribed, are in military, naval, or civil confinement or custody, or under bonds of the civil, military, or naval authorities or agents of the United States as prisoners of war, or persons detained for offenses of any kind, either before or after conviction.

Thirteenth. All persons who have voluntarily participated in said rebellion and the estimated value of whose taxable property is over $20,000.

Fourteenth. All persons who have taken the oath of amnesty as prescribed in the President's proclamation of December 8, A. D. 1863, or an oath of allegiance to the Government of the United States since the date of said proclamation and who have not thenceforward kept and maintained the same inviolate.

Provided, That special application may be made to the President for pardon by any person belonging to the excepted classes, and such clemency will be liberally extended as may be consistent with the facts of the case and the peace and dignity of the United States.

The Secretary of State will establish rules and regulations for administering and recording the said amnesty oath, so as to insure its benefit to the people and guard the Government against fraud.

In testimony whereof I have hereunto set my hand and caused the seal of the United States to be affixed.

[SEAL.]   Done at the city of Washington, the 29th day of May, A. D. 1865, and of the Independence of the United States the eighty-ninth.

ANDREW JOHNSON.

By the President:

WILLIAM H. SEWARD,
Secretary of State.

BY THE PRESIDENT OF THE UNITED STATES OF AMERICA.

A PROCLAMATION.

Whereas the fourth section of the fourth article of the Constitution of the United States declares that the United States shall guarantee to every State in the Union a republican form of government and shall protect each of them against invasion and domestic violence; and

Whereas the President of the United States is by the Constitution made Commander in Chief of the Army and Navy, as well as chief civil executive officer of the United States, and is bound by solemn oath faithfully to execute the office of President of the United States and to take care that the laws be faithfully executed; and

Whereas the rebellion which has been waged by a portion of the people of the United States against the properly constituted authorities of the Government thereof in the most violent and revolting form, but whose organized and armed forces have now been almost entirely overcome, has in its revolutionary progress deprived the people of the State of North Carolina of all civil government; and

Whereas it becomes necessary and proper to carry out and enforce the obligations of the United States to the people of North Carolina in securing them in the enjoyment of a republican form of government:

Now, therefore, in obedience to the high and solemn duties imposed upon me by the Constitution of the United States and for the purpose of enabling the loyal people of said State to organize a State government whereby justice may be established, domestic tranquillity insured, and loyal citizens protected in all their rights of life, liberty, and property, I, Andrew Johnson, President of the United States and Commander in Chief of the Army and Navy of the United States, do hereby appoint William W. Holden provisional governor of the State of North Carolina, whose duty it shall be, at the earliest practicable period, to prescribe such rules and regulations as may be necessary and proper for convening a convention composed of delegates to be chosen by that portion of the people of said State who are loyal to the United States, and no others, for the purpose of altering or amending the constitution thereof, and with authority to exercise within the limits of said State all the powers necessary and proper to enable such loyal people of the State of North Carolina to restore said State to its constitutional relations to the Federal Government and to present such a republican form of State government as will entitle the State to the guaranty of the United States therefor and its people to protection by the United States against invasion, insurrection, and domestic violence: *Provided*, That in any election that may be hereafter held for choosing delegates to any State convention as aforesaid no person shall be qualified as an elector or shall be eligible as a member of such convention unless he shall have previously taken and subscribed the oath of amnesty as set forth in the President's proclamation of May 29, A. D. 1865, and is a voter qualified as prescribed by the constitution and laws of the State of North Carolina in force immediately before the 20th day of May, A. D. 1861, the date of the so-called ordinance of secession; and the said convention, when convened, or the legislature that may be thereafter assembled, will prescribe the qualification of electors and the eligibility of persons to hold office under the constitution and laws of the State—a power the people of the several States composing the Federal Union have rightfully exercised from the origin of the Government to the present time.

And I do hereby direct—

First. That the military commander of the department and all officers and persons in the military and naval service aid and assist the said provisional governor in carrying into effect this proclamation; and they are enjoined to abstain from in any way hindering, impeding, or discouraging the loyal people from the organization of a State government as herein authorized.

Second. That the Secretary of State proceed to put in force all laws of the United States the administration whereof belongs to the State Department applicable to the geographical limits aforesaid.

Third. That the Secretary of the Treasury proceed to nominate for appointment assessors of taxes and collectors of customs and internal revenue and such other officers of the Treasury Department as are authorized by law and put in execution the revenue laws of the United

States within the geographical limits aforesaid. In making appointments the preference shall be given to qualified loyal persons residing within the districts where their respective duties are to be performed; but if suitable residents of the districts shall not be found, then persons residing in other States or districts shall be appointed.

Fourth. That the Postmaster-General proceed to establish post-offices and post routes and put into execution the postal laws of the United States within the said State, giving to loyal residents the preference of appointment; but if suitable residents are not found, then to appoint agents, etc., from other States.

Fifth. That the district judge for the judicial district in which North Carolina is included proceed to hold courts within said State in accordance with the provisions of the act of Congress. The Attorney-General will instruct the proper officers to libel and bring to judgment, confiscation, and sale property subject to confiscation and enforce the administration of justice within said State in all matters within the cognizance and jurisdiction of the Federal courts.

Sixth. That the Secretary of the Navy take possession of all public property belonging to the Navy Department within said geographical limits and put in operation all acts of Congress in relation to naval affairs having application to the said State.

Seventh. That the Secretary of the Interior put in force the laws relating to the Interior Department applicable to the geographical limits aforesaid.

In testimony whereof I have hereunto set my hand and caused the seal of the United States to be affixed.

[SEAL.]   Done at the city of Washington, this 29th day of May, A. D. 1865, and of the Independence of the United States the eighty-ninth.

ANDREW JOHNSON.

By the President:

WILLIAM H. SEWARD,
Secretary of State.

BY THE PRESIDENT OF THE UNITED STATES OF AMERICA.

A PROCLAMATION.

Whereas the fourth section of the fourth article of the Constitution of the United States declares that the United States shall guarantee to every State in the Union a republican form of government and shall protect each of them against invasion and domestic violence; and

Whereas the President of the United States is by the Constitution made Commander in Chief of the Army and Navy, as well as chief civil

executive officer of the United States, and is bound by solemn oath faithfully to execute the office of President of the United States and to take care that the laws be faithfully executed; and

Whereas the rebellion which has been waged by a portion of the people of the United States against the properly constituted authorities of the Government thereof in the most violent and revolting form, but whose organized and armed forces have now been almost entirely overcome, has in its revolutionary progress deprived the people of the State of Mississippi of all civil government; and

Whereas it becomes necessary and proper to carry out and enforce the obligations of the United States to the people of Mississippi in securing them in the enjoyment of a republican form of government:

Now, therefore, in obedience to the high and solemn duties imposed upon me by the Constitution of the United States and for the purpose of enabling the loyal people of said State to organize a State government whereby justice may be established, domestic tranquillity insured, and loyal citizens protected in all their rights of life, liberty, and property, I, Andrew Johnson, President of the United States and Commander in Chief of the Army and Navy of the United States, do hereby appoint William L. Sharkey, of Mississippi, provisional governor of the State of Mississippi, whose duty it shall be, at the earliest practicable period, to prescribe such rules and regulations as may be necessary and proper for convening a convention composed of delegates to be chosen by that portion of the people of said State who are loyal to the United States, and no others, for the purpose of altering or amending the constitution thereof, and with authority to exercise within the limits of said State all the powers necessary and proper to enable such loyal people of the State of Mississippi to restore said State to its constitutional relations to the Federal Government and to present such a republican form of State government as will entitle the State to the guaranty of the United States therefor and its people to protection by the United States against invasion, insurrection, and domestic violence: *Provided*, That in any election that may be hereafter held for choosing delegates to any State convention as aforesaid no person shall be qualified as an elector or shall be eligible as a member of such convention unless he shall have previously taken and subscribed the oath of amnesty as set forth in the President's proclamation of May 29, A. D. 1865, and is a voter qualified as prescribed by the constitution and laws of the State of Mississippi in force immediately before the 9th of January, A. D. 1861, the date of the so-called ordinance of secession; and the said convention, when convened, or the legislature that may be thereafter assembled, will prescribe the qualification of electors and the eligibility of persons to hold office under the constitution and laws of the State—a power the people of the several States composing the Federal Union have rightfully exercised from the origin of the Government to the present time.

And I do hereby direct—

First. That the military commander of the department and all officers and persons in the military and naval service aid and assist the said provisional governor in carrying into effect this proclamation; and they are enjoined to abstain from in any way hindering, impeding, or discouraging the loyal people from the organization of a State government as herein authorized.

Second. That the Secretary of State proceed to put in force all laws of the United States the administration whereof belongs to the State Department applicable to the geographical limits aforesaid.

Third. That the Secretary of the Treasury proceed to nominate for appointment assessors of taxes and collectors of customs and internal revenue and such other officers of the Treasury Department as are authorized by law and put in execution the revenue laws of the United States within the geographical limits aforesaid. In making appointments the preference shall be given to qualified loyal persons residing within the districts where their respective duties are to be performed; but if suitable residents of the districts shall not be found, then persons residing in other States or districts shall be appointed.

Fourth. That the Postmaster-General proceed to establish post-offices and post routes and put into execution the postal laws of the United States within the said State, giving to loyal residents the preference of appointment; but if suitable residents are not found, then to appoint agents, etc., from other States.

Fifth. That the district judge for the judicial district in which Mississippi is included proceed to hold courts within said State in accordance with the provisions of the act of Congress. The Attorney-General will instruct the proper officers to libel and bring to judgment, confiscation, and sale property subject to confiscation and enforce the administration of justice within said State in all matters within the cognizance and jurisdiction of the Federal courts.

Sixth. That the Secretary of the Navy take possession of all public property belonging to the Navy Department within said geographical limits and put in operation all acts of Congress in relation to naval affairs having application to the said State.

Seventh. That the Secretary of the Interior put in force the laws relating to the Interior Department applicable to the geographical limits aforesaid.

In testimony whereof I have hereunto set my hand and caused the seal of the United States to be affixed.

[SEAL.]   Done at the city of Washington, this 13th day of June, A. D. 1865, and of the Independence of the United States the eighty-ninth.

ANDREW JOHNSON.

By the President:

WILLIAM H. SEWARD, *Secretary of State.*

BY THE PRESIDENT OF THE UNITED STATES OF AMERICA.

A PROCLAMATION.

Whereas by my proclamation* of the 29th of April, 1865, all restrictions upon internal, domestic, and commercial intercourse, with certain exceptions therein specified and set forth, were removed "in such parts of the States of Tennessee, Virginia, North Carolina, South Carolina, Georgia, Florida, Alabama, Mississippi, and so much of Louisiana as lies east of the Mississippi River as shall be embraced within the lines of national military occupation;" and

Whereas by my proclamation of the 22d of May, 1865, for reasons therein given, it was declared that certain ports of the United States which had been previously closed against foreign commerce should, with certain specified exceptions, be reopened to such commerce on and after the 1st day of July next, subject to the laws of the United States, and in pursuance of such regulations as might be prescribed by the Secretary of the Treasury; and

Whereas I am satisfactorily informed that dangerous combinations against the laws of the United States no longer exist within the State of Tennessee; that the insurrection heretofore existing within said State has been suppressed; that within the boundaries thereof the authority of the United States is undisputed, and that such officers of the United States as have been duly commissioned are in the undisturbed exercise of their official functions:

Now, therefore, be it known that I, Andrew Johnson, President of the United States, do hereby declare that all restrictions upon internal, domestic, and coastwise intercourse and trade and upon the removal of products of States heretofore declared in insurrection, reserving and excepting only those relating to contraband of war, as hereinafter recited, and also those which relate to the reservation of the rights of the United States to property purchased in the territory of an enemy heretofore imposed in the territory of the United States east of the Mississippi River, are annulled, and I do hereby direct that they be forthwith removed; and that on and after the 1st day of July next all restrictions upon foreign commerce with said ports, with the exception and reservation aforesaid, be likewise removed; and that the commerce of said States shall be conducted under the supervision of the regularly appointed officers of the customs provided by law, and such officers of the customs shall receive any captured and abandoned property that may be turned over to them under the law by the military or naval forces of the United States and dispose of such property as shall be directed by the Secretary of the Treasury. The following articles, contraband of war, are excepted from the effect of this proclamation: Arms, ammunition, all articles from which ammunition is made, and gray uniforms and cloth.

* Executive order.

And I hereby also proclaim and declare that the insurrection, so far as it relates to and within the State of Tennessee and the inhabitants of the said State of Tennessee as reorganized and constituted under their recently adopted constitution and reorganization and accepted by them, is suppressed, and therefore, also, that all the disabilities and disqualifications attaching to said State and the inhabitants thereof consequent upon any proclamation issued by virtue of the fifth section of the act entitled "An act further to provide for the collection of duties on imports and for other purposes," approved the 13th day of July, 1861, are removed.

But nothing herein contained shall be considered or construed as in any wise changing or impairing any of the penalties and forfeitures for treason heretofore incurred under the laws of the United States or any of the provisions, restrictions, or disabilities set forth in my proclamation bearing date the 29th day of May, 1865, or as impairing existing regulations for the suspension of the *habeas corpus* and the exercise of military law in cases where it shall be necessary for the general public safety and welfare during the existing insurrection; nor shall this proclamation affect or in any way impair any laws heretofore passed by Congress and duly approved by the President or any proclamations or orders issued by him during the aforesaid insurrection abolishing slavery or in any way affecting the relations of slavery, whether of persons or property; but, on the contrary, all such laws and proclamations heretofore made or issued are expressly saved and declared to be in full force and virtue.

In testimony whereof I have hereunto set my hand and caused the seal of the United States to be affixed.

[SEAL.] Done at the city of Washington, this 13th day of June, A. D. 1865, and of the Independence of the United States of America the eighty-ninth.

ANDREW JOHNSON.

By the President:

WILLIAM H. SEWARD,
Secretary of State.

BY THE PRESIDENT OF THE UNITED STATES OF AMERICA.

A PROCLAMATION.

Whereas the fourth section of the fourth article of the Constitution of the United States declares that the United States shall guarantee to every State in the Union a republican form of government and shall protect each of them against invasion and domestic violence; and

Whereas the President of the United States is by the Constitution made Commander in Chief of the Army and Navy, as well as chief civil

executive officer of the United States, and is bound by solemn oath faithfully to execute the office of President of the United States and to take care that the laws be faithfully executed; and

Whereas the rebellion which has been waged by a portion of the people of the United States against the properly constituted authorities of the Government thereof in the most violent and revolting form, but whose organized and armed forces have now been almost entirely overcome, has in its revolutionary progress deprived the people of the State of Georgia of all civil government; and

Whereas it becomes necessary and proper to carry out and enforce the obligations of the United States to the people of Georgia in securing them in the enjoyment of a republican form of government:

Now, therefore, in obedience to the high and solemn duties imposed upon me by the Constitution of the United States and for the purpose of enabling the loyal people of said State to organize a State government whereby justice may be established, domestic tranquillity insured, and loyal citizens protected in all their rights of life, liberty, and property, I, Andrew Johnson, President of the United States and Commander in Chief of the Army and Navy of the United States, do hereby appoint James Johnson, of Georgia, provisional governor of the State of Georgia, whose duty it shall be, at the earliest practicable period, to prescribe such rules and regulations as may be necessary and proper for convening a convention composed of delegates to be chosen by that portion of the people of said State who are loyal to the United States, and no others, for the purpose of altering or amending the constitution thereof, and with authority to exercise within the limits of said State all the powers necessary and proper to enable such loyal people of the State of Georgia to restore said State to its constitutional relations to the Federal Government and to present such a republican form of State government as will entitle the State to the guaranty of the United States therefor and its people to protection by the United States against invasion, insurrection, and domestic violence: *Provided*, That in any election that may be hereafter held for choosing delegates to any State convention as aforesaid no person shall be qualified as an elector or shall be eligible as a member of such convention unless he shall have previously taken and subscribed the oath of amnesty as set forth in the President's proclamation of May 29, A. D. 1865, and is a voter qualified as prescribed by the constitution and laws of the State of Georgia in force immediately before the 19th of January, A. D. 1861, the date of the so-called ordinance of secession; and the said convention, when convened, or the legislature that may be thereafter assembled, will prescribe the qualification of electors and the eligibility of persons to hold office under the constitution and laws of the State—a power the people of the several States composing the Federal Union have rightfully exercised from the origin of the Government to the present time.

And I do hereby direct—

First. That the military commander of the department and all officers and persons in the military and naval service aid and assist the said provisional governor in carrying into effect this proclamation; and they are enjoined to abstain from in any way hindering, impeding, or discouraging the loyal people from the organization of a State government as herein authorized.

Second. That the Secretary of State proceed to put in force all laws of the United States the administration whereof belongs to the State Department applicable to the geographical limits aforesaid.

Third. That the Secretary of the Treasury proceed to nominate for appointment assessors of taxes and collectors of customs and internal revenue and such other officers of the Treasury Department as are authorized by law and put in execution the revenue laws of the United States within the geographical limits aforesaid. In making appointments the preference shall be given to qualified loyal persons residing within the districts where their respective duties are to be performed; but if suitable residents of the districts shall not be found, then persons residing in other States or districts shall be appointed.

Fourth. That the Postmaster-General proceed to establish post-offices and post routes and put into execution the postal laws of the United States within the said State, giving to loyal residents the preference of appointment; but if suitable residents are not found, then to appoint agents, etc., from other States.

Fifth. That the district judge for the judicial district in which Georgia is included proceed to hold courts within said State in accordance with the provisions of the act of Congress. The Attorney-General will instruct the proper officers to libel and bring to judgment, confiscation, and sale property subject to confiscation and enforce the administration of justice within said State in all matters within the cognizance and jurisdiction of the Federal courts.

Sixth. That the Secretary of the Navy take possession of all public property belonging to the Navy Department within said geographical limits and put in operation all acts of Congress in relation to naval affairs having application to the said State.

Seventh. That the Secretary of the Interior put in force the laws relating to the Interior Department applicable to the geographical limits aforesaid.

In testimony whereof I have hereunto set my hand and caused the seal of the United States to be affixed.

[SEAL.]   Done at the city of Washington, this 17th day of June, A. D. 1865, and of the Independence of the United States the eighty-ninth.

ANDREW JOHNSON.

By the President:

WILLIAM H. SEWARD, *Secretary of State.*

By the President of the United States of America.

A PROCLAMATION.

Whereas the fourth section of the fourth article of the Constitution of the United States declares that the United States shall guarantee to every State in the Union a republican form of government and shall protect each of them against invasion and domestic violence; and

Whereas the President of the United States is by the Constitution made Commander in Chief of the Army and Navy, as well as chief civil executive officer of the United States, and is bound by solemn oath faithfully to execute the office of President of the United States and to take care that the laws be faithfully executed; and

Whereas the rebellion which has been waged by a portion of the people of the United States against the properly constituted authorities of the Government thereof in the most violent and revolting form, but whose organized and armed forces have now been almost entirely overcome, has in its revolutionary progress deprived the people of the State of Texas of all civil government; and

Whereas it becomes necessary and proper to carry out and enforce the obligations of the United States to the people of the State of Texas in securing them in the enjoyment of a republican form of government:

Now, therefore, in obedience to the high and solemn duties imposed upon me by the Constitution of the United States and for the purpose of enabling the loyal people of said State to organize a State government whereby justice may be established, domestic tranquillity insured, and loyal citizens protected in all their rights of life, liberty, and property, I, Andrew Johnson, President of the United States and Commander in Chief of the Army and Navy of the United States, do hereby appoint Andrew J. Hamilton, of Texas, provisional governor of the State of Texas, whose duty it shall be, at the earliest practicable period, to prescribe such rules and regulations as may be necessary and proper for convening a convention composed of delegates to be chosen by that portion of the people of said State who are loyal to the United States, and no others, for the purpose of altering or amending the constitution thereof, and with authority to exercise within the limits of said State all the powers necessary and proper to enable such loyal people of the State of Texas to restore said State to its constitutional relations to the Federal Government and to present such a republican form of State government as will entitle the State to the guaranty of the United States therefor and its people to protection by the United States against invasion, insurrection, and domestic violence: *Provided*, That in any election that may be hereafter held for choosing delegates to any State convention as aforesaid no person shall be qualified as an elector or shall be eligible as a member of such convention unless he shall have previously taken and subscribed the oath of amnesty as set forth in the

President's proclamation of May 29, A. D. 1865, and is a voter qualified as prescribed by the constitution and laws of the State of Texas in force immediately before the 1st day of February, A. D. 1861, the date of the so-called ordinance of secession; and the said convention, when convened, or the legislature that may be thereafter assembled, will prescribe the qualification of electors and the eligibility of persons to hold office under the constitution and laws of the State—a power the people of the several States composing the Federal Union have rightfully exercised from the origin of the Government to the present time.

And I do hereby direct—

First. That the military commander of the department and all officers and persons in the military and naval service aid and assist the said provisional governor in carrying into effect this proclamation; and they are enjoined to abstain from in any way hindering, impeding, or discouraging the loyal people from the organization of a State government as herein authorized.

Second. That the Secretary of State proceed to put in force all laws of the United States the administration whereof belongs to the State Department applicable to the geographical limits aforesaid.

Third. That the Secretary of the Treasury proceed to nominate for appointment assessors of taxes and collectors of customs and internal revenue and such other officers of the Treasury Department as are authorized by law and put in execution the revenue laws of the United States within the geographical limits aforesaid. In making appointments the preference shall be given to qualified loyal persons residing within the districts where their respective duties are to be performed; but if suitable residents of the districts shall not be found, then persons residing in other States or districts shall be appointed.

Fourth. That the Postmaster-General proceed to establish post-offices and post routes and put into execution the postal laws of the United States within the said State, giving to loyal residents the preference of appointment; but if suitable residents are not found, then to appoint agents, etc., from other States.

Fifth. That the district judge for the judicial district in which Texas is included proceed to hold courts within said State in accordance with the provisions of the act of Congress. The Attorney-General will instruct the proper officers to libel and bring to judgment, confiscation, and sale property subject to confiscation and enforce the administration of justice within said State in all matters within the cognizance and jurisdiction of the Federal courts.

Sixth. That the Secretary of the Navy take possession of all public property belonging to the Navy Department within said geographical limits and put in operation all acts of Congress in relation to naval affairs having application to the said State.

Seventh. That the Secretary of the Interior put in force the laws relating to the Interior Department applicable to the geographical limits aforesaid.

In testimony whereof I have hereunto set my hand and caused the seal of the United States to be affixed.

[SEAL.] Done at the city of Washington, this 17th day of June, A. D. 1865, and of the Independence of the United States the eighty-ninth.

ANDREW JOHNSON.

By the President:

WILLIAM H. SEWARD, *Secretary of State.*

BY THE PRESIDENT OF THE UNITED STATES OF AMERICA.

A PROCLAMATION.

Whereas the fourth section of the fourth article of the Constitution of the United States declares that the United States shall guarantee to every State in the Union a republican form of government and shall protect each of them against invasion and domestic violence; and

Whereas the President of the United States is by the Constitution made Commander in Chief of the Army and Navy, as well as chief civil executive officer of the United States, and is bound by solemn oath faithfully to execute the office of President of the United States and to take care that the laws be faithfully executed; and

Whereas the rebellion which has been waged by a portion of the people of the United States against the properly constituted authorities of the Government thereof in the most violent and revolting form, but whose organized and armed forces have now been almost entirely overcome, has in its revolutionary progress deprived the people of the State of Alabama of all civil government; and

Whereas it becomes necessary and proper to carry out and enforce the obligations of the United States to the people of Alabama in securing them in the enjoyment of a republican form of government:

Now, therefore, in obedience to the high and solemn duties imposed upon me by the Constitution of the United States and for the purpose of enabling the loyal people of said State to organize a State government whereby justice may be established, domestic tranquillity insured, and loyal citizens protected in all their rights of life, liberty, and property, I, Andrew Johnson, President of the United States and Commander in Chief of the Army and Navy of the United States, do hereby appoint Lewis E. Parsons, of Alabama, provisional governor of the State of Alabama, whose duty it shall be, at the earliest practicable period, to prescribe such rules and regulations as may be necessary and proper for convening a convention composed of delegates to be chosen by that portion of the people of said State who are loyal to the United States, and no others, for the purpose of altering or amending the constitution thereof, and with authority to exercise within the limits of said State all the powers necessary and proper to enable such loyal people of the State of Alabama to restore said State to its constitutional relations to the Federal Government and to present such a republican form of State government as will entitle the State to the guaranty of the United States therefor and its people to protection by the United States against invasion, insurrection, and domestic violence: *Provided*, That in any election that may be hereafter held for choosing delegates to any State convention as aforesaid no person shall be qualified as an elector or shall be eligible as a member of such convention unless he shall have previously taken and subscribed the oath of amnesty as set forth in the President's proclamation of May 29, A. D. 1865, and is a voter qualified as prescribed by the constitution and laws of the State of Alabama in force immediately before the 11th day of January, A. D. 1861, the date of the so-called ordinance of secession; and the said convention, when convened, or the legislature that may be thereafter assembled, will prescribe the qualification of electors and the eligibility of persons to hold office under the constitution and laws of the State, a power the people of the several States composing the Federal Union have rightfully exercised from the origin of the Government to the present time.

And I do hereby direct—

First. That the military commander of the department and all officers and persons in the military and naval service aid and assist the said provisional governor in carrying into effect this proclamation; and they are enjoined to abstain from in any way hindering, impeding, or discouraging the loyal people from the organization of a State government as herein authorized.

Second. That the Secretary of State proceed to put in force all laws of the United States the administration whereof belongs to the State Department applicable to the geographical limits aforesaid.

Third. That the Secretary of the Treasury proceed to nominate for appointment assessors of taxes and collectors of customs and internal revenue and such other officers of the Treasury Department as are authorized by law and put in execution the revenue laws of the United States within the geographical limits aforesaid. In making appointments the preference shall be given to qualified loyal persons residing within the districts where their respective duties are to be performed; but if suitable residents of the districts shall not be found, then persons residing in other States or districts shall be appointed.

Fourth. That the Postmaster-General proceed to establish post-offices and post routes and put into execution the postal laws of the United States within the said State, giving to loyal residents the preference of appointment; but if suitable residents are not found, then to appoint agents, etc., from other States.

Fifth. That the district judge for the judicial district in which Alabama is included proceed to hold courts within said State in accordance with the provisions of the act of Congress. The Attorney-General will instruct the proper officers to libel and bring to judgment, confiscation, and sale property subject to confiscation and enforce the administration of justice within said State in all matters within the cognizance and jurisdiction of the Federal courts.

Sixth. That the Secretary of the Navy take possession of all public property belonging to the Navy Department within said geographical limits and put in operation all acts of Congress in relation to naval affairs having application to the said State.

Seventh. That the Secretary of the Interior put in force the laws relating to the Interior Department applicable to the geographical limits aforesaid.

In testimony whereof I have hereunto set my hand and caused the seal of the United States to be affixed.

[SEAL.]   Done at the city of Washington, this 21st day of June, A. D. 1865, and of the Independence of the United States the eighty-ninth.   ANDREW JOHNSON.

By the President:

WILLIAM H. SEWARD, *Secretary of State.*

BY THE PRESIDENT OF THE UNITED STATES OF AMERICA.

A PROCLAMATION.

Whereas by the proclamations of the President of the 19th and 27th of April, 1861, a blockade of certain ports of the United States was set on foot; but

Whereas the reasons for that measure have ceased to exist:

Now, therefore, be it known that I, Andrew Johnson, President of the United States, do hereby declare and proclaim the blockade aforesaid to be rescinded as to all the ports aforesaid, including that of Galveston and other ports west of the Mississippi River, which ports will be open to foreign commerce on the 1st of July next on the terms and conditions set forth in my proclamation of the 22d of May last.

It is to be understood, however, that the blockade thus rescinded was an international measure for the purpose of protecting the sovereign rights of the United States. The greater or less subversion of civil authority in the region to which it applied and the impracticability of at once restoring that in due efficiency may for a season make it advisable to employ the Army and Navy of the United States toward carrying the laws into effect wherever such employment may be necessary.

In testimony whereof I have hereunto set my hand and caused the seal of the United States to be affixed.

[SEAL.]   Done at the city of Washington, this 23d day of June, A. D. 1865, and of the Independence of the United States of America the eighty-ninth.   ANDREW JOHNSON.

By the President:

W. HUNTER, *Acting Secretary of State.*

By the President of the United States.

A PROCLAMATION.

Whereas it has been the desire of the General Government of the United States to restore unrestricted commercial intercourse between and in the several States as soon as the same could be safely done in view of resistance to the authority of the United States by combinations of armed insurgents; and

Whereas that desire has been shown in my proclamations of the 29th of April, 1865, the 13th of June, 1865, and the 23d of June, 1865; and

Whereas it now seems expedient and proper to remove restrictions upon internal, domestic, and coastwise trade and commercial intercourse between and within the States and Territories west of the Mississippi River:

Now, therefore, be it known that I, Andrew Johnson, President of the United States, do hereby declare that all restrictions upon internal, domestic, and coastwise intercourse and trade and upon the purchase and removal of products of States and parts of States and Territories heretofore declared in insurrection, lying west of the Mississippi River (excepting only those relating to property heretofore purchased by the agents or captured by or surrendered to the forces of the United States and to the transportation thereto or therein on private account of arms, ammunition, all articles from which ammunition is made, gray uniforms, and gray cloth), are annulled; and I do hereby direct that they be forthwith removed, and also that the commerce of such States and parts of States shall be conducted under the supervision of the regularly appointed officers of the customs, [who] shall receive any captured and abandoned property that may be turned over to them under the law by the military or naval forces of the United States and dispose of the same in accordance with instructions on the subject issued by the Secretary of the Treasury.

In testimony whereof I have hereunto set my hand and caused the seal of the United States to be affixed.

[SEAL.]　　Done at the city of Washington, this 24th day of June, A. D. 1865, and of the Independence of the United States of America the eighty-ninth.　　ANDREW JOHNSON.

By the President:

W. HUNTER, *Acting Secretary of State.*

By the President of the United States of America.

A PROCLAMATION.

Whereas the fourth section of the fourth article of the Constitution of the United States declares that the United States shall guarantee to every State in the Union a republican form of government and shall protect each of them against invasion and domestic violence; and

Whereas the President of the United States is by the Constitution made Commander in Chief of the Army and Navy, as well as chief civil

executive officer of the United States, and is bound by solemn oath faithfully to execute the office of President of the United States and to take care that the laws be faithfully executed; and

Whereas the rebellion which has been waged by a portion of the people of the United States against the properly constituted authorities of the Government thereof in the most violent and revolting form, but whose organized and armed forces have now been almost entirely overcome, has in its revolutionary progress deprived the people of the State of South Carolina of all civil government; and

Whereas it becomes necessary and proper to carry out and enforce the obligations of the United States to the people of South Carolina in securing them in the enjoyment of a republican form of government:

Now, therefore, in obedience to the high and solemn duties imposed upon me by the Constitution of the United States and for the purpose of enabling the loyal people of said State to organize a State government whereby justice may be established, domestic tranquillity insured, and loyal citizens protected in all their rights of life, liberty, and property, I, Andrew Johnson, President of the United States and Commander in Chief of the Army and Navy of the United States, do hereby appoint Benjamin F. Perry, of South Carolina, provisional governor of the State of South Carolina, whose duty it shall be, at the earliest practicable period, to prescribe such rules and regulations as may be necessary and proper for convening a convention composed of delegates to be chosen by that portion of the people of said State who are loyal to the United States, and no others, for the purpose of altering or amending the constitution thereof, and with authority to exercise within the limits of said State all the powers necessary and proper to enable such loyal people of the State of South Carolina to restore said State to its constitutional relations to the Federal Government and to present such a republican form of State government as will entitle the State to the guaranty of the United States therefor and its people to protection by the United States against invasion, insurrection, and domestic violence: *Provided*, That in any election that may be hereafter held for choosing delegates to any State convention as aforesaid no person shall be qualified as an elector or shall be eligible as a member of such convention unless he shall have previously taken and subscribed the oath of amnesty as set forth in the President's proclamation of May 29, A. D. 1865, and is a voter qualified as prescribed by the constitution and laws of the State of South Carolina in force immediately before the 17th day of November, A. D. 1860, the date of the so-called ordinance of secession; and the said convention, when convened, or the legislature that may be thereafter assembled, will prescribe the qualification of electors and the eligibility of persons to hold office under the constitution and laws of the State—a power the people of the several States composing the Federal Union have rightfully exercised from the origin of the Government to the present time.

And I do hereby direct—

First. That the military commander of the department and all officers and persons in the military and naval service aid and assist the said provisional governor in carrying into effect this proclamation; and they are enjoined to abstain from in any way hindering, impeding, or discouraging the loyal people from the organization of a State government as herein authorized.

Second. That the Secretary of State proceed to put in force all laws of the United States the administration whereof belongs to the State Department applicable to the geographical limits aforesaid.

Third. That the Secretary of the Treasury proceed to nominate for appointment assessors of taxes and collectors of customs and internal revenue and such other officers of the Treasury Department as are authorized by law and put in execution the revenue laws of the United States within the geographical limits aforesaid. In making appointments the preference shall be given to qualified loyal persons residing within the districts where their respective duties are to be performed; but if suitable residents of the districts shall not be found, then persons residing in other States or districts shall be appointed.

Fourth. That the Postmaster-General proceed to establish post-offices and post routes and put into execution the postal laws of the United States within the said State, giving to loyal residents the preference of appointment; but if suitable residents are not found, then to appoint agents, etc., from other States.

Fifth. That the district judge for the judicial district in which South Carolina is included proceed to hold courts within said State in accordance with the provisions of the act of Congress. The Attorney-General will instruct the proper officers to libel and bring to judgment, confiscation, and sale property subject to confiscation and enforce the administration of justice within said State in all matters within the cognizance and jurisdiction of the Federal courts.

Sixth. That the Secretary of the Navy take possession of all public property belonging to the Navy Department within said geographical limits and put in operation all acts of Congress in relation to naval affairs having application to the said State.

Seventh. That the Secretary of the Interior put in force the laws relating to the Interior Department applicable to the geographical limits aforesaid.

In testimony whereof I have hereunto set my hand and caused the seal of the United States to be affixed.

[SEAL.]   Done at the city of Washington, this 30th day of June, A. D. 1865, and of the Independence of the United States the eighty-ninth.

ANDREW JOHNSON.

By the President:

WILLIAM H. SEWARD, *Secretary of State.*

By the President of the United States of America.

A PROCLAMATION.

Whereas the fourth section of the fourth article of the Constitution of the United States declares that the United States shall guarantee to every State in the Union a republican form of government and shall protect each of them against invasion and domestic violence; and

Whereas the President of the United States is by the Constitution made Commander in Chief of the Army and Navy, as well as chief civil executive officer of the United States, and is bound by solemn oath faithfully to execute the office of President of the United States and to take care that the laws be faithfully executed; and

Whereas the rebellion which has been waged by a portion of the people of the United States against the properly constituted authorities of the Government thereof in the most violent and revolting form, but whose organized and armed forces have now been almost entirely overcome, has in its revolutionary progress deprived the people of the State of Florida of all civil government; and

Whereas it becomes necessary and proper to carry out and enforce the obligations of the United States to the people of Florida in securing them in the enjoyment of a republican form of government:

Now, therefore, in obedience to the high and solemn duties imposed upon me by the Constitution of the United States and for the purpose of enabling the loyal people of said State to organize a State government whereby justice may be established, domestic tranquillity insured, and loyal citizens protected in all their rights of life, liberty, and property, I, Andrew Johnson, President of the United States and Commander in Chief of the Army and Navy of the United States, do hereby appoint William Marvin provisional governor of the State of Florida, whose duty it shall be, at the earliest practicable period, to prescribe such rules and regulations as may be necessary and proper for convening a convention composed of delegates to be chosen by that portion of the people of said State who are loyal to the United States, and no others, for the purpose of altering or amending the constitution thereof, and with authority to exercise within the limits of said State all the powers necessary and proper to enable such loyal people of the State of Florida to restore said State to its constitutional relations to the Federal Government and to present such a republican form of State government as will entitle the State to the guaranty of the United States therefor and its people to protection by the United States against invasion, insurrection, and domestic violence: *Provided*, That in any election that may be hereafter held for choosing delegates to any State convention as aforesaid no person shall be qualified as an elector or shall be eligible as a member of such convention unless he shall have previously taken and subscribed the oath of amnesty as set forth in the President's proclamation of May 29, A. D. 1865, and is a voter qualified as prescribed by the constitution and laws of the State of Florida in force immediately before the 10th day of January, A. D. 1861, the date of the so-called ordinance of secession; and the said convention, when convened, or the legislature that may be thereafter assembled, will prescribe the qualification of electors and the eligibility of persons to hold office under the constitution and laws of the State—a power the people of the several States composing the Federal Union have rightfully exercised from the origin of the Government to the present time.

And I do hereby direct—

First. That the military commander of the department and all officers and persons in the military and naval service aid and assist the said provisional governor in carrying into effect this proclamation; and they are enjoined to abstain from in any way hindering, impeding, or discouraging the loyal people from the organization of a State government as herein authorized.

Second. That the Secretary of State proceed to put in force all laws of the United States the administration whereof belongs to the State Department applicable to the geographical limits aforesaid.

Third. That the Secretary of the Treasury proceed to nominate for appointment assessors of taxes and collectors of customs and internal revenue and such other officers of the Treasury Department as are authorized by law and put in execution the revenue laws of the United States within the geographical limits aforesaid. In making appointments the preference shall be given to qualified loyal persons residing within the districts where their respective duties are to be performed; but if suitable residents of the districts shall not be found, then persons residing in other States or districts shall be appointed.

Fourth. That the Postmaster-General proceed to establish post-offices and post routes and put into execution the postal laws of the United States within the said State, giving to loyal residents the preference of appointment; but if suitable residents are not found, then to appoint agents, etc., from other States.

Fifth. That the district judge for the judicial district in which Florida is included proceed to hold courts within said State in accordance with the provisions of the act of Congress. The Attorney-General will instruct the proper officers to libel and bring to judgment, confiscation, and sale property subject to confiscation and enforce the administration of justice within said State in all matters within the cognizance and jurisdiction of the Federal courts.

Sixth. That the Secretary of the Navy take possession of all public property belonging to the Navy Department within said geographical limits and put in operation all acts of Congress in relation to naval affairs having application to the said State.

Seventh. That the Secretary of the Interior put in force the laws relating to the Interior Department applicable to the geographical limits aforesaid.

In testimony whereof I have hereunto set my hand and caused the seal of the United States to be affixed.

[SEAL.] Done at the city of Washington, this 13th day of July, A. D. 1865, and of the Independence of the United States the nine-tieth.

ANDREW JOHNSON.

By the President:
WILLIAM H. SEWARD,
Secretary of State.

BY THE PRESIDENT OF THE UNITED STATES OF AMERICA.

A PROCLAMATION.

Whereas by my proclamations of the 13th and 24th of June, 1865, removing restrictions, in part, upon internal, domestic, and coastwise intercourse and trade with those States recently declared in insurrection, certain articles were excepted from the effect of said proclamations as contraband of war; and

Whereas the necessity for restricting trade in said articles has now in a great measure ceased:

It is hereby ordered that on and after the 1st day of September, 1865, all restrictions aforesaid be removed, so that the articles declared by the said proclamations to be contraband of war may be imported into and sold in said States, subject only to such regulations as the Secretary of the Treasury may prescribe.

In testimony whereof I have hereunto set my hand and caused the seal of the United States to be affixed.

[SEAL.] Done at the city of Washington, this 29th day of August, A. D. 1865, and of the Independence of the United States of America the ninetieth.

ANDREW JOHNSON.

By the President:
WILLIAM H. SEWARD,
Secretary of State.

BY THE PRESIDENT OF THE UNITED STATES OF AMERICA.

A PROCLAMATION.

Whereas by a proclamation of the 5th day of July, 1864, the President of the United States, when the civil war was flagrant and when combinations were in progress in Kentucky for the purpose of inciting insurgent raids into that State, directed that the proclamation suspending the privilege of the writ of *habeas corpus* should be made effectual in

Kentucky and that martial law should be established there and continue until said proclamation should be revoked or modified; and

Whereas since then the danger from insurgent raids into Kentucky has substantially passed away:

Now, therefore, be it known that I, Andrew Johnson, President of the United States, by virtue of the authority vested in me by the Constitution, do hereby declare that the said proclamation of the 5th day of July, 1864, shall be, and is hereby, modified in so far that martial law shall be no longer in force in Kentucky from and after the date hereof.

In testimony whereof I have hereunto set my hand and caused the seal of the United States to be affixed.

[SEAL.] Done at the city of Washington, this 12th day of October, A. D. 1865, and of the Independence of the United States of America the ninetieth. ANDREW JOHNSON.

By the President:

W. HUNTER, *Acting Secretary of State.*

BY THE PRESIDENT OF THE UNITED STATES OF AMERICA.

A PROCLAMATION.

Whereas it has pleased Almighty God during the year which is now coming to an end to relieve our beloved country from the fearful scourge of civil war and to permit us to secure the blessings of peace, unity, and harmony, with a great enlargement of civil liberty; and

Whereas our Heavenly Father has also during the year graciously averted from us the calamities of foreign war, pestilence, and famine, while our granaries are full of the fruits of an abundant season; and

Whereas righteousness exalteth a nation, while sin is a reproach to any people:

Now, therefore, be it known that I, Andrew Johnson, President of the United States, do hereby recommend to the people thereof that they do set apart and observe the first Thursday of December next as a day of national thanksgiving to the Creator of the Universe for these great deliverances and blessings.

And I do further recommend that on that occasion the whole people make confession of our national sins against His infinite goodness, and with one heart and one mind implore the divine guidance in the ways of national virtue and holiness.

In testimony whereof I have hereunto set my hand and caused the seal of the United States to be affixed.

[SEAL.] Done at the city of Washington, this 28th day of October, A. D. 1865, and of the Independence of the United States of America the ninetieth. ANDREW JOHNSON.

By the President:

WILLIAM H. SEWARD, *Secretary of State.*

By the President of the United States of America.

A PROCLAMATION.

Whereas by the proclamation of the President of the United States of the 15th day of September, 1863, the privilege of the writ of *habeas corpus* was, in certain cases therein set forth, suspended throughout the United States; and

Whereas the reasons for that suspension may be regarded as having ceased in some of the States and Territories:

Now, therefore, be it known that I, Andrew Johnson, President of the United States, do hereby proclaim and declare that the suspension aforesaid and all other proclamations and orders suspending the privilege of the writ of *habeas corpus* in the States and Territories of the United States are revoked and annulled, excepting as to the States of Virginia, Kentucky, Tennessee, North Carolina, South Carolina, Georgia, Florida, Alabama, Mississippi, Louisiana, Arkansas, and Texas, the District of Columbia, and the Territories of New Mexico and Arizona.

In witness whereof I have hereunto set my hand and caused the seal of the United States to be affixed.

[SEAL.] Done at the city of Washington, this 1st day of December, A. D. 1865, and of the Independence of the United States of America the ninetieth.   ANDREW JOHNSON.

By the President:
    WILLIAM H. SEWARD,
            Secretary of State.

EXECUTIVE ORDERS.

EXECUTIVE CHAMBER,
Washington, April 29, 1865.

Being desirous to relieve all loyal citizens and well-disposed persons residing in insurrectionary States from unnecessary commercial restrictions and to encourage them to return to peaceful pursuits—

It is hereby ordered, I. That all restrictions upon internal, domestic, and coastwise commercial intercourse be discontinued in such parts of the States of Tennessee, Virginia, North Carolina, South Carolina, Georgia, Florida, Alabama, Mississippi, and so much of Louisiana as lies east of the Mississippi River as shall be embraced within the lines of national military occupation, excepting only such restrictions as are imposed by acts of Congress and regulations in pursuance thereof prescribed by the Secretary of the Treasury and approved by the President, and excepting also from the effect of this order the following articles contraband of war, to wit: Arms, ammunition, all articles from which ammunition is manufactured, gray uniforms and cloth, locomotives, cars, railroad iron, and machinery for operating railroads, telegraph wires, insulators, and instruments for operating telegraphic lines.

II. That all existing military and naval orders in any manner restricting internal, domestic, and coastwise commercial intercourse and trade with or in the localities above named be, and the same are hereby, revoked, and that no military or naval officer in any manner interrupt or interfere with the same, or with any boats or other vessels engaged therein under proper authority, pursuant to the regulations of the Secretary of the Treasury.

ANDREW JOHNSON.

WAR DEPARTMENT,
Washington City, April 29, 1865.

The Executive order of January 20, 1865, prohibiting the exportation of hay, is rescinded from and after the 1st day of May, 1865.

By order of the President:

EDWIN M. STANTON,
Secretary of War.

EXECUTIVE CHAMBER,
Washington City, May 1, 1865.

Whereas the Attorney-General of the United States hath given his opinion that the persons implicated in the murder of the late President, Abraham Lincoln, and the attempted assassination of the Hon. William H. Seward, Secretary of State, and in an alleged conspiracy to assassinate other officers of the Federal Government at Washington City, and their aiders and abettors, are subject to the jurisdiction of and lawfully triable before a military commission—

It is ordered:

First. That the assistant adjutant-general detail nine competent military officers to serve as a commission for the trial of said parties, and that the Judge-Advocate-General proceed to prefer charges against said parties for their alleged offenses and bring them to trial before said military commission; that said trial or trials be conducted by the said Judge-Advocate-General, and as recorder thereof, in person, aided by such assistant or special judge-advocate as he may designate, and that said trials be conducted with all diligence consistent with the ends of justice; the said commission to sit without regard to hours.

Second. That Brevet Major-General Hartranft be assigned to duty as special provost-marshal-general for the purpose of said trial, and attendance upon said commission, and the execution of its mandates.

Third. That the said commission establish such order or rules of proceeding as may avoid unnecessary delay and conduce to the ends of public justice.

ANDREW JOHNSON.

Official copy:

W. A. NICHOLS,
Assistant Adjutant-General.

WAR DEPARTMENT,
Washington, D. C., May 3, 1865.

ORDER RESCINDING REGULATIONS PROHIBITING THE EXPORTATION OF ARMS, AMMUNITION, HORSES, MULES, AND LIVE STOCK.

The Executive order of November 21, 1862, prohibiting the exportation of arms and ammunition from the United States, and the Executive order of May 13, 1863,* prohibiting the exportation of horses, mules, and live stock, being no longer required by public necessities, the aforesaid orders are hereby rescinded and annulled.

By order of the President of the United States:

EDWIN M. STANTON,
Secretary of War.

EXECUTIVE MANSION,
Washington, May 4, 1865.

This being the day of the funeral of the late President, Abraham Lincoln, at Springfield, Ill., the Executive Office and the various Departments will be closed at 12 m. to-day.

ANDREW JOHNSON,
President of the United States.

SPECIAL ORDERS, No. 211.

WAR DEPARTMENT,
ADJUTANT-GENERAL'S OFFICE,
Washington, May 6, 1865.

*   *   *   *   *   *   *

4. A military commission is hereby appointed to meet at Washington, D. C., on Monday, the 8th day of May, 1865, at 9 o'clock a. m., or as soon thereafter as practicable, for the trial of David E. Herold, George A. Atzerodt, Lewis Payne, Michael O'Laughlin, Edward Spangler, Samuel Arnold, Mary E. Surratt, Samuel A. Mudd, and such other prisoners as may be brought before it, implicated in the murder of the late President, Abraham Lincoln, and the attempted assassination of the Hon. William

---

*Order of Secretary of War.

H. Seward, Secretary of State, and in an alleged conspiracy to assassinate other officers of the Federal Government at Washington City, and their aiders and abettors.

Detail for the court.

Major-General David Hunter, United States Volunteers.

Major-General Lewis Wallace, United States Volunteers.

Brevet Major-General August V. Kautz, United States Volunteers.

Brigadier-General Albion P. Howe, United States Volunteers.

Brigadier-General Robert S. Foster, United States Volunteers.

Brevet Brigadier-General Cyrus B. Comstock,* United States Volunteers.

Brigadier-General T. M. Harris, United States Volunteers.

Brevet Colonel Horace Porter,† aid-de-camp.

Lieutenant-Colonel David R. Clendenin, Eighth Illinois Cavalry.

Brigadier-General Joseph Holt, Judge-Advocate-General, United States Army, is appointed the judge-advocate and recorder of the commission, to be aided by such assistant or special judge-advocate as he may designate.

The commission will sit without regard to hours.

By order of the President of the United States:

E. D. TOWNSEND,
Assistant Adjutant-General.

WAR DEPARTMENT, *Washington City, May 7, 1865.*

Brigadier-General Holt, Judge-Advocate-General, having designated the Hon. John A. Bingham as a special judge-advocate, whose aid he requires in the prosecution of Herold and others before the military commission of which Major-General Hunter is presiding officer:

It is ordered, That the said John A. Bingham be, and he is hereby, appointed special judge-advocate for the purpose aforesaid, to aid the Judge-Advocate-General, pursuant to the order of the President in respect to said military commission.

By order of the President:

EDWIN M. STANTON,
Secretary of War.

SPECIAL ORDERS, No. 216.

WAR DEPARTMENT,
ADJUTANT-GENERAL'S OFFICE,
Washington, May 9, 1865.

*   *   *   *   *   *   *

91. Brevet Brigadier-General Cyrus B. Comstock, United States Volunteers, and Brevet Colonel Horace Porter, aid-de-camp, are hereby relieved

---

* Brevet Brigadier-General James A. Ekin substituted; see Special Orders, No. 216.

† Brevet Colonel C. H. Tompkins substituted; see Special Orders, No. 216.

from duty as members of the military commission appointed in Special Orders, No. 211, paragraph 4, dated "War Department, Adjutant-General's Office, Washington, May 6, 1865," and Brevet Brigadier-General James A. Ekin, United States Volunteers, and Brevet Colonel C. H. Tompkins, United States Army, are detailed in their places, respectively.

The commission will be composed as follows:

Major-General David Hunter, United States Volunteers.
Major-General Lewis Wallace, United States Volunteers.
Brevet Major-General August V. Kautz, United States Volunteers.
Brigadier-General Albion P. Howe, United States Volunteers.
Brigadier-General Robert S. Foster, United States Volunteers.
Brevet Brigadier-General James A. Ekin, United States Volunteers.
Brigadier-General T. M. Harris, United States Volunteers.
Brevet Colonel C. H. Tompkins, United States Army.
Lieutenant-Colonel David R. Clendenin, Eighth Illinois Cavalry.
Brigadier-General Joseph Holt, judge-advocate and recorder.

By order of the President of the United States:

E. D. TOWNSEND,
Assistant Adjutant-General.

EXECUTIVE CHAMBER,
Washington City, May 9, 1865.

EXECUTIVE ORDER TO REESTABLISH THE AUTHORITY OF THE UNITED STATES AND EXECUTE THE LAWS WITHIN THE GEOGRAPHICAL LIMITS KNOWN AS THE STATE OF VIRGINIA.

Ordered, first. That all acts and proceedings of the political, military, and civil organizations which have been in a state of insurrection and rebellion within the State of Virginia against the authority and laws of the United States, and of which Jefferson Davis, John Letcher, and William Smith were late the respective chiefs, are declared null and void. All persons who shall exercise, claim, pretend, or attempt to exercise any political, military, or civil power, authority, jurisdiction, or right by, through, or under Jefferson Davis, late of the city of Richmond, and his confederates, or under John Letcher or William Smith and their confederates, or under any pretended political, military, or civil commission or authority issued by them or either of them since the 17th day of April, 1861, shall be deemed and taken as in rebellion against the United States, and shall be dealt with accordingly.

Second. That the Secretary of State proceed to put in force all laws of the United States the administration whereof belongs to the Department of State applicable to the geographical limits aforesaid.

Third. That the Secretary of the Treasury proceed without delay to nominate for appointment assessors of taxes and collectors of customs and internal revenue and such other officers of the Treasury Department as are authorized by law, and shall put in execution the revenue laws of the United States within the geographical limits aforesaid. In making appointments the preference shall be given to qualified loyal persons residing within the districts where their respective duties are to be performed; but if suitable persons shall not be found residents of the districts, then persons residing in other States or districts shall be appointed.

Fourth. That the Postmaster-General shall proceed to establish post-offices and post routes and put into execution the postal laws of the United States within the said State, giving to loyal residents the preference of appointment; but if suitable persons are not found, then to appoint agents, etc., from other States.

Fifth. That the district judge of said district proceed to hold courts within said State in accordance with the provisions of the act of Congress. The Attorney-General will instruct the proper officers to libel and bring to judgment, confiscation, and sale property subject to confiscation, and enforce the administration of justice within said State in all matters, civil and criminal, within the cognizance and jurisdiction of the Federal courts.

Sixth. That the Secretary of War assign such assistant provost-marshal-general and such provost-marshals in each district of said State as he may deem necessary.

Seventh. The Secretary of the Navy will take possession of all public property belonging to the Navy Department within said geographical limits and put in operation all acts of Congress in relation to naval affairs having application to the said State.

Eighth. The Secretary of the Interior will also put in force the laws relating to the Department of the Interior.

Ninth. That to carry into effect the guaranty by the Federal Constitution of a republican form of State government and afford the advantage and security of domestic laws, as well as to complete the reestablishment of the authority and laws of the United States and the full and complete restoration of peace within the limits aforesaid, Francis H. Peirpoint, governor of the State of Virginia, will be aided by the Federal Government so far as may be necessary in the lawful measures which he may take for the extension and administration of the State government throughout the geographical limits of said State.

In testimony whereof I have hereunto set my hand and caused the seal of the United States to be affixed.

[SEAL.]   ANDREW JOHNSON.

By the President:
> W. HUNTER,
>   *Acting Secretary of State.*

WAR DEPARTMENT,
Washington City, May 27, 1865.

Ordered, That in all cases of sentences by military tribunals of imprisonment during the war the sentence be remitted and that the prisoners be discharged. The Adjutant-General will issue immediately the necessary instructions to carry this order into effect.

By order of the President of the United States:

EDWIN M. STANTON, *Secretary of War.*

EXECUTIVE OFFICE,
Washington, D. C., May 31, 1865.

To-morrow, the 1st of June, being the day appointed for special humiliation and prayer in consequence of the assassination of Abraham Lincoln, late President of the United States, the Executive Office and the various Departments will be closed during the day.

ANDREW JOHNSON,
President of the United States.

GENERAL ORDERS, NO. 107.

WAR DEPARTMENT,
ADJUTANT-GENERAL'S OFFICE,
Washington, June 2, 1865.

Ordered, That all military restrictions upon trade in any of the States or Territories of the United States, except in articles contraband of war— to wit, arms, ammunition, gray cloth, and all articles from which ammunition is manufactured; locomotives, cars, railroad iron, and machinery for operating railroads; telegraph wires, insulators, and instruments for operating telegraphic lines—shall cease from and after the present date.

By order of the President of the United States:

E. D. TOWNSEND, *Assistant Adjutant-General.*

DEPARTMENT OF STATE,
Washington, June 2, 1865.

Whereas, pursuant to the order of the President and as a means required by the public safety, directions were issued from this Department, under date of the 17th of December, 1864, requiring passports from all travelers entering the United States, except immigrant passengers directly entering an American port from a foreign country; and

Whereas the necessities which required the adoption of that measure are believed no longer to exist:

Now, therefore, the President directs that from and after this date the order above referred to shall be, and the same is hereby, rescinded.

Nothing in this regulation, however, will be construed to relieve from due accountability any enemies of the United States or offenders against their peace and dignity who may hereafter seek to enter the country or at any time be found within its lawful jurisdiction.

WILLIAM H. SEWARD.

EXECUTIVE MANSION,
Washington, D. C., June 2, 1865.

Whereas by an act of Congress approved March 3, 1865, there was established in the War Department a Bureau of Refugees, Freedmen, and Abandoned Lands, and to which, in accordance with the said act of Congress, is committed the supervision and management of all abandoned lands and the control of all subjects relating to refugees and freedmen from rebel States, or from any district of country within the territory embraced in the operations of the Army, under such rules and regulations as may be prescribed by the head of the Bureau and approved by the President; and

Whereas it appears that the management of abandoned lands and subjects relating to refugees and freedmen, as aforesaid, have been and still are, by orders based on military exigencies or legislation based on previous statutes, partly in the hands of military officers disconnected with said Bureau and partly in charge of officers of the Treasury Department: It is therefore

Ordered, That all officers of the Treasury Department, all military officers, and all others in the service of the United States turn over to the authorized officers of said Bureau all abandoned lands and property contemplated in said act of Congress approved March 3, 1865, establishing the Bureau of Refugees, Freedmen, and Abandoned Lands, that may now be under or within their control. They will also turn over to such officers all funds collected by tax or otherwise for the benefit of refugees or freedmen or accruing from abandoned lands or property set apart for their use, and will transfer to them all official records connected with the administration of affairs which pertain to said Bureau.

ANDREW JOHNSON.

GENERAL ORDERS, NO. 109.

WAR DEPARTMENT,
ADJUTANT-GENERAL'S OFFICE,
Washington, June 6, 1865.

ORDER FOR THE DISCHARGE OF CERTAIN PRISONERS OF WAR.

The prisoners of war at the several depots in the North will be discharged under the following regulations and restrictions:

I. All enlisted men of the rebel army and petty officers and seamen of the rebel navy will be discharged upon taking the oath of allegiance.

II. Officers of the rebel army not above the grade of captain and of the rebel navy not above the grade of lieutenant, except such as have graduated at the United States Military or Naval academies and such as held a commission in either the United States Army or Navy at the beginning of the rebellion, may be discharged upon taking the oath of allegiance.

III. When the discharges hereby ordered are completed, regulations will be issued in respect to the discharge of officers having higher rank than captain in the army or lieutenant in the navy.

IV. The several commanders of prison stations will discharge each day as many of the prisoners hereby authorized to be discharged as proper rolls can be prepared for, beginning with those who have been longest in prison and from the most remote points of the country; and certified rolls will be forwarded daily to the Commissary-General of Prisoners of those so discharged. The oath of allegiance only will be administered, but notice will be given that all who desire will be permitted to take the oath of amnesty after their release, in accordance with the regulations of the Department of State respecting the amnesty.

V. The Quartermaster's Department will furnish transportation to all released prisoners to the nearest accessible point to their homes, by rail or by steamboat.

By order of the President of the United States:

E. D. TOWNSEND,
Assistant Adjutant-General.

EXECUTIVE MANSION,
Washington, June 6, 1865.

Whereas circumstances of recent occurrence have made it no longer necessary to continue the prohibition of the departure for her destination of the gunboat *Fusyama*, built at New York for the Japanese Government, it is consequently ordered that that prohibition be removed. The Secretary of the Treasury will therefore cause a clearance to be issued to the *Fusyama*, and the Secretary of the Navy will not allow any obstacle thereto.

ANDREW JOHNSON.

[From the Daily National Intelligencer, June 13, 1865.]

CIRCULAR.

ATTORNEY-GENERAL'S OFFICE,
Washington, June 7, 1865.

By direction of the President, all persons belonging to the excepted classes enumerated in the President's amnesty proclamation of May 29, 1865, who may make special applications to the President for pardon are hereby notified that before their respective applications will be considered it must be shown that they have respectively taken and subscribed the oath (or affirmation) in said proclamation prescribed. Every such person desiring a special pardon should make personal application in writing therefor, and should transmit with such application the original oath (or affirmation) as taken and subscribed before an officer authorized under the rules and regulations promulgated by the Secretary of State to administer the amnesty oath prescribed in the said proclamation of the President.

JAMES SPEED,
Attorney-General.

EXECUTIVE OFFICE,
Washington, D. C., June 9, 1865.

It is represented to me in a communication from the Secretary of the Interior that Indians in New Mexico have been seized and reduced into slavery, and it is recommended that the authority of the executive branch of the Government should be exercised for the effectual suppression of a practice which is alike in violation of the rights of the Indians and of the provisions of the organic law of the said Territory.

Concurring in this recommendation, I do hereby order that the heads of the several Executive Departments do enjoin upon the subordinates, agents, and employees under their respective orders or supervision in that Territory to discountenance the practice aforesaid and to take all lawful means to suppress the same.

ANDREW JOHNSON.

GENERAL COURT-MARTIAL ORDERS, No. 356.

WAR DEPARTMENT,
ADJUTANT-GENERAL'S OFFICE,
Washington, July 5, 1865.

I. Before a military commission which convened at Washington, D. C., May 9, 1865, pursuant to paragraph 4 of Special Orders, No. 211, dated May 6, 1865, and paragraph 91 of Special Orders, No. 216, dated May 9, 1865, War Department, Adjutant-General's Office, Washington, and of which Major-General David Hunter, United States Volunteers, is president, were arraigned and tried David E. Herold, G. A. Atzerodt, Lewis Payne, Mary E. Surratt, Michael O'Laughlin, Edward Spangler, Samuel Arnold, and Samuel A. Mudd.

CHARGE I.

For maliciously, unlawfully, and traitorously, and in aid of the existing armed rebellion against the United States of America, on or before the 6th day of March, A. D. 1865, and on divers other days between that day and the 15th day of April, A. D. 1865, combining, confederating, and conspiring together with one John H. Surratt, John Wilkes Booth, Jefferson Davis, George N. Sanders, Beverley Tucker, Jacob Thompson, William C. Cleary, Clement C. Clay, George Harper, George Young, and others unknown to kill and murder, within the Military Department of Washington, and within the fortified and intrenched lines thereof, Abraham Lincoln, late, and at the time of said combining, confederating, and conspiring, President of the United States of America and Commander in Chief of the Army and Navy thereof; Andrew Johnson, now Vice-President of the United States aforesaid; William H. Seward, Secretary of State of the United States aforesaid; and Ulysses S. Grant, Lieutenant-General of the Army of the United States aforesaid, then in command of the armies of the United States, under the direction of the said Abraham Lincoln; and in pursuance of and in prosecuting said malicious, unlawful, and traitorous conspiracy aforesaid, and in aid of said rebellion, afterwards, to wit, on the 14th day of April, A. D. 1865, within the Military Department of Washington aforesaid, and within the fortified and intrenched lines of said military department, together with said John Wilkes Booth and John H. Surratt, maliciously, unlawfully, and traitorously murdering the said Abraham Lincoln, then President of the United States and Commander in Chief of the Army and Navy of the United States as aforesaid; and maliciously, unlawfully, and traitorously assaulting, with intent to kill and murder, the said William H. Seward, then Secretary of State of the United States as aforesaid; and lying in wait, with intent maliciously, unlawfully, and traitorously to kill and murder the said Andrew Johnson, then being Vice-President of the United States, and the said Ulysses S. Grant, then being Lieutenant-General and in command of the armies of the United States as aforesaid.

SPECIFICATION FIRST.

In this, that they, the said David E. Herold, Edward Spangler, Lewis Payne, Michael O'Laughlin, Samuel Arnold, Mary E. Surratt, George A. Atzerodt, and Samuel A. Mudd, together with the said John H. Surratt and John Wilkes Booth, incited and encouraged thereunto by Jefferson Davis, George N. Sanders, Beverley Tucker, Jacob Thompson, William C. Cleary, Clement C. Clay, George Harper, George Young, and others unknown, citizens of the United States aforesaid, and who were then engaged in armed rebellion against the United States of America, within the limits thereof, did, in aid of said armed rebellion, on or before the 6th day of March, A. D. 1865, and on divers other days and times between that day and the 15th day of April, A. D. 1865, combine, confederate, and conspire together at Washington City, within the Military Department of Washington, and within the intrenched fortifications and military lines of the said United States there being, unlawfully, maliciously, and traitorously to kill and murder Abraham Lincoln, then President of the United States aforesaid and Commander in Chief of the Army and Navy thereof; and unlawfully, maliciously, and traitorously to kill and murder Andrew Johnson, now Vice-President of the said United States, upon whom, on the death of said Abraham Lincoln, after the 4th day of March, A. D. 1865, the office of President of the said United States and Commander in Chief of the Army and Navy thereof would devolve; and to unlawfully, maliciously, and traitorously kill and murder Ulysses S. Grant, then Lieutenant-General, and, under the direction of the said Abraham Lincoln, in command of the armies of the United States aforesaid; and unlawfully, maliciously, and traitorously to kill and murder William H. Seward, then Secretary of State of the United States aforesaid, whose duty it was by law, upon the death of said President and Vice-President of the United States aforesaid, to cause an election to be held for electors of President of the United States—the conspirators aforesaid designing and intending by the killing and murder of the said Abraham Lincoln, Andrew Johnson, Ulysses S. Grant, and William H. Seward, as aforesaid, to deprive the Army and Navy of the said United States of a constitutional Commander in Chief, and to deprive the armies of the United States of their lawful commander, and to prevent a lawful election of President and Vice-President of the United States aforesaid, and by the means aforesaid to aid and comfort the insurgents engaged in armed rebellion against the said United States as aforesaid, and thereby to aid in the subversion and overthrow of the Constitution and laws of the said United States.

And being so combined, confederated, and conspiring together in the prosecution of said unlawful and traitorous conspiracy, on the night of the 14th day of April, A.D. 1865, at the hour of about 10 o'clock and 15 minutes p. m., at Ford's Theater, on Tenth street, in the city of Washington, and within the military department and military lines aforesaid, John Wilkes Booth, one of the conspirators aforesaid, in pursuance of said unlawful and traitorous conspiracy, did then and there unlawfully, maliciously, and traitorously, and with intent to kill and murder the said Abraham Lincoln, discharge a pistol then held in the hands of him, the said Booth, the same being then loaded with powder and a leaden ball, against and upon the left and posterior side of the head of the said Abraham Lincoln, and did thereby then and there inflict upon him, the said Abraham Lincoln, then President of the said United States and Commander in Chief of the Army and Navy thereof, a mortal wound, whereof afterwards, to wit, on the 15th day of April, A. D. 1865, at Washington City aforesaid, the said Abraham Lincoln died; and thereby then and there, and in pursuance of said conspiracy, the said defendants and the said John Wilkes Booth and John H. Surratt did unlawfully, traitorously, and maliciously, and with the intent to aid the rebellion as aforesaid, kill and murder the said Abraham Lincoln, President of the United States as aforesaid.

And in further prosecution of the unlawful and traitorous conspiracy aforesaid and of the murderous and traitorous intent of said conspiracy, the said Edward Spangler, on said 14th day of April, A. D. 1865, at about the same hour of that day as aforesaid, within said military department and the military lines aforesaid, did aid and assist the said John Wilkes Booth to obtain entrance to the box in said theater in which said Abraham Lincoln was sitting at the time he was assaulted and shot, as aforesaid, by John Wilkes Booth; and also did then and there aid said Booth in barring and obstructing the door of the box of said theater, so as to hinder and prevent any assistance to or rescue of the said Abraham Lincoln against the murderous assault of the said John Wilkes Booth, and did aid and abet him in making his escape after the said Abraham Lincoln had been murdered in manner aforesaid.

And in further prosecution of said unlawful, murderous, and traitorous conspiracy, and in pursuance thereof, and with the intent as aforesaid, the said David E. Herold did, on the night of the 14th of April, A. D. 1865, within the military department and military lines aforesaid, aid, abet, and assist the said John Wilkes Booth in the killing and murder of the said Abraham Lincoln, and did then and there aid and abet and assist him, the said John Wilkes Booth, in attempting to escape through the military lines aforesaid, and did accompany and assist the said John Wilkes Booth in attempting to conceal himself and escape from justice after killing and murdering said Abraham Lincoln, as aforesaid.

And in further prosecution of said unlawful and traitorous conspiracy and of the intent thereof as aforesaid, the said Lewis Payne did, on the same night of the 14th day of April, A. D. 1865, about the same hour of 10 o'clock and 15 minutes p. m., at the city of Washington, and within the military department and the military lines aforesaid, unlawfully and maliciously make an assault upon the said William H. Seward, Secretary of State, as aforesaid, in the dwelling house and bedchamber of him, the said William H. Seward, and the said Payne did then and there, with a large knife held in his hand, unlawfully, traitorously, and in pursuance of said conspiracy, strike, stab, cut, and attempt to kill and murder the said William H. Seward, and did thereby then and there, and with the intent aforesaid, with said knife, inflict upon the face and throat of the said William H. Seward divers grievous wounds; and the said Lewis Payne, in further prosecution of said conspiracy, at the same time and place last aforesaid, did attempt, with the knife aforesaid and a pistol held in his hand, to kill and murder Frederick W. Seward, Augustus H. Seward, Emrick W,

Hansell, and George F. Robinson, who were then striving to protect and rescue the said William H. Seward from murder by the said Lewis Payne, and did then and there, with said knife and pistol held in his hands, inflict upon the head of said Frederick W. Seward and upon the persons of said Augustus H. Seward, Emrick W. Hansell, and George F. Robinson divers grievous and dangerous wounds, with intent then and there to kill and murder the said Frederick W. Seward, Augustus H. Seward, Emrick W. Hansell, and George F. Robinson.

And in further prosecution of said conspiracy and its traitorous and murderous designs, the said George A. Atzerodt did, on the night of the 14th of April, A. D. 1865, and about the same hour of the night aforesaid, within the military department and the military lines aforesaid, lie in wait for Andrew Johnson, then Vice-President of the United States aforesaid, with the intent unlawfully and maliciously to kill and murder him, the said Andrew Johnson.

And in the further prosecution of the conspiracy aforesaid and of its murderous and treasonable purposes aforesaid, on the nights of the 13th and 14th of April, A. D. 1865, at Washington City, and within the military department and military lines aforesaid, the said Michael O'Laughlin did then and there lie in wait for Ulysses S. Grant, then Lieutenant-General and commander of the armies of the United States as aforesaid, with intent then and there to kill and murder the said Ulysses S. Grant.

And in further prosecution of said conspiracy, the said Samuel Arnold did, within the military department and military lines aforesaid, on or before the 6th day of March, A. D. 1865, and on divers other days and times between that day and the 15th day of April, A. D. 1865, combine, conspire with, and aid, counsel, abet, comfort, and support the said John Wilkes Booth, Lewis Payne, George A. Atzerodt, Michael O'Laughlin, and their confederates in said unlawful, murderous, and traitorous conspiracy and in the execution thereof, as aforesaid.

And in further prosecution of the said conspiracy, Mary E. Surratt did, at Washington City, and within the military department and military lines aforesaid, on or before the 6th day of March, A. D. 1865, and on divers other days and times between that day and the 20th day of April, A. D. 1865, receive, entertain, harbor and conceal, aid and assist, the said John Wilkes Booth, David E. Herold, Lewis Payne, John H. Surratt, Michael O'Laughlin, George A. Atzerodt, Samuel Arnold, and their confederates, with knowledge of the murderous and traitorous conspiracy aforesaid, and with intent to aid, abet, and assist them in the execution thereof and in escaping from justice after the murder of the said Abraham Lincoln, as aforesaid.

And in further prosecution of said conspiracy, the said Samuel A. Mudd did, at Washington City, and within the military department and military lines aforesaid, on or before the 6th day of March, A. D. 1865, and on divers other days and times between that day and the 20th day of April, A. D. 1865, advise, encourage, receive, entertain, harbor and conceal, aid and assist, the said John Wilkes Booth, David E. Herold, Lewis Payne, John H. Surratt, Michael O'Laughlin, George A. Atzerodt, Mary E. Surratt, and Samuel Arnold, and their confederates, with knowledge of the murderous and traitorous conspiracy aforesaid, and with intent to aid, abet, and assist them in the execution thereof and in escaping from justice after the murder of the said Abraham Lincoln, in pursuance of said conspiracy, in manner aforesaid.

To which charge and specification the accused, David E. Herold, G. A. Atzerodt, Lewis Payne, Mary E. Surratt, Michael O'Laughlin, Edward Spangler, Samuel Arnold, and Samuel A. Mudd, pleaded "not guilty."

FINDINGS AND SENTENCES.

1. In the case of David E. Herold, the commission, having maturely considered the evidence adduced, finds the accused as follows:

Of the specification, "Guilty, except combining, confederating, and conspiring with Edward Spangler; as to which part thereof, not guilty."

Of the charge, "Guilty, except the words of the charge that he combined, confederated, and conspired with Edward Spangler; as to which part of said charge, not guilty."

And the commission does therefore sentence him, the said David E. Herold, "To be hanged by the neck until he be dead, at such time and place as the President of the United States shall direct; two-thirds of the members of the commission concurring therein."

2. In the case of George A. Atzerodt, the commission, having maturely considered the evidence adduced, finds the accused as follows:

Of the specification, "Guilty, except combining, confederating, and conspiring with Edward Spangler; of this, not guilty."

Of the charge, "Guilty, except combining, confederating, and conspiring with Edward Spangler; of this, not guilty."

And the commission does therefore sentence him, the said George A. Atzerodt, "To be hung by the neck until he be dead, at such time and place as the President of the United States shall direct; two-thirds of the members of the commission concurring therein."

3. In the case of Lewis Payne, the commission, having maturely considered the evidence adduced, finds the accused as follows:

Of the specification, "Guilty, except combining, confederating, and conspiring with Edward Spangler; of this, not guilty."

Of the charge, "Guilty, except combining, confederating, and conspiring with Edward Spangler; of this, not guilty."

And the commission does therefore sentence him, the said Lewis Payne, "To be hung by the neck until he be dead, at such time and place as the President of the United States shall direct; two-thirds of the members of the commission concurring therein."

4. In the case of Mary E. Surratt, the commission, having maturely considered the evidence adduced, finds the accused as follows:

Of the specification, "Guilty, except as to receiving, entertaining, harboring, and concealing Samuel Arnold and Michael O'Laughlin, and except as to combining, confederating, and conspiring with Edward Spangler; of this, not guilty."

Of the charge, "Guilty, except as to combining, confederating, and conspiring with Edward Spangler; of this, not guilty."

And the commission does therefore sentence her, the said Mary E. Surratt, "To be hung by the neck until she be dead, at such time and place as the President of the United States shall direct; two-thirds of the members of the commission concurring therein."

5. In the case of Michael O'Laughlin, the commission, having maturely considered the evidence adduced, finds the accused as follows:

Of the specification, "Guilty, except the words thereof as follows: 'And in the further prosecution of the conspiracy aforesaid and of its murderous and treasonable purposes aforesaid, on the nights of the 13th and 14th of April, A. D. 1865, at Washington City, and within the military department and military lines aforesaid, the said Michael O'Laughlin did then and there lie in wait for Ulysses S. Grant, then Lieutenant-General and commander of the armies of the United States, with intent then and there to kill and murder the said Ulysses S. Grant;' of said words, not guilty; and except combining, confederating, and conspiring with Edward Spangler; of this, not guilty."

Of the charge, "Guilty, except combining, confederating, and conspiring with Edward Spangler; of this, not guilty."

And the commission does therefore sentence him, the said Michael O'Laughlin, "To be imprisoned at hard labor for life at such penitentiary as the President of the United States shall designate."

6. In the case of Edward Spangler, the commission, having maturely considered the evidence adduced, finds the accused as follows:

Of the specification, "Not guilty, except as to the words, 'The said Edward Spangler, on said 14th day of April, A. D. 1865, at about the same hour of that day as aforesaid, within said military department and the military lines aforesaid, did aid and abet him (meaning John Wilkes Booth) in making his escape after the said Abraham Lincoln had been murdered in manner aforesaid;' and of these words, guilty."

Of the charge, "Not guilty, but guilty of having feloniously and traitorously aided and abetted John Wilkes Booth in making his escape after having killed and murdered Abraham Lincoln, President of the United States, he the said Edward Spangler, at the time of aiding and abetting as aforesaid, well knowing that the said Abraham Lincoln, President as aforesaid, had been murdered by the said John Wilkes Booth, as aforesaid."

And the commission does therefore sentence him, the said Edward Spangler, "To be confined at hard labor for the period of six years at such penitentiary as the President of the United States shall designate."

7. In the case of Samuel Arnold, the commission, having maturely considered the evidence adduced, finds the accused as follows:

Of the specification, "Guilty, except combining, confederating, and conspiring with Edward Spangler; of this, not guilty."

Of the charge, "Guilty, except combining, confederating, and conspiring with Edward Spangler; of this, not guilty."

And the commission does therefore sentence him, the said Samuel Arnold, "To be imprisoned at hard labor for life at such penitentiary as the President of the United States shall designate."

8. In the case of Samuel A. Mudd, the commission, having maturely considered the evidence adduced, finds the accused as follows:

Of the specification, "Guilty, except combining, confederating, and conspiring with Edward Spangler; of this, not guilty; and except receiving, entertaining, harboring, and concealing Lewis Payne, John H. Surratt, Michael O'Laughlin, George A. Atzerodt, Mary E. Surratt, and Samuel Arnold; of this, not guilty."

Of the charge, "Guilty, except combining, confederating, and conspiring with Edward Spangler; of this, not guilty."

And the commission does therefore sentence him, the said Samuel A. Mudd, "To be imprisoned at hard labor for life at such penitentiary as the President of the United States shall designate."

II. The proceedings, findings, and sentences in the foregoing cases having been submitted to the President of the United States, the following are his orders:

EXECUTIVE MANSION, *July 5, 1865.*

The foregoing sentences in the cases of David E. Herold, George A. Atzerodt, Lewis Payne, Michael O'Laughlin, Edward Spangler, Samuel Arnold, Mary E. Surratt, and Samuel A. Mudd are hereby approved, and it is ordered that the sentences in the cases of David E. Herold, G. A. Atzerodt, Lewis Payne, and Mary E. Surratt be carried into execution by the proper military authority, under the direction of the Secretary of War, on the 7th day of July, 1865, between the hours of 10 o'clock a. m. and 2 o'clock p. m. of that day. It is further ordered that the prisoners Samuel Arnold, Samuel A. Mudd, Edward Spangler, and Michael

O'Laughlin be confined at hard labor in the penitentiary at Albany, N. Y., during the period designated in their respective sentences.

ANDREW JOHNSON, President.

III. Major-General W. S. Hancock, United States Volunteers, commanding Middle Military Division, is commanded to cause the foregoing sentences in the cases of David E. Herold, G. A. Atzerodt, Lewis Payne, and Mary E. Surratt to be duly executed in accordance with the President's order.

EXECUTIVE MANSION, July 15, 1865.

IV. The Executive order dated July 5, 1865, approving the sentences in the cases of Samuel Arnold, Samuel A. Mudd, Edward Spangler, and Michael O'Laughlin, is hereby modified so as to direct that the said Arnold, Mudd, Spangler, and O'Laughlin be confined at hard labor in the military prison at Dry Tortugas, Florida, during the period designated in their respective sentences.

The Adjutant-General of the Army is directed to issue orders for the said prisoners to be transported to the Dry Tortugas, and to be confined there accordingly.

ANDREW JOHNSON, President.

V. Major-General W. S. Hancock, United States Volunteers, commanding Middle Military Division, is commanded to send the prisoners Samuel Arnold, Samuel A. Mudd, Edward Spangler, and Michael O'Laughlin, under charge of a commissioned officer, with a sufficient guard, to the Dry Tortugas, Florida, where they will be delivered to the commanding officer of the post, who is hereby ordered to confine the said Arnold, Mudd, Spangler, and O'Laughlin at hard labor during the periods designated in their respective sentences.

VI. The military commission of which Major-General David Hunter is president is hereby dissolved.

By command of the President of the United States:

E. D. TOWNSEND, Assistant Adjutant-General.

WASHINGTON, August 7, 1865.

An impression seems to prevail that the interests of persons having business with the executive government require that they should have personal interviews with the President or heads of Departments. As this impression is believed to be entirely unfounded, it is expected that applications relating to such business will hereafter be made in writing to the head of that Department to which the business may have been assigned by law. Those applications will in their order be considered and disposed of by heads of Departments, subject to the approval of the President. This order is made necessary by the unusual numbers of persons visiting the seat of Government. It is impracticable to grant personal interviews to all of them, and desirable that there should be no invidious distinction in this respect. Similar business of persons who can not conveniently leave their homes must be neglected if the time of the executive officers here is engrossed by personal interviews with others. ANDREW JOHNSON.

[From the Daily National Intelligencer, August 26, 1865.]

DEPARTMENT OF STATE,
Washington, August 25, 1865.

Paroled prisoners asking passports as citizens of the United States, and against whom no special charges may be pending, will be furnished with passports upon application therefor to the Department of State in the usual form. Such passports will, however, be issued upon the condition that the applicants do not return to the United States without leave of the President. Other persons implicated in the rebellion who may wish to go abroad will apply to the Department of State for passports, and the applications will be disposed of according to the merits of the several cases.

By the President of the United States:

WILLIAM H. SEWARD.

EXECUTIVE OFFICE, *September 7, 1865.*

It is hereby ordered, That so much of the Executive order bearing date the 7th [2d] day of June, 1865, as made it the duty of all officers of the Treasury Department, military officers, and all others in the service of the United States to turn over to the authorized officers of the Bureau of Refugees, Freedmen, and Abandoned Lands all funds collected by tax or otherwise for the benefit of refugees or freedmen, or accruing from abandoned lands or property set apart for their use, be, and the same is hereby, suspended. ANDREW JOHNSON,
President.

GENERAL ORDERS, No. 138.

WAR DEPARTMENT,
ADJUTANT-GENERAL'S OFFICE,
Washington, September 16, 1865.

To provide for the transportation required by the Bureau of Refugees, Freedmen, and Abandoned Lands—

It is ordered, That upon the requisition of the Commissioner or the assistant commissioners of the Bureau transportation be furnished such destitute refugees and freedmen as are dependent upon the Government for support to points where they can procure employment and subsistence and support themselves, and thus relieve the Government, provided such transportation be confined by assistant commissioners within the limits of their jurisdiction.

Second. Free transportation on Government transports and United States military railroads will be furnished to such teachers only of refugees and freedmen, and persons laboring voluntarily in behalf of refugees and freedmen, as may be duly accredited by the Commissioner or assistant commissioners of the Bureau.

All stores and schoolbooks necessary to the subsistence, comfort, and instruction of dependent refugees and freedmen may be transported at Government expense, when such stores and books shall be turned over to the officers of the Quartermaster's Department, with the approval of the assistant commissioners, Commissioner, or department commander, the same to be transported as public stores, consigned to the quartermaster of the post to which they are destined, who, after inspection, will turn them over to the assistant commissioners or Bureau agent for whom they are intended for distribution.

All army officers traveling on public duty, under the orders of the commissioners, within the limits of their respective jurisdictions, will be entitled to mileage or actual cost of transportation, according to the revised Army Regulations, when transportation has not been furnished them by the Quartermaster's Department.

By order of the President of the United States:

E. D. TOWNSEND, *Assistant Adjutant-General.*

SPECIAL ORDERS, No. 503.

WAR DEPARTMENT,
ADJUTANT-GENERAL'S OFFICE,
Washington, September 19, 1865.

*　　*　　*　　*　　*　　*　　*

It has been represented to the Department that commanders of military posts and districts in Georgia, and particularly Brevet Brigadier-General C. H. Grosvenor, provost-marshal-general, and Brevet Major-General King, commanding in the district of Augusta, have assumed to decide questions of contracts and conflicting claims of property between individuals, and to order the delivery, surrender, or transfer of property and documents of title as between private persons, in which the Government is not concerned.

All such acts and proceedings on the part of military authorities in said State are declared by the President to be without authority and null and void.

All military commanders and authorities within said State are strictly ordered to abstain from any such acts, and not in any way to interfere with or assume to adjudicate any right, title, or claim of property between private individuals, and to suspend all action upon any orders heretofore made in respect to the ownership or delivery of property and the validity of contracts between private persons.

They are also forbidden from being directly or indirectly interested in any sales or contracts for cotton or other products of said State, and from using or suffering to be used any Government transportation for the transporting of cotton or other products of said State for or in behalf of private persons on any pretense whatever.

Military officers have no authority to interfere in any way in questions of sale or contracts of any kind between individuals or to decide any question of property between them without special instructions from this Department authorizing their action, and the usurpation of such power will be treated as a grave military offense.

Major-General Steedman, commanding the Department of Georgia, is specially charged with the enforcement of this order, and directed to make report as to any acts, proceedings, or orders of Brevet Major-General King and Brevet Brigadier-General Grosvenor, provost-marshal-general, in regard to contracts or conflicting claims of individuals in relation to cotton or other products, and to suspend all action upon any such orders until further instructions.

By order of the President of the United States.

E. D. TOWNSEND,
Assistant Adjutant-General.

GENERAL ORDERS, No. 145.

WAR DEPARTMENT,
ADJUTANT-GENERAL'S OFFICE,
Washington, October 9, 1865.

Whereas certain tracts of land, situated on the coast of South Carolina, Georgia, and Florida, at the time for the most part vacant, were set apart by Major-General W. T. Sherman's special field order No. 15 for the benefit of refugees and freedmen that had been congregated by the operations of war or had been left to take care of themselves by their former owners; and

Whereas an expectation was thereby created that they would be able to retain possession of said lands; and

Whereas a large number of the former owners are earnestly soliciting the restoration of the same and promising to absorb the labor and care for the freedmen:

It is ordered, That Major-General Howard, Commissioner of the Bureau of Refugees, Freedmen, and Abandoned Lands, proceed to the several above-named States and endeavor to effect an arrangement mutually satisfactory to the freedmen and the landowners, and make report. And in case a mutually satisfactory arrangement can be effected, he is duly empowered and directed to issue such orders as may become necessary, after a full and careful investigation of the interests of the parties concerned.

By order of the President of the United States:

E. D. TOWNSEND,
Assistant Adjutant-General.

EXECUTIVE OFFICE, *October 11, 1865.*

Whereas the following-named persons, to wit, John A. Campbell, of Alabama; John H. Reagan, of Texas; Alexander H. Stephens, of Georgia; George A. Trenholm, of South Carolina, and Charles Clark, of Mississippi, lately engaged in rebellion against the United States Government, who are now in close custody, have made their submission to the authority of the United States and applied to the President for pardon under his proclamation; and

Whereas the authority of the Federal Government is sufficiently restored in the aforesaid States to admit of the enlargement of said persons from close custody:

It is ordered, That they be released on giving their respective paroles to appear at such time and place as the President may designate to answer any charge that he may direct to be preferred against them, and also that they will respectively abide until further orders in the places herein designated, and not depart therefrom, to wit:

John A. Campbell, in the State of Alabama; John H. Reagan, in the State of Texas; Alexander H. Stephens, in the State of Georgia; George A. Trenholm, in the State of South Carolina; and Charles Clark, in the State of Mississippi. And if the President should grant his pardon to any of said persons, such person's parole will be thereby discharged.

ANDREW JOHNSON,
President.

EXECUTIVE OFFICE,
Washington City, November 11, 1865.

Ordered, That the civil and military agents of the Government transfer to the assistant commissioner of the Bureau of Refugees, Freedmen, and Abandoned Lands for Alabama the use and custody of all real estate, buildings, or other property, except cotton, seized or held by them in that State as belonging to the late rebel government, together with all such funds as may arise or have arisen from the rent, sale, or disposition of such property which have not been finally paid into the Treasury of the United States.

ANDREW JOHNSON,
President.

GENERAL ORDERS, NO. 164.

WAR DEPARTMENT,
ADJUTANT-GENERAL'S OFFICE,
Washington, November 24, 1865.

Ordered, That—

I. All persons claiming reward for the apprehension of John Wilkes Booth, Lewis Payne, G. A. Atzerodt, and David E. Herold, and Jefferson Davis, or either of them, are notified to file their claims and their proofs with the Adjutant-General for final adjudication by the special commission appointed to award and determine upon the validity of such claims before the 1st day of January next, after which time no claims will be received.

II. The rewards offered for the arrest of Jacob Thompson, Beverley Tucker, George N. Sanders, William G. Cleary, and John H. Surratt are revoked.

By order of the President of the United States:

E. D. TOWNSEND,
Assistant Adjutant-General.

FIRST ANNUAL MESSAGE.

WASHINGTON, *December 4, 1865.*

Fellow-Citizens of the Senate and House of Representatives:

To express gratitude to God in the name of the people for the preservation of the United States is my first duty in addressing you. Our thoughts next revert to the death of the late President by an act of parricidal treason. The grief of the nation is still fresh. It finds some solace in the consideration that he lived to enjoy the highest proof of its confidence by entering on the renewed term of the Chief Magistracy to which he had been elected; that he brought the civil war substantially to a close; that his loss was deplored in all parts of the Union, and that foreign nations have rendered justice to his memory. His removal cast upon me a heavier weight of cares than ever devolved upon any one of his predecessors. To fulfill my trust I need the support and confidence of all who are associated with me in the various departments of Government and the support and confidence of the people. There is but one way in which I can hope to gain their necessary aid. It is to state with frankness the principles which guide my conduct, and their application to the present state of affairs, well aware that the efficiency of my labors will in a great measure depend on your and their undivided approbation.

The Union of the United States of America was intended by its authors to last as long as the States themselves shall last. "The Union shall be perpetual" are the words of the Confederation. "To form a more perfect Union," by an ordinance of the people of the United States, is the declared purpose of the Constitution. The hand of Divine Providence was never more plainly visible in the affairs of men than in the framing and the adopting of that instrument. It is beyond comparison the greatest event in American history, and, indeed, is it not of all events in modern times the most pregnant with consequences for every people of the earth? The members of the Convention which prepared it brought to their work the experience of the Confederation, of their several States, and of other republican governments, old and new; but they needed and they obtained a wisdom superior to experience. And when for its validity it required the approval of a people that occupied a large part of a continent and acted separately in many distinct conventions, what is more wonderful than that, after earnest contention and long discussion, all feelings and all opinions were ultimately drawn in one way to its support? The Constitution to which life was thus imparted contains within itself ample resources for its own preservation. It has power to enforce the laws, punish treason, and insure domestic tranquillity. In case of the usurpation of the government of a State by one man or an oligarchy, it becomes a duty of the United States to make good the guaranty to that State of a republican form of government, and so to maintain the homogeneousness of all. Does the lapse of time reveal defects? A simple mode of amendment is provided in the Constitution itself, so that its conditions can always be made to conform to the requirements of advancing civilization. No room is allowed even for the thought of a possibility of its coming to an end. And these powers of self-preservation have always been asserted in their complete integrity by every patriotic Chief Magistrate—by Jefferson and Jackson not less than by Washington and Madison. The parting advice of the Father of his Country, while yet President, to the people of the United States was that the free Constitution, which was the work of their hands, might be sacredly maintained; and the inaugural words of President Jefferson held up "the preservation of the General Government in its whole constitutional vigor as the sheet anchor of our peace at home and safety abroad." The Constitution is the work of "the people of the United States," and it should be as indestructible as the people.

It is not strange that the framers of the Constitution, which had no model in the past, should not have fully comprehended the excellence of their own work. Fresh from a struggle against arbitrary power, many patriots suffered from harassing fears of an absorption of the State governments by the General Government, and many from a dread that the States would break away from their orbits. But the very greatness of our country should allay the apprehension of encroachments by the General Government. The subjects that come unquestionably within its jurisdiction are so numerous that it must ever naturally refuse to be embarrassed by questions that lie beyond it. Were it otherwise the Executive would sink beneath the burden, the channels of justice would be choked, legislation would be obstructed by excess, so that there is a greater temptation to exercise some of the functions of the General Government through the States than to trespass on their rightful sphere. The "absolute acquiescence in the decisions of the majority" was at the beginning of the century enforced by Jefferson as "the vital principle of republics;" and the events of the last four years have established, we will hope forever, that there lies no appeal to force.

The maintenance of the Union brings with it "the support of the State governments in all their rights," but it is not one of the rights of any State government to renounce its own place in the Union or to nullify the laws of the Union. The largest liberty is to be maintained in the discussion of the acts of the Federal Government, but there is no appeal from its laws except to the various branches of that Government itself, or to the people, who grant to the members of the legislative and of the executive departments no tenure but a limited one, and in that manner always retain the powers of redress.

"The sovereignty of the States" is the language of the Confederacy, and not the language of the Constitution. The latter contains the emphatic words—   .

This Constitution and the laws of the United States which shall be made in pursuance thereof, and all treaties made or which shall be made under the authority of the United States, shall be the supreme law of the land, and the judges in every State shall be bound thereby, anything in the constitution or laws of any State to the contrary notwithstanding.

Certainly the Government of the United States is a limited government, and so is every State government a limited government. With us this idea of limitation spreads through every form of administration— general, State, and municipal—and rests on the great distinguishing principle of the recognition of the rights of man. The ancient republics absorbed the individual in the state—prescribed his religion and controlled his activity. The American system rests on the assertion of the equal right of every man to life, liberty, and the pursuit of happiness, to freedom of conscience, to the culture and exercise of all his faculties. As a consequence the State government is limited—as to the General Government in the interest of union, as to the individual citizen in the interest of freedom.

States, with proper limitations of power, are essential to the existence of the Constitution of the United States. At the very commencement, when we assumed a place among the powers of the earth, the Declaration of Independence was adopted by States; so also were the Articles of Confederation; and when "the people of the United States" ordained and established the Constitution it was the assent of the States, one by one, which gave it vitality.　In the event, too, of any amendment to the Constitution, the proposition of Congress needs the confirmation of States. Without States one great branch of the legislative government would be wanting.　And if we look beyond the letter of the Constitution to the character of our country, its capacity for comprehending within its jurisdiction a vast continental empire is due to the system of States.　The best security for the perpetual existence of the States is the "supreme authority" of the Constitution of the United States.　The perpetuity of the Constitution brings with it the perpetuity of the States; their mutual relation makes us what we are, and in our political system their connection is indissoluble.　The whole can not exist without the parts, nor the parts without the whole.　So long as the Constitution of the United States endures, the States will endure.　The destruction of the one is the destruction of the other; the preservation of the one is the preservation of the other.

I have thus explained my views of the mutual relations of the Constitution and the States, because they unfold the principles on which I have sought to solve the momentous questions and overcome the appalling difficulties that met me at the very commencement of my Administration.　It has been my steadfast object to escape from the sway of momentary passions and to derive a healing policy from the fundamental and unchanging principles of the Constitution.

I found the States suffering from the effects of a civil war.　Resistance to the General Government appeared to have exhausted itself.　The United States had recovered possession of their forts and arsenals, and their armies were in the occupation of every State which had attempted to secede.　Whether the territory within the limits of those States should be held as conquered territory, under military authority emanating from the President as the head of the Army, was the first question that presented itself for decision.

Now military governments, established for an indefinite period, would have offered no security for the early suppression of discontent, would have divided the people into the vanquishers and the vanquished, and would have envenomed hatred rather than have restored affection.　Once established, no precise limit to their continuance was conceivable.　They would have occasioned an incalculable and exhausting expense.　Peaceful emigration to and from that portion of the country is one of the best means that can be thought of for the restoration of harmony, and that emigration would have been prevented; for what emigrant from abroad, what industrious citizen at home, would place himself willingly under military rule?　The chief persons who would have followed in the train of the Army would have been dependents on the General Government or men who expected profit from the miseries of their erring fellow-citizens. The powers of patronage and rule which would have been exercised, under the President, over a vast and populous and naturally wealthy region are greater than, unless under extreme necessity, I should be willing to intrust to any one man. They are such as, for myself, I could never, unless on occasions of great emergency, consent to exercise. The willful use of such powers, if continued through a period of years, would have endangered the purity of the general administration and the liberties of the States which remained loyal.

Besides, the policy of military rule over a conquered territory would have implied that the States whose inhabitants may have taken part in the rebellion had by the act of those inhabitants ceased to exist. But the true theory is that all pretended acts of secession were from the beginning null and void. The States can not commit treason nor screen the individual citizens who may have committed treason any more than they can make valid treaties or engage in lawful commerce with any foreign power. The States attempting to secede placed themselves in a condition where their vitality was impaired, but not extinguished; their functions suspended, but not destroyed.

But if any State neglects or refuses to perform its offices there is the more need that the General Government should maintain all its authority and as soon as practicable resume the exercise of all its functions. On this principle I have acted, and have gradually and quietly, and by almost imperceptible steps, sought to restore the rightful energy of the General Government and of the States. To that end provisional governors have been appointed for the States, conventions called, governors elected, legislatures assembled, and Senators and Representatives chosen to the Congress of the United States. At the same time the courts of the United States, as far as could be done, have been reopened, so that the laws of the United States may be enforced through their agency. The blockade has been removed and the custom-houses reestablished in ports of entry, so that the revenue of the United States may be collected. The Post-Office Department renews its ceaseless activity, and the General Government is thereby enabled to communicate promptly with its officers and agents. The courts bring security to persons and property; the opening of the ports invites the restoration of industry and commerce; the post-office renews the facilities of social intercourse and of business. And is it not happy for us all that the restoration of each one of these functions of the General Government brings with it a blessing to the States over which they are extended? Is it not a sure promise of harmony and renewed attachment to the Union that after all that has happened the return of the General Government is known only as a beneficence?

I know very well that this policy is attended with some risk; that for its success it requires at least the acquiescence of the States which it concerns; that it implies an invitation to those States, by renewing their allegiance to the United States, to resume their functions as States of the Union. But it is a risk that must be taken. In the choice of difficulties it is the smallest risk; and to diminish and if possible to remove all danger, I have felt it incumbent on me to assert one other power of the General Government—the power of pardon. As no State can throw a defense over the crime of treason, the power of pardon is exclusively vested in the executive government of the United States. In exercising that power I have taken every precaution to connect it with the clearest recognition of the binding force of the laws of the United States and an unqualified acknowledgment of the great social change of condition in regard to slavery which has grown out of the war.

The next step which I have taken to restore the constitutional relations of the States has been an invitation to them to participate in the high office of amending the Constitution. Every patriot must wish for a general amnesty at the earliest epoch consistent with public safety. For this great end there is need of a concurrence of all opinions and the spirit of mutual conciliation. All parties in the late terrible conflict must work together in harmony. It is not too much to ask, in the name of the whole people, that on the one side the plan of restoration shall proceed in conformity with a willingness to cast the disorders of the past into oblivion, and that on the other the evidence of sincerity in the future maintenance of the Union shall be put beyond any doubt by the ratification of the proposed amendment to the Constitution, which provides for the abolition of slavery forever within the limits of our country. So long as the adoption of this amendment is delayed, so long will doubt and jealousy and uncertainty prevail. This is the measure which will efface the sad memory of the past: this is the measure which will most certainly call population and capital and security to those parts of the Union that need them most. Indeed, it is not too much to ask of the States which are now resuming their places in the family of the Union to give this pledge of perpetual loyalty and peace. Until it is done the past, however much we may desire it, will not be forgotten. The adoption of the amendment reunites us beyond all power of disruption; it heals the wound that is still imperfectly closed; it removes slavery, the element which has so long perplexed and divided the country; it makes of us once more a united people, renewed and strengthened, bound more than ever to mutual affection and support.

The amendment to the Constitution being adopted, it would remain for the States whose powers have been so long in abeyance to resume their places in the two branches of the National Legislature, and thereby complete the work of restoration. Here it is for you, fellow-citizens of the Senate, and for you, fellow-citizens of the House of Representatives, to judge, each of you for yourselves, of the elections, returns, and qualifications of your own members.

The full assertion of the powers of the General Government requires the holding of circuit courts of the United States within the districts where their authority has been interrupted. In the present posture of our public affairs strong objections have been urged to holding those courts in any of the States where the rebellion has existed; and it was ascertained by inquiry that the circuit court of the United States would not be held within the district of Virginia during the autumn or early winter, nor until Congress should have "an opportunity to consider and act on the whole subject." To your deliberations the restoration of this branch of the civil authority of the United States is therefore necessarily referred, with the hope that early provision will be made for the resumption of all its functions. It is manifest that treason, most flagrant in character, has been committed. Persons who are charged with its commission should have fair and impartial trials in the highest civil tribunals of the country, in order that the Constitution and the laws may be fully vindicated, the truth clearly established and affirmed that treason is a crime, that traitors should be punished and the offense made infamous, and, at the same time, that the question may be judicially settled, finally and forever, that no State of its own will has the right to renounce its place in the Union.

The relations of the General Government toward the 4,000,000 inhabitants whom the war has called into freedom have engaged my most serious consideration. On the propriety of attempting to make the freedmen electors by the proclamation of the Executive I took for my counsel the Constitution itself, the interpretations of that instrument by its authors and their contemporaries, and recent legislation by Congress. When, at the first movement toward independence, the Congress of the United States instructed the several States to institute governments of their own, they left each State to decide for itself the conditions for the enjoyment of the elective franchise. During the period of the Confederacy there continued to exist a very great diversity in the qualifications of electors in the several States, and even within a State a distinction of qualifications prevailed with regard to the officers who were to be chosen. The Constitution of the United States recognizes these diversities when it enjoins that in the choice of members of the House of Representatives of the United States "the electors in each State shall have the qualifications requisite for electors of the most numerous branch of the State legislature." After the formation of the Constitution it remained, as before, the uniform usage for each State to enlarge the body of its electors according to its own judgment, and under this system one State after another has proceeded to increase the number of its electors, until now universal suffrage, or something very near it, is the general rule. So fixed was this reservation of power in the habits of the people and so unquestioned has been the interpretation of the Constitution that during the civil war the late President never harbored the purpose—certainly never avowed the purpose—of disregarding it; and in the acts of Congress during that period nothing can be found which, during the continuance of hostilities, much less after their close, would have sanctioned any departure by the Executive from a policy which has so uniformly obtained. Moreover, a concession of the elective franchise to the freedmen by act of the President of the United States must have been extended to all colored men, wherever found, and so must have established a change of suffrage in the Northern, Middle, and Western States, not less than in the Southern and Southwestern. Such an act would have created a new class of voters, and would have been an assumption of power by the President which nothing in the Constitution or laws of the United States would have warranted.

On the other hand, every danger of conflict is avoided when the settlement of the question is referred to the several States. They can, each for itself, decide on the measure, and whether it is to be adopted at once and absolutely or introduced gradually and with conditions. In my judgment the freedmen, if they show patience and manly virtues, will sooner obtain a participation in the elective franchise through the States than through the General Government, even if it had power to intervene. When the tumult of emotions that have been raised by the suddenness of the social change shall have subsided, it may prove that they will receive the kindest usage from some of those on whom they have heretofore most closely depended.

But while I have no doubt that now, after the close of the war, it is not competent for the General Government to extend the elective franchise in the several States, it is equally clear that good faith requires the security of the freedmen in their liberty and their property, their right to labor, and their right to claim the just return of their labor. I can not too strongly urge a dispassionate treatment of this subject, which should be carefully kept aloof from all party strife. We must equally avoid hasty assumptions of any natural impossibility for the two races to live side by side in a state of mutual benefit and good will. The experiment involves us in no inconsistency; let us, then, go on and make that experiment in good faith, and not be too easily disheartened. The country is in need of labor, and the freedmen are in need of employment, culture, and protection. While their right of voluntary migration and expatriation is not to be questioned, I would not advise their forced removal and colonization. Let us rather encourage them to honorable and useful industry, where it may be beneficial to themselves and to the country; and, instead of hasty anticipations of the certainty of failure, let there be nothing wanting to the fair trial of the experiment. The change in their condition is the substitution of labor by contract for the status of slavery. The freedman can not fairly be accused of unwillingness to work so long as a doubt remains about his freedom of choice in his pursuits and the certainty of his recovering his stipulated wages. In this the interests of the employer and the employed coincide. The employer desires in his workmen spirit and alacrity, and these can be permanently secured in no other way. And if the one ought to be able to enforce the contract, so ought the other. The public interest will be best promoted if the several States will provide adequate protection and remedies for the freedmen. Until this is in some way accomplished there is no chance for the advantageous use of their labor, and the blame of ill success will not rest on them.

I know that sincere philanthropy is earnest for the immediate realization of its remotest aims; but time is always an element in reform. It is one of the greatest acts on record to have brought 4,000,000 people into freedom. The career of free industry must be fairly opened to them, and then their future prosperity and condition must, after all, rest mainly on themselves. If they fail, and so perish away, let us be careful that the failure shall not be attributable to any denial of justice. In all that relates to the destiny of the freedmen we need not be too anxious to read the future; many incidents which, from a speculative point of view, might raise alarm will quietly settle themselves. Now that slavery is at an end, or near its end, the greatness of its evil in the point of view of public economy becomes more and more apparent. Slavery was essentially a monopoly of labor, and as such locked the States where it prevailed against the incoming of free industry. Where labor was the property of the capitalist, the white man was excluded from employment, or had but the second best chance of finding it; and the foreign emigrant turned away from the region where his condition would be so precarious. With the destruction of the monopoly free labor will hasten from all parts of the civilized world to assist in developing various and immeasurable resources which have hitherto lain dormant. The eight or nine States nearest the Gulf of Mexico have a soil of exuberant fertility, a climate friendly to long life, and can sustain a denser population than is found as yet in any part of our country. And the future influx of population to them will be mainly from the North or from the most cultivated nations in Europe. From the sufferings that have attended them during our late struggle let us look away to the future, which is sure to be laden for them with greater prosperity than has ever before been known. The removal of the monopoly of slave labor is a pledge that those regions will be peopled by a numerous and enterprising population, which will vie with any in the Union in compactness, inventive genius, wealth, and industry.

Our Government springs from and was made for the people—not the people for the Government. To them it owes allegiance; from them it must derive its courage, strength, and wisdom. But while the Government is thus bound to defer to the people, from whom it derives its existence, it should, from the very consideration of its origin, be strong in its power of resistance to the establishment of inequalities. Monopolies, perpetuities, and class legislation are contrary to the genius of free government, and ought not to be allowed. Here there is no room for favored classes or monopolies; the principle of our Government is that of equal laws and freedom of industry. Wherever monopoly attains a foothold, it is sure to be a source of danger, discord, and trouble. We shall but fulfill our duties as legislators by according "equal and exact justice to all men," special privileges to none. The Government is subordinate to the people; but, as the agent and representative of the people, it must be held superior to monopolies, which in themselves ought never to be granted, and which, where they exist, must be subordinate and yield to the Government.

The Constitution confers on Congress the right to regulate commerce among the several States. It is of the first necessity, for the maintenance of the Union, that that commerce should be free and unobstructed. No State can be justified in any device to tax the transit of travel and commerce between States. The position of many States is such that if they were allowed to take advantage of it for purposes of local revenue the commerce between States might be injuriously burdened, or even virtually prohibited. It is best, while the country is still young and while the tendency to dangerous monopolies of this kind is still feeble, to use the power of Congress so as to prevent any selfish impediment to the free circulation of men and merchandise. A tax on travel and merchandise in their transit constitutes one of the worst forms of monopoly, and the evil is increased if coupled with a denial of the choice of route. When the vast extent of our country is considered, it is plain that every obstacle to the free circulation of commerce between the States ought to be sternly guarded against by appropriate legislation within the limits of the Constitution.

The report of the Secretary of the Interior explains the condition of the public lands, the transactions of the Patent Office and the Pension Bureau, the management of our Indian affairs, the progress made in the construction of the Pacific Railroad, and furnishes information in reference to matters of local interest in the District of Columbia. It also presents evidence of the successful operation of the homestead act, under the provisions of which 1,160,533 acres of the public lands were entered during the last fiscal year—more than one-fourth of the whole number of acres sold or otherwise disposed of during that period. It is estimated that the receipts derived from this source are sufficient to cover the expenses incident to the survey and disposal of the lands entered under this act, and that payments in cash to the extent of from 40 to 50 per cent will be made by settlers who may thus at any time acquire title before the expiration of the period at which it would otherwise vest. The homestead policy was established only after long and earnest resistance; experience proves its wisdom. The lands in the hands of industrious settlers, whose labor creates wealth and contributes to the public resources, are worth more to the United States than if they had been reserved as a solitude for future purchasers.

The lamentable events of the last four years and the sacrifices made by the gallant men of our Army and Navy have swelled the records of the Pension Bureau to an unprecedented extent. On the 30th day of June last the total number of pensioners was 85,986, requiring for their annual pay, exclusive of expenses, the sum of $8,023,445. The number of applications that have been allowed since that date will require a large increase of this amount for the next fiscal year. The means for the payment of the stipends due under existing laws to our disabled soldiers and sailors and to the families of such as have perished in the service of the country will no doubt be cheerfully and promptly granted. A grateful people will not hesitate to sanction any measures having for their object the relief of soldiers mutilated and families made fatherless in the efforts to preserve our national existence.

The report of the Postmaster-General presents an encouraging exhibit of the operations of the Post-Office Department during the year. The revenues of the past year, from the loyal States alone, exceeded the maximum annual receipts from all the States previous to the rebellion in the sum of $6,038,091; and the annual average increase of revenue during the last four years, compared with the revenues of the four years immediately preceding the rebellion, was $3,533,845. The revenues of the last fiscal year amounted to $14,556,158 and the expenditures to $13,694,728, leaving a surplus of receipts over expenditures of $861,430. Progress has been made in restoring the postal service in the Southern States. The views presented by the Postmaster-General against the policy of granting subsidies to the ocean mail steamship lines upon established routes and in favor of continuing the present system, which limits the compensation for ocean service to the postage earnings, are recommended to the careful consideration of Congress.

It appears from the report of the Secretary of the Navy that while at the commencement of the present year there were in commission 530 vessels of all classes and descriptions, armed with 3,000 guns and manned by 51,000 men, the number of vessels at present in commission is 117, with 830 guns and 12,128 men. By this prompt reduction of the naval forces the expenses of the Government have been largely diminished, and a number of vessels purchased for naval purposes from the merchant marine have been returned to the peaceful pursuits of commerce. Since the suppression of active hostilities our foreign squadrons have been reestablished, and consist of vessels much more efficient than those employed on similar service previous to the rebellion. The suggestion for the enlargement of the navy-yards, and especially for the establishment of one in fresh water for ironclad vessels, is deserving of consideration, as is also the recommendation for a different location and more ample grounds for the Naval Academy.

In the report of the Secretary of War a general summary is given of the military campaigns of 1864 and 1865, ending in the suppression of armed resistance to the national authority in the insurgent States. The operations of the general administrative bureaus of the War Department during the past year are detailed and an estimate made of the appropriations that will be required for military purposes in the fiscal year commencing the 1st day of July, 1866. The national military force on the 1st of May, 1865, numbered 1,000,516 men. It is proposed to reduce the military establishment to a peace footing, comprehending 50,000 troops of all arms, organized so as to admit of an enlargement by filling up the ranks to 82,600 if the circumstances of the country should require an augmentation of the Army. The volunteer force has already been reduced by the discharge from service of over 800,000 troops, and the Department is proceeding rapidly in the work of further reduction. The war estimates are reduced from $516,240,131 to $33,814,461, which amount, in the opinion of the Department, is adequate for a peace establishment. The measures of retrenchment in each bureau and branch of the service exhibit a diligent economy worthy of commendation. Reference is also made in the report to the necessity of providing for a uniform militia system and to the propriety of making suitable provision for wounded and disabled officers and soldiers.

The revenue system of the country is a subject of vital interest to its honor and prosperity, and should command the earnest consideration of Congress. The Secretary of the Treasury will lay before you a full and detailed report of the receipts and disbursements of the last fiscal year, of the first quarter of the present fiscal year, of the probable receipts and expenditures for the other three quarters, and the estimates for the year following the 30th of June, 1866. I might content myself with a reference to that report, in which you will find all the information required for your deliberations and decision, but the paramount importance of the subject so presses itself on my own mind that I can not but lay before you my views of the measures which are required for the good character, and I might almost say for the existence, of this people. The life of a republic lies certainly in the energy, virtue, and intelligence of its citizens; but it is equally true that a good revenue system is the life of an organized government. I meet you at a time when the nation has voluntarily burdened itself with a debt unprecedented in our annals. Vast as is its amount, it fades away into nothing when compared with the countless blessings that will be conferred upon our country and upon man by the preservation of the nation's life. Now, on the first occasion of the meeting of Congress since the return of peace, it is of the utmost importance to inaugurate a just policy, which shall at once be put in motion, and which shall commend itself to those who come after us for its continuance. We must aim at nothing less than the complete effacement of the financial evils that necessarily followed a state of civil war. We must endeavor to apply the earliest remedy to the deranged state of the currency, and not shrink from devising a policy which, without being oppressive to the people, shall immediately begin to effect a reduction of the debt, and, if persisted in, discharge it fully within a definitely fixed number of years.

It is our first duty to prepare in earnest for our recovery from the ever-increasing evils of an irredeemable currency without a sudden revulsion, and yet without untimely procrastination. For that end we must each, in our respective positions, prepare the way. I hold it the duty of the Executive to insist upon frugality in the expenditures, and a sparing economy is itself a great national resource. Of the banks to which authority has been given to issue notes secured by bonds of the United States we may require the greatest moderation and prudence, and the law must be rigidly enforced when its limits are exceeded. We may each one of us counsel our active and enterprising countrymen to be constantly on their guard, to liquidate debts contracted in a paper currency, and by conducting business as nearly as possible on a system of cash payments or short credits to hold themselves prepared to return to the standard of gold and silver. To aid our fellow-citizens in the prudent management of their monetary affairs, the duty devolves on us to diminish by law the amount of paper money now in circulation. Five years ago the bank-note circulation of the country amounted to not much more than two hundred millions; now the circulation, bank and national, exceeds seven hundred millions. The simple statement of the fact recommends more strongly than any words of mine could do the necessity of our restraining this expansion. The gradual reduction of the currency is the only measure that can save the business of the country from disastrous calamities, and this can be almost imperceptibly accomplished by gradually funding the national circulation in securities that may be made redeemable at the pleasure of the Government.

Our debt is doubly secure—first in the actual wealth and still greater undeveloped resources of the country, and next in the character of our institutions. The most intelligent observers among political economists have not failed to remark that the public debt of a country is safe in proportion as its people are free; that the debt of a republic is the safest of all. Our history confirms and establishes the theory, and is, I firmly believe, destined to give it a still more signal illustration. The secret of this superiority springs not merely from the fact that in a republic the national obligations are distributed more widely through countless numbers in all classes of society; it has its root in the character of our laws. Here all men contribute to the public welfare and bear their fair share of the public burdens. During the war, under the impulses of patriotism, the men of the great body of the people, without regard to their own comparative want of wealth, thronged to our armies and filled our fleets of war, and held themselves ready to offer their lives for the public good. Now, in their turn, the property and income of the country should bear their just proportion of the burden of taxation, while in our impost system, through means of which increased vitality is incidentally imparted to all the industrial interests of the nation, the duties should be so adjusted as to fall most heavily on articles of luxury, leaving the necessaries of life as free from taxation as the absolute wants of the Government economically administered will justify. No favored class should demand freedom from assessment, and the taxes should be so distributed as not to fall unduly on the poor, but rather on the accumulated wealth of the country. We should look at the national debt just as it is—not as a national blessing, but as a heavy burden on the industry of the country, to be discharged without unnecessary delay.

It is estimated by the Secretary of the Treasury that the expenditures for the fiscal year ending the 30th of June, 1866, will exceed the receipts $112,194,947. It is gratifying, however, to state that it is also estimated that the revenue for the year ending the 30th of June, 1867, will exceed the expenditures in the sum of $111,682,818. This amount, or so much as may be deemed sufficient for the purpose, may be applied to the reduction of the public debt, which on the 31st day of October, 1865, was $2,740,854,750. Every reduction will diminish the total amount of interest to be paid, and so enlarge the means of still further reductions, until the whole shall be liquidated; and this, as will be seen from the estimates of the Secretary of the Treasury, may be accomplished by annual payments even within a period not exceeding thirty years. I have faith that we shall do all this within a reasonable time; that as we have amazed the world by the suppression of a civil war which was thought to be beyond the control of any government, so we shall equally show the superiority of our institutions by the prompt and faithful discharge of our national obligations.

The Department of Agriculture under its present direction is accomplishing much in developing and utilizing the vast agricultural capabilities of the country, and for information respecting the details of its management reference is made to the annual report of the Commissioner.

I have dwelt thus fully on our domestic affairs because of their transcendent importance. Under any circumstances our great extent of territory and variety of climate, producing almost everything that is necessary for the wants and even the comforts of man, make us singularly independent of the varying policy of foreign powers and protect us against every temptation to "entangling alliances," while at the present moment the reestablishment of harmony and the strength that comes from harmony will be our best security against "nations who feel power and forget right." For myself, it has been and it will be my constant aim to promote peace and amity with all foreign nations and powers, and I have every reason to believe that they all, without exception, are animated by the same disposition. Our relations with the Emperor of China, so recent in their origin, are most friendly. Our commerce with his dominions is receiving new developments, and it is very pleasing to find that the Government of that great Empire manifests satisfaction with our policy and reposes just confidence in the fairness which marks our intercourse. The unbroken harmony between the United States and the Emperor of Russia is receiving a new support from an enterprise designed to carry telegraphic lines across the continent of Asia, through his dominions, and so to connect us with all Europe by a new channel of intercourse. Our commerce with South America is about to receive encouragement by a direct line of mail steamships to the rising Empire of Brazil. The distinguished party of men of science who have recently left our country to make a scientific exploration of the natural history and rivers and mountain ranges of that region have received from the Emperor that generous welcome which was to have been expected from his constant friendship for the United States and his well-known zeal in promoting the advancement of knowledge. A hope is entertained that our commerce with the rich and populous countries that border the Mediterranean Sea may be largely increased. Nothing will be wanting on the part of this Government to extend the protection of our flag over the enterprise of our fellow-citizens. We receive from the powers in that region assurances of good will; and it is worthy of note that a special envoy has brought us messages of condolence on the death of our late Chief Magistrate from the Bey of Tunis, whose rule includes the old dominions of Carthage, on the African coast.

Our domestic contest, now happily ended, has left some traces in our relations with one at least of the great maritime powers. The formal accordance of belligerent rights to the insurgent States was unprecedented, and has not been justified by the issue. But in the systems of neutrality pursued by the powers which made that concession there was a marked difference. The materials of war for the insurgent States were furnished, in a great measure, from the workshops of Great Britain, and British ships, manned by British subjects and prepared for receiving British armaments, sallied from the ports of Great Britain to make war on American commerce under the shelter of a commission from the insurgent States. These ships, having once escaped from British ports, ever afterwards entered them in every part of the world to refit, and so to renew their depredations. The consequences of this conduct were most disastrous to the States then in rebellion, increasing their desolation and misery by the prolongation of our civil contest. It had, moreover, the effect, to a great extent, to drive the American flag from the sea, and to transfer much of our shipping and our commerce to the very power whose subjects had created the necessity for such a change. These events took place before I was called to the administration of the Government. The sincere desire for peace by which I am animated led me to approve the proposal, already made, to submit the question which had thus arisen between the countries to arbitration. These questions are of such moment that they must have commanded the attention of the great powers, and are so interwoven with the peace and interests of every one of them as to have insured an impartial decision. I regret to inform you that Great Britain declined the arbitrament, but, on the other hand, invited us to the formation of a joint commission to settle mutual claims between the two countries, from which those for the depredations before mentioned should be excluded. The proposition, in that very unsatisfactory form, has been declined.

The United States did not present the subject as an impeachment of the good faith of a power which was professing the most friendly dispositions, but as involving questions of public law of which the settlement is essential to the peace of nations; and though pecuniary reparation to their injured citizens would have followed incidentally on a decision against Great Britain, such compensation was not their primary object. They had a higher motive, and it was in the interests of peace and justice to establish important principles of international law. The correspondence will be placed before you. The ground on which the British minister rests his justification is, substantially, that the municipal law of a nation and the domestic interpretations of that law are the measure of its duty as a neutral, and I feel bound to declare my opinion before you and before the world that that justification can not be sustained before the tribunal of nations. At the same time, I do not advise to any present attempt at redress by acts of legislation. For the future, friendship between the two countries must rest on the basis of mutual justice.

From the moment of the establishment of our free Constitution the civilized world has been convulsed by revolutions in the interests of democracy or of monarchy, but through all those revolutions the United States have wisely and firmly refused to become propagandists of republicanism. It is the only government suited to our condition; but we have never sought to impose it on others, and we have consistently followed the advice of Washington to recommend it only by the careful preservation and prudent use of the blessing. During all the intervening period the policy of European powers and of the United States has, on the whole, been harmonious. Twice, indeed, rumors of the invasion of some parts of America in the interest of monarchy have prevailed; twice my predecessors have had occasion to announce the views of this nation in respect to such interference. On both occasions the remonstrance of the United States was respected from a deep conviction on the part of European Governments that the system of noninterference and mutual abstinence from propagandism was the true rule for the two hemispheres. Since those times we have advanced in wealth and power, but we retain the same purpose to leave the nations of Europe to choose their own dynasties and form their own systems of government. This consistent moderation may justly demand a corresponding moderation. We should regard it as a great calamity to ourselves, to the cause of good government, and to the peace of the world should any European power challenge the American people, as it were, to the defense of republicanism against foreign interference. We can not foresee and are unwilling to consider what opportunities might present themselves, what combinations might offer to protect ourselves against designs inimical to our form of government. The United States desire to act in the future as they have ever acted heretofore; they never will be driven from that course but by the aggression of European powers, and we rely on the wisdom and justice of those powers to respect the system of noninterference which has so long been sanctioned by time, and which by its good results has approved itself to both continents.

The correspondence between the United States and France in reference to questions which have become subjects of discussion between the two Governments will at a proper time be laid before Congress.

When, on the organization of our Government under the Constitution, the President of the United States delivered his inaugural address to the two Houses of Congress, he said to them, and through them to the country and to mankind, that—

The preservation of the sacred fire of liberty and the destiny of the republican model of government are justly considered, perhaps, as *deeply*, as *finally*, staked on the experiment intrusted to the hands of the American people.

And the House of Representatives answered Washington by the voice of Madison:

We adore the Invisible Hand which has led the American people, through so many difficulties, to cherish a conscious responsibility for the destiny of republican liberty.

More than seventy-six years have glided away since these words were spoken; the United States have passed through severer trials than were foreseen; and now, at this new epoch in our existence as one nation, with our Union purified by sorrows and strengthened by conflict and established by the virtue of the people, the greatness of the occasion invites us once more to repeat with solemnity the pledges of our fathers to hold ourselves answerable before our fellow-men for the success of the republican form of government. Experience has proved its sufficiency in peace and in war; it has vindicated its authority through dangers and afflictions, and sudden and terrible emergencies, which would have crushed any system that had been less firmly fixed in the hearts of the people. At the inauguration of Washington the foreign relations of the country were few and its trade was repressed by hostile regulations; now all the civilized nations of the globe welcome our commerce, and their governments profess toward us amity. Then our country felt its way hesitatingly along an untried path, with States so little bound together by rapid means of communication as to be hardly known to one another, and with historic traditions extending over very few years; now intercourse between the States is swift and intimate; the experience of centuries has been crowded into a few generations, and has created an intense, indestructible nationality. Then our jurisdiction did not reach beyond the inconvenient boundaries of the territory which had achieved independence; now, through cessions of lands, first colonized by Spain and France, the country has acquired a more complex character, and has for its natural limits the chain of lakes, the Gulf of Mexico, and on the east and the west the two great oceans.   Other nations were wasted by civil wars for ages before they could establish for themselves the necessary degree of unity; the latent conviction that our form of government is the best ever known to the world has enabled us to emerge from civil war within four years with a complete vindication of the constitutional authority of the General Government and with our local liberties and State institutions unimpaired.

The throngs of emigrants that crowd to our shores are witnesses of the confidence of all peoples in our permanence.   Here is the great land of free labor, where industry is blessed with unexampled rewards and the bread of the workingman is sweetened by the consciousness that the cause of the country "is his own cause, his own safety, his own dignity."   Here everyone enjoys the free use of his faculties and the choice of activity as a natural right.   Here, under the combined influence of a fruitful soil, genial climes, and happy institutions, population has increased fifteenfold within a century.   Here, through the easy development of boundless resources, wealth has increased with twofold greater rapidity than numbers, so that we have become secure against the financial vicissitudes of other countries and, alike in business and in opinion, are self-centered and truly independent.   Here more and more care is given to provide education for everyone born on our soil.   Here religion, released from political connection with the civil government, refuses to subserve the craft of statesmen, and becomes in its independence the spiritual life of the people.   Here toleration is extended to every opinion, in the quiet certainty that truth needs only a fair field to secure the victory.   Here the human mind goes forth unshackled in the pursuit of science, to collect stores of knowledge and acquire an ever-increasing mastery over the forces of nature.   Here the national domain is offered and held in millions of separate freeholds, so that our fellow-citizens, beyond the occupants of any other part of the earth, constitute in reality a people.   Here exists the democratic form of government; and that form of government, by the confession of European statesmen, "gives a power of which no other form is capable, because it incorporates every man with the state and arouses everything that belongs to the soul."

Where in past history does a parallel exist to the public happiness which is within the reach of the people of the United States?   Where in any part of the globe can institutions be found so suited to their habits or so entitled to their love as their own free Constitution?   Every one of them, then, in whatever part of the land he has his home, must wish its perpetuity.   Who of them will not now acknowledge, in the words of Washington, that "every step by which the people of the United States have advanced to the character of an independent nation seems to have been distinguished by some token of providential agency"?   Who will not join with me in the prayer that the Invisible Hand which has led us through the clouds that gloomed around our path will so guide us onward to a perfect restoration of fraternal affection that we of this day may be able to transmit our great inheritance of State governments in all their rights, of the General Government in its whole constitutional vigor, to our posterity, and they to theirs through countless generations?

ANDREW JOHNSON.

SPECIAL MESSAGES.

WASHINGTON, *December 11, 1865.*

To the Senate and House of Representatives of the United States:

I transmit a report of this date from the Secretary of State, and the papers referred to therein, concerning the Universal Exposition to be held at Paris in the year 1867, in which the United States have been invited by the Government of France to take part. I commend the subject to your early and favorable consideration.

ANDREW JOHNSON.

WASHINGTON, *December 13, 1865.*

To the Senate of the United States:

In answer to the resolution of the Senate of the 11th instant, requesting information on the subject of a decree of the so-called Emperor of Mexico of the 3d of October last, I transmit a report from the Secretary of State and the documents by which it was accompanied.

ANDREW JOHNSON.

WASHINGTON, *December 14, 1865.*

To the House of Representatives:

In answer to the resolution of the House of Representatives of the 11th instant, requesting information relative to a so-called decree concerning the reestablishment of slavery or peonage in the Republic of Mexico, I transmit a report from the Secretary of State and the documents by which it was accompanied.

ANDREW JOHNSON.

WASHINGTON, D. C., *December 18, 1865.*

To the Senate and House of Representatives of the United States:

In compliance with the requirements of the third section of the act approved March 3, 1865, I transmit herewith a communication from the Secretary of War, with the accompanying report and estimates of the Commissioner of the Bureau of Refugees, Freedmen, and Abandoned Lands.

ANDREW JOHNSON.

WASHINGTON, *December 18, 1865.*

To the Senate of the United States:

In reply to the resolution adopted by the Senate on the 12th instant, I have the honor to state that the rebellion waged by a portion of the people against the properly constituted authority of the Government of the United States has been suppressed; that the United States are in possession of every State in which the insurrection existed, and that, as far as it could be done, the courts of the United States have been restored, post-offices reestablished, and steps taken to put into effective operation the revenue laws of the country.

As the result of the measures instituted by the Executive with the view of inducing a resumption of the functions of the States comprehended in the inquiry of the Senate, the people of North Carolina, South Carolina, Georgia, Alabama, Mississippi, Louisiana, Arkansas, and Tennessee have reorganized their respective State governments, and "are yielding obedience to the laws and Government of the United States" with more willingness and greater promptitude than under the circumstances could reasonably have been anticipated. The proposed amendment to the Constitution, providing for the abolition of slavery forever within the limits of the country, has been ratified by each one of those States, with the exception of Mississippi, from which no official information has been received, and in nearly all of them measures have been adopted or are now pending to confer upon freedmen the privileges which are essential to their comfort, protection, and security. In Florida and Texas the people are making commendable progress in restoring their State governments, and no doubt is entertained that they will at an early period be in a condition to resume all of their practical relations with the General Government.

In "that portion of the Union lately in rebellion" the aspect of affairs is more promising than, in view of all the circumstances, could well have been expected. The people throughout the entire South evince a laudable desire to renew their allegiance to the Government and to repair the devastations of war by a prompt and cheerful return to peaceful pursuits, and abiding faith is entertained that their actions will conform to their professions, and that in acknowledging the supremacy of the Constitution and laws of the United States their loyalty will be unreservedly given to the Government, whose leniency they can not fail to appreciate and whose fostering care will soon restore them to a condition of prosperity. It is true that in some of the States the demoralizing effects of the war are to be seen in occasional disorders; but these are local in character, not frequent in occurrence, and are rapidly disappearing as the authority of civil law is extended and sustained. Perplexing questions are naturally to be expected from the great and sudden change in the relations between the two races; but systems are gradually developing themselves under which the freedman will receive the protection to which he is justly entitled, and, by means of his labor, make himself a useful and independent member in the community in which he has a home.

From all the information in my possession and from that which I have recently derived from the most reliable authority I am induced to cherish the belief that sectional animosity is surely and rapidly merging itself into a spirit of nationality, and that representation, connected with a properly adjusted system of taxation, will result in a harmonious restoration of the relation of the States to the National Union.

The report of Carl Schurz is herewith transmitted, as requested by the Senate. No reports from the Hon. John Covode have been received by the President. The attention of the Senate is invited to the accompanying report from Lieutenant-General Grant, who recently made a tour of inspection through several of the States whose inhabitants participated in the rebellion.
                                                    ANDREW JOHNSON.

                                WASHINGTON, *December 20, 1865.*
To the Senate of the United States:

In reply to the resolution of the Senate of the 19th instant, requesting that the President, if not inconsistent with the public service, communicate to the Senate the "report of General Howard of his observations of the condition of the seceded States and the operation of the Freedmen's Bureau therein," I have to state that the report of the Commissioner of the Bureau of Refugees, Freedmen, and Abandoned Lands was yesterday transmitted to both Houses of Congress, as required by the third section of the act approved March 3, 1865.   ANDREW JOHNSON.

                                WASHINGTON, *December 21, 1865.*
To the Senate:

In compliance with the resolution of the Senate of the 11th instant, respecting the occupation by the French troops of the Republic of Mexico and the establishment of a monarchy there, I transmit a report from the Secretary of State and the documents by which it was accompanied.
                                                    ANDREW JOHNSON.

                                WASHINGTON, *January 5, 1866.*
To the Senate of the United States:

In compliance with the resolution of the Senate of the 19th ultimo, requesting information in regard to any plans to induce the immigration of dissatisfied citizens of the United States into Mexico, their organization there with the view to create disturbances in the United States, and especially in regard to the plans of Dr. William M. Gwin and M. F. Maury, and to the action taken by the Government of the United States to prevent the success of such schemes, I transmit a report from the Acting Secretary of State and the papers by which it was accompanied.

ANDREW JOHNSON.

WASHINGTON, *January 5, 1866.*

To the Senate of the United States:

I have received the following preamble and resolution, adopted by the Senate on the 21st ultimo:

Whereas the Constitution declares that "in all criminal prosecutions the accused shall enjoy the right of a speedy and public trial by an impartial jury of the State or district wherein the crime shall have been committed;" and

Whereas several months have elapsed since Jefferson Davis, late president of the so-called Confederate States, was captured and confined for acts notoriously done by him as such, which acts, if duly proved, render him guilty of treason against the United States and liable to the penalties thereof; and

Whereas hostilities between the Government of the United States and the insurgents have ceased, and not one of the latter, so far as is known to the Senate, is now held in confinement for the part he may have acted in the rebellion except said Jefferson Davis: Therefore,

Resolved, That the President be respectfully requested, if compatible with the public safety, to inform the Senate upon what charges or for what reasons said Jefferson Davis is still held in confinement, and why he has not been put upon his trial.

In reply to the resolution I transmit the accompanying reports from the Secretary of War and the Attorney-General, and at the same time invite the attention of the Senate to that portion of my message dated the 4th day of December last which refers to Congress the questions connected with the holding of circuit courts of the United States within the districts where their authority has been interrupted.

ANDREW JOHNSON.

WASHINGTON, *January 5, 1866.*

To the House of Representatives:

In compliance with the resolution of the House of Representatives of the 18th ultimo, requesting information in regard to steps taken by the so-called Emperor of Mexico or by any European power to obtain from the United States a recognition of the so-called Empire of Mexico, and what action has been taken in the premises by the Government of the United States, I transmit a report from the Acting Secretary of State and the papers by which it was accompanied.

ANDREW JOHNSON.

WASHINGTON, *January 10, 1866.*

To the House of Representatives:

In answer to the resolution of the House of Representatives of the 8th instant, asking for information in regard to the alleged kidnaping in

Mexico of the child of an American lady, I transmit a report from the Acting Secretary of State, to whom the resolution was referred.

ANDREW JOHNSON.

WASHINGTON, D. C., *January 12, 1866.*

To the Senate and House of Representatives:

I transmit herewith a communication addressed to me by Messrs. John Evans and J. B. Chaffee as "United States Senators elect from the State of Colorado," together with the accompanying documents.

Under authority of the act of Congress approved the 21st day of March, 1864, the people of Colorado, through a convention, formed a constitution making provision for a State government, which, when submitted to the qualified voters of the Territory, was rejected.

In the summer of 1865 a second convention was called by the executive committees of the several political parties in the Territory, which assembled at Denver on the 8th of August, 1865. On the 12th of that month this convention adopted a State constitution, which was submitted to the people on the 5th of September, 1865, and ratified by a majority of 155 of the qualified voters. The proceedings in the second instance for the formation of a State government having differed in time and mode from those specified in the act of March 21, 1864, I have declined to issue the proclamation for which provision is made in the fifth section of the law, and therefore submit the question for the consideration and further action of Congress.

ANDREW JOHNSON.

EXECUTIVE OFFICE, *January 20, 1866.*

To the Senate of the United States:

I communicate to the Senate herewith, for its constitutional action thereon, the several treaties* with the Indians of the Southwest referred to in the accompanying communication from the Secretary of the Interior.

ANDREW JOHNSON.

EXECUTIVE OFFICE, *January 20, 1866.*

To the Senate of the United States:

I communicate to the Senate herewith, for its constitutional action thereon, the several treaties with bands of the Sioux Nation of Indians which are referred to in the accompanying communication from the Secretary of the Interior.

ANDREW JOHNSON.

---

* With the confederated tribes of the Arapahoe and Cheyenne Indians, concluded October 14, 1865; with the Apache, Cheyenne, and Arapahoe tribes, respectively, concluded October 17, 1865; with the several bands of the Comanche tribe, concluded October 18, 1865.

EXECUTIVE MANSION, *January 20, 1866.*

To the Senate of the United States:

I communicate to the Senate herewith, for its constitutional action thereon, the treaties with the Omaha and Winnebago Indians referred to in the accompanying communication from the Secretary of the Interior.

ANDREW JOHNSON.

WASHINGTON, *January 26, 1866.*

To the Senate of the United States:

In compliance with the resolution of the Senate of the 11th instant, requesting information in regard to a negotiation for the transit of United States troops in 1861 through Mexican territory, I transmit a report from the Acting Secretary of State and the papers by which it was accompanied.

ANDREW JOHNSON.

WASHINGTON, *January 26, 1866.*

To the Senate of the United States:

I transmit to the Senate, for its consideration with a view to ratification, a convention between the United States and the Empire of Japan for the reduction of import duties, which was signed at Yedo the 28th of January, 1864.

ANDREW JOHNSON.

WASHINGTON, *January 26, 1866.*

To the Senate of the United States:

I transmit to the Senate, for its consideration with a view to ratification, a convention between the Empire of Japan and the Governments of the United States, Great Britain, France, and Holland, providing for the payment to said Governments of the sum of $3,000,000 for indemnities and expenses, which was signed by the respective parties at Yokohama on the 22d of October, 1864.

ANDREW JOHNSON.

WASHINGTON, *January 26, 1866.*

To the Senate of the United States:

In answer to the resolution of the Senate of the 17th instant, requesting the President "to communicate to the Senate, if in his opinion not inconsistent with the public interest, any letters from Major-General Sheridan, commanding the Military Division of the Gulf, or from any other officer of the Department of Texas, in regard to the present condition of affairs on the southeastern frontier of the United States, and especially in regard to any violation of neutrality on the part of the army now occupying the right bank of the Rio Grande," I transmit herewith a report from the Secretary of War, bearing date the 24th instant.

Concurring in his opinion that the publication of the correspondence at this time is not consistent with the public interest, the papers referred to in the accompanying report are for the present withheld.

ANDREW JOHNSON.

WASHINGTON, *January 26, 1866.*

To the House of Representatives:

In compliance with the resolution of the House of Representatives of the 22d instant, requesting the communication of any correspondence or other information in regard to a demonstration by the Congress of the United States of Colombia, or any other country, in honor of President Juarez, of the Republic of Mexico, I transmit herewith a report from the Acting Secretary of State, with the papers by which it was accompanied.

ANDREW JOHNSON.

WASHINGTON, *January 26, 1866.*

To the House of Representatives:

In answer to the resolution of the House of Representatives of the 8th instant, asking for information in regard to the reported surrender of the rebel pirate vessel called the *Shenandoah*, I transmit a report from the Acting Secretary of State, to whom the resolution was referred.

ANDREW JOHNSON.

WASHINGTON, *January 30, 1866.*

To the Senate and House of Representatives:

Believing that the commercial interests of our country would be promoted by a formal recognition of the independence of the Dominican Republic, while such a recognition would be in entire conformity with the settled policy of the United States, I have with that view nominated to the Senate an officer of the same grade with the one now accredited to the Republic of Hayti; and I recommend that an appropriation be made by Congress toward providing for his compensation.

ANDREW JOHNSON.

WASHINGTON, *February 1, 1866.*

To the House of Representatives:

In compliance with the resolution of the House of Representatives of the 10th ultimo, requesting information in regard to the organization in the city of New York of the "Imperial Mexican Express Company" under a grant from the so-called Emperor of Mexico, I transmit a report from the Secretary of State and the papers by which it was accompanied.

ANDREW JOHNSON.

WASHINGTON, *February 2, 1866.*
To the Senate of the United States:

The accompanying correspondence is transmitted to the Senate in compliance with its resolution of the 16th ultimo, requesting the President, "if not inconsistent with the public interest, to communicate to the Senate any correspondence which may have taken place between himself and any of the judges of the Supreme Court touching the holding of the civil courts of the United States in the insurrectionary States for the trial of crimes against the United States."

ANDREW JOHNSON.

WASHINGTON, *February 2, 1866.*
To the Senate of the United States:

In answer to the resolution of the Senate of the 30th ultimo, requesting the President, "if not incompatible with the public interests, to communicate to the Senate a copy of the late report of Major-General Sherman upon the condition of the States in his department, in which he has lately made a tour of inspection," I transmit herewith a copy of a communication, dated December 22, 1865, addressed to the Headquarters of the Army by Major-General Sherman, commanding the Military Division of the Mississippi

ANDREW JOHNSON.

WASHINGTON, *February 9, 1866.*
To the House of Representatives:

In reply to the resolution of the House of Representatives of the 10th ultimo, requesting the President of the United States, "if not incompatible with the public interest, to communicate to the House any report or reports made by the Judge-Advocate-General or any other officer of the Government as to the grounds, facts, or accusations upon which Jefferson Davis, Clement C. Clay, jr., Stephen R. Mallory, and David L. Yulee, or either of them, are held in confinement," I transmit herewith reports from the Secretary of War and the Attorney-General, and concur in the opinion therein expressed that the publication of the papers called for by the resolution is not at the present time compatible with the public interest.

ANDREW JOHNSON.

WASHINGTON, *February 10, 1866.*
To the Senate and House of Representatives:

I transmit, for the consideration of Congress, a correspondence between the Secretary of State and the minister of France accredited to this Government, and also other papers, relative to a proposed international conference at Constantinople upon the subject of cholera.

ANDREW JOHNSON.

WASHINGTON, *March 5, 1866.*

To the House of Representatives:

I transmit the accompanying report from the Secretary of War, in answer to the resolution of the House of Representatives of the 27th ultimo, requesting information in regard to the distribution of the rewards offered by the Government for the arrest of the assassins of the late President Lincoln. ANDREW JOHNSON.

WASHINGTON, *March 5, 1866.*

To the Senate of the United States:

In compliance with the resolution of the Senate of the 27th ultimo, I transmit herewith a communication from the Secretary of War, together with the reports of the assistant commissioners of the Freedmen's Bureau made since December 1, 1865. ANDREW JOHNSON.

WASHINGTON, *March 6, 1866.*

To the Senate of the United States:

In answer to the resolutions of the Senate of the 5th of January and 27th of February last, requesting information in regard to provisional governors of States, I transmit reports from the Secretary of State and the Secretary of War, to whom the resolutions were referred.

ANDREW JOHNSON.

WASHINGTON, D. C., *March 6, 1866.*

To the Senate of the United States:

I transmit to the Senate, for its constitutional action thereon, a treaty with the Utah, Yampah-Ute, Pah-Vant, San-Pete-Ute, Tim-p-nogs, and Cum-um-bah bands of the Utah Indians, referred to in the accompanying papers from the Secretary of the Interior. ANDREW JOHNSON.

WASHINGTON, *March 6, 1866.*

To the House of Representatives:

In answer to the resolution of the House of Representatives of the 12th of January last, requesting information in regard to provisional governments of certain States, I transmit a report from the Secretary of State, to whom the resolution was referred. ANDREW JOHNSON.

WASHINGTON, *March 6, 1866.*

To the House of Representatives:

In answer to the resolution of the House of Representatives of the 27th ultimo, requesting certain information in relation to President Benito Juarez, of Mexico, I transmit a report from the Secretary of State.

ANDREW JOHNSON.

WASHINGTON, *March 8, 1866.*

To the Senate of the United States:

I transmit, for the consideration of the Senate, a copy of a letter of the 21st ultimo from the governor of the Territory of Colorado to the Secretary of State, with the memorial to which it refers, relative to the location of the Pacific Railroad.

ANDREW JOHNSON.

WASHINGTON, *March 12, 1866.*

To the Senate and House of Representatives:

I transmit, for your consideration, a copy of two communications from the minister of the United States at Paris, in regard to a proposed exhibition of fishery and water culture, to be held at Arcachon, near Bordeaux, in France, in July next.

ANDREW JOHNSON.

WASHINGTON, *March 15, 1866.*

To the Senate of the United States:

In answer to the resolution of the Senate of the 5th instant, upon the subject of the supposed kidnaping of colored persons in the Southern States for the purpose of selling them as slaves in Cuba, I transmit a report from the Secretary of State, to whom the resolution was referred.

ANDREW JOHNSON.

WASHINGTON, D. C., *March 19, 1866.*

To the House of Representatives:

In answer to the resolution of the House of Representatives dated January 5, 1866, requesting information as to the number of men and officers in the regular and volunteer service of the United States, I transmit a report from the Secretary of War, with the papers by which it was accompanied.

ANDREW JOHNSON.

WASHINGTON, *March 20, 1866.*

To the House of Representatives:

In compliance with the resolution of the House of Representatives of the 11th of December last, requesting information upon the present condition of affairs in the Republic of Mexico, I transmit a report from the Secretary of State and the papers by which it was accompanied.

ANDREW JOHNSON.

WASHINGTON, *March 21, 1866.*

To the Senate of the United States:

I transmit to the Senate, for its constitutional action thereon, a treaty made with the Great and Little Osage Indians on the 29th September, 1865, together with the accompanying papers.

ANDREW JOHNSON.

WASHINGTON, *March 21, 1866.*

To the Senate of the United States:

I transmit to the Senate, for its constitutional action thereon, a treaty made with the Woll-pah-pe tribe of Snake Indians on the 12th of August, 1865, together with the accompanying papers.

ANDREW JOHNSON.

WASHINGTON, D. C., *March 26, 1866.*

To the Senate of the United States:

I transmit to the Senate a memorial of the legislature of Alabama, asking an extension of time for the completion of certain railroads in said State.

ANDREW JOHNSON.

WASHINGTON, *March 30, 1866.*

To the Senate of the United States:

I transmit herewith, for the constitutional action of the Senate, a treaty negotiated with the Shawnee Indians, dated March 1, 1866, with supplemental article, dated March 14, 1866, with accompanying communications from the honorable Secretary of the Interior and Commissioner of Indian Affairs.

ANDREW JOHNSON.

WASHINGTON, *April 3, 1866.*

To the Senate of the United States:

I transmit herewith a report by the Secretary of War, in compliance with the Senate resolution of the 7th March, 1866, respecting the improvement of the Washington City Canal, to promote the health of the metropolis.

ANDREW JOHNSON.

WASHINGTON, D. C., *April 3, 1866.*

To the House of Representatives:

I transmit a communication from the Secretary of the Treasury, dated the 22d ultimo, together with a letter addressed to him by the governor of Alabama, asking that the State of Alabama may be allowed to assume and pay in State bonds the direct tax now due from that State to the United States, or that delay of payment may be authorized until the State can by the sale of its bonds or by taxation make provision for the liquidation of the indebtedness.

I concur in the opinion of the Secretary of the Treasury "that it is desirable that the State of Alabama and the other Southern States should be allowed to assume and pay their proportion of the direct taxes now due," and therefore recommend the necessary legislation by Congress.

ANDREW JOHNSON.

WASHINGTON, *April 4, 1866.*

To the Senate and House of Representatives:

I transmit to Congress a report from the Secretary of State, with the accompanying papers, relative to the claim on this Government of the owners of the British vessel *Magicienne,* and recommend an appropriation for the satisfaction of the claim, pursuant to the award of the arbitrators.

ANDREW JOHNSON.

WASHINGTON, *April 5, 1866.*

To the Senate and House of Representatives:

I herewith transmit communications from the Secretary of the Treasury and the Postmaster-General, suggesting a modification of the oath of office prescribed by the act of Congress approved July 2, 1862. I fully concur in their recommendation, and as the subject pertains to the efficient administration of the revenue and postal laws in the Southern States I earnestly commend it to the early consideration of Congress.

ANDREW JOHNSON.

WASHINGTON, *April 6, 1866.*

To the Senate of the United States:

I transmit, for the constitutional action of the Senate, a supplemental article to the Pottawatomie treaty of November 15, 1861, concluded on the 29th ultimo, together with the accompanying communications from the Secretary of the Interior and Commissioner of Indian Affairs.

ANDREW JOHNSON.

WASHINGTON, D. C., *April 7, 1866.*

To the House of Representatives of the United States:

I transmit a communication from the Secretary of the Interior, with the accompanying papers, in reference to grants of land made by acts of Congress passed in the years 1850, 1853, and 1856 to the States of Mississippi, Alabama, Arkansas, Florida, and Louisiana, to aid in the construction of certain railroads. As these acts will expire by limitation on the 11th day of August, 1866, leaving the roads for whose benefit they were conferred in an unfinished condition, it is recommended that the time within which they may be completed be extended for a period of five years.

ANDREW JOHNSON.

WASHINGTON, *April 11, 1866.*

To the Senate of the United States:

In compliance with the resolution of the Senate of the 27th ultimo, in relation to the seizure and detention at New York of the steamship

Meteor, I transmit herewith a report from the Secretary of State and the papers by which it was accompanied.

ANDREW JOHNSON.

WASHINGTON, *April 13, 1866.*

To the Senate of the United States: .

I transmit herewith, for the constitutional action of the Senate, a treaty concluded with the Bois Forte band of Chippewa Indians on the 7th instant, together with the accompanying communications from the Secretary of the Interior and Commissioner of Indian Affairs.

ANDREW JOHNSON.

WASHINGTON, *April 13, 1866.*

To the House of Representatives:

In answer to the resolution of the House of Representatives of the 10th instant, requesting information in regard to the rights and interests of American citizens in the fishing grounds adjacent to the British Provinces, I transmit a report from the Secretary of State, to whom the resolution was referred.

ANDREW JOHNSON.

WASHINGTON, *April 20, 1866.*

To the Senate of the United States:

In compliance with the Senate's resolution of the 8th January, 1866, I transmit herewith a communication from the Secretary of War of the 19th instant, covering copies of the correspondence respecting General Orders, No. 17,* issued by the commander of the Department of California, and also the Attorney-General's opinion as to the question whether the order involves a breach of neutrality toward Mexico.

ANDREW JOHNSON.

WASHINGTON, D. C., *April 20, 1866.*

To the House of Representatives:

In reply to the resolution of the House of Representatives of the 2d instant, requesting information respecting the collection of the remains of officers and soldiers killed and buried on the various battlefields about Atlanta, I transmit herewith a report on the subject from the Secretary of War.

ANDREW JOHNSON.

---

*Instructing commanders on the southern frontiers within the Department of California "to take the necessary measures to preserve the neutrality of the United States with respect to the parties engaged in the existing war in Mexico, and to suffer no armed parties to pass the frontier from the United States, nor suffer any arms or munitions of war to be sent over the frontier to either belligerent," etc.

WASHINGTON, *April 21, 1866.*

To the Senate of the United States:

I transmit herewith a communication of this date from the Secretary of War, covering a copy of the proceedings of a board of officers in relation to brevet appointments in the Regular Army, requested in the Senate's resolution of the 18th April, 1866.

ANDREW JOHNSON.

WASHINGTON, *April 23, 1866.*

To the Senate of the United States:

I transmit to the Senate, for its consideration with a view to ratification, a convention which was signed at Tangier on the 31st of May last between the United States and other powers on the one part and the Sultan of Morocco on the other part, concerning the administration and maintenance of a light-house on Cape Spartel.

ANDREW JOHNSON.

WASHINGTON, *April 23, 1866.*

To the House of Representatives:

In answer to the resolution of the House of Representatives of the 16th instant, requesting information relative to the proposed evacuation of Mexico by French military forces, I transmit a report from the Secretary of State and the documents by which it was accompanied.

ANDREW JOHNSON.

EXECUTIVE MANSION,
Washington, D. C., April 24, 1866.

To the Senate and House of Representatives:

I submit herewith, for the consideration of Congress, the accompanying communication from the Secretary of the Interior, in relation to the Union Pacific Railroad Company, eastern division.

It appears that the company were required to complete 100 miles of their road within three years after their acceptance of the conditions of the original act of Congress. This period expired December 22, 1865. Sixty-two miles had been previously accepted by the Government. Since that date an additional section of 23 miles has been completed. Commissioners appointed for that purpose have examined and reported upon it, and an application has been made for its acceptance.

The failure to complete 100 miles of road within the period prescribed renders it questionable whether the executive officers of the Government are authorized to issue the bonds and patents to which the company would be entitled if this as well as the other requirements of the act had been faithfully observed.

This failure may to some extent be ascribed to the financial condition of the country incident to the recent civil war. As the company appear to be engaged in the energetic prosecution of their work and manifest a disposition to comply with the conditions of the grant, I recommend that the time for the completion of this part of the road be extended and that authority be given for the issue of bonds and patents on account of the section now offered for acceptance notwithstanding such failure, should the company in other respects be thereunto entitled.

ANDREW JOHNSON.

WASHINGTON, D. C., *April 28, 1866.*

To the Senate of the United States:

I transmit herewith, for the constitutional action of the Senate, a treaty this day concluded with the Choctaw and Chickasaw nations of Indians.

ANDREW JOHNSON.

WASHINGTON, *April 30, 1866.*

To the House of Representatives:

In answer to the resolution of the House of Representatives of the 25th instant, requesting information in regard to the rebel debt known as the cotton loan, I transmit a report from the Secretary of State, to whom the resolution was referred. ANDREW JOHNSON.

WASHINGTON, D. C., *May 2, 1866.*

To the House of Representatives:

In reply to the resolution of the House of Representatives of the 23d ultimo, I transmit a report from the Secretary of War, from which it will be perceived that it is not deemed compatible with the public interests to communicate to the House the report made by General Smith and the Hon. James T. Brady of their investigations at New Orleans, La.

ANDREW JOHNSON.

WASHINGTON, D. C., *May 4, 1866.*

To the House of Representatives:

In answer to the resolution of the House of Representatives of the 5th of March, 1866, requesting the names of persons worth more than $20,000 to whom special pardons have been issued, and a statement of the amount of property which has been seized as belonging to the enemies of the Government, or as abandoned property, and returned to those who claimed to be the original owners, I transmit herewith reports from the Secretary of State, the Secretary of the Treasury, the Secretary of

War, and the Attorney-General, together with a copy of the amnesty proclamation of the 29th of May, 1865, and a copy of the warrants issued in cases in which special pardons are granted. The second, third, and fourth conditions of the warrant prescribe the terms, so far as property is concerned, upon which all such pardons are granted and accepted.

ANDREW JOHNSON.

WASHINGTON, *May 4, 1866.*

To the Senate and House of Representatives:

Referring to my message of the 12th of March last, communicating information in regard to a proposed exposition of fishery and water culture at Arcachon, in France, I communicate a copy of another dispatch from the minister of the United States in Paris to the Secretary of State, and again invite the attention of Congress to the subject.

ANDREW JOHNSON.

WASHINGTON, *May 7, 1866.*

To the Senate of the United States:

In compliance with the resolution of the Senate of the 19th ultimo, I transmit herewith a report from Benjamin C. Truman, relative to the condition of the Southern people and the States in which the rebellion existed.

ANDREW JOHNSON.

WASHINGTON, *May 9, 1866.*

To the Senate and House of Representatives:

I transmit to Congress a copy of a correspondence between the Secretary of State and the acting chargé d'affaires of the United States at Guayaquil, in the Republic of Ecuador, from which it appears that the Government of that Republic has failed to pay the first installment of the award of the commissioners under the convention between the United States and Ecuador of the 25th November, 1862, which installment was due on the 17th of February last.

As debts of this character from one government to another are justly regarded as of a peculiarly sacred character, and as further diplomatic measures are not in this instance likely to be successful, the expediency of authorizing other proceedings in case they should ultimately prove to be indispensable is submitted to your consideration.

ANDREW JOHNSON.

WASHINGTON, D. C., *May 10, 1866.*

To the House of Representatives:

I transmit herewith a report from the Secretary of the Treasury, in answer to the resolution of the House of Representatives of the 3d instant, requesting information concerning discriminations made by the so-called Maximilian Government of Mexico against American commerce, or against commerce from particular American ports.

ANDREW JOHNSON.

WASHINGTON, May 11, 1866.

To the House of Representatives:

I transmit a report from the Secretary of State, in answer to that part of the resolution of the House of Representatives of the 7th instant which calls for information in regard to the clerks employed in the Department of State.

ANDREW JOHNSON.

WASHINGTON, May 16, 1866.

To the Senate and House of Representatives:

I transmit to Congress a copy of the correspondence between the Secretary of State and Cornelius Vanderbilt, of New York, relative to the joint resolution of the 28th of January, 1864, upon the subject of the gift of the steamer *Vanderbilt* to the United States.

ANDREW JOHNSON.

EXECUTIVE MANSION,
Washington, May 17, 1866.

Hon. SCHUYLER COLFAX,
 Speaker of the House of Representatives.

SIR: I have the honor to submit herewith a communication of the Secretary of War, inclosing one from the Lieutenant-General, relative to the necessity for legislation upon the subject of the Army.

ANDREW JOHNSON.

WASHINGTON, D. C., May 17, 1866.

To the House of Representatives:

In further response to the resolution of the House of Representatives of the 7th instant, calling for information in regard to clerks employed in the several Executive Departments, I transmit herewith reports from the Secretary of the Navy and the Secretary of the Interior and the Postmaster-General.

ANDREW JOHNSON.

WASHINGTON, D. C., May 22, 1866.

To the House of Representatives:

I transmit herewith a report from the Secretary of the Treasury, made in compliance with the resolution of the House of Representatives of the 7th instant, calling for information in respect to clerks employed in the several Executive Departments of the Government.

ANDREW JOHNSON.

WASHINGTON, D. C., *May 22, 1866.*

To the House of Representatives:

In answer to the resolution of the House of Representatives of the 27th ultimo, requesting a collation of the provisions in reference to freedmen contained in the amended constitutions of the Southern States and in the laws of those States passed since the suppression of the rebellion, I transmit a report from the Secretary of State, to whom the resolution was referred.

ANDREW JOHNSON.

WASHINGTON, D. C., *May 24, 1866.*

To the House of Representatives:

I transmit herewith a report from the Postmaster-General, made in answer to the resolution of the House of Representatives of the 14th instant, calling for information relative to the proposed mail steamship service between the United States and Brazil.

ANDREW JOHNSON.

WASHINGTON, D. C., *May 25, 1866.*

To the House of Representatives:

In compliance with the resolution of the House of Representatives of the 21st instant, I transmit herewith a report from the Secretary of War, with the accompanying papers, in reference to the operations of the Bureau of Refugees, Freedmen, and Abandoned Lands.

ANDREW JOHNSON.

WASHINGTON, *May 30, 1866.*

To the Senate and House of Representatives:

With sincere regret I announce to Congress that Winfield Scott, late Lieutenant-General in the Army of the United States, departed this life at West Point, in the State of New York, on the 29th day of May instant, at 11 o'clock in the forenoon. I feel well assured that Congress will share in the grief of the nation which must result from its bereavement of a citizen whose high fame is identified with the military history of the Republic.

ANDREW JOHNSON.

WASHINGTON, D. C., *May 30, 1866.*

To the House of Representatives:

I transmit a communication from the Secretary of War, covering a supplemental report to that already made to the House of Representatives, in answer to its resolution of the 21st instant, requesting the reports of General Steedman and others in reference to the operations of the Bureau of Refugees, Freedmen, and Abandoned Lands.

ANDREW JOHNSON.

WASHINGTON, *June 5, 1866.*

To the Senate of the United States:

I transmit to the Senate, for its consideration with a view to ratification, a convention between the United States and the Republic of Venezuela on the subject of the claims of citizens of the United States upon the Government of that Republic, which convention was signed by the plenipotentiaries of the parties at the city of Caracas on the 25th of April last.
ANDREW JOHNSON.

WASHINGTON, *June 9, 1866.*

To the House of Representatives:

I transmit herewith a report from the Acting Secretary of the Interior, communicating the information requested by a resolution of the House of Representatives of the 21st ultimo, in relation to the removal of the Sioux Indians of Minnesota and the provisions made for their accommodation in the Territory of Nebraska.
ANDREW JOHNSON.

WASHINGTON, *June 9, 1866.*

To the Senate of the United States:

In compliance with a call of the Senate, as expressed in a resolution adopted on the 6th instant, I transmit a copy of the report of the Board of Visitors to the United States Naval Academy for the year 1866.
ANDREW JOHNSON.

WASHINGTON, *June 11, 1866.*

To the House of Representatives:

In answer to the resolution of the House of Representatives of the 10th ultimo, calling for information relative to the claims of citizens of the United States against the Republic of Venezuela, I transmit a report from the Secretary of State.
ANDREW JOHNSON.

WASHINGTON, *June 11, 1866.*

To the Senate and House of Representatives:

It is proper that I should inform Congress that a copy of an act of the legislature of Georgia of the 10th of March last has been officially communicated to me, by which that State accepts the donation of lands for the benefit of colleges for agriculture and the mechanic arts, which donation was provided for by the acts of Congress of the 2d of July, 1862, and 14th of April, 1864.
ANDREW JOHNSON.

WASHINGTON, *June 11, 1866.*

To the Senate and House of Representatives:

I communicate and invite the attention of Congress to a copy of joint resolutions of the senate and house of representatives of the State of Georgia, requesting a suspension of the collection of the internal-revenue tax due from that State pursuant to the act of Congress of the 5th of August, 1861.

ANDREW JOHNSON.

WASHINGTON, *June 13, 1866.*

To the House of Representatives:

In answer to the resolution of the House of Representatives of the 11th instant, requesting information concerning the provisions of the laws and ordinances of the late insurgent States on the subject of the rebel debt, so called, I transmit a report from the Secretary of State and the document by which it was accompanied.

ANDREW JOHNSON.

WASHINGTON, *June 14, 1866.*

To the House of Representatives:

In answer to a resolution of the House of Representatives of the 28th of May, requesting information as to what progress has been made in completing the maps connected with the boundary survey under the treaty of Washington, with copies of any correspondence on this subject not heretofore printed, I transmit a report from the Secretary of State and the documents which accompanied it.

ANDREW JOHNSON.

WASHINGTON, *June 15, 1866.*

To the Senate of the United States:

In compliance with a resolution of the Senate of the 13th instant, calling for information in regard to the departure of troops from Austria to Mexico, I transmit a report from the Secretary of State and the documents by which it was accompanied.

ANDREW JOHNSON.

WASHINGTON, *June 16, 1866.*

To the Senate of the United States:

I communicate herewith a report from the Acting Secretary of the Interior, furnishing, as requested by a resolution of the Senate of the 25th ultimo, information touching the transactions of the executive branch of the Government respecting the transportation, settlement, and colonization of persons of the African race.

ANDREW JOHNSON.

WASHINGTON, *June 18, 1866.*

To the House of Representatives:

In reply to a resolution of the House of Representatives of the 11th instant, requesting information in regard to the dispatch of military forces from Austria for service in Mexico, I transmit a report from the Secretary of State on the subject.

ANDREW JOHNSON.

WASHINGTON, D. C., *June 20, 1866.*

To the House of Representatives:

In compliance with the resolution of the House of Representatives of the 21st ultimo, requesting information as to the collection of the direct tax in the States whose inhabitants participated in the rebellion, I transmit a communication from the Secretary of the Treasury, accompanied by a report from the Deputy Commissioner of Internal Revenue.

ANDREW JOHNSON.

WASHINGTON, D. C., *June 22, 1866.*

To the Senate and House of Representatives:

I submit to Congress a report of the Secretary of State, to whom was referred the concurrent resolution of the 18th instant, respecting a submission to the legislatures of the States of an additional article to the Constitution of the United States. It will be seen from this report that the Secretary of State had, on the 16th instant, transmitted to the governors of the several States certified copies of the joint resolution passed on the 13th instant, proposing an amendment to the Constitution.

Even in ordinary times any question of amending the Constitution must be justly regarded as of paramount importance. This importance is at the present time enhanced by the fact that the joint resolution was not submitted by the two Houses for the approval of the President and that of the thirty-six States which constitute the Union eleven are excluded from representation in either House of Congress, although, with the single exception of Texas, they have been entirely restored to all their functions as States in conformity with the organic law of the land, and have appeared at the national capital by Senators and Representatives, who have applied for and have been refused admission to the vacant seats. Nor have the sovereign people of the nation been afforded an opportunity of expressing their views upon the important questions which the amendment involves. Grave doubts, therefore, may naturally and justly arise as to whether the action of Congress is in harmony with the sentiments of the people, and whether State legislatures, elected without reference to such an issue, should be called upon by Congress to decide respecting the ratification of the proposed amendment.

Waiving the question as to the constitutional validity of the proceedings of Congress upon the joint resolution proposing the amendment or as to the merits of the article which it submits through the executive department to the legislatures of the States, I deem it proper to observe that the steps taken by the Secretary of State, as detailed in the accompanying report, are to be considered as purely ministerial, and in no sense whatever committing the Executive to an approval or a recommendation of the amendment to the State legislatures or to the people. On the contrary, a proper appreciation of the letter and spirit of the Constitution, as well as of the interests of national order, harmony, and union, and a due deference for an enlightened public judgment may at this time well suggest a doubt whether any amendment to the Constitution ought to be proposed by Congress and pressed upon the legislatures of the several States for final decision until after the admission of such loyal Senators and Representatives of the now unrepresented States as have been or as may hereafter be chosen in conformity with the Constitution and laws of the United States.

ANDREW JOHNSON.

WASHINGTON, *June 22, 1866.*

To the Senate and House of Representatives:

In further answer to recent resolutions of the Senate and House of Representatives, requesting information in regard to the employment of European troops in Mexico, I transmit to Congress a copy of a dispatch of the 4th of this month addressed to the Secretary of State by the minister of the United States at Paris.

ANDREW JOHNSON.

WASHINGTON, *June 22, 1866.*

To the House of Representatives:

In answer to a resolution of the House of Representatives of the 18th instant, calling for information in regard to the arrest and imprisonment in Ireland of American citizens, I transmit herewith a report from the Secretary of State on the subject.

ANDREW JOHNSON.

WASHINGTON CITY, *June 23, 1866.*

To the House of Representatives:

I transmit herewith a report from the Secretary of the Interior, communicating in part the information requested by a resolution of the House of Representatives of the 23d of April last, in relation to appropriations and expenditures connected with the Indian service.

ANDREW JOHNSON.

WASHINGTON, D. C., *June 28, 1866.*

To the Senate and House of Representatives:

I transmit a communication from the Secretary of the Navy and the accompanying copy of a report and maps prepared by a board of examiners appointed under authority of the joint resolution approved June 1, 1866, "to examine a site for a fresh-water basin for ironclad vessels of the United States Navy."   ANDREW JOHNSON.

WASHINGTON, D. C., *June 28, 1866.*

To the House of Representatives:

I transmit herewith reports from the heads of the several Executive Departments, made in answer to the resolution of the House of Representatives of the 4th instant, requesting information as to whether any of the civil or military employees of the Government have assisted in the rendition of public honors to the rebel living or dead.

ANDREW JOHNSON.

WASHINGTON, *July 7, 1866.*

To the Senate of the United States:

The accompanying report of the Secretary of the Treasury is transmitted to the Senate in compliance with its resolution of the 20th ultimo, calling for a statement of the expenditures of the United States for the various public works of the Government in each State and Territory of the Union and in the District of Columbia from the year 1860 to the close of the year 1865.   ANDREW JOHNSON.

WASHINGTON, D. C., *July 7, 1866.*

To the Senate of the United States:

I transmit herewith, for the constitutional action of the Senate, a treaty concluded with the Seminole Nation of Indians on the 21st day of March, 1866, together with the accompanying communications from the Secretary of the Interior and the Commissioner of Indian Affairs.

ANDREW JOHNSON.

WASHINGTON, D. C., *July 7, 1866.*

To the Senate of the United States:

I transmit herewith, for the constitutional action of the Senate, a treaty concluded with the Creek Nation of Indians on the 14th day of June, 1866, together with the accompanying communications from the Secretary of the Interior and the Commissioner of Indian Affairs.

ANDREW JOHNSON.

WASHINGTON, *July 17, 1866.*

To the House of Representatives:

In answer to a resolution of the House of Representatives of yesterday, requesting information relative to proposed international movements in connection with the Paris Universal Exposition for the reform of systems of coinage, weights, and measures, I transmit a report from the Secretary of State and the documents by which it was accompanied.

ANDREW JOHNSON.

WASHINGTON, *July 17, 1866.*

To the Senate and House of Representatives:

I herewith transmit to Congress a report, dated 12th instant, with the accompanying papers, received from the Secretary of State, in compliance with the requirements of the eighteenth section of the act entitled "An act to regulate the diplomatic and consular systems of the United States," approved August 18, 1856.

ANDREW JOHNSON.

WASHINGTON, *July 20, 1866.*

To the Senate of the United States:

I transmit, for the constitutional action of the Senate, certain articles of agreement made at the Delaware Agency, Kans., on the 4th instant between the United States and the Delaware Indians.

ANDREW JOHNSON.

WASHINGTON, *July 20, 1866.*

To the Senate:

I herewith submit, for the constitutional action of the Senate, a treaty negotiated at the city of Washington, D. C., on the 19th instant, between the United States, represented by Dennis N. Cooley, Commissioner of Indian Affairs, and Elijah Sells, superintendent of Indian affairs for the southern superintendency, and the Cherokee Nation of Indians, represented by its delegates, James McDaniel, Smith Christie, White Catcher, L. H. Benge, J. B. Jones, and Daniel H. Ross.

The distracted condition of the Cherokee Nation and the peculiar relation of many of its members to this Government during the rebellion presented almost insuperable difficulties to treating with them. The treaty now submitted is a result of protracted negotiations. Its stipulations are, it is believed, as satisfactory to the contracting parties and furnish as just provisions for the welfare of the Indians and as strong guaranties for the maintenance of peaceful relations with them as under the circumstances could be expected.

ANDREW JOHNSON.

WASHINGTON, D. C., *July 24, 1866.*

To the Senate of the United States:

I hereby transmit, for the constitutional action of the Senate, a treaty concluded on the 15th of November, 1865, between the United States and the confederate tribes and bands of Indians of middle Oregon, the same being amendatory and supplemental to the treaty with said Indians of the 25th of June, 1855.

ANDREW JOHNSON.

WASHINGTON, D. C., *July 24, 1866.*

To the House of Representatives:

The following "Joint resolution, restoring Tennessee to her relations in the Union," was last evening presented for my approval:

Whereas in the year 1861 the government of the State of Tennessee was seized upon and taken possession of by persons in hostility to the United States, and the inhabitants of said State, in pursuance of an act of Congress, were declared to be in a state of insurrection against the United States; and

Whereas said State government can only be restored to its former political relations in the Union by the consent of the lawmaking power of the United States; and

Whereas the people of said State did, on the 22d day of February, 1865, by a large popular vote, adopt and ratify a constitution of government whereby slavery was abolished and all ordinances and laws of secession and debts contracted under the same were declared void; and

Whereas a State government has been organized under said constitution which has ratified the amendment to the Constitution of the United States abolishing slavery, also the amendment proposed by the Thirty-ninth Congress, and has done other acts proclaiming and denoting loyalty: Therefore,

Be it resolved by the Senate and House of Representatives of the United States in Congress assembled, That the State of Tennessee is hereby restored to her former proper practical relations to the Union, and is again entitled to be represented by Senators and Representatives in Congress.

The preamble simply consists of statements, some of which are assumed, while the resolution is merely a declaration of opinion. It comprises no legislation, nor does it confer any power which is binding upon the respective Houses, the Executive, or the States. It does not admit to their seats in Congress the Senators and Representatives from the State of Tennessee, for, notwithstanding the passage of the resolution, each House, in the exercise of the constitutional right to judge for itself of the elections, returns, and qualifications of its members, may, at its discretion, admit them or continue to exclude them. If a joint resolution of this kind were necessary and binding as a condition precedent to the admission of members of Congress, it would happen, in the event of a veto by the Executive, that Senators and Representatives could only be admitted to the halls of legislation by a two-thirds vote of each of the Houses.

Among other reasons recited in the preamble for the declaration contained in the resolution is the ratification by the State government of Tennessee of "the amendment to the Constitution of the United States abolishing slavery, also the amendment proposed by the Thirty-ninth Congress." If, as is also declared in the preamble, "said State government can only be restored to its former political relations in the Union by the consent of the lawmaking power of the United States," it would really seem to follow that the joint resolution which at this late day has received the sanction of Congress should have been passed, approved, and placed on the statute books before any amendment to the Constitution was submitted to the legislature of Tennessee for ratification. Otherwise the inference is plainly deducible that while, in the opinion of Congress, the people of a State may be too strongly disloyal to be entitled to representation, they may nevertheless, during the suspension of their "former proper practical relations to the Union," have an equally potent voice with other and loyal States in propositions to amend the Constitution, upon which so essentially depend the stability, prosperity, and very existence of the nation.

A brief reference to my annual message of the 4th of December last will show the steps taken by the Executive for the restoration to their constitutional relations to the Union of the States that had been affected by the rebellion. Upon the cessation of active hostilities provisional governors were appointed, conventions called, governors elected by the people, legislatures assembled, and Senators and Representatives chosen to the Congress of the United States. At the same time the courts of the United States were reopened, the blockade removed, the custom-houses reestablished, and postal operations resumed. The amendment to the Constitution abolishing slavery forever within the limits of the country was also submitted to the States, and they were thus invited to and did participate in its ratification, thus exercising the highest functions pertaining to a State. In addition nearly all of these States, through their conventions and legislatures, had adopted and ratified constitutions "of government whereby slavery was abolished and all ordinances and laws of secession and debts contracted under the same were declared void." So far, then, the political existence of the States and their relations to the Federal Government had been fully and completely recognized and acknowledged by the executive department of the Government; and the completion of the work of restoration, which had progressed so favorably, was submitted to Congress, upon which devolved all questions pertaining to the admission to their seats of the Senators and Representatives chosen from the States whose people had engaged in the rebellion.

All these steps had been taken when, on the 4th day of December, 1865, the Thirty-ninth Congress assembled. Nearly eight months have elapsed since that time; and no other plan of restoration having been proposed by Congress for the measures instituted by the Executive, it is now declared, in the joint resolution submitted for my approval, "that the State of Tennessee is hereby restored to her former proper practical relations to the Union, and is again entitled to be represented by Senators and Representatives in Congress.'' Thus, after the lapse of nearly eight months, Congress proposes to pave the way to the admission to representation of one of the eleven States whose people arrayed themselves in rebellion against the constitutional authority of the Federal Government.

Earnestly desiring to remove every cause of further delay, whether real or imaginary, on the part of Congress to the admission to seats of loyal Senators and Representatives from the State of Tennessee, I have, notwithstanding the anomalous character of this proceeding, affixed my signature to the resolution. My approval, however, is not to be construed as an acknowledgment of the right of Congress to pass laws preliminary to the admission of duly qualified Representatives from any of the States. Neither is it to be considered as committing me to all the statements made in the preamble, some of which are, in my opinion, without foundation in fact, especially the assertion that the State of Tennessee has ratified the amendment to the Constitution of the United States proposed by the Thirty-ninth Congress. No official notice of such ratification has been received by the Executive or filed in the Department of State; on the contrary, unofficial information from the most reliable sources induces the belief that the amendment has not yet been constitutionally sanctioned by the legislature of Tennessee. The right of each House under the Constitution to judge of the elections, returns, and qualifications of its own members is undoubted, and my approval or disapproval of the resolution could not in the slightest degree increase or diminish the authority in this respect conferred upon the two branches of Congress.

In conclusion I can not too earnestly repeat my recommendation for the admission of Tennessee, and all other States, to a fair and equal participation in national legislation when they present themselves in the persons of loyal Senators and Representatives who can comply with all the requirements of the Constitution and the laws. By this means harmony and reconciliation will be effected, the practical relations of all the States to the Federal Government reestablished, and the work of restoration, inaugurated upon the termination of the war, successfully completed. ANDREW JOHNSON.

WASHINGTON, *July 25, 1866.*

To the Senate of the United States:

I nominate Lieutenant-General Ulysses S. Grant to be General of the Army of the United States. ANDREW JOHNSON,

WASHINGTON, *July 26, 1866.*

To the House of Representatives:

In answer to two resolutions of the House of Representatives of the 23d instant, in the following words, respectively—

Resolved, That the House of Representatives respectfully request the President of the United States to urge upon the Canadian authorities, and also the British Government, the release of the Fenian prisoners recently captured in Canada;

Resolved, That this House respectfully request the President to cause the prosecutions instituted in the United States courts against the Fenians to be discontinued, if compatible with the public interest—

I transmit a report on the subject from the Secretary of State, together with the documents which accompany it.

ANDREW JOHNSON.

VETO MESSAGES.

WASHINGTON, *February 19, 1866.*

To the Senate of the United States:

I have examined with care the bill, which originated in the Senate and has been passed by the two Houses of Congress, to amend an act entitled "An act to establish a bureau for the relief of freedmen and refugees," and for other purposes. Having with much regret come to the conclusion that it would not be consistent with the public welfare to give my approval to the measure, I return the bill to the Senate with my objections to its becoming a law.

I might call to mind in advance of these objections that there is no immediate necessity for the proposed measure. The act to establish a bureau for the relief of freedmen and refugees, which was approved in the month of March last, has not yet expired. It was thought stringent and extensive enough for the purpose in view in time of war. Before it ceases to have effect further experience may assist to guide us to a wise conclusion as to the policy to be adopted in time of peace.

I share with Congress the strongest desire to secure to the freedmen the full enjoyment of their freedom and property and their entire independence and equality in making contracts for their labor, but the bill before me contains provisions which in my opinion are not warranted by the Constitution and are not well suited to accomplish the end in view.

The bill proposes to establish by authority of Congress military jurisdiction over all parts of the United States containing refugees and freedmen. It would by its very nature apply with most force to those parts of the United States in which the freedmen most abound, and it expressly extends the existing temporary jurisdiction of the Freedmen's Bureau, with greatly enlarged powers, over those States "in which the ordinary course of judicial proceedings has been interrupted by the rebellion." The source from which this military jurisdiction is to emanate is none other than the President of the United States, acting through the War Department and the Commissioner of the Freedmen's Bureau. The agents to carry out this military jurisdiction are to be selected either from the Army or from civil life; the country is to be divided into districts and subdistricts, and the number of salaried agents to be employed may be equal to the number of counties or parishes in all the United States where freedmen and refugees are to be found.

The subjects over which this military jurisdiction is to extend in every part of the United States include protection to "all employees, agents, and officers of this bureau in the exercise of the duties imposed" upon them by the bill. In eleven States it is further to extend over all cases affecting freedmen and refugees discriminated against "by local law, custom, or prejudice." In those eleven States the bill subjects any white person who may be charged with depriving a freedman of "any civil rights or immunities belonging to white persons" to imprisonment or fine, or both, without, however, defining the "civil rights and immunities" which are thus to be secured to the freedmen by military law. This military jurisdiction also extends to all questions that may arise respecting contracts. The agent who is thus to exercise the office of a military judge may be a stranger, entirely ignorant of the laws of the place, and exposed to the errors of judgment to which all men are liable. The exercise of power over which there is no legal supervision by so vast a number of agents as is contemplated by the bill must, by the very nature of man, be attended by acts of caprice, injustice, and passion.

The trials having their origin under this bill are to take place without the intervention of a jury and without any fixed rules of law or evidence. The rules on which offenses are to be "heard and determined" by the numerous agents are such rules and regulations as the President, through the War Department, shall prescribe. No previous presentment is required nor any indictment charging the commission of a crime against the laws; but the trial must proceed on charges and specifications. The punishment will be, not what the law declares, but such as a court-martial may think proper; and from these arbitrary tribunals there lies no appeal, no writ of error to any of the courts in which the Constitution of the United States vests exclusively the judicial power of the country.

While the territory and the classes of actions and offenses that are made subject to this measure are so extensive, the bill itself, should it become a law, will have no limitation in point of time, but will form a part of the permanent legislation of the country. I can not reconcile a system of military jurisdiction of this kind with the words of the Constitution which declare that "no person shall be held to answer for a capital or otherwise infamous crime unless on a presentment or indictment of a grand jury, except in cases arising in the land or naval forces, or in the militia when in actual service in time of war or public danger," and that "in all criminal prosecutions the accused shall enjoy the right to a speedy and public trial by an impartial jury of the State and district wherein the crime shall have been committed." The safeguards which the experience and wisdom of ages taught our fathers to establish as securities for the protection of the innocent, the punishment of the guilty, and the equal administration of justice are to be set aside, and for the sake of a more vigorous interposition in behalf of justice we are to take the risks of the many acts of injustice that would necessarily follow from an almost countless number of agents established in every parish or county in nearly a third of the States of the Union, over whose decisions there is to be no supervision or control by the Federal courts. The power that would be thus placed in the hands of the President is such as in time of peace certainly ought never to be intrusted to any one man.

If it be asked whether the creation of such a tribunal within a State is warranted as a measure of war, the question immediately presents itself whether we are still engaged in war. Let us not unnecessarily disturb the commerce and credit and industry of the country by declaring to the American people and to the world that the United States are still in a condition of civil war. At present there is no part of our country in which the authority of the United States is disputed. Offenses that may be committed by individuals should not work a forfeiture of the rights of whole communities. The country has returned, or is returning, to a state of peace and industry, and the rebellion is in fact at an end. The measure, therefore, seems to be as inconsistent with the actual condition of the country as it is at variance with the Constitution of the United States.

If, passing from general considerations, we examine the bill in detail, it is open to weighty objections.

In time of war it was eminently proper that we should provide for those who were passing suddenly from a condition of bondage to a state of freedom. But this bill proposes to make the Freedmen's Bureau, established by the act of 1865 as one of many great and extraordinary military measures to suppress a formidable rebellion, a permanent branch of the public administration, with its powers greatly enlarged. I have no reason to suppose, and I do not understand it to be alleged, that the act of March, 1865, has proved deficient for the purpose for which it was passed, although at that time and for a considerable period thereafter the Government of the United States remained unacknowledged in most of the States whose inhabitants had been involved in the rebellion. The institution of slavery, for the military destruction of which the Freedmen's Bureau was called into existence as an auxiliary, has been already effectually and finally abrogated throughout the whole country by an amendment of the Constitution of the United States, and practically its eradication has received the assent and concurrence of most of those States in which it at any time had an existence. I am not, therefore, able to discern in the condition of the country anything to justify an apprehension that the powers and agencies of the Freedmen's Bureau, which were effective for the protection of freedmen and refugees during the actual continuance of hostilities and of African servitude, will now, in a time of peace and after the abolition of slavery, prove inadequate to the same proper ends. If I am correct in these views, there can be no necessity for the enlargement of the powers of the Bureau, for which provision is made in the bill.

The third section of the bill authorizes a general and unlimited grant of support to the destitute and suffering refugees and freedmen, their wives and children. Succeeding sections make provision for the rent or purchase of landed estates for freedmen, and for the erection for their benefit of suitable buildings for asylums and schools, the expenses to be defrayed from the Treasury of the whole people. The Congress of the United States has never heretofore thought itself empowered to establish asylums beyond the limits of the District of Columbia, except for the benefit of our disabled soldiers and sailors. It has never founded schools for any class of our own people, not even for the orphans of those who have fallen in the defense of the Union, but has left the care of education to the much more competent and efficient control of the States, of communities, of private associations, and of individuals. It has never deemed itself authorized to expend the public money for the rent or purchase of homes for the thousands, not to say millions, of the white race who are honestly toiling from day to day for their subsistence. A system for the support of indigent persons in the United States was never contemplated by the authors of the Constitution; nor can any good reason be advanced why, as a permanent establishment, it should be founded for one class or color of our people more than another. Pending the war many refugees and freedmen received support from the Government, but it was never intended that they should thenceforth be fed, clothed, educated, and sheltered by the United States. The idea on which the slaves were assisted to freedom was that on becoming free they would be a self-sustaining population. Any legislation that shall imply that they are not expected to attain a self-sustaining condition must have a tendency injurious alike to their character and their prospects.

The appointment of an agent for every county and parish will create an immense patronage, and the expense of the numerous officers and their clerks, to be appointed by the President, will be great in the beginning, with a tendency steadily to increase. The appropriations asked by the Freedmen's Bureau as now established, for the year 1866, amount to $11,745,000. It may be safely estimated that the cost to be incurred under the pending bill will require double that amount—more than the entire sum expended in any one year under the Administration of the second Adams. If the presence of agents in every parish and county is to be considered as a war measure, opposition, or even resistance, might be provoked; so that to give effect to their jurisdiction troops would have to be stationed within reach of every one of them, and thus a large standing force be rendered necessary. Large appropriations would therefore be required to sustain and enforce military jurisdiction in every county or parish from the Potomac to the Rio Grande. The condition of our fiscal affairs is encouraging, but in order to sustain the present measure of public confidence it is necessary that we practice not merely customary economy, but, as far as possible, severe retrenchment.

In addition to the objections already stated, the fifth section of the bill proposes to take away land from its former owners without any legal proceedings being first had, contrary to that provision of the Constitution which declares that no person shall ''be deprived of life, liberty, or property without due process of law.'' It does not appear that a part of the lands to which this section refers may not be owned by minors or persons of unsound mind, or by those who have been faithful to all their obligations as citizens of the United States. If any portion of the land is held by such persons, it is not competent for any authority to deprive them of it. If, on the other hand, it be found that the property is liable to confiscation, even then it can not be appropriated to public purposes until by due process of law it shall have been declared forfeited to the Government.

There is still further objection to the bill, on grounds seriously affecting the class of persons to whom it is designed to bring relief. It will tend to keep the mind of the freedman in a state of uncertain expectation and restlessness, while to those among whom he lives it will be a source of constant and vague apprehension.

Undoubtedly the freedman should be protected, but he should be protected by the civil authorities, especially by the exercise of all the constitutional powers of the courts of the United States and of the States. His condition is not so exposed as may at first be imagined. He is in a portion of the country where his labor can not well be spared. Competition for his services from planters, from those who are constructing or repairing railroads, and from capitalists in his vicinage or from other States will enable him to command almost his own terms. He also possesses a perfect right to change his place of abode, and if, therefore, he does not find in one community or State a mode of life suited to his desires or proper remuneration for his labor, he can move to another where that labor is more esteemed and better rewarded. In truth, however, each State, induced by its own wants and interests, will do what is necessary and proper to retain within its borders all the labor that is needed for the development of its resources. The laws that regulate supply and demand will maintain their force, and the wages of the laborer will be regulated thereby. There is no danger that the exceedingly great demand for labor will not operate in favor of the laborer.

Neither is sufficient consideration given to the ability of the freedmen to protect and take care of themselves. It is no more than justice to them to believe that as they have received their freedom with moderation and forbearance, so they will distinguish themselves by their industry and thrift, and soon show the world that in a condition of freedom they are self-sustaining, capable of selecting their own employment and their own places of abode, of insisting for themselves on a proper remuneration, and of establishing and maintaining their own asylums and schools. It is earnestly hoped that instead of wasting away they will by their own efforts establish for themselves a condition of respectability and prosperity. It is certain that they can attain to that condition only through their own merits and exertions.

In this connection the query presents itself whether the system proposed by the bill will not, when put into complete operation, practically transfer the entire care, support, and control of 4,000,000 emancipated slaves to agents, overseers, or taskmasters, who, appointed at Washington, are to be located in every county and parish throughout the United States containing freedmen and refugees. Such a system would inevitably tend to a concentration of power in the Executive which would enable him, if so disposed, to control the action of this numerous class and use them for the attainment of his own political ends.

I can not but add another very grave objection to this bill. The Constitution imperatively declares, in connection with taxation, that each State *shall* have at least one Representative, and fixes the rule for the number to which, in future times, each State shall be entitled. It also provides that the Senate of the United States *shall* be composed of two Senators from each State, and adds with peculiar force "that no State, without its consent, shall be deprived of its equal suffrage in the Senate." The original act was necessarily passed in the absence of the States chiefly to be affected, because their people were then contumaciously engaged in the rebellion. Now the case is changed, and some, at least, of those States are attending Congress by loyal representatives, soliciting the allowance of the constitutional right for representation. At the time, however, of the consideration and the passing of this bill there was no Senator or Representative in Congress from the eleven States which are to be mainly affected by its provisions. The very fact that reports were and are made against the good disposition of the people of that portion of the country is an additional reason why they need and should have representatives of their own in Congress to explain their condition, reply to accusations, and assist by their local knowledge in the perfecting of measures immediately affecting themselves. While the liberty of deliberation would then be free and Congress would have full power to decide according to its judgment, there could be no objection urged that the States most interested had not been permitted to be heard. The principle is firmly fixed in the minds of the American people that there should be no taxation without representation. Great burdens have now to be borne by all the country, and we may best demand that they shall be borne without murmur when they are voted by a majority of the representatives of all the people. I would not interfere with the unquestionable right of Congress to judge, each House for itself, "of the elections, returns, and qualifications of its own members;" but that authority can not be construed as including the right to shut out in time of peace any State from the representation to which it is entitled by the Constitution. At present all the people of eleven States are excluded—those who were most faithful during the war not less than others. The State of Tennessee, for instance, whose authorities engaged in rebellion, was restored to all her constitutional relations to the Union by the patriotism and energy of her injured and betrayed people. Before the war was brought to a termination they had placed themselves in relations with the General Government, had established a State government of their own, and, as they were not included in the emancipation proclamation, they by their own act had amended their constitution so as to abolish slavery within the limits of their State. I know no reason why the State of Tennessee, for example, should not fully enjoy "all her constitutional relations to the United States."

The President of the United States stands toward the country in a somewhat different attitude from that of any member of Congress. Each member of Congress is chosen from a single district or State; the President is chosen by the people of all the States. As eleven States are not at this time represented in either branch of Congress, it would seem to be his duty on all proper occasions to present their just claims to Congress. There always will be differences of opinion in the community, and individuals may be guilty of transgressions of the law, but these do not constitute valid objections against the right of a State to representation. I would in no wise interfere with the discretion of Congress with regard to the qualifications of members; but I hold it my duty to recommend to you, in the interests of peace and the interests of union, the admission of every State to its share in public legislation when, however insubordinate, insurgent, or rebellious its people may have been, it presents itself, not only in an attitude of loyalty and harmony, but in the persons of representatives whose loyalty can not be questioned under any existing constitutional or legal test. It is plain that an indefinite or permanent exclusion of any part of the country from representation must be attended by a spirit of disquiet and complaint. It is unwise and dangerous to pursue a course of measures which will unite a very large section of the country against another section of the country, however much the latter may preponderate. The course of emigration, the development of industry and business, and natural causes will raise up at the South men as devoted to the Union as those of any other part of the land; but if they are all excluded from Congress, if in a permanent statute they are declared not to be in full constitutional relations to the country, they may think they have cause to become a unit in feeling and sentiment against the Government. Under the political education of the American people the idea is inherent and ineradicable that the consent of the majority of the whole people is necessary to secure a willing acqui-escence in legislation.

The bill under consideration refers to certain of the States as though they had not "been fully restored in all their constitutional relations to the United States." If they have not, let us at once act together to secure that desirable end at the earliest possible moment. It is hardly neces-sary for me to inform Congress that in my own judgment most of those States, so far, at least, as depends upon their own action, have already been fully restored, and are to be deemed as entitled to enjoy their con-stitutional rights as members of the Union. Reasoning from the Consti-tution itself and from the actual situation of the country, I feel not only entitled but bound to assume that with the Federal courts restored and those of the several States in the full exercise of their functions the rights and interests of all classes of people will, with the aid of the military in cases of resistance to the laws, be essentially protected against unconsti-tutional infringement or violation. Should this expectation unhappily fail, which I do not anticipate, then the Executive is already fully armed with the powers conferred by the act of March, 1865, establishing the Freedmen's Bureau, and hereafter, as heretofore, he can employ the land and naval forces of the country to suppress insurrection or to overcome obstructions to the laws.

In accordance with the Constitution, I return the bill to the Senate, in the earnest hope that a measure involving questions and interests so important to the country will not become a law, unless upon deliberate consideration by the people it shall receive the sanction of an enlightened public judgment.

ANDREW·JOHNSON.

WASHINGTON, D. C., *March 27, 1866.*

To the Senate of the United States:

I regret that the bill, which has passed both Houses of Congress, en-titled "An act to protect all persons in the United States in their civil rights and furnish the means of their vindication," contains provisions which I can not approve consistently with my sense of duty to the whole people and my obligations to the Constitution of the United States. I am therefore constrained to return it to the Senate, the House in which it originated, with my objections to its becoming a law.

By the first section of the bill all persons born in the United States and not subject to any foreign power, excluding Indians not taxed, are declared to be citizens of the United States. This provision comprehends the Chinese of the Pacific States, Indians subject to taxation, the people called gypsies, as well as the entire race designated as blacks, people of color, negroes, mulattoes, and persons of African blood. Every individual of these races born in the United States is by the bill made a citizen of the United States. It does not purport to declare or confer any other right of citizenship than Federal citizenship. It does not purport to give these classes of persons any status as citizens of States, except that which may result from their status as citizens of the United States. The power to confer the right of State citizenship is just as exclusively with the several States as the power to confer the right of Federal citizenship is with Congress.

The right of Federal citizenship thus to be conferred on the several excepted races before mentioned is now for the first time proposed to be given by law. If, as is claimed by many, all persons who are native born already are, by virtue of the Constitution, citizens of the United States, the passage of the pending bill can not be necessary to make them such. If, on the other hand, such persons are not citizens, as may be assumed from the proposed legislation to make them such, the grave question presents itself whether, when eleven of the thirty-six States are unrepresented in Congress at the present time, it is sound policy to make our entire colored population and all other excepted classes citizens of the United States. Four millions of them have just emerged from slavery into freedom. Can it be reasonably supposed that they possess the requisite qualifications to entitle them to all the privileges and immunities of citizens of the United States? Have the people of the several States expressed such a conviction? It may also be asked whether it is necessary that they should be declared citizens in order that they may be secured in the enjoyment of the civil rights proposed to be conferred by the bill. Those rights are, by Federal as well as State laws, secured to all domiciled aliens and foreigners, even before the completion of the process of naturalization; and it may safely be assumed that the same enactments are sufficient to give like protection and benefits to those for whom this bill provides special legislation. Besides, the policy of the Government from its origin to the present time seems to have been that persons who are strangers to and unfamiliar with our institutions and our laws should pass through a certain probation, at the end of which, before attaining the coveted prize, they must give evidence of their fitness to receive and to exercise the rights of citizens as contemplated by the Constitution of the United States. The bill in effect proposes a discrimination against large numbers of intelligent, worthy, and patriotic foreigners, and in favor of the negro, to whom, after long years of bondage, the avenues to freedom and intelligence have just now been suddenly opened. He must of necessity, from his previous unfortunate condition of servitude, be less informed as to the nature and character of our institutions than he who, coming from abroad, has, to some extent at least, familiarized himself with the principles of a Government to which he voluntarily intrusts "life, liberty, and the pursuit of happiness." Yet it is now proposed, by a single legislative enactment, to confer the rights of citizens upon all persons of African descent born within the extended limits of the United States, while persons of foreign birth who make our land their home must undergo a probation of five years, and can only then become citizens upon proof that they are "of good moral character, attached to the principles of the Constitution of the United States, and well disposed to the good order and happiness of the same."

The first section of the bill also contains an enumeration of the rights to be enjoyed by these classes so made citizens "in every State and Territory in the United States." These rights are "to make and enforce contracts; to sue, be parties, and give evidence; to inherit, purchase, lease, sell, hold, and convey real and personal property," and to have "full and equal benefit of all laws and proceedings for the security of person and property as is enjoyed by white citizens." So, too, they are made subject to the same punishment, pains, and penalties in common with white citizens, and to none other. Thus a perfect equality of the white and colored races is attempted to be fixed by Federal law in every State of the Union over the vast field of State jurisdiction covered by these enumerated rights. In no one of these can any State ever exercise any power of discrimination between the different races. In the exercise of State policy over matters exclusively affecting the people of each State it has frequently been thought expedient to discriminate between the two races. By the statutes of some of the States, Northern as well as Southern, it is enacted, for instance, that no white person shall intermarry with a negro or mulatto. Chancellor Kent says, speaking of the blacks, that—

Marriages between them and the whites are forbidden in some of the States where slavery does not exist, and they are prohibited in all the slaveholding States; and when not absolutely contrary to law, they are revolting, and regarded as an offense against public decorum.

I do not say that this bill repeals State laws on the subject of marriage between the two races, for as the whites are forbidden to intermarry with the blacks, the blacks can only make such contracts as the whites themselves are allowed to make, and therefore can not under this bill enter into the marriage contract with the whites. I cite this discrimination, however, as an instance of the State policy as to discrimination, and to inquire whether if Congress can abrogate all State laws of discrimination between the two races in the matter of real estate, of suits, and of contracts generally Congress may not also repeal the State laws as to the contract of marriage between the two races. Hitherto every subject embraced in the enumeration of rights contained in this bill has been considered as exclusively belonging to the States. They all relate to the internal police and economy of the respective States. They are matters which in each State concern the domestic condition of its people, varying in each according to its own peculiar circumstances and the safety and well-being of its own citizens. I do not mean to say that upon all these subjects there are not Federal restraints—as, for instance, in the State power of legislation over contracts there is a Federal limitation that no State shall pass a law impairing the obligations of contracts; and, as to crimes, that no State shall pass an *ex post facto* law; and, as to money, that no State shall make anything but gold and silver a legal tender; but where can we find a Federal prohibition against the power of any State to discriminate, as do most of them, between aliens and citizens, between artificial persons, called corporations, and natural persons, in the right to hold real estate? If it be granted that Congress can repeal all State laws discriminating between whites and blacks in the subjects covered by this bill, why, it may be asked, may not Congress repeal in the same way all State laws discriminating between the two races on the subjects of suffrage and office? If Congress can declare by law who shall hold lands, who shall testify, who shall have capacity to make a contract in a State, then Congress can by law also declare who, without regard to color or race, shall have the right to sit as a juror or as a judge, to hold any office, and, finally, to vote "in every State and Territory of the United States." As respects the Territories, they come within the power of Congress, for as to them the lawmaking power is the Federal power; but as to the States no similar provision exists vesting in Congress the power "to make rules and regulations" for them.

The object of the second section of the bill is to afford discriminating protection to colored persons in the full enjoyment of all the rights secured to them by the preceding section. It declares—

That any person who, under color of any law, statute, ordinance, regulation, or custom, shall subject, or cause to be subjected, any inhabitant of any State or Territory to the deprivation of any right secured or protected by this act, or to different punishment, pains, or penalties on account of such person having at any time been held in a condition of slavery or involuntary servitude, except as a punishment for crime whereof the party shall have been duly convicted, or by reason of his color or race, than is prescribed for the punishment of white persons, shall be deemed guilty of a misdemeanor, and on conviction shall be punished by fine not exceeding $1,000, or imprisonment not exceeding one year, or both, in the discretion of the court.

This section seems to be designed to apply to some existing or future law of a State or Territory which may conflict with the provisions of the bill now under consideration. It provides for counteracting such forbidden legislation by imposing fine and imprisonment upon the legislators who may pass such conflicting laws, or upon the officers or agents who shall put or attempt to put them into execution. It means an official offense, not a common crime committed against law upon the persons or property of the black race. Such an act may deprive the black man of his property, but not of the *right* to hold property. It means a deprivation of the right itself, either by the State judiciary or the State legislature It is therefore assumed that under this section members of State legislatures who should vote for laws conflicting with the provisions of the bill, that judges of the State courts who should render judgments in antagonism with its terms, and that marshals and sheriffs who should, as ministerial officers, execute processes sanctioned by State laws and issued by State judges in execution of their judgments could be brought before other tribunals and there subjected to **fine** and imprisonment for the performance of the duties which such State laws might impose. The legislation thus proposed invades the judicial power of the State. It says to every State court or judge, If you decide that this act is unconstitutional; if you refuse, under the prohibition of a State law, to allow a negro to testify; if you hold that over such a subject-matter the State law is paramount, and "under color" of a State law refuse the exercise of the right to the negro, your error of judgment, however conscientious, shall subject you to fine and imprisonment. I do not apprehend that the conflicting legislation which the bill seems to contemplate is so likely to occur as to render it necessary at this time to adopt a measure of such doubtful constitutionality.

In the next place, this provision of the bill seems to be unnecessary, as adequate judicial remedies could be adopted to secure the desired end without invading the immunities of legislators, always important to be preserved in the interest of public liberty; without assailing the independence of the judiciary, always essential to the preservation of individual rights; and without impairing the efficiency of ministerial officers, always necessary for the maintenance of public peace and order. The remedy proposed by this section seems to be in this respect not only anomalous, but unconstitutional; for the Constitution guarantees nothing with certainty if it does not insure to the several States the right of making and executing laws in regard to all matters arising within their jurisdiction, subject only to the restriction that in cases of conflict with the Constitution and constitutional laws of the United States the latter should be held to be the supreme law of the land.

The third section gives the district courts of the United States exclusive "cognizance of all crimes and offenses committed against the provisions of this act," and concurrent jurisdiction with the circuit courts of the United States of all civil and criminal cases "affecting persons who are denied or can not enforce in the courts or judicial tribunals of the State or locality where they may be any of the rights secured to them by the first section." The construction which I have given to the second section is strengthened by this third section, for it makes clear what kind of denial or deprivation of the rights secured by the first section was in contemplation. It is a denial or deprivation of such rights "in the courts or judicial tribunals of the State." It stands, therefore, clear of doubt that the offense and the penalties provided in the second section are intended for the State judge who, in the clear exercise of his functions as a judge, not acting ministerially but judicially, shall decide contrary to this Federal law. In other words, when a State judge, acting upon a question involving a conflict between a State law and a Federal law, and bound, according to his own judgment and responsibility, to give an impartial decision between the two, comes to the conclusion that the State law is valid and the Federal law is invalid, he must not follow the dictates of his own judgment, at the peril of fine and imprisonment. The legislative department of the Government of the United States thus takes from the judicial department of the States the sacred and exclusive duty of judicial decision, and converts the State judge into a mere ministerial officer, bound to decide according to the will of Congress.

It is clear that in States which deny to persons whose rights are secured by the first section of the bill any one of those rights all criminal and civil cases affecting them will, by the provisions of the third section, come under the exclusive cognizance of the Federal tribunals. It follows that if, in any State which denies to a colored person any one of all those rights, that person should commit a crime against the laws of a State— murder, arson, rape, or any other crime—all protection and punishment through the courts of the State are taken away, and he can only be tried and punished in the Federal courts. How is the criminal to be tried? If the offense is provided for and punished by Federal law, that law, and not the State law, is to govern. It is only when the offense does not happen to be within the purview of Federal law that the Federal courts are to try and punish him under any other law. Then resort is to be had to "the common law, as modified and changed" by State legislation, "so far as the same is not inconsistent with the Constitution and laws of the United States." So that over this vast domain of criminal jurisprudence provided by each State for the protection of its own citizens and for the punishment of all persons who violate its criminal laws, Federal law, whenever it can be made to apply, displaces State law. The question here naturally arises, from what source Congress derives the power to transfer to Federal tribunals certain classes of cases embraced in this section. The Constitution expressly declares that the judicial power of the United States "shall extend to all cases, in law and equity, arising under this Constitution, the laws of the United States, and treaties made or which shall be made under their authority; to all cases affecting ambassadors, other public ministers, and consuls; to all cases of admiralty and maritime jurisdiction; to controversies to which the United States shall be a party; to controversies between two or more States, between a State and citizens of another State, between citizens of different States, between citizens of the same State claiming lands under grants of different States, and between a State, or the citizens thereof, and foreign states, citizens, or subjects." Here the judicial power of the United States is expressly set forth and defined; and the act of September 24, 1789, establishing the judicial courts of the United States, in conferring upon the Federal courts jurisdiction over cases originating in State tribunals, is careful to confine them to the classes enumerated in the above-recited clause of the Constitution. This section of the bill undoubtedly comprehends cases and authorizes the exercise of powers that are not, by the Constitution, within the jurisdiction of the courts of the United States. To transfer them to those courts would be an exercise of authority well calculated to excite distrust and alarm on the part of all the States, for the bill applies alike to all of them—as well to those that have as to those that have not been engaged in rebellion.

It may be assumed that this authority is incident to the power granted to Congress by the Constitution, as recently amended, to enforce, by appropriate legislation, the article declaring that—

Neither slavery nor involuntary servitude, except as a punishment for crime whereof the party shall have been duly convicted, shall exist within the United States or any place subject to their jurisdiction.

It can not, however, be justly claimed that, with a view to the enforcement of this article of the Constitution, there is at present any necessity for the exercise of all the powers which this bill confers. Slavery has been abolished, and at present nowhere exists within the jurisdiction of the United States; nor has there been, nor is it likely there will be, any attempt to revive it by the people or the States. If, however, any such attempt shall be made, it will then become the duty of the General Government to exercise any and all incidental powers necessary and proper to maintain inviolate this great constitutional law of freedom.

The fourth section of the bill provides that officers and agents of the Freedmen's Bureau shall be empowered to make arrests, and also that other officers may be specially commissioned for that purpose by the President of the United States. It also authorizes circuit courts of the United States and the superior courts of the Territories to appoint, without limitation, commissioners, who are to be charged with the performance of *quasi* judicial duties. The fifth section empowers the commissioners so to be selected by the courts to appoint in writing, under their hands, one or more suitable persons from time to time to execute warrants and other processes described by the bill. These numerous official agents are made to constitute a sort of police, in addition to the military, and are authorized to summon a *posse comitatus*, and even to call to their aid such portion of the land and naval forces of the United States, or of the militia, "as may be necessary to the performance of the duty with which they are charged." This extraordinary power is to be conferred upon agents irresponsible to the Government and to the people, to whose number the discretion of the commissioners is the only limit, and in whose hands such authority might be made a terrible engine of wrong, oppression, and fraud. The general statutes regulating the land and naval forces of the United States, the militia, and the execution of the laws are believed to be adequate for every emergency which can occur in time of peace. If it should prove otherwise, Congress can at any time amend those laws in such manner as, while subserving the public welfare, not to jeopard the rights, interests, and liberties of the people.

The seventh section provides that a fee of $10 shall be paid to each commissioner in every case brought before him, and a fee of $5 to his deputy or deputies "for each person he or they may arrest and take before any such commissioner," "with such other fees as may be deemed reasonable by such commissioner," "in general for performing such other duties as may be required in the premises." All these fees are to be "paid out of the Treasury of the United States," whether there is a conviction or not; but in case of conviction they are to be recoverable from the defendant. It seems to me that under the influence of such temptations bad men might convert any law, however beneficent, into an instrument of persecution and fraud.

By the eighth section of the bill the United States courts, which sit only in one place for white citizens, must migrate with the marshal and district attorney (and necessarily with the clerk, although he is not mentioned) to any part of the district upon the order of the President, and there hold a court, "for the purpose of the more speedy arrest and trial of persons charged with a violation of this act;" and there the judge and officers of the court must remain, upon the order of the President, "for the time therein designated."

The ninth section authorizes the President, or such person as he may empower for that purpose, "to employ such part of the land or naval forces of the United States, or of the militia, as shall be necessary to prevent the violation and enforce the due execution of this act." This language seems to imply a permanent military force, that is to be always at hand, and whose only business is to be the enforcement of this measure over the vast region where it is intended to operate.

I do not propose to consider the policy of this bill. To me the details of the bill seem fraught with evil. The white race and the black race of the South have hitherto lived together under the relation of master and slave—capital owning labor. Now, suddenly, that relation is changed, and as to ownership capital and labor are divorced. They stand now each master of itself. In this new relation, one being necessary to the other, there will be a new adjustment, which both are deeply interested in making harmonious. Each has equal power in settling the terms, and if left to the laws that regulate capital and labor it is confidently believed that they will satisfactorily work out the problem. Capital, it is true, has more intelligence, but labor is never so ignorant as not to understand its own interests, not to know its own value, and not to see that capital must pay that value.

This bill frustrates this adjustment. It intervenes between capital and labor and attempts to settle questions of political economy through the agency of numerous officials whose interest it will be to foment discord between the two races, for as the breach widens their employment will continue, and when it is closed their occupation will terminate.

In all our history, in all our experience as a people living under Federal and State law, no such system as that contemplated by the details of this bill has ever before been proposed or adopted. They establish for the security of the colored race safeguards which go infinitely beyond any that the General Government has ever provided for the white race. In fact, the distinction of race and color is by the bill made to operate in favor of the colored and against the white race. They interfere with the municipal legislation of the States, with the relations existing exclusively between a State and its citizens, or between inhabitants of the same State—an absorption and assumption of power by the General Government which, if acquiesced in, must sap and destroy our federative system of limited powers and break down the barriers which preserve the rights of the States. It is another step, or rather stride, toward centralization and the concentration of all legislative powers in the National Government. The tendency of the bill must be to resuscitate the spirit of rebellion and to arrest the progress of those influences which are more closely drawing around the States the bonds of union and peace.

My lamented predecessor, in his proclamation of the 1st of January, 1863, ordered and declared that all persons held as slaves within certain States and parts of States therein designated were and thenceforward should be free; and further, that the executive government of the United States, including the military and naval authorities thereof, would recognize and maintain the freedom of such persons. This guaranty has been rendered especially obligatory and sacred by the amendment of the Constitution abolishing slavery throughout the United States. I therefore fully recognize the obligation to protect and defend that class of our people whenever and wherever it shall become necessary, and to the full extent compatible with the Constitution of the United States.

Entertaining these sentiments, it only remains for me to say that I will cheerfully cooperate with Congress in any measure that may be necessary for the protection of the civil rights of the freedmen, as well as those of all other classes of persons throughout the United States, by judicial process, under equal and impartial laws, in conformity with the provisions of the Federal Constitution.

I now return the bill to the Senate, and regret that in considering the bills and joint resolutions—forty-two in number—which have been thus far submitted for my approval I am compelled to withhold my assent from a second measure that has received the sanction of both Houses of Congress.
                                                    ANDREW JOHNSON.

WASHINGTON, D. C., *May 15, 1866.*

To the Senate of the United States:

I return to the Senate, in which House it originated, the bill, which has passed both Houses of Congress, entitled "An act for the admission of the State of Colorado into the Union," with my objections to its becoming a law at this time.

First. From the best information which I have been able to obtain I do not consider the establishment of a State government at present necessary for the welfare of the people of Colorado. Under the existing Territorial government all the rights, privileges, and interests of the citizens are protected and secured. The qualified voters choose their own legislators and their own local officers, and are represented in Congress by a Delegate of their own selection. They make and execute their own municipal laws, subject only to revision by Congress—an authority not likely to be exercised unless in extreme or extraordinary cases. The population is small, some estimating it so low as 25,000, while advocates of the bill reckon the number at from 35,000 to 40,000 souls. The people are principally recent settlers, many of whom are understood to be ready for removal to other mining districts beyond the limits of the Territory if circumstances shall render them more inviting. Such a population can not but find relief from excessive taxation if the Territorial system, which devolves the expenses of the executive, legislative, and judicial departments upon the United States, is for the present continued. They can not but find the security of person and property increased by their reliance upon the national executive power for the maintenance of law and order against the disturbances necessarily incident to all newly organized communities.

Second. It is not satisfactorily established that a majority of the citizens of Colorado desire or are prepared for an exchange of a Territorial for a State government. In September, 1864, under the authority of Congress, an election was lawfully appointed and held for the purpose of ascertaining the views of the people upon this particular question. Six thousand one hundred and ninety-two votes were cast, and of this number a majority of 3,152 was given against the proposed change. In September, 1865, without any legal authority, the question was again presented to the people of the Territory, with the view of obtaining a reconsideration of the result of the election held in compliance with the act of Congress approved March 21, 1864. At this second election 5,905 votes were polled, and a majority of 155 was given in favor of a State organization. It does not seem to me entirely safe to receive this, the last-mentioned, result, so irregularly obtained, as sufficient to outweigh the one which had been legally obtained in the first election. Regularity and conformity to law are essential to the preservation of order and stable government, and should, as far as practicable, always be observed in the formation of new States.

Third. The admission of Colorado at this time as a State into the Federal Union appears to me to be incompatible with the public interests of the country. While it is desirable that Territories, when sufficiently matured, should be organized as States, yet the spirit of the Constitution seems to require that there should be an approximation toward equality among the several States composing the Union. No State can have less or more than two Senators in Congress. The largest State has a population of 4,000,000; several of the States have a population exceeding 2,000,000, and many others have a population exceeding 1,000,000. A population of 127,000 is the ratio of apportionment of Representatives among the several States.

If this bill should become a law, the people of Colorado, 30,000 in number, would have in the House of Representatives one member, while New York, with a population of 4,000,000, has but thirty-one; Colorado would have in the electoral college three votes, while New York has only thirty-three; Colorado would have in the Senate two votes, while New York has no more.

Inequalities of this character have already occurred, but it is believed that none have happened where the inequality was so great. When such inequality has been allowed, Congress is supposed to have permitted it on the ground of some high public necessity and under circumstances which promised that it would rapidly disappear through the growth and development of the newly admitted State. Thus, in regard to the several States in what was formerly called the "Northwest Territory," lying east of the Mississippi, their rapid advancement in population rendered it certain that States admitted with only one or two Representatives in Congress would in a very short period be entitled to a great increase of representation. So, when California was admitted, on the ground of commercial and political exigencies, it was well foreseen that that State was destined rapidly to become a great, prosperous, and important mining and commercial community. In the case of Colorado, I am not aware that any national exigency, either of a political or commercial nature, requires a departure from the law of equality which has been so generally adhered to in our history.

If information submitted in connection with this bill is reliable, Colorado, instead of increasing, has declined in population. At an election for members of a Territorial legislature held in 1861, 10,580 votes were cast; at the election before mentioned, in 1864, the number of votes cast was 6,192; while at the irregular election held in 1865, which is assumed as a basis for legislative action at this time, the aggregate of votes was 5,905. Sincerely anxious for the welfare and prosperity of every Territory and State, as well as for the prosperity and welfare of the whole Union, I regret this apparent decline of population in Colorado; but it is manifest that it is due to emigration which is going on from that Territory into other regions within the United States, which either are in fact or are believed by the inhabitants of Colorado to be richer in mineral wealth and agricultural resources. If, however, Colorado has not really declined in population, another census or another election under the authority of Congress would place the question beyond doubt, and cause but little delay in the ultimate admission of the Territory as a State if desired by the people.

The tenor of these objections furnishes the reply which may be expected to an argument in favor of the measure derived from the enabling act which was passed by Congress on the 21st day of March, 1864. Although Congress then supposed that the condition of the Territory was such as to warrant its admission as a State, the result of two years' experience shows that every reason which existed for the institution of a Territorial instead of a State government in Colorado at its first organization still continues in force.

The condition of the Union at the present moment is calculated to inspire caution in regard to the admission of new States. Eleven of the old States have been for some time, and still remain, unrepresented in Congress. It is a common interest of all the States, as well those represented as those unrepresented, that the integrity and harmony of the Union should be restored as completely as possible, so that all those who are expected to bear the burdens of the Federal Government shall be consulted concerning the admission of new States; and that in the meantime no new State shall be prematurely and unnecessarily admitted to a participation in the political power which the Federal Government wields, not for the benefit of any individual State or section, but for the common safety, welfare, and happiness of the whole country.

ANDREW JOHNSON.

WASHINGTON, D. C., *June 15, 1866.*
To the Senate of the United States:

The bill entitled "An act to enable the New York and Montana Iron Mining and Manufacturing Company to purchase a certain amount of the public lands not now in market" is herewith returned to the Senate, in which it originated, with the objections which induce me to withhold my approval.

By the terms of this bill the New York and Montana Iron Mining and Manufacturing Company are authorized, at any time within one year after the date of approval, to *preempt* two tracts of land in the Territory of Montana, not exceeding in the aggregate twenty sections, and not included in any Indian reservation or in any Government reservation for military or other purposes. Three of these sections may be selected from lands containing *iron ore and coal*, and the remainder from *timber* lands lying near thereto. These selections are to be made under regulations from the Secretary of the Interior and be subject to his approval. The company, on the selection of the lands, may acquire immediate possession by permanently marking their boundaries and publishing description thereof in any two newspapers of general circulation in the Territory of Montana. Patents are to be issued on the performance, within two years, of the following conditions:

First. The lands to be surveyed at the expense of the company, and each tract to be "as nearly in a square form as may be practicable."

Second. The company to furnish evidence satisfactory to the Secretary of the Interior that they have erected and have in operation in one or more places on said lands iron works capable of manufacturing at least 1,500 tons of iron per annum.

Third. The company to have paid for said lands the minimum price of $1.25 per acre.

It is also provided that the "patents shall convey no title to any mineral lands except iron and coal, or to any lands held by right of possession, or by any other title, *except Indian title*, valid at the time of the selection of the said lands." The company are to have the privileges of *ordinary preemptors* and be subject to the same restrictions as such preemptors with reference to wood and timber on the lands, with the exception of so much as may be necessarily used in the erection of buildings and in the legitimate business of manufacturing iron.

The parties upon whom these privileges are conferred are designated in the bill as "The New York and Montana Iron Mining and Manufacturing Company." Their names and residence not being disclosed, it must be inferred that this company is a corporation, which, under color of corporate powers derived from some State or Territorial legislative authority, proposes to carry on the business of mining and manufacturing iron, and to accomplish these ends seeks this grant of public land in Montana. Two questions thus arise, viz, whether the privileges the bill would confer should be granted to any person or persons, and, secondly, whether, if unobjectionable in other respects, they should be conferred upon a corporation.

The public domain is a national trust, set apart and held for the general welfare upon principles of equal justice, and not to be bestowed as a special privilege upon a favored class. The proper rules for the disposal of public land have from the earliest period been the subject of earnest inquiry, grave discussion, and deliberate judgment. The purpose of *direct* revenue was the first object, and this was attained by public sale to the highest bidder, and subsequently by the right of private purchase at a fixed minimum. It was soon discovered that the surest and most speedy means of promoting the wealth and prosperity of the country was by encouraging actual settlement and occupation, and hence a system of preemption rights, resulting most beneficially, in all the Western Territories. By progressive steps it has advanced to the homestead principle, securing to every head of a family, widow, and single man 21 years of age and to every soldier who has borne arms for his country a landed estate sufficient, with industry, for the purpose of independent support.

Without tracing the system of preemption laws through the several stages, it is sufficient to observe that it rests upon certain just and plain principles, firmly established in all our legislation. The object of these laws is to encourage the expansion of population and the development of agricultural interests, and hence they have been invariably restricted to settlers. Actual residence and cultivation are made indispensable conditions; and, to guard the privilege from abuses of speculation or monopoly, the law is rigid as to the mode of establishing claims by adequate testimony, with penalties for perjury. Mining, trading, or any pursuit other than culture of the soil is interdicted, mineral lands being expressly excluded from preemption privileges, excepting those containing coal, which, in quantities not exceeding 160 acres, are restricted to individuals in actual possession and commerce, with an enhanced minimum of $20 per acre.

For a quarter of a century the quantity of land subject to agricultural preemption has been limited so as not to exceed a quarter section, or 160 acres; and, still further to guard against monopoly, the privilege of preemption is not allowed to any person who owns 320 acres of land in any State or Territory of the United States, nor is any person entitled to more than one preemptive right, nor is it extended to lands to which the Indian usufruct has not been extinguished. To restrict the privilege within reasonable limits, credit to the ordinary preemptor on *offered* land is not extended beyond twelve months, within which time the minimum price must be paid. Where the settlement is upon *unoffered* territory, the time for payment is limited to the day of public offering designated by proclamation of the President; while, to prevent depreciation of the land by waste or destruction of what may constitute its value, penal enactments have been made for the punishment of persons depredating upon public timber.

Now, supposing the New York and Montana Iron Mining and Manufacturing Company to be entitled to all the preemption rights which it has been found just and expedient to bestow upon natural persons, it will be seen that the privileges conferred by the bill in question are in direct conflict with every principle heretofore observed in respect to the disposal of the public lands.

The bill confers preemption right to *mineral lands*, which, excepting coal lands, at an enhanced minimum, have heretofore, as a general principle, been carefully excluded from preemption. The object of the company is not to cultivate the soil or to promote agriculture, but is for the sole purpose of mining and manufacturing iron. The company is not limited, like ordinary preemptors, to one preemptive claim of a quarter section, but may preempt two bodies of land, amounting in the aggregate to twenty sections, containing 12,800 acres, or eighty ordinary individual preemption rights. The timber is not protected, but, on the contrary, is devoted to speedy destruction; for even before the consummation of title the company are allowed to consume whatever may be necessary in the erection of buildings and the business of manufacturing iron. For these special privileges, in contravention of the land policy of so many years, the company are required to pay only the minimum price of $1.25 per acre, or one-sixteenth of the established minimum, and are granted a credit of two years, or twice the time allowed ordinary preemptors on offered lands.

Nor is this all. The preemption right in question covers three sections of land containing iron ore and *coal*. The act passed on the 1st of July, 1864, made it lawful for the President to cause tracts embracing coal beds or coal fields to be offered at public sale in suitable legal subdivisions to the highest bidder, after public notice of not less than three months, at a minimum price of $20 per acre, and any lands not thus disposed of were thereafter to be liable to private entry at said minimum. By the act of March 3, 1865, the right of preemption to coal lands is granted to any citizen of the United States who at that date was engaged in the business of coal mining on the public domain for purposes of commerce; and he is authorized to enter, according to legal subdivisions, at the minimum price of $20 per acre, a quantity of land not exceeding 160 acres, to embrace his improvements and mining premises. Under these acts the minimum price of three sections of coal lands would be thirty-eight thousand four hundred dollars ($38,400).

By the bill now in question these sections containing *coal and iron* are bestowed on this company at the nominal price of $1.25 per acre, or two thousand four hundred dollars ($2,400), thus making a gratuity or gift to the New York and Montana Iron Mining and Manufacturing Company of thirty-six thousand dollars ($36,000).

On what ground can such a gratuity to this company be justified, especially at a time when the burdens of taxation bear so heavily upon all classes of the people?

Less than two years ago it appears to have been the deliberate judgment of Congress that tracts of land containing coal beds or coal fields should be sold, after three months' notice, to the bidder at public auction who would give the highest price over $20 per acre, and that a citizen engaged in the business of actual coal mining on the public domain should only secure a tract of 160 acres, at private entry, upon payment of $20 per acre and formal and satisfactory proof that he in all respects came within the requirements of the statute. It can not be that the coal fields of Montana have depreciated nearly twentyfold in value since July, 1864. So complete a revolution in the land policy as is manifested by this act can only be ascribed, therefore, to an inadvertence, which Congress will, I trust, promptly correct.

Believing that the preemption policy—so deliberately adopted, so long practiced, so carefully guarded with a view to the disposal of the public lands in a manner that would promote the population and prosperity of the country—should not be perverted to the purposes contemplated by this bill, I would be constrained to withhold my sanction even if this company were, as natural persons, entitled to the privileges of ordinary preemptors; for if a corporation, as the name and the absence of any designation of individuals would denote, the measure before me is liable to another fatal objection.

Why should incorporated companies have the privileges of individual preemptors? What principle of justice requires such a policy? What motive of public welfare can fail to condemn it? Lands held by corporations were regarded by ancient laws as held in mortmain, or by ''dead hand,'' and from the time of Magna Charta corporations required the royal license to hold land, because such holding was regarded as in derogation of public policy and common right. Preemption is itself a special privilege, only authorized by its supposed public benefit in promoting the settlement and cultivation of vacant territory and in rewarding the enterprise of the persons upon whom the privilege is bestowed. ''Preemption rights,'' as declared by the Supreme Court of the United States, ''are founded in an enlightened public policy, rendered necessary by the enterprise of our citizens. The adventurous pioneer, who is found in advance of our settlements, encounters many hardships, and not unfrequently dangers from savage incursions. He is generally poor, and it is fit that his enterprise should be rewarded by the privilege of purchasing the spot selected by him, not to exceed 160 acres.''

It may be said that this company, before they obtain a patent, must prove that within two years they ''have erected and have in operation in one or more places on the said lands iron works with a capacity for manufacturing at least 1,500 tons of iron per annum.'' On the other hand, they are to have possession for two years of more than 12,000 acres of the choice land of the Territory, of which nearly 2,000 acres are to contain *iron ore and coal* and over 10,000 acres to be of *timber* land selected by themselves. They will thus have the first and exclusive choice. In fact, they are the only parties who at this time would have any privilege whatever in the way of obtaining titles in that Territory. Inasmuch as Montana has not yet been organized into a land district, the general preemption laws for the benefit of individual settlers have not yet been extended to that country, nor has a single acre of public land in the Territory yet been surveyed. With such exclusive and extraordinary privileges, how many companies would be willing to undertake furnaces that would produce 5 tons per day in much less time than two years?

It is plain the pretended consideration on which the patent is to issue bears no just proportion to that of the ordinary preemptor, and that this bill is but the precursor of a system of land distribution to a privileged class, unequal, unjust, and which ought not to receive the sanction of the General Government. Many thousand pioneers have turned their steps to the Western Territories, seeking, with their wives and children, homesteads to be acquired by sturdy industry under the preemption laws. On their arrival they should not find the timbered lands and the tracts containing iron ore and coal already surveyed and claimed by corporate companies, favored by the special legislation of Congress, and with boundaries fixed even in advance of the public surveys—a departure from the salutary provision requiring a settler upon unsurveyed lands to limit the boundaries of his claim to the lines of the public survey after they shall have been established. He receives a title only to a legal subdivision, including his residence and improvements. The survey of the company may not accord with that which will hereafter be made by the Government, while the patent that issues will be descriptive of and confer a title to the tract as surveyed by the company.

I am aware of no precedent for granting such exclusive rights to a manufacturing company for a nominal consideration. Congress have made concessions to railway companies of alternate sections within given limits of the lines of their roads. This policy originated in the belief that the facilities afforded by reaching the parts of the country remote from the great centers of population would expedite the settlement and sale of the public domain. These incidental advantages were secured without pecuniary loss to the Government, by reason of the enhanced value of the reserved sections, which are held at the double minimum. Mining and manufacturing companies, however, have always been distinguished from public-improvement corporations. The former are, in law and in fact, only private associations for trade and business on individual account and for personal benefit. Admitting the proposition that railroad grants can stand on sound principle, it is plain that such can not be the case with concessions to companies like that contemplated by this measure. In view of the strong temptation to monopolize the public lands, with the pernicious results, it would seem at least of doubtful expediency to lift corporations above all competition with actual settlers by authorizing them to become purchasers of public lands in the Territories for any purpose, and particularly when clothed with the special benefits of this bill. For myself, I am convinced that the privileges of ordinary preemptors ought not to be extended to incorporated companies.

A third objection may be mentioned, as it exemplifies the spirit in which special privileges are sought by incorporated companies.

Land subject to Indian occupancy has always been scrupulously guarded by law from preemption settlement or encroachment under any pretext until the Indian title should be extinguished. In the fourth section of this act, however, lands held by "Indian title" are excepted from prohibition against the patent to be issued to the New York and Montana Iron Mining and Manufacturing Company.

The bill provides that the patent "shall convey no title to any mineral lands *except iron and coal*, or to any lands held by right of possession, or by any other title, *except Indian title*, valid at the time of the selection of the said lands." It will be seen that by the first section lands in "Indian reservations" are excluded from individual preemption right, but by the fourth section the patent may cover any Indian title except a *reservation;* so that no matter what may be the nature of the Indian title, unless it be in a reservation, it is unprotected from the privilege conceded by this bill.

Without further pursuing the subject, I return the bill to the Senate without my signature, and with the following as prominent objections to its becoming a law:

First. That it gives to the New York and Montana Iron Mining and Manufacturing Company preemption privileges to iron and coal lands on a large scale and at the ordinary minimum—a privilege denied to ordinary preemptors. It bestows upon the company large tracts of *coal* lands at one-sixteenth of the minimum price required from ordinary preemptors. It also relieves the company from restrictions imposed upon ordinary preemptors in respect to *timber lands;* allows double the time for payment granted to preemptors on offered lands; and these privileges are for purposes not heretofore authorized by the preemption laws, but for trade and manufacturing.

Second. Preemption rights on such a scale to private corporations are unequal and hostile to the policy and principles which sanction preemption laws.

Third. The bill allows this company to take possession of land, use it, and acquire a patent thereto before the Indian title is extinguished, and thus violates the good faith of the Government toward the aboriginal tribes.

ANDREW JOHNSON.

WASHINGTON, D. C., *July 16, 1866.*

To the House of Representatives:

A careful examination of the bill passed by the two Houses of Congress entitled "An act to continue in force and to amend 'An act to establish a bureau for the relief of freedmen and refugees, and for other purposes'" has convinced me that the legislation which it proposes would not be consistent with the welfare of the country, and that it falls clearly within the reasons assigned in my message of the 19th of February last, returning, without my signature, a similar measure which originated in the Senate. It is not my purpose to repeat the objections which I then urged. They are yet fresh in your recollection, and can be readily examined as a part of the records of one branch of the National Legislature. Adhering to the principles set forth in that message, I now reaffirm them and the line of policy therein indicated.

The only ground upon which this kind of legislation can be justified is that of the war-making power. The act of which this bill is intended as amendatory was passed during the existence of the war. By its own provisions it is to terminate within one year from the cessation of hostilities and the declaration of peace. It is therefore yet in existence, and it is likely that it will continue in force as long as the freedmen may require the benefit of its provisions. It will certainly remain in operation as a law until some months subsequent to the meeting of the next session of Congress, when, if experience shall make evident the necessity of additional legislation, the two Houses will have ample time to mature and pass the requisite measures. In the meantime the questions arise, Why should this war measure be continued beyond the period designated in the original act, and why in time of peace should military tribunals be created to continue until each "State shall be fully restored in its constitutional relations to the Government and shall be duly represented in the Congress of the United States"?

It was manifest, with respect to the act approved March 3, 1865, that prudence and wisdom alike required that jurisdiction over all cases concerning the free enjoyment of the immunities and rights of citizenship, as well as the protection of person and property, should be conferred upon some tribunal in every State or district where the ordinary course of judicial proceedings was interrupted by the rebellion, and until the same should be fully restored. At that time, therefore, an urgent necessity existed for the passage of some such law. Now, however, war has substantially ceased; the ordinary course of judicial proceedings is no longer interrupted; the courts, both State and Federal, are in full, complete, and successful operation, and through them every person, regardless of race and color, is entitled to and can be heard. The protection granted to the white citizen is already conferred by law upon the freedman; strong and stringent guards, by way of penalties and punishments, are thrown around his person and property, and it is believed that ample protection will be afforded him by due process of law, without resort to the dangerous expedient of "military tribunals," now that the war has been brought to a close. The necessity no longer existing for such tribunals, which had their origin in the war, grave objections to their continuance must present themselves to the minds of all reflecting and dispassionate men. Independently of the danger, in representative republics, of conferring upon the military, in time of peace, extraordinary powers—so carefully guarded against by the patriots and statesmen of the earlier days of the Republic, so frequently the ruin of governments founded upon the same free principles, and subversive of the rights and liberties of the citizen— the question of practical economy earnestly commends itself to the consideration of the lawmaking power. With an immense debt already burdening the incomes of the industrial and laboring classes, a due regard for their interests, so inseparably connected with the welfare of the country, should prompt us to rigid economy and retrenchment, and influence us to abstain from all legislation that would unnecessarily increase the public indebtedness. Tested by this rule of sound political wisdom, I can see no reason for the establishment of the "military jurisdiction" conferred upon the officials of the Bureau by the fourteenth section of the bill.

By the laws of the United States and of the different States competent courts, Federal and State, have been established and are now in full practical operation. By means of these civil tribunals ample redress is afforded for all private wrongs, whether to the person or the property of the citizen, without denial or unnecessary delay. They are open to all, without regard to color or race.   I feel well assured that it will be better to trust the rights, privileges, and immunities of the citizen to tribunals thus established, and presided over by competent and impartial judges, bound by fixed rules of law and evidence, and where the right of trial by jury is guaranteed and secured, than to the caprice or judgment of an officer of the Bureau, who it is possible may be entirely ignorant of the principles that underlie the just administration of the law.   There is danger, too, that conflict of jurisdiction will frequently arise between the civil courts and these military tribunals, each having concurrent jurisdiction over the person and the cause of action—the one judicature administered and controlled by civil law, the other by the military.   How is the conflict to be settled, and who is to determine between the two tribunals when it arises?   In my opinion, it is wise to guard against such conflict by leaving to the courts and juries the protection of all civil rights and the redress of all civil grievances.

The fact can not be denied that since the actual cessation of hostilities many acts of violence, such, perhaps, as had never been witnessed in their previous history, have occurred in the States involved in the recent rebellion.   I believe, however, that public sentiment will sustain me in the assertion that such deeds of wrong are not confined to any particular State or section, but are manifested over the entire country, demonstrating that the cause that produced them does not depend upon any particular locality, but is the result of the agitation and derangement incident to a long and bloody civil war.   While the prevalence of such disorders must be greatly deplored, their occasional and temporary occurrence would seem to furnish no necessity for the extension of the Bureau beyond the period fixed in the original act.

Besides the objections which I have thus briefly stated, I may urge upon your consideration the additional reason that recent developments in regard to the practical operations of the Bureau in many of the States show that in numerous instances it is used by its agents as a means of promoting their individual advantage, and that the freedmen are employed for the advancement of the personal ends of the officers instead of their own improvement and welfare, thus confirming the fears originally entertained by many that the continuation of such a Bureau for any unnecessary length of time would inevitably result in fraud, corruption, and oppression.   It is proper to state that in cases of this character investigations have been promptly ordered, and the offender punished whenever his guilt has been satisfactorily established.

As another reason against the necessity of the legislation contemplated by this measure, reference may be had to the "civil-rights bill," now a law of the land, and which will be faithfully executed so long as it shall remain unrepealed and may not be declared unconstitutional by courts of competent jurisdiction.   By that act it is enacted—

That all persons born in the United States and not subject to any foreign power, excluding Indians not taxed, are hereby declared to be citizens of the United States;

and such citizens, of every race and color, without regard to any previous condition of slavery or involuntary servitude, except as a punishment for crime whereof the party shall have been duly convicted, shall have the same right in every State and Territory in the United States to make and enforce contracts; to sue, be parties, and give evidence; to inherit, purchase, lease, sell, hold, and convey real and personal property, and to full and equal benefit of all laws and proceedings for the security of person and property, as is enjoyed by white citizens, and shall be subject to like punishment, pains, and penalties, and to none other, any law, statute, ordinance, regulation, or custom to the contrary notwithstanding.

By the provisions of the act full protection is afforded through the district courts of the United States to all persons injured, and whose privileges, as thus declared, are in any way impaired; and heavy penalties are denounced against the person who willfully violates the law. I need not state that that law did not receive my approval; yet its remedies are far more preferable than those proposed in the present bill—the one being civil and the other military.

By the sixth section of the bill herewith returned certain proceedings by which the lands in the "parishes of St. Helena and St. Luke, South Carolina," were sold and bid in, and afterwards disposed of by the tax commissioners, are ratified and confirmed. By the seventh, eighth, ninth, tenth, and eleventh sections provisions by law are made for the disposal of the lands thus acquired to a particular class of citizens. While the quieting of titles is deemed very important and desirable, the discrimination made in the bill seems objectionable, as does also the attempt to confer upon the commissioners judicial powers by which citizens of the United States are to be deprived of their property in a mode contrary to that provision of the Constitution which declares that no person shall "be deprived of life, liberty, or property without due process of law." As a general principle, such legislation is unsafe, unwise, partial, and unconstitutional. It may deprive persons of their property who are equally deserving objects of the nation's bounty as those whom by this legislation Congress seeks to benefit. The title to the land thus to be portioned out to a favored class of citizens must depend upon the regularity of the tax sales under the law as it existed at the time of the sale, and no subsequent legislation can give validity to the right thus acquired as against the original claimants. The attention of Congress is therefore invited to a more mature consideration of the measures proposed in these sections of the bill.

In conclusion I again urge upon Congress the danger of class legislation, so well calculated to keep the public mind in a state of uncertain expectation, disquiet, and restlessness and to encourage interested hopes and fears that the National Government will continue to furnish to classes of citizens in the several States means for support and maintenance regardless of whether they pursue a life of indolence or of labor, and regardless also of the constitutional limitations of the national authority in times of peace and tranquillity.

The bill is herewith returned to the House of Representatives, in which it originated, for its final action.

ANDREW JOHNSON.

WASHINGTON, D. C., *July 28, 1866.*

To the House of Representatives:

I herewith return, without my approval, the bill entitled "An act erecting the Territory of Montana into a surveying district, and for other purposes."

The bill contains four sections, the first of which erects the Territory into a surveying district and authorizes the appointment of a surveyor-general; the second constitutes the Territory a land district; the third authorizes the appointment of a register and receiver for said district; and the fourth requires the surveyor-general to—

select and survey eighteen alternate odd sections of nonmineral timber lands within said district for the New York and Montana Iron Mining and Manufacturing Company, incorporated under the laws of the State of New York, which lands the said company shall have immediate possession of on the payment of $1.25 per acre, and shall have a patent for the same whenever, within two years after their selection, they shall have furnished evidence satisfactory to the Secretary of the Interior that they have erected and have in operation on the said lands iron works with a capacity for manufacturing 1,500 tons of iron per annum: *Provided,* That the said lands shall revert to the United States in case the above-mentioned iron works be not erected within the specified time: *And provided,* That until the title to the said lands shall have been perfected the timber shall not be cut off from more than one section of the said lands.

To confer the special privileges specified in this fourth section appears to be the chief object of the bill, the provisions of which are subject to some of the most important objections that induced me to return to the Senate with my disapproval the bill entitled "An act to enable the New York and Montana Iron Mining and Manufacturing Company to purchase a certain amount of the public lands not now in market." That bill authorized the same corporation to select and survey in the Territory of Montana, in square form, twenty-one sections of land, three of which might contain coal and iron ore, for which the minimum rate of $1.25 per acre was to be paid. The present bill omits these sections of mineral lands, and directs the surveyor-general to select and survey the timber lands; but it contains the objectionable feature of granting to a private mining and manufacturing corporation exclusive rights and privileges in the public domain which are by law denied to individuals. The first choice of timber land in the Territory is bestowed upon a corporation foreign to the Territory and over which Congress has no control. The surveyor-general of the district, a public officer who should have no connection with any purchase of public land, is made the agent of the corporation to select the land, the selections to be made in the absence of all competition; and over 11,000 acres are bestowed at the lowest price of public lands. It is by no means certain that the substitution of alternate sections for the compact body of lands contemplated by the other bill is any less injurious to the public interest, for alternate sections stripped of timber are not likely to enhance the value of those reserved by the Government. Be this as it may, this bill bestows a large monopoly of public lands without adequate consideration; confers a right and privilege in quantity equivalent to seventy-two preemption rights; introduces a dangerous system of privileges to private trading corporations; and is an unjust discrimination in favor of traders and speculators against individual settlers and pioneers who are seeking homes and improving our Western Territories. Such a departure from the long-established, wise, and just policy which has heretofore governed the disposition of the public funds [lands] can not receive my sanction. The objections enumerated apply to the fourth section of the bill. The first, second, and third sections, providing for the appointment of a surveyor-general, register, and receiver, are unobjectionable if any necessity requires the creation of these offices and the additional expenses of a new surveying land district. But they appear in this instance to be only needed as a part of the machinery to enable the "New York and Montana Iron Mining and Manufacturing Company" to secure these privileges; for I am informed by the proper Department, in a communication hereto annexed, that there is no public necessity for a surveyor-general, register, or receiver in Montana Territory, since it forms part of an existing surveying and land district, wherein the public business is, under present laws, transacted with adequate facility, so that the provisions of the first, second, and third sections would occasion needless expense to the General Government. ANDREW JOHNSON.

PROCLAMATIONS.

ANDREW JOHNSON, PRESIDENT OF THE UNITED STATES OF AMERICA.

To all whom it may concern:

An exequatur, bearing date the 13th day of October, 1864, having been issued to Esteban Rogers, recognizing him as consul *ad interim* of the Republic of Chile for the port of New York and its dependencies and declaring him free to exercise and enjoy such functions, powers, and privileges as are allowed to consuls by the law of nations or by the laws of the United States and existing treaty stipulations between the Government of Chile and the United States; but as it is deemed advisable that the said Esteban Rogers should no longer be permitted to continue in the exercise of said functions, powers, and privileges:

These are therefore to declare that I no longer recognize the said

Esteban Rogers as consul *ad interim* of the Republic of Chile for the port of New York and its dependencies and will not permit him to exercise or enjoy any of the functions, powers, or privileges allowed to a consular officer of that nation; and that I do hereby wholly revoke and annul the said exequatur heretofore given and do declare the same to be absolutely null and void from this day forward.

In testimony whereof I have caused these letters to be made patent and the seal of the United States of America to be hereunto affixed.

[SEAL.]   Given under my hand, at Washington, this 12th day of February, A. D. 1866, and of the Independence of the United States of America the ninetieth.

ANDREW JOHNSON.

By the President:

WILLIAM H. SEWARD,
Secretary of State.

ANDREW JOHNSON, PRESIDENT OF THE UNITED STATES OF AMERICA.

To all whom it may concern:

An exequatur, bearing date the 7th day of October, 1864, having been issued to Claudius Edward Habicht, recognizing him as consul of Sweden and Norway at New York and declaring him free to exercise and enjoy such functions, powers, and privileges as are allowed to consuls by the law of nations or by the laws of the United States and existing treaty stipulations between the Government of Sweden and Norway and the United States; but as it is deemed advisable that the said Claudius Edward Habicht should no longer be permitted to continue in the exercise of said functions, powers, and privileges:

These are therefore to declare that I no longer recognize the said Claudius Edward Habicht as consul of Sweden and Norway at New York and will not permit him to exercise or enjoy any of the functions, powers, or privileges allowed to a consular officer of that nation; and that I do hereby wholly revoke and annul the said exequatur heretofore given and do declare the same to be absolutely null and void from this day forward.

In testimony whereof I have caused these letters to be made patent and the seal of the United States of America to be hereunto affixed.

[SEAL.]   Given under my hand, at Washington, the 26th day of March, A. D. 1866, and of the Independence of the United States of America the ninetieth.

ANDREW JOHNSON.

By the President:

WILLIAM H. SEWARD,
Secretary of State.

ANDREW JOHNSON, PRESIDENT OF THE UNITED STATES OF AMERICA.

To all whom it may concern:

An exequatur, bearing date the 1st day of July, 1865, having been issued to S. M. Svenson, recognizing him as vice-consul of Sweden and Norway at New Orleans and declaring him free to exercise and enjoy such functions, powers, and privileges as are allowed to vice-consuls by the law of nations or by the laws of the United States and existing treaty stipulations between the Government of Sweden and Norway and the United States; but as it is deemed advisable that the said S. M. Svenson should no longer be permitted to continue in the exercise of said functions, powers, and privileges:

These are therefore to declare that I no longer recognize the said S. M. Svenson as vice-consul of Sweden and Norway at New Orleans and will not permit him to exercise or enjoy any of the functions, powers, or privileges allowed to a consular officer of that nation; and that I do hereby wholly revoke and annul the said exequatur heretofore given and do declare the same to be absolutely null and void from this day forward.

In testimony whereof I have caused these letters to be made patent and the seal of the United States of America to be hereunto affixed.

[SEAL.]   Given under my hand, at Washington, the 26th day of March, A. D. 1866, and of the Independence of the United States of America the ninetieth.

ANDREW JOHNSON.

By the President:

WILLIAM H. SEWARD,
Secretary of State.

BY THE PRESIDENT OF THE UNITED STATES OF AMERICA.

A PROCLAMATION.

Whereas by proclamations of the 15th and 19th of April, 1861, the President of the United States, in virtue of the power vested in him by the Constitution and the laws, declared that the laws of the United States were opposed and the execution thereof obstructed in the States of South Carolina, Georgia, Alabama, Florida, Mississippi, Louisiana, and Texas by combinations too powerful to be suppressed by the ordinary course of judicial proceedings or by the powers vested in the marshals by law; and

Whereas by another proclamation, made on the 16th day of August, in the same year, in pursuance of an act of Congress approved July 13, 1861, the inhabitants of the States of Georgia, South Carolina, Virginia,

North Carolina, Tennessee, Alabama, Louisiana, Texas, Arkansas, Mississippi, and Florida (except the inhabitants of that part of the State of Virginia lying west of the Alleghany Mountains and of such other parts of that State and the other States before named as might maintain a loyal adhesion to the Union and the Constitution or might be from time to time occupied and controlled by forces of the United States engaged in the dispersion of insurgents) were declared to be in a state of insurrection against the United States; and

Whereas by another proclamation, of the 1st day of July, 1862, issued in pursuance of an act of Congress approved June 7, in the same year, the insurrection was declared to be still existing in the States aforesaid, with the exception of certain specified counties in the State of Virginia; and

Whereas by another proclamation, made on the 2d day of April, 1863, in pursuance of the act of Congress of July 13, 1861, the exceptions named in the proclamation of August 16, 1861, were revoked and the inhabitants of the States of Georgia, South Carolina, North Carolina, Tennessee, Alabama, Louisiana, Texas, Arkansas, Mississippi, Florida, and Virginia (except the forty-eight counties of Virginia designated as West Virginia and the ports of New Orleans, Key West, Port Royal, and Beaufort, in North Carolina) were declared to be still in a state of insurrection against the United States; and

Whereas the House of Representatives, on the 22d day of July, 1861, adopted a resolution in the words following, namely:

Resolved by the House of Representatives of the Congress of the United States, That the present deplorable civil war has been forced upon the country by the disunionists of the Southern States now in revolt against the constitutional Government and in arms around the capital; that in this national emergency Congress, banishing all feelings of mere passion or resentment, will recollect only its duty to the whole country; that this war is not waged upon our part in any spirit of oppression, nor for any purpose of conquest or subjugation, nor purpose of overthrowing or interfering with the rights or established institutions of those States, but to defend and maintain the supremacy of the Constitution and to preserve the Union, with all the dignity, equality, and rights of the several States unimpaired; and that as soon as these objects are accomplished the war ought to cease.

And whereas the Senate of the United States, on the 25th day of July, 1861, adopted a resolution in the words following, to wit:

Resolved, That the present deplorable civil war has been forced upon the country by the disunionists of the Southern States now in revolt against the constitutional Government and in arms around the capital; that in this national emergency Congress, banishing all feeling of mere passion or resentment, will recollect only its duty to the whole country; that this war is not prosecuted upon our part in any spirit of oppression, nor for any purpose of conquest or subjugation, nor purpose of overthrowing or interfering with the rights or established institutions of those States, but to defend and maintain the supremacy of the Constitution and all laws made in pursuance thereof and to preserve the Union, with all the dignity, equality, and rights of the several States unimpaired; that as soon as these objects are accomplished the war ought to cease.

And whereas these resolutions, though not joint or concurrent in form, are substantially identical, and as such may be regarded as having expressed the sense of Congress upon the subject to which they relate; and

Whereas by my proclamation of the 13th day of June last the insurrection in the State of Tennessee was declared to have been suppressed, the authority of the United States therein to be undisputed, and such United States officers as had been duly commissioned to be in the undisturbed exercise of their official functions; and

Whereas there now exists no organized armed resistance of misguided citizens or others to the authority of the United States in the States of Georgia, South Carolina, Virginia, North Carolina, Tennessee, Alabama, Louisiana, Arkansas, Mississippi, and Florida, and the laws can be sustained and enforced therein by the proper civil authority, State or Federal, and the people of said States are well and loyally disposed and have conformed or will conform in their legislation to the condition of affairs growing out of the amendment to the Constitution of the United States prohibiting slavery within the limits and jurisdiction of the United States; and

Whereas, in view of the before-recited premises, it is the manifest determination of the American people that no State of its own will has the right or the power to go out of, or separate itself from, or be separated from, the American Union, and that therefore each State ought to remain and constitute an integral part of the United States; and

Whereas the people of the several before-mentioned States have, in the manner aforesaid, given satisfactory evidence that they acquiesce in this sovereign and important resolution of national unity; and

Whereas it is believed to be a fundamental principle of government that people who have revolted and who have been overcome and subdued must either be dealt with so as to induce them voluntarily to become friends or else they must be held by absolute military power or devastated so as to prevent them from ever again doing harm as enemies, which last-named policy is abhorrent to humanity and to freedom; and

Whereas the Constitution of the United States provides for constituent communities only as States, and not as Territories, dependencies, provinces, or protectorates; and

Whereas such constituent States must necessarily be, and by the Constitution and laws of the United States are, made equals and placed upon a like footing as to political rights, immunities, dignity, and power with the several States with which they are united; and

Whereas the observance of political equality, as a principle of right and justice, is well calculated to encourage the people of the aforesaid States to be and become more and more constant and persevering in their renewed allegiance; and

Whereas standing armies, military occupation, martial law, military tribunals, and the suspension of the privilege of the writ of *habeas corpus* are in time of peace dangerous to public liberty, incompatible with the individual rights of the citizen, contrary to the genius and spirit of our free institutions, and exhaustive of the national resources, and ought not, therefore, to be sanctioned or allowed except in cases of actual necessity for repelling invasion or suppressing insurrection or rebellion; and

Whereas the policy of the Government of the United States from the beginning of the insurrection to its overthrow and final suppression has been in conformity with the principles herein set forth and enumerated:

Now, therefore, I, Andrew Johnson, President of the United States, do hereby proclaim and declare that the insurrection which heretofore existed in the States of Georgia, South Carolina, Virginia, North Carolina, Tennessee, Alabama, Louisiana, Arkansas, Mississippi, and Florida is at an end and is henceforth to be so regarded.

In testimony whereof I have hereunto set my hand and caused the seal of the United States to be affixed.

[SEAL.]   Done at the city of Washington, this 2d day of April, A. D. 1866, and of the Independence of the United States of America the ninetieth.

                                    ANDREW JOHNSON.

By the President:
    WILLIAM H. SEWARD, *Secretary of State.*

ANDREW JOHNSON, PRESIDENT OF THE UNITED STATES OF AMERICA.

To all whom it may concern:

Whereas the exequatur of Claudius Edward Habicht, recognizing him as consul of Sweden and Norway at New York, and that of S. M. Svenson as vice-consul of Sweden and Norway at New Orleans were formally revoked on the 26th day of March last; and

Whereas representations have been made to me since that date which have effectually relieved those gentlemen from the charges of unlawful and unfriendly conduct heretofore entertained against them:

Now, therefore, be it known that I, Andrew Johnson, President of the United States of America, do hereby annul the revocation of the exequaturs of the said Claudius Edward Habicht and S. M. Svenson and restore to them the right to exercise the functions and privileges heretofore granted as consular officers of the Government of Sweden and Norway.

In testimony whereof I have hereunto signed my name and caused the seal of the United States to be affixed.

[SEAL.]   Done at the city of Washington, this 30th day of May, A. D. 1866, and of the Independence of the United States the ninetieth.

                                    ANDREW JOHNSON.

By the President:
    WILLIAM H. SEWARD, *Secretary of State.*

BY THE PRESIDENT OF THE UNITED STATES OF AMERICA.

A PROCLAMATION.

Whereas it has become known to me that certain evil-disposed persons have, within the territory and jurisdiction of the United States, begun and set on foot and have provided and prepared, and are still engaged in providing and preparing, means for a military expedition and enterprise, which expedition and enterprise is to be carried on from the territory and jurisdiction of the United States against colonies, districts, and people of British North America, within the dominions of the United Kingdom of Great Britain and Ireland, with which said colonies, districts, and people and Kingdom the United States are at peace; and

Whereas the proceedings aforesaid constitute a high misdemeanor, forbidden by the laws of the United States as well as by the law of nations:

Now, therefore, for the purpose of preventing the carrying on of the unlawful expedition and enterprise aforesaid from the territory and jurisdiction of the United States and to maintain the public peace as well as the national honor and enforce obedience and respect to the laws of the United States, I, Andrew Johnson, President of the United States, do admonish and warn all good citizens of the United States against taking part in or in any wise aiding, countenancing, or abetting said unlawful proceedings; and I do exhort all judges, magistrates, marshals, and officers in the service of the United States to employ all their lawful authority and power to prevent and defeat the aforesaid unlawful proceedings and to arrest and bring to justice all persons who may be engaged therein.

And, pursuant to the act of Congress in such case made and provided, I do furthermore authorize and empower Major-General George G. Meade, commander of the Military Division of the Atlantic, to employ the land and naval forces of the United States and the militia thereof to arrest and prevent the setting on foot and carrying on the expedition and enterprise aforesaid.

In testimony whereof I have hereunto set my hand and caused the seal of the United States to be affixed.

[SEAL.] Done at the city of Washington, this 6th day of June, A. D. 1866, and of the Independence of the United States the ninetieth.

ANDREW JOHNSON.

By the President:

WILLIAM H. SEWARD, *Secretary of State.*

BY THE PRESIDENT OF THE UNITED STATES OF AMERICA.

A PROCLAMATION.

Whereas a war is existing in the Republic of Mexico, aggravated by foreign military intervention; and

Whereas the United States, in accordance with their settled habits and policy, are a neutral power in regard to the war which thus afflicts the Republic of Mexico; and

Whereas it has become known that one of the belligerents in the said war, namely, the Prince Maximilian, who asserts himself to be Emperor in Mexico, has issued a decree in regard to the port of Matamoras and other Mexican ports which are in the occupation and possession of another of the said belligerents, namely, the United States of Mexico, which decree is in the following words:

The port of Matamoras and all those of the northern frontier which have withdrawn from their obedience to the Government are closed to foreign and coasting traffic during such time as the empire of the law shall not be therein reinstated.

ART. 2. Merchandise proceeding from the said ports, on arriving at any other where the excise of the Empire is collected, shall pay the duties on importation, introduction, and consumption, and, on satisfactory proof of contravention, shall be irremissibly confiscated. Our minister of the treasury is charged with the punctual execution of this decree.

Given at Mexico, the 9th of July, 1866.

And whereas the decree thus recited, by declaring a belligerent blockade unsupported by competent military or naval force, is in violation of the neutral rights of the United States as defined by the law of nations as well as of the treaties existing between the United States of America and the aforesaid United States of Mexico:

Now, therefore, I, Andrew Johnson, President of the United States, do hereby proclaim and declare that the aforesaid decree is held and will be held by the United States to be absolutely null and void as against the Government and citizens of the United States, and that any attempt which shall be made to enforce the same against the Government or the citizens of the United States will be disallowed.

In witness whereof I have hereunto set my hand and caused the seal of the United States to be affixed.

[SEAL.] Done at the city of Washington, the 17th day of August, A. D. 1866, and of the Independence of the United States of America the ninety-first. ANDREW JOHNSON.

By the President:

WILLIAM H. SEWARD,
Secretary of State.

BY THE PRESIDENT OF THE UNITED STATES OF AMERICA.

A PROCLAMATION.

Whereas by proclamations of the 15th and 19th of April, 1861, the President of the United States, in virtue of the power vested in him by the Constitution and the laws, declared that the laws of the United States were opposed and the execution thereof obstructed in the States of South Carolina, Georgia, Alabama, Florida, Mississippi, Louisiana, and Texas by combinations too powerful to be suppressed by the ordinary course of judicial proceedings or by the powers vested in the marshals by law; and

Whereas by another proclamation, made on the 16th day of August, in the same year, in pursuance of an act of Congress approved July 13, 1861, the inhabitants of the States of Georgia, South Carolina, Virginia, North Carolina, Tennessee, Alabama, Louisiana, Texas, Arkansas, Mississippi, and Florida (except the inhabitants of that part of the State of Virginia lying west of the Alleghany Mountains, and except also the inhabitants of such other parts of that State and the other States before named as might maintain a loyal adhesion to the Union and the Constitution or might be from time to time occupied and controlled by forces of the United States engaged in the dispersion of insurgents) were declared to be in a state of insurrection against the United States; and

Whereas by another proclamation, of the 1st day of July, 1862, issued in pursuance of an act of Congress approved June 7, in the same year, the insurrection was declared to be still existing in the States aforesaid, with the exception of certain specified counties in the State of Virginia; and

Whereas by another proclamation, made on the 2d day of April, 1863, in pursuance of the act of Congress of July 13, 1861, the exceptions named in the proclamation of August 16, 1861, were revoked and the inhabitants of the States of Georgia, South Carolina, North Carolina, Tennessee, Alabama, Louisiana, Texas, Arkansas, Mississippi, Florida, and Virginia (except the forty-eight counties of Virginia designated as West Virginia and the ports of New Orleans, Key West, Port Royal, and Beaufort, in North Carolina) were declared to be still in a state of insurrection against the United States; and

Whereas by another proclamation, of the 15th day of September, 1863, made in pursuance of the act of Congress approved March 3, 1863, the rebellion was declared to be still existing and the privilege of the writ of *habeas corpus* was in certain specified cases suspended throughout the United States, said suspension to continue throughout the duration of the rebellion or until said proclamation should, by a subsequent one to be issued by the President of the United States, be modified or revoked; and

Whereas the House of Representatives, on the 22d day of July, 1861, adopted a resolution in the words following, namely:

Resolved by the House of Representatives of the Congress of the United States, That the present deplorable civil war has been forced upon the country by the disunionists of the Southern States now in revolt against the constitutional Government and in arms around the capital; that in this national emergency Congress, banishing all feelings of mere passion or resentment, will recollect only its duty to the whole country; that this war is not waged upon our part in any spirit of oppression, nor for any purpose of conquest or subjugation, nor purpose of overthrowing or interfering with the rights or established institutions of those States, but to defend and maintain the supremacy of the Constitution and to preserve the Union, with all the dignity, equality, and rights of the several States unimpaired; and that as soon as these objects are accomplished the war ought to cease.

And whereas the Senate of the United States, on the 25th day of July, 1861, adopted a resolution in the words following, to wit:

Resolved, That the present deplorable civil war has been forced upon the country by the disunionists of the Southern States now in revolt against the constitutional Government and in arms around the capital; that in this national emergency Congress, banishing all feeling of mere passion or resentment, will recollect only its duty to the whole country; that this war is not prosecuted upon our part in any spirit of oppression, nor for any purpose of conquest or subjugation, nor purpose of overthrowing or interfering with the rights or established institutions of those States, but to defend and maintain the supremacy of the Constitution and all laws made in pursuance thereof and to preserve the Union, with all the dignity, equality, and rights of the several States unimpaired; that as soon as these objects are accomplished the war ought to cease.

And whereas these resolutions, though not joint or concurrent in form, are substantially identical, and as such have hitherto been and yet are regarded as having expressed the sense of Congress upon the subject to which they relate; and

Whereas the President of the United States, by proclamation of the 13th of June, 1865, declared that the insurrection in the State of Tennessee had been suppressed, and that the authority of the United States therein was undisputed, and that such United States officers as had been duly commissioned were in the undisturbed exercise of their official functions; and

Whereas the President of the United States, by further proclamation, issued on the 2d day of April, 1866, did promulgate and declare that there no longer existed any armed resistance of misguided citizens or others to the authority of the United States in any or in all the States before mentioned, excepting only the State of Texas, and did further promulgate and declare that the laws could be sustained and enforced in the several States before mentioned, except Texas, by the proper civil authorities, State or Federal, and that the people of the said States, except Texas, are well and loyally disposed and have conformed or will conform in their legislation to the condition of affairs growing out of the amendment to the Constitution of the United States prohibiting slavery within the limits and jurisdiction of the United States;

And did further declare in the same proclamation that it is the manifest determination of the American people that no State, of its own will, has a right or power to go out of, or separate itself from, or be separated from, the American Union; and that, therefore, each State ought to remain and constitute an integral part of the United States;

And did further declare in the same last-mentioned proclamation that the several aforementioned States, excepting Texas, had in the manner aforesaid given satisfactory evidence that they acquiesce in this sovereign and important resolution of national unity; and

Whereas the President of the United States in the same proclamation did further declare that it is believed to be a fundamental principle of government that the people who have revolted and who have been overcome and subdued must either be dealt with so as to induce them voluntarily to become friends or else they must be held by absolute military power or devastated so as to prevent them from ever again doing harm as enemies, which last-named policy is abhorrent to humanity and to freedom; and

Whereas the President did in the same proclamation further declare that the Constitution of the United States provides for constituent communities only as States, and not as Territories, dependencies, provinces, or protectorates;

And further, that such constituent States must necessarily be, and by the Constitution and laws of the United States are, made equals and placed upon a like footing as to political rights, immunities, dignity, and power with the several States with which they are united;

And did further declare that the observance of political equality, as a principle of right and justice, is well calculated to encourage the people of the before-named States, except Texas, to be and to become more and more constant and persevering in their renewed allegiance; and

Whereas the President did further declare that standing armies, military occupation, martial law, military tribunals, and the suspension of the writ of *habeas corpus* are in time of peace dangerous to public liberty, incompatible with the individual rights of the citizen, contrary to the genius and spirit of our free institutions, and exhaustive of the national resources, and ought not, therefore, to be sanctioned or allowed except in cases of actual necessity for repelling invasion or suppressing insurrection or rebellion;

And the President did further, in the same proclamation, declare that the policy of the Government of the United States from the beginning of the insurrection to its overthrow and final suppression had been conducted in conformity with the principles in the last-named proclamation recited; and

Whereas the President, in the said proclamation of the 13th of June, 1865, upon the grounds therein stated and hereinbefore recited, did then and thereby proclaim and declare that the insurrection which heretofore existed in the several States before named, except in Texas, was at an end and was henceforth to be so regarded; and

Whereas subsequently to the said 2d day of April, 1866, the insurrection in the State of Texas has been completely and everywhere suppressed and ended and the authority of the United States has been successfully and completely established in the said State of Texas and now remains therein unresisted and undisputed, and such of the proper United States officers as have been duly commissioned within the limits of the said State are now in the undisturbed exercise of their official functions; and

Whereas the laws can now be sustained and enforced in the said State of Texas by the proper civil authority, State or Federal, and the people of the said State of Texas, like the people of the other States before named, are well and loyally disposed and have conformed or will conform in their legislation to the condition of affairs growing out of the amendment of the Constitution of the United States prohibiting slavery within the limits and jurisdiction of the United States; and

Whereas all the reasons and conclusions set forth in regard to the several States therein specially named now apply equally and in all respects to the State of Texas, as well as to the other States which had been involved in insurrection; and

Whereas adequate provision has been made by military orders to enforce the execution of the acts of Congress, aid the civil authorities, and secure obedience to the Constitution and laws of the United States within the State of Texas if a resort to military force for such purpose should at any time become necessary:

Now, therefore, I, Andrew Johnson, President of the United States, do hereby proclaim and declare that the insurrection which heretofore existed in the State of Texas is at an end and is to be henceforth so regarded in that State as in the other States before named in which the said insurrection was proclaimed to be at an end by the aforesaid proclamation of the 2d day of April, 1866.

And I do further proclaim that the said insurrection is at an end and that peace, order, tranquillity, and civil authority now exist in and throughout the whole of the United States of America.

In testimony whereof I have hereunto set my hand and caused the seal of the United States to be affixed.

[SEAL.]   Done at the city of Washington, this 20th day of August, A. D. 1866, and of the Independence of the United States of America the ninety-first.

ANDREW JOHNSON.

By the President:

WILLIAM H. SEWARD,
    Secretary of State.

BY THE PRESIDENT OF THE UNITED STATES.

A PROCLAMATION.

Almighty God, our Heavenly Father, has been pleased to vouchsafe to us as a people another year of that national life which is an indispensable condition of peace, security, and progress. That year has, moreover, been crowned with many peculiar blessings.

The civil war that so recently closed among us has not been anywhere reopened; foreign intervention has ceased to excite alarm or apprehension; intrusive pestilence has been benignly mitigated; domestic tranquillity has improved, sentiments of conciliation have largely prevailed, and affections of loyalty and patriotism have been widely renewed; our fields have yielded quite abundantly, our mining industry has been richly rewarded, and we have been allowed to extend our railroad system far into the interior recesses of the country, while our commerce has resumed its customary activity in foreign seas.

These great national blessings demand a national acknowledgment.

Now, therefore, I, Andrew Johnson, President of the United States, do hereby recommend that Thursday, the 29th day of November next, be set apart and be observed everywhere in the several States and Territories of the United States by the people thereof as a day of thanksgiving and praise to Almighty God, with due remembrance that "in His temple doth every man speak of His honor." I recommend also that on the same solemn occasion they do humbly and devoutly implore Him to grant to our national councils and to our whole people that divine wisdom which alone can lead any nation into the ways of all good.

In offering these national thanksgivings, praises, and supplications we have the divine assurance that "the Lord remaineth a king forever; them that are meek shall He guide in judgment and such as are gentle shall He learn His way; the Lord shall give strength to His people, and the Lord shall give to His people the blessing of peace."

In witness whereof I have hereunto set my hand and caused the seal of the United States to be affixed.

[SEAL.] Done at the city of Washington, this 8th day of October, A. D. 1866, and of the Independence of the United States the ninety-first. ANDREW JOHNSON.

By the President:

WILLIAM H. SEWARD, *Secretary of State.*

EXECUTIVE ORDERS.

[From the Daily National Intelligencer, April 9, 1866.]

EXECUTIVE MANSION, *April 7, 1866.*

It is eminently right and proper that the Government of the United States should give earnest and substantial evidence of its just appreciation of the services of the patriotic men who when the life of the nation was imperiled entered the Army and Navy to preserve the integrity of the Union, defend the Government, and maintain and perpetuate unimpaired its free institutions.

It is therefore directed—

First. That in appointments to office in the several Executive Departments of the General Government and the various branches of the public service connected with said Departments preference shall be given to such meritorious and honorably discharged soldiers and sailors—particularly those who have been disabled by wounds received or diseases contracted in the line of duty—as may possess the proper qualifications.

Second. That in all promotions in said Departments and the several branches of the public service connected therewith such persons shall have preference, when equally eligible and qualified, over those who have not faithfully and honorably served in the land or naval forces of the United States.

ANDREW JOHNSON.

DEPARTMENT OF STATE,
Washington, April 13, 1866.

On the 14th of April, 1865, great affliction was brought upon the American people by the assassination of the lamented Abraham Lincoln, then President of the United States. The undersigned is therefore directed by the President to announce that in commemoration of that event the public offices will be closed to-morrow, the 14th instant.

WILLIAM H. SEWARD.

GENERAL ORDERS, No. 26.

WAR DEPARTMENT,
ADJUTANT-GENERAL'S OFFICE,
Washington, May 1, 1866.

ORDER IN RELATION TO TRIALS BY MILITARY COURTS AND COMMISSIONS.

Whereas some military commanders are embarrassed by doubts as to the operation of the proclamation of the President dated the 2d day of April, 1866, upon trials by military courts-martial and military officers; to remove such doubts—

It is ordered by the President, That hereafter, whenever offenses committed by civilians are to be tried where civil tribunals are in existence which can try them, their cases are not authorized to be, and will not be, brought before military courts-martial or commissions, but will be committed to the proper civil authorities. This order is not applicable to camp followers, as provided for under the sixtieth article of war, or to contractors and others specified in section 16, act of July 17, 1862, and sections 1 and 2, act of March 2, 1863. Persons and offenses cognizable by the Rules and Articles of War and by the acts of Congress above cited will continue to be tried and punished by military tribunals as prescribed by the Rules and Articles of War and acts of Congress hereinafter cited, to wit:

[Sixtieth of the Rules and Articles of War.]

60. All sutlers and retainers to the camp, and all persons whatsoever serving with the armies of the United States in the field, though not enlisted soldiers, are to be subject to orders, according to the rules and discipline of war.

[Extract from "An act to define the pay and emoluments of certain officers of the Army, and for other purposes," approved July 17, 1862.]

SEC. 16. *And be it further enacted*, That whenever any contractor for subsistence, clothing, arms, ammunition, munitions of war, and for every description of supplies for the Army or Navy of the United States, shall be found guilty by a court-martial of fraud or willful neglect of duty, he shall be punished by fine, imprisonment, or such other punishment as the court-martial shall adjudge; and any person who shall contract to furnish supplies of any kind or description for the Army or Navy, *he* shall be deemed and taken as a part of the land or naval forces of the United States for which he shall contract to furnish said supplies, and be subject to the rules and regulations for the government of the land and naval forces of the United States.

[Extract from "An act to prevent and punish frauds upon the Government of the United States," approved March 2, 1863.]

Be it enacted by the Senate and House of Representatives of the United States of America in Congress assembled, That any person in the land or naval forces of the United States, or in the militia in actual service of the United States in time of war, who shall make or cause to be made, or present or cause to be presented for payment or approval to or by any person or officer in the civil or military service of the United States, any claim upon or against the Government of the United States, or any department or officer thereof, knowing such claim to be false, fictitious, or fraudulent; any person in such forces or service who shall, for the purpose of obtaining or aiding in obtaining the approval or payment of such claim, make, use, or cause to be made or used, any false bill, receipt, voucher, entry, roll, account, claim, statement, certificate, affidavit, or deposition, knowing the same to contain any false or fraudulent statement or entry; any person in said forces or service who shall make or procure to be made, or knowingly advise the making of, any false oath to any fact, statement, or certificate, voucher or entry, for the purpose of obtaining or of aiding to obtain any approval or payment of any claim against the United States, or any department or officer thereof; any person in said forces or service who, for the purpose of obtaining or enabling any other person to obtain from the Government of the United States, or any department or officer thereof, any payment or allowance, or the approval or signature of any person in the military, naval, or civil service of the United States of or to any false, fraudulent, or fictitious claim, shall forge or counterfeit, or cause or procure to be forged or counterfeited, any signature upon any bill, receipt, voucher, account, claim, roll, statement, affidavit, or deposition; and any person in said forces or service who shall utter or use the same as true or genuine, knowing the same to have been forged or counterfeited; any person in said forces or service who shall enter into any agreement, combination, or conspiracy to cheat or defraud the Government of the United States, or any department or officer thereof, by obtaining or aiding and assisting to obtain the payment or allowance of any false or fraudulent claim; any person in said forces or service who shall steal, embezzle, or knowingly and willfully misappropriate or apply to his own use or benefit, or who shall wrongfully and knowingly sell, convey, or dispose of any ordnance, arms, ammunition, clothing, subsistence stores, money, or other property of the United States, furnished or to be used for the military or naval service of the United States; any contractor, agent, paymaster, quartermaster, or other person whatsoever in said forces or service having charge, possession, custody, or control of any money or other public property used or to be used in the military or naval service of the United States, who shall, with intent to defraud the United States, or willfully to conceal such money or other property, deliver or cause to be delivered to any other person having authority to receive the same any amount of such money or other public property less than that for which he shall receive a certificate or receipt; any person in said forces or service who is or shall be authorized to make or deliver any certificate, voucher, or receipt, or other paper certifying the receipt of arms, ammunition, provisions, clothing, or other public property so used or to be used, who shall make or deliver the same to any person without having full knowledge of the truth of the facts stated therein, and with intent to cheat, defraud, or injure the United States; any person in said forces or service who shall knowingly purchase or receive, in pledge for any obligation or indebtedness, from any soldier, officer, or other person called into or employed in said forces or service, any arms, equipments, ammunition, clothes, or military stores, or other public property, such soldier, officer, or other person not having the lawful right to pledge or sell the same, shall be deemed guilty of a criminal offense, and shall be subject to the rules and regulations made for the government of the military and naval forces of the United States, and of the militia when called into and employed in the actual service of the United States in time of war, and to the provisions of this act. And every person so offending may be arrested and held for trial by a court-martial, and if found guilty shall be punished by fine and imprisonment, or such other punishment as the court-martial may adjudge, save the punishment of death.

SEC. 2. *And be it further enacted,* That any person heretofore called or hereafter to be called into or employed in such forces or service who shall commit any violation of this act, and shall afterwards receive his discharge or be dismissed from the service, shall, notwithstanding such discharge or dismissal, continue to be liable to be arrested and held for trial and sentence by a court-martial in the same manner and to the same extent as if he had not received such discharge or been dismissed.

*   *   *   *   *   *   *

By order of the Secretary of War:

E. D. TOWNSEND,
Assistant Adjutant-General.

EXECUTIVE MANSION, *May 29, 1866.*

The President with profound sorrow announces to the people of the United States the death of Winfield Scott, the late Lieutenant-General of the Army. On the day which may be appointed for his funeral the several Executive Departments of the Government will be closed.

The heads of the War and Navy Departments will respectively give orders for paying appropriate honors to the memory of the deceased.

ANDREW JOHNSON.

[From the Daily National Intelligencer, June 6, 1866.]

ATTORNEY-GENERAL'S OFFICE,
Washington, D. C., June 5, 1866.

By direction of the President, you* are hereby instructed to cause the arrest of all prominent, leading, or conspicuous persons called "Fenians" who you may have probable cause to believe have been or may be guilty of violations of the neutrality laws of the United States.

JAMES SPEED,
Attorney-General.

*Addressed to district attorneys and marshals of the United States.

DEPARTMENT OF STATE,
Washington, June 18, 1866.

The President directs the undersigned to perform the painful duty of announcing to the people of the United States that Lewis Cass, distinguished not more by faithful service in varied public trusts than by exalted patriotism at a recent period of political disorder, departed this life at 4 o'clock yesterday morning. The several Executive Departments of the Government will cause appropriate honors to be rendered to the memory of the deceased at home and abroad wherever the national name and authority are acknowledged.

WILLIAM H. SEWARD.

EXECUTIVE MANSION,
Washington, D. C., October 26, 1866.

Hon. EDWIN M. STANTON,
Secretary of War.

SIR: Recent advices indicate an early evacuation of Mexico by the French expeditionary forces and that the time has arrived when our minister to Mexico should place himself in communication with that Republic.

In furtherance of the objects of his mission and as evidence of the earnest desire felt by the United States for the proper adjustment of the questions involved, I deem it of great importance that General Grant should by his presence and advice cooperate with our minister.

I have therefore to ask that you will request General Grant to proceed to some point on our Mexican frontier most suitable and convenient for communication with our minister, or (if General Grant deems it best) to accompany him to his destination in Mexico, and to give him the aid of his advice in carrying out the instructions of the Secretary of State, a copy of which is herewith sent for the General's information.

General Grant will make report to the Secretary of War of such matters as, in his discretion, ought to be communicated to the Department.

Very respectfully, yours,

ANDREW JOHNSON.

EXECUTIVE MANSION,
Washington, D. C., October 30, 1866.

Hon. EDWIN M. STANTON,
Secretary of War.

SIR: General Ulysses S. Grant having found it inconvenient to assume the duties specified in my letter to you of the 26th instant, you will please relieve him from the same and assign them in all respects to William T. Sherman, Lieutenant-General of the Army of the United States. By way of guiding General Sherman in the performance of his duties, you will furnish him with a copy of your special orders to General Grant, made in compliance with my letter of the 26th instant, together with a copy of the instructions of the Secretary of State to Lewis D. Campbell, esq., therein mentioned. The Lieutenant-General will proceed to the execution of his duties without delay.

Very respectfully, yours,

ANDREW JOHNSON.

EXECUTIVE MANSION,
Washington, D. C., November 1, 1866.

Hon. EDWIN M. STANTON,
Secretary of War.

SIR: In the report of General Grant of the 27th ultimo, inclosed in your communication of that date, reference is made to the force at present stationed in the Military Department of Washington (which embraces the District of Columbia, the counties of Alexander and Fairfax, Va., and the States of Maryland and Delaware), and it is stated that the entire number of troops comprised in the command is 2,224, of which only 1,550 are enumerated as "effective." In view of the prevalence in various portions of the country of a revolutionary and turbulent disposition, which might at any moment assume insurrectionary proportions and lead to serious disorders, and of the duty of the Government to be at all times prepared to act with decision and effect, this force is not deemed adequate for the protection and security of the seat of Government.

I therefore request that you will at once take such measures as will insure its safety, and thus discourage any attempt for its possession by insurgent or other illegal combinations.

Very respectfully, yours,

ANDREW JOHNSON.

EXECUTIVE MANSION,
Washington, D. C., November 2, 1866.

Hon. EDWIN M. STANTON,
Secretary of War.

SIR: There is ground to apprehend danger of an insurrection in Baltimore against the constituted authorities of the State of Maryland on or about the day of the election soon to be held in that city, and that in such contingency the aid of the United States might be invoked under the acts of Congress which pertain to that subject. While I am averse to any military demonstration that would have a tendency to interfere with the free exercise of the elective franchise in Baltimore or be construed into any interference in local questions, I feel great solicitude that should an insurrection take place the Government should be prepared to meet and promptly put it down. I accordingly desire you to call General Grant's attention to the subject, leaving to his own discretion and judgment the measures of preparation and precaution that should be adopted.

Very respectfully, yours,

ANDREW JOHNSON.

SECOND ANNUAL MESSAGE.

WASHINGTON, *December 3, 1866.*

Fellow-Citizens of the Senate and House of Representatives:

After a brief interval the Congress of the United States resumes its annual legislative labors. An all-wise and merciful Providence has abated the pestilence which visited our shores, leaving its calamitous traces upon some portions of our country. Peace, order, tranquillity, and civil authority have been formally declared to exist throughout the whole of the United States. In all of the States civil authority has superseded the coercion of arms, and the people, by their voluntary action, are maintaining their governments in full activity and complete operation. The enforcement of the laws is no longer "obstructed in any State by combinations too powerful to be suppressed by the ordinary course of judicial proceedings," and the animosities engendered by the war are rapidly yielding to the beneficent influences of our free institutions and to the kindly effects of unrestricted social and commercial intercourse. An entire restoration of fraternal feeling must be the earnest wish of every patriotic heart; and we will have accomplished our grandest national achievement when, forgetting the sad events of the past and remembering only their instructive lessons, we resume our onward career as a free, prosperous, and united people.

In my message of the 4th of December, 1865, Congress was informed of the measures which had been instituted by the Executive with a view to the gradual restoration of the States in which the insurrection occurred to their relations with the General Government. Provisional governors had been appointed, conventions called, governors elected, legislatures assembled, and Senators and Representatives chosen to the Congress of the United States. Courts had been opened for the enforcement of laws long in abeyance. The blockade had been removed, custom-houses reestablished, and the internal-revenue laws put in force, in order that the people might contribute to the national income. Postal operations had been renewed, and efforts were being made to restore them to their former condition of efficiency. The States themselves had been asked to take part in the high function of amending the Constitution, and of thus sanctioning the extinction of African slavery as one of the legitimate results of our internecine struggle.

Having progressed thus far, the executive department found that it had accomplished nearly all that was within the scope of its constitutional authority. One thing, however, yet remained to be done before the work of restoration could be completed, and that was the admission to Congress of loyal Senators and Representatives from the States whose people had rebelled against the lawful authority of the General Government. This question devolved upon the respective Houses, which by the Constitution are made the judges of the elections, returns, and qualifications of their own members, and its consideration at once engaged the attention of Congress.

In the meantime the executive department—no other plan having been proposed by Congress—continued its efforts to perfect, as far as was practicable, the restoration of the proper relations between the citizens of the respective States, the States, and the Federal Government, extending from time to time, as the public interests seemed to require, the judicial, revenue, and postal systems of the country. With the advice and consent of the Senate, the necessary officers were appointed and appropriations made by Congress for the payment of their salaries. The proposition to amend the Federal Constitution, so as to prevent the existence of slavery within the United States or any place subject to their jurisdiction, was ratified by the requisite number of States, and on the 18th day of December, 1865, it was officially declared to have become valid as a part of the Constitution of the United States. All of the States in which the insurrection had existed promptly amended their constitutions so as to make them conform to the great change thus effected in the organic law of the land; declared null and void all ordinances and laws of secession; repudiated all pretended debts and obligations created for the revolutionary purposes of the insurrection, and proceeded in good faith to the enactment of measures for the protection and amelioration of the condition of the colored race. Congress, however, yet hesitated to admit any of these States to representation, and it was not until toward the close of the eighth month of the session that an exception was made in favor of Tennessee by the admission of her Senators and Representatives.

I deem it a subject of profound regret that Congress has thus far failed to admit to seats loyal Senators and Representatives from the other States whose inhabitants, with those of Tennessee, had engaged in the rebellion. Ten States—more than one-fourth of the whole number— remain without representation; the seats of fifty members in the House of Representatives and of twenty members in the Senate are yet vacant, not by their own consent, not by a failure of election, but by the refusal of Congress to accept their credentials. Their admission, it is believed, would have accomplished much toward the renewal and strengthening of our relations as one people and removed serious cause for discontent on the part of the inhabitants of those States. It would have accorded with the great principle enunciated in the Declaration of American Independence that no people ought to bear the burden of taxation and yet be denied the right of representation. It would have been in consonance with the express provisions of the Constitution that "each State shall have at least one Representative" and "that no State, without its consent, shall be deprived of its equal suffrage in the Senate." These provisions were intended to secure to every State and to the people of every

State the right of representation in each House of Congress; and so important was it deemed by the framers of the Constitution that the equality of the States in the Senate should be preserved that not even by an amendment of the Constitution can any State, without its consent, be denied a voice in that branch of the National Legislature.

It is true it has been assumed that the existence of the States was terminated by the rebellious acts of their inhabitants, and that, the insurrection having been suppressed, they were thenceforward to be considered merely as conquered territories. The legislative, executive, and judicial departments of the Government have, however, with great distinctness and uniform consistency, refused to sanction an assumption so incompatible with the nature of our republican system and with the professed objects of the war. Throughout the recent legislation of Congress the undeniable fact makes itself apparent that these ten political communities are nothing less than States of this Union. At the very commencement of the rebellion each House declared, with a unanimity as remarkable as it was significant, that the war was not "waged upon our part in any spirit of oppression, nor for any purpose of conquest or subjugation, nor purpose of overthrowing or interfering with the rights or established institutions of those States, but to defend and maintain the supremacy of the Constitution and all laws made in pursuance thereof, and to preserve the Union, with all the dignity, equality, and rights of the several States unimpaired; and that as soon as these objects" were "accomplished the war ought to cease." In some instances Senators were permitted to continue their legislative functions, while in other instances Representatives were elected and admitted to seats after their States had formally declared their right to withdraw from the Union and were endeavoring to maintain that right by force of arms. All of the States whose people were in insurrection, as States, were included in the apportionment of the direct tax of $20,000,000 annually laid upon the United States by the act approved 5th August, 1861. Congress, by the act of March 4, 1862, and by the apportionment of representation thereunder also recognized their presence as States in the Union; and they have, for judicial purposes, been divided into districts, as States alone can be divided. The same recognition appears in the recent legislation in reference to Tennessee, which evidently rests upon the fact that the functions of the State were not destroyed by the rebellion, but merely suspended; and that principle is of course applicable to those States which, like Tennessee, attempted to renounce their places in the Union.

The action of the executive department of the Government upon this subject has been equally definite and uniform, and the purpose of the war was specifically stated in the proclamation issued by my predecessor on the 22d day of September, 1862. It was then solemnly proclaimed and declared "that hereafter, as heretofore, the war will be prosecuted for the object of practically restoring the constitutional relation between the

United States and each of the States and the people thereof in which States that relation is or may be suspended or disturbed."

The recognition of the States by the judicial department of the Government has also been clear and conclusive in all proceedings affecting them as States had in the Supreme, circuit, and district courts.

In the admission of Senators and Representatives from any and all of the States there can be no just ground of apprehension that persons who are disloyal will be clothed with the powers of legislation, for this could not happen when the Constitution and the laws are enforced by a vigilant and faithful Congress. Each House is made the "judge of the elections, returns, and qualifications of its own members," and may, "with the concurrence of two-thirds, expel a member." When a Senator or Representative presents his certificate of election, he may at once be admitted or rejected; or, should there be any question as to his eligibility, his credentials may be referred for investigation to the appropriate committee. If admitted to a seat, it must be upon evidence satisfactory to the House of which he thus becomes a member that he possesses the requisite constitutional and legal qualifications. If refused admission as a member for want of due allegiance to the Government and returned to his constituents, they are admonished that none but persons loyal to the United States will be allowed a voice in the legislative councils of the nation, and the political power and moral influence of Congress are thus effectively exerted in the interests of loyalty to the Government and fidelity to the Union. Upon this question, so vitally affecting the restoration of the Union and the permanency of our present form of government, my convictions, heretofore expressed, have undergone no change, but, on the contrary, their correctness has been confirmed by reflection and time. If the admission of loyal members to seats in the respective Houses of Congress was wise and expedient a year ago, it is no less wise and expedient now. If this anomalous condition is right now—if in the exact condition of these States at the present time it is lawful to exclude them from representation—I do not see that the question will be changed by the efflux of time. Ten years hence, if these States remain as they are, the right of representation will be no stronger, the right of exclusion will be no weaker.

The Constitution of the United States makes it the duty of the President to recommend to the consideration of Congress "such measures as he shall judge necessary and expedient." I know of no measure more imperatively demanded by every consideration of national interest, sound policy, and equal justice than the admission of loyal members from the now unrepresented States. This would consummate the work of restoration and exert a most salutary influence in the reestablishment of peace, harmony, and fraternal feeling. It would tend greatly to renew the confidence of the American people in the vigor and stability of their institutions. It would bind us more closely together as a nation and enable us to show to the world the inherent and recuperative power of a government founded upon the will of the people and established upon the principles of liberty, justice, and intelligence. Our increased strength and enhanced prosperity would irrefragably demonstrate the fallacy of the arguments against free institutions drawn from our recent national disorders by the enemies of republican government. The admission of loyal members from the States now excluded from Congress, by allaying doubt and apprehension, would turn capital now awaiting an opportunity for investment into the channels of trade and industry. It would alleviate the present troubled condition of those States, and by inducing emigration aid in the settlement of fertile regions now uncultivated and lead to an increased production of those staples which have added so greatly to the wealth of the nation and commerce of the world. New fields of enterprise would be opened to our progressive people and soon the devastations of war would be repaired and all traces of our domestic differences effaced from the minds of our countrymen.

In our efforts to preserve "the unity of government which constitutes us one people" by restoring the States to the condition which they held prior to the rebellion, we should be cautious, lest, having rescued our nation from perils of threatened disintegration, we resort to consolidation, and in the end absolute despotism, as a remedy for the recurrence of similar troubles. The war having terminated, and with it all occasion for the exercise of powers of doubtful constitutionality, we should hasten to bring legislation within the boundaries prescribed by the Constitution and to return to the ancient landmarks established by our fathers for the guidance of succeeding generations.

The constitution which at any time exists till changed by an explicit and authentic act of the whole people is sacredly obligatory upon all. * * * If in the opinion of the people the distribution or modification of the constitutional powers be in any particular wrong, let it be corrected by an amendment in the way which the Constitution designates; but let there be no change by usurpation, for * * * it is the customary weapon by which free governments are destroyed.

Washington spoke these words to his countrymen when, followed by their love and gratitude, he voluntarily retired from the cares of public life. "To keep in all things within the pale of our constitutional powers and cherish the Federal Union as the only rock of safety" were prescribed by Jefferson as rules of action to endear to his "countrymen the true principles of their Constitution and promote a union of sentiment and action, equally auspicious to their happiness and safety." Jackson held that the action of the General Government should always be strictly confined to the sphere of its appropriate duties, and justly and forcibly urged that our Government is not to be maintained nor our Union preserved "by invasions of the rights and powers of the several States. In thus attempting to make our General Government strong we make it weak. Its true strength consists in leaving individuals and States as much as possible to themselves; in making itself felt, not in its power, but in its beneficence; not in its control, but in its protection; not in binding the States more closely to the center, but leaving each to move unobstructed in its proper constitutional orbit." These are the teachings of men whose deeds and services have made them illustrious, and who, long since withdrawn from the scenes of life, have left to their country the rich legacy of their example, their wisdom, and their patriotism. Drawing fresh inspiration from their lessons, let us emulate them in love of country and respect for the Constitution and the laws.

The report of the Secretary of the Treasury affords much information respecting the revenue and commerce of the country. His views upon the currency and with reference to a proper adjustment of our revenue system, internal as well as impost, are commended to the careful consideration of Congress. In my last annual message I expressed my general views upon these subjects. I need now only call attention to the necessity of carrying into every department of the Government a system of rigid accountability, thorough retrenchment, and wise economy. With no exceptional nor unusual expenditures, the oppressive burdens of taxation can be lessened by such a modification of our revenue laws as will be consistent with the public faith and the legitimate and necessary wants of the Government.

The report presents a much more satisfactory condition of our finances than one year ago the most sanguine could have anticipated. During the fiscal year ending the 30th June, 1865 (the last year of the war), the public debt was increased $941,902,537, and on the 31st of October, 1865, it amounted to $2,740,854,750. On the 31st day of October, 1866, it had been reduced to $2,551,310,006, the diminution during a period of fourteen months, commencing September 1, 1865, and ending October 31, 1866, having been $206,379,565. In the last annual report on the state of the finances it was estimated that during the three quarters of the fiscal year ending the 30th of June last the debt would be increased $112,194,947. During that period, however, it was reduced $31,196,387, the receipts of the year having been $89,905,905 more and the expenditures $200,529,235 less than the estimates. Nothing could more clearly indicate than these statements the extent and availability of the national resources and the rapidity and safety with which, under our form of government, great military and naval establishments can be disbanded and expenses reduced from a war to a peace footing.

During the fiscal year ending June 30, 1866, the receipts were $558,-032,620 and the expenditures $520,750,940, leaving an available surplus of $37,281,680. It is estimated that the receipts for the fiscal year ending the 30th June, 1867, will be $475,061,386, and that the expenditures will reach the sum of $316,428,078, leaving in the Treasury a surplus of $158,633,308. For the fiscal year ending June 30, 1886, it is estimated that the receipts will amount to $436,000,000 and that the expenditures will be $350,247,641, showing an excess of $85,752,359 in favor of the Government. These estimated receipts may be diminished by a reduction of excise and import duties, but after all necessary reductions shall have been made the revenue of the present and of following years will doubtless be sufficient to cover all legitimate charges upon the Treasury and leave a large annual surplus to be applied to the payment of the principal of the debt. There seems now to be no good reason why taxes may not be reduced as the country advances in population and wealth, and yet the debt be extinguished within the next quarter of a century.

The report of the Secretary of War furnishes valuable and important information in reference to the operations of his Department during the past year. Few volunteers now remain in the service, and they are being discharged as rapidly as they can be replaced by regular troops. The Army has been promptly paid, carefully provided with medical treatment, well sheltered and subsisted, and is to be furnished with breech-loading small arms. The military strength of the nation has been unimpaired by the discharge of volunteers, the disposition of unserviceable or perishable stores, and the retrenchment of expenditure. Sufficient war material to meet any emergency has been retained, and from the disbanded volunteers standing ready to respond to the national call large armies can be rapidly organized, equipped, and concentrated. Fortifications on the coast and frontier have received or are being prepared for more powerful armaments; lake surveys and harbor and river improvements are in course of energetic prosecution. Preparations have been made for the payment of the additional bounties authorized during the recent session of Congress, under such regulations as will protect the Government from fraud and secure to the honorably discharged soldier the well-earned reward of his faithfulness and gallantry. More than 6,000 maimed soldiers have received artificial limbs or other surgical apparatus, and 41 national cemeteries, containing the remains of 104,526 Union soldiers, have already been established. The total estimate of military appropriations is $25,205,669.

It is stated in the report of the Secretary of the Navy that the naval force at this time consists of 278 vessels, armed with 2,351 guns. Of these, 115 vessels, carrying 1,029 guns, are in commission, distributed chiefly among seven squadrons. The number of men in the service is 13,600. Great activity and vigilance have been displayed by all the squadrons, and their movements have been judiciously and efficiently arranged in such manner as would best promote American commerce and protect the rights and interests of our countrymen abroad. The vessels unemployed are undergoing repairs or are laid up until their services may be required. Most of the ironclad fleet is at League Island, in the vicinity of Philadelphia, a place which, until decisive action should be taken by Congress, was selected by the Secretary of the Navy as the most eligible location for that class of vessels. It is important that a suitable public station should be provided for the ironclad fleet. It is intended that these vessels shall be in proper condition for any emergency, and it is desirable that the bill accepting League Island for naval purposes, which passed the House of Representatives at its last session, should receive final action at an early period, in order that there may be a suitable public station for this class of vessels, as well as a navy-yard of area sufficient for the wants of the service on the Delaware River. The naval pension fund amounts to $11,750,000, having been increased $2,750,000 during the year. The expenditures of the Department for the fiscal year ending 30th June last were $43,324,526, and the estimates for the coming year amount to $23,568,436. Attention is invited to the condition of our seamen and the importance of legislative measures for their relief and improvement. The suggestions in behalf of this deserving class of our fellow-citizens are earnestly recommended to the favorable attention of Congress.

The report of the Postmaster-General presents a most satisfactory condition of the postal service and submits recommendations which deserve the consideration of Congress. The revenues of the Department for the year ending June 30, 1866, were $14,386,986 and the expenditures $15,352,079, showing an excess of the latter of $965,093. In anticipation of this deficiency, however, a special appropriation was made by Congress in the act approved July 28, 1866. Including the standing appropriation of $700,000 for free mail matter as a legitimate portion of the revenues, yet remaining unexpended, the actual deficiency for the past year is only $265,093—a sum within $51,141 of the amount estimated in the annual report of 1864. The decrease of revenue compared with the previous year was $1\frac{1}{5}$ per cent, and the increase of expenditures, owing principally to the enlargement of the mail service in the South, was 12 per cent. On the 30th of June last there were in operation 6,930 mail routes, with an aggregate length of 180,921 miles, an aggregate annual transportation of 71,837,914 miles, and an aggregate annual cost, including all expenditures, of $8,410,184. The length of railroad routes is 32,092 miles and the annual transportation 30,609,467 miles. The length of steamboat routes is 14,346 miles and the annual transportation 3,411,962 miles. The mail service is rapidly increasing throughout the whole country, and its steady extension in the Southern States indicates their constantly improving condition. The growing importance of the foreign service also merits attention. The post-office department of Great Britain and our own have agreed upon a preliminary basis for a new postal convention, which it is believed will prove eminently beneficial to the commercial interests of the United States, inasmuch as it contemplates a reduction of the international letter postage to one-half the existing rates; a reduction of postage with all other countries to and from which correspondence is transmitted in the British mail, or in closed mails through the United Kingdom; the establishment of uniform and reasonable charges for the sea and territorial transit of correspondence in closed mails; and an allowance to each post-office department of the right to use all mail communications established under the authority of the other for the dispatch of correspondence, either in open or closed mails, on the same terms as those applicable to the inhabitants of the country providing the means of transmission.

The report of the Secretary of the Interior exhibits the condition of those branches of the public service which are committed to his supervision. During the last fiscal year 4,629,312 acres of public land were disposed of, 1,892,516 acres of which were entered under the homestead act. The policy originally adopted relative to the public lands has undergone essential modifications. Immediate revenue, and not their rapid settlement, was the cardinal feature of our land system. Long experience and earnest discussion have resulted in the conviction that the early development of our agricultural resources and the diffusion of an energetic population over our vast territory are objects of far greater importance to the national growth and prosperity than the proceeds of the sale of the land to the highest bidder in open market. The preemption laws confer upon the pioneer who complies with the terms they impose the privilege of purchasing a limited portion of "unoffered lands" at the minimum price. The homestead enactments relieve the settler from the payment of purchase money, and secure him a permanent home upon the condition of residence for a term of years. This liberal policy invites emigration from the Old and from the more crowded portions of the New World. Its propitious results are undoubted, and will be more signally manifested when time shall have given to it a wider development.

Congress has made liberal grants of public land to corporations in aid of the construction of railroads and other internal improvements. Should this policy hereafter prevail, more stringent provisions will be required to secure a faithful application of the fund. The title to the lands should not pass, by patent or otherwise, but remain in the Government and subject to its control until some portion of the road has been actually built. Portions of them might then from time to time be conveyed to the corporation, but never in a greater ratio to the whole quantity embraced by the grant than the completed parts bear to the entire length of the projected improvement. This restriction would not operate to the prejudice of any undertaking conceived in good faith and executed with reasonable energy, as it is the settled practice to withdraw from market the lands falling within the operation of such grants, and thus to exclude the inception of a subsequent adverse right. A breach of the conditions which Congress may deem proper to impose should work a forfeiture of claim to the lands so withdrawn but unconveyed, and of title to the lands conveyed which remain unsold.

Operations on the several lines of the Pacific Railroad have been prosecuted with unexampled vigor and success. Should no unforeseen causes of delay occur, it is confidently anticipated that this great thoroughfare will be completed before the expiration of the period designated by Congress.

During the last fiscal year the amount paid to pensioners, including the expenses of disbursement, was $13,459,996, and 50,177 names were added to the pension rolls. The entire number of pensioners June 30, 1866, was 126,722. This fact furnishes melancholy and striking proof of the sacrifices made to vindicate the constitutional authority of the Federal Government and to maintain inviolate the integrity of the Union. They impose upon us corresponding obligations. It is estimated that $33,000,000 will be required to meet the exigencies of this branch of the service during the next fiscal year.

Treaties have been concluded with the Indians, who, enticed into armed opposition to our Government at the outbreak of the rebellion, have unconditionally submitted to our authority and manifested an earnest desire for a renewal of friendly relations.

During the year ending September 30, 1866, 8,716 patents for useful inventions and designs were issued, and at that date the balance in the Treasury to the credit of the patent fund was $228,297.

As a subject upon which depends an immense amount of the production and commerce of the country, I recommend to Congress such legislation as may be necessary for the preservation of the levees of the Mississippi River. It is a matter of national importance that early steps should be taken, not only to add to the efficiency of these barriers against destructive inundations, but for the removal of all obstructions to the free and safe navigation of that great channel of trade and commerce.

The District of Columbia under existing laws is not entitled to that representation in the national councils which from our earliest history has been uniformly accorded to each Territory established from time to time within our limits. It maintains peculiar relations to Congress, to whom the Constitution has granted the power of exercising exclusive legislation over the seat of Government. Our fellow-citizens residing in the District, whose interests are thus confided to the special guardianship of Congress, exceed in number the population of several of our Territories, and no just reason is perceived why a Delegate of their choice should not be admitted to a seat in the House of Representatives. No mode seems so appropriate and effectual of enabling them to make known their peculiar condition and wants and of securing the local legislation adapted to them. I therefore recommend the passage of a law authorizing the electors of the District of Columbia to choose a Delegate, to be allowed the same rights and privileges as a Delegate representing a Territory. The increasing enterprise and rapid progress of improvement in the District are highly gratifying, and I trust that the efforts of the municipal authorities to promote the prosperity of the national metropolis will receive the efficient and generous cooperation of Congress.

The report of the Commissioner of Agriculture reviews the operations of his Department during the past year, and asks the aid of Congress in its efforts to encourage those States which, scourged by war, are now earnestly engaged in the reorganization of domestic industry.

It is a subject of congratulation that no foreign combinations against our domestic peace and safety or our legitimate influence among the nations have been formed or attempted. While sentiments of reconciliation, loyalty, and patriotism have increased at home, a more just consideration of our national character and rights has been manifested by foreign nations.

The entire success of the Atlantic telegraph between the coast of Ireland and the Province of Newfoundland is an achievement which has been justly celebrated in both hemispheres as the opening of an era in the progress of civilization. There is reason to expect that equal success will attend and even greater results follow the enterprise for connecting the two continents through the Pacific Ocean by the projected line of telegraph between Kamchatka and the Russian possessions in America.

The resolution of Congress protesting against pardons by foreign governments of persons convicted of infamous offenses on condition of emigration to our country has been communicated to the states with which we maintain intercourse, and the practice, so justly the subject of complaint on our part, has not been renewed.

The congratulations of Congress to the Emperor of Russia upon his escape from attempted assassination have been presented to that humane and enlightened ruler and received by him with expressions of grateful appreciation.

The Executive, warned of an attempt by Spanish American adventurers to induce the emigration of freedmen of the United States to a foreign country, protested against the project as one which, if consummated, would reduce them to a bondage even more oppressive than that from which they have just been relieved. Assurance has been received from the Government of the State in which the plan was matured that the proceeding will meet neither its encouragement nor approval. It is a question worthy of your consideration whether our laws upon this subject are adequate to the prevention or punishment of the crime thus meditated.

In the month of April last, as Congress is aware, a friendly arrangement was made between the Emperor of France and the President of the United States for the withdrawal from Mexico of the French expeditionary military forces. This withdrawal was to be effected in three detachments, the first of which, it was understood, would leave Mexico in November, now past, the second in March next, and the third and last in November, 1867. Immediately upon the completion of the evacuation the French Government was to assume the same attitude of nonintervention in regard to Mexico as is held by the Government of the United

States. Repeated assurances have been given by the Emperor since that agreement that he would complete the promised evacuation within the period mentioned, or sooner.

It was reasonably expected that the proceedings thus contemplated would produce a crisis of great political interest in the Republic of Mexico. The newly appointed minister of the United States, Mr. Campbell, was therefore sent forward on the 9th day of November last to assume his proper functions as minister plenipotentiary of the United States to that Republic. It was also thought expedient that he should be attended in the vicinity of Mexico by the Lieutenant-General of the Army of the United States, with the view of obtaining such information as might be important to determine the course to be pursued by the United States in reestablishing and maintaining necessary and proper intercourse with the Republic of Mexico. Deeply interested in the cause of liberty and humanity, it seemed an obvious duty on our part to exercise whatever influence we possessed for the restoration and permanent establishment in that country of a domestic and republican form of government.

Such was the condition of our affairs in regard to Mexico when, on the 22d of November last, official information was received from Paris that the Emperor of France had some time before decided not to withdraw a detachment of his forces in the month of November past, according to engagement, but that this decision was made with the purpose of withdrawing the whole of those forces in the ensuing spring. Of this determination, however, the United States had not received any notice or intimation, and so soon as the information was received by the Government care was taken to make known its dissent to the Emperor of France.

I can not forego the hope that France will reconsider the subject and adopt some resolution in regard to the evacuation of Mexico which will conform as nearly as practicable with the existing engagement, and thus meet the just expectations of the United States. The papers relating to the subject will be laid before you. It is believed that with the evacuation of Mexico by the expeditionary forces no subject for serious differences between France and the United States would remain. The expressions of the Emperor and people of France warrant a hope that the traditionary friendship between the two countries might in that case be renewed and permanently restored.

A claim of a citizen of the United States for indemnity for spoliations committed on the high seas by the French authorities in the exercise of a belligerent power against Mexico has been met by the Government of France with a proposition to defer settlement until a mutual convention for the adjustment of all claims of citizens and subjects of both countries arising out of the recent wars on this continent shall be agreed upon by the two countries. The suggestion is not deemed unreasonable, but it belongs to Congress to direct the manner in which claims for indemnity by foreigners as well as by citizens of the United States arising out of the late civil war shall be adjudicated and determined. I have no doubt that the subject of all such claims will engage your attention at a convenient and proper time.

It is a matter of regret that no considerable advance has been made toward an adjustment of the differences between the United States and Great Britain arising out of the depredations upon our national commerce and other trespasses committed during our civil war by British subjects, in violation of international law and treaty obligations. The delay, however, may be believed to have resulted in no small degree from the domestic situation of Great Britain. An entire change of ministry occurred in that country during the last session of Parliament. The attention of the new ministry was called to the subject at an early day, and there is some reason to expect that it will now be considered in a becoming and friendly spirit. The importance of an early disposition of the question can not be exaggerated. Whatever might be the wishes of the two Governments, it is manifest that good will and friendship between the two countries can not be established until a reciprocity in the practice of good faith and neutrality shall be restored between the respective nations.

On the 6th of June last, in violation of our neutrality laws, a military expedition and enterprise against the British North American colonies was projected and attempted to be carried on within the territory and jurisdiction of the United States. In obedience to the obligation imposed upon the Executive by the Constitution to see that the laws are faithfully executed, all citizens were warned by proclamation against taking part in or aiding such unlawful proceedings, and the proper civil, military, and naval officers were directed to take all necessary measures for the enforcement of the laws. The expedition failed, but it has not been without its painful consequences. Some of our citizens who, it was alleged, were engaged in the expedition were captured, and have been brought to trial as for a capital offense in the Province of Canada. Judgment and sentence of death have been pronounced against some, while others have been acquitted. Fully believing in the maxim of government that severity of civil punishment for misguided persons who have engaged in revolutionary attempts which have disastrously failed is unsound and unwise, such representations have been made to the British Government in behalf of the convicted persons as, being sustained by an enlightened and humane judgment, will, it is hoped, induce in their cases an exercise of clemency and a judicious amnesty to all who were engaged in the movement. Counsel has been employed by the Government to defend citizens of the United States on trial for capital offenses in Canada, and a discontinuance of the prosecutions which were instituted in the courts of the United States against those who took part in the expedition has been directed.

I have regarded the expedition as not only political in its nature, but as also in a great measure foreign from the United States in its causes, character, and objects. The attempt was understood to be made in sympathy with an insurgent party in Ireland, and by striking at a British Province on this continent was designed to aid in obtaining redress for political grievances which, it was assumed, the people of Ireland had suffered at the hands of the British Government during a period of several centuries. The persons engaged in it were chiefly natives of that country, some of whom had, while others had not, become citizens of the United States under our general laws of naturalization. Complaints of misgovernment in Ireland continually engage the attention of the British nation, and so great an agitation is now prevailing in Ireland that the British Government have deemed it necessary to suspend the writ of *habeas corpus* in that country. These circumstances must necessarily modify the opinion which we might otherwise have entertained in regard to an expedition expressly prohibited by our neutrality laws. So long as those laws remain upon our statute books they should be faithfully executed, and if they operate harshly, unjustly, or oppressively Congress alone can apply the remedy by their modification or repeal.

Political and commercial interests of the United States are not unlikely to be affected in some degree by events which are transpiring in the eastern regions of Europe, and the time seems to have come when our Government ought to have a proper diplomatic representation in Greece.

This Government has claimed for all persons not convicted or accused or suspected of crime an absolute political right of self-expatriation and a choice of new national allegiance. Most of the European States have dissented from this principle, and have claimed a right to hold such of their subjects as have emigrated to and been naturalized in the United States and afterwards returned on transient visits to their native countries to the performance of military service in like manner as resident subjects. Complaints arising from the claim in this respect made by foreign states have heretofore been matters of controversy between the United States and some of the European powers, and the irritation consequent upon the failure to settle this question increased during the war in which Prussia, Italy, and Austria were recently engaged. While Great Britain has never acknowledged the right of expatriation, she has not for some years past practically insisted upon the opposite doctrine. France has been equally forbearing, and Prussia has proposed a compromise, which, although evincing increased liberality, has not been accepted by the United States. Peace is now prevailing everywhere in Europe, and the present seems to be a favorable time for an assertion by Congress of the principle so long maintained by the executive department that naturalization by one state fully exempts the native-born subject of any other state from the performance of military service under any foreign government, so long as he does not voluntarily renounce its rights and benefits.

In the performance of a duty imposed upon me by the Constitution I have thus submitted to the representatives of the States and of the people such information of our domestic and foreign affairs as the public interests seem to require. Our Government is now undergoing its most trying ordeal, and my earnest prayer is that the peril may be successfully and finally passed without impairing its original strength and symmetry. The interests of the nation are best to be promoted by the revival of fraternal relations, the complete obliteration of our past differences, and the reinauguration of all the pursuits of peace. Directing our efforts to the early accomplishment of these great ends, let us endeavor to preserve harmony between the coordinate departments of the Government, that each in its proper sphere may cordially cooperate with the other in securing the maintenance of the Constitution, the preservation of the Union, and the perpetuity of our free institutions.

ANDREW JOHNSON.

SPECIAL MESSAGES.

WASHINGTON, *December 8, 1866.*

To the House of Representatives:

In reply to a resolution of the House of Representatives of the 5th instant, inquiring if any portion of Mexican territory has been occupied by United States troops, I transmit the accompanying report upon the subject from the Secretary of War.

ANDREW JOHNSON.

WASHINGTON, *December 8, 1866.*

To the House of Representatives:

I have the honor to communicate a report of the Secretary of State relating to the discovery and arrest of John H. Surratt.

ANDREW JOHNSON.

WASHINGTON, D. C., *December 11, 1866.*

To the House of Representatives:

I transmit herewith reports from the Secretary of War and the Attorney-General, in compliance with a resolution of the 3d instant, requesting the President to communicate to the House, "if not in his opinion incompatible with the public interests, the information asked for in a resolution of this House dated the 23d June last, and which resolution he has up to this time failed to answer, as to whether any application has been made to him for the pardon of G. E. Pickett, who acted as a major-general of the rebel forces in the late war for the suppression of insurrection, and, if so, what has been the action thereon; and also to communicate copies of all papers, entries, indorsements, and other documentary evidence in relation to any proceeding in connection with such application; and that he also inform this House whether, since the adjournment at Raleigh, N. C., on the 30th of March last, of the last board or court of inquiry convened to investigate the facts attending the hanging of a number of United States soldiers for alleged desertion from the rebel army, any further measures have been taken to bring the said Pickett or other perpetrators of that crime to punishment.''

In transmitting the accompanying papers containing the information requested by the House of Representatives it is proper to state that, instead of bearing date the 23d of June last, the first resolution was dated the 23d of July, and was received by the Executive only four days before the termination of the session.

ANDREW JOHNSON.

WASHINGTON, *December 14, 1866.*

To the Senate and House of Representatives:

I communicate a translation of a letter of the 17th of August last addressed to me by His Majesty Alexander, Emperor of Russia, in reply to the joint resolution of Congress approved on the 16th day of May, 1866, relating to the attempted assassination of the Emperor, a certified copy of which was, in compliance with the request of Congress, forwarded to His Majesty by the hands of Gustavus V. Fox, late Assistant Secretary of the Navy of the United States.

ANDREW JOHNSON.

WASHINGTON, *December 15, 1866.*

To the House of Representatives:

I transmit herewith a report from the Secretary of the Interior, in answer to a resolution of the House of Representatives of the 10th instant, in relation to the Atchison and Pikes Peak Railroad Company.

ANDREW JOHNSON.

WASHINGTON, *December 20, 1866.*

To the House of Representatives:

In compliance with the resolution of the House of Representatives of December 4 last, requesting information ''relating to the attempt of Santa Anna and Ortega to organize armed expeditions within the United States for the purpose of overthrowing the National Government of the Republic of Mexico,'' I transmit a report from the Secretary of State and the papers accompanying it.

ANDREW JOHNSON.

WASHINGTON, *December 21, 1866.*

To the House of Representatives:

In answer to a resolution of the House of Representatives of the 19th instant, calling for a copy of certain correspondence relating to the joint occupancy of the island of San Juan, in Washington Territory, I transmit a report from the Secretary of State on the subject.

ANDREW JOHNSON.

WASHINGTON, *January 3, 1867.*

To the House of Representatives:

I have the honor to communicate an additional report of the Secretary of State relating to the discovery and arrest of John H. Surratt.

ANDREW JOHNSON.

WASHINGTON, *January 8, 1867.*

To the House of Representatives:

I transmit herewith a report from the Secretary of War and the accompanying papers, in reply to the resolution of the House of Representatives of the 13th ultimo, requesting copies of all official documents, orders, letters, and papers of every description relative to the trial by a military commission and conviction of Crawford Keys and others for the murder of Emory Smith and others, and to the respite of the sentence in the case of said Crawford Keys or either of his associates, their transfer to Fort Delaware, and subsequent release upon a writ of *habeas corpus.*

ANDREW JOHNSON.

WASHINGTON, *January 8, 1867.*

To the House of Representatives:

I transmit the accompanying report from the Attorney-General as a partial reply to the resolution of the House of Representatives of the 10th ultimo, requesting a "list of names of all persons engaged in the late rebellion against the United States Government who have been pardoned by the President from April 15, 1865, to this date; that said list shall also state the rank of each person who has been so pardoned, if he has been engaged in the military service of the so-called Confederate government, and the position if he shall have held any civil office under said so-called Confederate government; and shall also further state whether such person has at any time prior to April 14, 1861, held any office under the United States Government, and, if so, what office, together with the reasons for granting such pardons and also the names of the person or persons at whose solicitation such pardon was granted."

ANDREW JOHNSON.

WASHINGTON, *January 9, 1867.*

To the House of Representatives:

I transmit herewith a communication from the Secretary of the Navy, in answer to a resolution of the House of the 19th ultimo, requesting a statement of the amounts charged to the State Department since May 1, 1865, for services rendered by naval vessels.

ANDREW JOHNSON.

WASHINGTON, *January 9, 1867.*

To the Senate of the United States:

I transmit herewith a communication from the Secretary of the Navy, with the accompanying documents, in answer to a resolution of the Senate of the 5th ultimo, calling for copies of orders, instructions, and directions issued from that Department in relation to the employment of officers and others in the navy-yards of the United States, and all communications received in relation to employment at the Norfolk Navy-Yard.

ANDREW JOHNSON.

WASHINGTON, *January 10, 1867.*

To the House of Representatives:

I transmit to the House of Representatives, in answer to a resolution of the 17th ultimo, calling for information relative to the revolution in Candia, a report of the Secretary of State, with accompanying documents.

ANDREW JOHNSON.

EXECUTIVE MANSION,
Washington, January 14, 1867.

To the House of Representatives:

In compliance with the resolution of the House of the 19th ultimo, requesting information regarding the occupation of Mexican territory by the troops of the United States, I transmit a report of the Secretary of State and one of the Secretary of War, and the documents by which they were accompanied.

ANDREW JOHNSON.

WASHINGTON, *January 18, 1867.*

To the Senate of the United States:

In compliance with a resolution of the 19th ultimo, requesting certain information in regard to the Universal Exposition to be held at Paris during the present year, I transmit a report from the Secretary of State and the documents to which it refers.

ANDREW JOHNSON.

WASHINGTON, D. C., *January 19, 1867.*

To the House of Representatives:

I herewith communicate a report from the Secretary of the Interior, in answer to a resolution of the House of Representatives of the 16th instant, in relation to the clerks of the Federal courts and the marshal of the United States for the district of North Carolina.

ANDREW JOHNSON.

To the House of Representatives:

I transmit herewith a report from the Secretary of War and the accompanying papers, in compliance with the resolution of the House of Representatives of the 19th ultimo, requesting copies of all papers in possession of the President touching the case of George St. Leger Grenfel.

JANUARY 21, 1867.   ANDREW JOHNSON.

WASHINGTON, *January 23, 1867.*

To the Senate of the United States:

I transmit to the Senate, in answer to their resolution of the 21st instant, a report from the Secretary of State, with accompanying papers.*

ANDREW JOHNSON.

WASHINGTON, *January 28, 1867.*

To the Senate of the United States:

I transmit herewith a report† from the Secretary of State, with accompanying papers, in answer to the Senate's resolution of the 7th instant.

ANDREW JOHNSON.

WASHINGTON, *January 28, 1867.*

To the House of Representatives of the United States:

In compliance with a resolution of the House of Representatives of the 7th instant, in relation to the attempted compromise of certain suits instituted in the English courts in behalf of the United States against Fraser, Trenholm & Co., alleged agents of the so-called Confederate government, I transmit a report from the Secretary of State and the documents by which it was accompanied.

ANDREW JOHNSON.

---

*Correspondence with Mr. Motley, envoy extraordinary and minister plenipotentiary at Vienna, relative to his reported resignation.

†Relating to an alleged emigration of citizens of the United States to the dominions of the Sublime Porte for the purpose of settling and acquiring landed property there.

WASHINGTON, *January 29, 1867.*

To the House of Representatives of the United States:

I transmit herewith a report* from the Secretary of State, in answer to the resolution of the House of Representatives of the 24th instant.

ANDREW JOHNSON.

WASHINGTON, *January 29, 1867.*

To the House of Representatives:

In compliance with the resolution of the House of Representatives of the 12th ultimo and its request of the 28th instant for all correspondence, reports, and information in my possession in relation to the riot which occurred in the city of New Orleans on the 30th day of July last, I transmit herewith copies of telegraphic dispatches upon the subject, and reports from the Secretary of War, with the papers accompanying the same.

ANDREW JOHNSON.

WASHINGTON, *January 29, 1867.*

To the House of Representatives:

In compliance with the resolution of the House of Representatives of the 4th of December last, requesting information upon the present condition of affairs in the Republic of Mexico, and of one of the 18th of the same month, desiring me to communicate to the House of Representatives copies of all correspondence on the subject of the evacuation of Mexico by the French troops not before officially published, I transmit a report from the Secretary of State and the papers accompanying it.

ANDREW JOHNSON.

WASHINGTON, *January 31, 1867.*

To the House of Representatives:

I transmit herewith reports from the heads of the several Executive Departments, containing the information in reference to appointments to office requested in the resolution adopted by the House of Representatives on the 6th of December last.

ANDREW JOHNSON.

EXECUTIVE MANSION, *January 31, 1867.*

To the House of Representatives:

I transmit herewith a report by the Secretary of War of January 30, containing the information asked for in a resolution of the House of

---

*Stating that the Department of State has received no information concerning the removal of the Protestant Church or religious assembly meeting at the American embassy from the city of Rome by an order of that Government.

Representatives of January 25, 1867, hereto annexed, respecting the execution of "An act providing for the appointment of a commissioner to examine and report upon certain claims of the State of Iowa," approved July 25, 1866.

ANDREW JOHNSON.

WASHINGTON, *January 31, 1867.*

To the Senate of the United States:

The accompanying reports from the heads of the several Executive Departments of the Government are submitted in compliance with a resolution of the Senate dated the 12th ultimo, inquiring whether any person appointed to an office required by law to be filled by and with the advice and consent of the Senate, and who was commissioned during the recess of the Senate, previous to the assembling of the present Congress, to fill a vacancy, has been continued in such office and permitted to discharge its functions, either by the granting of a new commission or otherwise, since the end of the session of the Senate on the 28th day of July last, without the submission of the name of such person to the Senate for its confirmation; and particularly whether a surveyor or naval officer of the port of Philadelphia has thus been continued in office without the consent of the Senate, and, if any such officer has performed the duties of that office, whether he has received any salary or compensation therefor.

ANDREW JOHNSON.

WASHINGTON, *February 1, 1867.*

To the Senate of the United States:

I herewith lay before the Senate, for its constitutional action thereon, a treaty concluded the 29th day of August, 1866, between Alexander Cummings, governor of Colorado Territory and *ex officio* superintendent of Indian affairs, Hon. A. C. Hunt, and D. C. Oakes, United States Indian agent, duly authorized and appointed as commissioners for the purpose, and the chiefs and warriors of the Uintah Jampa, or Grand River, bands of Utah Indians.

A letter of the Secretary of the Interior of the 31st of January, with copy of letter from the Commissioner of Indian Affairs of the 28th of January, 1867, together with a map showing the tract of country claimed by said Indians, accompany the treaty.

ANDREW JOHNSON.

WASHINGTON, *February 4, 1867.*

To the Senate of the United States:

In answer to the resolution of the Senate of the 2d instant, requesting the Secretary of State to report what steps have been taken by him to secure to the United States the right to make the necessary surveys for an interoceanic ship canal through the territory of Colombia, I transmit herewith the report of the Secretary of State.

ANDREW JOHNSON.

WASHINGTON, *February 4, 1867.*

To the Senate of the United States:

I herewith communicate a report from the Secretary of the Interior of this date, in answer to a resolution of the Senate of the 31st ultimo, in relation to the deputy marshals, bailiffs, and criers in the District of Columbia who have received compensation for the year 1866.

ANDREW JOHNSON.

WASHINGTON, *February 4, 1867.*

To the Senate of the United States:

I transmit a report of the Secretary of the Treasury, in answer to a resolution of the Senate of the 31st ultimo, on the subject of a treaty of reciprocity with the Hawaiian Islands.

ANDREW JOHNSON.

WASHINGTON, *February 5, 1867.*

To the Senate of the United States:

I transmit herewith, in answer to the Senate's resolution of the 2d instant, a report from the Secretary of State, with an accompanying document.*

ANDREW JOHNSON.

WASHINGTON, *February 5, 1867.*

To the House of Representatives:

I transmit a report from the Secretary of State, in answer to a resolution of the House of Representatives of yesterday, making inquiry as to the States which have ratified the amendment to the Constitution proposed by the Thirty-ninth Congress.

ANDREW JOHNSON.

WASHINGTON, *February 7, 1867.*

To the House of Representatives:

In answer to the resolution of the House of Representatives of the 4th instant, requesting me to communicate to that body any official correspondence which may have taken place with regard to the visit of Professor Agassiz to Brazil, I transmit herewith the report of the Secretary of State and the papers accompanying it.

ANDREW JOHNSON.

*Copy of the letter on which the Secretary of State founded his inquiries addressed to Mr. Motley, United States minister at Vienna, with regard to his reported conversation and opinions.

WASHINGTON, *February 7, 1867.*

To the House of Representatives:

I herewith communicate a report of the Secretary of the Interior, in answer to a resolution of the House of Representatives of the 22d ultimo, requesting information relative to the condition, occupancy, and area of the Hot Springs Reservation, in the State of Arkansas.

ANDREW JOHNSON.

WASHINGTON, *February 9, 1867.*

To the Senate of the United States:

I transmit herewith, in answer to the Senate's resolution of the 7th instant, a report* from the Secretary of State, with an accompanying document.

ANDREW JOHNSON.

WASHINGTON, *February 11, 1867.*

To the Senate of the United States:

In compliance with the resolution of the Senate of the 6th of February, 1867, requesting me to transmit copies of all correspondence not heretofore communicated on the subject of grants to American citizens for railroad and telegraph lines across the territory of the Republic of Mexico, I submit herewith the report of the Secretary of State and the papers accompanying it.

ANDREW JOHNSON.

WASHINGTON, *February 16, 1867.*

To the House of Representatives:

I transmit a report from the Secretary of State, in answer to a resolution of the House of Representatives of yesterday, making further inquiry as to the States which have ratified the amendment to the Constitution proposed by the Thirty-ninth Congress.

ANDREW JOHNSON.

WASHINGTON, *February 16, 1867.*

To the Senate of the United States:

In answer to the resolution of the Senate of the 27th of July last, relative to the practicability of establishing equal reciprocal relations between the United States and the British North American Provinces and to the actual condition of the question of the fisheries, I transmit a report on the subject from the Secretary of State, with the papers to which it refers.

ANDREW JOHNSON.

---

*Relating to the reported transfer of the United States minister from Stockholm to Bogota.

WASHINGTON, *February 18, 1867.*

To the Senate of the United States:

I have received a resolution of the Senate dated the 8th day of January last, requesting the President to inform the Senate if any violations of the act entitled ''An act to protect all persons in the United States in their civil rights and furnish the means of their vindication'' have come to his knowledge, and, if so, what steps, if any, have been taken by him to enforce the law and punish the offenders.

Not being cognizant of any cases which came within the purview of the resolution, in order that the inquiry might have the fullest range I referred it to the heads of the several Executive Departments, whose reports are herewith communicated for the information of the Senate.

With the exception of the cases mentioned in the reports of the Secretary of War and the Attorney-General, no violations, real or supposed, of the act to which the resolution refers have at any time come to the knowledge of the Executive. The steps taken in these cases to enforce the law appear in these reports.

The Secretary of War, under date of the 15th instant, submitted a series of reports from the General Commanding the armies of the United States and other military officers as to supposed violations of the act alluded to in the resolution, with the request that they should be referred to the Attorney-General ''for his investigation and report, to the end that the cases may be designated which are cognizant by the civil authorities and such as are cognizant by military tribunals.'' I have directed the reference so to be made.

ANDREW JOHNSON.

WASHINGTON, *February 18, 1867.*

To the House of Representatives:

I transmit a letter of the 26th ultimo, addressed to me by W. F. M. Arny, secretary and acting governor of the Territory of New Mexico, with the memorials to Congress by which it was accompanied, requesting certain appropriations for that Territory. The attention of the House of Representatives is invited to the subject.

ANDREW JOHNSON.

WASHINGTON, *February 19, 1867.*

To the House of Representatives:

I transmit the accompanying reports from the Secretary of the Treasury and the Secretary of War, in answer to the resolution of the House of Representatives of the 28th May last, requesting certain information in regard to captured and forfeited cotton.

ANDREW JOHNSON.

WASHINGTON, *February 20, 1867.*

To the House of Representatives:

I transmit a report from the Secretary of State, giving information of States which have ratified the amendment to the Constitution proposed by the Thirty-ninth Congress in addition to those named in his report which was communicated in my message of the 16th instant, in answer to a resolution of the House of Representatives of the 15th instant.

ANDREW JOHNSON.

WASHINGTON, *February 21, 1867.*

To the Senate of the United States:

I transmit to the Senate, in answer to their resolution of the 11th instant, a report from the Secretary of State, with accompanying documents.*

ANDREW JOHNSON.

WASHINGTON, *February 21, 1867.*

To the Senate of the United States:

I transmit to the Senate, in answer to their resolution of the 31st ultimo, a report from the Secretary of State, with accompanying documents.†

ANDREW JOHNSON.

WASHINGTON, *February 21, 1867.*

To the Senate of the United States:

I transmit to the Senate, in answer to their resolution of the 19th instant, a report from the Secretary of State, with accompanying documents.‡

ANDREW JOHNSON.

WASHINGTON, *February 21, 1867.*

To the House of Representatives:

I transmit to the House of Representatives, in answer to their resolution of the 14th instant, a report § from the Secretary of State of this date.

ANDREW JOHNSON.

WASHINGTON, *February 21, 1867.*

To the Senate of the United States:

For the reasons stated‖ in the accompanying communication from the Secretary of the Interior, I withdraw the treaty concluded with the New

---

*Correspondence relative to the refusal of the United States consul at Cadiz, Spain, to certify invoices of wines shipped from that port, etc.

†Correspondence with foreign ministers of the United States relative to the policy of the President toward the States lately in rebellion.

‡Correspondence relative to the salary of the United States minister to Portugal.

§Stating that the correspondence relative to the refusal of the United States consul at Cadiz, Spain, to certify invoices of wines shipped from that port had been sent to the Senate.

‖For the purpose of concluding a new treaty.

York Indians in Kansas and submitted to the Senate in the month of December, 1863, but upon which I am informed no action has yet been taken.

ANDREW JOHNSON.

WASHINGTON CITY, D. C., *February 23, 1867.*

To the Senate of the United States:

I herewith lay before the Senate, for its constitutional action thereon, a treaty concluded in the city of Washington on the 19th of February, 1867, between the United States and the Sac and Fox tribes of Indians of Missouri.

A letter of the Secretary of the Interior of the 23d and copy of a letter of the Commissioner of Indian Affairs of the 19th of February, 1867, accompany the treaty.

ANDREW JOHNSON.

WASHINGTON CITY, D. C., *February 23, 1867.*

To the Senate of the United States:

I herewith lay before the Senate, for its constitutional action thereon, a treaty concluded in the city of Washington on the 18th February, 1867, between the United States and the Sac and Fox tribes of Indians of the Mississippi.

A letter of the Secretary of the Interior of the 23d and a copy of a letter of the Commissioner of Indian Affairs of the 19th February, 1867, accompany the treaty.

ANDREW JOHNSON.

WASHINGTON CITY, D. C., *February 23, 1867.*

To the Senate of the United States:

I herewith lay before the Senate, for its constitutional action thereon, a treaty concluded on the 19th February, 1867, between the United States and the Sisseton and Wahpeton bands of Indians.

A letter of the Secretary of the Interior of the 23d instant and accompanying copies of letters of the Commissioner of Indian Affairs and Major T. R. Brown, in relation to said treaty, are also herewith transmitted.

ANDREW JOHNSON.

WASHINGTON, *February 23, 1867.*

To the Senate and House of Representatives:

I transmit a copy of a letter of the 12th instant addressed to me by His Excellency Lucius Fairchild, governor of the State of Wisconsin, and of the memorial to Congress concerning the Paris Exposition adopted by the legislature of that State during its present session.

ANDREW JOHNSON.

EXECUTIVE MANSION, *February 25, 1867.*

To the House of Representatives:

I transmit herewith a report from the Secretary of the Interior, in reply to the resolution of the House of Representatives of the 11th instant, calling for certain information relative to removals and appointments in his Department since the adjournment of the first session of the Thirty-ninth Congress.   ANDREW JOHNSON.

WASHINGTON, D. C., *February 26, 1867.*

To the Senate and House of Representatives:

I transmit to Congress a copy of a correspondence between the Secretary of State and G. V. Fox, esq., relative to the presentation by the latter to the Emperor of Russia of the resolution of Congress expressive of the feelings of the people of the United States in reference to the providential escape of that sovereign from an attempted assassination.

ANDREW JOHNSON.

WASHINGTON, *February 26, 1867.*

To the Senate of the United States:

I transmit to the Senate, with a view to ratification, a general convention of amity, commerce, and navigation and for the surrender of fugitive criminals between the United States and the Dominican Republic, signed by the plenipotentiaries of the parties at the city of St. Domingo on the 8th of this month.   ANDREW JOHNSON.

WASHINGTON, D. C., *February 27, 1867.*

To the House of Representatives:

I transmit herewith a communication from the Secretary of the Navy, in answer to a resolution of the House of Representatives of the 21st instant, calling for a copy of a letter addressed by Richard M. Boynton and Harriet M. Fisher to the Secretary of the Navy in the month of February, 1863, together with the indorsement made thereon by the Chief of the Bureau of Ordnance.   ANDREW JOHNSON.

WASHINGTON, *March 2, 1867.*

To the House of Representatives:

I transmit herewith a report of the Attorney-General, additional to the one submitted by him December 13, 1866, in reply to the resolution of the House of Representatives of December 10, 1866, requesting "a list of names of all persons who have been engaged in the late rebellion against the United States Government who have been pardoned by the President from April 15, 1865, to this date; that said list shall also state the rank of each person who has been so pardoned, if he has been engaged in the military service of the so-called Confederate States, and the position if he shall have held any civil office under said so-called Confederate government; and shall also further state whether such person has at any time prior to April 14, 1861, held any office under the United States Government, and, if so, what office, together with the reasons for granting such pardons, and also the names of the person or persons at whose solicitation such pardon was granted.''

ANDREW JOHNSON.

MARCH 2, 1867.

To the House of Representatives:

The act entitled "An act making appropriations for the support of the Army for the year ending June 30, 1868, and for other purposes'' contains provisions to which I must call attention. Those provisions are contained in the second section, which in certain cases virtually deprives the President of his constitutional functions as Commander in Chief of the Army, and in the sixth section, which denies to ten States of this Union their constitutional right to protect themselves in any emergency by means of their own militia. Those provisions are out of place in an appropriation act. I am compelled to defeat these necessary appropriations if I withhold my signature to the act. Pressed by these considerations, I feel constrained to return the bill with my signature, but to accompany it with my protest against the sections which I have indicated.

ANDREW JOHNSON.

VETO MESSAGES.

WASHINGTON, *January 5, 1867.*

To the Senate of the United States:

I have received and considered a bill entitled "An act to regulate the elective franchise in the District of Columbia,'' passed by the Senate on the 13th of December and by the House of Representatives on the succeeding day. It was presented for my approval on the 26th ultimo—six days after the adjournment of Congress—and is now returned with my objections to the Senate, in which House it originated.

Measures having been introduced at the commencement of the first session of the present Congress for the extension of the elective franchise to persons of color in the District of Columbia, steps were taken by the corporate authorities of Washington and Georgetown to ascertain and make known the opinion of the people of the two cities upon a subject so immediately affecting their welfare as a community. The question was submitted to the people at special elections held in the month of December, 1865, when the qualified voters of Washington and Georgetown, with great unanimity of sentiment, expressed themselves opposed to the contemplated legislation. In Washington, in a vote of 6,556—the largest, with but two exceptions, ever polled in that city—only thirty-five ballots were cast for negro suffrage, while in Georgetown, in an aggregate of 813 votes—a number considerably in excess of the average vote at the four preceding annual elections—but one was given in favor of the proposed extension of the elective franchise. As these elections seem to have been conducted with entire fairness, the result must be accepted as a truthful expression of the opinion of the people of the District upon the question which evoked it. Possessing, as an organized community, the same popular right as the inhabitants of a State or Territory to make known their will upon matters which affect their social and political condition, they could have selected no more appropriate mode of memorializing Congress upon the subject of this bill than through the suffrages of their qualified voters.

Entirely disregarding the wishes of the people of the District of Columbia, Congress has deemed it right and expedient to pass the measure now submitted for my signature. It therefore becomes the duty of the Executive, standing between the legislation of the one and the will of the other, fairly expressed, to determine whether he should approve the bill, and thus aid in placing upon the statute books of the nation a law against which the people to whom it is to apply have solemnly and with such unanimity protested, or whether he should return it with his objections in the hope that upon reconsideration Congress, acting as the representatives of the inhabitants of the seat of Government, will permit them to regulate a purely local question as to them may seem best suited to their interests and condition.

The District of Columbia was ceded to the United States by Maryland and Virginia in order that it might become the permanent seat of Government of the United States. Accepted by Congress, it at once became subject to the "exclusive legislation" for which provision is made in the Federal Constitution. It should be borne in mind, however, that in exercising its functions as the lawmaking power of the District of Columbia the authority of the National Legislature is not without limit, but that Congress is bound to observe the letter and spirit of the Constitution as well in the enactment of local laws for the seat of Government as in legislation common to the entire Union. Were it to be admitted that the right "to exercise exclusive legislation in all cases whatsoever" conferred upon Congress unlimited power within the District of Columbia, titles of nobility might be granted within its boundaries; laws might be made "respecting an establishment of religion or prohibiting the free exercise thereof, or abridging the freedom of speech or of the press, or the right of the people peaceably to assemble and to petition the Government for a redress of grievances.'' Despotism would thus reign at the seat of government of a free republic, and as a place of permanent residence it would be avoided by all who prefer the blessings of liberty to the mere emoluments of official position.

It should also be remembered that in legislating for the District of Columbia under the Federal Constitution the relation of Congress to its inhabitants is analogous to that of a legislature to the people of a State under their own local constitution. It does not, therefore, seem to be asking too much that in matters pertaining to the District Congress should have a like respect for the will and interest of its inhabitants as is entertained by a State legislature for the wishes and prosperity of those for whom they legislate. The spirit of our Constitution and the genius of our Government require that in regard to any law which is to affect and have a permanent bearing upon a people their will should exert at least a reasonable influence upon those who are acting in the capacity of their legislators. Would, for instance, the legislature of the State of New York, or of Pennsylvania, or of Indiana, or of any State in the Union, in opposition to the expressed will of a large majority of the people whom they were chosen to represent, arbitrarily force upon them as voters all persons of the African or negro race and make them eligible for office without any other qualification than a certain term of residence within the State? In neither of the States named would the colored population, when acting together, be able to produce any great social or political result. Yet in New York, before he can vote, the man of color must fulfill conditions that are not required of the white citizen; in Pennsylvania the elective franchise is restricted to white freemen, while in Indiana negroes and mulattoes are expressly excluded from the right of suffrage. It hardly seems consistent with the principles of right and justice that representatives of States where suffrage is either denied the colored man or granted to him on qualifications requiring intelligence or property should compel the people of the District of Columbia to try an experiment which their own constituents have thus far shown an unwillingness to test for themselves. Nor does it accord with our republican ideas that the principle of self-government should lose its force when applied to the residents of the District merely because their legislators are not, like those of the States, responsible through the ballot to the people for whom they are the lawmaking power.

The great object of placing the seat of Government under the exclusive legislation of Congress was to secure the entire independence of the General Government from undue State influence and to enable it to discharge without danger of interruption or infringement of its authority the high functions for which it was created by the people. For this important purpose it was ceded to the United States by Maryland and Virginia, and it certainly never could have been contemplated as one of the objects to be attained by placing it under the exclusive jurisdiction of Congress that it would afford to propagandists or political parties a place for an experimental test of their principles and theories. While, indeed, the residents of the seat of Government are not citizens of any State and are not, therefore, allowed a voice in the electoral college or representation in the councils of the nation, they are, nevertheless, American citizens, entitled as such to every guaranty of the Constitution, to every benefit of the laws, and to every right which pertains to citizens of our common country. In all matters, then, affecting their domestic affairs, the spirit of our democratic form of government demands that their wishes should be consulted and respected and they taught to feel that although not permitted practically to participate in national concerns, they are, nevertheless, under a paternal government regardful of their rights, mindful of their wants, and solicitous for their prosperity. It was evidently contemplated that all local questions would be left to their decision, at least to an extent that would not be incompatible with the object for which Congress was granted exclusive legislation over the seat of Government. When the Constitution was yet under consideration, it was assumed by Mr. Madison that its inhabitants would be allowed "a municipal legislature for local purposes, derived from their own suffrages." When for the first time Congress, in the year 1800, assembled at Washington, President Adams, in his speech at its opening, reminded the two Houses that it was for them to consider whether the local powers over the District of Columbia, vested by the Constitution in the Congress of the United States, should be immediately exercised, and he asked them to "consider it as the capital of a great nation, advancing with unexampled rapidity in arts, in commerce, in wealth, and in population, and possessing within itself those resources which, if not thrown away or lamentably misdirected, would secure to it a long course of prosperity and self-government." Three years had not elapsed when Congress was called upon to determine the propriety of retroceding to Maryland and Virginia the jurisdiction of the territory which they had respectively relinquished to the Government of the United States. It was urged on the one hand that exclusive jurisdiction was not necessary or useful to the Government; that it deprived the inhabitants of the District of their political rights; that much of the time of Congress was consumed in legislation pertaining to it; that its government was expensive; that Congress was not competent to legislate for the District, because the members were strangers to its local concerns; and that it was an example of a government without representation—an experiment dangerous to the liberties of the States. On the other hand it was held, among other reasons, and successfully, that the Constitution, the acts of cession of Virginia and Maryland, and the act of Congress accepting the grant all contemplated the exercise of exclusive legislation by Congress, and that its usefulness, if not its necessity, was inferred from the inconvenience which was felt for want of it by the Congress of the Confederation; that the people themselves, who, it was said, had been deprived of their political rights, had not complained and did not desire a retrocession; that the evil might be remedied by giving them a representation in Congress when the District should become sufficiently populous, and in the meantime a local legislature; that if the inhabitants had not political rights they had great political influence; that the trouble and expense of legislating for the District would not be great, but would diminish, and might in a great measure be avoided by a local legislature; and that Congress could not retrocede the inhabitants without their consent. Continuing to live substantially under the laws that existed at the time of the cession, and such changes only having been made as were suggested by themselves, the people of the District have not sought by a local legislature that which has generally been willingly conceded by the Congress of the nation.

As a general rule sound policy requires that the legislature should yield to the wishes of a people, when not inconsistent with the constitution and the laws. The measures suited to one community might not be well adapted to the condition of another; and the persons best qualified to determine such questions are those whose interests are to be directly affected by any proposed law. In Massachusetts, for instance, male persons are allowed to vote without regard to color, provided they possess a certain degree of intelligence. In a population in that State of 1,231,066 there were, by the census of 1860, only 9,602 persons of color, and of the males over 20 years of age there were 339,086 white to 2,602 colored. By the same official enumeration there were in the District of Columbia 60,764 whites to 14,316 persons of the colored race. Since then, however, the population of the District has largely increased, and it is estimated that at the present time there are nearly 100,000 whites to 30,000 negroes. The cause of the augmented numbers of the latter class needs no explanation. Contiguous to Maryland and Virginia, the District during the war became a place of refuge for those who escaped from servitude, and it is yet the abiding place of a considerable proportion of those who sought within its limits a shelter from bondage. Until then held in slavery and denied all opportunities for mental culture, their first knowledge of the Government was acquired when, by conferring upon them freedom, it became the benefactor of their race. The test of their capability for improvement began when for the first time the career of free industry and the avenues to intelligence were opened to them. Possessing these advantages but a limited time—the greater number perhaps having entered the District of Columbia during the later years of the war, or since its termination—we may well pause to inquire whether, after so brief a probation, they are as a class capable of an intelligent exercise of the right of suffrage and qualified to discharge the duties of official position. The people who are daily witnesses of their mode of living, and who have become familiar with their habits of thought, have expressed the conviction that they are not yet competent to serve as electors, and thus become eligible for office in the local governments under which they live. Clothed with the elective franchise, their numbers, already largely in excess of the demand for labor, would be soon increased by an influx from the adjoining States. Drawn from fields where employment is abundant, they would in vain seek it here, and so add to the embarrassments already experienced from the large class of idle persons congregated in the District. Hardly yet capable of forming correct judgments upon the important questions that often make the issues of a political contest, they could readily be made subservient to the purposes of designing persons. While in Massachusetts, under the census of 1860, the proportion of white to colored males over 20 years of age was 130 to 1, here the black race constitutes nearly one-third of the entire population, whilst the same class surrounds the District on all sides, ready to change their residence at a moment's notice, and with all the facility of a nomadic people, in order to enjoy here, after a short residence, a privilege they find nowhere else. It is within their power in one year to come into the District in such numbers as to have the supreme control of the white race, and to govern them by their own officers and by the exercise of all the municipal authority—among the rest, of the power of taxation over property in which they have no interest. In Massachusetts, where they have enjoyed the benefits of a thorough educational system, a qualification of intelligence is required, while here suffrage is extended to all without discrimination—as well to the most incapable who can prove a residence in the District of one year as to those persons of color who, comparatively few in number, are permanent inhabitants, and, having given evidence of merit and qualification, are recognized as useful and responsible members of the community. Imposed upon an unwilling people placed by the Constitution under the exclusive legislation of Congress, it would be viewed as an arbitrary exercise of power and as an indication by the country of the purpose of Congress to compel the acceptance of negro suffrage by the States. It would engender a feeling of opposition and hatred between the two races, which, becoming deep rooted and ineradicable, would prevent them from living together in a state of mutual friendliness. Carefully avoiding every measure that might tend to produce such a result, and following the clear and well-ascertained popular will, we should assiduously endeavor to promote kindly relations between them, and thus, when that popular will leads the way, prepare for the gradual and harmonious introduction of this new element into the political power of the country.

It can not be urged that the proposed extension of suffrage in the District of Columbia is necessary to enable persons of color to protect either their interests or their rights. They stand here precisely as they stand in Pennsylvania, Ohio, and Indiana. Here as elsewhere, in all that pertains to civil rights, there is nothing to distinguish this class of persons from citizens of the United States, for they possess the "full and equal benefit of all laws and proceedings for the security of person and property as is enjoyed by white citizens," and are made "subject to like punishment, pains, and penalties, and to none other, any law, statute, ordinance, regulation, or custom to the contrary notwithstanding." Nor, as has been assumed, are their suffrages necessary to aid a loyal sentiment here, for local governments already exist of undoubted fealty to the Government, and are sustained by communities which were among the first to testify their devotion to the Union, and which during the struggle furnished their full quotas of men to the military service of the country.

The exercise of the elective franchise is the highest attribute of an American citizen, and when guided by virtue, intelligence, patriotism, and a proper appreciation of our institutions constitutes the true basis of a democratic form of government, in which the sovereign power is lodged in the body of the people. Its influence for good necessarily depends upon the elevated character and patriotism of the elector, for if exercised by persons who do not justly estimate its value and who are indifferent as to its results it will only serve as a means of placing power in the hands of the unprincipled and ambitious, and must eventuate in the complete destruction of that liberty of which it should be the most powerful conservator. Great danger is therefore to be apprehended from an untimely extension of the elective franchise to any new class in our country, especially when the large majority of that class, in wielding the power thus placed in their hands, can not be expected correctly to comprehend the duties and responsibilities which pertain to suffrage. Yesterday, as it were, 4,000,000 persons were held in a condition of slavery that had existed for generations; to-day they are freemen and are assumed by law to be citizens. It can not be presumed, from their previous condition of servitude, that as a class they are as well informed as to the nature of our Government as the intelligent foreigner who makes our land the home of his choice. In the case of the latter neither a residence of five years and the knowledge of our institutions which it gives nor attachment to the principles of the Constitution are the only conditions upon which he can be admitted to citizenship; he must prove in addition a good moral character, and thus give reasonable ground for the belief that he will be faithful to the obligations which he assumes as a citizen of the Republic. Where a people—the source of all political power—speak by their suffrages through the instrumentality of the ballot box, it must be carefully guarded against the control of those who are corrupt in principle and enemies of free institutions, for it can only become to our political and social system a safe conductor of healthy popular sentiment when kept free from demoralizing influences. Controlled through fraud and usurpation by the designing, anarchy and despotism must inevitably follow.

In the hands of the patriotic and worthy our Government will be preserved upon the principles of the Constitution inherited from our fathers. It follows, therefore, that in admitting to the ballot box a new class of voters not qualified for the exercise of the elective franchise we weaken our system of government instead of adding to its strength and durability.

In returning this bill to the Senate I deeply regret that there should be any conflict of opinion between the legislative and executive departments of the Government in regard to measures that vitally affect the prosperity and peace of the country. Sincerely desiring to reconcile the States with one another and the whole people to the Government of the United States, it has been my earnest wish to cooperate with Congress in all measures having for their object a proper and complete adjustment of the questions resulting from our late civil war. Harmony between the coordinate branches of the Government, always necessary for the public welfare, was never more demanded than at the present time, and it will therefore be my constant aim to promote as far as possible concert of action between them. The differences of opinion that have already occurred have rendered me only the more cautious, lest the Executive should encroach upon any of the prerogatives of Congress, or by exceeding in any manner the constitutional limit of his duties destroy the equilibrium which should exist between the several coordinate departments, and which is so essential to the harmonious working of the Government. I know it has been urged that the executive department is more likely to enlarge the sphere of its action than either of the other two branches of the Government, and especially in the exercise of the veto power conferred upon it by the Constitution. It should be remembered, however, that this power is wholly negative and conservative in its character, and was intended to operate as a check upon unconstitutional, hasty, and improvident legislation and as a means of protection against invasions of the just powers of the executive and judicial departments. It is remarked by Chancellor Kent that—

To enact laws is a transcendent power, and if the body that possesses it be a full and equal representation of the people there is danger of its pressing with destructive weight upon all the other parts of the machinery of Government. It has therefore been thought necessary by the most skillful and most experienced artists in the science of civil polity that strong barriers should be erected for the protection and security of the other necessary powers of the Government. Nothing has been deemed more fit and expedient for the purpose than the provision that the head of the executive department should be so constituted as to secure a requisite share of independence and that he should have a negative upon the passing of laws; and that the judiciary power, resting on a still more permanent basis, should have the right of determining upon the validity of laws by the standard of the Constitution.

The necessity of some such check in the hands of the Executive is shown by reference to the most eminent writers upon our system of government, who seem to concur in the opinion that encroachments are most to be apprehended from the department in which all legislative powers are vested by the Constitution.　Mr. Madison, in referring to the diffi-culty of providing some practical security for each against the invasion of the others, remarks that "the legislative department is everywhere extending the sphere of its activity and drawing all power into its impet-uous vortex." "The founders of our Republic * * * seem never to have recollected the danger from legislative usurpations, which by assem-bling all power in the same hands must lead to the same tyranny as is threatened by Executive usurpations." "In a representative republic, where the executive magistracy is carefully limited both in the extent and the duration of its power, and where the legislative power is exer-cised by an assembly which is inspired, by a supposed influence over the people, with an intrepid confidence in its own strength, which is suffi-ciently numerous to feel all the passions which actuate a multitude, yet not so numerous as to be incapable of pursuing the objects of its passions by means which reason prescribes, it is against the enterprising ambi-tion of this department that the people ought to indulge all their jealousy and exhaust all their precautions." "The legislative department derives a superiority in our governments from other circumstances.　Its consti-tutional powers being at once more extensive and less susceptible of pre-cise limits, it can with the greater facility mask, under complicated and indirect measures, the encroachments which it makes on the coordinate departments." "On the other side, the Executive power being restrained within a narrower compass and being more simple in its nature, and the judiciary being described by landmarks still less uncertain, projects of usurpation by either of these departments would immediately betray and defeat themselves.　Nor is this all.　As the legislative department alone has access to the pockets of the people and has in some constitutions full discretion and in all a prevailing influence over the pecuniary rewards of those who fill the other departments, a dependence is thus created in the latter which gives still greater facility to encroachments of the former." "We have seen that the tendency of republican governments is to an ag-grandizement of the legislative at the expense of the other departments."

Mr. Jefferson, in referring to the early constitution of Virginia, objected that by its provisions all the powers of government—legislative, execu-tive, and judicial—resulted to the legislative body, holding that "the concentrating these in the same hands is precisely the definition of despotic government.　It will be no alleviation that these powers will be exercised by a plurality of hands, and not by a single one.　One hundred and seventy-three despots would surely be as oppressive as one." "As little will it avail us that they are chosen by ourselves.　An elective despo-tism was not the government we fought for, but one which should not only be founded on free principles, but in which the powers of govern-ment should be so divided and balanced among several bodies of magis-tracy as that no one could transcend their legal limits without being effectually checked and restrained by the others.　For this reason that convention which passed the ordinance of government laid its foundation on this basis, that the legislative, executive, and judicial departments should be separate and distinct, so that no person should exercise the powers of more than one of them at the same time. But no barrier was provided between these several powers. The judiciary and executive members were left dependent on the legislative for their subsistence in office, and some of them for their continuance in it. If, therefore, the legislature assumes executive and judiciary powers, no opposition is likely to be made, nor, if made, can be effectual, because in that case they may put their proceedings into the form of an act of assembly, which will render them obligatory on the other branches. They have accordingly in many instances decided rights which should have been left to judiciary controversy; and the direction of the executive, during the whole time of their session, is becoming habitual and familiar.''

Mr. Justice Story, in his Commentaries on the Constitution, reviews the same subject, and says:

The truth is that the legislative power is the great and overruling power in every free government. * * * The representatives of the people will watch with jealousy every encroachment of the executive magistrate, for it trenches upon their own authority. But who shall watch the encroachment of these representatives themselves? Will they be as jealous of the exercise of power by themselves as by others? * * *

There are many reasons which may be assigned for the engrossing influence of the legislative department. In the first place, its constitutional powers are more extensive, and less capable of being brought within precise limits than those of either the other departments. The bounds of the executive authority are easily marked out and defined. It reaches few objects, and those are known. It can not transcend them without being brought in contact with the other departments. Laws may check and restrain and bound its exercise. The same remarks apply with still greater force to the judiciary. The jurisdiction is, or may be, bounded to a few objects or persons; or, however general and unlimited, its operations are necessarily confined to the mere administration of private and public justice. It can not punish without law. It can not create controversies to act upon. It can decide only upon rights and cases as they are brought by others before it. It can do nothing for itself. It must do everything for others. It must obey the laws, and if it corruptly administers them it is subjected to the power of impeachment. On the other hand, the legislative power, except in the few cases of constitutional prohibition, is unlimited. It is forever varying its means and its ends. It governs the institutions and laws and public policy of the country. It regulates all its vast interests. It disposes of all its property. Look but at the exercise of two or three branches of its ordinary powers. It levies all taxes; it directs and appropriates all supplies; it gives the rules for the descent, distribution, and devises of all property held by individuals; it controls the sources and the resources of wealth; it changes at its will the whole fabric of the laws; it molds at its pleasure almost all the institutions which give strength and comfort and dignity to society.

In the next place, it is the direct visible representative of the will of the people in all the changes of times and circumstances. It has the pride as well as the power of numbers. It is easily moved and steadily moved by the strong impulses of popular feeling and popular odium. It obeys without reluctance the wishes and the will of the majority for the time being. The path to public favor lies open by such obedience, and it finds not only support but impunity in whatever measures the majority advises, even though they transcend the constitutional limits.   It has no motive, therefore, to be jealous or scrupulous in its own use of power; and it finds its ambition stimulated and its arm strengthened by the countenance and the courage of numbers.   These views are not alone those of men who look with apprehension upon the fate of republics, but they are also freely admitted by some of the strongest advocates for popular rights and the permanency of republican institutions.   *   *   *

*   *   *   Each department should have a will of its own.   *   *   *   Each should have its own independence secured beyond the power of being taken away by either or both of the others.   But at the same time the relations of each to the other should be so strong that there should be a mutual interest to sustain and protect each other. There should not only be constitutional means, but personal motives to resist encroachments of one or either of the others.   Thus ambition would be made to counteract ambition, the desire of power to check power, and the pressure of interest to balance an opposing interest.

*   *   *   The judiciary is naturally and almost necessarily, as has been already said, the weakest department.   It can have no means of influence by patronage. Its powers can never be wielded for itself.   It has no command over the purse or the sword of the nation.   It can neither lay taxes, nor appropriate money, nor command armies, nor appoint to office.   It is never brought into contact with the people by constant appeals and solicitations and private intercourse, which belong to all the other departments of Government.   It is seen only in controversies or in trials and punishments.   Its rigid justice and impartiality give it no claims to favor, however they may respect.   It stands solitary and unsupported, except by that portion of public opinion which is interested only in the strict administration of justice.   It can rarely secure the sympathy or zealous support either of the Executive or the Legislature.   If they are not, as is not unfrequently the case, jealous of its prerogatives, the constant necessity of scrutinizing the acts of each, upon the application of any private person, and the painful duty of pronouncing judgment that these acts are a departure from the law or Constitution can have no tendency to conciliate kindness or nourish influence.   It would seem, therefore, that some additional guards would, under the circumstances, be necessary to protect this department from the absolute dominion of the others.   Yet rarely have any such guards been applied, and every attempt to introduce them has been resisted with a pertinacity which demonstrates how slow popular leaders are to introduce checks upon their own power and how slow the people are to believe that the judiciary is the real bulwark of their liberties.   *   *   *

*   *   *   If any department of the Government has undue influence or absorbing power, it certainly has not been the executive or judiciary.

In addition to what has been said by these distinguished writers, it may also be urged that the dominant party in each House may, by the expulsion of a sufficient number of members or by the exclusion from representation of a requisite number of States, reduce the minority to less than one-third.   Congress by these means might be enabled to pass a law, the objections of the President to the contrary notwithstanding, which would render impotent the other two departments of the Government and make inoperative the wholesome and restraining power which it was intended by the framers of the Constitution should be exerted by them.   This would be a practical concentration of all power in the Congress of the United States; this, in the language of the author of the Declaration of Independence, would be "precisely the definition of despotic government."

I have preferred to reproduce these teachings of the great statesmen and constitutional lawyers of the early and later days of the Republic rather than to rely simply upon an expression of my own opinions. We can not too often recur to them, especially at a conjuncture like the present. Their application to our actual condition is so apparent that they now come to us a living voice, to be listened to with more attention than at any previous period of our history. We have been and are yet in the midst of popular commotion. The passions aroused by a great civil war are still dominant. It is not a time favorable to that calm and deliberate judgment which is the only safe guide when radical changes in our institutions are to be made. The measure now before me is one of those changes. It initiates an untried experiment for a people who have said, with one voice, that it is not for their good. This alone should make us pause, but it is not all. The experiment has not been tried, or so much as demanded, by the people of the several States for themselves. In but few of the States has such an innovation been allowed as giving the ballot to the colored population without any other qualification than a residence of one year, and in most of them the denial of the ballot to this race is absolute and by fundamental law placed beyond the domain of ordinary legislation. In most of those States the evil of such suffrage would be partial, but, small as it would be, it is guarded by constitutional barriers. Here the innovation assumes formidable proportions, which may easily grow to such an extent as to make the white population a subordinate element in the body politic.

After full deliberation upon this measure, I can not bring myself to approve it, even upon local considerations, nor yet as the beginning of an experiment on a larger scale. I yield to no one in attachment to that rule of general suffrage which distinguishes our policy as a nation. But there is a limit, wisely observed hitherto, which makes the ballot a privilege and a trust, and which requires of some classes a time suitable for probation and preparation. To give it indiscriminately to a new class, wholly unprepared by previous habits and opportunities to perform the trust which it demands, is to degrade it, and finally to destroy its power, for it may be safely assumed that no political truth is better established than that such indiscriminate and all-embracing extension of popular suffrage must end at last in its destruction.

ANDREW JOHNSON.

WASHINGTON, *January 28, 1867.*

To the Senate of the United States:

I return to the Senate, in which House it originated, a bill entitled "An act to admit the State of Colorado into the Union," to which I can not, consistently with my sense of duty, give my approval. With the exception of an additional section, containing new provisions, it is substantially the same as the bill of a similar title passed by Congress during the last session, submitted to the President for his approval, returned with the objections contained in a message bearing date the 15th of May last, and yet awaiting the reconsideration of the Senate.

A second bill, having in view the same purpose, has now passed both Houses of Congress and been presented for my signature. Having again carefully considered the subject, I have been unable to perceive any reason for changing the opinions which have already been communicated to Congress. I find, on the contrary, that there are many objections to the proposed legislation of which I was not at that time aware, and that while several of those which I then assigned have in the interval gained in strength, yet others have been created by the altered character of the measures now submitted.

The constitution under which the State government is proposed to be formed very properly contains a provision that all laws in force at the time of its adoption and the admission of the State into the Union shall continue as if the constitution had not been adopted. Among those laws is one absolutely prohibiting negroes and mulattoes from voting. At the recent session of the Territorial legislature a bill for the repeal of this law, introduced into the council, was almost unanimously rejected; and at the very time when Congress was engaged in enacting the bill now under consideration the legislature passed an act excluding negroes and mulattoes from the right to sit as jurors. This bill was vetoed by the governor of the Territory, who held that by the laws of the United States negroes and mulattoes are citizens, and subject to the duties, as well as entitled to the rights, of citizenship. The bill, however, was passed, the objections of the governor to the contrary notwithstanding, and is now a law of the Territory. Yet in the bill now before me, by which it is proposed to admit the Territory as a State, it is provided that "there shall be no denial of the elective franchise or any other rights to any person by reason of race or color, excepting Indians not taxed."

The incongruity thus exhibited between the legislation of Congress and that of the Territory, taken in connection with the protest against the admission of the State hereinafter referred to, would seem clearly to indicate the impolicy and injustice of the proposed enactment.

It might, indeed, be a subject of grave inquiry, and doubtless will result in such inquiry if this bill becomes a law, whether it does not attempt to exercise a power not conferred upon Congress by the Federal Constitution. That instrument simply declares that Congress may admit new States into the Union. It nowhere says that Congress may make new States for the purpose of admitting them into the Union or for any other purpose; and yet this bill is as clear an attempt to make the institutions as any in which the people themselves could engage.

In view of this action of Congress, the house of representatives of the Territory have earnestly protested against being forced into the Union without first having the question submitted to the people. Nothing could be more reasonable than the position which they thus assume; and it certainly can not be the purpose of Congress to force upon a community against their will a government which they do not believe themselves capable of sustaining.

The following is a copy of the protest alluded to as officially transmitted to me:

Whereas it is announced in the public prints that it is the intention of Congress to admit Colorado as a State into the Union: Therefore,

Resolved by the house of representatives of the Territory, That, representing, as we do, the last and only legal expression of public opinion on this question, we earnestly protest against the passage of a law admitting the State without first having the question submitted to a vote of the people, for the reasons, first, that we have a right to a voice in the selection of the character of our government; second, that we have not a sufficient population to support the expenses of a State government. For these reasons we trust that Congress will not force upon us a government against our will.

Upon information which I considered reliable, I assumed in my message of the 15th of May last that the population of Colorado was not more than 30,000, and expressed the opinion that this number was entirely too small either to assume the responsibilities or to enjoy the privileges of a State.

It appears that previous to that time the legislature, with a view to ascertain the exact condition of the Territory, had passed a law authorizing a census of the population to be taken. The law made it the duty of the assessors in the several counties to take the census in connection with the annual assessments, and, in order to secure a correct enumeration of the population, allowed them a liberal compensation for the service by paying them for every name returned, and added to their previous oath of office an oath to perform this duty with fidelity.

From the accompanying official report it appears that returns have been received from fifteen of the eighteen counties into which the State is divided, and that their population amounts in the aggregate to 24,909. The three remaining counties are estimated to contain 3,000, making a total population of 27,909.

This census was taken in the summer season, when it is claimed that the population is much larger than at any other period, as in the autumn miners in large numbers leave their work and return to the East with the results of their summer enterprise.

The population, it will be observed, is but slightly in excess of one-fifth of the number required as the basis of representation for a single Congressional district in any of the States—the number being 127,000.

I am unable to perceive any good reason for such great disparity in the right of representation, giving, as it would, to the people of Colorado not only this vast advantage in the House of Representatives, but an equality in the Senate, where the other States are represented by millions. With perhaps a single exception, no such inequality as this has ever before been attempted. I know that it is claimed that the population of the different States at the time of their admission has varied at different periods, but it has not varied much more than the population of each decade and the corresponding basis of representation for the different periods.

The obvious intent of the Constitution was that no State should be admitted with a less population than the ratio for a Representative at the time of application. The limitation in the second section of the first article of the Constitution, declaring that "each State shall have at least one Representative," was manifestly designed to protect the States which originally composed the Union from being deprived, in the event of a waning population, of a voice in the popular branch of Congress, and was never intended as a warrant to force a new State into the Union with a representative population far below that which might at the time be required of sister members of the Confederacy. This bill, in view of the prohibition of the same section, which declares that "the number of Representatives shall not exceed one for every 30,000," is at least a violation of the spirit if not the letter of the Constitution.

It is respectfully submitted that however Congress, under the pressure of circumstances, may have admitted two or three States with less than a representative population at the time, there has been no instance in which an application for admission has ever been entertained when the population, as officially ascertained, was below 30,000.

Were there any doubt of this being the true construction of the Constitution, it would be dispelled by the early and long-continued practice of the Federal Government. For nearly sixty years after the adoption of the Constitution no State was admitted with a population believed at the time to be less than the current ratio for a Representative, and the first instance in which there appears to have been a departure from the principle was in 1845, in the case of Florida. Obviously the result of sectional strife, we would do well to regard it as a warning of evil rather than as an example for imitation; and I think candid men of all parties will agree that the inspiring cause of the violation of this wholesome principle of restraint is to be found in a vain attempt to balance these antagonisms, which refused to be reconciled except through the bloody arbitrament of arms. The plain facts of our history will attest that the great and leading States admitted since 1845, viz, Iowa, Wisconsin, California, Minnesota, and Kansas, including Texas, which was admitted that year, have all come with an ample population for one Representative, and some of them with nearly or quite enough for two.

To demonstrate the correctness of my views on this question, I subjoin a table containing a list of the States admitted since the adoption of the

Federal Constitution, with the date of admission, the ratio of representation, and the representative population when admitted, deduced from the United States census tables, the calculation being made for the period of the decade corresponding with the date of admission.

Colorado, which it is now proposed to admit as a State, contains, as has already been stated, a population less than 28,000, while the present ratio of representation is 127,000.

There can be no reason that I can perceive for the admission of Colorado that would not apply with equal force to nearly every other Territory now organized; and I submit whether, if this bill become a law, it will be possible to resist the logical conclusion that such Territories as Dakota, Montana, and Idaho must be received as States whenever they present themselves, without regard to the number of inhabitants they may respectively contain. Eight or ten new Senators and four or five new members of the House of Representatives would thus be admitted to represent a population scarcely exceeding that which in any other portion of the nation is entitled to but a single member of the House of Representatives, while the average for two Senators in the Union, as now constituted, is at least 1,000,000 people. It would surely be unjust to all other sections of the Union to enter upon a policy with regard to the admission of new States which might result in conferring such a disproportionate share of influence in the National Legislature upon communities which, in pursuance of the wise policy of our fathers, should for some years to come be retained under the fostering care and protection of the National Government. If it is deemed just and expedient now to depart from the settled policy of the nation during all its history, and to admit all the Territories to the rights and privileges of States, irrespective of their population or fitness for such government, it is submitted whether it would not be well to devise such measures as will bring the subject before the country for consideration and decision. This would seem to be eminently wise, because, as has already been stated, if it is right to admit Colorado now there is no reason for the exclusion of the other Territories.

It is no answer to these suggestions that an enabling act was passed authorizing the people of Colorado to take action on this subject. It is well known that that act was passed in consequence of representations that the population reached, according to some statements, as high as 80,000, and to none less than 50,000, and was growing with a rapidity which by the time the admission could be consummated would secure a population of over 100,000. These representations proved to have been wholly fallacious, and in addition the people of the Territory by a deliberate vote decided that they would not assume the responsibilities of a State government. By that decision they utterly exhausted all power that was conferred by the enabling act, and there has been no step taken since in relation to the admission that has had the slightest sanction or warrant of law.

The proceeding upon which the present application is based was in the utter absence of all law in relation to it, and there is no evidence that the votes on the question of the formation of a State government bear any relation whatever to the sentiment of the Territory. The protest of the house of representatives previously quoted is conclusive evidence to the contrary.

But if none of these reasons existed against this proposed enactment, the bill itself, besides being inconsistent in its provisions in conferring power upon a person unknown to the laws and who may never have a legal existence, is so framed as to render its execution almost impossible. It is, indeed, a question whether it is not in itself a nullity. To say the least, it is of exceedingly doubtful propriety to confer the power proposed in this bill upon the "governor elect," for as by its own terms the constitution is not to take effect until after the admission of the State, he in the meantime has no more authority than any other private citizen. But even supposing him to be clothed with sufficient authority to convene the legislature, what constitutes the "State legislature" to which is to be referred the submission of the conditions imposed by Congress? Is it a new body to be elected and convened by proclamation of the "governor elect," or is it that body which met more than a year ago under the provisions of the State constitution? By reference to the second section of the schedule and to the eighteenth section of the fourth article of the State constitution it will be seen that the term of the members of the house of representatives and that of one-half of the members of the senate expired on the first Monday of the present month. It is clear that if there were no intrinsic objections to the bill itself in relation to purposes to be accomplished this objection would be fatal, as it is apparent that the provisions of the third section of the bill to admit Colorado have reference to a period and a state of facts entirely different from the present and affairs as they now exist, and if carried into effect must necessarily lead to confusion.

Even if it were settled that the old and not a new body were to act, it would be found impracticable to execute the law, because a considerable number of the members, as I am informed, have ceased to be residents of the Territory, and in the sixty days within which the legislature is to be convened after the passage of the act there would not be sufficient time to fill the vacancies by new elections, were there any authority under which they could be held.

It may not be improper to add that if these proceedings were all regular and the result to be obtained were desirable, simple justice to the people of the Territory would require a longer period than sixty days within which to obtain action on the conditions proposed by the third section of the bill. There are, as is well known, large portions of the Territory with which there is and can be no general communication, there being several counties which from November to May can only be reached by persons traveling on foot, while with other regions of the Territory, occupied by a large portion of the population, there is very little more freedom of access. Thus, if this bill should become a law, it would be impracticable to obtain any expression of public sentiment in reference to its provisions, with a view to enlighten the legislature, if the old body were called together, and, of course, equally impracticable to procure the election of a new body. This defect might have been remedied by an extension of the time and a submission of the question to the people, with a fair opportunity to enable them to express their sentiments.

The admission of a new State has generally been regarded as an epoch in our history marking the onward progress of the nation; but after the most careful and anxious inquiry on the subject I can not perceive that the proposed proceeding is in conformity with the policy which from the origin of the Government has uniformly prevailed in the admission of new States. I therefore return the bill to the Senate without my signature.

ANDREW JOHNSON.

States.	Admitted.	Ratio.	Population.
Vermont	1791	33,000	92,320
Kentucky	1792	33,000	95,638
Tennessee	1796	33,000	73,864
Ohio	1802	33,000	82,443
Louisiana	1812	35,000	75,212
Indiana	1816	35,000	98,110
Mississippi	1817	35,000	53,677
Illinois	1818	35,000	46,274
Alabama	1819	35,000	111,150
Maine	1820	35,000	298,335
Missouri	1821	35,000	69,260
Arkansas	1836	47,700	65,175
Michigan	1837	47,700	158,073
Florida	1845	70,680	57,951
Texas	1845	70,680	*189,327
Iowa	1846	70,680	132,527
Wisconsin	1848	70,680	250,497
California	1850	70,680	92,597
Oregon	1858	93,492	44,630
Minnesota	1859	93,492	138,909
Kansas	1861	93,492	107,206
West Virginia	1862	93,492	349,628
Nevada	1864	127,000	Not known.

*In 1850.

WASHINGTON, *January 29, 1867.*

To the Senate of the United States:

I return for reconsideration a bill entitled "An act for the admission of the State of Nebraska into the Union," which originated in the Senate and has received the assent of both Houses of Congress. A bill having in view the same object was presented for my approval a few hours prior to the adjournment of the last session, but, submitted at a time when there was no opportunity for a proper consideration of the subject, I withheld my signature and the measure failed to become a law.

It appears by the preamble of this bill that the people of Nebraska, availing themselves of the authority conferred upon them by the act passed on the 19th day of April, 1864, "have adopted a constitution which, upon due examination, is found to conform to the provisions and comply with the conditions of said act, and to be republican in its form of government, and that they now ask for admission into the Union." This proposed law would therefore seem to be based upon the declaration contained in the enabling act that upon compliance with its terms the people of Nebraska should be admitted into the Union upon an equal footing with the original States. Reference to the bill, however, shows that while by the first section Congress distinctly accepts, ratifies, and confirms the Constitution and State government which the people of the Territory have formed for themselves, declares Nebraska to be one of the United States of America, and admits her into the Union upon an equal footing with the original States in all respects whatsoever, the third section provides that this measure "shall not take effect except upon the fundamental condition that within the State of Nebraska there shall be no denial of the elective franchise, or of any other right, to any person by reason of race or color, excepting Indians not taxed; and upon the further fundamental condition that the legislature of said State, by a solemn public act, shall declare the assent of said State to the said fundamental condition, and shall transmit to the President of the United States an authentic copy of said act, upon receipt whereof the President, by proclamation, shall forthwith announce the fact, whereupon said fundamental condition shall be held as a part of the organic law of the State; and thereupon, and without any further proceeding on the part of Congress, the admission of said State into the Union shall be considered as complete." This condition is not mentioned in the original enabling act; was not contemplated at the time of its passage; was not sought by the people themselves; has not heretofore been applied to the inhabitants of any State asking admission, and is in direct conflict with the constitution adopted by the people and declared in the preamble "to be republican in its form of government," for in that instrument the exercise of the elective franchise and the right to hold office are expressly limited to white citizens of the United States. Congress thus undertakes to authorize and compel the legislature to change a constitution which, it is declared in the preamble, has received the sanction of the people, and which by this bill is "accepted, ratified, and confirmed" by the Congress of the nation.

The first and third sections of the bill exhibit yet further incongruity. By the one Nebraska is "admitted into the Union upon an equal footing with the original States in all respects whatsoever," while by the other Congress demands as a condition precedent to her admission requirements which in our history have never been asked of any people when presenting a constitution and State government for the acceptance of the lawmaking power. It is expressly declared by the third section that the bill "shall not take effect except upon the fundamental condition that within the State of Nebraska there shall be no denial of the elective franchise, or of any other right, to any person by reason of race or color, excepting Indians not taxed." Neither more nor less than the assertion of the right of Congress to regulate the elective franchise of any State hereafter to be admitted, this condition is in clear violation of the Federal Constitution, under the provisions of which, from the very foundation of the Government, each State has been left free to determine for itself the qualifications necessary for the exercise of suffrage within its limits. Without precedent in our legislation, it is in marked contrast with those limitations which, imposed upon States that from time to time have become members of the Union, had for their object the single purpose of preventing any infringement of the Constitution of the country.

If Congress is satisfied that Nebraska at the present time possesses sufficient population to entitle her to full representation in the councils of the nation, and that her people desire an exchange of a Territorial for a State government, good faith would seem to demand that she should be admitted without further requirements than those expressed in the enabling act, with all of which, it is asserted in the preamble, her inhabitants have complied. Congress may, under the Constitution, admit new States or reject them, but the people of a State can alone make or change their organic law and prescribe the qualifications requisite for electors. Congress, however, in passing the bill in the shape in which it has been submitted for my approval, does not merely reject the application of the people of Nebraska for present admission as a State into the Union, on the ground that the constitution which they have submitted restricts the exercise of the elective franchise to the white population, but imposes conditions which, if accepted by the legislature, may, without the consent of the people, so change the organic law as to make electors of all persons within the State without distinction of race or color. In view of this fact, I suggest for the consideration of Congress whether it would not be just, expedient, and in accordance with the principles of our Government to allow the people, by popular vote or through a convention chosen by themselves for that purpose, to declare whether or not they will accept the terms upon which it is now proposed to admit them into the Union. This course would not occasion much greater delay than that which the bill contemplates when it requires that the legislature shall be convened within thirty days after this measure shall have become a law for the purpose of considering and deciding the conditions which it imposes, and gains additional force when we consider that the proceedings attending the formation of the State constitution were not in conformity with the provisions of the enabling act; that in an aggregate vote of 7,776 the majority in favor of the constitution did not exceed 100; and that it is alleged that, in consequence of frauds, even this result can not be received as a fair expression of the wishes of the people.   As upon them must fall the burdens of a State organization, it is but just that they should be permitted to determine for themselves a question which so materially affects their interests.   Possessing a soil and a climate admirably adapted to those industrial pursuits which bring prosperity and greatness to a people, with the advantage of a central position on the great highway that will soon connect the Atlantic and Pacific States, Nebraska is rapidly gaining in numbers and wealth, and may within a very brief period claim admission on grounds which will challenge and secure universal assent.   She can therefore wisely and patiently afford to wait.   Her population is said to be steadily and even rapidly increasing, being now generally conceded as high as 40,000, and estimated by some whose judgment is entitled to respect at a still greater number.   At her present rate of growth she will in a very short time have the requisite population for a Representative in Congress, and, what is far more important to her own citizens, will have realized such an advance in material wealth as will enable the expenses of a State government to be borne without oppression to the taxpayer.   Of new communities it may be said with special force—and it is true of old ones—that the inducement to emigrants; other things being equal, is in almost the precise ratio of the rate of taxation.   The great States of the Northwest owe their marvelous prosperity largely to the fact that they were continued as Territories until they had grown to be wealthy and populous communities.

ANDREW JOHNSON.

WASHINGTON, *March 2, 1867.*

To the Senate of the United States:

I have carefully examined the bill "to regulate the tenure of certain civil offices."   The material portion of the bill is contained in the first section, and is of the effect following, namely:

That every person holding any civil office to which he has been appointed, by and with the advice and consent of the Senate, and every person who shall hereafter be appointed to any such office and shall become duly qualified to act therein, is and shall be entitled to hold such office until a successor shall have been appointed by the President, with the advice and consent of the Senate, and duly qualified; and that the Secretaries of State, of the Treasury, of War, of the Navy, and of the Interior, the Postmaster-General, and the Attorney-General shall hold their offices respectively for and during the term of the President by whom they may have been appointed and for one month thereafter, subject to removal by and with the advice and consent of the Senate.

These provisions are qualified by a reservation in the fourth section, "that nothing contained in the bill shall be construed to extend the term of any office the duration of which is limited by law." In effect the bill provides that the President shall not remove from their places any of the civil officers whose terms of service are not limited by law without the advice and consent of the Senate of the United States. The bill in this respect conflicts, in my judgment, with the Constitution of the United States. The question, as Congress is well aware, is by no means a new one. That the power of removal is constitutionally vested in the President of the United States is a principle which has been not more distinctly declared by judicial authority and judicial commentators than it has been uniformly practiced upon by the legislative and executive departments of the Government. The question arose in the House of Representatives so early as the 16th of June, 1789, on the bill for establishing an Executive Department denominated "the Department of Foreign Affairs." The first clause of the bill, after recapitulating the functions of that officer and defining his duties, had these words: "To be removable from office by the President of the United States." It was moved to strike out these words and the motion was sustained with great ability and vigor. It was insisted that the President could not constitutionally exercise the power of removal exclusively of the Senate; that the Federalist so interpreted the Constitution when arguing for its adoption by the several States; .hat the Constitution had nowhere given the President power of removal, either expressly or by strong implication, but, on the contrary, had distinctly provided for removals from office by impeachment only.

A construction which denied the power of removal by the President was further maintained by arguments drawn from the danger of the abuse of the power; from the supposed tendency of an exposure of public officers to capricious removal to impair the efficiency of the civil service; from the alleged injustice and hardship of displacing incumbents dependent upon their official stations without sufficient consideration; from a supposed want of responsibility on the part of the President, and from an imagined defect of guaranties against a vicious President who might incline to abuse the power. On the other hand, an exclusive power of removal by the President was defended as a true exposition of the text of the Constitution. It was maintained that there are certain causes for which persons ought to be removed from office without being guilty of treason, bribery, or malfeasance, and that the nature of things demands that it should be so. "Suppose," it was said, "a man becomes insane by the visitation of God and is likely to ruin our affairs; are the hands of the Government to be confined from warding off the evil? Suppose a person in office not possessing the talents he was judged to have at the time of the appointment; is the error not to be corrected? Suppose he acquires vicious habits and incurable indolence or total neglect of the duties of his office, which shall work mischief to the public welfare; is there no way to arrest the threatened danger? Suppose he becomes odious and unpopular by reason of the measures he pursues—and this he may do without committing any positive offense against the law; must he preserve his office in despite of the popular will? Suppose him grasping for his own aggrandizement and the elevation of his connections by every means short of the treason defined by the Constitution, hurrying your affairs to the precipice of destruction, endangering your domestic tranquillity, plundering you of the means of defense, alienating the affections of your allies and promoting the spirit of discord; must the tardy, tedious, desultory road by way of impeachment be traveled to overtake the man who, barely confining himself within the letter of the law, is employed in drawing off the vital principle of the Government? The nature of things, the great objects of society, the express objects of the Constitution itself, require that this thing should be otherwise. To unite the Senate with the President in the exercise of the power," it was said, "would involve us in the most serious difficulty. Suppose a discovery of any of those events should take place when the Senate is not in session; how is the remedy to be applied? The evil could be avoided in no other way than by the Senate sitting always." In regard to the danger of the power being abused if exercised by one man it was said "that the danger is as great with respect to the Senate, who are assembled from various parts of the continent, with different impressions and opinions;" "that such a body is more likely to misuse the power of removal than the man whom the united voice of America calls to the Presidential chair. As the nature of government requires the power of removal," it was maintained "that it should be exercised in this way by the hand capable of exerting itself with effect; and the power must be conferred on the President by the Constitution as the executive officer of the Government."

Mr. Madison, whose adverse opinion in the Federalist had been relied upon by those who denied the exclusive power, now participated in the debate. He declared that he had reviewed his former opinions, and he summed up the whole case as follows:

The Constitution affirms that the executive power is vested in the President. Are there exceptions to this proposition? Yes; there are. The Constitution says that in appointing to office the Senate shall be associated with the President, unless in the case of inferior officers, when the law shall otherwise direct. Have we (that is, Congress) a right to extend this exception? I believe not. If the Constitution has invested all executive power in the President, I venture to assert that the Legislature has no right to diminish or modify his executive authority. The question now resolves itself into this: Is the power of displacing an executive power? I conceive that if any power whatsoever is in the Executive it is the power of appointing, overseeing, and controlling those who execute the laws. If the Constitution had not qualified the power of the President in appointing to office by associating the Senate with him in that business, would it not be clear that he would have the right by virtue of his executive power to make such appointment? Should we be authorized in defiance of that clause in the Constitution, "The executive power shall be vested in the President," to unite the Senate with the President in the appointment to office? I conceive not. If it is admitted that we should not be authorized to do this,

I think it may be disputed whether we have a right to associate them in removing persons from office, the one power being as much of an executive nature as the other; and the first one is authorized by being excepted out of the general rule established by the Constitution in these words: "The executive power shall be vested in the President."

The question, thus ably and exhaustively argued, was decided by the House of Representatives, by a vote of 34 to 20, in favor of the principle that the executive power of removal is vested by the Constitution in the Executive, and in the Senate by the casting vote of the Vice-President.

The question has often been raised in subsequent times of high excitement, and the practice of the Government has, nevertheless, conformed in all cases to the decision thus early made.

The question was revived during the Administration of President Jackson, who made, as is well recollected, a very large number of removals, which were made an occasion of close and rigorous scrutiny and remonstrance. The subject was long and earnestly debated in the Senate, and the early construction of the Constitution was, nevertheless, freely accepted as binding and conclusive upon Congress.

The question came before the Supreme Court of the United States in January, 1839, *ex parte* Hennen. It was declared by the court on that occasion that the power of removal from office was a subject much disputed, and upon which a great diversity of opinion was entertained in the early history of the Government. This related, however, to the power of the President to remove officers appointed with the concurrence of the Senate, and the great question was whether the removal was to be by the President alone or with the concurrence of the Senate, both constituting the appointing power. No one denied the power of the President and Senate jointly to remove where the tenure of the office was not fixed by the Constitution, which was a full recognition of the principle that the power of removal was incident to the power of appointment; but it was very early adopted as a practical construction of the Constitution that this power was vested in the President alone, and such would appear to have been the legislative construction of the Constitution, for in the organization of the three great Departments of State, War, and Treasury, in the year 1789, provision was made for the appointment of a subordinate officer by the head of the Department, who should have charge of the records, books, and papers appertaining to the office when the head of the Department should be removed from office by the President of the United States. When the Navy Department was established, in the year 1798, provision was made for the charge and custody of the books, records, and documents of the Department in case of vacancy in the office of Secretary by removal or otherwise. It is not here said "by removal of the President," as is done with respect to the heads of the other Departments, yet there can be no doubt that he holds his office with the same tenure as the other Secretaries and is removable by the

President. The change of phraseology arose, probably, from its having become the settled and well-understood construction of the Constitution that the power of removal was vested in the President alone in such cases, although the appointment of the officer is by the President and Senate. (13 Peters, p. 139.)

Our most distinguished and accepted commentators upon the Constitution concur in the construction thus early given by Congress, and thus sanctioned by the Supreme Court. After a full analysis of the Congressional debate to which I have referred, Mr. Justice Story comes to this conclusion:

After a most animated discussion, the vote finally taken in the House of Representatives was affirmative of the power of removal in the President, without any cooperation of the Senate, by the vote of 34 members against 20. In the Senate the clause in the bill affirming the power was carried by the casting vote of the Vice-President. That the final decision of this question so made was greatly influenced by the exalted character of the President then in office was asserted at the time and has always been believed; yet the doctrine was opposed as well as supported by the highest talents and patriotism of the country. The public have acquiesced in this decision, and it constitutes, perhaps, the most extraordinary case in the history of the Government of a power conferred by implication on the Executive by the assent of a bare majority of Congress which has not been questioned on many other occasions.

The commentator adds:

Nor is this general acquiescence and silence without a satisfactory explanation.

Chancellor Kent's remarks on the subject are as follows:

On the first organization of the Government it was made a question whether the power of removal in case of officers appointed to hold at pleasure resided nowhere but in the body which appointed, and, of course, whether the consent of the Senate was not requisite to remove. This was the construction given to the Constitution, while it was pending for ratification before the State conventions, by the author of the Federalist. But the construction which was given to the Constitution by Congress, after great consideration and discussion, was different. The words of the act [establishing the Treasury Department] are: "And whenever the same shall be removed from office by the President of the United States, or in any other case of vacancy in the office, the assistant shall act." This amounted to a legislative construction of the Constitution, and it has ever since been acquiesced in and acted upon as a decisive authority in the case. It applies equally to every other officer of the Government appointed by the President, whose term of duration is not specially declared. It is supported by the weighty reason that the subordinate officers in the executive department ought to hold at the pleasure of the head of the department, because he is invested generally with the executive authority, and the participation in that authority by the Senate was an exception to a general principle and ought to be taken strictly. The President is the great responsible officer for the faithful execution of the law, and the power of removal was incidental to that duty, and might often be requisite to fulfill it.

Thus has the important question presented by this bill been settled, in the language of the late Daniel Webster (who, while dissenting from it, admitted that it was settled), by construction, settled by precedent, settled by the practice of the Government, and settled by statute. The events of the last war furnished a practical confirmation of the wisdom of the Constitution as it has hitherto been maintained in many of its parts, including that which is now the subject of consideration. When the war broke out, rebel enemies, traitors, abettors, and sympathizers were found in every Department of the Government, as well in the civil service as in the land and naval military service. They were found in Congress and among the keepers of the Capitol; in foreign missions; in each and all the Executive Departments; in the judicial service; in the post-office, and among the agents for conducting Indian affairs. Upon probable suspicion they were promptly displaced by my predecessor, so far as they held their offices under executive authority, and their duties were confided to new and loyal successors. No complaints against that power or doubts of its wisdom were entertained in any quarter. I sincerely trust and believe that no such civil war is likely to occur again. I can not doubt, however, that in whatever form and on whatever occasion sedition can raise an effort to hinder or embarrass or defeat the legitimate action of this Government, whether by preventing the collection of revenue, or disturbing the public peace, or separating the States, or betraying the country to a foreign enemy, the power of removal from office by the Executive, as it has heretofore existed and been practiced, will be found indispensable.

Under these circumstances, as a depositary of the executive authority of the nation, I do not feel at liberty to unite with Congress in reversing it by giving my approval to the bill. At the early day when this question was settled, and, indeed, at the several periods when it has subsequently been agitated, the success of the Constitution of the United States, as a new and peculiar system of free representative government, was held doubtful in other countries, and was even a subject of patriotic apprehension among the American people themselves. A trial of nearly eighty years, through the vicissitudes of foreign conflicts and of civil war, is confidently regarded as having extinguished all such doubts and apprehensions for the future. During that eighty years the people of the United States have enjoyed a measure of security, peace, prosperity, and happiness never surpassed by any nation. It can not be doubted that the triumphant success of the Constitution is due to the wonderful wisdom with which the functions of government were distributed between the three principal departments—the legislative, the executive, and the judicial—and to the fidelity with which each has confined itself or been confined by the general voice of the nation within its peculiar and proper sphere. While a just, proper, and watchful jealousy of executive power constantly prevails, as it ought ever to prevail, yet it is equally true that an efficient Executive, capable, in the language of the oath prescribed to the President, of executing the laws and, within the sphere of executive action, of preserving, protecting, and defending the Constitution of the United States, is an indispensable security for tranquillity at home and peace, honor, and safety abroad. Governments have been erected in many countries upon our model. If one or many of them have thus far failed in fully securing to their people the benefits which we have derived from our system, it may be confidently asserted that their misfortune has resulted from their unfortunate failure to maintain the integrity of each of the three great departments while preserving harmony among them all.

Having at an early period accepted the Constitution in regard to the Executive office in the sense in which it was interpreted with the concurrence of its founders, I have found no sufficient grounds in the arguments now opposed to that construction or in any assumed necessity of the times for changing those opinions. For these reasons I return the bill to the Senate, in which House it originated, for the further consideration of Congress which the Constitution prescribes. Insomuch as the several parts of the bill which I have not considered are matters chiefly of detail and are based altogether upon the theory of the Constitution from which I am obliged to dissent, I have not thought it necessary to examine them with a view to make them an occasion of distinct and special objections.

Experience, I think, has shown that it is the easiest, as it is also the most attractive, of studies to frame constitutions for the self-government of free states and nations. But I think experience has equally shown that it is the most difficult of all political labors to preserve and maintain such free constitutions of self-government when once happily established. I know no other way in which they can be preserved and maintained except by a constant adherence to them through the various vicissitudes of national existence, with such adaptations as may become necessary, always to be effected, however, through the agencies and in the forms prescribed in the original constitutions themselves.

Whenever administration fails or seems to fail in securing any of the great ends for which republican government is established, the proper course seems to be to renew the original spirit and forms of the Constitution itself.

ANDREW JOHNSON.

WASHINGTON, *March 2, 1867.*

To the House of Representatives:

I have examined the bill "to provide for the more efficient government of the rebel States" with the care and anxiety which its transcendent importance is calculated to awaken. I am unable to give it my assent, for reasons so grave that I hope a statement of them may have some influence on the minds of the patriotic and enlightened men with whom the decision must ultimately rest.

The bill places all the people of the ten States therein named under the absolute domination of military rulers; and the preamble undertakes to give the reason upon which the measure is based and the ground upon which it is justified. It declares that there exists in those States no legal governments and no adequate protection for life or property, and asserts the necessity of enforcing peace and good order within their limits. Is this true as matter of fact?

It is not denied that the States in question have each of them an actual government, with all the powers—executive, judicial, and legislative—which properly belong to a free state. They are organized like the other States of the Union, and, like them, they make, administer, and execute the laws which concern their domestic affairs. An existing *de facto* government, exercising such functions as these, is itself the law of the state upon all matters within its jurisdiction. To pronounce the supreme law-making power of an established state illegal is to say that law itself is unlawful.

The provisions which these governments have made for the preservation of order, the suppression of crime, and the redress of private injuries are in substance and principle the same as those which prevail in the Northern States and in other civilized countries. They certainly have not succeeded in preventing the commission of all crime, nor has this been accomplished anywhere in the world. There, as well as elsewhere, offenders sometimes escape for want of vigorous prosecution, and occasionally, perhaps, by the inefficiency of courts or the prejudice of jurors. It is undoubtedly true that these evils have been much increased and aggravated, North and South, by the demoralizing influences of civil war and by the rancorous passions which the contest has engendered. But that these people are maintaining local governments for themselves which habitually defeat the object of all government and render their own lives and property insecure is in itself utterly improbable, and the averment of the bill to that effect is not supported by any evidence which has come to my knowledge. All the information I have on the subject convinces me that the masses of the Southern people and those who control their public acts, while they entertain diverse opinions on questions of Federal policy, are completely united in the effort to reorganize their society on the basis of peace and to restore their mutual prosperity as rapidly and as completely as their circumstances will permit.

The bill, however, would seem to show upon its face that the establishment of peace and good order is not its real object. The fifth section declares that the preceding sections shall cease to operate in any State where certain events shall have happened. These events are, first, the selection of delegates to a State convention by an election at which negroes shall be allowed to vote; second, the formation of a State constitution by the convention so chosen; third, the insertion into the State constitution of a provision which will secure the right of voting at all elections to negroes and to such white men as may not be disfranchised for rebellion or felony; fourth, the submission of the constitution for ratification to negroes and white men not disfranchised, and its actual ratification by their vote; fifth, the submission of the State constitution to Congress for examination and approval, and the actual approval of it by that body; sixth, the adoption of a certain amendment to the Federal Constitution by a vote of the legislature elected under the new constitution; seventh, the adoption of said amendment by a sufficient number of other States to make it a part of the Constitution of the United States. All these conditions must be fulfilled before the people of any of these States can be relieved from the bondage of military domination; but when they are fulfilled, then immediately the pains and penalties of the bill are to cease, no matter whether there be peace and order or not, and without any reference to the security of life or property. The excuse given for the bill in the preamble is admitted by the bill itself not to be real. The military rule which it establishes is plainly to be used, not for any purpose of order or for the prevention of crime, but solely as a means of coercing the people into the adoption of principles and measures to which it is known that they are opposed, and upon which they have an undeniable right to exercise their own judgment.

I submit to Congress whether this measure is not in its whole character, scope, and object without precedent and without authority, in palpable conflict with the plainest provisions of the Constitution, and utterly destructive to those great principles of liberty and humanity for which our ancestors on both sides of the Atlantic have shed so much blood and expended so much treasure.

The ten States named in the bill are divided into five districts. For each district an officer of the Army, not below the rank of a brigadier-general, is to be appointed to rule over the people; and he is to be supported with an efficient military force to enable him to perform his duties and enforce his authority. Those duties and that authority, as defined by the third section of the bill, are ''to protect all persons in their rights of person and property, to suppress insurrection, disorder, and violence, and to punish or cause to be punished all disturbers of the public peace or criminals.'' The power thus given to the commanding officer over all the people of each district is that of an absolute monarch. His mere will is to take the place of all law. The law of the States is now the only rule applicable to the subjects placed under his control, and that is completely displaced by the clause which declares all interference of State authority to be null and void. He alone is permitted to determine what are rights of person or property, and he may protect them in such way as in his discretion may seem proper. It places at his free disposal all the lands and goods in his district, and he may distribute them without let or hindrance to whom he pleases. Being bound by no State law, and there being no other law to regulate the subject, he may make a criminal code of his own; and he can make it as bloody as any recorded in history, or he can reserve the privilege of acting upon the impulse of his private passions in each case that arises. He is bound by no rules of evidence; there is, indeed, no provision by which he is authorized or required to take any evidence at all. Everything is a crime which he chooses to call so, and all persons are condemned whom he pronounces to be guilty. He is not bound to keep any record or make any report of his proceedings. He may arrest his victims wherever he finds them, without warrant, accusation, or proof of probable cause. If he gives them a trial before he inflicts the punishment, he gives it of his grace and mercy, not because he is commanded so to do.

To a casual reader of the bill it might seem that some kind of trial was secured by it to persons accused of crime, but such is not the case. The officer "may allow local civil tribunals to try offenders," but of course this does not require that he shall do so. If any State or Federal court presumes to exercise its legal jurisdiction by the trial of a malefactor without his special permission, he can break it up and punish the judges and jurors as being themselves malefactors. He can save his friends from justice, and despoil his enemies contrary to justice.

It is also provided that "he shall have power to organize military commissions or tribunals;" but this power he is not commanded to exercise. It is merely permissive, and is to be used only "when in his judgment it may be necessary for the trial of offenders." Even if the sentence of a commission were made a prerequisite to the punishment of a party, it would be scarcely the slightest check upon the officer, who has authority to organize it as he pleases, prescribe its mode of proceeding, appoint its members from his own subordinates, and revise all its decisions. Instead of mitigating the harshness of his single rule, such a tribunal would be used much more probably to divide the responsibility of making it more cruel and unjust.

Several provisions dictated by the humanity of Congress have been inserted in the bill, apparently to restrain the power of the commanding officer; but it seems to me that they are of no avail for that purpose. The fourth section provides: First. That trials shall not be unnecessarily delayed; but I think I have shown that the power is given to punish without trial; and if so, this provision is practically inoperative. Second. Cruel or unusual punishment is not to be inflicted; but who is to decide what is cruel and what is unusual? The words have acquired a legal meaning by long use in the courts. Can it be expected that military officers will understand or follow a rule expressed in language so purely technical and not pertaining in the least degree to their profession? If not, then each officer may define cruelty according to his own temper, and if it is not usual he will make it usual. Corporal punishment, imprisonment, the gag, the ball and chain, and all the almost insupportable forms of torture invented for military punishment lie within the range of choice. Third. The sentence of a commission is not to be executed without being approved by the commander, if it affects life or liberty, and a sentence of death must be approved by the President. This applies to cases in which there has been a trial and sentence. I take it to be clear, under this bill, that the military commander may condemn to death without even the form of a trial by a military commission, so that the life of the condemned may depend upon the will of two men instead of one.

It is plain that the authority here given to the military officer amounts to absolute despotism. But to make it still more unendurable, the bill provides that it may be delegated to as many subordinates as he chooses to appoint, for it declares that he shall "punish or cause to be punished." Such a power has not been wielded by any monarch in England for more than five hundred years. In all that time no people who speak the English language have borne such servitude. It reduces the whole population of the ten States—all persons, of every color, sex, and condition, and every stranger within their limits—to the most abject and degrading slavery. No master ever had a control so absolute over the slaves as this bill gives to the military officers over both white and colored persons.

It may be answered to this that the officers of the Army are too magnanimous, just, and humane to oppress and trample upon a subjugated people. I do not doubt that army officers are as well entitled to this kind of confidence as any other class of men. But the history of the world has been written in vain if it does not teach us that unrestrained authority can never be safely trusted in human hands. It is almost sure to be more or less abused under any circumstances, and it has always resulted in gross tyranny where the rulers who exercise it are strangers to their subjects and come among them as the representatives of a distant power, and more especially when the power that sends them is unfriendly. Governments closely resembling that here proposed have been fairly tried in Hungary and Poland, and the suffering endured by those people roused the sympathies of the entire world. It was tried in Ireland, and, though tempered at first by principles of English law, it gave birth to cruelties so atrocious that they are never recounted without just indignation. The French Convention armed its deputies with this power and sent them to the southern departments of the Republic. The massacres, murders, and other atrocities which they committed show what the passions of the ablest men in the most civilized society will tempt them to do when wholly unrestrained by law.

The men of our race in every age have struggled to tie up the hands of their governments and keep them within the law, because their own experience of all mankind taught them that rulers could not be relied on to concede those rights which they were not legally bound to respect. The head of a great empire has sometimes governed it with a mild and paternal sway, but the kindness of an irresponsible deputy never yields what the law does not extort from him. Between such a master and the people subjected to his domination there can be nothing but enmity;

he punishes them if they resist his authority, and if they submit to it he hates them for their servility.

I come now to a question which is, if possible, still more important. Have we the power to establish and carry into execution a measure like this? I answer, Certainly not, if we derive our authority from the Constitution and if we are bound by the limitations which it imposes.

This proposition is perfectly clear, that no branch of the Federal Government—executive, legislative, or judicial—can have any just powers except those which it derives through and exercises under the organic law of the Union. Outside of the Constitution we have no legal authority more than private citizens, and within it we have only so much as that instrument gives us. This broad principle limits all our functions and applies to all subjects. It protects not only the citizens of States which are within the Union, but it shields every human being who comes or is brought under our jurisdiction. We have no right to do in one place more than in another that which the Constitution says we shall not do at all. If, therefore, the Southern States were in truth out of the Union, we could not treat their people in a way which the fundamental law forbids.

Some persons assume that the success of our arms in crushing the opposition which was made in some of the States to the execution of the Federal laws reduced those States and all their people—the innocent as well as the guilty—to the condition of vassalage and gave us a power over them which the Constitution does not bestow or define or limit. No fallacy can be more transparent than this. Our victories subjected the insurgents to legal obedience, not to the yoke of an arbitrary despotism. When an absolute sovereign reduces his rebellious subjects, he may deal with them according to his pleasure, because he had that power before. But when a limited monarch puts down an insurrection, he must still govern according to law. If an insurrection should take place in one of our States against the authority of the State government and end in the overthrow of those who planned it, would that take away the rights of all the people of the counties where it was favored by a part or a majority of the population? Could they for such a reason be wholly outlawed and deprived of their representation in the legislature? I have always contended that the Government of the United States was sovereign within its constitutional sphere; that it executed its laws, like the States themselves, by applying its coercive power directly to individuals, and that it could put down insurrection with the same effect as a State and no other. The opposite doctrine is the worst heresy of those who advocated secession, and can not be agreed to without admitting that heresy to be right.

Invasion, insurrection, rebellion, and domestic violence were anticipated when the Government was framed, and the means of repelling and suppressing them were wisely provided for in the Constitution; but it was not thought necessary to declare that the States in which they might occur should be expelled from the Union. Rebellions, which were invariably suppressed, occurred prior to that out of which these questions grow; but the States continued to exist and the Union remained unbroken. In Massachusetts, in Pennsylvania, in Rhode Island, and in New York, at different periods in our history, violent and armed opposition to the United States was carried on; but the relations of those States with the Federal Government were not supposed to be interrupted or changed thereby after the rebellious portions of their population were defeated and put down. It is true that in these earlier cases there was no formal expression of a determination to withdraw from the Union, but it is also true that in the Southern States the ordinances of secession were treated by all the friends of the Union as mere nullities and are now acknowledged to be so by the States themselves. If we admit that they had any force or validity or that they did in fact take the States in which they were passed out of the Union, we sweep from under our feet all the grounds upon which we stand in justifying the use of Federal force to maintain the integrity of the Government.

This is a bill passed by Congress in time of peace. There is not in any one of the States brought under its operation either war or insurrection. The laws of the States and of the Federal Government are all in undisturbed and harmonious operation. The courts, State and Federal, are open and in the full exercise of their proper authority. Over every State comprised in these five military districts, life, liberty, and property are secured by State laws and Federal laws, and the National Constitution is everywhere in force and everywhere obeyed. What, then, is the ground on which this bill proceeds? The title of the bill announces that it is intended "for the more efficient government" of these ten States. It is recited by way of preamble that no legal State governments "nor adequate protection for life or property" exist in those States, and that peace and good order should be thus enforced. The first thing which arrests attention upon these recitals, which prepare the way for martial law, is this, that the only foundation upon which martial law can exist under our form of government is not stated or so much as pretended. Actual war, foreign invasion, domestic insurrection—none of these appear; and none of these, in fact, exist. It is not even recited that any sort of war or insurrection is threatened. Let us pause here to consider, upon this question of constitutional law and the power of Congress, a recent decision of the Supreme Court of the United States in *ex parte* Milligan.

I will first quote from the opinion of the majority of the court:

Martial law can not arise from a threatened invasion. The necessity must be actual and present, the invasion real, such as effectually closes the courts and deposes the civil administration.

We see that martial law comes in only when actual war closes the courts and deposes the civil authority; but this bill, in time of peace, makes martial law operate as though we were in actual war, and becomes the *cause* instead of the *consequence* of the abrogation of civil authority. One more quotation:

> It follows from what has been said on this subject that there are occasions when martial law can be properly applied. If in foreign invasion or civil war the courts are actually closed, and it is impossible to administer criminal justice according to law, *then*, on the theater of active military operations, where war really prevails, there is a necessity to furnish a substitute for the civil authority thus overthrown, to preserve the safety of the army and society; and as no power is left but the military, it is allowed to govern by martial rule until the laws can have their free course.

I now quote from the opinion of the minority of the court, delivered by Chief Justice Chase:

> We by no means assert that Congress can establish and apply the laws of war where no war has been declared or exists. Where peace exists, the laws of peace must prevail.

This is sufficiently explicit. Peace exists in all the territory to which this bill applies. It asserts a power in Congress, in time of peace, to set aside the laws of peace and to substitute the laws of war. The minority, concurring with the majority, declares that Congress does not possess that power. Again, and, if possible, more emphatically, the Chief Justice, with remarkable clearness and condensation, sums up the whole matter as follows:

> There are under the Constitution three kinds of military jurisdiction—one to be exercised both in peace and war; another to be exercised in time of foreign war without the boundaries of the United States, or in time of rebellion and civil war within States or districts occupied by rebels treated as belligerents; and a third to be exercised in time of invasion or insurrection within the limits of the United States, or during rebellion within the limits of the States maintaining adhesion to the National Government, when the public danger requires its exercise. The first of these may be called jurisdiction under military law, and is found in acts of Congress prescribing rules and articles of war or otherwise providing for the government of the national forces; the second may be distinguished as military government, superseding as far as may be deemed expedient the local law, and exercised by the military commander under the direction of the President, with the express or implied sanction of Congress; while the third may be denominated martial law proper, and is called into action by Congress, or temporarily, when the action of Congress can not be invited, and in the case of justifying or excusing peril, by the President, in times of insurrection or invasion or of civil or foreign war, within districts or localities where ordinary law no longer adequately secures public safety and private rights.

It will be observed that of the three kinds of military jurisdiction which can be exercised or created under our Constitution there is but one that can prevail in time of peace, and that is the code of laws enacted by Congress for the government of the national forces. That body of military law has no application to the citizen, nor even to the citizen soldier enrolled in the militia in time of peace. But this bill is not a part of that sort of military law, for that applies only to the soldier and not to the citizen, whilst, contrariwise, the military law provided by this bill applies only to the citizen and not to the soldier.

I need not say to the representatives of the American people that their Constitution forbids the exercise of judicial power in any way but one— that is, by the ordained and established courts. It is equally well known that in all criminal cases a trial by jury is made indispensable by the express words of that instrument. I will not enlarge on the inestimable value of the right thus secured to every freeman or speak of the danger to public liberty in all parts of the country which must ensue from a denial of it anywhere or upon any pretense. A very recent decision of the Supreme Court has traced the history, vindicated the dignity, and made known the value of this great privilege so clearly that nothing more is needed. To what extent a violation of it might be excused in time of war or public danger·may admit of discussion, but we are providing now for a time of profound peace, when there is not an armed soldier within our borders except those who are in the service of the Government. It is in such a condition of things that an act of Congress is proposed which, if carried out, would deny a trial by the lawful courts and juries to 9,000,000 American citizens and to their posterity for an indefinite period. It seems to be scarcely possible that anyone should seriously believe this consistent with a Constitution which declares in simple, plain, and unambiguous language that all persons shall have that right and that no person shall ever in any case be deprived of it. The Constitution also forbids the arrest of the citizen without judicial warrant, founded on probable cause. This bill authorizes an arrest without warrant, at the pleasure of a military commander. The Constitution declares that "no person shall be held to answer for a capital or otherwise·infamous crime unless on presentment by a grand jury." This bill holds every person not a soldier answerable for all crimes and all charges without any presentment. The Constitution declares that "no person shall be deprived of life, liberty, or property without due process of law." This bill sets aside all process of law, and makes the citizen answerable in his person and property to the will of one man, and as to his life to the will of two. Finally, the Constitution declares that "the privilege of the writ of *habeas corpus* shall not be suspended unless when, in case of rebellion or invasion, the public safety may require it;" whereas this bill declares martial law (which of itself suspends this great writ) in time of peace, and authorizes the military to make the arrest, and gives to the prisoner only one privilege, and that is a trial "without unnecessary delay." He has no hope of release from custody, except the hope, such as it is, of release by acquittal before a military commission.

The United States are bound to guarantee to each State a republican form of government. Can it be pretended that this obligation is not palpably broken if we carry out a measure like this, which wipes away every vestige of republican government in ten States and puts the life, property, liberty, and honor of all the people in each of them under the domination of a single person clothed with unlimited authority?

The Parliament of England, exercising the omnipotent power which it claimed, was accustomed to pass bills of attainder; that is to say, it would convict men of treason and other crimes by legislative enactment. The person accused had a hearing, sometimes a patient and fair one, but generally party prejudice prevailed instead of justice. It often became necessary for Parliament to acknowledge its error and reverse its own action. The fathers of our country determined that no such thing should occur here. They withheld the power from Congress, and thus forbade its exercise by that body, and they provided in the Constitution that no State should pass any bill of attainder. It is therefore impossible for any person in this country to be constitutionally convicted or punished for any crime by a legislative proceeding of any sort. Nevertheless, here is a bill of attainder against 9,000,000 people at once. It is based upon an accusation so vague as to be scarcely intelligible and found to be true upon no credible evidence. Not one of the 9,000,000 was heard in his own defense. The representatives of the doomed parties were excluded from all participation in the trial. The conviction is to be followed by the most ignominious punishment ever inflicted on large masses of men. It disfranchises them by hundreds of thousands and degrades them all, even those who are admitted to be guiltless, from the rank of freemen to the condition of slaves.

The purpose and object of the bill—the general intent which pervades it from beginning to end—is to change the entire structure and character of the State governments and to compel them by force to the adoption of organic laws and regulations which they are unwilling to accept if left to themselves. The negroes have not asked for the privilege of voting; the vast majority of them have no idea what it means. This bill not only thrusts it into their hands, but compels them, as well as the whites, to use it in a particular way. If they do not form a constitution with prescribed articles in it and afterwards elect a legislature which will act upon certain measures in a prescribed way, neither blacks nor whites can be relieved from the slavery which the bill imposes upon them. Without pausing here to consider the policy or impolicy of Africanizing the southern part of our territory, I would simply ask the attention of Congress to that manifest, well-known, and universally acknowledged rule of constitutional law which declares that the Federal Government has no jurisdiction, authority, or power to regulate such subjects for any State. To force the right of suffrage out of the hands of the white people and into the hands of the negroes is an arbitrary violation of this principle.

This bill imposes martial law at once, and its operations will begin so soon as the general and his troops can be put in place. The dread alternative between its harsh rule and compliance with the terms of this measure is not suspended, nor are the people afforded any time for free deliberation. The bill says to them, take martial law first, *then* deliberate. And when they have done all that this measure requires them to do other conditions and contingencies over which they have no control yet remain to be fulfilled before they can be relieved from martial law. Another Congress must first approve the Constitution made in conformity with the will of this Congress and must declare these States entitled to representation in both Houses. The whole question thus remains open and unsettled and must again occupy the attention of Congress; and in the meantime the agitation which now prevails will continue to disturb all portions of the people.

The bill also denies the legality of the governments of ten of the States which participated in the ratification of the amendment to the Federal Constitution abolishing slavery forever within the jurisdiction of the United States and practically excludes them from the Union. If this assumption of the bill be correct, their concurrence can not be considered as having been legally given, and the important fact is made to appear that the consent of three-fourths of the States—the requisite number—has not been constitutionally obtained to the ratification of that amendment, thus leaving the question of slavery where it stood before the amendment was officially declared to have become a part of the Constitution.

That the measure proposed by this bill does violate the Constitution in the particulars mentioned and in many other ways which I forbear to enumerate is too clear to admit of the least doubt. It only remains to consider whether the injunctions of that instrument ought to be obeyed or not. I think they ought to be obeyed, for reasons which I will proceed to give as briefly as possible.

In the first place, it is the only system of free government which we can hope to have as a nation. When it ceases to be the rule of our conduct, we may perhaps take our choice between complete anarchy, a consolidated despotism, and a total dissolution of the Union; but national liberty regulated by law will have passed beyond our reach.

It is the best frame of government the world ever saw. No other is or can be so well adapted to the genius, habits, or wants of the American people. Combining the strength of a great empire with unspeakable blessings of local self-government, having a central power to defend the general interests, and recognizing the authority of the States as the guardians of industrial rights, it is "the sheet anchor of our safety abroad and our peace at home." It was ordained "to form a more perfect union, establish justice, insure domestic tranquillity, promote the general welfare, provide for the common defense, and secure the blessings of liberty to ourselves and to our posterity." These great ends have been attained heretofore, and will be again by faithful obedience to it; but they are certain to be lost if we treat with disregard its sacred obligations.

It was to punish the gross crime of defying the Constitution and to vindicate its supreme authority that we carried on a bloody war of four years' duration. Shall we now acknowledge that we sacrificed a million of lives and expended billions of treasure to enforce a Constitution which is not worthy of respect and preservation?

Those who advocated the right of secession alleged in their own justification that we had no regard for law and that their rights of property, life, and liberty would not be safe under the Constitution as administered by us. If we now verify their assertion, we prove that they were in truth and in fact fighting for their liberty, and instead of branding their leaders with the dishonoring name of traitors against a righteous and legal government we elevate them in history to the rank of self-sacrificing patriots, consecrate them to the admiration of the world, and place them by the side of Washington, Hampden, and Sidney. No; let us leave them to the infamy they deserve, punish them as they should be punished, according to law, and take upon ourselves no share of the odium which they should bear alone.

It is a part of our public history which can never be forgotten that both Houses of Congress, in July, 1861, declared in the form of a solemn resolution that the war was and should be carried on for no purpose of subjugation, but solely to enforce the Constitution and laws, and that when this was yielded by the parties in rebellion the contest should cease, with the constitutional rights of the States and of individuals unimpaired. This resolution was adopted and sent forth to the world unanimously by the Senate and with only two dissenting voices in the House. It was accepted by the friends of the Union in the South as well as in the North as expressing honestly and truly the object of the war. On the faith of it many thousands of persons in both sections gave their lives and their fortunes to the cause. To repudiate it now by refusing to the States and to the individuals within them the rights which the Constitution and laws of the Union would secure to them is a breach of our plighted honor for which I can imagine no excuse and to which I can not voluntarily become a party.

The evils which spring from the unsettled state of our Government will be acknowledged by all. Commercial intercourse is impeded, capital is in constant peril, public securities fluctuate in value, peace itself is not secure, and the sense of moral and political duty is impaired. To avert these calamities from our country it is imperatively required that we should immediately decide upon some course of administration which can be steadfastly adhered to. I am thoroughly convinced that any settlement or compromise or plan of action which is inconsistent with the principles of the Constitution will not only be unavailing, but mischievous; that it will but multiply the present evils, instead of removing them. The Constitution, in its whole integrity and vigor, throughout the length and breadth of the land, is the best of all compromises. Besides, our duty does not, in my judgment, leave us a choice between that and any other. I believe that it contains the remedy that is so much needed, and that if the coordinate branches of the Government would unite upon its provisions they would be found broad enough and strong enough to sustain in time of peace the nation which they bore safely through the ordeal of a protracted civil war. Among the most sacred guaranties of that instrument are those which declare that ''each State shall have at least one Representative,'' and that ''no State, without its consent, shall be deprived of its equal suffrage in the Senate.'' Each House is made the ''judge of the elections, returns, and qualifications of its own members,'' and may, ''with the concurrence of two-thirds, expel a member.'' Thus, as heretofore urged, ''in the admission of Senators and Representatives from any and all of the States there can be no just ground of apprehension that persons who are disloyal will be clothed with the powers of legislation, for this could not happen when the Constitution and the laws are enforced by a vigilant and faithful Congress.'' ''When a Senator or Representative presents his certificate of election, he may at once be admitted or rejected; or, should there be any question as to his eligibility, his credentials may be referred for investigation to the appropriate committee. If admitted to a seat, it must be upon evidence satisfactory to the House of which he thus becomes a member that he possesses the requisite constitutional and legal qualifications. If refused admission as a member for want of due allegiance to the Government, and returned to his constituents, they are admonished that none but persons loyal to the United States will be allowed a voice in the legislative councils of the nation, and the political power and moral influence of Congress are thus effectively exerted in the interests of loyalty to the Government and fidelity to the Union.'' And is it not far better that the work of restoration should be accomplished by simple compliance with the plain requirements of the Constitution than by a recourse to measures which in effect destroy the States and threaten the subversion of the General Government? All that is necessary to settle this simple but important question without further agitation or delay is a willingness on the part of all to sustain the Constitution and carry its provisions into practical operation. If to-morrow either branch of Congress would declare that upon the presentation of their credentials members constitutionally elected and loyal to the General Government would be admitted to seats in Congress, while all others would be excluded and their places remain vacant until the selection by the people of loyal and qualified persons, and if at the same time assurance were given that this policy would be continued until all the States were represented in Congress, it would send a thrill of joy throughout the entire land, as indicating the inauguration of a system which must speedily bring tranquillity to the public mind.

While we are legislating upon subjects which are of great importance to the whole people, and which must affect all parts of the country, not only during the life of the present generation, but for ages to come, we should remember that all men are entitled at least to a hearing in the councils which decide upon the destiny of themselves and their children.

At present ten States are denied representation, and when the Fortieth Congress assembles on the 4th day of the present month sixteen States will be without a voice in the House of Representatives. This grave fact, with the important questions before us, should induce us to pause in a course of legislation which, looking solely to the attainment of political ends, fails to consider the rights it transgresses, the law which it violates, or the institutions which it imperils.   ANDREW JOHNSON.

PROCLAMATIONS.

ANDREW JOHNSON, PRESIDENT OF THE UNITED STATES OF AMERICA.

To all whom it may concern:

Whereas exequaturs were heretofore issued to the following-named persons at the dates mentioned and for the places specified, recognizing them as consular officers, respectively, of the Kingdom of Hanover, of the Electorate of Hesse, of the Duchy of Nassau, and of the city of Frankfort, and declaring them free to exercise and enjoy functions, powers, and privileges under the said exequaturs, viz:

FOR THE KINGDOM OF HANOVER.

Julius Frederich, consul at Galveston, Tex., July 28, 1848.
Otto Frank, consul at San Francisco, Cal., July 9, 1850.
Augustus Reichard, consul at New Orleans, La., January 22, 1853.
Kauffmann H. Muller, consul at Savannah, Ga., June 28, 1854.
G. C. Baurmeister, consul at Charleston, S. C., April 21, 1856.
Adolph Gosling, consul-general at New York, November 7, 1859.
G. W. Hennings, vice-consul at New York, July 2, 1860.
George Papendiek, consul at Boston, November 3, 1863.
Francis A. Hoffmann, consul at Chicago, July 26, 1864.
Carl C. Schöttler, consul at Philadelphia, Pa., September 23, 1864.
A. Rettberg, consul at Cleveland, Ohio, September 27, 1864.
A. C. Wilmaus, consul at Milwaukee, Wis., October 7, 1864.
Adolph Meier, consul at St. Louis, Mo., October 7, 1864.
Theodor Schwartz, consul at Louisville, Ky., October 12, 1864.
Carl F. Adae, consul at Cincinnati, Ohio, October 20, 1864.
Werner Dresel, consul at Baltimore, Md., July 25, 1866.

FOR THE ELECTORATE OF HESSE.

Theodor Wagner, consul at Galveston, Tex., March 7, 1857.
Clamor Friedrich Hagedorn, consul at Philadelphia, February 14, 1862.
Werner Dresel, consul at Baltimore, Md., September 26, 1864.
Friedrich Kuhne, consul at New York, September 30, 1864.
Richard Thiele, consul at New Orleans, La., October 18, 1864.
Carl Adae, consul at Cincinnati, Ohio, October 20, 1864.
Robert Barth, consul at St. Louis, Mo., April 11, 1865.
C. F. Mebius, consul at San Francisco, Cal., May 3, 1865.

FOR THE DUCHY OF NASSAU.

Wilhelm A. Kobbe, consul-general for the United States at New York, November 19, 1846.

Friedrich Wilhelm Freudenthal, consul for Louisiana at New Orleans, January 22, 1852.

Franz Moureau, consul for the western half of Texas at New Braunfels, April 6, 1857.

Carl C. Finkler, consul for California at San Francisco, May 21, 1864.

Ludwig von Baumbach, consul for Wisconsin, September 27, 1864.

Otto Cuntz, consul for Massachusetts at Boston, October 7, 1864.

Friedrich Kuhne, consul at New York, September 30, 1864.

Carl F. Adae, consul for the State of Ohio, October 20, 1864.

Robert Barth, consul for Missouri, April 18, 1865.

FOR THE CITY OF FRANKFORT.

John H. Harjes, consul at Philadelphia, Pa., September 27, 1864.

F. A. Reuss, consul at St. Louis, Mo., September 30, 1864.

A. C. Wilmanns, consul for Wisconsin at Milwaukee, October 7, 1864.

Francis A. Hoffmann, consul for Chicago, Ill., October 12, 1864.

Carl F. Adae, consul for Ohio and Indiana, October 20, 1864.

Jacob Julius de Neufville, consul in New York, July 3, 1866.

And whereas the said countries, namely, the Kingdom of Hanover, the Electorate of Hesse, the Duchy of Nassau, and the city of Frankfort, have, in consequence of the late war between Prussia and Austria, been united to the Crown of Prussia; and

Whereas His Majesty the King of Prussia has requested of the President of the United States that the aforesaid exequaturs may, in consequence of the before-recited premises, be revoked:

Now, therefore, these presents do declare that the above-named consular officers are no longer recognized, and that the exequaturs heretofore granted to them are hereby declared to be absolutely null and void from this day forward.

In testimony whereof I have caused these letters to be made patent and the seal of the United States of America to be hereunto affixed.

[SEAL.]　　Given under my hand at the city of Washington, this 19th day of December, A. D. 1866, and of the Independence of the United States of America the ninety-first.

By the President:　　　　　　　　　　　　ANDREW JOHNSON.

WILLIAM H. SEWARD, *Secretary of State.*

ANDREW JOHNSON, PRESIDENT OF THE UNITED STATES OF AMERICA.

To all whom it may concern:

An exequatur, bearing date the 22d day of March, 1866, having been issued to Gerhard Janssen, recognizing him as consul of Oldenburg for New York and declaring him free to exercise and enjoy such functions, powers, and privileges as are allowed to consuls by the law of nations or by the laws of the United States and existing treaty stipulations between the Government of Oldenburg and the United States, and the said Janssen having refused to appear in the supreme court of the State of New York to answer in a suit there pending against himself and others on the plea that he is a consular officer of Oldenburg, thus seeking to use his official position to defeat the ends of justice, it is deemed advisable that the said Gerhard Janssen should no longer be permitted to continue in the exercise of said functions, powers, and privileges.

These are therefore to declare that I no longer recognize the said Gerhard Janssen as consul of Oldenburg for New York and will not permit him to exercise or enjoy any of the functions, powers, or privileges allowed to consuls of that nation; and that I do hereby wholly revoke and annul the said exequatur heretofore given and do declare the same to be absolutely null and void from this day forward.

In testimony whereof I have caused these letters to be made patent and the seal of the United States of America to be hereunto affixed.

[SEAL.]   Given under my hand at Washington, this 26th day of December, A. D. 1866, and of the Independence of the United States of America the ninety-first.

ANDREW JOHNSON.

By the President:
WILLIAM H. SEWARD, *Secretary of State.*

BY THE PRESIDENT OF THE UNITED STATES OF AMERICA.

A PROCLAMATION.

Whereas satisfactory evidence has been received by me from His Imperial Majesty the Emperor of France, through the Marquis de Montholon, his envoy extraordinary and minister plenipotentiary, that vessels belonging to citizens of the United States entering any port of France or of its dependencies on or after the 1st day of January, 1867, will not be subjected to the payment of higher duties on tonnage than are levied upon vessels belonging to citizens of France entering the said ports:

Now, therefore, I, Andrew Johnson, President of the United States of America, by virtue of the authority vested in me by an act of Congress of the 7th day of January, 1824, entitled "An act concerning discriminating duties of tonnage and impost," and by an act in addition thereto of the 24th day of May, 1828, do hereby declare and proclaim that on and after the said 1st day of January, 1867, so long as vessels of the United States shall be admitted to French ports on the terms aforesaid, French vessels entering ports of the United States will be subject to no higher rates of duty on tonnage than are levied upon vessels of the United States in the ports thereof.

In testimony whereof I have hereunto set my hand and caused the seal of the United States to be affixed.

[SEAL.]   Done at the city of Washington, this 28th day of December, A. D. 1866, and of the Independence of the United States of America the ninety-first.   ANDREW JOHNSON.

By the President:

WILLIAM H. SEWARD, *Secretary of State.*

BY THE PRESIDENT OF THE UNITED STATES OF AMERICA.

A PROCLAMATION.

Whereas, in virtue of the power conferred by the act of Congress approved June 22, 1860, sections 15 and 24 of which act were designed by proper provisions to secure the strict neutrality of citizens of the United States residing in or visiting the Empires of China and Japan, a notification was issued on the 4th of August last by the legation of the United States in Japan, through the consulates of the open ports of that Empire, requesting American shipmasters not to approach the coasts of Suwo and Nagato pending the then contemplated hostilities between the Tycoon of Japan and the Daimio of the said Provinces; and

Whereas authentic information having been received by the said legation that such hostilities had actually commenced, a regulation in furtherance of the aforesaid notification and pursuant to the act referred to was issued by the minister resident of the United States in Japan forbidding American merchant vessels from stopping or anchoring at any port or roadstead in that country except the three opened ports, viz, Kanagawa (Yokohama), Nagasaki, and Hakodate, unless in distress or forced by stress of weather, as provided by treaty, and giving notice that masters of vessels committing a breach of the regulation would thereby render themselves liable to prosecution and punishment and also to forfeiture of the protection of the United States if the visit to such nonopened port or roadstead should either involve a breach of treaty or be construed as an act in aid of insurrection or rebellion:

Now, therefore, be it known that I, Andrew Johnson, President of the United States of America, with a view to prevent acts which might injuriously affect the relations existing between the Government of the United States and that of Japan, do hereby call public attention to the aforesaid notification and regulation, which are hereby sanctioned and confirmed.

In testimony whereof I have hereunto set my hand and caused the seal of the United States to be affixed.

[SEAL.]   Done at the city of Washington, this 12th day of January, A. D. 1867, and of the Independence of the United States the ninety-first.   ANDREW JOHNSON.

By the President:

WILLIAM H. SEWARD, *Secretary of State.*

BY THE PRESIDENT OF THE UNITED STATES OF AMERICA.

A PROCLAMATION.

Whereas by an act of the Congress of the United States of the 24th of May, 1828, entitled "An act in addition to an act entitled 'An act concerning discriminating duties of tonnage and impost' and to equalize the duties on Prussian vessels and their cargoes," it is provided that, upon satisfactory evidence being given to the President of the United States by the government of any foreign nation that no discriminating duties of tonnage or impost are imposed or levied in the ports of the said nation upon vessels wholly belonging to citizens of the United States or upon the produce, manufactures, or merchandise imported in the same from the United States or from any foreign country, the President is thereby authorized to issue his proclamation declaring that the foreign discriminating duties of tonnage and impost within the United States are and shall be suspended and discontinued so far as respects the vessels of the said foreign nation and the produce, manufactures, or merchandise imported into the United States in the same from the said foreign nation or from any other foreign country, the said suspension to take effect from the time of such notification being given to the President of the United States and to continue so long as the reciprocal exemption of vessels belonging to citizens of the United States and their cargoes, as aforesaid, shall be continued, and no longer; and

Whereas satisfactory evidence has lately been received by me from His Majesty the King of the Hawaiian Islands, through an official communication of His Majesty's minister of foreign relations under date of the 10th of December, 1866, that no other or higher duties of tonnage and impost are imposed or levied in the ports of the Hawaiian Islands upon vessels wholly belonging to citizens of the United States and upon the produce, manufactures, or merchandise imported in the same from the United States and from any foreign country whatever than are levied on Hawaiian ships and their cargoes in the same ports under like circumstances:

Now, therefore, I, Andrew Johnson, President of the United States of America, do hereby declare and proclaim that so much of the several acts imposing discriminating duties of tonnage and impost within the United States are and shall be suspended and discontinued so far as respects the vessels of the Hawaiian Islands and the produce, manufactures, and merchandise imported into the United States in the same from the dominions of the Hawaiian Islands and from any other foreign country whatever, the said suspension to take effect from the said 10th day of December and to continue thenceforward so long as the reciprocal exemption of the vessels of the United States and the produce, manufactures, and merchandise imported into the dominions of the Hawaiian

Islands in the same, as aforesaid, shall be continued on the part of the Government of His Majesty the King of the Hawaiian Islands.

In testimony whereof I have hereunto set my hand and caused the seal of the United States to be affixed.

[SEAL.]   Done at the city of Washington, the 29th day of January, A. D. 1867, and of the Independence of the United States of America the ninety-first.

ANDREW JOHNSON.

By the President:

WILLIAM H. SEWARD,
Secretary of State.

BY THE PRESIDENT OF THE UNITED STATES OF AMERICA.

A PROCLAMATION.

Whereas the Congress of the United States did by an act approved on the 19th day of April, 1864, authorize the people of the Territory of Nebraska to form a constitution and State government and for the admission of such State into the Union on an equal footing with the original States upon certain conditions in said act specified; and

Whereas said people did adopt a constitution conforming to the provisions and conditions of said act and ask admission into the Union; and

Whereas the Congress of the United States did on the 8th and 9th days of February, 1867, in mode prescribed by the Constitution, pass a further act for the admission of the State of Nebraska into the Union, in which last-named act it was provided that it should not take effect except upon the fundamental condition that within the State of Nebraska there should be no denial of the elective franchise or of any other right to any person by reason of race or color, excepting Indians not taxed, and upon the further fundamental condition that the legislature of said State, by a solemn public act, should declare the assent of said State to the said fundamental condition and should transmit to the President of the United States an authenticated copy of said act of the legislature of said State, upon receipt whereof the President, by proclamation, should forthwith announce the fact, whereupon said fundamental condition should be held as a part of the organic law of the State, and thereupon, and without any further proceeding on the part of Congress, the admission of said State into the Union should be considered as complete; and

Whereas within the time prescribed by said act of Congress of the 8th and 9th of February, 1867, the legislature of the State of Nebraska did pass an act ratifying the said act of Congress of the 8th and 9th of February, 1867, and declaring that the aforenamed provisions of the third section of said last-named act of Congress should be a part of the organic law of the State of Nebraska; and

Whereas a duly authenticated copy of said act of the legislature of the State of Nebraska has been received by me:

Now, therefore, I, Andrew Johnson, President of the United States of America, do, in accordance with the provisions of the act of Congress last herein named, declare and proclaim the fact that the fundamental conditions imposed by Congress on the State of Nebraska to entitle that State to admission to the Union have been ratified and accepted and that the admission of the said State into the Union is now complete.

In testimony whereof I have hereto set my hand and have caused the seal of the United States to be affixed.

[SEAL.]   Done at the city of Washington, this 1st day of March, A. D. 1867, and of the Independence of the United States of America the ninety-first.

ANDREW JOHNSON.

By the President:
> WILLIAM H. SEWARD,
> *Secretary of State.*

[NOTE.—The Fortieth Congress, first session, met March 4, 1867, in accordance with the act of January 22, 1867, and on March 30, in accordance with the concurrent resolution of March 29, adjourned to July 3. The Senate met in special session April 1, in conformity to the proclamation of the President of the United States of March 30, and on April 20 adjourned without day. The Fortieth Congress, first session, again met July 3, and on July 20, in accordance with the concurrent resolution of the latter date, adjourned to November 21; again met November 21, and on December 2, 1867, in accordance with the concurrent resolution of November 26, adjourned without day.]

SPECIAL MESSAGES.

MARCH 11, 1867.

To the Senate of the United States:

I transmit to the Senate, in answer to their resolution of the 28th of July last, a report from the Secretary of State, with accompanying documents.*

ANDREW JOHNSON.

---

*Correspondence since March 4, 1857, touching the claim to military service asserted by France and Prussia in reference to persons born in those countries, but who have since become citizens of the United States.

WASHINGTON CITY, *March 13, 1867.*

To the Senate of the United States:

I herewith lay before the Senate, for its constitutional action thereon, a treaty concluded this day between the United States and the chiefs and headmen of the Kickapoo tribe of Indians.

A letter of the Secretary of the Interior and a copy of a letter of the Commissioner of Indian Affairs, explanatory of said treaty, are also herewith transmitted.

ANDREW JOHNSON.

WASHINGTON CITY, D. C.,
March 13, 1867.

To the Senate of the United States:

I herewith lay before the Senate, for its constitutional action thereon, a treaty concluded in this city on the 15th instant [ultimo] between the United States and the Stockbridge and Munsee tribes of Indians.

A letter of the Secretary of the Interior of the 25th instant [ultimo] and a copy of a communication from the Commissioner of Indian Affairs of the 19th instant [ultimo], explanatory of the said treaty, are also herewith transmitted.

ANDREW JOHNSON.

WASHINGTON CITY, D. C.,
March 13, 1867.

To the Senate of the United States:

I herewith lay before the Senate, for its constitutional action thereon, a treaty concluded in this city on the 23d instant [ultimo] between the United States and the following tribes of Indians, viz: The Senecas, the confederated Senecas and Shawnees, the Quapaws, the Ottawas, the confederated Peorias, Kaskaskias, Weas and Piankeshaws, and the Miamis.

A letter of the Secretary of the Interior of the 26th instant [ultimo] and a copy of a letter of the Commissioner of Indian Affairs of the 25th instant [ultimo], explanatory of said treaty, are also herewith transmitted.

ANDREW JOHNSON.

WASHINGTON CITY, D. C.,
March 13, 1867.

To the Senate of the United States:

I herewith lay before the Senate, for its constitutional action thereon, a treaty concluded on the 2d March, 1866, between the United States and the Shawnee tribe of Indians of Kansas.

A letter of the Secretary of the Interior of the 6th instant and a copy of a communication from the Commissioner of Indian Affairs of the 2d instant, explanatory of the said treaty, are also herewith transmitted.

ANDREW JOHNSON.

WASHINGTON CITY, D. C.,
March 13, 1867.

To the Senate of the United States:

I herewith lay before the Senate, for its constitutional action thereon, a treaty concluded on the 27th instant [ultimo] between the United States and the Pottawatomie tribe of Indians.

A letter of the Secretary of the Interior of the 28th instant [ultimo] and a copy of a communication from the Commissioner of Indian Affairs of the 27th instant [ultimo], explanatory of the said treaty, are also herewith transmitted.

ANDREW JOHNSON.

WASHINGTON CITY, D. C.,
March 13, 1867.

To the Senate of the United States:

I herewith lay before the Senate, for its constitutional action thereon a treaty concluded in this city on the 13th instant [ultimo] between the United States and the Kansas or Kaw tribe of Indians.

A letter of the Secretary of the Interior of the 25th instant [ultimo] and a copy of a communication of the 19th instant [ultimo] from the Commissioner of Indian Affairs, explanatory of said treaty, are also herewith transmitted.

ANDREW JOHNSON.

WASHINGTON CITY, *March 13, 1867.*

To the Senate of the United States:

I herewith lay before the Senate, for its constitutional action thereon, a treaty this day concluded between the United States and the Cherokee Nation of Indians, providing for the sale of their lands in Kansas, known as the "Cherokee neutral lands."

A letter of the Secretary of the Interior and accompanying copy of a letter from the Commissioner of Indian Affairs of this date, in relation to the treaty, are also herewith transmitted.

ANDREW JOHNSON.

WASHINGTON, *March 14, 1867.*

To the House of Representatives:

I transmit herewith a report from the Secretary of State, in further answer to the resolution* of the House of Representatives of the 24th of January last.

ANDREW JOHNSON.

*Requesting information "in relation to a removal of the Protestant Church or religious assembly meeting at the American embassy from the city of Rome by an order of that Government."

WASHINGTON, *March 15, 1867.*

To the Senate of the United States:

I transmit to the Senate, in further answer to their resolution of the 31st of January last, a report from the Secretary of State, with accompanying documents.*

ANDREW JOHNSON.

WASHINGTON, *March 20, 1867.*

To the House of Representatives:

I transmit to the House of Representatives, in answer to their resolution of the 18th instant, a report † from the Secretary of State, with its accompanying papers.

ANDREW JOHNSON.

WASHINGTON, *March 20, 1867.*

To the House of Representatives:

I transmit to the House of Representatives, in answer to their resolution of the 18th instant, a report ‡ from the Secretary of State, with an accompanying paper.

ANDREW JOHNSON.

WASHINGTON, *March 20, 1867.*

To the Senate of the United States:

I transmit to the Senate, in answer to their resolution of the 15th instant, reports§ from the Secretary of State and the Secretary of the Treasury, with accompanying papers.

ANDREW JOHNSON.

WASHINGTON, *March 20, 1867.*

To the House of Representatives:

In answer to a resolution of the House of Representatives of the 7th instant, relative to the arrest, imprisonment, and treatment of American citizens in Great Britain or its Provinces, I transmit a report from the Secretary of State on the subject.

ANDREW JOHNSON.

WASHINGTON, D. C., *March 21, 1867.*

To the Senate of the United States:

I herewith lay before the Senate, for its constitutional action thereon, a treaty concluded on the 19th of March, 1867, between the United States and the Chippewa tribe of Indians of the Mississippi.

---

*Dispatch from the United States consul at Geneva, with an inclosure, refuting charges against his moral character, etc.

† Relating to trials in Canada of citizens of the United States for complicity in the Fenian invasion of that country.

‡ Relating to the withdrawal of French troops from the Mexican Republic.

§ Relating to the fees of consular agents within the districts of salaried consuls, etc.

A letter of the Secretary of the Interior and a copy of a letter of Hon. Lewis V. Bogy, special commissioner, of the 20th instant, explanatory of the said treaty, are also herewith transmitted.

ANDREW JOHNSON.

WASHINGTON, D. C., *March 30, 1867.*

To the House of Representatives:

In giving my approval to the joint resolution providing for the expenses of carrying into full effect an act entitled "An act to provide for the more efficient government of the rebel States," I am moved to do so for the following reason: The seventh section of the act supplementary to the act for the more efficient government of the rebel States provides that the expenses incurred under or by virtue of that act shall be paid out of any moneys in the Treasury not otherwise appropriated. This provision is wholly unlimited as to the amount to be expended, whereas the resolution now before me limits the appropriation to $500,000. I consider this limitation as a very necessary check against unlimited expenditure and liabilities. Yielding to that consideration, I feel bound to approve this resolution, without modifying in any manner any objections heretofore stated against the original and supplemental acts.

ANDREW JOHNSON.

WASHINGTON, *March 30, 1867.*

To the Senate of the United States:

I transmit to the Senate, for its consideration with a view to ratification, a treaty between the United States and His Majesty the Emperor of all the Russias upon the subject of a cession of territory by the latter to the former, which treaty was this day signed in this city by the plenipotentiaries of the parties.

ANDREW JOHNSON.

PROCLAMATION.

BY THE PRESIDENT OF THE UNITED STATES OF AMERICA.

A PROCLAMATION.

Whereas objects of interest to the United States require that the Senate should be convened at 12 o'clock on Monday, the 1st day of April next, to receive and act upon such communications as may be made to it on the part of the Executive:

Now, therefore, I, Andrew Johnson, President of the United States, have considered it to be my duty to issue this my proclamation, declaring that an extraordinary occasion requires the Senate of the United States to convene for the transaction of business at the Capitol, in the city of Washington, on Monday, the 1st day of April next, at 12 o'clock on that day, of which all who shall at that time be entitled to act as members of that body are hereby required to take notice.

Given under my hand and the seal of the United States, at Washington, the 30th day of March, A. D. 1867, and of the Independence of the United States of America the ninety-first.

[SEAL.]

By the President: ANDREW JOHNSON.

WILLIAM H. SEWARD,
     Secretary of State.

SPECIAL MESSAGES.

[The following messages were sent to the special session of the Senate.]

WASHINGTON, *March 28, 1867.*

To the Senate of the United States:

I transmit to the Senate, in answer to their resolution of the 20th instant, a report * from the Secretary of State, with accompanying documents.

ANDREW JOHNSON.

WASHINGTON, *April 12, 1867.*

To the Senate of the United States:

I transmit to the Senate, in answer to their resolution of the 10th instant, calling for information relative to prisoners of war taken by belligerents in the Mexican Republic, a report from the Secretary of State, with accompanying papers.

ANDREW JOHNSON.

WASHINGTON, *April 13, 1867.*

To the Senate of the United States:

In compliance with a resolution of the Senate of the 28th of January last, requesting certain information in regard to governors, secretaries, and judges of Territories, I transmit herewith reports † from the Secretary of State, the Secretary of the Interior, and the Attorney-General.

ANDREW JOHNSON.

*Relating to the exequatur of the consul of the Grand Duchy of Oldenburg residing at New York.

†Relating to the absence of Territorial officers from their posts of duty.

WASHINGTON, *April 15, 1867.*

To the Senate of the United States:

I transmit to the Senate, in answer to their resolution of the 13th instant, a report* from the Secretary of State.

ANDREW JOHNSON.

WASHINGTON, *April 16, 1867.*

To the Senate of the United States:

I transmit herewith reports from the heads of the several Executive Departments, in answer to the resolution of the Senate of the 11th instant, requesting "copies of any official opinions which may have been given by the Attorney-General, the Solicitor of the Treasury, or by any other officer of the Government on the interpretation of the act of Congress regulating the tenure of office, and especially with regard to appointments by the President during the recess of Congress."

ANDREW JOHNSON.

[The following messages were sent to the Fortieth Congress, first session.]

WASHINGTON, *July 5, 1867.*

To the Senate of the United States:

I transmit to the Senate, for its consideration with a view to ratification, a convention for commercial reciprocity between the United States and His Majesty the King of the Hawaiian Islands, which convention was signed by the plenipotentiaries of the parties in the city of San Francisco on the 21st day of May last.

ANDREW JOHNSON.

WASHINGTON, *July 5, 1867.*

To the Senate and House of Representatives:

I transmit to Congress a copy of a convention between the United States and the Republic of Venezuela for the adjustment of claims of citizens of the United States on the Government of that Republic. The ratifications of this convention were exchanged at Caracas on the 10th of April last. As its first article stipulates that the commissioners shall meet in that city within four months from that date, the expediency of passing the usual act for the purpose of carrying the convention into effect will, of course, engage the attention of Congress.

ANDREW JOHNSON.

*Relating to the absence of Governor Alexander Cumming from the Territory of Colorado since his appointment as governor.

WASHINGTON, *July 6, 1867.*

To the Senate and House of Representatives:

I transmit to Congress a copy of a treaty between the United States and His Majesty the Emperor of all the Russias, the ratifications of which were exchanged in this city on the 20th day of June last.

This instrument provides for a cession of territory to the United States in consideration of the payment of $7,200,000 in gold. The attention of Congress is invited to the subject of an appropriation for this payment, and also to that of proper legislation for the occupation and government of the territory as a part of the dominion of the United States.

ANDREW JOHNSON.

WASHINGTON, *July 6, 1867.*

To the Senate of the United States:

I transmit to the Senate, for its consideration with a view to ratification, a convention between the United States, Great Britain, France, the Netherlands, and Japan, concluded at Yedo on the 25th of June, 1866.

ANDREW JOHNSON.

To the House of Representatives: WASHINGTON, *July 8, 1867.*

I transmit herewith a report from the Attorney-General, additional to the reports submitted by him December 31, 1866, and March 2, 1867, in reply to a resolution of the House of Representatives of December 10, 1866, requesting "a list of names of all persons engaged in the late rebellion against the United States Government who have been pardoned by the President from April 15, 1865, to this date; that said list shall also state the rank of each person who has been so pardoned, if he has been engaged in the military service of the so-called Confederate government, and the position if he shall have held any civil office under said so-called Confederate government; and shall also further state whether such person has at any time prior to April 14, 1861, held any office under the United States Government, and, if so, what office, together with the reasons for granting such pardon, and also the names of the person or persons at whose solicitation such pardon was granted."

ANDREW JOHNSON.

To the House of Representatives WASHINGTON, *July 9, 1867.*

In compliance with the resolution of the House of Representatives of the 5th of July, requesting the President "to inform the House what States have ratified the amendment to the Constitution of the United States proposed by concurrent resolution of the two Houses of Congress, June 16, 1866," I transmit a report from the Secretary of State.

ANDREW JOHNSON.

WASHINGTON, *July 10, 1867.*

To the House of Representatives:

In compliance with so much of the resolution of the House of Representatives of the 8th instant as requests information in regard to certain agreements said to have been entered into between the United States, European and West Virginia Land and Mining Company and certain reputed agents of the Republic of Mexico, I transmit a report from the Secretary of State and the papers accompanying it.

ANDREW JOHNSON.

WASHINGTON, *July 11, 1867.*

To the House of Representatives:

In compliance with the resolution of the House of Representatives of the 3d instant, requesting me to transmit all the official correspondence between the Department of State and the Hon. Lewis D. Campbell, late minister to Mexico, and also that with his successor, I communicate a report from the Secretary of State and the papers accompanying it.

ANDREW JOHNSON.

WASHINGTON, *July 12, 1867.*

To the Senate of the United States:

In compliance with the resolution of the Senate of the 8th instant, requesting me to transmit "all the official correspondence between the Department of State and the Hon. Lewis D. Campbell, late minister of the United States to the Republic of Mexico, from the time of his appointment, also the correspondence of the Department with his successor," I communicate herewith a report on the subject from the Secretary of State, from which it appears that the correspondence called for by the Senate has already been communicated to the House of Representatives.

ANDREW JOHNSON.

WASHINGTON, D. C., *July 15, 1867.*

To the Senate of the United States:

I transmit herewith reports from the Secretary of War and the Attorney-General, containing the information called for by the resolution of the Senate of the 3d instant, requesting the President "to communicate to the Senate copies of all orders, instructions, circular letters, or letters of advice issued to the respective military officers assigned to the command of the several military districts under the act passed March 2, 1867, entitled 'An act to provide for the more efficient government of the rebel States,' and the act supplementary thereto, passed March 23, 1867; also copies of all opinions given to him by the Attorney-General of the United States touching the construction and interpretation of said acts, and of all correspondence relating to the operation, construction, or execution of said acts that may have taken place between himself and any of said commanders, or between him and the General of the Army, or between the latter and any of said commanders, touching the same subjects; also copies of all orders issued by any of said commanders in carrying out the provisions of said acts or either of them; also that he inform the Senate what progress has been made in the matter of registration under said acts, and whether the sum of money heretofore appropriated for carrying them out is probably sufficient.''

In answer to that portion of the resolution which inquires whether the sum of money heretofore appropriated for carrying these acts into effect is probably sufficient, reference is made to the accompanying report of the Secretary of War. It will be seen from that report that the appropriation of $500,000 made in the act approved March 30, 1867, for the purpose of carrying into effect the ''Act to provide for the more efficient government of the rebel States,'' passed March 2, 1867, and the act supplementary thereto, passed March 23, 1867, has already been expended by the commanders of the several military districts, and that, in addition, the sum of $1,648,277 is required for present purposes.

It is exceedingly difficult at the present time to estimate the probable expense of carrying into full effect the two acts of March last and the bill which passed the two Houses of Congress on the 13th instant. If the existing governments of ten States of the Union are to be deposed and their entire machinery is to be placed under the exclusive control and authority of the respective district commanders, all the expenditures incident to the administration of such governments must necessarily be incurred by the Federal Government. It is believed that, in addition to the $2,100,000 already expended or estimated for, the sum which would be required for this purpose would not be less than $14,000,000—the aggregate amount expended prior to the rebellion in the administration of their respective governments by the ten States embraced in the provisions of these acts. This sum would no doubt be considerably augmented if the machinery of these States is to be operated by the Federal Government, and would be largely increased if the United States, by abolishing the existing State governments, should become responsible for liabilities incurred by them before the rebellion in laudable efforts to develop their resources, and in no wise created for insurrectionary or revolutionary purposes. The debts of these States, thus legitimately incurred, when accurately ascertained will, it is believed, approximate $100,000,000; and they are held not only by our own citizens, among whom are residents of portions of the country which have ever remained loyal to the Union, but by persons who are the subjects of foreign governments. It is worthy the consideration of Congress and the country whether, if the Federal Government by its action were to assume such obligations, so large an addition to our public expenditures would not seriously impair the credit of the nation, or, on the other hand, whether the refusal of Congress to guarantee the payment of the debts of these States, after having displaced or abolished their State governments, would not be viewed as a violation of good faith and a repudiation by the national legislature of liabilities which these States had justly and legally incurred.

ANDREW JOHNSON.

WASHINGTON, *July 18, 1867.*

To the Senate of the United States:

In compliance with the resolution of the Senate of the 8th instant, requesting me to furnish to that body copies of any correspondence on the files of the Department of State relating to any recent events in Mexico, I communicate a report from the Secretary of State, with the papers accompanying it.

ANDREW JOHNSON.

WASHINGTON, *July 18, 1867.*

To the House of Representatives:

In compliance with that part of the resolution of the House of Representatives of the 8th instant which requests me to transmit to the House of Representatives any official correspondence or other information relating to the capture and execution of Maximilian and the arrest and reported execution of Santa Anna in Mexico, I inclose herewith a report from the Secretary of State, from which it appears that the correspondence called for by the House of Representatives has already been communicated to the Senate of the United States.

ANDREW JOHNSON.

WASHINGTON, *July 20, 1867.*

To the House of Representatives:

I have received a resolution adopted by the House of Representatives on the 8th instant, inquiring "whether the publication which appeared in the National Intelligencer and other public prints on the 21st of June last, and which contained a statement of the proceedings of the President and Cabinet in respect to an interpretation of the acts of Congress commonly known as the reconstruction acts, was made by the authority of the President or with his knowledge and consent," and "whether the full and complete record or minute of all the proceedings, conclusions, and determinations of the President and Cabinet relating to said acts of Congress and their interpretation is embraced or given in said publication," and also requesting that "a true copy of the full and complete record or minute of such proceedings, conclusions, and determinations in regard to the interpretation of said reconstruction acts" be furnished to the House.

In compliance with the request of the House of Representatives, I have to state that the publication to which the resolution refers was made by proper authority, and that it comprises the proceedings in Cabinet relating to the acts of Congress mentioned in the inquiry, upon which, after tak-ing the opinions of the heads of the several Executive Departments of the Government, I had announced my own conclusions.   Other questions arising from these acts have been under consideration, upon which, how-ever, no final conclusion has been reached.   No publication in reference to them has, therefore, been authorized by me; but should it at any time be deemed proper and advantageous to the interests of the country to make public those or any other proceedings of the Cabinet, authority for their promulgation will be given by the President.

A correct copy of the record of the proceedings, published in the National Intelligencer and other newspapers on the 21st ultimo, is here-with transmitted, together with a copy of the instructions based upon the conclusions of the President and Cabinet and sent to the commanders of the several military districts created by act of Congress of March 2, 1867.

ANDREW JOHNSON.

In Cabinet, *June 18, 1867.*

Present: The President, the Secretary of State, the Secretary of the Treasury, the Secretary of War, the Secretary of the Navy, the Postmaster-General, the Attorney-General, the Acting Secretary of the Interior.

The President announced that he had under consideration the two opinions from the Attorney-General as to the legal questions arising upon the acts of Congress com-monly known as the reconstruction acts, and that in view of the great magnitude of the subject and of the various interests involved he deemed it proper to have it considered fully in the Cabinet and to avail himself of all the light which could be afforded by the opinions and advice of the members of the Cabinet, to enable him to see that these laws be faithfully executed and to decide what orders and instruc-tions are necessary and expedient to be given to the military commanders.

The President said further that the branch of the subject that seemed to him first in order for consideration was as to the instructions to be sent to the military com-manders for their guidance and for the guidance of persons offering for registration. The instructions proposed by the Attorney-General, as set forth in the summary con-tained in his last opinion, will therefore be now considered.

The summary was then read at length.

The reading of the summary having been concluded, each section was then con-sidered, discussed, and voted upon as follows:

1. The oath prescribed in the supplemental act defines all the qualifications re-quired, and every person who can take that oath is entitled to have his name entered upon the list of voters.

All vote "aye" except the Secretary of War, who votes "nay."

2. The board of registration have no authority to administer any other oath to the person applying for registration than this prescribed oath, nor to administer any oath to any other person touching the qualifications of the applicant or the falsity of the oath so taken by him.

No provision is made for challenging the qualifications of the applicant or enter-ing upon any trial or investigation of his qualifications, either by witnesses or any other form of proof.

All vote "aye" except the Secretary of War, who votes "nay."

3. As to citizenship and residence:

The applicant for registration must be a citizen of the State and of the United

States, and must be a resident of a county or parish included in the election district. He may be registered if he has been such citizen for a period less than twelve months at the time he applies for registration, but he can not vote at any election unless his citizenship has then extended to the full term of one year. As to such a person, the exact length of his citizenship should be noted opposite his name on the list, so that it may appear on the day of election, upon reference to the list, whether the full term has then been accomplished.

Concurred in unanimously.

4. An unnaturalized person can not take this oath, but an alien who has been naturalized can take it, and no other proof of naturalization can be required from him.

All vote "aye" except the Secretary of War, who votes "nay."

5. No one who is not 21 years of age at the time of registration can take the oath, for he must swear that he has then attained that age.

Concurred in unanimously.

6. No one who has been disfranchised for participation in any rebellion against the United States or for felony committed against the laws of any State or of the United States can take this oath.

The actual participation in a rebellion or the actual commission of a felony does not amount to disfranchisement. The sort of disfranchisement here meant is that which is declared by law passed by competent authority, or which has been fixed upon the criminal by the sentence of the court which tried him for the crime.

No law of the United States has declared the penalty of disfranchisement for participation in rebellion alone; nor is it known that any such law exists in either of these ten States, except, perhaps, Virginia, as to which State special instructions will be given.

- All vote "aye" except the Secretary of War, who dissents as to the second and third paragraphs.

7. As to disfranchisement arising from having held office followed by participation in rebellion:

This is the most important part of the oath, and requires strict attention to arrive at its meaning. The applicant must swear or affirm as follows:

"That I have never been a member of any State legislature, nor held any executive or judicial office in any State, and afterwards engaged in an insurrection or rebellion against the United States or given aid or comfort to the enemies thereof; that I have never taken an oath as a member of Congress of the United States, or as an officer of the United States, or as a member of any State legislature, or as an executive or judicial officer of any State, to support the Constitution of the United States, and afterwards engaged in insurrection or rebellion against the United States or given aid or comfort to the enemies thereof."

Two elements must concur in order to disqualify a person under these clauses: First, the office and official oath to support the Constitution of the United States; second, engaging afterwards in rebellion. Both must exist to work disqualification, and must happen in the order of time mentioned.

A person who has held an office and taken the oath to support the Federal Constitution and has not afterwards engaged in rebellion is not disqualified. So, too, a person who has engaged in rebellion, but has not theretofore held an office and taken that oath, is not disqualified.

All vote "aye" except the Secretary of War, who votes "nay."

8. Officers of the United States:

As to these the language is without limitation. The person who has at any time prior to the rebellion held any office, civil or military, under the United States, and has taken an official oath to support the Constitution of the United States, is subject to disqualification.

Concurred in unanimously.

9. Militia officers of any State prior to the rebellion are not subject to disqualification.

All vote "aye" except the Secretary of War, who votes "nay."

10. Municipal officers—that is to say, officers of incorporated cities, towns, and villages, such as mayors, aldermen, town council, police, and other city or town officers—are not subject to disqualification.

Concurred in unanimously.

11. Persons who have prior to the rebellion been members of the Congress of the United States or members of a State legislature are subject to disqualification, but those who have been members of conventions framing or amending the constitution of a State prior to the rebellion are not subject to disqualification.

Concurred in unanimously.

12. All the executive or judicial officers of any State who took an oath to support the Constitution of the United States are subject to disqualification, including county officers. They are subject to disqualification if they were required to take as a part of their official oath the oath to support the Constitution of the United States.

Concurred in unanimously.

13. Persons who exercised mere employments under State authority are not disqualified; such as commissioners to lay out roads, commissioners of public works, visitors of State institutions, directors of State institutions, examiners of banks, notaries public, commissioners to take acknowledgments of deeds.

Concurred in unanimously; but the Secretary of State, the Secretary of the Treasury, and the Secretary of War express the opinion that lawyers are such officers as are disqualified if they participated in the rebellion. Two things must exist as to any person to disqualify him from voting: First, the office held prior to the rebellion, and, afterwards, participation in the rebellion.

14. An act to fix upon a person the offense of engaging in rebellion under this law must be an overt and voluntary act, done with the intent of aiding or furthering the common unlawful purpose. A person forced into the rebel service by conscription or under a paramount authority which he could not safely disobey, and who would not have entered such service if left to the free exercise of his own will, can not be held to be disqualified from voting.

All vote "aye" except the Secretary of War, who votes "nay" as the proposition is stated.

15. Mere acts of charity, where the intent is to relieve the wants of the object of such charity, and not done in aid of the cause in which he may have been engaged, do not disqualify; but organized contributions of food and clothing for the general relief of persons engaged in the rebellion, and not of a merely sanitary character, but contributed to enable them to perform their unlawful object, may be classed with acts which do disqualify. Forced contributions to the rebel cause in the form of taxes or military assessments, which a person was compelled to pay or contribute, do not disqualify; but voluntary contributions to the rebel cause, even such indirect contributions as arise from the voluntary loan of money to the rebel authorities or purchase of bonds or securities created to afford the means of carrying on the rebellion, will work disqualification.

Concurred in unanimously.

16. All those who in legislative or other official capacity were engaged in the furtherance of the common unlawful purpose, where the duties of the office necessarily had relation to the support of the rebellion, such as members of the rebel conventions, congresses, and legislatures, diplomatic agents of the rebel Confederacy, and other officials whose offices were created for the purpose of more effectually carrying on hostilities or whose duties appertained to the support of the rebel cause, must be held to be disqualified; but officers who during the rebellion discharged official duties not incident to war, but only such duties as belong even to a state of peace and were

necessary to the preservation of order and the administration of law, are not to be considered as thereby engaging in rebellion or as disqualified. Disloyal sentiments, opinions, or sympathies would not disqualify, but where a person has by speech or writing incited others to engage in rebellion he must come under the disqualification.

All vote "aye" except the Secretary of War, who dissents to the second paragraph, with the exception of the words "where a person has by speech or by writing incited others to engage in rebellion he must come under the disqualification."

17. The duties of the board appointed to superintend the elections.

This board, having the custody of the list of registered voters in the district for which it is constituted, must see that the name of the person offering to vote is found upon the registration list, and if such proves to be the fact it is the duty of the board to receive his vote if then qualified by residence. They can not receive the vote of any person whose name is not upon the list, though he may be ready to take the registration oath, and although he may satisfy them that he was unable to have his name registered at the proper time, in consequence of absence, sickness, or other cause.

The board can not enter into any inquiry as to the qualifications of any person whose name is not on the registration list, or as to the qualifications of any person whose name is on that list.

Concurred in unanimously.

18. The mode of voting is provided in the act to be by ballot. The board will keep a record and poll book of the election, showing the votes, list of voters, and the persons elected by a plurality of the votes cast at the election, and make returns of these to the commanding general of the district.

Concurred in unanimously.

19. The board appointed for registration and for superintending the elections must take the oath prescribed by the act of Congress approved July 2, 1862, entitled "An act to prescribe an oath of office."

Concurred in unanimously.

IN CABINET, *June 20, 1867.*

Present: The same Cabinet officers as on the 18th, except the Acting Secretary of the Interior.

The President announced to the Cabinet that after full deliberation he concurred with the majority upon the sections of the summary upon which the Secretary of War expressed his dissent, and that he concurred with the Cabinet upon those sections approved by unanimous vote; that as it appeared the military commanders entertained doubts upon the points covered by the summary, and as their action hitherto had not been uniform, he deemed it proper, without further delay, to communicate in a general order* to the respective commanders the points set forth in the summary.

VETO MESSAGES.

WASHINGTON, *March 23, 1867.*

To the House of Representatives:

I have considered the bill entitled "An act supplementary to an act entitled 'An act to provide for the more efficient government of the rebel States,' passed March 2, 1867, and to facilitate restoration," and now return it to the House of Representatives with my objections.

This bill provides for elections in the ten States brought under the operation of the original act to which it is supplementary. Its details are

*See Executive order of June 20, 1867, pp. 552–556.

principally directed to the elections for the formation of the State constitutions, but by the sixth section of the bill "all elections" in these States occurring while the original act remains in force are brought within its purview. Referring to these details, it will be found that, first of all, there is to be a registration of the voters. No one whose name has not been admitted on the list is to be allowed to vote at any of these elections. To ascertain who is entitled to registration, reference is made necessary, by the express language of the supplement, to the original act and to the pending bill. The fifth section of the original act provides, as to voters, that they shall be "male citizens of the State, 21 years old and upward, of whatever race, color, or previous condition, who have been residents of said State for one year." This is the general qualification, followed, however, by many exceptions. No one can be registered, according to the original act, "who may be disfranchised for participation in the rebellion"—a provision which left undetermined the question as to what amounted to disfranchisement, and whether without a judicial sentence the act itself produced that effect. This supplemental bill superadds an oath, to be taken by every person before his name can be admitted upon the registration, that he has "not been disfranchised for participation in any rebellion or civil war against the United States." It thus imposes upon every person the necessity and responsibility of deciding for himself, under the peril of punishment by a military commission if he makes a mistake, what works disfranchisement by participation in rebellion and what amounts to such participation. Almost every man— the negro as well as the white—above 21 years of age who was resident in these ten States during the rebellion, voluntarily or involuntarily, at some time and in some way did participate in resistance to the lawful authority of the General Government. The question with the citizen to whom this oath is to be proposed must be a fearful one, for while the bill does not declare that perjury may be assigned for such false swearing nor fix any penalty for the offense, we must not forget that martial law prevails; that every person is answerable to a military commission, without previous presentment by a grand jury, for any charge that may be made against him, and that the supreme authority of the military commander determines the question as to what is an offense and what is to be the measure of punishment.

The fourth section of the bill provides "that the commanding general of each district shall appoint as many boards of registration as may be necessary, consisting of three loyal officers or persons." The only qualification stated for these officers is that they must be "loyal." They may be persons in the military service or civilians, residents of the State or strangers. Yet these persons are to exercise most important duties and are vested with unlimited discretion. They are to decide what names shall be placed upon the register and from their decision there is to be no appeal. They are to superintend the elections and to decide all questions which may arise. They are to have the custody of the ballots and to make return of the persons elected. Whatever frauds or errors they may commit must pass without redress. All that is left for the commanding general is to receive the returns of the elections, open the same, and ascertain who are chosen "according to the returns of the officers who conducted said elections." By such means and with this sort of agency are the conventions of delegates to be constituted.

As the delegates are to speak for the people, common justice would seem to require that they should have authority from the people themselves. No convention so constituted will in any sense represent the wishes of the inhabitants of these States, for under the all-embracing exceptions of these laws, by a construction which the uncertainty of the clause as to disfranchisement leaves open to the board of officers, the great body of the people may be excluded from the polls and from all opportunity of expressing their own wishes or voting for delegates who will faithfully reflect their sentiments.

I do not deem it necessary further to investigate the details of this bill. No consideration could induce me to give my approval to such an election law for any purpose, and especially for the great purpose of framing the constitution of a State. If ever the American citizen should be left to the free exercise of his own judgment it is when he is engaged in the work of forming the fundamental law under which he is to live. That work is his work, and it can not properly be taken out of his hands. All this legislation proceeds upon the contrary assumption that the people of each of these States shall have no constitution except such as may be arbitrarily dictated by Congress and formed under the restraint of military rule. A plain statement of facts makes this evident.

In all these States there are existing constitutions, framed in the accustomed way by the people. Congress, however, declares that these constitutions are not "loyal and republican," and requires the people to form them anew. What, then, in the opinion of Congress, is necessary to make the constitution of a State "loyal and republican"? The original act answers the question: It is universal negro suffrage—a question which the Federal Constitution leaves exclusively to the States themselves. All this legislative machinery of martial law, military coercion, and political disfranchisement is avowedly for that purpose and none other. The existing constitutions of the ten States conform to the acknowledged standards of loyalty and republicanism. Indeed, if there are degrees in republican forms of government, their constitutions are more republican now than when these States, four of which were members of the original thirteen, first became members of the Union.

Congress does not now demand that a single provision of their constitutions be changed except such as confine suffrage to the white population. It is apparent, therefore, that these provisions do not conform to the standard of republicanism which Congress seeks to establish. That there may be no mistake, it is only necessary that reference should be made to the original act, which declares "such constitution shall provide that the elective franchise shall be enjoyed by all such persons as have the qualifications herein stated for electors of delegates." What class of persons is here meant clearly appears in the same section; that is to say, "the male citizens of said State 21 years old and upward, of whatever race, color, or previous condition, who have been resident in said State for one year previous to the day of such election."

Without these provisions no constitution which can be framed in any one of the ten States will be of any avail with Congress. This, then, is the test of what the constitution of a State of this Union must contain to make it republican. Measured by such a standard, how few of the States now composing the Union have republican constitutions! If in the exercise of the constitutional guaranty that Congress shall secure to every State a republican form of government universal suffrage for blacks as well as whites is a *sine qua non*, the work of reconstruction may as well begin in Ohio as in Virginia, in Pennsylvania as in North Carolina.

When I contemplate the millions of our fellow-citizens of the South with no alternative left but to impose upon themselves this fearful and untried experiment of complete negro enfranchisement—and white disfranchisement, it may be, almost as complete—or submit indefinitely to the rigor of martial law, without a single attribute of freemen, deprived of all the sacred guaranties of our Federal Constitution, and threatened with even worse wrongs, if any worse are possible, it seems to me their condition is the most deplorable to which any people can be reduced. It is true that they have been engaged in rebellion and that their object being a separation of the States and a dissolution of the Union there was an obligation resting upon every loyal citizen to treat them as enemies and to wage war against their cause.

Inflexibly opposed to any movement imperiling the integrity of the Government, I did not hesitate to urge the adoption of all measures necessary for the suppression of the insurrection. After a long and terrible struggle the efforts of the Government were triumphantly successful, and the people of the South, submitting to the stern arbitrament, yielded forever the issues of the contest. Hostilities terminated soon after it became my duty to assume the responsibilities of the chief executive officer of the Republic, and I at once endeavored to repress and control the passions which our civil strife had engendered, and, no longer regarding these erring millions as enemies, again acknowledged them as our friends and our countrymen. The war had accomplished its objects. The nation was saved and that seminal principle of mischief which from the birth of the Government had gradually but inevitably brought on the rebellion was totally eradicated. Then, it seemed to me, was the auspicious time to commence the work of reconciliation; then, when these people sought once more our friendship and protection, I considered it our duty generously to meet them in the spirit of charity and for-giveness and to conquer them even more effectually by the magnanim-ity of the nation than by the force of its arms. I yet believe that if the policy of reconciliation then inaugurated, and which contemplated an early restoration of these people to all their political rights, had received the support of Congress, every one of these ten States and all their peo-ple would at this moment be fast anchored in the Union and the great work which gave the war all its sanction and made it just and holy would have been accomplished. Then over all the vast and fruitful regions of the South peace and its blessings would have prevailed, while now millions are deprived of rights guaranteed by the Constitution to every citizen and after nearly two years of legislation find themselves placed under an absolute military despotism. "A military republic, a govern-ment founded on mock elections and supported only by the sword," was nearly a quarter of a century since pronounced by Daniel Webster, when speaking of the South American States, as "a movement, indeed, but a retrograde and disastrous movement, from the regular and old-fashioned monarchical systems;" and he added:

If men would enjoy the blessings of republican government, they must govern themselves by reason, by mutual counsel and consultation, by a sense and feeling of general interest, and by the acquiescence of the minority in the will of the major-ity, properly expressed; and, above all, the military must be kept, according to the language of our bill of rights, in strict subordination to the civil authority. Wher-ever this lesson is not both learned and practiced there can be no political freedom. Absurd, preposterous is it, a scoff and a satire on free forms of constitutional liberty, for frames of government to be prescribed by military leaders and the right of suf-frage to be exercised at the point of the sword.

I confidently believe that a time will come when these States will again occupy their true positions in the Union. The barriers which now seem so obstinate must yield to the force of an enlightened and just public opinion, and sooner or later unconstitutional and oppressive legislation will be effaced from our statute books. When this shall have been con-summated, I pray God that the errors of the past may be forgotten and that once more we shall be a happy, united, and prosperous people, and that at last, after the bitter and eventful experience through which the nation has passed, we shall all come to know that our only safety is in the pres-ervation of our Federal Constitution and in according to every American citizen and to every State the rights which that Constitution secures.

ANDREW JOHNSON.

WASHINGTON, D. C., *April 10, 1867.**

The first session of the Fortieth Congress adjourned on the 30th day of March, 1867. This bill,† which was passed during that session, was not

---

*Pocket veto. Was never sent to Congress, but was deposited in the Department of State.

†"Joint resolution placing certain troops of Missouri on an equal footing with others as to bounties."

presented for my approval by the Hon. Edmund G. Ross, of the Senate of the United States, and a member of the Committee on Enrolled Bills, until Monday, the 1st day of April, 1867, two days after the adjournment. It is not believed that the approval of any bill after the adjournment of Congress, whether presented before or after such adjournment, is authorized by the Constitution of the United States, that instrument expressly declaring that no bill shall become a law the return of which may have been prevented by the adjournment of Congress. To concede that under the Constitution the President, after the adjournment of Congress, may, without limitation in respect to time, exercise the power of approval, and thus determine at his discretion whether or not bills shall become laws, might subject the executive and legislative departments of the Government to influences most pernicious to correct legislation and sound public morals, and—with a single exception, occurring during the prevalence of civil war—would be contrary to the established practice of the Government from its inauguration to the present time. This bill will therefore be filed in the office of the Secretary of State without my approval.

ANDREW JOHNSON.

WASHINGTON, D. C., *July 19, 1867.*

To the House of Representatives of the United States:

I return herewith the bill entitled "An act supplementary to an act entitled 'An act to provide for the more efficient government of the rebel States,' passed on the 2d day of March, 1867, and the act supplementary thereto, passed on the 23d day of March, 1867," and will state as briefly as possible some of the reasons which prevent me from giving it my approval.

This is one of a series of measures passed by Congress during the last four months on the subject of reconstruction. The message returning the act of the 2d of March last states at length my objections to the passage of that measure. They apply equally well to the bill now before me, and I am content merely to refer to them and to reiterate my conviction that they are sound and unanswerable.

There are some points peculiar to this bill, which I will proceed at once to consider.

The first section purports to declare "the true intent and meaning," in some particulars, of the two prior acts upon this subject.

It is declared that the intent of those acts was, first, that the existing governments in the ten "rebel States" "were not legal State governments," and, second, "that thereafter said governments, if continued, were to be continued subject in all respects to the military commanders of the respective districts and to the paramount authority of Congress."

Congress may by a declaratory act fix upon a prior act a construction altogether at variance with its apparent meaning, and from the time, at

least, when such a construction is fixed the original act will be construed
to mean exactly what it is stated to mean by the declaratory statute.
There will be, then, from the time this bill may become a law no doubt,
no question, as to the relation in which the "existing governments" in
those States, called in the original act "the provisional governments,"
stand toward the military authority.   As those relations stood before
the declaratory act, these "governments," it is true, were made subject
to absolute military authority in many important respects, but not in all,
the language of the act being "subject to the military authority of the
United States, as hereinafter prescribed."   By the sixth section of the
original act these governments were made "in all respects subject to
the paramount authority of the United States."

Now by this declaratory act it appears that Congress did not by the
original act intend to limit the military authority to any particulars or
subjects therein "prescribed," but meant to make it universal.   Thus
over all of these ten States this military government is now declared to
have unlimited authority.   It is no longer confined to the preservation
of the public peace, the administration of criminal law, the registration
of voters, and the superintendence of elections, but "in all respects" is
asserted to be paramount to the existing civil governments.

It is impossible to conceive any state of society more intolerable than
this; and yet it is to this condition that 12,000,000 American citizens
are reduced by the Congress of the United States.   Over every foot of
the immense territory occupied by these American citizens the Constitution of the United States is theoretically in full operation.   It binds all
the people there and should protect them; yet they are denied every one
of its sacred guaranties.

Of what avail will it be to any one of these Southern people when
seized by a file of soldiers to ask for the cause of arrest or for the production of the warrant?   Of what avail to ask for the privilege of bail
when in military custody, which knows no such thing as bail?   Of what
avail to demand a trial by jury, process for witnesses, a copy of the
indictment, the privilege of counsel, or that greater privilege, the writ of
habeas corpus?

The veto of the original bill of the 2d of March was based on two distinct grounds—the interference of Congress in matters strictly appertaining to the reserved powers of the States and the establishment of military
tribunals for the trial of citizens in time of peace.   The impartial reader
of that message will understand that all that it contains with respect to
military despotism and martial law has reference especially to the fearful
power conferred on the district commanders to displace the criminal
courts and assume jurisdiction to try and to punish by military boards;
that, potentially, the suspension of the *habeas corpus* was martial law and
military despotism.   The act now before me not only declares that the
intent was to confer such military authority, but also to confer unlimited

military authority over all the other courts of the State and over all the officers of the State—legislative, executive, and judicial. Not content with the general grant of power, Congress, in the second section of this bill, specifically gives to each military commander the power ''to. suspend or remove from office, or from the performance of official duties and the exercise of official powers, any officer or person holding or exercising, or professing to hold or exercise, any civil or military office or duty in such district under any power, election, appointment, or authority derived from, or granted by, or claimed under any so-called State, or the government thereof, or any municipal or other division thereof.''

A power that hitherto all the departments of the Federal Government, acting in concert or separately, have not dared to exercise is here attempted to be conferred on a subordinate military officer. To him, as a military officer of the Federal Government, is given the power, supported by '' a sufficient military force,'' to remove every civil officer of the State. What next? The district commander, who has thus displaced the civil officer, is authorized to fill the vacancy by the detail of an officer or soldier of the Army, or by the appointment of '' some other person.''

This military appointee, whether an officer, a soldier, or '' some other person,'' is to perform ''the duties of such officer or person so suspended or removed.'' In other words, an officer or soldier of the Army is thus transformed into a civil officer. He may be made a governor, a legislator, or a judge. However unfit he may deem himself for such civil duties, he must obey the order. The officer of the Army must, if ''detailed,'' go upon the supreme bench of the State with the same prompt obedience as if he were detailed to go upon a court-martial. The soldier, if detailed to act as a justice of the peace, must obey as quickly as if he were detailed for picket duty.

What is the character of such a military civil officer? This bill declares that he shall perform the duties of the civil office to which he is detailed. It is clear, however, that he does not lose his position in the military service. He is still an officer or soldier of the Army; he is still subject to the rules and regulations which govern it, and must yield due deference, respect, and obedience toward his superiors.

The clear intent of this section is that the officer or soldier detailed to fill a civil office must execute its duties according to the laws of the State. If he is appointed a governor of a State, he is to execute the duties as provided by the laws of that State, and for the time being his military character is to be suspended in his new civil capacity. If he is appointed a State treasurer, he must at once assume the custody and disbursement of the funds of the State, and must perform those duties precisely according to the laws of the State, for he is intrusted with no other official duty or other official power. Holding the office of treasurer and intrusted with funds, it happens that he is required by the State laws to enter into bond with security and to take an oath of office; yet from the beginning of the bill to the end there is no provision for any bond or oath of office, or for any single qualification required under the State law, such as residence, citizenship, or anything else. The only oath is that provided for in the ninth section, by the terms of which everyone detailed or appointed to any civil office in the State is required "to take and to subscribe the oath of office prescribed by law for officers of the United States." Thus an officer of the Army of the United States detailed to fill a civil office in one of these States gives no official bond and takes no official oath for the performance of his new duties, but as a civil officer of the State only takes the same oath which he had already taken as a military officer of the United States. He is, at last, a military officer performing civil duties, and the authority under which he acts is Federal authority only; and the inevitable result is that the Federal Government, by the agency of its own sworn officers, in effect assumes the civil government of the State.

A singular contradiction is apparent here. Congress declares these local State governments to be illegal governments, and then provides that these illegal governments shall be carried on by Federal officers, who are to perform the very duties imposed on its own officers by this illegal State authority. It certainly would be a novel spectacle if Congress should attempt to carry on a *legal* State government by the agency of its own officers. It is yet more strange that Congress attempts to sustain and carry on an *illegal* State government by the same Federal agency.

In this connection I must call attention to the tenth and eleventh sections of the bill, which provide that none of the officers or appointees of these military commanders "shall be bound in his action by any opinion of any civil officer of the United States," and that all the provisions of the act "shall be construed liberally, to the end that all the intents thereof may be fully and perfectly carried out."

It seems Congress supposed that this bill might require construction, and they fix, therefore, the rule to be applied. But where is the construction to come from? Certainly no one can be more in want of instruction than a soldier or an officer of the Army detailed for a civil service, perhaps the most important in a State, with the duties of which he is altogether unfamiliar. This bill says he shall not be bound in his action by the opinion of any civil officer of the United States. The duties of the office are altogether civil, but when he asks for an opinion he can only ask the opinion of another military officer, who, perhaps, understands as little of his duties as he does himself; and as to his "action," he is answerable to the military authority, and to the military authority alone. Strictly, no opinion of any civil officer other than a judge has a binding force.

But these military appointees would not be bound even by a judicial opinion. They might very well say, even when their action is in conflict with the Supreme Court of the United States, "That court is composed of civil officers of the United States, and we are not bound to conform our action to any opinion of any such authority."

This bill and the acts to which it is supplementary are all founded upon the assumption that these ten communities are not States and that their existing governments are not legal. Throughout the legislation upon this subject they are called "rebel States," and in this particular bill they are denominated "so-called States," and the vice of illegality is declared to pervade all of them. The obligations of consistency bind a legislative body as well as the individuals who compose it. It is now too late to say that these ten political communities are not States of this Union. Declarations to the contrary made in these three acts are contradicted again and again by repeated acts of legislation enacted by Congress from the year 1861 to the year 1867.

During that period, while these States were in actual rebellion, and after that rebellion was brought to a close, they have been again and again recognized as States of the Union. Representation has been apportioned to them as States. They have been divided into judicial districts for the holding of district and circuit courts of the United States, as States of the Union only can be districted. The last act on this subject was passed July 23, 1866, by which every one of these ten States was arranged into districts and circuits.

They have been called upon by Congress to act through their legislatures upon at least two amendments to the Constitution of the United States. As States they have ratified one amendment, which required the vote of twenty-seven States of the thirty-six then composing the Union. When the requisite twenty-seven votes were given in favor of that amendment—seven of which votes were given by seven of these ten States—it was proclaimed to be a part of the Constitution of the United States, and slavery was declared no longer to exist within the United States or any place subject to their jurisdiction. If these seven States were not legal States of the Union, it follows as an inevitable consequence that in some of the States slavery yet exists. It does not exist in these seven States, for they have abolished it also in their State constitutions; but Kentucky not having done so, it would still remain in that State. But, in truth, if this assumption that these States have no legal State governments be true, then the abolition of slavery by these illegal governments binds no one, for Congress now denies to these States the power to abolish slavery by denying to them the power to elect a legal State legislature, or to frame a constitution for any purpose, even for such a purpose as the abolition of slavery.

As to the other constitutional amendment, having reference to suffrage, it happens that these States have not accepted it. The consequence is that it has never been proclaimed or understood, even by Congress, to be a part of the Constitution of the United States. The Senate of the United

States has repeatedly given its sanction to the appointment of judges, district attorneys, and marshals for every one of these States; yet, if they are not legal States, not one of these judges is authorized to hold a court. So, too, both Houses of Congress have passed appropriation bills to pay all these judges, attorneys, and officers of the United States for exercising their functions in these States. Again, in the machinery of the internal-revenue laws all these States are districted, not as "Territories," but as "States."

So much for continuous legislative recognition. The instances cited, however, fall far short of all that might be enumerated. Executive recognition, as is well known, has been frequent and unwavering. The same may be said as to judicial recognition through the Supreme Court of the United States. That august tribunal, from first to last, in the administration of its duties *in banc* and upon the circuit, has never failed to recognize these ten communities as legal States of the Union. The cases depending in that court upon appeal and writ of error from these States when the rebellion began have not been dismissed upon any idea of the cessation of jurisdiction. They were carefully continued from term to term until the rebellion was entirely subdued and peace reestablished, and then they were called for argument and consideration as if no insurrection had intervened. New cases, occurring since the rebellion, have come from these States before that court by writ of error and appeal, and even by original suit, where only "a State" can bring such a suit. These cases are entertained by that tribunal in the exercise of its acknowledged jurisdiction, which could not attach to them if they had come from any political body other than a State of the Union. Finally, in the allotment of their circuits made by the judges at the December term, 1865, every one of these States is put on the same footing of legality with all the other States of the Union. Virginia and North Carolina, being a part of the fourth circuit, are allotted to the Chief Justice. South Carolina, Georgia, Alabama, Mississippi, and Florida constitute the fifth circuit, and are allotted to the late Mr. Justice Wayne. Louisiana, Arkansas, and Texas are allotted to the sixth judicial circuit, as to which there is a vacancy on the bench.

The Chief Justice, in the exercise of his circuit duties, has recently held a circuit court in the State of North Carolina. If North Carolina is not a State of this Union, the Chief Justice had no authority to hold a court there, and every order, judgment, and decree rendered by him in that court were *coram non judice* and void.

Another ground on which these reconstruction acts are attempted to be sustained is this: That these ten States are conquered territory; that the constitutional relation in which they stood as States toward the Federal Government prior to the rebellion has given place to a new relation; that their territory is a conquered country and their citizens a conquered people, and that in this new relation Congress can govern them by military power.

A title by conquest stands on clear ground; it is a new title acquired by war; it applies only to territory; for goods or movable things regularly captured in war are called "booty," or, if taken by individual soldiers, "plunder."

There is not a foot of the land in any one of these ten States which the United States holds by conquest, save only such land as did not belong to either of these States or to any individual owner. I mean such lands as did belong to the pretended government called the Confederate States. These lands we may claim to hold by conquest. As to all other land or territory, whether belonging to the States or to individuals, the Federal Government has now no more title or right to it than it had before the rebellion. Our own forts, arsenals, navy-yards, custom-houses, and other Federal property situate in those States we now hold, not by the title of conquest, but by our old title, acquired by purchase or condemnation for public use, with compensation to former owners. We have not conquered these places, but have simply "repossessed" them.

If we require more sites for forts, custom-houses, or other public use, we must acquire the title to them by purchase or appropriation in the regular mode. At this moment the United States, in the acquisition of sites for national cemeteries in these States, acquires title in the same way. The Federal courts sit in court-houses owned or leased by the United States, not in the court-houses of the States. The United States pays each of these States for the use of its jails. Finally, the United States levies its direct taxes and its internal revenue upon the property in these States, including the productions of the lands within their territorial limits, not by way of levy and contribution in the character of a conqueror, but in the regular way of taxation, under the same laws which apply to all the other States of the Union.

From first to last, during the rebellion and since, the title of each of these States to the lands and public buildings owned by them has never been disturbed, and not a foot of it has ever been acquired by the United States, even under a title by confiscation, and not a foot of it has ever been taxed under Federal law.

In conclusion I must respectfully ask the attention of Congress to the consideration of one more question arising under this bill. It vests in the military commander, subject only to the approval of the General of the Army of the United States, an unlimited power to remove from office any civil or military officer in each of these ten States, and the further power, subject to the same approval, to detail or appoint any military officer or soldier of the United States to perform the duties of the officer so removed, and to fill all vacancies occurring in those States by death, resignation, or otherwise.

The military appointee thus required to perform the duties of a civil office according to the laws of the State, and, as such, required to take an oath, is for the time being a civil officer. What is his character? Is he a civil officer of the State or a civil officer of the United States? If he is a civil officer of the State, where is the Federal power under our Constitution which authorizes his appointment by any Federal officer? If, however, he is to be considered a civil officer of the United States, as his appointment and oath would seem to indicate, where is the authority for his appointment vested by the Constitution? The power of appointment of all officers of the United States, civil or military, where not provided for in the Constitution, is vested in the President, by and with the advice and consent of the Senate, with this exception, that Congress "may by law vest the appointment of such inferior officers as they think proper in the President alone, in the courts of law, or in the heads of Departments." But this bill, if these are to be considered inferior officers within the meaning of the Constitution, does not provide for their appointment by the President alone, or by the courts of law, or by the heads of Departments, but vests the appointment in one subordinate executive officer, subject to the approval of another subordinate executive officer. So that, if we put this question and fix the character of this military appointee either way, this provision of the bill is equally opposed to the Constitution.

Take the case of a soldier or officer appointed to perform the office of judge in one of these States, and, as such, to administer the proper laws of the State. Where is the authority to be found in the Constitution for vesting in a military or an executive officer strict judicial functions to be exercised under State law? It has been again and again decided by the Supreme Court of the United States that acts of Congress which have attempted to vest *executive* powers in the *judicial* courts or judges of the United States are not warranted by the Constitution. If Congress can not clothe *a judge* with merely *executive* duties, how can they clothe *an officer* or *soldier* of the Army with *judicial* duties over citizens of the United States who are not in the military or naval service? So, too, it has been repeatedly decided that Congress can not require a State officer, executive or judicial, to perform any duty enjoined upon him by a law of the United States. How, then, can Congress confer power upon an executive officer of the United States to perform such duties in a State? If Congress could not vest in a judge of one of these States any judicial authority under the United States by direct enactment, how can it accomplish the same thing indirectly, by removing the State judge and putting an officer of the United States in his place?

To me these considerations are conclusive of the unconstitutionality of this part of the bill now before me, and I earnestly commend their consideration to the deliberate judgment of Congress.

Within a period less than a year the legislation of Congress has attempted to strip the executive department of the Government of some of its essential powers. The Constitution and the oath provided in it devolve upon the President the power and duty to see that the laws are faithfully executed. The Constitution, in order to carry out this power, gives him the choice of the agents, and makes them subject to his control and supervision. But in the execution of these laws the constitutional obligation upon the President remains, but the power to exercise that constitutional duty is effectually taken away. The military commander is as to the power of appointment made to take the place of the President, and the General of the Army the place of the Senate; and any attempt on the part of the President to assert his own constitutional power may, under pretense of law, be met by official insubordination. It is to be feared that these military officers, looking to the authority given by these laws rather than to the letter of the Constitution, will recognize no authority but the commander of the district and the General of the Army.

If there were no other objection than this to this proposed legislation, it would be sufficient. Whilst I hold the chief executive authority of the United States, whilst the obligation rests upon me to see that all the laws are faithfully executed, I can never willingly surrender that trust or the powers given for its execution. I can never give my assent to be made responsible for the faithful execution of laws, and at the same time surrender that trust and the powers which accompany it to any other executive officer, high or low, or to any number of executive officers. If this executive trust, vested by the Constitution in the President, is to be taken from him and vested in a subordinate officer, the responsibility will be with Congress in clothing the subordinate with unconstitutional power and with the officer who assumes its exercise.

This interference with the constitutional authority of the executive department is an evil that will inevitably sap the foundations of our federal system; but it is not the worst evil of this legislation. It is a great public wrong to take from the President powers conferred on him alone by the Constitution, but the wrong is more flagrant and more dangerous when the powers so taken from the President are conferred upon subordinate executive officers, and especially upon military officers. Over nearly one-third of the States of the Union military power, regulated by no fixed law, rules supreme. Each one of the five district commanders, though not chosen by the people or responsible to them, exercises at this hour more executive power, military and civil, than the people have ever been willing to confer upon the head of the executive department, though chosen by and responsible to themselves. The remedy must come from the people themselves. They know what it is and how it is to be applied. At the present time they can not, according to the forms of the Constitution, repeal these laws; they can not remove or control this military despotism. The remedy is, nevertheless, in their hands; it is to be found in the ballot, and is a sure one if not controlled by fraud, overawed by arbitrary power, or, from apathy on their part, too long delayed. With abiding confidence in their patriotism, wisdom, and integrity, I am still hopeful of the future, and that in the end the rod of despotism will be broken, the armed heel of power lifted from the necks of the people, and the principles of a violated Constitution preserved.

ANDREW JOHNSON.

WASHINGTON, D. C., *July 19, 1867.*

To the House of Representatives:

For reasons heretofore stated in my several veto messages to Congress upon the subject of reconstruction, I return without my approval the "Joint resolution to carry into effect the several acts providing for the more efficient government of the rebel States," and appropriating for that purpose the sum of $1,000,000.

ANDREW JOHNSON.

PROCLAMATIONS.

BY THE PRESIDENT OF THE UNITED STATES.

A PROCLAMATION.

Whereas by the Constitution of the United States the executive power is vested in a President of the United States of America, who is bound by solemn oath faithfully to execute the office of President and to the best of his ability to preserve, protect, and defend the Constitution of the United States, and is by the same instrument made Commander in Chief of the Army and Navy of the United States and is required to take care that the laws be faithfully executed; and

Whereas by the same Constitution it is provided that the said Constitution and the laws of the United States which shall be made in pursuance thereof shall be the supreme law of the land, and the judges in every State shall be bound thereby; and

Whereas in and by the same Constitution the judicial power of the United States is vested in one Supreme Court and in such inferior courts as Congress may from time to time ordain and establish, and the aforesaid judicial power is declared to extend to all cases in law and equity arising under the Constitution, the laws of the United States, and the treaties which shall be made under their authority; and

Whereas all officers, civil and military, are bound by oath that they will support and defend the Constitution against all enemies, foreign and domestic, and will bear true faith and allegiance to the same; and

Whereas all officers of the Army and Navy of the United States, in accepting their commissions under the laws of Congress and the Rules and Articles of War, incur an obligation to observe, obey, and follow such directions as they shall from time to time receive from the President or the General or other superior officers set over them according to the rules and discipline of war; and

Whereas it is provided by law that whenever, by reason of unlawful obstructions, combinations, or assemblages of persons or rebellion against the authority of the Government of the United States, it shall become impracticable, in the judgment of the President of the United States, to enforce by the ordinary course of judicial proceedings the laws of the United States within any State or Territory, the Executive in that case is authorized and required to secure their faithful execution by the employment of the land and naval forces; and

Whereas impediments and obstructions, serious in their character, have recently been interposed in the States of North Carolina and South Carolina, hindering and preventing for a time a proper enforcement there of the laws of the United States and of the judgments and decrees of a lawful court thereof, in disregard of the command of the President of the United States; and

Whereas reasonable and well-founded apprehensions exist that such ill-advised and unlawful proceedings may be again attempted there or elsewhere:

Now, therefore, I, Andrew Johnson, President of the United States, do hereby warn all persons against obstructing or hindering in any manner whatsoever the faithful execution of the Constitution and the laws; and I do solemnly enjoin and command all officers of the Government, civil and military, to render due submission and obedience to said laws and to the judgments and decrees of the courts of the United States, and to give all the aid in their power necessary to the prompt enforcement and execution of such laws, decrees, judgments, and processes.

And I do hereby enjoin upon the officers of the Army and Navy to assist and sustain the courts and other civil authorities of the United States in a faithful administration of the laws thereof and in the judgments, decrees, mandates, and processes of the courts of the United States; and I call upon all good and well-disposed citizens of the United States to remember that upon the said Constitution and laws, and upon the judgments, decrees, and processes of the courts made in accordance with the same, depend the protection of the lives, liberty, property, and happiness of the people. And I exhort them everywhere to testify their devotion to their country, their pride in its prosperity and greatness, and their determination to uphold its free institutions by a hearty cooperation in the efforts of the Government to sustain the authority of the law, to maintain the supremacy of the Federal Constitution, and to preserve unimpaired the integrity of the National Union.

In testimony whereof I have caused the seal of the United States to be affixed to these presents and sign the same with my hand.

[SEAL.]   Done at the city of Washington, the 3d day of September, in the year 1867.

ANDREW JOHNSON.

By the President:

WILLIAM H. SEWARD,
Secretary of State.

By the President of the United States of America.

A PROCLAMATION.

Whereas in the month of July, A. D. 1861, the two Houses of Congress, with extraordinary unanimity, solemnly declared that the war then existing was not waged on the part of the Government in any spirit of oppression nor for any purpose of conquest or subjugation, nor purpose of overthrowing or interfering with the rights or established institutions of the States, but to defend and maintain the supremacy of the Constitution and to preserve the Union, with all the dignity, equality, and rights of the several States unimpaired, and that as soon as these objects should be accomplished the war ought to cease; and

Whereas the President of the United States, on the 8th day of December, A. D. 1863, and on the 26th day of March, A. D. 1864, did, with the objects of suppressing the then existing rebellion, of inducing all persons to return to their loyalty, and of restoring the authority of the United States, issue proclamations offering amnesty and pardon to all persons who had, directly or indirectly, participated in the then existing rebellion, except as in those proclamations was specified and reserved; and

Whereas the President of the United States did on the 29th day of May, A. D. 1865, issue a further proclamation, with the same objects before mentioned, and to the end that the authority of the Government of the United States might be restored and that peace, order, and freedom might be established, and the President did by the said last-mentioned proclamation proclaim and declare that he thereby granted to all persons who had, directly or indirectly, participated in the then existing rebellion, except as therein excepted, amnesty and pardon, with restoration of all rights of property, except as to slaves, and except in certain cases where legal proceedings had been instituted, but upon condition that such persons should take and subscribe an oath therein prescribed, which oath should be registered for permanent preservation; and

Whereas in and by the said last-mentioned proclamation of the 29th day of May, A. D. 1865, fourteen extensive classes of persons therein specially described were altogether excepted and excluded from the benefits thereof; and

Whereas the President of the United States did, on the 2d day of April, A. D. 1866, issue a proclamation declaring that the insurrection was at an end and was thenceforth to be so regarded; and

Whereas there now exists no organized armed resistance of misguided citizens or others to the authority of the United States in the States of Georgia, South Carolina, Virginia, North Carolina, Tennessee, Alabama, Louisiana, Arkansas, Mississippi, Florida, and Texas, and the laws can be sustained and enforced therein by the proper civil authority, State or Federal, and the people of said States are well and loyally disposed, and have contormed, or, if permitted to do so, will conform in their legislation to the condition of affairs growing out of the amendment to the Constitution of the United States prohibiting slavery within the limits and jurisdiction of the United States; and

Whereas there no longer exists any reasonable ground to apprehend within the States which were involved in the late rebellion any renewal thereof or any unlawful resistance by the people of said States to the Constitution and laws of the United States; and

Whereas large standing armies, military occupation, martial law, military tribunals, and the suspension of the privilege of the writ of *habeas corpus* and the right of trial by jury are in time of peace dangerous to public liberty, incompatible with the individual rights of the citizen, contrary to the genius and spirit of our free institutions, and exhaustive of the national resources, and ought not, therefore, to be sanctioned or allowed except in cases of actual necessity for repelling invasion or suppressing insurrection or rebellion; and

Whereas a retaliatory or vindictive policy, attended by unnecessary disqualifications, pains, penalties, confiscations, and disfranchisements, now, as always, could only tend to hinder reconciliation among the people and national restoration, while it must seriously embarrass, obstruct, and repress popular energies and national industry and enterprise; and

Whereas for these reasons it is now deemed essential to the public welfare and to the more perfect restoration of constitutional law and order that the said last-mentioned proclamation so as aforesaid issued on the 29th day of May, A. D. 1865, should be modified, and that the full and beneficent pardon conceded thereby should be opened and further extended to a large number of the persons who by its aforesaid exceptions have been hitherto excluded from Executive clemency:

Now, therefore, be it known that I, Andrew Johnson, President of the United States, do hereby proclaim and declare that the full pardon described in the said proclamation of the 29th day of May, A. D. 1865, shall henceforth be opened and extended to all persons who, directly or indirectly, participated in the late rebellion, with the restoration of all privileges, immunities, and rights of property, except as to property with regard to slaves, and except in cases of legal proceedings under the laws of the United States; but upon this condition, nevertheless, that every such person who shall seek to avail himself of this proclamation shall take and subscribe the following oath and shall cause the same to be registered for permanent preservation in the same manner and with the same effect as with the oath prescribed in the said proclamation of the 29th day of May, 1865, namely:

I, —— ——, do solemnly swear (or affirm), in presence of Almighty God, that I will henceforth faithfully support, protect, and defend the Constitution of the United States and the Union of the States thereunder, and that I will in like manner abide by and faithfully support all laws and proclamations which have been made during the late rebellion with reference to the emancipation of slaves. So help me God.

The following persons, and no others, are excluded from the benefits of this proclamation and of the said proclamation of the 29th day of May, 1865, namely:

First. The chief or pretended chief executive officers, including the President, the Vice-President, and all heads of departments of the pretended Confederate or rebel government, and all who were agents thereof in foreign states and countries, and all who held or pretended to hold in the service of the said pretended Confederate government a military rank or title above the grade of brigadier-general or naval rank or title above that of captain, and all who were or pretended to be governors of States while maintaining, aiding, abetting, or submitting to and acquiescing in the rebellion.

Second. All persons who in any way treated otherwise than as lawful prisoners of war persons who in any capacity were employed or engaged in the military or naval service of the United States.

Third. All persons who at the time they may seek to obtain the benefits of this proclamation are actually in civil, military, or naval confinement or custody, or legally held to bail, either before or after conviction, and all persons who were engaged, directly or indirectly, in the assassination of the late President of the United States or in any plot or conspiracy in any manner therewith connected.

In testimony whereof I have signed these presents with my hand and have caused the seal of the United States to be hereunto affixed.

[SEAL.]   Done at the city of Washington, the 7th day of September, A. D. 1867, and of the Independence of the United States of America the ninety-second.

ANDREW JOHNSON.

By the President:

WILLIAM H. SEWARD,
Secretary of State.

BY THE PRESIDENT OF THE UNITED STATES OF AMERICA.

A PROCLAMATION.

Whereas it has been ascertained that in the nineteenth paragraph of the proclamation of the President of the United States of the 20th of August, 1866, declaring the insurrection at an end which had theretofore existed in the State of Texas, the previous proclamation of the 13th of June, 1865, instead of that of the 2d day of April, 1866, was referred to:

Now, therefore, be it known that I, Andrew Johnson, President of the United States, do hereby declare and proclaim that the said words "13th of June, 1865," are to be regarded as erroneous in the paragraph adverted to, and that the words "2d day of April, 1866," are to be considered as substituted therefor.

In testimony whereof I have hereunto set my hand and caused the seal of the United States to be affixed.

[SEAL.] Done at the city of Washington, this 7th day of October, A. D. 1867, and of the Independence of the United States of America the ninety-second.

ANDREW JOHNSON.

By the President:

WILLIAM H. SEWARD,
Secretary of State.

BY THE PRESIDENT OF THE UNITED STATES OF AMERICA.

A PROCLAMATION.

In conformity with a recent custom that may now be regarded as established on national consent and approval, I, Andrew Johnson, President of the United States, do hereby recommend to my fellow-citizens that Thursday, the 28th day of November next, be set apart and observed throughout the Republic as a day of national thanksgiving and praise to the Almighty Ruler of Nations, with whom are dominion and fear, who maketh peace in His high places.

Resting and refraining from secular labors on that day, let us reverently and devoutly give thanks to our Heavenly Father for the mercies and blessings with which He has crowned the now closing year. Especially let us remember that He has covered our land through all its extent with greatly needed and very abundant harvests; that He has caused industry to prosper, not only in our fields, but also in our workshops, in our mines, and in our forests. He has permitted us to multiply ships upon our lakes and rivers and upon the high seas, and at the same time to extend our iron roads so far into the secluded places of the continent as to guarantee speedy overland intercourse between the two oceans. He has inclined our hearts to turn away from domestic contentions and commotions consequent upon a distracting and desolating civil war, and to walk more and more in the ancient ways of loyalty, conciliation, and brotherly love. He has blessed the peaceful efforts with which we have established new and important commercial treaties with foreign nations, while we have at the same time strengthened our national defenses and greatly enlarged our national borders.

While thus rendering the unanimous and heartfelt tribute of national praise and thanksgiving which is so justly due to Almighty God, let us not fail to implore Him that the same divine protection and care which we have hitherto so undeservedly and yet so constantly enjoyed may be continued to our country and our people throughout all their generations forever.

In witness whereof I have hereunto set my hand and caused the seal of the United States to be affixed.

[SEAL.]   Done at the city of Washington, this 26th day of October, A. D. 1867, and of the Independence of the United States the ninety-second.

ANDREW JOHNSON.

By the President:
> WILLIAM H. SEWARD,
> *Secretary of State.*

EXECUTIVE ORDERS.

GENERAL ORDERS, No. 10.

HEADQUARTERS OF THE ARMY,
ADJUTANT-GENERAL'S OFFICE,
Washington, March 11, 1867.

*   *   *   *   *   *   *

II. In pursuance of the act of Congress entitled "An act to provide for the more efficient government of the rebel States," the President directs the following assignments to be made:

First District, State of Virginia, to be commanded by Brevet Major-General J. M. Schofield. Headquarters, Richmond, Va.

Second District, consisting of North Carolina and South Carolina, to be commanded by Major-General D. E. Sickles. Headquarters, Columbia, S. C.

Third District, consisting of the States of Georgia, Florida, and Alabama, to be commanded by Major-General G. H. Thomas. Headquarters, Montgomery, Ala.

Fourth District, consisting of the States of Mississippi and Arkansas, to be commanded by Brevet Major-General E. O. C. Ord. Headquarters, Vicksburg, Miss.

Fifth District, consisting of the States of Louisiana and Texas, to be commanded by Major-General P. H. Sheridan. Headquarters, New Orleans, La.

The powers of departmental commanders are hereby delegated to the above-named district commanders.

By command of General Grant:

E. D. TOWNSEND,
Assistant Adjutant-General.

GENERAL ORDERS, NO. 18.

HEADQUARTERS OF THE ARMY,
ADJUTANT-GENERAL'S OFFICE,
Washington, March 15, 1867.

The President directs that the following change be made, at the request of Major-General Thomas, in the assignment announced in General Orders, No. 10, of March 11, 1867, of commanders of districts, under the act of Congress entitled "An act to provide for the more efficient government of the rebel States," and of the Department of the Cumberland, created in General Orders, No. 14, of March 12, 1867:

Brevet Major-General John Pope to command the Third District, consisting of the States of Georgia, Florida, and Alabama; and Major-General George H. Thomas to command the Department of the Cumberland.

By command of General Grant:

E. D. TOWNSEND,
Assistant Adjutant-General.

WAR DEPARTMENT,
ADJUTANT-GENERAL'S OFFICE,
Washington, June 20, 1867.

Whereas several commanders of military districts created by the acts of Congress known as the reconstruction acts have expressed doubts as to the proper construction thereof and in respect to some of their powers and duties under said acts, and have applied to the Executive for information in relation thereto; and

Whereas the said acts of Congress have been referred to the Attorney-General for his opinion thereon, and the said acts and the opinion of the Attorney-General have been fully and carefully considered by the President in conference with the heads of the respective Departments:

The President accepts the following as a practical interpretation of the aforesaid acts of Congress on the points therein presented, and directs the same to be transmitted to the respective military commanders for their information, in order that there may be uniformity in the execution of said acts:

1. The oath prescribed in the supplemental act defines all the qualifications required, and every person who can take that oath is entitled to have his name entered upon the list of voters.

2. The board of registration have no authority to administer any other oath to the person applying for registration than this prescribed oath, nor to administer an oath to any other person touching the qualifications of the applicant or the falsity of the oath so taken by him. The act, to guard against falsity in the oath, provides that if false the person taking it shall be tried and punished for perjury.

No provision is made for challenging the qualifications of the applicant or entering upon any trial or investigation of his qualifications, either by witnesses or any other form of proof.

3. *As to citizenship and residence:*

The applicant for registration must be a citizen of the State and of the United States, and must be a resident of a county or parish included in the election district. He may be registered if he has been such citizen for a period less than twelve months at the time he applies for registration, but he can not vote at any election unless his citizenship has *then* extended to the full term of one year. As to such a person, the exact length of his citizenship should be noted opposite his name on the list, so that it may appear on the day of election, upon reference to the list, whether the full term has then been accomplished.

4. An unnaturalized person can not take this oath, but an alien who has been naturalized can take it, and no other proof of naturalization can be required from him.

5. No one who is not 21 years of age at the time of registration can take the oath, for he must swear that he has then attained that age.

6. No one who has been disfranchised for participation in any rebellion against the United States or for felony committed against the laws of any State or of the United States can take this oath.

The actual participation in a rebellion or the actual commission of a felony does not amount to disfranchisement. The sort of disfranchisement here meant is that which is declared by law passed by competent authority, or which has been fixed upon the criminal by the sentence of the court which tried him for the crime.

No law of the United States has declared the penalty of disfranchisement for participation in rebellion alone; nor is it known that any such law exists in either of these ten States, except, perhaps, Virginia, as to which State special instructions will be given.

7. *As to disfranchisement arising from having held office followed by participation in rebellion:*

This is the most important part of the oath, and requires strict attention to arrive at its meaning. The applicant must swear or affirm as follows:

That I have never been a member of any State legislature, nor held any executive or judicial office in any State, and afterwards engaged in an insurrection or rebellion against the United States or given aid or comfort to the enemies thereof; that I have never taken an oath as a member of Congress of the United States, or as an officer of the United States, or as a member of any State legislature, or as an executive or judicial officer of any State, to support the Constitution of the United States, and afterwards engaged in insurrection or rebellion against the United States or given aid or comfort to the enemies thereof.

Two elements must concur in order to disqualify a person under these clauses: First, the office and official oath to support the Constitution of the United States; second, engaging afterwards in rebellion. Both must exist to work disqualification, and must happen in the order of time mentioned.

A person who has held an office and taken the oath to support the Federal Constitution and has not afterwards engaged in rebellion is not disqualified. So, too, a person who has engaged in rebellion, but has not theretofore held an office and taken that oath, is not disqualified.

8. *Officers of the United States:*

As to these the language is without limitation. The person who has at any time prior to the rebellion held an office, civil or military, under the United States, and has taken an official oath to support the Constitution of the United States, is subject to disqualification.

9. *Militia officers* of any State prior to the rebellion are not subject to disqualification.

10. *Municipal officers*—that is to say, officers of incorporated cities, towns, and villages, such as mayors, aldermen, town council, police, and other city or town officers—are not subject to disqualification.

11. Persons who have prior to the rebellion been members of the Congress of the United States or members of a State legislature are subject to disqualification, but those who have been members of conventions framing or amending the Constitution of a State prior to the rebellion are not subject to disqualification.

12. All the executive or judicial officers of any State who took an oath to support the Constitution of the United States are subject to disqualification, including county officers. They are subject to disqualification if they were required to take as a part of their official oath *the oath to support the Constitution of the United States.*

13. Persons who exercised mere employment under State authority are not disqualified; such as commissioners to lay out roads, commissioners of public works, visitors of State institutions, directors of State institutions, examiners of banks, notaries public, and commissioners to take acknowledgments of deeds.

ENGAGING IN REBELLION.

Having specified what offices held by anyone prior to the rebellion come within the meaning of the law, it is necessary next to set forth what subsequent conduct fixes upon such person the offense of engaging in rebellion. Two things must exist as to any person to disqualify him from voting: First, the office held prior to the rebellion, and, afterwards, participation in the rebellion.

14. An act to fix upon a person the offense of engaging in the rebellion under this law must be an overt and voluntary act, done with the intent of aiding or furthering the common unlawful purpose. A person forced into the rebel service by conscription or under a paramount authority which he could not safely disobey, and who would not have entered

such service if left to the free exercise of his own will, can not be held to be disqualified from voting.

15. Mere acts of charity, where the intent is to relieve the wants of the object of such charity, and not done in aid of the cause in which he may have been engaged, do not disqualify; but organized contributions of food and clothing for the general relief of persons engaged in the rebellion, and not of a merely sanitary character, but contributed to enable them to perform their unlawful object, may be classed with acts which do disqualify.

Forced contributions to the rebel cause in the form of taxes or military assessments, which a person was compelled to pay or contribute, do not disqualify; but voluntary contributions to the rebel cause, even such indirect contributions as arise from the voluntary loan of money to rebel authorities or purchase of bonds or securities created to afford the means of carrying on the rebellion, will work disqualification.

16. All those who in legislative or other official capacity were engaged in the furtherance of the common unlawful purpose, where the duties of the office necessarily had relation to the support of the rebellion, such as members of the rebel conventions, congresses, and legislatures, diplomatic agents of the rebel Confederacy, and other officials whose offices were created for the purpose of more effectually carrying on hostilities or whose duties appertained to the support of the rebel cause, must be held to be disqualified.

But officers who during the rebellion discharged official duties not incident to war, but only such duties as belong even to a state of peace and were necessary to the preservation of order and the administration of law, are not to be considered as thereby engaging in rebellion or as disqualified. Disloyal sentiments, opinions, or sympathies would not disqualify, but where a person has by speech or by writing incited others to engage in rebellion he must come under the disqualification.

17. *The duties of the board appointed to superintend the elections:*

This board, having the custody of the list of registered voters in the district for which it is constituted, must see that the name of the person offering to vote is found upon the registration list, and if such proves to be the fact it is the duty of the board to receive his vote if then qualified by residence. They can not receive the vote of any person whose name is not upon the list, though he may be ready to take the registration oath, and although he may satisfy them that he was unable to have his name registered at the proper time, in consequence of absence, sickness, or other cause.

The board can not enter into any inquiry as to the qualifications of any person whose name is not on the registration list, or as to the qualifications of any person whose name is on the list.

18. *The mode of voting* is provided in the act to be *by ballot.* The board will keep a record and poll book of the election, showing the votes,

list of voters, and the persons elected by a plurality of the votes cast at the election, and make returns of these to the commanding general of the district.

19. The board appointed for registration and for superintending the elections must take the oath prescribed by the act of Congress approved July 2, 1862, entitled "An act to prescribe an oath of office."

By order of the President:

E. D. TOWNSEND,
Assistant Adjutant-General.

EXECUTIVE MANSION,
Washington, August 12, 1867.

Hon. EDWIN M. STANTON,
Secretary of War.

SIR: By virtue of the power and authority vested in me as President by the Constitution and laws of the United States, you are hereby suspended from office as Secretary of War, and will cease to exercise any and all functions pertaining to the same.

You will at once transfer to General Ulysses S. Grant, who has this day been authorized and empowered to act as Secretary of War *ad interim*, all records, books, and other property now in your custody and charge.

ANDREW JOHNSON.

EXECUTIVE MANSION,
Washington, D. C., August 12, 1867.

General ULYSSES S. GRANT,
Washington, D. C.

SIR: The Hon. Edwin M. Stanton having been this day suspended as Secretary of War, you are hereby authorized and empowered to act as Secretary of War *ad interim*, and will at once enter upon the discharge of the duties of the office.

The Secretary of War has been instructed to transfer to you all the records, books, papers, and other public property now in his custody and charge.

ANDREW JOHNSON.

EXECUTIVE MANSION,
Washington, D. C., August 17, 1867.

Major-General George H. Thomas is hereby assigned to the command of the Fifth Military District, created by the act of Congress passed on the 2d day of March, 1867.

Major-General P. H. Sheridan is hereby assigned to the command of the Department of the Missouri.

Major-General Winfield S. Hancock is hereby assigned to the command of the Department of the Cumberland.

The Secretary of War *ad interim* will give the necessary instructions to carry this order into effect.

ANDREW JOHNSON.

EXECUTIVE MANSION,
Washington, D. C., August 26, 1867.

General U. S. GRANT,
 Secretary of War ad interim.

SIR: In consequence of the unfavorable condition of the health of Major-General George H. Thomas, as reported to you in Surgeon Hasson's dispatch of the 21st instant, my order dated August 17, 1867, is hereby modified so as to assign Major-General Winfield S. Hancock to the command of the Fifth Military District, created by the act of Congress passed March 2, 1867, and of the military department comprising the States of Louisiana and Texas. On being relieved from the command of the Department of the Missouri by Major-General P. H. Sheridan, Major-General Hancock will proceed directly to New Orleans, La., and, assuming the command to which he is hereby assigned, will, when necessary to a faithful execution of the laws, exercise any and all powers conferred by acts of Congress upon district commanders and any and all authority pertaining to officers in command of military departments.

Major-General P. H. Sheridan will at once turn over his present command to the officer next in rank to himself, and, proceeding without delay to Fort Leavenworth, Kans., will relieve Major-General Hancock of the command of the Department of the Missouri.

Major-General George H. Thomas will until further orders remain in command of the Department of the Cumberland.

 Very respectfully, yours,

ANDREW JOHNSON.

EXECUTIVE MANSION,
Washington, D. C., August 26, 1867.

Brevet Major-General Edward R. S. Canby is hereby assigned to the command of the Second Military District, created by the act of Congress of March 2, 1867, and of the Military Department of the South, embracing the States of North Carolina and South Carolina. He will, as soon as practicable, relieve Major-General Daniel E. Sickles, and, on assuming the command to which he is hereby assigned, will, when necessary to a faithful execution of the laws, exercise any and all powers conferred by acts of Congress upon district commanders and any and all authority pertaining to officers in command of military departments.

Major-General Daniel E. Sickles is hereby relieved from the command of the Second Military District.

The Secretary of War *ad interim* will give the necessary instructions to carry this order into effect.

ANDREW JOHNSON.

EXECUTIVE MANSION,
Washington, D. C., September 4, 1867.

The heads of the several Executive Departments of the Government are instructed to furnish each person holding an appointment in their respective Departments with an official copy of the proclamation of the President bearing date the 3d instant, with directions strictly to observe its requirements for an earnest support of the Constitution of the United States and a faithful execution of the laws which have been made in pursuance thereof.

ANDREW JOHNSON.

[NOTE.—The Fortieth Congress, second session, met December 2, 1867, in conformity to the Constitution of the United States, and on July 27, 1868, in accordance with the concurrent resolution of July 24, adjourned to September 21; again met September 21, and adjourned to October 16; again met October 16, and adjourned to November 10; again met November 10 and adjourned to December 7, 1868; the latter meetings and adjournments being in accordance with the concurrent resolution of September 21.]

THIRD ANNUAL MESSAGE.

WASHINGTON, *December 3, 1867.*

Fellow-Citizens of the Senate and House of Representatives:

The continued disorganization of the Union, to which the President has so often called the attention of Congress, is yet a subject of profound and patriotic concern. We may, however, find some relief from that anxiety in the reflection that the painful political situation, although before untried by ourselves, is not new in the experience of nations. Political science, perhaps as highly perfected in our own time and country as in any other, has not yet disclosed any means by which civil wars can be absolutely prevented. An enlightened nation, however, with a wise and beneficent constitution of free government, may diminish their frequency and mitigate their severity by directing all its proceedings in accordance with its fundamental law.

When a civil war has been brought to a close, it is manifestly the first interest and duty of the state to repair the injuries which the war has inflicted, and to secure the benefit of the lessons it teaches as fully and as speedily as possible. This duty was, upon the termination of the rebellion, promptly accepted, not only by the executive department, but by the insurrectionary States themselves, and restoration in the first moment of peace was believed to be as easy and certain as it was indispensable. The expectations, however, then so reasonably and confidently entertained were disappointed by legislation from which I felt constrained by my obligations to the Constitution to withhold my assent.

It is therefore a source of profound regret that in complying with the obligation imposed upon the President by the Constitution to give to Congress from time to time information of the state of the Union I am unable to communicate any definitive adjustment, satisfactory to the American people, of the questions which since the close of the rebellion have agitated the public mind. On the contrary, candor compels me to declare that at this time there is no Union as our fathers understood the term, and as they meant it to be understood by us. The Union which they established can exist only where all the States are represented in both Houses of Congress; where one State is as free as another to regulate its internal concerns according to its own will, and where the laws of the central Government, strictly confined to matters of national jurisdiction, apply with equal force to all the people of every section. That such is not the present "state of the Union" is a melancholy fact, and we must all acknowledge that the restoration of the States to their proper legal relations with the Federal Government and with one another, according to the terms of the original compact, would be the greatest temporal blessing which God, in His kindest providence, could bestow upon this nation. It becomes our imperative duty to consider whether or not it is impossible to effect this most desirable consummation.

The Union and the Constitution are inseparable. As long as one is obeyed by all parties, the other will be preserved; and if one is destroyed, both must perish together. The destruction of the Constitution will be followed by other and still greater calamities. It was ordained not only to form a more perfect union between the States, but to "establish justice, insure domestic tranquillity, provide for the common defense, promote the general welfare, and secure the blessings of liberty to ourselves and our posterity." Nothing but implicit obedience to its requirements in all parts of the country will accomplish these great ends. Without that obedience we can look forward only to continual outrages upon individual rights, incessant breaches of the public peace, national weakness, financial dishonor, the total loss of our prosperity, the general corruption of morals, and the final extinction of popular freedom. To save our country from evils so appalling as these, we should renew our efforts again and again.

To me the process of restoration seems perfectly plain and simple. It consists merely in a faithful application of the Constitution and laws. The execution of the laws is not now obstructed or opposed by physical force. There is no military or other necessity, real or pretended, which can prevent obedience to the Constitution, either North or South. All the rights and all the obligations of States and individuals can be protected and enforced by means perfectly consistent with the fundamental law. The courts may be everywhere open, and if open their process would be unimpeded. Crimes against the United States can be prevented or punished by the proper judicial authorities in a manner entirely practicable and legal. There is therefore no reason why the Constitution should not be obeyed, unless those who exercise its powers have determined that it shall be disregarded and violated. The mere naked will of this Government, or of some one or more of its branches, is the only obstacle that can exist to a perfect union of all the States.

On this momentous question and some of the measures growing out of it I have had the misfortune to differ from Congress, and have expressed my convictions without reserve, though with becoming deference to the opinion of the legislative department. Those convictions are not only unchanged, but strengthened by subsequent events and further reflection. The transcendent importance of the subject will be a sufficient excuse for calling your attention to some of the reasons which have so strongly influenced my own judgment. The hope that we may all finally concur in a mode of settlement consistent at once with our true interests and with our sworn duties to the Constitution is too natural and too just to be easily relinquished.

It is clear to my apprehension that the States lately in rebellion are still members of the National Union. When did they cease to be so? The "ordinances of secession" adopted by a portion (in most of them a very small portion) of their citizens were mere nullities. If we admit now that they were valid and effectual for the purpose intended by their authors, we sweep from under our feet the whole ground upon which we justified the war. Were those States afterwards expelled from the Union by the war? The direct contrary was averred by this Government to be its purpose, and was so understood by all those who gave their blood and treasure to aid in its prosecution. It can not be that a successful war, waged for the preservation of the Union, had the legal effect of dissolving it. The victory of the nation's arms was not the disgrace of her policy; the defeat of secession on the battlefield was not the triumph of its lawless principle. Nor could Congress, with or without the consent of the Executive, do anything which would have the effect, directly or indirectly, of separating the States from each other. To dissolve the Union is to repeal the Constitution which holds it together, and that is a power which does not belong to any department of this Government, or to all of them united.

This is so plain that it has been acknowledged by all branches of the Federal Government. The Executive (my predecessor as well as myself) and the heads of all the Departments have uniformly acted upon the principle that the Union is not only undissolved, but indissoluble. Congress submitted an amendment of the Constitution to be ratified by the Southern States, and accepted their acts of ratification as a necessary and lawful exercise of their highest function. If they were not States, or were States out of the Union, their consent to a change in the fundamental law of the Union would have been nugatory, and Congress in asking it committed a political absurdity. The judiciary has also given the solemn sanction of its authority to the same view of the case. The judges of the Supreme Court have included the Southern States in their circuits, and they are constantly, *in banc* and elsewhere, exercising jurisdiction which does not belong to them unless those States are States of the Union.

If the Southern States are component parts of the Union, the Constitution is the supreme law for them, as it is for all the other States. They are bound to obey it, and so are we. The right of the Federal Government, which is clear and unquestionable, to enforce the Constitution upon them implies the correlative obligation on our part to observe its limitations and execute its guaranties. Without the Constitution we are nothing; by, through, and under the Constitution we are what it makes us. We may doubt the wisdom of the law, we may not approve of its provisions, but we can not violate it merely because it seems to confine our powers within limits narrower than we could wish. It is not a question of individual or class or sectional interest, much less of party predominance, but of duty—of high and sacred duty—which we are all sworn to perform. If we can not support the Constitution with the cheerful alacrity of those who love and believe in it, we must give to it at least the fidelity of public servants who act under solemn obligations and commands which they dare not disregard.

The constitutional duty is not the only one which requires the States to be restored. There is another consideration which, though of minor importance, is yet of great weight. On the 22d day of July, 1861, Congress declared by an almost unanimous vote of both Houses that the war should be conducted solely for the purpose of preserving the Union and maintaining the supremacy of the Federal Constitution and laws, without impairing the dignity, equality, and rights of the States or of individuals, and that when this was done the war should cease. I do not say that this declaration is personally binding on those who joined in making it, any more than individual members of Congress are personally bound to pay a public debt created under a law for which they voted. But it was a solemn, public, official pledge of the national honor, and I can not imagine upon what grounds the repudiation of it is to be justified. If it be said that we are not bound to keep faith with rebels, let it be remembered that this promise was not made to rebels only. Thousands of true men in the South were drawn to our standard by it, and hundreds of thousands in the North gave their lives in the belief that it would be carried out. It was made on the day after the first great battle of the war had been fought and lost. All patriotic and intelligent men then saw the necessity of giving such an assurance, and believed that without it the war would end in disaster to our cause. Having given that assurance in the extremity of our peril, the violation of it now, in the day of our power, would be a rude rending of that good faith which holds the moral world together; our country would cease to have any claim upon the confidence of men; it would make the war not only a failure, but a fraud.

Being sincerely convinced that these views are correct, I would be unfaithful to my duty if I did not recommend the repeal of the acts of Congress which place ten of the Southern States under the domination of military masters. If calm reflection shall satisfy a majority of your honorable bodies that the acts referred to are not only a violation of the national faith, but in direct conflict with the Constitution, I dare not permit myself to doubt that you will immediately strike them from the statute book.

To demonstrate the unconstitutional character of those acts I need do no more than refer to their general provisions. It must be seen at once that they are not authorized. To dictate what alterations shall be made in the constitutions of the several States; to control the elections of State legislators and State officers, members of Congress and electors of President and Vice-President, by arbitrarily declaring who shall vote and who shall be excluded from that privilege; to dissolve State legislatures or prevent them from assembling; to dismiss judges and other civil functionaries of the State and appoint others without regard to State law; to organize and operate all the political machinery of the States; to regulate the whole administration of their domestic and local affairs according to the mere will of strange and irresponsible agents, sent among them for that purpose—these are powers not granted to the Federal Government or to any one of its branches. Not being granted, we violate our trust by assuming them as palpably as we would by acting in the face of a positive interdict; for the Constitution forbids us to do whatever it does not affirmatively authorize, either by express words or by clear implication. If the authority we desire to use does not come to us through the Constitution, we can exercise it only by usurpation, and usurpation is the most dangerous of political crimes. By that crime the enemies of free government in all ages have worked out their designs against public liberty and private right. It leads directly and immediately to the establishment of absolute rule, for undelegated power is always unlimited and unrestrained.

The acts of Congress in question are not only objectionable for their assumption of ungranted power, but many of their provisions are in conflict with the direct prohibitions of the Constitution. The Constitution commands that a republican form of government shall be guaranteed to all the States; that no person shall be deprived of life, liberty, or property without due process of law, arrested without a judicial warrant, or punished without a fair trial before an impartial jury; that the privilege of *habeas corpus* shall not be denied in time of peace, and that no bill of attainder shall be passed even against a single individual. Yet the system of measures established by these acts of Congress does totally subvert and destroy the form as well as the substance of republican government in the ten States to which they apply. It binds them hand and foot in absolute slavery, and subjects them to a strange and hostile power, more unlimited and more likely to be abused than any other now known among civilized men. It tramples down all those rights in which the essence of liberty consists, and which a free government is always most careful to protect. It denies the *habeas corpus* and the trial by jury. Personal freedom, property, and life, if assailed by the passion, the prejudice, or the rapacity of the ruler, have no security whatever. It has the effect of a bill of attainder or bill of pains and penalties, not upon a few individuals, but upon whole masses, including the millions who inhabit the subject States, and even their unborn children. These wrongs, being expressly forbidden, can not be constitutionally inflicted upon any portion of our people, no matter how they may have come within our jurisdiction, and no matter whether they live in States, Territories, or districts.

I have no desire to save from the proper and just consequences of their great crime those who engaged in rebellion against the Government, but as a mode of punishment the measures under consideration are the most unreasonable that could be invented. Many of those people are perfectly innocent; many kept their fidelity to the Union untainted to the last; many were incapable of any legal offense; a large proportion even of the persons able to bear arms were forced into rebellion against their will, and of those who are guilty with their own consent the degrees of guilt are as various as the shades of their character and temper. But these acts of Congress confound them all together in one common doom. Indiscriminate vengeance upon classes, sects, and parties, or upon whole communities, for offenses committed by a portion of them against the governments to which they owed obedience was common in the barbarous ages of the world; but Christianity and civilization have made such progress that recourse to a punishment so cruel and unjust would meet with the condemnation of all unprejudiced and right-minded men. The punitive justice of this age, and especially of this country, does not consist in stripping whole States of their liberties and reducing all their people, without distinction, to the condition of slavery. It deals separately with each individual, confines itself to the forms of law, and vindicates its own purity by an impartial examination of every case before a competent judicial tribunal. If this does not satisfy all our desires with regard to Southern rebels, let us console ourselves by reflecting that a free Constitution, triumphant in war and unbroken in peace, is worth far more to us and our children than the gratification of any present feeling.

I am aware it is assumed that this system of government for the Southern States is not to be perpetual. It is true this military government is to be only provisional, but it is through this temporary evil that a greater evil is to be made perpetual.   If the guaranties of the Constitution can be broken provisionally to serve a temporary purpose, and in a part only of the country, we can destroy them everywhere and for all time.   Arbitrary measures often change, but they generally change for the worse. It is the curse of despotism that it has no halting place.   The intermitted exercise of its power brings no sense of security to its subjects, for they can never know what more they will be called to endure when its red right hand is armed to plague them again.   Nor is it possible to conjecture how or where power, unrestrained by law, may seek its next victims. The States that are still free may be enslaved at any moment; for if the Constitution does not protect all, it protects none.

It is manifestly and avowedly the object of these laws to confer upon negroes the privilege of voting and to disfranchise such a number of white citizens as will give the former a clear majority at all elections in the Southern States.   This, to the minds of some persons, is so important that a violation of the Constitution is justified as a means of bringing it about.   The morality is always false which excuses a wrong because it proposes to accomplish a desirable end.   We are not permitted to do evil that good may come.   But in this case the end itself is evil, as well as the means.   The subjugation of the States to negro domination would be worse than the military despotism under which they are now suffering. It was believed beforehand that the people would endure any amount of military oppression for any length of time rather than degrade themselves by subjection to the negro race.   Therefore they have been left without a choice.   Negro suffrage was established by act of Congress, and the military officers were commanded to superintend the process of clothing the negro race with the political privileges torn from white men.

The blacks in the South are entitled to be well and humanely governed, and to have the protection of just laws for all their rights of person and property.   If it were practicable at this time to give them a Government exclusively their own, under which they might manage their own affairs in their own way, it would become a grave question whether we ought to do so, or whether common humanity would not require us to save them from themselves.   But under the circumstances this is only a speculative point.   It is not proposed merely that they shall govern themselves, but that they shall rule the white race, make and administer State laws, elect Presidents and members of Congress, and shape to a greater or less extent the future destiny of the whole country.   Would such a trust and power be safe in such hands?

The peculiar qualities which should characterize any people who are fit to decide upon the management of public affairs for a great state have seldom been combined.   It is the glory of white men to know that they have had these qualities in sufficient measure to build upon this continent a great political fabric and to preserve its stability for more than ninety years, while in every other part of the world all similar experiments have failed. But if anything can be proved by known facts, if all reasoning upon evidence is not abandoned, it must be acknowledged that in the progress of nations negroes have shown less capacity for government than any other race of people. No independent government of any form has ever been successful in their hands. On the contrary, wherever they have been left to their own devices they have shown a constant tendency to relapse into barbarism. In the Southern States, however, Congress has undertaken to confer upon them the privilege of the ballot. Just released from slavery, it may be doubted whether as a class they know more than their ancestors how to organize and regulate civil society. Indeed, it is admitted that the blacks of the South are not only regardless of the rights of property, but so utterly ignorant of public affairs that their voting can consist in nothing more than carrying a ballot to the place where they are directed to deposit it. I need not remind you that the exercise of the elective franchise is the highest attribute of an American citizen, and that when guided by virtue, intelligence, patriotism, and a proper appreciation of our free institutions it constitutes the true basis of a democratic form of government, in which the sovereign power is lodged in the body of the people. A trust artificially created, not for its own sake, but solely as a means of promoting the general welfare, its influence for good must necessarily depend upon the elevated character and true allegiance of the elector. It ought, therefore, to be reposed in none except those who are fitted morally and mentally to administer it well; for if conferred upon persons who do not justly estimate its value and who are indifferent as to its results, it will only serve as a means of placing power in the hands of the unprincipled and ambitious, and must eventuate in the complete destruction of that liberty of which it should be the most powerful conservator. I have therefore heretofore urged upon your attention the great danger—

to be apprehended from an untimely extension of the elective franchise to any new class in our country, especially when the large majority of that class, in wielding the power thus placed in their hands, can not be expected correctly to comprehend the duties and responsibilities which pertain to suffrage. Yesterday, as it were, 4,000,000 persons were held in a condition of slavery that had existed for generations; to-day they are freemen and are assumed by law to be citizens. It can not be presumed, from their previous condition of servitude, that as a class they are as well informed as to the nature of our Government as the intelligent foreigner who makes our land the home of his choice. In the case of the latter neither a residence of five years and the knowledge of our institutions which it gives nor attachment to the principles of the Constitution are the only conditions upon which he can be admitted to citizenship; he must prove in addition a good moral character, and thus give reasonable ground for the belief that he will be faithful to the obligations which he assumes as a citizen of the Republic. Where a people—the source of all political power—speak by their suffrages through the instrumentality of the ballot box, it must be carefully guarded against the control of those who are corrupt in principle and enemies of free institutions, for it can only become to our political and social system a safe conductor of healthy popular sentiment when kept free from demoralizing influences. Controlled through fraud and usurpation by the designing, anarchy and despotism must inevitably follow. In the hands of the patriotic and worthy our Government will be preserved upon the principles of the Constitution inherited from our fathers. It follows, therefore, that in admitting to the ballot box a new class of voters not qualified for the exercise of the elective franchise we weaken our system of government instead of adding to its strength and durability.

*   *   *   *   *   *   *

I yield to no one in attachment to that rule of general suffrage which distinguishes our policy as a nation. But there is a limit, wisely observed hitherto, which makes the ballot a privilege and a trust, and which requires of some classes a time suitable for probation and preparation. To give it indiscriminately to a new class, wholly unprepared by previous habits and opportunities to perform the trust which it demands, is to degrade it, and finally to destroy its power, for it may be safely assumed that no political truth is better established than that such indiscriminate and all-embracing extension of popular suffrage must end at last in its destruction.

I repeat the expression of my willingness to join in any plan within the scope of our constitutional authority which promises to better the condition of the negroes in the South, by encouraging them in industry, enlightening their minds, improving their morals, and giving protection to all their just rights as freedmen. But the transfer of our political inheritance to them would, in my opinion, be an abandonment of a duty which we owe alike to the memory of our fathers and the rights of our children.

The plan of putting the Southern States wholly and the General Government partially into the hands of negroes is proposed at a time peculiarly unpropitious. The foundations of society have been broken up by civil war. Industry must be reorganized, justice reestablished, public credit maintained, and order brought out of confusion. To accomplish these ends would require all the wisdom and virtue of the great men who formed our institutions originally. I confidently believe that their descendants will be equal to the arduous task before them, but it is worse than madness to expect that negroes will perform it for us. Certainly we ought not to ask their assistance till we despair of our own competency.

The great difference between the two races in physical, mental, and moral characteristics will prevent an amalgamation or fusion of them together in one homogeneous mass. If the inferior obtains the ascendency over the other, it will govern with reference only to its own interests—for it will recognize no common interest—and create such a tyranny as this continent has never yet witnessed. Already the negroes are influenced by promises of confiscation and plunder. They are taught to regard as an enemy every white man who has any respect for the rights of his own race. If this continues it must become worse and worse, until all order will be subverted, all industry cease, and the fertile fields of the South grow up into a wilderness. Of all the dangers which our nation has yet encountered, none are equal to those which must result from the success of the effort now making to Africanize the half of our country.

I would not put considerations of money in competition with justice and right; but the expenses incident to ''reconstruction'' under the system adopted by Congress aggravate what I regard as the intrinsic wrong of the measure itself. It has cost uncounted millions already, and if persisted in will add largely to the weight of taxation, already too oppressive to be borne without just complaint, and may finally reduce the Treasury of the nation to a condition of bankruptcy. We must not delude ourselves. It will require a strong standing army and probably more than $200,000,000 per annum to maintain the supremacy of negro governments after they are established. The sum thus thrown away would, if properly used, form a sinking fund large enough to pay the whole national debt in less than fifteen years. It is vain to hope that negroes will maintain their ascendency themselves. Without military power they are wholly incapable of holding in subjection the white people of the South.

I submit to the judgment of Congress whether the public credit may not be injuriously affected by a system of measures like this. With our debt and the vast private interests which are complicated with it, we can not be too cautious of a policy which might by possibility impair the confidence of the world in our Government. That confidence can only be retained by carefully inculcating the principles of justice and honor on the popular mind and by the most scrupulous fidelity to all our engagements of every sort. Any serious breach of the organic law, persisted in for a considerable time, can not but create fears for the stability of our institutions. Habitual violation of prescribed rules, which we bind ourselves to observe, must demoralize the people. Our only standard of civil duty being set at naught, the sheet anchor of our political morality is lost, the public conscience swings from its moorings and yields to every impulse of passion and interest. If we repudiate the Constitution, we will not be expected to care much for mere pecuniary obligations. The violation of such a pledge as we made on the 22d day of July, 1861, will assuredly diminish the market value of our other promises. Besides, if we acknowledge that the national debt was created, not to hold the States in the Union, as the taxpayers were led to suppose, but to expel them from it and hand them over to be governed by negroes, the moral duty to pay it may seem much less clear. I say it may *seem* so, for I do not admit that this or any other argument in favor of repudiation can be entertained as sound; but its influence on some classes of minds may well be apprehended. The financial honor of a great commercial nation, largely indebted and with a republican form of government administered by agents of the popular choice, is a thing of such delicate texture and the destruction of it would be followed by such unspeakable calamity that every true patriot must desire to avoid whatever might expose it to the slightest danger.

The great interests of the country require immediate relief from these enactments. Business in the South is paralyzed by a sense of general insecurity, by the terror of confiscation, and the dread of negro supremacy.

The Southern trade, from which the North would have derived so great a profit under a government of law, still languishes, and can never be revived until it ceases to be fettered by the arbitrary power which makes all its operations unsafe.   That rich country—the richest in natural resources the world ever saw—is worse than lost if it be not soon placed under the protection of a free constitution.   Instead of being, as it ought to be, a source of wealth and power, it will become an intolerable burden upon the rest of the nation.

Another reason for retracing our steps will doubtless be seen by Congress in the late manifestations of public opinion upon this subject.   We live in a country where the popular will always enforces obedience to itself, sooner or later.   It is vain to think of opposing it with anything short of legal authority backed by overwhelming force.   It can not have escaped your attention that from the day on which Congress fairly and formally presented the proposition to govern the Southern States by military force, with a view to the ultimate establishment of negro supremacy, every expression of the general sentiment has been more or less adverse to it.   The affections of this generation can not be detached from the institutions of their ancestors.   Their determination to preserve the inheritance of free government in their own hands and transmit it undivided and unimpaired to their own posterity is too strong to be successfully opposed.   Every weaker passion will disappear before that love of liberty and law for which the American people are distinguished above all others in the world.

How far the duty of the President "to preserve, protect, and defend the Constitution" requires him to go in opposing an unconstitutional act of Congress is a very serious and important question, on which I have deliberated much and felt extremely anxious to reach a proper conclusion.   Where an act has been passed according to the forms of the Constitution by the supreme legislative authority, and is regularly enrolled among the public statutes of the country, Executive resistance to it, especially in times of high party excitement, would be likely to produce violent collision between the respective adherents of the two branches of the Government.   This would be simply civil war, and civil war must be resorted to only as the last remedy for the worst of evils. Whatever might tend to provoke it should be most carefully avoided. A faithful and conscientious magistrate will concede very much to honest error, and something even to perverse malice, before he will endanger the public peace; and he will not adopt forcible measures, or such as might lead to force, as long as those which are peaceable remain open to him or to his constituents.   It is true that cases may occur in which the Executive would be compelled to stand on its rights, and maintain them regardless of all consequences.   If Congress should pass an act which is not only in palpable conflict with the Constitution, but will certainly, if carried out, produce immediate and irreparable injury to the organic structure of the Government, and if there be neither judicial remedy for the wrongs it inflicts nor power in the people to protect themselves without the official aid of their elected defender—if, for instance, the legislative department should pass an act even through all the forms of law to abolish a coordinate department of the Government—in such a case the President must take the high responsibilities of his office and save the life of the nation at all hazards. The so-called reconstruction acts, though as plainly unconstitutional as any that can be imagined, were not believed to be within the class last mentioned. The people were not wholly disarmed of the power of self-defense. In all the Northern States they still held in their hands the sacred right of the ballot, and it was safe to believe that in due time they would come to the rescue of their own institutions. It gives me pleasure to add that the appeal to our common constituents was not taken in vain, and that my confidence in their wisdom and virtue seems not to have been misplaced.

It is well and publicly known that enormous frauds have been perpetrated on the Treasury and that colossal fortunes have been made at the public expense. This species of corruption has increased, is increasing, and if not diminished will soon bring us into total ruin and disgrace. The public creditors and the taxpayers are alike interested in an honest administration of the finances, and neither class will long endure the large-handed robberies of the recent past. For this discreditable state of things there are several causes. Some of the taxes are so laid as to present an irresistible temptation to evade payment. The great sums which officers may win by connivance at fraud create a pressure which is more than the virtue of many can withstand, and there can be no doubt that the open disregard of constitutional obligations avowed by some of the highest and most influential men in the country has greatly weakened the moral sense of those who serve in subordinate places. The expenses of the United States, including interest on the public debt, are more than six times as much as they were seven years ago. To collect and disburse this vast amount requires careful supervision as well as systematic vigilance. The system, never perfected, was much disorganized by the "tenure-of-office bill," which has almost destroyed official accountability. The President may be thoroughly convinced that an officer is incapable, dishonest, or unfaithful to the Constitution, but under the law which I have named the utmost he can do is to complain to the Senate and ask the privilege of supplying his place with a better man. If the Senate be regarded as personally or politically hostile to the President, it is natural, and not altogether unreasonable, for the officer to expect that it will take his part as far as possible, restore him to his place, and give him a triumph over his Executive superior. The officer has other chances of impunity arising from accidental defects of evidence, the mode of investigating it, and the secrecy of the hearing. It is not wonderful that official malfeasance should become bold in proportion as the delinquents learn to think themselves safe.   I am entirely persuaded that under such a rule the President can not perform the great duty assigned to him of seeing the laws faithfully executed, and that it disables him most especially from enforcing that rigid accountability which is necessary to the due execution of the revenue laws.

The Constitution invests the President with authority to *decide* whether a removal should be made in any given case; the act of Congress declares in substance that he shall only *accuse* such as he supposes to be unworthy of their trust.   The Constitution makes him sole *judge* in the premises, but the statute takes away his jurisdiction, transfers it to the Senate, and leaves him nothing but the odious and sometimes impracticable duty of becoming a *prosecutor*.   The prosecution is to be conducted before a tribunal whose members are not, like him, responsible to the whole people, but to separate constituent bodies, and who may hear his accusation with great disfavor.   The Senate is absolutely without any known standard of decision applicable to such a case.   Its judgment can not be anticipated, for it is not governed by any rule.   The law does not define what shall be deemed good cause for removal.   It is impossible even to conjecture what may or may not be so considered by the Senate.   The nature of the subject forbids clear proof.   If the charge be incapacity, what evidence will support it?   Fidelity to the Constitution may be understood or misunderstood in a thousand different ways, and by violent party men, in violent party times, unfaithfulness to the Constitution may even come to be considered meritorious.   If the officer be accused of dishonesty, how shall it be made out?   Will it be inferred from acts unconnected with public duty, from private history, or from general reputation, or must the President await the commission of an actual misdemeanor in office?   Shall he in the meantime risk the character and interest of the nation in the hands of men to whom he can not give his confidence?   Must he forbear his complaint until the mischief is done and can not be prevented?   If his zeal in the public service should impel him to anticipate the overt act, must he move at the peril of being tried himself for the offense of slandering his subordinate?   In the present circumstances of the country someone must be held responsible for official delinquency of every kind. It is extremely difficult to say where that responsibility should be thrown if it be not left where it has been placed by the Constitution.   But all just men will admit that the President ought to be entirely relieved from such responsibility if he can not meet it by reason of restrictions placed by law upon his action.

The unrestricted power of removal from office is a very great one to be trusted even to a magistrate chosen by the general suffrage of the whole people and accountable directly to them for his acts.   It is undoubtedly liable to abuse, and at some periods of our history perhaps has been abused.   If it be thought desirable and constitutional that it should be so limited as to make the President merely a common informer against other public agents, he should at least be permitted to act in that capacity before some open tribunal, independent of party politics, ready to investigate the merits of every case, furnished with the means of taking evidence, and bound to decide according to established rules. This would guarantee the safety of the accuser when he acts in good faith, and at the same time secure the rights of the other party. I speak, of course, with all proper respect for the present Senate, but it does not seem to me that any legislative body can be so constituted as to insure its fitness for these functions.

It is not the theory of this Government that public offices are the property of those who hold them. They are given merely as a trust for the public benefit, sometimes for a fixed period, sometimes during good behavior, but generally they are liable to be terminated at the pleasure of the appointing power, which represents the collective majesty and speaks the will of the people. The forced retention in office of a single dishonest person may work great injury to the public interests. The danger to the public service comes not from the power to remove, but from the power to appoint. Therefore it was that the framers of the Constitution left the power of removal unrestricted, while they gave the Senate a right to reject all appointments which in its opinion were not fit to be made. A little reflection on this subject will probably satisfy all who have the good of the country at heart that our best course is to take the Constitution for our guide, walk in the path marked out by the founders of the Republic, and obey the rules made sacred by the observance of our great predecessors.

The present condition of our finances and circulating medium is one to which your early consideration is invited.

The proportion which the currency of any country should bear to the whole value of the annual produce circulated by its means is a question upon which political economists have not agreed. Nor can it be controlled by legislation, but must be left to the irrevocable laws which everywhere regulate commerce and trade. The circulating medium will ever irresistibly flow to those points where it is in greatest demand. The law of demand and supply is as unerring as that which regulates the tides of the ocean; and, indeed, currency, like the tides, has its ebbs and flows throughout the commercial world.

At the beginning of the rebellion the bank-note circulation of the country amounted to not much more than $200,000,000; now the circulation of national-bank notes and those known as ''legal-tenders'' is nearly seven hundred millions. While it is urged by some that this amount should be increased, others contend that a decided reduction is absolutely essential to the best interests of the country. In view of these diverse opinions, it may be well to ascertain the real value of our paper issues when compared with a metallic or convertible currency. For this purpose let us inquire how much gold and silver could be purchased by the seven hundred millions of paper money now in circulation. Probably not more than half the amount of the latter, showing that when our paper currency is compared with gold and silver its commercial value is compressed into three hundred and fifty millions. This striking fact makes it the obvious duty of the Government, as early as may be consistent with the principles of sound political economy, to take such measures as will enable the holder of its notes and those of the national banks to convert them without loss into specie or its equivalent. A reduction of our paper circulating medium need not necessarily follow. This, however, would depend upon the law of demand and supply, though it should be borne in mind that by making legal-tender and bank notes convertible into coin or its equivalent their present specie value in the hands of their holders would be enhanced 100 per cent.

Legislation for the accomplishment of a result so desirable is demanded by the highest public considerations. The Constitution contemplates that the circulating medium of the country shall be uniform in quality and value. At the time of the formation of that instrument the country had just emerged from the War of the Revolution, and was suffering from the effects of a redundant and worthless paper currency. The sages of that period were anxious to protect their posterity from the evils that they themselves had experienced. Hence in providing a circulating medium they conferred upon Congress the power to coin money and regulate the value thereof, at the same time prohibiting the States from making anything but gold and silver a tender in payment of debts.

The anomalous condition of our currency is in striking contrast with that which was originally designed. Our circulation now embraces, first, notes of the national banks, which are made receivable for all dues to the Government, excluding imposts, and by all its creditors, excepting in payment of interest upon its bonds and the securities themselves; second, legal-tender notes, issued by the United States, and which the law requires shall be received as well in payment of all debts between citizens as of all Government dues, excepting imposts; and, third, gold and silver coin. By the operation of our present system of finance, however, the metallic currency, when collected, is reserved only for one class of Government creditors, who, holding its bonds, semiannually receive their interest in coin from the National Treasury. They are thus made to occupy an invidious position, which may be used to strengthen the arguments of those who would bring into disrepute the obligations of the nation. In the payment of all its debts the plighted faith of the Government should be inviolably maintained. But while it acts with fidelity toward the bondholder who loaned his money that the integrity of the Union might be preserved, it should at the same time observe good faith with the great masses of the people, who, having rescued the Union from the perils of rebellion, now bear the burdens of taxation, that the Government may be able to fulfill its engagements. There is no reason which will be accepted as satisfactory by the people why those who defend us on the land and protect us on the sea; the pensioner upon the gratitude of the nation, bearing the scars and wounds received while in its service; the public servants in the various Departments of the Government; the farmer who supplies the soldiers of the Army and the sailors of the Navy; the artisan who toils in the nation's workshops, or the mechanics and laborers who build its edifices and construct its forts and vessels of war, should, in payment of their just and hard-earned dues, receive depreciated paper, while another class of their countrymen, no more deserving, are paid in coin of gold and silver. Equal and exact justice requires that all the creditors of the Government should be paid in a currency possessing a uniform value. This can only be accomplished by the restoration of the currency to the standard established by the Constitution; and by this means we would remove a discrimination which may, if it has not already done so, create a prejudice that may become deep rooted and widespread and imperil the national credit.

The feasibility of making our currency correspond with the constitutional standard may be seen by reference to a few facts derived from our commercial statistics.

The production of precious metals in the United States from 1849 to 1857, inclusive, amounted to $579,000,000; from 1858 to 1860, inclusive, to $137,500,000, and from 1861 to 1867, inclusive, to $457,500,000—making the grand aggregate of products since 1849 $1,174,000,000. The amount of specie coined from 1849 to 1857 inclusive, was $439,000,000; from 1858 to 1860, inclusive, $125,000,000, and from 1861 to 1867, inclusive, $310,000,000—making the total coinage since 1849 $874,000,000. From 1849 to 1857, inclusive, the net exports of specie amounted to $271,000,000; from 1858 to 1860, inclusive, to $148,000,000, and from 1861 to 1867, inclusive, $322,000,000—making the aggregate of net exports since 1849 $741,000,000. These figures show an excess of product over net exports of $433,000,000. There are in the Treasury $111,000,000 in coin, something more than $40,000,000 in circulation on the Pacific Coast, and a few millions in the national and other banks—in all about $160,000,000. This, however, taking into account the specie in the country prior to 1849, leaves more than $300,000,000 which have not been accounted for by exportation, and therefore may yet remain in the country.

These are important facts and show how completely the inferior currency will supersede the better, forcing it from circulation among the masses and causing it to be exported as a mere article of trade, to add to the money capital of foreign lands. They show the necessity of retiring our paper money, that the return of gold and silver to the avenues of trade may be invited and a demand created which will cause the retention at home of at least so much of the productions of our rich and inexhaustible gold-bearing fields as may be sufficient for purposes of circulation. It is unreasonable to expect a return to a sound currency so long as the Government by continuing to issue irredeemable notes fills the channels of circulation with depreciated paper. Notwithstanding a coinage by our mints, since 1849, of $874,000,000, the people are now strangers to the currency which was designed for their use and benefit, and specimens of the precious metals bearing the national device are seldom seen, except when produced to gratify the interest excited by their novelty. If depreciated paper is to be continued as the permanent currency of the country, and all our coin is to become a mere article of traffic and speculation, to the enhancement in price of all that is indispensable to the comfort of the people, it would be wise economy to abolish our mints, thus saving the nation the care and expense incident to such establishments, and let all our precious metals be exported in bullion. The time has come, however, when the Government and national banks should be required to take the most efficient steps and make all necessary arrangements for a resumption of specie payments at the earliest practicable period. Specie payments having been once resumed by the Government and banks, all notes or bills of paper issued by either of a less denomination than $20 should by law be excluded from circulation, so that the people may have the benefit and convenience of a gold and silver currency which in all their business transactions will be uniform in value at home and abroad.

Every man of property or industry, every man who desires to preserve what he honestly possesses or to obtain what he can honestly earn, has a direct interest in maintaining a safe circulating medium—such a medium as shall be real and substantial, not liable to vibrate with opinions, not subject to be blown up or blown down by the breath of speculation, but to be made stable and secure. A disordered currency is one of the greatest political evils. It undermines the virtues necessary for the support of the social system and encourages propensities destructive of its happiness; it wars against industry, frugality, and economy, and it fosters the evil spirits of extravagance and speculation.

It has been asserted by one of our profound and most gifted statesmen that—

Of all the contrivances for cheating the laboring classes of mankind, none has been more effectual than that which deludes them with paper money. This is the most effectual of inventions to fertilize the rich man's fields by the sweat of the poor man's brow. Ordinary tyranny, oppression, excessive taxation—these bear lightly on the happiness of the mass of the community compared with a fraudulent currency and the robberies committed by depreciated paper. Our own history has recorded for our instruction enough, and more than enough, of the demoralizing tendency, the injustice, and the intolerable oppression on the virtuous and well disposed of a degraded paper currency authorized by law or in any way countenanced by government.

It is one of the most successful devices, in times of peace or war, expansions or revulsions, to accomplish the transfer of all the precious metals from the great mass of the people into the hands of the few, where they are hoarded in secret places or deposited in strong boxes under bolts and bars, while the people are left to endure all the inconvenience, sacrifice, and demoralization resulting from the use of a depreciated and worthless paper money.

The condition of our finances and the operations of our revenue system are set forth and fully explained in the able and instructive report of the Secretary of the Treasury. On the 30th of June, 1866, the public debt amounted to $2,783,425,879; on the 30th of June last it was $2,692,199,215, showing a reduction during the fiscal year of $91,226,664. During the fiscal year ending June 30, 1867, the receipts were $490,634,010 and the expenditures $346,729,129, leaving an available surplus of $143,904,880. It is estimated that the receipts for the fiscal year ending June 30, 1868, will be $417,161,928 and that the expenditures will reach the sum of $393,269,226, leaving in the Treasury a surplus of $23,892,702. For the fiscal year ending June 30, 1869, it is estimated that the receipts will amount to $381,000,000 and that the expenditures will be $372,000,000, showing an excess of $9,000,000 in favor of the Government.

The attention of Congress is earnestly invited to the necessity of a thorough revision of our revenue system. Our internal-revenue laws and impost system should be so adjusted as to bear most heavily on articles of luxury, leaving the necessaries of life as free from taxation as may be consistent with the real wants of the Government, economically administered. Taxation would not then fall unduly on the man of moderate means; and while none would be entirely exempt from assessment, all, in proportion to their pecuniary abilities, would contribute toward the support of the State. A modification of the internal-revenue system, by a large reduction in the number of articles now subject to tax, would be followed by results equally advantageous to the citizen and the Government. It would render the execution of the law less expensive and more certain, remove obstructions to industry, lessen the temptations to evade the law, diminish the violations and frauds perpetrated upon its provisions, make its operations less inquisitorial, and greatly reduce in numbers the army of taxgatherers created by the system, who "take from the mouth of honest labor the bread it has earned." Retrenchment, reform, and economy should be carried into every branch of the public service, that the expenditures of the Government may be reduced and the people relieved from oppressive taxation; a sound currency should be restored, and the public faith in regard to the national debt sacredly observed. The accomplishment of these important results, together with the restoration of the Union of the States upon the principles of the Constitution, would inspire confidence at home and abroad in the stability of our institutions and bring to the nation prosperity, peace, and good will.

The report of the Secretary of War *ad interim* exhibits the operations of the Army and of the several bureaus of the War Department. The aggregate strength of our military force on the 30th of September last was 56,315. The total estimate for military appropriations is $77,124,707, including a deficiency in last year's appropriation of $13,600,000. The payments at the Treasury on account of the service of the War Department from January 1 to October 29, 1867—a period of ten months— amounted to $109,807,000. The expenses of the military establishment, as well as the numbers of the Army, are now three times as great as they have ever been in time of peace, while the discretionary power is vested in the Executive to add millions to this expenditure by an increase of the Army to the maximum strength allowed by the law.

The comprehensive report of the Secretary of the Interior furnishes interesting information in reference to the important branches of the public service connected with his Department. The menacing attitude of some of the warlike bands of Indians inhabiting the district of country between the Arkansas and Platte rivers and portions of Dakota Territory required the presence of a large military force in that region. Instigated by real or imaginary grievances, the Indians occasionally committed acts of barbarous violence upon emigrants and our frontier settlements; but a general Indian war has been providentially averted. The commissioners under the act of 20th July, 1867, were invested with full power to adjust existing difficulties, negotiate treaties with the disaffected bands, and select for them reservations remote from the traveled routes between the Mississippi and the Pacific. They entered without delay upon the execution of their trust, but have not yet made any official report of their proceedings. It is of vital importance that our distant Territories should be exempt from Indian outbreaks, and that the construction of the Pacific Railroad, an object of national importance, should not be interrupted by hostile tribes. These objects, as well as the material interests and the moral and intellectual improvement of the Indians, can be most effectually secured by concentrating them upon portions of country set apart for their exclusive use and located at points remote from our highways and encroaching white settlements.

Since the commencement of the second session of the Thirty-ninth Congress 510 miles of road have been constructed on the main line and branches of the Pacific Railway. The line from Omaha is rapidly approaching the eastern base of the Rocky Mountains, while the terminus of the last section of constructed road in California, accepted by the Government on the 24th day of October last, was but 11 miles distant from the summit of the Sierra Nevada. The remarkable energy evinced by the companies offers the strongest assurance that the completion of the road from Sacramento to Omaha will not be long deferred.

During the last fiscal year 7,041,114 acres of public land were disposed of, and the cash receipts from sales and fees exceeded by one-half million dollars the sum realized from those sources during the preceding year. The amount paid to pensioners, including expenses of disbursements, was $18,619,956, and 36,482 names were added to the rolls. The entire number of pensioners on the 30th of June last was 155,474. Eleven thousand six hundred and fifty-five patents and designs were issued during the year ending September 30, 1867, and at that date the balance in the Treasury to the credit of the patent fund was $286,607.

The report of the Secretary of the Navy states that we have seven squadrons actively and judiciously employed, under efficient and able commanders, in protecting the persons and property of American citizens, maintaining the dignity and power of the Government, and promoting the commerce and business interests of our countrymen in every part of the world. Of the 238 vessels composing the present Navy of the United States, 56, carrying 507 guns, are in squadron service. During the year the number of vessels in commission has been reduced 12, and there are 13 less on squadron duty than there were at the date of the last report. A large number of vessels were commenced and in the course of construction when the war terminated, and although Congress had made the necessary appropriations for their completion, the Department has either suspended work upon them or limited the slow completion of the steam vessels, so as to meet the contracts for machinery made with private establishments. The total expenditures of the Navy Department for the fiscal year ending June 30, 1867, were $31,034,011. No appropriations have been made or required since the close of the war for the construction and repair of vessels, for steam machinery, ordnance, provisions and clothing, fuel, hemp, etc., the balances under these several heads having been more than sufficient for current expenditures. It should also be stated to the credit of the Department that, besides asking no appropriations for the above objects for the last two years, the Secretary of the Navy, on the 30th of September last, in accordance with the act of May 1, 1820, requested the Secretary of the Treasury to carry to the surplus fund the sum of $65,000,000, being the amount received from the sales of vessels and other war property and the remnants of former appropriations.

The report of the Postmaster-General shows the business of the Post-Office Department and the condition of the postal service in a very favorable light, and the attention of Congress is called to its practical recommendations. The receipts of the Department for the year ending June 30, 1867, including all special appropriations for sea and land service and for free mail matter, were $19,978,693. The expenditures for all purposes were $19,235,483, leaving an unexpended balance in favor of the Department of $743,210, which can be applied toward the expenses of the Department for the current year. The increase of postal revenue, independent of specific appropriations, for the year 1867 over that of 1866 was $850,040. The increase of revenue from the sale of stamps and stamped envelopes was $783,404. The increase of expenditures for 1867 over those of the previous year was owing chiefly to the extension of the land and ocean mail service. During the past year new postal conventions have been ratified and exchanged with the United Kingdom of Great Britain and Ireland, Belgium, the Netherlands, Switzerland, the North German Union, Italy, and the colonial government at Hong Kong, reducing very largely the rates of ocean and land postages to and from and within those countries.

The report of the Acting Commissioner of Agriculture concisely presents the condition, wants, and progress of an interest eminently worthy the fostering care of Congress, and exhibits a large measure of useful results achieved during the year to which it refers.

The reestablishment of peace at home and the resumption of extended trade, travel, and commerce abroad have served to increase the number and variety of questions in the Department for Foreign Affairs. None of these questions, however, have seriously disturbed our relations with other states.

The Republic of Mexico, having been relieved from foreign intervention, is earnestly engaged in efforts to reestablish her constitutional system of government. A good understanding continues to exist between our Government and the Republics of Hayti and San Domingo, and our cordial relations with the Central and South American States remain unchanged. The tender, made in conformity with a resolution of Congress, of the good offices of the Government with a view to an amicable adjustment of peace between Brazil and her allies on one side and Paraguay on the other, and between Chile and her allies on the one side and Spain on the other, though kindly received, has in neither case been fully accepted by the belligerents. The war in the valley of the Parana is still vigorously maintained. On the other hand, actual hostilities between the Pacific States and Spain have been more than a year suspended. I shall, on any proper occasion that may occur, renew the conciliatory recommendations which have been already made. Brazil, with enlightened sagacity and comprehensive statesmanship, has opened the great channels of the Amazon and its tributaries to universal commerce. One thing more seems needful to assure a rapid and cheering progress in South America. I refer to those peaceful habits without which states and nations can not in this age well expect material prosperity or social advancement.

The Exposition of Universal Industry at Paris has passed, and seems to have fully realized the high expectations of the French Government. If due allowance be made for the recent political derangement of industry here, the part which the United States has borne in this exhibition of invention and art may be regarded with very high satisfaction. During the exposition a conference was held of delegates from several nations, the United States being one, in which the inconveniences of commerce and social intercourse resulting from the diverse standards of money value were very fully discussed, and plans were developed for establishing by universal consent a common principle for the coinage of gold. These conferences are expected to be renewed, with the attendance of many foreign states not hitherto represented. A report of these interesting proceedings will be submitted to Congress, which will, no doubt, justly appreciate the great object and be ready to adopt any measure which may tend to facilitate its ultimate accomplishment.

On the 25th of February, 1862, Congress declared by law that Treasury notes, without interest, authorized by that act should be legal tender in payment of all debts, public and private, within the United States. An annual remittance of $30,000, less stipulated expenses, accrues to claimants under the convention made with Spain in 1834. These remittances, since the passage of that act, have been paid in such notes. The claimants insist that the Government ought to require payment in coin. The subject may be deemed worthy of your attention.

No arrangement has yet been reached for the settlement of our claims for British depredations upon the commerce of the United States. I have felt it my duty to decline the proposition of arbitration made by Her Majesty's Government, because it has hitherto been accompanied by reservations and limitations incompatible with the rights, interest, and honor of our country. It is not to be apprehended that Great Britain will persist in her refusal to satisfy these just and reasonable claims, which involve the sacred principle of nonintervention—a principle henceforth not more important to the United States than to all other commercial nations.

The West India islands were settled and colonized by European States simultaneously with the settlement and colonization of the American continent. Most of the colonies planted here became independent nations in the close of the last and the beginning of the present century. Our own country embraces communities which at one period were colonies of Great Britain, France, Spain, Holland, Sweden, and Russia. The people in the West Indies, with the exception of those of the island of Hayti, have neither attained nor aspired to independence, nor have they become prepared for self-defense. Although possessing considerable commercial value, they have been held by the several European States which colonized or at some time conquered them, chiefly for purposes of military and naval strategy in carrying out European policy and designs in regard to this continent. In our Revolutionary War ports and harbors in the West India islands were used by our enemy, to the great injury and embarrassment of the United States. We had the same experience in our second war with Great Britain. The same European policy for a long time excluded us even from trade with the West Indies, while we were at peace with all nations. In our recent civil war the rebels and their piratical and blockade-breaking allies found facilities in the same ports for the work, which they too successfully accomplished, of injuring and devastating the commerce which we are now engaged in rebuilding. We labored especially under this disadvantage, that European steam vessels employed by our enemies found friendly shelter, protection, and supplies in West Indian ports, while our naval operations were necessarily carried on from our own distant shores. There was then a universal feeling of the want of an advanced naval outpost between the Atlantic coast and Europe. The duty of obtaining such an outpost peacefully and lawfully, while neither doing nor menacing injury to other states, earnestly engaged the attention of the executive department before the close of the war, and it has not been lost sight of since that time. A not entirely dissimilar naval want revealed itself during the same period on the Pacific coast. The required foothold there was fortunately secured by our late treaty with the Emperor of Russia, and it now seems imperative that the more obvious necessities of the Atlantic coast should not be less carefully provided for. A good and convenient port and harbor, capable of easy defense, will supply that want. With the possession of such a station by the United States, neither we nor any other American nation need longer apprehend injury or offense from any transatlantic enemy. I agree with our early statesmen that the West Indies naturally gravitate to, and may be expected ultimately to be absorbed by, the continental States, including our own. I agree with them also that it is wise to leave the question of such absorption to this process of natural political gravitation. The islands of St. Thomas and St. John, which constitute a part of the group called the Virgin Islands, seemed to offer us advantages immediately desirable, while their acquisition could be secured in harmony with the principles to which I have alluded. A treaty has therefore been concluded with the King of Denmark for the cession of those islands, and will be submitted to the Senate for consideration.

It will hardly be necessary to call the attention of Congress to the subject of providing for the payment to Russia of the sum stipulated in the treaty for the cession of Alaska. Possession having been formally delivered to our commissioner, the territory remains for the present in care of a military force, awaiting such civil organization as shall be directed by Congress.

The annexation of many small German States to Prussia and the reorganization of that country under a new and liberal constitution have induced me to renew the effort to obtain a just and prompt settlement of the long-vexed question concerning the claims of foreign states for military service from their subjects naturalized in the United States.

In connection with this subject the attention of Congress is respectfully called to a singular and embarrassing conflict of laws. The executive department of this Government has hitherto uniformly held, as it now holds, that naturalization in conformity with the Constitution and laws of the United States absolves the recipient from his native allegiance. The courts of Great Britain hold that allegiance to the British Crown is indefeasible, and is not absolved by our laws of naturalization. British judges cite courts and law authorities of the United States in support of that theory against the position held by the executive authority of the United States. This conflict perplexes the public mind concerning the rights of naturalized citizens and impairs the national authority abroad.

I called attention to this subject in my last annual message, and now again respectfully appeal to Congress to declare the national will unmistakably upon this important question.

The abuse of our laws by the clandestine prosecution of the African slave trade from American ports or by American citizens has altogether ceased, and under existing circumstances no apprehensions of its renewal in this part of the world are entertained. Under these circumstances it becomes a question whether we shall not propose to Her Majesty's Government a suspension or discontinuance of the stipulations for maintaining a naval force for the suppression of that trade.

ANDREW JOHNSON.

SPECIAL MESSAGES.

WASHINGTON, *December 3, 1867.*

To the Senate of the United States:

I transmit, for consideration with a view to ratification, a treaty between the United States and His Majesty the King of Denmark, stipulating for the cession of the islands of St. Thomas and St. John, in the West Indies.

ANDREW JOHNSON.

WASHINGTON, *December 3, 1867.*

To the Senate of the United States:

I transmit, for consideration with a view to ratification, a treaty of friendship, commerce, and navigation between the United States and the Republic of Nicaragua, signed at the city of Managua on the 21st day of June last. This instrument has been framed pursuant to the amendments of the Senate of the United States to the previous treaty between the parties of the 16th of March, 1859.

ANDREW JOHNSON.

WASHINGTON, *December 4, 1867.*

To the House of Representatives:

I transmit herewith a final report from the Attorney-General, additional to the reports submitted by him December 31, 1866, March 2, 1867, and July 8, 1867, in reply to a resolution of the House of Representatives December 10, 1866, requesting " a list of the names of all persons engaged in the late rebellion against the United States Government who have been pardoned by the President from April 15, 1865, to this date; that said list shall also state the rank of each person who has been so pardoned, if he has been engaged in the military service of the so-called Confederate government, and the position if he shall have held any civil office under said so-called Confederate government; and shall also state whether such person has at any time prior to April 14, 1861, held any office under the United States Government, and, if so, what office, together with the reason for granting such pardon, and also the names of the person or persons at whose solicitation such pardon was granted.''

ANDREW JOHNSON.

WASHINGTON, *December 4, 1867.*

To the Senate of the United States:

I transmit to the Senate, in answer to their resolution of the 26th ultimo, a report * from the Secretary of State, with accompanying papers.

ANDREW JOHNSON.

WASHINGTON, *December 5, 1867.*

To the House of Representatives:

In compliance with the resolution of the House of Representatives of the 17th July last, requesting me to communicate all information received at the several Departments of the Government touching the organization within or near the territory of the United States of armed bodies of men for the purpose of avenging the death of the Archduke Maximilian or of intervening in Mexican affairs, and what measures have been taken to prevent the organization or departure of such organized bodies for the purpose of carrying out such objects, I transmit a report from the Secretary of State and the papers accompanying it.

ANDREW JOHNSON.

WASHINGTON, *December 5, 1867.*

To the Senate of the United States:

I submit to the Senate, for its consideration with a view to ratification, a commercial treaty between the United States of America and Her Majesty the Queen of Madagascar, signed at Antananarivo on the 14th of February last.

ANDREW JOHNSON.

WASHINGTON, *December 10, 1867.*

To the Senate of the United States:

I transmit to the Senate, in answer to their resolution of the 25th ultimo, a report † from the Secretary of State, with accompanying papers.

ANDREW JOHNSON.

---

*Relating to the removal of J. Lothrop Motley from his post as minister of the United States at Vienna.

†Relating to the formation and the functions of the Government of the united States of North Germany.

WASHINGTON, *December 10, 1867.*

To the Senate of the United States:

I transmit a copy of a dispatch of the 17th of July last, addressed to the Secretary of State, and of the papers which accompanied it, from Anson Burlingame, esq., minister of the United States to China, relating to a proposed modification of the existing treaty between this Government and that of China.

The Senate is aware that the original treaty is chiefly *ex parte* in its character. The proposed modification, though not of sufficient importance to warrant all the usual forms, does not seem to be objectionable; but it can not be legally accepted by the executive government without the advice and consent of the Senate. If this should be given, it may be indicated by a resolution, upon the adoption of which the United States minister to China will be instructed to inform the Government of that country that the modification has been assented to.

ANDREW JOHNSON.

WASHINGTON, *December 12, 1867.*

To the Senate of the United States:

On the 12th of August last I suspended Mr. Stanton from the exercise of the office of Secretary of War, and on the same day designated General Grant to act as Secretary of War *ad interim*.

The following are copies of the Executive orders:

EXECUTIVE MANSION,
Washington, August 12, 1867.

Hon. EDWIN M. STANTON,
    Secretary of War.

SIR: By virtue of the power and authority vested in me as President by the Constitution and laws of the United States, you are hereby suspended from office as Secretary of War, and will cease to exercise any and all functions pertaining to the same.

You will at once transfer to General Ulysses S. Grant, who has this day been authorized and empowered to act as Secretary of War *ad interim*, all records, books, and other property now in your custody and charge.

EXECUTIVE MANSION,
Washington, D. C., August 12, 1867.

General ULYSSES S. GRANT,
    Washington, D. C.

SIR: The Hon. Edwin M. Stanton having been this day suspended as Secretary of War, you are hereby authorized and empowered to act as Secretary of War *ad interim*, and will at once enter upon the discharge of the duties of the office.

The Secretary of War has been instructed to transfer to you all the records, books, papers, and other public property now in his custody and charge.

The following communication was received from Mr. Stanton:

WAR DEPARTMENT,
Washington City, August 12, 1867.

The PRESIDENT.

SIR: Your note of this date has been received, informing me that by virtue of the powers and authority vested in you as President by the Constitution and laws of the United States I am suspended from office as Secretary of War, and will cease to exercise any and all functions pertaining to the same, and also directing me at once to transfer to General Ulysses S. Grant, who has this day been authorized and empowered to act as Secretary of War *ad interim*, all records, books, papers, and other public property now in my custody and charge.

Under a sense of public duty I am compelled to deny your right under the Constitution and laws of the United States, without the advice and consent of the Senate and without any legal cause, to suspend me from office as Secretary of War or the exercise of any or all functions pertaining to the same, or without such advice and consent to compel me to transfer to any person the records, books, papers, and public property in my custody as Secretary.

But inasmuch as the General Commanding the armies of the United States has been appointed *ad interim*, and has notified me that he has accepted the appointment, I have no alternative but to submit, under protest, to superior force.

The suspension has not been revoked, and the business of the War Department is conducted by the Secretary *ad interim*.

Prior to the date of this suspension I had come to the conclusion that the time had arrived when it was proper Mr. Stanton should retire from my Cabinet. The mutual confidence and general accord which should exist in such a relation had ceased. I supposed that Mr. Stanton was well advised that his continuance in the Cabinet was contrary to my wishes, for I had repeatedly given him so to understand by every mode short of an express request that he should resign. Having waited full time for the voluntary action of Mr. Stanton, and seeing no manifestation on his part of an intention to resign, I addressed him the following note on the 5th of August:

SIR: Public considerations of a high character constrain me to say that your resignation as Secretary of War will be accepted.

To this note I received the following reply:

WAR DEPARTMENT,
Washington, August 5, 1867.

SIR: Your note of this day has been received, stating that public considerations of a high character constrain you to say that my resignation as Secretary of War will be accepted.

In reply I have the honor to say that public considerations of a high character, which alone have induced me to continue at the head of this Department, constrain me not to resign the office of Secretary of War before the next meeting of Congress.

This reply of Mr. Stanton was not merely a disinclination of compliance with the request for his resignation; it was a defiance, and something more. Mr. Stanton does not content himself with assuming that public considerations bearing upon his continuance in office form as fully a rule of action for himself as for the President, and that upon so delicate a question as the fitness of an officer for continuance in his office the officer is as competent and as impartial to decide as his superior, who is responsible for his conduct. But he goes further, and plainly intimates what he means by "public considerations of a high character," and this is nothing else than his loss of confidence in his superior. He says that these public considerations have "alone induced me to continue at the head of this Department," and that they "constrain me not to resign the office of Secretary of War before the next meeting of Congress."

This language is very significant. Mr. Stanton holds the position unwillingly. He continues in office only under a sense of high public duty. He is ready to leave when it is safe to leave, and as the danger he apprehends from his removal then will not exist when Congress is here, he is constrained to remain during the interim. What, then, is that danger which can only be averted by the presence of Mr. Stanton or of Congress? Mr. Stanton does not say that "public considerations of a high character" constrain him to hold on to the office indefinitely. He does not say that no one other than himself can at any time be found to take his place and perform its duties. On the contrary, he expresses a desire to leave the office at the earliest moment consistent with these high public considerations. He says, in effect, that while Congress is away he must remain, but that when Congress is here he can go. In other words, he has lost confidence in the President. He is unwilling to leave the War Department in his hands or in the hands of anyone the President may appoint or designate to perform its duties. If he resigns, the President may appoint a Secretary of War that Mr. Stanton does not approve; therefore he will not resign. But when Congress is in session the President can not appoint a Secretary of War which the Senate does not approve; consequently when Congress meets Mr. Stanton is ready to resign.

Whatever cogency these "considerations" may have had on Mr. Stanton, whatever right he may have had to entertain such considerations, whatever propriety there might be in the expression of them to others, one thing is certain, it was official misconduct, to say the least of it, to parade them before his superior officer.

Upon the receipt of this extraordinary note I only delayed the order of suspension long enough to make the necessary arrangements to fill the office. If this were the only cause for his suspension, it would be ample. Necessarily it must end our most important official relations, for I can not imagine a degree of effrontery which would embolden the head of a Department to take his seat at the council table in the Executive Mansion after such an act; nor can I imagine a President so forgetful of the proper respect and dignity which belong to his office as to submit to such intrusion. I will not do Mr. Stanton the wrong to suppose that he entertained any idea of offering to act as one of my constitutional advisers after that note was written. There was an interval of a week between that date and the order of suspension, during which two Cabinet meetings were held. Mr. Stanton did not present himself at either, nor was he expected.

On the 12th of August Mr. Stanton was notified of his suspension and that General Grant had been authorized to take charge of the Department.

In his answer to this notification, of the same date, Mr. Stanton expresses himself as follows:

Under a sense of public duty I am compelled to deny your right under the Constitution and laws of the United States, without the advice and consent of the Senate and without any legal cause, to suspend me from office as Secretary of War or the exercise of any or all functions pertaining to the same, or without such advice and consent to compel me to transfer to any person the records, books, papers, and public property in my custody as Secretary.

But inasmuch as the General Commanding the armies of the United States has been appointed *ad interim*, and has notified me that he has accepted the appointment, I have no alternative but to submit, under protest, to superior force.

It will not escape attention that in his note of August 5 Mr. Stanton stated that he had been constrained to continue in the office, even before he was requested to resign, by considerations of a high public character. In this note of August 12 a new and different sense of public duty compels him to deny the President's right to suspend him from office without the consent of the Senate. This last is the public duty of resisting an act contrary to law, and he charges the President with violation of the law in ordering his suspension.

Mr. Stanton refers generally to the Constitution and laws of the "United States," and says that a sense of public duty "under" these compels him to deny the right of the President to suspend him from office. As to his sense of duty under the Constitution, that will be considered in the sequel. As to his sense of duty under "the laws of the United States," he certainly can not refer to the law which creates the War Department, for that expressly confers upon the President the unlimited right to remove the head of the Department. The only other law bearing upon the question is the tenure-of-office act, passed by Congress over the Presidential veto March 2, 1867. This is the law which, under a sense of public duty, Mr. Stanton volunteers to defend.

There is no provision in this law which compels any officer coming within its provisions to remain in office. It forbids removals—not resignations. Mr. Stanton was perfectly free to resign at any moment, either upon his own motion or in compliance with a request or an order. It was a matter of choice or of taste. There was nothing compulsory in the nature of legal obligation. Nor does he put his action upon that imperative ground. He says he acts under a "sense of public duty," not of legal obligation, compelling him to hold on and leaving him no choice. The public duty which is upon him arises from the respect which he owes to the Constitution and the laws, violated in his own case. He is therefore compelled by this sense of public duty to vindicate violated law and to stand as its champion.

This was not the first occasion in which Mr. Stanton, in discharge of a public duty, was called upon to consider the provisions of that law. That tenure-of-office law did not pass without notice. Like other acts, it was sent to the President for approval. As is my custom, I submitted its consideration to my Cabinet for their advice upon the question whether I should approve it or not. It was a grave question of constitutional law, in which I would, of course, rely most upon the opinion of the Attorney-General and of Mr. Stanton, who had once been Attorney-General.

Every member of my Cabinet advised me that the proposed law was unconstitutional. All spoke without doubt or reservation, but Mr. Stanton's condemnation of the law was the most elaborate and emphatic. He referred to the constitutional provisions, the debates in Congress, especially to the speech of Mr. Buchanan when a Senator, to the decisions of the Supreme Court, and to the usage from the beginning of the Government through every successive Administration, all concurring to establish the right of removal as vested by the Constitution in the President. To all these he added the weight of his own deliberate judgment, and advised me that it was my duty to defend the power of the President from usurpation and to veto the law.

I do not know when a sense of public duty is more imperative upon a head of Department than upon such an occasion as this. He acts then under the gravest obligations of law, for when he is called upon by the President for advice it is the Constitution which speaks to him. All his other duties are left by the Constitution to be regulated by statute, but this duty was deemed so momentous that it is imposed by the Constitution itself.

After all this I was not prepared for the ground taken by Mr. Stanton in his note of August 12. I was not prepared to find him compelled by a new and indefinite sense of public duty, under "the Constitution," to assume the vindication of a law which, under the solemn obligations of public duty imposed by the Constitution itself, he advised me was a violation of that Constitution. I make great allowance for a change of opinion, but such a change as this hardly falls within the limits of greatest indulgence.

Where our opinions take the shape of advice, and influence the action of others, the utmost stretch of charity will scarcely justify us in repudiating them when they come to be applied to ourselves.

But to proceed with the narrative. I was so much struck with the full mastery of the question manifested by Mr. Stanton, and was at the time so fully occupied with the preparation of another veto upon the pending reconstruction act, that I requested him to prepare the veto upon this tenure-of-office bill. This he declined, on the ground of physical disability to undergo at the time the labor of writing, but stated his readiness to furnish what aid might be required in the preparation of materials for the paper.

At the time this subject was before the Cabinet it seemed to be taken for granted that as to those members of the Cabinet who had been appointed by Mr. Lincoln their tenure of office was not fixed by the provisions of the act. I do not remember that the point was distinctly decided, but I well recollect that it was suggested by one member of the Cabinet who was appointed by Mr. Lincoln, and that no dissent was expressed.

Whether the point was well taken or not did not seem to me of any consequence, for the unanimous expression of opinion against the constitutionality and policy of the act was so decided that I felt no concern, so far as the act had reference to the gentlemen then present, that I would be embarrassed in the future. The bill had not then become a law. The limitation upon the power of removal was not yet imposed, and there was yet time to make any changes. If any one of these gentlemen had then said to me that he would avail himself of the provisions of that bill in case it became a law, I should not have hesitated a moment as to his removal. No pledge was then expressly given or required. But there are circumstances when to give an expressed pledge is not necessary, and when to require it is an imputation of possible bad faith. I felt that if these gentlemen came within the purview of the bill it was as to them a dead letter, and that none of them would ever take refuge under its provisions.

I now pass to another subject. When, on the 15th of April, 1865, the duties of the Presidential office devolved upon me, I found a full Cabinet of seven members, all of them selected by Mr. Lincoln. I made no change. On the contrary, I shortly afterwards ratified a change determined upon by Mr. Lincoln, but not perfected at his death, and admitted his appointee, Mr. Harlan, in the place of Mr. Usher, who was in office at the time.

The great duty of the time was to reestablish government, law, and order in the insurrectionary States. Congress was then in recess, and the sudden overthrow of the rebellion required speedy action. This grave subject had engaged the attention of Mr. Lincoln in the last days of his life, and the plan according to which it was to be managed had been prepared and was ready for adoption. A leading feature of that plan was that it should be carried out by the Executive authority, for, so far as I have been informed, neither Mr. Lincoln nor any member of his Cabinet doubted his authority to act or proposed to call an extra session of Congress to do the work. The first business transacted in Cabinet after I became President was this unfinished business of my predecessor. A plan or scheme of reconstruction was produced which had been prepared for Mr. Lincoln by Mr. Stanton, his Secretary of War. It was approved, and at the earliest moment practicable was applied in the form of a proclamation to the State of North Carolina, and afterwards became the basis of action in turn for the other States.

Upon the examination of Mr. Stanton before the Impeachment Committee he was asked the following question:

Did any one of the Cabinet express a doubt of the power of the executive branch of the Government to reorganize State governments which had been in rebellion without the aid of Congress?

He answered:

None whatever. I had myself entertained no doubt of the authority of the President to take measures for the organization of the rebel States on the plan proposed during the vacation of Congress and agreed in the plan specified in the proclamation in the case of North Carolina.

There is perhaps no act of my Administration for which I have been more denounced than this. It was not originated by me, but I shrink from no responsibility on that account, for the plan approved itself to my own judgment, and I did not hesitate to carry it into execution.

Thus far and upon this vital policy there was perfect accord between the Cabinet and myself, and I saw no necessity for a change. As time passed on there was developed an unfortunate difference of opinion and of policy between Congress and the President upon this same subject and upon the ultimate basis upon which the reconstruction of these States should proceed, especially upon the question of negro suffrage. Upon this point three members of the Cabinet found themselves to be in sympathy with Congress. They remained only long enough to see that the difference of policy could not be reconciled. They felt that they should remain no longer, and a high sense of duty and propriety constrained them to resign their positions. We parted with mutual respect for the sincerity of each other in opposite opinions, and mutual regret that the difference was on points so vital as to require a severance of official relations. This was in the summer of 1866. The subsequent sessions of Congress developed new complications, when the suffrage bill for the District of Columbia and the reconstruction acts of March 2 and March 23, 1867, all passed over the veto. It was in Cabinet consultations upon these bills that a difference of opinion upon the most vital points was developed. Upon these questions there was perfect accord between all the members of the Cabinet and myself, except Mr. Stanton. He stood alone, and the difference of opinion could not be reconciled. That unity of opinion which, upon great questions of public policy or administration, is so essential to the Executive was gone.

I do not claim that a head of Department should have no other opinions than those of the President. He has the same right, in the conscientious discharge of duty, to entertain and express his own opinions as has the President. What I do claim is that the President is the responsible head of the Administration, and when the opinions of a head of Department are irreconcilably opposed to those of the President in grave matters of policy and administration there is but one result which can solve the difficulty, and that is a severance of the official relation. This in the past history of the Government has always been the rule, and it is a wise one, for such differences of opinion among its members must impair the efficiency of any Administration.

I have now referred to the general grounds upon which the withdrawal of Mr. Stanton from my Administration seemed to me to be proper and necessary, but I can not omit to state a special ground, which, if it stood alone, would vindicate my action.

The sanguinary riot which occurred in the city of New Orleans on the 30th of August, 1866, justly aroused public indignation and public inquiry, not only as to those who were engaged in it, but as to those who, more or less remotely, might be held to responsibility for its occurrence. I need not remind the Senate of the effort made to fix that responsibility on the President. The charge was openly made, and again and again reiterated all through the land, that the President was warned in time, but refused to interfere.

By telegrams from the lieutenant-governor and attorney-general of Louisiana, dated the 27th and 28th of August, I was advised that a body of delegates claiming to be a constitutional convention were about to assemble in New Orleans; that the matter was before the grand jury, but that it would be impossible to execute civil process without a riot; and this question was asked:

Is the military to interfere to prevent process of court?

This question was asked at a time when the civil courts were in the full exercise of their authority, and the answer sent by telegraph on the same 28th of August was this:

The military will be expected to sustain, and not to interfere with, the proceedings of the courts.

On the same 28th of August the following telegram was sent to Mr. Stanton by Major-General Baird, then (owing to the absence of General Sheridan) in command of the military at New Orleans:

Hon. EDWIN M. STANTON,
  Secretary of War:

A convention has been called, with the sanction of Governor Wells, to meet here on Monday. The lieutenant-governor and city authorities think it unlawful, and propose to break it up by arresting the delegates. I have given no orders on the subject, but have warned the parties that I could not countenance or permit such action without instructions to that effect from the President. Please instruct me at once by telegraph.

The 28th of August was on Saturday. The next morning, the 29th, this dispatch was received by Mr. Stanton at his residence in this city. He took no action upon it, and neither sent instructions to General Baird himself nor presented it to me for such instructions. On the next day (Monday) the riot occurred. I never saw this dispatch from General Baird until some ten days or two weeks after the riot, when, upon my call for all the dispatches, with a view to their publication, Mr. Stanton sent it to me.

These facts all appear in the testimony of Mr. Stanton before the Judiciary Committee in the impeachment investigation.

On the 30th, the day of the riot, and after it was suppressed, General Baird wrote to Mr. Stanton a long letter, from which I make the following extract:

SIR: I have the honor to inform you that a very serious riot has occurred here to-day. I had not been applied to by the convention for protection, but the lieutenant-governor and the mayor had freely consulted with me, and I was so fully convinced that it was so strongly the intent of the city authorities to preserve the peace, in order to prevent military interference, that I did not regard an outbreak as a thing to be apprehended. The lieutenant-governor had assured me that even if a writ of arrest was issued by the court the sheriff would not attempt to serve it without my permission, and for to-day they designed to suspend it. I inclose herewith copies of my correspondence with the mayor and of a dispatch which the lieutenant-governor claims to have received from the President. I regret that no reply to my dispatch to you of Saturday has yet reached me. General Sheridan is still absent in Texas.

The dispatch of General Baird of the 28th asks for immediate instructions, and his letter of the 30th, after detailing the terrible riot which had just happened, ends with the expression of regret that the instructions which he asked for were not sent. It is not the fault or the error or the omission of the President that this military commander was left without instructions; but for all omissions, for all errors, for all failures to instruct when instruction might have averted this calamity, the President was openly and persistently held responsible. Instantly, without waiting for proof, the delinquency of the President was heralded in every form of utterance. Mr. Stanton knew then that the President was not responsible for this delinquency. The exculpation was in his power, but it was not given by him to the public, and only to the President in obedience to a requisition for all the dispatches.

No one regrets more than myself that General Baird's request was not brought to my notice. It is clear from his dispatch and letter that if the Secretary of War had given him proper instructions the riot which arose on the assembling of the convention would have been averted.

There may be those ready to say that I would have given no instructions even if the dispatch had reached me in time, but all must admit that I ought to have had the opportunity.

The following is the testimony given by Mr. Stanton before the impeachment investigation committee as to this dispatch:

Q. Referring to the dispatch of the 28th of July by General Baird, I ask you whether that dispatch on its receipt was communicated?

A. I received that dispatch on Sunday forenoon. I examined it carefully, and considered the question presented. I did not see that I could give any instructions different from the line of action which General Baird proposed, and made no answer to the dispatch.

Q. I see it stated that this was received at 10.20 p. m. Was that the hour at which it was received by you?

A. That is the date of its reception in the telegraph office Saturday night. I received it on Sunday forenoon at my residence. A copy of the dispatch was furnished to the President several days afterwards, along with all the other dispatches and communications on that subject, but it was not furnished by me before that time. I suppose it may have been ten or fifteen days afterwards.

Q. The President himself being in correspondence with those parties upon the same subject, would it not have been proper to have advised him of the reception of that dispatch?

A. I know nothing about his correspondence, and know nothing about any correspondence except this one dispatch. We had intelligence of the riot on Thursday morning. The riot had taken place on Monday.

It is a difficult matter to define all the relations which exist between the heads of Departments and the President. The legal relations are well enough defined. The Constitution places these officers in the relation of his advisers when he calls upon them for advice. The acts of Congress go further. Take, for example, the act of 1789 creating the War Department. It provides that—

There shall be a principal officer therein to be called the Secretary for the Department of War, who shall perform and execute such duties as shall from time to time be enjoined on or intrusted to him by the President of the United States; and, furthermore, the said principal officer shall conduct the business of the said Department in such manner as the President of the United States shall from time to time order and instruct.

Provision is also made for the appointment of an inferior officer by the head of the Department, to be called the chief clerk, "who, whenever said principal officer shall be removed from office by the President of the United States," shall have the charge and custody of the books, records, and papers of the Department.

The legal relation is analogous to that of principal and agent. It is the President upon whom the Constitution devolves, as head of the executive department, the duty to see that the laws are faithfully executed; but as he can not execute them in person, he is allowed to select his agents, and is made responsible for their acts within just limits. So complete is this presumed delegation of authority in the relation of a head of Department to the President that the Supreme Court of the United States have decided that an order made by a head of Department is presumed to be made by the President himself.

The principal, upon whom such responsibility is placed for the acts of a subordinate, ought to be left as free as possible in the matter of selection and of dismissal. To hold him to responsibility for an officer beyond his control; to leave the question of the fitness of such an agent to be decided *for* him and not *by* him; to allow such a subordinate, when the President, moved by "public considerations of a high character," requests his resignation, to assume for himself an equal right to act upon his own views of "public considerations" and to make his own conclusions paramount to those of the President—to allow all this is to reverse the just order of administration and to place the subordinate above the superior.

There are, however, other relations between the President and a head of Department beyond these defined legal relations, which necessarily attend them, though not expressed. Chief among these is mutual confidence. This relation is so delicate that it is sometimes hard to say when or how it ceases. A single flagrant act may end it at once, and then there is no difficulty. But confidence may be just as effectually destroyed by a series of causes too subtle for demonstration. As it is a plant of slow growth, so, too, it may be slow in decay. Such has been the process here. I will not pretend to say what acts or omissions have broken up this relation. They are hardly susceptible of statement, and still less of formal proof. Nevertheless, no one can read the correspondence of the 5th of August without being convinced that this relation was effectually gone on both sides, and that while the President was unwilling to allow Mr. Stanton to remain in his Administration, Mr. Stanton was equally unwilling to allow the President to carry on his Administration without his presence.

In the great debate which took place in the House of Representatives in 1789, in the first organization of the principal Departments, Mr. Madison spoke as follows:

It is evidently the intention of the Constitution that the first magistrate should be responsible for the executive department. So far, therefore, as we do not make the officers who are to aid him in the duties of that department responsible to him, he is not responsible to the country. Again: Is there no danger that an officer, when he is appointed by the concurrence of the Senate and has friends in that body, may choose rather to risk his establishment on the favor of that branch than rest it upon the discharge of his duties to the satisfaction of the executive branch, which is constitutionally authorized to inspect and control his conduct? And if it should happen that the officers connect themselves with the Senate, they may mutually support each other, and for want of efficacy reduce the power of the President to a mere vapor, in which case his responsibility would be annihilated, and the expectation of it is unjust. The high executive officers, joined in cabal with the Senate, would lay the foundation of discord, and end in an assumption of the executive power only to be removed by a revolution in the Government.

Mr. Sedgwick, in the same debate, referring to the proposition that a head of Department should only be removed or suspended by the concurrence of the Senate, used this language:

But if proof be necessary, what is then the consequence? Why, in nine cases out of ten, where the case is very clear to the mind of the President that the man ought to be removed, the effect can not be produced, because it is absolutely impossible to produce the necessary evidence. Are the Senate to proceed without evidence? Some gentlemen contend not. Then the object will be lost. Shall a man under these circumstances be saddled upon the President who has been appointed for no other purpose but to aid the President in performing certain duties? Shall he be continued, I ask again, against the will of the President? If he is, where is the responsibility? Are you to look for it in the President, who has no control over the officer, no power to remove him if he acts unfeelingly or unfaithfully? Without you make him responsible you weaken and destroy the strength and beauty of your system. What is to be done in cases which can only be known from a long acquaintance with the conduct of an officer?

I had indulged the hope that upon the assembling of Congress Mr. Stanton would have ended this unpleasant complication according to his intimation given in his note of August 12. The duty which I have felt myself called upon to perform was by no means agreeable, but I feel that I am not responsible for the controversy or for the consequences.

Unpleasant as this necessary change in my Cabinet has been to me upon personal considerations, I have the consolation to be assured that so far as the public interests are involved there is no cause for regret.

Salutary reforms have been introduced by the Secretary *ad interim*, and great reductions of expenses have been effected under his administration of the War Department, to the saving of millions to the Treasury.

ANDREW JOHNSON.

WASHINGTON, *December 14, 1867.*
To the House of Representatives:

In compliance with the resolution of the House of Representatives of the 9th instant, I transmit herewith a copy of the papers relating to the trial by a military commission of Albert M. D. C. Lusk, of Louisiana. No action in the case has yet been taken by the President.

ANDREW JOHNSON.

WASHINGTON, *December 17, 1867.*
To the House of Representatives:

I transmit for the information of the House of Representatives a report from the Secretary of State, with an accompanying paper.*

ANDREW JOHNSON.

WASHINGTON, *December 17, 1867.*
To the Senate of the United States:

In answer to the resolution of the Senate of the 6th instant, concerning the International Monetary Conference held at Paris in June last, I transmit a report from the Secretary of State, which is accompanied by the papers called for by the resolution.

ANDREW JOHNSON.

WASHINGTON, *December 17, 1867.*
To the Senate of the United States:

I transmit, for the consideration of the Senate, an agreement between the diplomatic representatives of certain foreign powers in Japan, including the minister of the United States, on the one part, and plenipotentiaries on the part of the Japanese Government, relative to the settlement of Yokohama.

---

* Report of George H. Sharpe relative to the assassination of President Lincoln and the attempted assassination of Secretary Seward.

This instrument can not be legally binding upon the United States unless sanctioned by the Senate. There appears to be no objection to its approval.

A copy of General Van Valkenburgh's dispatch to the Secretary of State, by which the agreement was accompanied, and of the map to which it refers, are also herewith transmitted. ANDREW JOHNSON.

WASHINGTON, D. C., *December 18, 1867.*

Gentlemen of the Senate and of the House of Representatives:

An official copy of the order issued by Major-General Winfield S. Hancock, commander of the Fifth Military District, dated headquarters in New Orleans, La., on the 29th day of November, has reached me through the regular channels of the War Department, and I herewith communicate it to Congress for such action as may seem to be proper in view of all the circumstances.

It will be perceived that General Hancock announces that he will make the law the rule of his conduct; that he will uphold the courts and other civil authorities in the performance of their proper duties, and that he will use his military power only to preserve the peace and enforce the law. He declares very explicitly that the sacred right of the trial by jury and the privilege of the writ of *habeas corpus* shall not be crushed out or trodden under foot. He goes further, and in one comprehensive sentence asserts that the principles of American liberty are still the inheritance of this people and ever should be.

When a great soldier, with unrestricted power in his hands to oppress his fellow-men, voluntarily foregoes the chance of gratifying his selfish ambition and devotes himself to the duty of building up the liberties and strengthening the laws of his country, he presents an example of the highest public virtue that human nature is capable of practicing. The strongest claim of Washington to be "first in war, first in peace, and first in the hearts of his countrymen" is founded on the great fact that in all his illustrious career he scrupulously abstained from violating the legal and constitutional rights of his fellow-citizens. When he surrendered his commission to Congress, the President of that body spoke his highest praise in saying that he had "always regarded the rights of the civil authorities through all dangers and disasters." Whenever power above the law courted his acceptance, he calmly put the temptation aside. By such magnanimous acts of forbearance he won the universal admiration of mankind and left a name which has no rival in the history of the world.

I am far from saying that General Hancock is the only officer of the American Army who is influenced by the example of Washington. Doubtless thousands of them are faithfully devoted to the principles for which the men of the Revolution laid down their lives. But the distinguished honor belongs to him of being the first officer in high command south of the Potomac, since the close of the civil war, who has given utterance to these noble sentiments in the form of a military order.

I respectfully suggest to Congress that some public recognition of General Hancock's patriotic conduct is due, if not to him, to the friends of law and justice throughout the country. Of such an act as his at such a time it is but fit that the dignity should be vindicated and the virtue proclaimed, so that its value as an example may not be lost to the nation.

ANDREW JOHNSON.

WASHINGTON, *December 19, 1867.*

To the Senate of the United States:

I transmit to the Senate, in answer to a resolution of that body of the 16th instant, a report* from the Secretary of State, with accompanying papers.

ANDREW JOHNSON.

WASHINGTON, *December 20, 1867.*

To the Senate and House of Representatives:

I herewith transmit to Congress a report, dated the 20th instant, with the accompanying papers, received from the Secretary of State in compliance with the requirements of the eighteenth section of the act entitled "An act to regulate the diplomatic and consular systems of the United States," approved August 18, 1856.

ANDREW JOHNSON.

WASHINGTON, *December 31, 1867.*

To the House of Representatives:

In answer to a resolution of the House of Representatives of the 18th instant, requesting information concerning alleged interference by Russian naval vessels with whaling vessels of the United States, I transmit a report from the Secretary of State and the papers referred to therein.

ANDREW JOHNSON.

WASHINGTON, *January 6, 1868.*

To the Senate of the United States:

I herewith transmit to the Senate a report from the Secretary of the Treasury, containing the information requested in their resolution of the 16th ultimo, relative to the amount of United States bonds issued to the Union Pacific Railroad Company and each of its branches, including the Central Pacific Railroad Company of California.

ANDREW JOHNSON.

---

* Relating to the removal of Governor Ballard, of the Territory of Idaho.

WASHINGTON, *January 7, 1868.*

To the House of Representatives:

I transmit a report from the Secretary of State, in answer to a resolution of the House of Representatives of yesterday, making inquiry how many and what State legislatures have ratified the proposed amendment to the Constitution of the United States known as the fourteenth article.

ANDREW JOHNSON.

WASHINGTON, *January 7, 1868.*

To the Senate and House of Representatives:

A Spanish steamer named *Nuestra Señora* being in the harbor of Port Royal, S. C., on the 1st of December, 1861, Brigadier-General T. W. Sherman, who was in command of the United States forces there, received information which he supposed justified him in seizing her, as she was on her way from Charleston to Havana with insurgent correspondence on board. The seizure was made accordingly, and during the ensuing spring the vessel was sent to New York, in order that the legality of the seizure might be tried.

By a decree of June 20, 1863, Judge Betts ordered the vessel to be restored, and by a subsequent decree, of October 15, 1863, he referred the adjustment of damages to amicable negotiations between the two Governments.

While the proceeding in admiralty was pending, the vessel was appraised and taken by the Navy Department at the valuation of $28,000, which sum that Department paid into the Treasury.

As the amount of this valuation can not legally be drawn from the Treasury without authority from Congress, I recommend an appropriation for that purpose.

It is proposed to appoint a commissioner on the part of this Government to adjust, informally in this case, with a similar commissioner on the part of Spain, the question of damages, the commissioners to name an arbiter for points upon which they may disagree. When the amount of the damages shall thus have been ascertained, application will be made to Congress for a further appropriation toward paying them.

ANDREW JOHNSON.

WASHINGTON, D. C., *January 14, 1868.*

To the House of Representatives:

I transmit herewith a communication from the Secretary of War *ad interim,* with the accompanying papers, prepared in compliance with a resolution of the House of Representatives of March 15, 1867, requesting information in reference to contracts for ordnance projectiles and small arms.

ANDREW JOHNSON.

WASHINGTON, D. C., *January 14, 1868.*

To the Senate and House of Representatives:

I transmit herewith the report made by the commissioners appointed under the act of Congress approved on the 20th day of July, 1867, entitled "An act to establish peace with certain hostile Indian tribes," together with the accompanying papers.

ANDREW JOHNSON.

WASHINGTON, *January 14, 1868.*

To the Senate of the United States:

In answer to the resolution of the Senate of yesterday, calling for information relating to the appointment of the American minister at Pekin to a diplomatic or other mission on behalf of the Chinese Government by the Emperor of China, I transmit a report from the Secretary of State upon the subject, together with the accompanying papers.

ANDREW JOHNSON.

WASHINGTON CITY, *January 14, 1868.*

To the Senate of the United States:

I herewith lay before the Senate, for its constitutional action thereon, the following treaties, concluded at "Medicine Lodge Creek," Kansas, between the Indian tribes therein named and the United States, by their commissioners appointed by the act of Congress approved July 20, 1867, entitled "An act to establish peace with certain hostile Indian tribes," viz:

A treaty with the Kiowa and Comanche tribes, concluded October 21, 1867.

A treaty with the Kiowa, Comanche, and Apache tribes, concluded October 28, 1867.

A treaty with the Arapahoe and Cheyenne tribes, dated October 28, 1867.

A letter of this date from the Secretary of the Interior, transmitting said treaties, is herewith inclosed.

ANDREW JOHNSON.

WASHINGTON, *January 17, 1868.*

To the Senate of the United States:

With reference to the convention between the United States and Denmark for the cession of the islands of St. Thomas and St. John, in the West Indies, I transmit a report from the Secretary of State on the subject of the vote of St. Thomas on the question of accepting the cession.

ANDREW JOHNSON.

WASHINGTON, D. C., *January 23, 1868.*

To the Senate of the United States:

In compliance with the request of the Senate of yesterday, I return herewith their resolution of the 21st instant, calling for information in reference to James A. Seddon, late Secretary of War of the so-called Confederate States. ANDREW JOHNSON.

WASHINGTON, *January 23, 1868.*

To the Senate of the United States:

I have received the following preamble and resolution, adopted by the Senate on the 8th instant:

Whereas Senate bill No. 141, and entitled "An act for the further security of equal rights in the District of Columbia," having at this present session passed both Houses of Congress, was afterwards, on the 11th day of December, 1867, duly presented to the President of the United States for his approval and signature; and

Whereas more than ten days, exclusive of Sundays, have since elapsed in this session without said bill having been returned, either approved or disapproved: Therefore,

Resolved, That the President of the United States be requested to inform the Senate whether said bill has been delivered to and received by the Secretary of State, as provided by the second section of the act of the 27th day of July, 1789.

As the act which the resolution mentions has no relevancy to the subject under inquiry, it is presumed that it was the intention of the Senate to refer to the law of the 15th September, 1789, the second section of which prescribes—

That whenever a bill, order, resolution, or vote of the Senate and House of Representatives, having been approved and signed by the President of the United States, or not having been returned by him with his objections, shall become a law or take effect, it shall forthwith thereafter be received by the said Secretary from the President; and whenever a bill, order, resolution, or vote shall be returned by the President with his objections, and shall, on being reconsidered, be agreed to be passed, and be approved by two-thirds of both Houses of Congress, and thereby become a law or take effect, it shall in such case be received by the said Secretary from the President of the Senate or the Speaker of the House of Representatives, in whichsoever House it shall last have been so approved.

Inasmuch as the bill "for the further security of equal rights in the District of Columbia" has not become a law in either of the modes designated in the section above quoted, it has not been delivered to the Secretary of State for record and promulgation. The Constitution expressly declares that—

If any bill shall not be returned by the President within ten days (Sundays excepted) after it shall have been presented to him, the same shall be a law in like manner as if he had signed it, unless the Congress by their adjournment prevent its return, in which case it shall not be a law.

As stated in the preamble to the resolution, the bill to which it refers was presented for my approval on the 11th day of December, 1867. On the 20th of same month, and before the expiration of the ten days after the presentation of the bill to the President, the two Houses, in accordance with a concurrent resolution adopted on the 3d [13th] of December, adjourned until the 6th of January, 1868. Congress by their adjournment thus prevented the return of the bill within the time prescribed by the Constitution, and it was therefore left in the precise condition in which that instrument positively declares a bill "shall not be a law."

If the adjournment in December did not cause the failure of this bill, because not such an adjournment as is contemplated by the Constitution in the clause which I have cited, it must follow that such was the nature of the adjournments during the past year, on the 30th day of March until the first Wednesday of July and from the 20th of July until the 21st of November. Other bills will therefore be affected by the decision which may be rendered in this case, among them one having the same title as that named in the resolution, and containing similar provisions, which, passed by both Houses in the month of July last, failed to become a law by reason of the adjournment of Congress before ten days for its consideration had been allowed the Executive.

ANDREW JOHNSON.

WASHINGTON, *January 27, 1868.*
To the House of Representatives of the United States:

In answer to a resolution of the House of Representatives of the 22d instant, calling for a copy of the report of Abram S. Hewitt, commissioner of the United States to the Paris Universal Exhibition of 1867, I transmit a report from the Secretary of State and the papers which accompany it.

ANDREW JOHNSON.

WASHINGTON, *January 27, 1868.*
To the Senate and House of Representatives:

I transmit a report from the Secretary of State and the documents to which it refers, in relation to the formal transfer of territory from Russia to the United States in accordance with the treaty of the 30th of March last.

ANDREW JOHNSON.

WASHINGTON, *January 28, 1868.*
To the Senate of the United States:

I transmit, for the consideration of the Senate with a view to its ratification, an additional article to the treaty of navigation and commerce with Russia of the 18th of December, 1832, which additional article was concluded and signed between the plenipotentiaries of the two Governments at Washington on the 27th instant.

ANDREW JOHNSON.

WASHINGTON, *February 3, 1868.*

To the Senate and House of Representatives:

I transmit to Congress a report from the Secretary of State, suggesting the necessity for a further appropriation toward defraying the expense of employing copying clerks, with a view to enable his Department seasonably to answer certain calls for information.

ANDREW JOHNSON.

WASHINGTON, *February 3, 1868.*

To the House of Representatives:

In answer to a resolution of the House of Representatives of the 27th ultimo, directing the Secretary of State to furnish information in regard to the trial of John H. Surratt, I transmit a report from the Secretary of State.

ANDREW JOHNSON.

WASHINGTON, *February 3, 1868.*

To the House of Representatives:

I transmit herewith a report* from the Secretary of State, in answer to a resolution of the House of Representatives of the 28th of January.

ANDREW JOHNSON.

WASHINGTON, *February 10, 1868.*

To the House of Representatives:

I transmit herewith a communication from the Secretary of the Navy, relative to depredations upon and the future care of the reservations of lands for the "purpose of supplying timber for the Navy of the United States."

ANDREW JOHNSON.

WASHINGTON, D. C., *February 10, 1868.*

To the House of Representatives:

In reply to the resolution of the House of Representatives of the 1st instant, I transmit herewith a report from the Postmaster-General, in reference to the appointment of a special agent to take charge of the post-office at Penn Yan, in the State of New York.

ANDREW JOHNSON.

WASHINGTON, *February 10, 1868.*

To the Senate of the United States:

I transmit a report from the Secretary of State, with the accompanying papers, on the subject of a transfer of the Peninsula and Bay of

*Relating to the famine in Sweden and Norway.

Samana to the United States.   The advice and consent of the Senate to the transfer, upon the terms proposed in the draft of a convention with the Dominican Republic, are requested.

ANDREW JOHNSON.

WASHINGTON, *February 10, 1868.*
To the Senate of the United States:

I submit to the Senate, for its consideration with a view to ratification, the accompanying consular convention between the United States and the Govenrment of His Majesty the King of Italy.

ANDREW JOHNSON.

WASHINGTON, D. C., *February 10, 1868.*
To the Senate of the United States:

I transmit herewith a report from the Attorney-General, prepared in compliance with the resolution of the Senate of the 30th ultimo, requesting information as to the number of justices of the peace now in commission in each ward, respectively, of the city of Washington.

ANDREW JOHNSON.

WASHINGTON, *February 10, 1868.*
To the House of Representatives:

In answer to the resolution of the House of Representatives of the 25th of November, 1867, calling for information in relation to the trial and conviction of American citizens in Great Britain and Ireland for the two years last past, I transmit a partial report from the Secretary of State, which is accompanied by a portion of the papers called for by the resolution.

ANDREW JOHNSON.

WASHINGTON, D. C., *February 11, 1868.*
To the House of Representatives:

In compliance with the resolution adopted yesterday by the House of Representatives, requesting any further correspondence the President "may have had with General U. S. Grant, in addition to that heretofore submitted, on the subject of the recent vacation by the latter of the War Office," I transmit herewith a copy of a communication addressed to General Grant on the 10th instant, together with a copy of the accompanying papers.

ANDREW JOHNSON

EXECUTIVE MANSION, *February 10, 1868.*

General U. S. GRANT,
  Commanding Armies of the United States, Washington, D. C.

GENERAL: The extraordinary character of your letter of the 3d instant* would seem to preclude any reply on my part; but the manner in which publicity has been given to the correspondence of which that letter forms a part and the grave questions which are involved induce me to take this mode of giving, as a proper sequel to the communications which have passed between us, the statements of the five members of the Cabinet who were present on the occasion of our conversation on the 14th ultimo. Copies of the letters which they have addressed to me upon the subject are accordingly herewith inclosed.

You speak of my letter of the 31st ultimo † as a reiteration of the "many and gross misrepresentations" contained in certain newspaper articles, and reassert the correctness of the statements contained in your communication of the 28th ultimo,‡ adding—and here I give your own words—"anything in yours in reply to it to the contrary notwithstanding."

When a controversy upon matters of fact reaches the point to which this has been brought, further assertion or denial between the immediate parties should cease, especially where upon either side it loses the character of the respectful discussion which is required by the relations in which the parties stand to each other and degenerates in tone and temper. In such a case, if there is nothing to rely upon but the opposing statements, conclusions must be drawn from those statements alone and from whatever intrinsic probabilities they afford in favor of or against either of the parties. I should not shrink from this test in this controversy; but, fortunately, it is not left to this test alone. There were five Cabinet officers present at the conversation the detail of which in my letter of the 28th [31st †] ultimo you allow yourself to say contains "many and gross misrepresentations." These gentlemen heard that conversation and have read my statement. They speak for themselves, and I leave the proof without a word of comment.

I deem it proper before concluding this communication to notice some of the statements contained in your letter.

You say that a performance of the promises alleged to have been made by you to the President "would have involved a resistance to law and an inconsistency with the whole history of my connection with the suspension of Mr. Stanton." You then state that you had fears the President would, on the removal of Mr. Stanton, appoint someone in his place who would embarrass the Army in carrying out the reconstruction acts, and add:

"It was to prevent such an appointment that I accepted the office of Secretary of War *ad interim*, and not for the purpose of enabling you to get rid of Mr. Stanton by withholding it from him in opposition to law, or, not doing so myself, surrendering it to one who would, as the statements and assumptions in your communication plainly indicate was sought."

First of all, you here admit that from the very beginning of what you term "the whole history" of your connection with Mr. Stanton's suspension you intended to circumvent the President. It was to carry out that intent that you accepted the appointment. This was in your mind at the time of your acceptance. It was not, then, in obedience to the order of your superior, as has heretofore been supposed, that you assumed the duties of the office. You knew it was the President's purpose to prevent Mr. Stanton from resuming the office of Secretary of War, and you intended to defeat that purpose. You accepted the office, not in the interest of the President, but of Mr. Stanton. If this purpose, so entertained by you, had been confined to yourself; if when accepting the office you had done so with a mental reservation to frustrate the President, it would have been a tacit deception. In the ethics of

---

*See pp. 618–620.   † See pp. 615–618.   ‡ See pp. 613–615.

some persons such a course is allowable. But you can not stand even upon that questionable ground. The "history" of your connection with this transaction, as written by yourself, places you in a different predicament, and shows that you not only concealed your design from the President, but induced him to suppose that you would carry out his purpose to keep Mr. Stanton out of office by retaining it yourself after an attempted restoration by the Senate, so as to require Mr. Stanton to establish his right by judicial decision.

I now give that part of this "history" as written by yourself in your letter of the 28th ultimo:*

"Some time after I assumed the duties of Secretary of War *ad interim* the President asked me my views as to the course Mr. Stanton would have to pursue, in case the Senate should not concur in his suspension, to obtain possession of his office. My reply was, in substance, that Mr. Stanton would have to appeal to the courts to reinstate him, illustrating my position by citing the ground I had taken in the case of the Baltimore police commissioners."

Now, at that time, as you admit in your letter of the 3d instant,† you held the office for the very object of defeating an appeal to the courts. In that letter you say that in accepting the office one motive was to prevent the President from appointing some other person who would retain possession, and thus make judicial proceedings necessary. You knew the President was unwilling to trust the office with anyone who would not by holding it compel Mr. Stanton to resort to the courts. You perfectly understood that in this interview, "some time" after you accepted the office, the President, not content with your silence, desired an expression of your views, and you answered him that Mr. Stanton "would have to appeal to the courts." If the President reposed confidence *before* he knew your views, and that confidence had been violated, it might have been said he made a mistake; but a violation of confidence reposed *after* that conversation was no mistake of his nor of yours. It is the fact only that needs be stated, that at the date of this conversation you did not intend to hold the office with the purpose of forcing Mr. Stanton into court, but did hold it then and had accepted it to prevent that course from being carried out. In other words, you said to the President, "That is the proper course," and you said to yourself, "I have accepted this office, and now hold it to defeat that course." The excuse you make in a subsequent paragraph of that letter of the 28th ultimo,* that afterwards you changed your views as to what would be a proper course, has nothing to do with the point now under consideration. The point is that *before* you changed your views you had secretly determined to do the very thing which at last you did— surrender the office to Mr. Stanton. You may have changed your views as to the law, but you certainly did not change your views as to the course you had marked out for yourself from the beginning.

I will only notice one more statement in your letter of the 3d instant †—that the performance of the promises which it is alleged were made by you would have involved you in the resistance of law. I know of no statute that would have been violated had you, carrying out your promises in good faith, tendered your resignation when you concluded not to be made a party in any legal proceedings. You add:

"I am in a measure confirmed in this conclusion by your recent orders directing me to disobey orders from the Secretary of War, *my superior* and your subordinate, without having countermanded his authority to issue the orders I am to disobey."

On the 24th ‡ ultimo you addressed a note to the President requesting in writing an order given to you verbally five days before to disregard orders from Mr. Stanton as Secretary of War until you "knew from the President himself that they were his orders."

On the 29th,§ in compliance with your request, I did give you instructions in writing "not to obey any order from the War Department assumed to be issued by the

*See pp. 613–615. †See pp. 618–620. ‡See p. 613. §See p. 615.

direction of the President unless such order is known by the General Commanding the armies of the United States to have been authorized by the Executive."

There are some orders which a Secretary of War may issue without the authority of the President; there are others which he issues simply as the agent of the President, and which purport to be "by direction" of the President. For such orders the President is responsible, and he should therefore know and understand what they are before giving such "direction." Mr. Stanton states in his letter of the 4th instant,* which accompanies the published correspondence, that he "has had no correspondence with the President since the 12th of August last;" and he further says that since he resumed the duties of the office he has continued to discharge them "without any personal or written communication with the President;" and he adds, "No orders have been issued from this Department in the name of the President with my knowledge, and I have received no orders from him."

It thus seems that Mr. Stanton now discharges the duties of the War Department without any reference to the President and without using his name.

My order to you had only reference to orders "assumed to be issued by the direction of the President." It would appear from Mr. Stanton's letter that you have received no such orders from him. However, in your note to the President of the 30th ultimo,† in which you acknowledge the receipt of the written order of the 29th,† you say that you have been informed by Mr. Stanton that he has not received any order limiting his authority to issue orders to the Army, according to the practice of the Department, and state that "while this authority to the War Department is not countermanded it will be satisfactory evidence to me that any orders issued from the War Department by direction of the President are authorized by the Executive."

The President issues an order to you to obey no order from the War Department purporting to be made "by the direction of the President" until you have referred it to him for his approval. You reply that you have received the President's order and will not obey it, but will obey an order purporting to be given by his direction *if it comes from the War Department.* You will not obey the direct order of the President, but will obey his indirect order. If, as you say, there has been a practice in the War Department to issue orders in the name of the President without his direction, does not the precise order you have requested and have received change the practice as to the General of the Army? Could not the President countermand any such order issued to you from the War Department? If you should receive an order from that Department, issued in the name of the President, to do a special act, and an order directly from the President himself not to do the act, is there a doubt which you are to obey? You answer the question when you say to the President, in your letter of the 3d instant,‡ the Secretary of War is "my superior and your subordinate," and yet you refuse obedience to the superior out of a deference to the subordinate.

Without further comment upon the insubordinate attitude which you have assumed, I am at a loss to know how you can relieve yourself from obedience to the orders of the President, who is made by the Constitution the Commander in Chief of the Army and Navy, and is therefore the official superior as well of the General of the Army as of the Secretary of War.

Respectfully, yours, ANDREW JOHNSON.

[Letter addressed to each of the members of the Cabinet present at the conversation between the President and General Grant on the 14th of January, 1868, and answers thereto.]

Executive Mansion, *Washington, D. C., February 5, 1868.*

Sir: The Chronicle of this morning contains a correspondence between the President and General Grant reported from the War Department in answer to a resolution of the House of Representatives.

*See pp. 612–613.   †See p. 615.   ‡See pp. 618–620.

I beg to call your attention to that correspondence, and especially to that part of it which refers to the conversation between the President and General Grant at the Cabinet meeting on Tuesday, the 14th of January, and to request you to state what was said in that conversation.

Very respectfully, yours,

ANDREW JOHNSON.

WASHINGTON, D. C., *February 5, 1868.*

The PRESIDENT.

SIR: Your note of this date was handed to me this evening. My recollection of the conversation at the Cabinet meeting on Tuesday, the 14th of January, corresponds with your statement of it in the letter of the 31st ultimo* in the published correspondence.

The three points specified in that letter, giving your recollection of the conversation, are correctly stated.

Very respectfully,

GIDEON WELLES.

TREASURY DEPARTMENT, *February 6, 1868.*

The PRESIDENT.

SIR: I have received your note of the 5th instant, calling my attention to the correspondence between yourself and General Grant as published in the Chronicle of yesterday, especially to that part of it which relates to what occurred at the Cabinet meeting on Tuesday, the 14th ultimo, and requesting me to state what was said in the conversation referred to.

I can not undertake to state the precise language used, but I have no hesitation in saying that your account of that conversation as given in your letter to General Grant under date of the 31st ultimo* substantially and in all important particulars accords with my recollection of it.

With great respect, your obedient servant,

HUGH McCULLOCH.

POST-OFFICE DEPARTMENT,
Washington, February 6, 1868.

The PRESIDENT.

SIR: I am in receipt of your letter of the 5th of February, calling my attention to the correspondence published in the Chronicle between the President and General Grant, and especially to that part of it which refers to the conversation between the President and General Grant at the Cabinet meeting on Tuesday, the 14th of January, with a request that I state what was said in that conversation.

In reply I have the honor to state that I have read carefully the correspondence in question, and particularly the letter of the President to General Grant dated January 31, 1868.* The following extract from your letter of the 31st January to General Grant is, according to my recollection, a correct statement of the conversation that took place between the President and General Grant at the Cabinet meeting on the 14th of January last. In the presence of the Cabinet the President asked General Grant whether, "in conversation which took place after his appointment as Secretary of War *ad interim,* he did not agree either to remain at the head of the War Department and abide any judicial proceedings that might follow the nonconcurrence by the Senate in Mr. Stanton's suspension, or, should he wish not to become involved in such a controversy, to put the President in the same position with respect to the office as he occupied previous to General Grant's appointment, by returning

*See pp. 615–618.

it to the President in time to anticipate such action by the Senate." This General Grant admitted.

The President then asked General Grant if at the conference on the preceding Saturday he had not, to avoid misunderstanding, requested General Grant to state what he intended to do, and, further, if in reply to that inquiry he (General Grant) had not referred to their former conversations, saying that from them the President understood his position, and that his (General Grant's) action would be consistent with the understanding which had been reached.

To these questions General Grant replied in the affirmative.

The President asked General Grant if at the conclusion of their interview on Saturday it was not understood that they were to have another conference on Monday before final action by the Senate in the case of Mr. Stanton.

General Grant replied that such was the understanding, but that he did not suppose the Senate would act so soon; that on Monday he had been engaged in a conference with General Sherman, and was occupied with "many little matters," and asked if General Sherman had not called on that day.

I take this mode of complying with the request contained in the President's letter to me, because my attention had been called to the subject before, when the conversation between the President and General Grant was under consideration.

Very respectfully, your obedient servant,

ALEX. W. RANDALL,
Postmaster-General.

DEPARTMENT OF THE INTERIOR,
Washington, D. C., February 6, 1868.

The PRESIDENT.

SIR: I am in receipt of yours of yesterday, calling my attention to a correspondence between yourself and General Grant published in the Chronicle newspaper, and especially to that part of said correspondence "which refers to the conversation between the President and General Grant at the Cabinet meeting on Tuesday, the 14th of January," and requesting me "to state what was said in that conversation."

In reply I submit the following statement: At the Cabinet meeting on Tuesday, the 14th of January, 1868, General Grant appeared and took his accustomed seat at the board. When he had been reached in the order of business, the President asked him, as usual, if he had anything to present.

In reply the General, after referring to a note which he had that morning addressed to the President, inclosing a copy of the resolution of the Senate refusing to concur in the reasons for the suspension of Mr. Stanton, proceeded to say that he regarded his duties as Secretary of War *ad interim* terminated by that resolution, and that he could not lawfully exercise such duties for a moment after the adoption of the resolution by the Senate; that the resolution reached him last night, and that this morning he had gone to the War Department, entered the Secretary's room, bolted one door on the inside, locked the other on the outside, delivered the key to the Adjutant-General, and proceeded to the Headquarters of the Army and addressed the note above mentioned to the President, informing him that he (General Grant) was no longer Secretary of War *ad interim*.

The President expressed great surprise at the course which General Grant had thought proper to pursue, and, addressing himself to the General, proceeded to say, in substance, that he had anticipated such action on the part of the Senate, and, being very desirous to have the constitutionality of the tenure-of-office bill tested and his right to suspend or remove a member of the Cabinet decided by the judicial tribunals of the country, he had some time ago, and shortly after General Grant's appointment as Secretary of War *ad interim*, asked the General what his action would be in the event that the Senate should refuse to concur in the suspension of

Mr. Stanton, and that the General had then agreed either to remain at the head of the War Department till a decision could be obtained from the court or resign the office into the hands of the President before the case was acted upon by the Senate, so as to place the President in the same situation he occupied at the time of his (Grant's) appointment.

The President further said that the conversation was renewed on the preceding Saturday, at which time he asked the General what he intended to do if the Senate should undertake to reinstate Mr. Stanton, in reply to which the General referred to their former conversation upon the same subject and said: "You understand my position, and my conduct will be conformable to that understanding;" that he (the General) then expressed a repugnance to being made a party to a judicial proceeding, saying that he would expose himself to fine and imprisonment by doing so, as his continuing to discharge the duties of Secretary of War *ad interim* after the Senate should have refused to concur in the suspension of Mr. Stanton would be a violation of the tenure-of-office bill; that in reply to this he (the President) informed General Grant he had not suspended Mr. Stanton under the tenure-of-office bill, but by virtue of the powers conferred on him by the Constitution; and that, as to the fine and imprisonment, he (the President) would pay whatever fine was imposed and submit to whatever imprisonment might be adjudged against him (the General); that they continued the conversation for some time, discussing the law at length, and that they finally separated without having reached a definite conclusion, and with the understanding that the General would see the President again on Monday.

In reply General Grant admitted that the conversations had occurred, and said that at the first conversation he had given it as his opinion to the President that in the event of nonconcurrence by the Senate in the action of the President in respect to the Secretary of War the question would have to be decided by the court—that Mr. Stanton would have to appeal to the court to reinstate him in office; that the *ins* would remain in till they could be displaced and the *outs* put in by legal proceedings; and that he *then* thought so, and had agreed that if he should change his mind he would notify the President in time to enable him to make another appointment, but that at the time of the first conversation he had not looked very closely into the law; that it had recently been discussed by the newspapers, and that this had induced him to examine it more carefully, and that he had come to the conclusion that if the Senate should refuse to concur in the suspension Mr. Stanton would thereby be reinstated, and that he (Grant) could not continue thereafter to act as Secretary of War *ad interim* without subjecting himself to fine and imprisonment, and that he came over on Saturday to inform the President of this change in his views, and did so inform him; that the President replied that he had not suspended Mr. Stanton under the tenure-of-office bill, but under the Constitution, and had appointed him (Grant) by virtue of the authority derived from the Constitution, etc.; that they continued to discuss the matter some time, and finally he left, without any conclusion having been reached, expecting to see the President again on Monday.

He then proceeded to explain why he had not called on the President on Monday, saying that he had had a long interview with General Sherman, that various little matters had occupied his time till it was late, and that he did not think the Senate would act so soon, and asked: "Did not General Sherman call on you on Monday?"

I do not know what passed between the President and General Grant on Saturday, except as I learned it from the conversation between them at the Cabinet meeting on Tuesday, and the foregoing is substantially what then occurred. The precise words used on the occasion are not, of course, given exactly in the order in which they were spoken, but the ideas expressed and the facts stated are faithfully preserved and presented.

I have the honor to be, sir, with great respect, your obedient servant,

O. H. BROWNING.

DEPARTMENT OF STATE,
Washington, February 6, 1868.

The PRESIDENT.

SIR: The meeting to which you refer in your letter was a regular Cabinet meeting. While the members were assembling, and before the President had entered the council chamber, General Grant on coming in said to me that he was in attendance there, not as a member of the Cabinet, but upon invitation, and I replied by the inquiry whether there was a change in the War Department. After the President had taken his seat, business went on in the usual way of hearing matters submitted by the several Secretaries. When the time came for the Secretary of War, General Grant said that he was now there, not as Secretary of War, but upon the President's invitation; that he had retired from the War Department. A slight difference then appeared about the supposed invitation, General Grant saying that the officer who had borne his letter to the President that morning announcing his retirement from the War Department had told him that the President desired to see him at the Cabinet, to which the President answered that when General Grant's communication was delivered to him the President simply replied that he supposed General Grant would be very soon at the Cabinet meeting. I regarded the conversation thus begun as an incidental one. It went on quite informally, and consisted of a statement on your part of your views in regard to the understanding of the tenure upon which General Grant had assented to hold the War Department *ad interim* and of his replies by way of answer and explanation. It was respectful and courteous on both sides. Being in this conversational form, its details could only have been preserved by verbatim report. So far as I know, no such report was made at the time. I can give only the general effect of the conversation. Certainly you stated that, although you had reported the reasons for Mr. Stanton's suspension to the Senate, you nevertheless held that he would not be entitled to resume the office of Secretary of War even if the Senate should disapprove of his suspension, and that you had proposed to have the question tested by judicial process, to be applied to the person who should be the incumbent of the Department under your designation of Secretary of War *ad interim* in the place of Mr. Stanton. You contended that this was well understood between yourself and General Grant; that when he entered the War Department as Secretary *ad interim* he expressed his concurrence in a belief that the question of Mr. Stanton's restoration would be a question for the courts; that in a subsequent conversation with General Grant you had adverted to the understanding thus had, and that General Grant expressed his concurrence in it; that at some conversation which had been previously held General Grant said he still adhered to the same construction of the law, but said if he should change his opinion he would give you seasonable notice of it, so that you should in any case be placed in the same position in regard to the War Department that you were while General Grant held it *ad interim*. I did not understand General Grant as denying nor as explicitly admitting these statements in the form and full extent to which you made them. His admission of them was rather indirect and circumstantial, though I did not understand it to be an evasive one. He said that, reasoning from what occurred in the case of the police in Maryland, which he regarded as a parallel one, he was of opinion, and so assured you, that it would be his right and duty under your instructions to hold the War Office after the Senate should disapprove of Mr. Stanton's suspension until the question should be decided upon by the courts; that he remained until very recently of that opinion, and that on the Saturday before the Cabinet meeting a conversation was held between yourself and him in which the subject was generally discussed.

General Grant's statement was that in that conversation he had stated to you the legal difficulties which might arise, involving fine and imprisonment, under the civil-tenure bill, and that he did not care to subject himself to those penalties; that you replied to this remark that you regarded the civil-tenure bill as unconstitutional and did not think its penalties were to be feared, or that you would voluntarily assume them; and you insisted that General Grant should either retain the office until relieved by yourself, according to what you claimed was the original understanding between yourself and him, or, by seasonable notice of change of purpose on his part, put you in the same situation which you would be if he adhered. You claimed that General Grant finally said in that Saturday's conversation that you understood his views, and his proceedings thereafter would be consistent with what had been so understood. General Grant did not controvert, nor can I say that he admitted, this last statement. Certainly General Grant did not at any time in the Cabinet meeting insist that he had in the Saturday's conversation, either distinctly or finally, advised you of his determination to retire from the charge of the War Department otherwise than under your own subsequent direction. He acquiesced in your statement that the Saturday's conversation ended with an expectation that there would be a subsequent conference on the subject, which he, as well as yourself, supposed could seasonably take place on Monday. You then alluded to the fact that General Grant did not call upon you on Monday, as you had expected from that conversation. General Grant admitted that it was his expectation or purpose to call upon you on Monday. General Grant assigned reasons for the omission. He said he was in conference with General Sherman; that there were many little matters to be attended to; he had conversed upon the matter of the incumbency of the War Department with General Sherman, and he expected that General Sherman would call upon you on Monday. My own mind suggested a further explanation, but I do not remember whether it was mentioned or not, namely, that it was not supposed by General Grant on Monday that the Senate would decide the question so promptly as to anticipate further explanation between yourself and him if delayed beyond that day. General Grant made another explanation—that he was engaged on Sunday with General Sherman, and I think, also, on Monday, in regard to the War Department matter, with a hope, though he did not say in an effort, to procure an amicable settlement of the affair of Mr. Stanton, and he still hoped that it would be brought about.

I have the honor to be, with great respect, your obedient servant,

WILLIAM H. SEWARD.

WASHINGTON, D. C., *February 11, 1868.*

To the House of Representatives:

The accompanying letter from General Grant, received since the transmission to the House of Representatives of my communication of this date, is submitted to the House as a part of the correspondence referred to in the resolution of the 10th instant.

ANDREW JOHNSON.

HEADQUARTERS ARMY OF THE UNITED STATES,
Washington, D. C., February 11, 1868.

His Excellency A. JOHNSON,
    President of the United States.

SIR: I have the honor to acknowledge the receipt of your communication of the 10th instant,* accompanied by statements of five Cabinet ministers of their recollection of what occurred in Cabinet meeting on the 14th of January. Without admitting anything in these statements where they differ from anything heretofore stated by me, I propose to notice only that portion of your communication wherein I am charged with insubordination. I think it will be plain to the reader of my letter of

* See pp. 603–610.

the 30th of January* that I did not propose to disobey any legal order of the President distinctly given, but only gave an interpretation of what would be regarded as satisfactory evidence of the President's sanction to orders communicated by the Secretary of War. I will say here that your letter of the 10th instant† contains the first intimation I have had that you did not accept that interpretation.

Now for reasons for giving that interpretation. It was clear to me before my letter of January 30* was written that I, the person having more public business to transact with the Secretary of War than any other of the President's subordinates, was the only one who had been instructed to disregard the authority of Mr. Stanton where his authority was derived as agent of the President.

On the 27th of January I received a letter from the Secretary of War (copy herewith) directing me to furnish escort to public treasure from the Rio Grande to New Orleans, etc., at the request of the Secretary of the Treasury to him. I also send two other inclosures, showing recognition of Mr. Stanton as Secretary of War by both the Secretary of the Treasury and the Postmaster-General, in all of which cases the Secretary of War had to call upon me to make the orders requested or give the information desired, and where his authority to do so is derived, in my view, as agent of the President.

With an order so clearly ambiguous as that of the President here referred to, it was my duty to inform the President of my interpretation of it and to abide by that interpretation until I received other orders.

Disclaiming any intention, now or heretofore, of disobeying any legal order of the President distinctly communicated,

I remain, very respectfully, your obedient servant,

U. S. GRANT, *General.*

WAR DEPARTMENT,
Washington City, January 27, 1868.

General U. S. GRANT,
   Commanding Army United States.

GENERAL: The Secretary of the Treasury has requested this Department to afford A. F. Randall, special agent of the Treasury Department, such military aid as may be necessary to secure and forward for deposit from Brownsville, Tex., to New Orleans public moneys in possession of custom-house officers at Brownsville, and which are deemed insecure at that place.

You will please give such directions as you may deem proper to the officer commanding at Brownsville to carry into effect the request of the Treasury Department, the instructions to be sent by telegraph to Galveston, to the care of A. F. Randall, special agent, who is at Galveston waiting telegraphic orders, there being no telegraphic communication with Brownsville, and the necessity for military protection to the public moneys represented as urgent.

Please favor me with a copy of such instructions as you may give, in order that they may be communicated to the Secretary of the Treasury.

Yours, truly,
   EDWIN M. STANTON,
      Secretary of War.

POST-OFFICE DEPARTMENT, CONTRACT OFFICE,
Washington, February 3, 1868.

The Honorable the SECRETARY OF WAR.

SIR: It has been represented to this Department that in October last a military commission was appointed to settle upon some general plan of defense for the Texas frontiers, and that the said commission has made a report recommending a line of posts from the Rio Grande to the Red River.

---

*See p. 615.   †See pp. 603–605.

An application is now pending in this Department for a change in the course of the San Antonio and El Paso mail, so as to send it by way of Forts Mason, Griffin, and Stockton instead of Camps Hudson and Lancaster. This application requires immediate decision, but before final action can be had thereon it is desired to have some official information as to the report of the commission above referred to.

Accordingly, I have the honor to request that you will cause this Department to be furnished as early as possible with the information desired in the premises, and also with a copy of the report, if any has been made by the commission.

Very respectfully, etc.,

GEO. W. McLELLAN,
Second Assistant Postmaster-General.

FEBRUARY 3, 1868.

Referred to the General of the Army for report.

EDWIN M. STANTON,
Secretary of War.

TREASURY DEPARTMENT, *January 29, 1868.*

The Honorable SECRETARY OF WAR.

SIR: It is represented to this Department that a band of robbers has obtained such a foothold in the section of country between Humboldt and Lawrence, Kans., committing depredations upon travelers, both by public and private conveyance, that the safety of the public money collected by the receiver of the land office at Humboldt requires that it should be guarded during its transit from Humboldt to Lawrence. I have therefore the honor to request that the proper commanding officer of the district may be instructed by the War Department, if in the opinion of the honorable Secretary of War it can be done without prejudice to the public interests, to furnish a sufficient military guard to protect such moneys as may be *in transitu* from the above office for the purpose of being deposited to the credit of the Treasurer of the United States. As far as we are now advised, such service will not be necessary oftener than once a month. Will you please advise me of the action taken, that I may instruct the receiver and the Commissioner of the General Land Office in the matter?

Very respectfully, your obedient servant,

H. McCULLOCH,
Secretary of the Treasury.

Respectfully referred to the General of the Army to give the necessary orders in this case and to furnish this Department a copy for the information of the Secretary of the Treasury.

By order of the Secretary of War:

ED. SCHRIVER,
Inspector-General.

[The following are inserted because they have direct bearing on the two messages from the President of February 11, 1868, and their inclosures.]

WAR DEPARTMENT,
Washington City, February 4, 1868.

Hon. SCHUYLER COLFAX,
Speaker of the House of Representatives.

SIR: In answer to the resolution of the House of Representatives of the 3d instant, I transmit herewith copies furnished me by General Grant of correspondence between him and the President relating to the Secretary of War, and which he reports to be all the correspondence he has had with the President on the subject.

I have had no correspondence with the President since the 12th of August last.

After the action of the Senate on his alleged reason for my suspension from the office of Secretary of War, I resumed the duties of that office, as required by the act of Congress, and have continued to discharge them without any personal or written communication with the President. No orders have been issued from this Department in the name of the President with my knowledge, and I have received no orders from him.

The correspondence sent herewith embraces all the correspondence known to me on the subject referred to in the resolution of the House of Representatives.

I have the honor to be, sir, with great respect, your obedient servant,

EDWIN M. STANTON,
Secretary of War.

General Grant to the President:

HEADQUARTERS ARMY OF THE UNITED STATES,
Washington, January 24, 1868.

His Excellency A. JOHNSON,
President of the United States.

SIR: I have the honor very respectfully to request to have in writing the order which the President gave me verbally on Sunday, the 19th instant, to disregard the orders of the Hon. E. M. Stanton as Secretary of War until I knew from the President himself that they were his orders.

I have the honor to be, very respectfully, your obedient servant,

U. S. GRANT, *General.*

General Grant to the President.

HEADQUARTERS ARMY OF THE UNITED STATES,
Washington, D. C., January 28, 1868.

His Excellency A. JOHNSON,
President of the United States.

SIR: On the 24th instant I requested you to give me in writing the instructions which you had previously given me verbally not to obey any order from Hon. E. M. Stanton, Secretary of War, unless I knew that it came from yourself. To this written request I received a message that has left doubt in my mind of your intentions. To prevent any possible misunderstanding, therefore, I renew the request that you will give me written instructions, and till they are received will suspend action on your verbal ones.

I am compelled to ask these instructions in writing in consequence of the many and gross misrepresentations affecting my personal honor circulated through the press for the last fortnight, purporting to come from the President, of conversations which occurred either with the President privately in his office or in Cabinet meeting. What is written admits of no misunderstanding.

In view of the misrepresentations referred to, it will be well to state the facts in the case.

Some time after I assumed the duties of Secretary of War *ad interim* the President asked me my views as to the course Mr. Stanton would have to pursue, in case the Senate should not concur in his suspension, to obtain possession of his office. My reply was, in substance, that Mr. Stanton would have to appeal to the courts to reinstate him, illustrating my position by citing the ground I had taken in the case of the Baltimore police commissioners.

In that case I did not doubt the technical right of Governor Swann to remove the old commissioners and to appoint their successors. As the old commissioners refused to give up, however, I contended that no resource was left but to appeal to the courts.

Finding that the President was desirous of keeping Mr. Stanton out of office, whether sustained in the suspension or not, I stated that I had not looked particularly into the tenure-of-office bill, but that what I had stated was a general principle, and if I should change my mind in this particular case I would inform him of the fact.

Subsequently, on reading the tenure-of-office bill closely, I found that I could not, without violation of the law, refuse to vacate the office of Secretary of War the moment Mr. Stanton was reinstated by the Senate, even though the President should order me to retain it, which he never did.

Taking this view of the subject, and learning on Saturday, the 11th instant, that the Senate had taken up the subject of Mr. Stanton's suspension, after some conversation with Lieutenant-General Sherman and some members of my staff, in which I stated that the law left me no discretion as to my action should Mr. Stanton be reinstated, and that I intended to inform the President, I went to the President for the sole purpose of making this decision known, and did so make it known.

In doing this I fulfilled the promise made in our last preceding conversation on the subject.

The President, however, instead of accepting my view of the requirements of the tenure-of-office bill, contended that he had suspended Mr. Stanton under the authority given by the Constitution, and that the same authority did not preclude him from reporting, as an act of courtesy, his reasons for the suspension to the Senate; that, having appointed me under the authority given by the Constitution, and not under any act of Congress, I could not be governed by the act. I stated that the law was binding on me, constitutional or not, until set aside by the proper tribunal. An hour or more was consumed, each reiterating his views on this subject, until, getting late, the President said he would see me again.

I did not agree to call again on Monday, nor at any other definite time, nor was I sent for by the President until the following Tuesday.

From the 11th to the Cabinet meeting on the 14th instant a doubt never entered my mind about the President's fully understanding my position, namely, that if the Senate refused to concur in the suspension of Mr. Stanton my powers as Secretary of War *ad interim* would cease and Mr. Stanton's right to resume at once the functions of his office would under the law be indisputable, and I acted accordingly. With Mr. Stanton I had no communication, direct nor indirect, on the subject of his reinstatement during his suspension.

I knew it had been recommended to the President to send in the name of Governor Cox, of Ohio, for Secretary of War, and thus save all embarrassment—a proposition that I sincerely hoped he would entertain favorably; General Sherman seeing the President at my particular request to urge this on the 13th instant.

On Tuesday (the day Mr. Stanton reentered the office of the Secretary of War) General Comstock, who had carried my official letter announcing that with Mr. Stanton's reinstatement by the Senate I had ceased to be Secretary of War *ad interim*, and who saw the President open and read the communication, brought back to me from the President a message that he wanted to see me that day at the Cabinet meeting, after I had made known the fact that I was no longer Secretary of War *ad interim*.

At this meeting, after opening it as though I were a member of the Cabinet, when reminded of the notification already given him that I was no longer Secretary of War *ad interim*, the President gave a version of the conversations alluded to already. In this statement it was asserted that in both conversations I had agreed to hold on to the office of Secretary of War until displaced by the courts, or resign, so as to place the President where he would have been had I never accepted the office. After hearing the President through, I stated our conversations substantially as given in this letter. I will add that my conversation before the Cabinet embraced other matter not pertinent here, and is therefore left out.

I in no wise admitted the correctness of the President's statement of our conversations, though, to soften the evident contradiction my statement gave, I said (alluding to our first conversation on the subject) the President might have understood
me the way he said, namely, that I had promised to resign if I did not resist the
reinstatement. I made no such promise.

I have the honor to be, very respectfully, your obedient servant,

U. S. GRANT, *General.*

HEADQUARTERS ARMY OF THE UNITED STATES,
January 30, 1868.

Respectfully forwarded to the Secretary of War for his information.

U. S. GRANT, *General.*

[Indorsement of the President on General Grant's note of January 24, 1868.*]

JANUARY 29, 1868.

As requested in this communication, General Grant is instructed in writing not
to obey any order from the War Department assumed to be issued by the direction of
the President unless such order is known by the General Commanding the armies
of the United States to have been authorized by the Executive.

ANDREW JOHNSON.

General Grant to the President.

HEADQUARTERS ARMY OF THE UNITED STATES,
Washington, January 30, 1868.

His Excellency A. JOHNSON,
President of the United States.

SIR: I have the honor to acknowledge the return of my note of the 24th instant,*
with your indorsement thereon, that I am not to obey any order from the War Department assumed to be issued by the direction of the President unless such order
is known by me to have been authorized by the Executive, and in reply thereto to
say that I am informed by the Secretary of War that he has not received from the
Executive any order or instructions limiting or impairing his authority to issue
orders to the Army, as has heretofore been his practice under the law and the customs of the Department. While this authority to the War Department is not countermanded it will be satisfactory evidence to me that any orders issued from the
War Department by direction of the President are authorized by the Executive.

I have the honor to be, very respectfully, your obedient servant,

U. S. GRANT, *General.*

HEADQUARTERS ARMY UNITED STATES,
January 30, 1868.

Respectfully forwarded to the Secretary of War for his information.

U. S. GRANT, *General.*

The President to General Grant.

EXECUTIVE MANSION, *January 31, 1868.*

General U. S. GRANT,
Commanding United States Armies.

GENERAL: I have received your communication of the 28th instant,† renewing your
request of the 24th,* that I should repeat in a written form my verbal instructions of

*See p. 613.   † See pp. 613–615.

the 19th instant, viz, that you obey no order from the Hon. Edwin M. Stanton as Secretary of War unless you have information that it was issued by the President's directions.

In submitting this request (with which I complied on the 29th instant*) you take occasion to allude to recent publications in reference to the circumstances connected with the vacation by yourself of the office of Secretary of War *ad interim*, and with the view of correcting statements which you term "gross misrepresentations" give at length your own recollection of the facts under which, without the sanction of the President, from whom you had received and accepted the appointment, you yielded the Department of War to the present incumbent.

As stated in your communication, some time after you had assumed the duties of Secretary of War *ad interim* we interchanged views respecting the course that should be pursued in the event of nonconcurrence by the Senate in the suspension from office of Mr. Stanton. I sought that interview, calling myself at the War Department. My sole object in then bringing the subject to your attention was to ascertain definitely what would be your own action should such an attempt be made for his restoration to the War Department. That object was accomplished, for the interview terminated with the distinct understanding that if upon reflection you should prefer not to become a party to the controversy or should conclude that it would be your duty to surrender the Department to Mr. Stanton upon action in his favor by the Senate you were to return the office to me prior to a decision by the Senate, in order that if I desired to do so I might designate someone to succeed you. It must have been apparent to you that had not this understanding been reached it was my purpose to relieve you from the further discharge of the duties of Secretary of War *ad interim* and to appoint some other person in that capacity.

Other conversations upon this subject ensued, all of them having on my part the same object and leading to the same conclusion as the first. It is not necessary, however, to refer to any of them excepting that of Saturday, the 11th instant, mentioned in your communication. As it was then known that the Senate had proceeded to consider the case of Mr. Stanton, I was anxious to learn your determination. After a protracted interview, during which the provisions of the tenure-of-office bill were freely discussed, you said that, as had been agreed upon in our first conference, you would either return the office to my possession in time to enable me to appoint a successor before final action by the Senate upon Mr. Stanton's suspension, or would remain as its head, awaiting a decision of the question by judicial proceedings. It was then understood that there would be a further conference on Monday, by which time I supposed you would be prepared to inform me of your final decision. You failed, however, to fulfill the engagement, and on Tuesday notified me in writing of the receipt by you of official notification of the action of the Senate in the case of Mr. Stanton, and at the same time informed me that according to the act regulating the tenure of certain civil offices your functions as Secretary of War *ad interim* ceased from the moment of the receipt of the notice. You thus, in disregard of the understanding between us, vacated the office without having given me notice of your intention to do so. It is but just, however, to say that in your communication you claim that you did inform me of your purpose, and thus "fulfilled the promise made in our last preceding conversation on this subject." The fact that such a promise existed is evidence of an arrangement of the kind I have mentioned. You had found in our first conference "that the President was desirous of keeping Mr. Stanton out of office whether sustained in the suspension or not." You knew what reasons had induced the President to ask from you a promise; you also knew that in case your views of duty did not accord with his own convictions it was his purpose to fill your place by another appointment. Even ignoring the existence of a positive understanding between us, these conclusions were plainly deducible from our various conversations. It is certain, however, that even under these circumstances you did not offer

*See p. 615.

to return the place to my possession, but, according to your own statement, placed yourself in a position where, could I have anticipated your action, I would have been compelled to ask of you, as I was compelled to ask of your predecessor in the War Department, a letter of resignation, or else to resort to the more disagreeable expedient of suspending you by a successor.

As stated in your letter, the nomination of Governor Cox, of Ohio, for the office of Secretary of War was suggested to me. His appointment as Mr. Stanton's successor was urged in your name, and it was said that his selection would save further embarrassment. I did not think that in the selection of a Cabinet officer I should be trammeled by such considerations. I was prepared to take the responsibility of deciding the question in accordance with my ideas of constitutional duty, and, having determined upon a course which I deemed right and proper, was anxious to learn the steps you would take should the possession of the War Department be demanded by Mr. Stanton. Had your action been in conformity to the understanding between us, I do not believe that the embarrassment would have attained its present proportions or that the probability of its repetition would have been so great.

I know that, with a view to an early termination of a state of affairs so detrimental to the public interests, you voluntarily offered, both on Wednesday, the 15th instant, and on the succeeding Sunday, to call upon Mr. Stanton and urge upon him that the good of the service required his resignation. I confess that I considered your proposal as a sort of reparation for the failure on your part to act in accordance with an understanding more than once repeated, which I thought had received your full assent, and under which you could have returned to me the office which I had conferred upon you, thus saving yourself from embarrassment and leaving the responsibility where it properly belonged—with the President, who is accountable for the faithful execution of the laws.

I have not yet been informed by you whether, as twice proposed by yourself, you have called upon Mr. Stanton and made an effort to induce him voluntarily to retire from the War Department.

You conclude your communication with a reference to our conversation at the meeting of the Cabinet held on Tuesday, the 14th instant. In your account of what then occurred you say that after the President had given his version of our previous conversations you stated them substantially as given in your letter; that you in no wise admitted the correctness of his statement of them, "though, to soften the evident contradiction my statement gave, I said (alluding to our first conversation on the subject) the President might have understood me the way he said, namely, that I had promised to resign if I did not resist the reinstatement. I made no such promise."

My recollection of what then transpired is diametrically the reverse of your narration. In the presence of the Cabinet I asked you—

First. If, in a conversation which took place shortly after your appointment as Secretary of War *ad interim*, you did not agree either to remain at the head of the War Department and abide any judicial proceedings that might follow nonconcurrence by the Senate in Mr. Stanton's suspension, or, should you wish not to become involved in such a controversy, to put me in the same position with respect to the office as I occupied previous to your appointment, by returning it to me in time to anticipate such action by the Senate. This you admitted.

Second. I then asked you if, at our conference on the preceding Saturday, I had not, to avoid misunderstanding, requested you to state what you intended to do, and, further, if in reply to that inquiry you had not referred to our former conversations, saying that from them I understood your position, and that your action would be consistent with the understanding which had been reached. To these questions you also replied in the affirmative.

Third. I next asked if at the conclusion of our interview on Saturday it was not understood that we were to have another conference on Monday before final action by the Senate in the case of Mr. Stanton. You replied that such was the under standing, but that you did not suppose the Senate would act so soon; that on Monday you had been engaged in a conference with General Sherman and were occupied with "many little matters," and asked if General Sherman had not called on that day. What relevancy General Sherman's visit to me on Monday had with the purpose for which you were then to have called I am at a loss to perceive, as he certainly did not inform me whether you had determined to retain possession of the office or to afford me an opportunity to appoint a successor in advance of any attempted reinstatement of Mr. Stanton.

This account of what passed between us at the Cabinet meeting on the 14th instant widely differs from that contained in your communication, for it shows that instead of having "stated our conversations as given in the letter" which has made this reply necessary you admitted that my recital of them was entirely accurate. Sincerely anxious, however, to be correct in my statements, I have to-day read this narration of what occurred on the 14th instant to the members of the Cabinet who were then present. They, without exception, agree in its accuracy.

It is only necessary to add that on Wednesday morning, the 15th instant, you called on me, in company with Lieutenant-General Sherman. After some preliminary conversation, you remarked that an article in the National Intelligencer of that date did you much injustice. I replied that I had not read the Intelligencer of that morning. You then first told me that it was your intention to urge Mr. Stanton to resign his office.

After you had withdrawn I carefully read the article of which you had spoken, and found that its statements of the understanding between us were substantially correct. On the 17th I caused it to be read to four of the five members of the Cabinet who were present at our conference on the 14th, and they concurred in the general accuracy of its statements respecting our conversation upon that occasion.

In reply to your communication, I have deemed it proper, in order to prevent further misunderstanding, to make this simple recital of facts.

Very respectfully, yours,

ANDREW JOHNSON.

General Grant to the President.

HEADQUARTERS ARMY OF THE UNITED STATES,
Washington, D. C., February 3, 1868.

His Excellency A. JOHNSON,
President of the United States.

SIR: I have the honor to acknowledge the receipt of your communication of the 31st ultimo,* in answer to mine of the 28th ultimo.† After a careful reading and comparison of it with the article in the National Intelligencer of the 15th ultimo and the article over the initials J. B. S. in the New York World of the 27th ultimo, purporting to be based upon your statement and that of the members of your Cabinet therein named, I find it to be but a reiteration, only somewhat more in detail, of the "many and gross misrepresentations" contained in these articles, and which my statement of the facts set forth in my letter of the 28th ultimo† was intended to correct; and I here reassert the correctness of my statements in that letter, anything in yours in reply to it to the contrary notwithstanding.

I confess my surprise that the Cabinet officers referred to should so greatly misapprehend the facts in the matter of admissions alleged to have been made by me at the Cabinet meeting of the 14th ultimo as to suffer their names to be made the

*See pp. 615–618.   †See pp. 613–615.

basis of the charges in the newspaper article referred to, or agree in the accuracy, as you affirm they do, of your account of what occurred at that meeting.

You know that we parted on Saturday, the 11th ultimo, without any promise on my part, either express or implied, to the effect that I would hold on to the office of Secretary of War *ad interim* against the action of the Senate, or, declining to do so myself, would surrender it to you before such action was had, or that I would see you again at any fixed time on the subject.

The performance of the promises alleged by you to have been made by me would have involved a resistance to law and an inconsistency with the whole history of my connection with the suspension of Mr. Stanton.

From our conversations and my written protest of August 1, 1867, against the removal of Mr. Stanton, you must have known that my greatest objection to his removal or suspension was the fear that someone would be appointed in his stead who would, by opposition to the laws relating to the restoration of the Southern States to their proper relations to the Government, embarrass the Army in the performance of duties especially imposed upon it by these laws; and it was to prevent such an appointment that I accepted the office of Secretary of War *ad interim*, and not for the purpose of enabling you to get rid of Mr. Stanton by my withholding it from him in opposition to law, or, not doing so myself, surrendering it to one who would, as the statement and assumptions in your communication plainly indicate was sought. And it was to avoid this same danger, as well as to relieve you from the personal embarrassment in which Mr. Stanton's reinstatement would place you, that I urged the appointment of Governor Cox, believing that it would be agreeable to you and also to Mr. Stanton, satisfied as I was that it was the good of the country, and not the office, the latter desired.

On the 15th ultimo, in presence of General Sherman, I stated to you that I thought Mr. Stanton would resign, but did not say that I would advise him to do so. On the 18th I did agree with General Sherman to go and advise him to that course, and on the 19th I had an interview alone with Mr. Stanton, which led me to the conclusion that any advice to him of the kind would be useless, and I so informed General Sherman.

Before I consented to advise Mr. Stanton to resign, I understood from him, in a conversation on the subject immediately after his reinstatement, that it was his opinion that the act of Congress entitled "An act temporarily to supply vacancies in the Executive Departments in certain cases," approved February 20, 1863, was repealed by subsequent legislation, which materially influenced my action. Previous to this time I had had no doubt that the law of 1863 was still in force, and, notwithstanding my action, a fuller examination of the law leaves a question in my mind whether it is or is not repealed. This being the case, I could not now advise his resignation, lest the same danger I apprehended on his first removal might follow.

The course you would have it understood I agreed to pursue was in violation of law and without orders from you, while the course I did pursue, and which I never doubted you fully understood, was in accordance with law and not in disobedience of any orders of my superior.

And now, Mr. President, when my honor as a soldier and integrity as a man have been so violently assailed, pardon me for saying that I can but regard this whole matter, from the beginning to the end, as an attempt to involve me in the resistance of law, for which you hesitated to assume the responsibility in orders, and thus to destroy my character before the country. I am in a measure confirmed in this conclusion by your recent orders directing me to disobey orders from the Secretary of War, my superior and your subordinate, without having countermanded his authority to issue the orders I am to disobey.

With the assurance, Mr. President, that nothing less than a vindication of my personal honor and character could have induced this correspondence on my part,

I have the honor to be, very respectfully, your obedient servant,

U. S. GRANT, *General.*

Respectfully forwarded to the Secretary of War for his information, and to be made a part of correspondence previously furnished on same subject.

U. S. GRANT, *General.*

WASHINGTON, *February 17, 1868.*

To the House of Representatives of the United States:

In reply to the resolution adopted by the House of Representatives on the 19th of December last, calling for correspondence and information in relation to Russian America, I transmit reports and accompanying documents from the Secretary of State and the Secretary of the Treasury, respectively.

ANDREW JOHNSON.

WASHINGTON, *February 18, 1868.*

To the House of Representatives of the United States:

In answer to a resolution of the House of Representatives of the 17th of January last, calling for information in regard to the execution of the treaty of 1858 with China, for the settlement of claims, I transmit a report of the Secretary of State and the papers which accompany it.

ANDREW JOHNSON.

WASHINGTON, D. C., *February 19, 1868.*

To the House of Representatives:

I transmit herewith a report from the Attorney-General, prepared in compliance with the resolution of the House of Representatives of the 26th November, 1867, requesting a list of all pardons ''granted since the 14th day of April, 1865, to any person or persons charged with or convicted of making or passing counterfeit money, or having counterfeit money or tools or instruments for making the same in his or their possession, or charged with or convicted of the crime of forgery or criminal alteration of papers, accounts, or other documents, or of the crime of perjury, and that such list be accompanied by a particular statement in each case of the reasons or grounds of the pardon, with a disclosure of the names of persons, if any, who recommended or advised the same.''

ANDREW JOHNSON.

WASHINGTON, D. C., *February 19, 1868.*

To the Senate of the United States:

I transmit herewith a report from the Attorney-General, prepared in compliance with a resolution adopted by the Senate on the 2d day of December last, requesting ''a full list of the names of all persons pardoned by the President since May 1, 1865, who have been convicted of counterfeiting United States bonds, greenbacks, national-bank currency, fractional currency, or the coin of the United States, with the date of issuing each pardon, reasons for issuing it, and by whom recommended.''

ANDREW JOHNSON.

WASHINGTON, *February 20, 1868.*

To the Senate of the United States:

In answer to a resolution of the Senate of the 18th of December last, requesting information in regard to the island of San Juan, on Puget Sound, I transmit a report from the Secretary of State and the papers which accompanied it.

ANDREW JOHNSON.

WASHINGTON, *February 20, 1868.*

To the Senate of the United States:

With reference to the convention between Denmark and the United States concluded on the 24th of October last, I transmit to the Senate a copy in translation of a note of the 19th instant addressed to the Secretary of State by His Danish Majesty's chargé d'affaires, announcing the ratification of the convention by the Government of Denmark and stating his readiness to proceed with the customary exchange of ratifications.

ANDREW JOHNSON.

WASHINGTON, *February 21, 1868.*

To the House of Representatives of the United States:

I transmit herewith a communication from the Chief of the Engineer Corps of the Army, accompanied by a report, in reference to ship canals around the Falls of the Ohio River, called for by the resolution of the House of Representatives of the 18th instant.

ANDREW JOHNSON.

WASHINGTON, D. C., *February 21, 1868.*

To the Senate of the United States:

On the 12th day of August, 1867, by virtue of the power and authority vested in the President by the Constitution and laws of the United States, I suspended Edwin M. Stanton from the office of Secretary of War.

In further exercise of the power and authority so vested in the President, I have this day removed Mr. Stanton from office and designated the Adjutant-General of the Army to act as Secretary of War *ad interim*.

Copies of the communications upon this subject addressed to Mr. Stanton and the Adjutant-General are herewith transmitted for the information of the Senate.

ANDREW JOHNSON.

WASHINGTON, D. C., *February 22, 1868.*

To the Senate of the United States:

I have received a copy of the resolution adopted by the Senate on the 21st instant, as follows:

Whereas the Senate have received and considered the communication of the President stating that he had removed Edwin M. Stanton, Secretary of War, and had designated the Adjutant-General of the Army to act as Secretary of War *ad interim:* Therefore,

Resolved by the Senate of the United States, That under the Constitution and laws of the United States the President has no power to remove the Secretary of War and designate any other officer to perform the duties of that office *ad interim.*

This resolution is confined to the power of the President to remove the Secretary of War and to designate another officer to perform the duties of the office *ad interim*, and by its preamble is made expressly applicable to the removal of Mr. Stanton and the designation to act *ad interim* of the Adjutant-General of the Army. Without, therefore, attempting to discuss the general power of removal as to all officers, upon which subject no expression of opinion is contained in the resolution, I shall confine myself to the question as thus limited—the power to remove the Secretary of War.

It is declared in the resolution—

That under the Constitution and laws of the United States the President has no power to remove the Secretary of War and designate any other officer to perform the duties of that office *ad interim.*

As to the question of power under the Constitution, I do not propose at present to enter upon its discussion.

The uniform practice from the beginning of the Government, as established by every President who has exercised the office, and the decisions of the Supreme Court of the United States have settled the question in favor of the power of the President to remove all officers excepting a class holding appointments of a judicial character. No practice nor any decision has ever excepted a Secretary of War from this general power of the President to make removals from office.

It is only necessary, then, that I should refer to the power of the Executive, under the laws of the United States, to remove from office a Secretary of War. The resolution denies that under these laws this power has any existence. In other words, it affirms that no such authority is recognized or given by the statutes of the country.

What, then, are the laws of the United States which deny the President the power to remove that officer? I know but two laws which bear upon this question. The first in order of time is the act of August 7, 1789, creating the Department of War, which, after providing for a Secretary as its principal officer, proceeds as follows:

SEC. 2. *And be it further enacted,* That there shall be in the said Department an inferior officer, to be appointed by the said principal officer, to be employed therein as he shall deem proper, and to be called the chief clerk in the Department of War, and who, whenever the said principal officer shall be removed from office by the President of the United States, or in any other case of vacancy, shall during such vacancy have the charge and custody of all records, books, and papers appertaining to the said Department.

It is clear that this act, passed by a Congress many of whose members participated in the formation of the Constitution, so far from denying the power of the President to remove the Secretary of War, recognizes it as existing in the Executive alone, without the concurrence of the Senate or of any other department of the Government. Furthermore, this act does not purport to confer the power by legislative authority, nor in fact was there any other existing legislation through which it was bestowed upon the Executive. The recognition of the power by this act is therefore complete as a recognition under the Constitution itself, for there was no other source or authority from which it could be derived.

The other act which refers to this question is that regulating the tenure of certain civil offices, passed by Congress on the 2d day of March, 1867. The first section of that act is in the following words:

That every person holding any civil office to which he has been appointed by and with the advice and consent of the Senate, and every person who shall hereafter be appointed to any such office, and shall become duly qualified to act therein, is and shall be entitled to hold such office until a successor shall have been in like manner appointed and duly qualified, except as herein otherwise provided: *Provided*, That the Secretaries of State, of the Treasury, of War, of the Navy, and of the Interior, the Postmaster-General, and the Attorney-General shall hold their offices, respectively, for and during the term of the President by whom they may have been appointed and for one month thereafter, subject to removal by and with the advice and consent of the Senate.

The fourth section of the same act restricts the term of offices to the limit prescribed by the law creating them.

That part of the first section which precedes the proviso declares that every person holding a civil office to which he has been or may be appointed by and with the advice and consent of the Senate shall hold such office until a successor shall have been in like manner appointed. It purports to take from the Executive, during the fixed time established for the tenure of the office, the independent power of removal, and to require for such removal the concurrent action of the President and the Senate.

The proviso that follows proceeds to fix the term of office of the seven heads of Departments, whose tenure never had been defined before, by prescribing that they "shall hold their offices, respectively, for and during the term of the President by whom they may have been appointed and for one month thereafter, subject to removal by and with the advice and consent of the Senate."

Thus, as to these enumerated officers, the proviso takes from the President the power of removal except with the advice and consent of the Senate. By its terms, however, before he can be deprived of the power to displace them it must appear that he himself has appointed them. It is only in that case that they have any tenure of office or any independent right to hold during the term of the President and for one month after the cessation of his official functions. The proviso, therefore, gives no tenure of office to any one of these officers who has been appointed by a former President beyond one month after the accession of his successor.

In the case of Mr. Stanton, the only appointment under which he held the office of Secretary of War was that conferred upon him by my immediate predecessor, with the advice and consent of the Senate. He has never held from me any appointment as the head of the War Department. Whatever right he had to hold the office was derived from that original appointment and my own sufferance. The law was not intended to protect such an incumbent of the War Department by taking from the President the power to remove him. This, in my judgment, is perfectly clear, and the law itself admits of no other just construction. We find in all that portion of the first section which precedes the proviso that as to civil officers generally the President is deprived of the power of removal, and it is plain that if there had been no proviso that power would just as clearly have been taken from him so far as it applies to the seven heads of Departments. But for reasons which were no doubt satisfactory to Congress these principal officers were specially provided for, and as to them the express and only requirement is that the President who has appointed them shall not without the advice and consent of the Senate remove them from office. The consequence is that as to my Cabinet, embracing the seven officers designated in the first section, the act takes from me the power, without the concurrence of the Senate, to remove any one of them that I have appointed, but it does not protect such of them as I did not appoint, nor give to them any tenure of office beyond my pleasure.

An examination of this act, then, shows that while in one part of the section provision is made for officers generally, in another clause there is a class of officers, designated by their official titles, who are excepted from the general terms of the law, and in reference to whom a clear distinction is made as to the general power of removal limited in the first clause of the section.

This distinction is that as to such of these enumerated officers as hold under the appointment of the President the power of removal can only be exercised by him with the consent of the Senate, while as to those who have not been appointed by him there is no like denial of his power to displace them. It would be a violation of the plain meaning of this enactment to place Mr. Stanton upon the same footing as those heads of Departments who have been appointed by myself. As to him, this law gives him no tenure of office. The members of my Cabinet who have been appointed by me are by this act entitled to hold for one month after the term of my office shall cease; but Mr. Stanton could not, against the wishes of my successor, hold a moment thereafter. If he were permitted by that successor to hold for the first two weeks, would that successor have no power to remove him? But the power of my successor over him could be no greater than my own. If my successor would have the power to remove Mr. Stanton after permitting him to remain a period of two weeks, because he was not appointed by him, but by his predecessor, I, who have tolerated Mr. Stanton for more than two years, certainly have the same right to remove him, and upon the same ground, namely, that he was not appointed by me, but by my predecessor.

Under this construction of the tenure-of-office act, I have never doubted my power to remove Mr. Stanton.

Whether the act were constitutional or not, it was always my opinion that it did not secure him from removal. I was, however, aware that there were doubts as to the construction of the law, and from the first I deemed it desirable that at the earliest possible moment those doubts should be settled and the true construction of the act fixed by decision of the Supreme Court of the United States. My order of suspension in August last was intended to place the case in such a position as would make a resort to a judicial decision both necessary and proper. My understanding and wishes, however, under that order of suspension were frustrated, and the late order for Mr. Stanton's removal was a further step toward the accomplishment of that purpose.

I repeat that my own convictions as to the true construction of the law and as to its constitutionality were well settled and were sustained by every member of my Cabinet, including Mr. Stanton himself. Upon the question of constitutionality, each one in turn deliberately advised me that the tenure-of-office act was unconstitutional. Upon the question whether, as to those members who were appointed by my predecessor, that act took from me the power to remove them, one of those members emphatically stated in the presence of the others sitting in Cabinet that they did not come within the provisions of the act, and it was no protection to them. No one dissented from this construction, and I understood them all to acquiesce in its correctness. In a matter of such grave consequence I was not disposed to rest upon my own opinions, though fortified by my constitutional advisers. I have therefore sought to bring the question at as early a day as possible before the Supreme Court of the United States for final and authoritative decision.

In respect to so much of the resolution as relates to the designation of an officer to act as Secretary of War *ad interim*, I have only to say that I have exercised this power under the provisions of the first section of the act of February 13, 1795, which, so far as they are applicable to vacancies caused by removals, I understand to be still in force.

The legislation upon the subject of *ad interim* appointments in the Executive Departments stands, as to the War Office, as follows:

The second section of the act of the 7th of August, 1789, makes provision for a vacancy in the very case of a removal of the head of the War

Department, and upon such a vacancy gives the charge and custody of the records, books, and papers to the chief clerk.   Next, by the act of the 8th of May, 1792, section 8, it is provided that in case of a vacancy occasioned by death, absence from the seat of Government, or sickness of the head of the War Department the President may authorize a person to perform the duties of the office until a successor is appointed or the disability removed.   The act, it will be observed, does not provide for the case of a vacancy caused by removal.   Then, by the first section of the act of February 13, 1795, it is provided that in case of any vacancy the President may appoint a person to perform the duties while the vacancy exists.

These acts are followed by that of the 20th of February, 1863, by the first section of which provision is again made for a vacancy caused by death, resignation, absence from the seat of Government, or sickness of the head of any Executive Department of the Government, and upon the occurrence of such a vacancy power is given to the President—

to authorize the head of any other Executive Department, or other officer in either of said Departments whose appointment is vested in the President, at his discretion, to perform the duties of the said respective offices until a successor be appointed or until such absence or inability by sickness shall cease: *Provided*, That no one vacancy shall be supplied in manner aforesaid for a longer term than six months.

This law, with some modifications, reenacts the act of 1792, and provides, as did that act, for the sort of vacancies so to be filled; but, like the act of 1792, it makes no provision for a vacancy occasioned by removal.   It has reference altogether to vacancies arising from other causes.

According to my construction of the act of 1863, while it impliedly repeals the act of 1792 regulating the vacancies therein described, it has no bearing whatever upon so much of the act of 1795 as applies to a vacancy caused by removal.   The act of 1795 therefore furnishes the rule for a vacancy occasioned by removal—one of the vacancies expressly referred to in the act of the 7th of August, 1789, creating the Department of War.   Certainly there is no express repeal by the act of 1863 of the act of 1795.   The repeal, if there is any, is by implication, and can only be admitted so far as there is a clear inconsistency between the two acts. The act of 1795 is inconsistent with that of 1863 as to a vacancy occasioned by death, resignation, absence, or sickness, but not at all inconsistent as to a vacancy caused by removal.

It is assuredly proper that the President should have the same power to fill temporarily a vacancy occasioned by removal as he has to supply a place made vacant by death or the expiration of a term.   If, for instance, the incumbent of an office should be found to be wholly unfit to exercise its functions, and the public service should require his immediate expulsion, a remedy should exist and be at once applied, and time be allowed the President to select and appoint a successor, as is permitted him in case of a vacancy caused by death or the termination of an official term.

The necessity, therefore, for an *ad interim* appointment is just as great, and, indeed, may be greater in cases of removal than in any others. Before it be held, therefore, that the power given by the act of 1795 in cases of removal is abrogated by succeeding legislation an express repeal ought to appear. So wholesome a power should certainly not be taken away by loose implication.

It may be, however, that in this, as in other cases of implied repeal, doubts may arise. It is confessedly one of the most subtle and debatable questions which arise in the construction of statutes. If upon such a question I have fallen into an erroneous construction, I submit whether it should be characterized as a violation of official duty and of law.

I have deemed it proper, in vindication of the course which I have considered it my duty to take, to place before the Senate the reasons upon which I have based my action. Although I have been advised by every member of my Cabinet that the entire tenure-of-office act is unconstitutional, and therefore void, and although I have expressly concurred in that opinion in the veto message which I had the honor to submit to Congress when I returned the bill for reconsideration, I have refrained from making a removal of any officer contrary to the provisions of the law, and have only exercised that power in the case of Mr. Stanton, which, in my judgment, did not come within its provisions. I have endeavored to proceed with the greatest circumspection, and have acted only in an extreme and exceptional case, carefully following the course which I have marked out for myself as a general rule, faithfully to execute all laws, though passed over my objections on the score of constitutionality. In the present instance I have appealed, or sought to appeal, to that final arbiter fixed by the Constitution for the determination of all such questions. To this course I have been impelled by the solemn obligations which rest upon me to sustain inviolate the powers of the high office committed to my hands.

Whatever may be the consequences merely personal to myself, I could not allow them to prevail against a public duty so clear to my own mind, and so imperative. If what was possible had been certain, if I had been fully advised when I removed Mr. Stanton that in thus defending the trust committed to my hands my own removal was sure to follow, I could not have hesitated. Actuated by public considerations of the highest character, I earnestly protest against the resolution of the Senate which charges me in what I have done with a violation of the Constitution and laws of the United States.

ANDREW JOHNSON.

WASHINGTON, *February 25, 1868.*

To the Senate of the United States:

In further answer of the resolution of the Senate of the 13th of January last, relative to the appointment of the Hon. Anson Burlingame to a diplomatic or other mission by the Emperor of China, I transmit a report from the Secretary of State and the communication which accompanied it.

ANDREW JOHNSON.

WASHINGTON, D. C., *February 26, 1868.*

To the Senate of the United States:

I transmit herewith a report from the General Commanding the Army of the United States, prepared in compliance with the resolution of the Senate of the 4th instant, requesting copies of all instructions relating to the Third Military District issued to General Pope and General Meade.

ANDREW JOHNSON.

WASHINGTON, *March 4, 1868.*

To the Senate of the United States:

In answer to the resolution of the Senate of the 17th February ultimo, concerning the alleged interference of the United States consul at Rome in the late difficulty in Italy, I transmit a report from the Secretary of State, containing the information called for by the resolution.

ANDREW JOHNSON.

WASHINGTON, *March 5, 1868.*

To the Senate of the United States:

I transmit a report of this date from the Secretary of State, and the accompanying papers, in regard to the revolution in the Dominican Republic.

ANDREW JOHNSON.

WASHINGTON, *March 5, 1868.*

To the Senate of the United States:

In answer to the resolution of the Senate of the 21st of February last, in relation to the abduction of one Allan Macdonald from Canada, I transmit a communication from the Secretary of State, accompanied by the papers relating to that subject.

ANDREW JOHNSON.

WASHINGTON, *March 5, 1868.*

To the House of Representatives of the United States:

In answer to the resolution of the House of Representatives of the 7th of January last, in relation to the claim of the late Benjamin W. Perkins against the Russian Government, I transmit a communication from the Secretary of State, which is accompanied by the papers called for by the resolution.

ANDREW JOHNSON.

WASHINGTON, *March 6, 1868.*

To the Senate of the United States:

I transmit to the Senate the accompanying report * of the Secretary of State, in answer to their resolution of the 13th January.

ANDREW JOHNSON.

WASHINGTON, *March 10, 1868.*

To the Senate of the United States:

I transmit, for the consideration of the Senate with a view to ratification, a treaty between the United States and His Majesty the King of Prussia, in the name of the North German Confederation, for the purpose of regulating the citizenship of those persons who emigrate from the Confederation to this country and from the United States to the North German Confederation.

ANDREW JOHNSON.

WASHINGTON, *March 11, 1868.*

To the House of Representatives:

In further answer to the resolution of the House of Representatives of the 25th of November, 1867, calling for information in relation to the trial and conviction of American citizens in Great Britain and Ireland for the last two years, I transmit a continuation of the report from the Secretary of State upon the subject.

ANDREW JOHNSON.

WASHINGTON, *March 14, 1868.*

To the Senate of the United States:

In answer to the resolution of the Senate of the 27th of January last, in relation to the arrest and trial of the Rev. John McMahon, Robert B. Lynch, and John Warren by the Government of Great Britain, and requesting to be informed what action has been taken by this Government in maintaining the rights of American citizens abroad, I transmit a report of the Secretary of State, which is accompanied by a copy of the papers called for by that resolution.

ANDREW JOHNSON.

WASHINGTON, D. C., *March 18, 1868.*

To the Senate of the United States:

I herewith lay before the Senate, for its constitutional action thereon, a treaty made on the 2d day of March, 1868, by and between Nathaniel G. Taylor, Commissioner of Indian Affairs; Alexander C. Hunt, governor and *ex officio* superintendent of Indian affairs of Colorado Territory, and Kit Carson, on the part of the United States, and the representatives of

---

*Relating to a claim, under the act of Congress of August 18, 1856, of citizens of the United States to guano on Alta Vela, an island in the vicinity of Santo Domingo.

the Tabeguache, Muache, Capote, Weeminuche, Yampa, Grand River, and Uintah bands of Ute Indians.

A letter of the Secretary of the Interior of the 17th instant and the papers therein referred to are also herewith transmitted.

ANDREW JOHNSON.

WASHINGTON, *March 24, 1868.*

To the Senate of the United States:

I transmit to the Senate, for its consideration with a view to ratification, a convention, signed on the 23d instant, for the surrender of criminals, between the United States and the Government of Italy.

ANDREW JOHNSON.

WASHINGTON, *March 24, 1868.*

To the House of Representatives:

I transmit herewith a report* and accompanying documents, in answer to a resolution of the House of Representatives of the 18th ultimo.

ANDREW JOHNSON.

WASHINGTON, *March 25, 1868.*

To the House of Representatives:

I transmit to the House of Representatives, in answer to a resolution of the 9th instant, the accompanying report † from the Secretary of State.

ANDREW JOHNSON.

WASHINGTON, *March 25, 1868.*

To the House of Representatives:

I transmit herewith a report and accompanying document,‡ in answer to a resolution of the House of Representatives of the 11th ultimo.

ANDREW JOHNSON.

WASHINGTON, *March 25, 1868.*

To the House of Representatives of the United States:

In answer to a resolution of the House of Representatives of the 18th ultimo, relating to the report of Mr. Cowdin, I transmit a report of the Secretary of State and the document§ to which it refers.

ANDREW JOHNSON.

---

*Relating to unexpended appropriations for contingent expenses of foreign intercourse; amount remaining on deposit with Baring Brothers & Co. September 30, 1867, etc.

†Declining to transmit copies of correspondence, negotiations, and treaties with German States since January 1, 1868, relative to the rights of naturalized citizens.

‡Statement of amounts paid for legal services by the Department of State during each year since 1860, with names of persons to whom paid.

§Report of Elliot C. Cowdin, United States commissioner to the Paris Exposition of 1867, on silk and silk manufactures.

WASHINGTON, *April 2, 1868.*

To the House of Representatives:

I transmit to the House of Representatives, in further answer to their resolution of the 9th ultimo, the accompanying report* from the Secretary of State.

ANDREW JOHNSON.

WASHINGTON, *April 2, 1868.*

To the House of Representatives:

In further reply to the resolution adopted by the House of Representatives on the 19th of December, 1867, calling for correspondence and information in relation to Russian America, I transmit a report from the Secretary of State and the papers which accompanied it.

ANDREW JOHNSON.

WASHINGTON, *April 3, 1868.*

To the House of Representatives:

I transmit a report from the Secretary of State and the papers accompanying it, in answer to a resolution of the House of Representatives of the 10th of February last, requesting information relative to the imprisonment and destruction of the property of Antonio Pelletier by the people and authorities of Hayti.

ANDREW JOHNSON.

WASHINGTON, *April 13, 1868.*

To the Senate of the United States:

In answer to the resolution of the Senate of the 5th of February last, calling for the correspondence upon the subject of the murder by the inhabitants of the island of Formosa of the ship's company of the American bark *Rover*, I transmit a report from the Secretary of State and a report from the Secretary of the Navy, with accompanying papers.

ANDREW JOHNSON.

WASHINGTON, *April 18, 1868.*

To the Senate of the United States:

In answer to the resolution of the Senate of the 14th of April instant, calling for information relative to any application by any party for exclusive privileges in connection with hunting, trading, and the fisheries in Alaska, I transmit herewith the report of the Secretary of State on the subject, with its accompanying papers.

ANDREW JOHNSON.

---

*Transmitting correspondence pertaining to the convention of February 22, 1868, with the North German Confederation, relative to naturalization.

WASHINGTON, D. C., *April 22, 1868.*

To the Senate of the United States:

In compliance with the resolution of the Senate of the 28th ultimo, requesting information as to the number and designations of military departments formed since the 1st day of August, 1867, and as to the statute or other authority under which they have been established, I transmit a report from the Adjutant-General's Office showing the organization since that date of the Department of Alaska and the Military Division of the Atlantic.

The orders issued by me upon this subject are in accordance with long-established usage and hitherto unquestioned authority. This will be readily seen from the accompanying report, which shows that, employing the authority vested by the Constitution in the President as Commander in Chief of the Army, it has been customary for my predecessors to create such military divisions and departments as from time to time they deemed advisable.

ANDREW JOHNSON.

WASHINGTON, *April 27, 1868.*

To the Senate and House of Representatives:

I submit a report of the Secretary of State, concerning the naturalization treaty recently negotiated between the United States and North Germany.

ANDREW JOHNSON.

WASHINGTON, D. C., *May 5, 1868.*

To the Senate and House of Representatives:

I transmit to Congress the accompanying documents, which I deem it proper to state are all the papers* that have been submitted to the President relating to the proceedings to which they refer in the States of South Carolina and Arkansas.

ANDREW JOHNSON.

WASHINGTON, *May 6, 1868.*

To the Senate of the United States:

I transmit to the Senate, in further answer to their resolution of the 14th of April last, the accompanying report† from the Secretary of State.

ANDREW JOHNSON.

WASHINGTON, D. C., *May 8, 1868.*

To the House of Representatives:

I transmit herewith reports from the Secretary of the Treasury and the Secretary of the Navy, prepared in compliance with a resolution

---

*Constitutions of South Carolina and Arkansas.

†Relating to application for exclusive privileges in connection with hunting, trading, and the fisheries in Alaska.

of the House of Representatives of the 12th of December last, requesting information respecting the sale of public vessels since the close of the rebellion. No report upon the subject has yet been received from the Department of War.

ANDREW JOHNSON.

WASHINGTON, *May 9, 1868.*

To the House of Representatives:

I transmit to the House of Representatives, in answer to their resolution of the 14th ultimo, a report from the Secretary of State, with accompanying papers.*

ANDREW JOHNSON.

WASHINGTON, *May 9, 1868.*

To the Senate of the United States:

I transmit herewith reports from the Secretary of the Treasury and the Attorney-General, prepared in compliance with the resolution of the Senate of the 17th December last, requesting information in reference to the seizure and confiscation of property. No report upon this subject has yet been received by me from the War Department.

ANDREW JOHNSON.

WASHINGTON, D. C.,
May 11, 1868.

To the Senate and House of Representatives:

I transmit to Congress the accompanying documents,† which embrace all the papers that have been submitted to me relating to the proceedings to which they refer in the States of North Carolina and Louisiana.

ANDREW JOHNSON.

WASHINGTON, *May 15, 1868.*

To the House of Representatives:

I transmit to the House of Representatives, in answer to their resolution of the 8th instant, a report ‡ from the Secretary of State, with accompanying papers.

ANDREW JOHNSON.

* Report of Freeman H. Morse, United States consul at London, on " The Foreign Maritime Commerce of the United States: Its Past, Present, and Future," etc.

† Constitutions of North Carolina and Louisiana.

‡ Relating to the detention, at the request of the House of Representatives, of the ironclad monitors *Oneoto* and *Catawba*, purchased from the United States by Swift & Co., and supposed to be intended for the Government of Peru, then at war with a power friendly to the United States.

WASHINGTON, D. C., *May 18, 1868.*

To the Senate and House of Representatives:

I transmit to Congress the accompanying document,* which is the only paper which has been submitted to me relating to the proceedings to which it refers in the State of Georgia.

ANDREW JOHNSON.

WASHINGTON, *May 23, 1868.*

To the Senate of the United States:

I transmit to the Senate a report from the Secretary of State, with accompaniments, in relation to recent events in the Empire of Japan.

ANDREW JOHNSON.

WASHINGTON, D. C., *May 27, 1868.*

To the Senate and House of Representatives:

I transmit to Congress the accompanying documents,† which are the only papers which have been submitted to me relating to the proceedings to which they refer in the State of Florida.

ANDREW JOHNSON.

WASHINGTON, *May 29, 1868.*

To the House of Representatives:

I transmit herewith a letter from the Secretary of the Navy, in reply to the resolution of the House of Representatives adopted on the 26th instant, making inquiries relative to a naval force at Hayti.

ANDREW JOHNSON.

WASHINGTON, *June 2, 1868.*

To the Senate of the United States:

I communicate, for the information of the Senate, in confidence, a report of the Secretary of State, accompanied by a copy of a dispatch recently received from the acting consul of the United States at San Jose, Costa Rica.

ANDREW JOHNSON.

WASHINGTON, *June 2, 1868.*

To the Senate of the United States:

I communicate, for the consideration of the Senate, a report from the Secretary of State, accompanied by a copy of a dispatch recently received from the acting United States consul in charge of the legation at San Jose, Costa Rica.

ANDREW JOHNSON.

---

* Constitution of Georgia.

† Letter from the president of the constitutional convention of Florida, transmitting a copy of the constitution of that State.

WASHINGTON, *June 5, 1868.*

To the House of Representatives:

In further answer to the resolution of the House of Representatives of the 25th of November, 1867, calling for information in relation to the trial and conviction of American citizens in Great Britain and Ireland for the last two years, I transmit the accompanying report from the Secretary of State upon the subject.

ANDREW JOHNSON.

WASHINGTON, *June 8, 1868.*

To the Senate of the United States:

In compliance with the resolution of the Senate of the 28th ultimo, I transmit herewith a communication from the Postmaster-General, with a copy of the correspondence recently had with the authorities of Great Britain in relation to a new postal treaty.

ANDREW JOHNSON.

WASHINGTON, D. C., *June 10, 1868.*

To the House of Representatives:

In reply to the resolution of the House of Representatives of the 1st instant, I transmit herewith a report from the Secretary of the Interior, in reference to a treaty now being negotiated between the Great and Little Osage Indians and the special Indian commissioners acting on the part of the United States.

ANDREW JOHNSON.

WASHINGTON, D. C., *June 13, 1868.*

To the Senate of the United States:

I herewith submit to the Senate, for its constitutional action thereon, a treaty concluded on the 27th ultimo between commissioners on the part of the United States and the Great and Little Osage tribe of Indians of Kansas, together with a communication from the Secretary of the Interior suggesting an amendment to the fourteenth article, and a copy of the report of the commissioners.

ANDREW JOHNSON.

WASHINGTON, D. C., *June 15, 1868.*

To the House of Representatives:

I transmit herewith a report from the Secretary of the Interior, made in reply to the resolution adopted by the House of Representatives on the 13th instant.

The treaty recently concluded with the Great and Little Osage Indians, to which the accompanying report refers, was submitted to the Senate prior to the receipt of the resolution of the House upon the subject.

ANDREW JOHNSON.

WASHINGTON, *June 19, 1868.*

To the Senate of the United States:

I transmit to the Senate, for its consideration with a view to its ratification, a treaty between the United States and His Majesty the King of Bavaria, signed at Munich on the 26th ultimo, concerning the citizenship of persons emigrating from Bavaria to the United States and from the United States to the Kingdom of Bavaria. I transmit also a copy of the letter of the United States minister communicating the treaty, of the protocol which accompanied it, and a translation of the Bavarian military law referred to in the latter paper.

ANDREW JOHNSON.

WASHINGTON, D. C., *June 20, 1868.*

To the Senate of the United States:

I herewith transmit to the Senate, for its constitutional action thereon, a treaty concluded at Fort Sumner, N. Mex., on the 1st instant, between Lieutenant-General W. T. Sherman and Colonel Samuel F. Tappan, on the part of the United States, and the chiefs and headmen of the Navajo Indians, on the part of the latter. I also transmit a communication upon the subject from the Secretary of the Interior, with the accompanying papers.

ANDREW JOHNSON.

WASHINGTON, *June 22, 1868.*

To the Senate of the United States:

I transmit to the Senate, in answer to their resolution of the 28th ultimo, a report from the Secretary of State, with accompanying papers.*

ANDREW JOHNSON.

WASHINGTON, *June 23, 1868.*

To the House of Representatives:

I transmit a report from the Secretary of State, in answer to a resolution of the House of Representatives of the 15th instant, upon the subject of Messrs. Warren and Costello, who have been convicted and sentenced to penal imprisonment in Great Britain.

ANDREW JOHNSON.

WASHINGTON, *June 23, 1868.*

To the Senate of the United States:

I transmit to the Senate a copy of a dispatch addressed to the Department of State by the consul of the United States at Bangkok, Siam, dated

---

* Correspondence relative to the act of Congress of March 27, 1867, prohibiting persons in the diplomatic service of the United States from wearing any uniform or official costume not previously authorized by Congress.

December 31, 1867, with a view to its consideration and the ratification thereof, of the modification proposed by the royal counselors of the Kingdom of Siam in Article I of the general regulations which form a part of the treaty between the United States and that Kingdom concluded May 29, 1856, of which a printed copy is also herewith transmitted.

ANDREW JOHNSON.

WASHINGTON, *June 29, 1868.*

To the Senate and House of Representatives:

I transmit to Congress a copy of a dispatch from the United States consul at Elsinore, and of an instruction from the Secretary of State to the United States minister at Copenhagen, relative to an alleged practice of the Danish authorities to banish convicts to this country. The expediency of making it a penal offense to bring such persons to the United States is submitted to your consideration.

ANDREW JOHNSON.

To the House of Representatives: WASHINGTON, *July 2, 1868.*

I transmit herewith a report from the Secretary of State of the 2d instant, together with accompanying papers.*

ANDREW JOHNSON.

WASHINGTON, D. C., *July 7, 1868.*

To the Senate of the United States:

I herewith lay before the Senate, for its constitutional action thereon, a treaty concluded at Fort Laramie, Dakota Territory, on the 7th of May, 1868, between the United States and the chiefs and headmen of the Crow Indians of Montana, and a treaty concluded at Fort Laramie, Dakota Territory, on the 10th of May, 1868, between the United States and the chiefs and headmen of the Northern Cheyenne and Northern Arapahoe tribes of Indians.

A letter from the Secretary of the Interior suggesting amendments to said treaties, and the papers to which he refers in his communication, are also herewith transmitted.

ANDREW JOHNSON.

WASHINGTON, D. C., *July 7, 1868.*

To the Senate of the United States:

I herewith lay before the Senate, for its constitutional action thereon, a treaty made and concluded at Ottawa, Kans., on the 1st day of June,

---

*Petitions of merchants and shipowners of New York and Boston relative to the detention, at the request of the House of Representatives, of the ironclad monitors *Oneoto* and *Catawba*, purchased from the United States by Swift & Co., and supposed to be intended for the Government of Peru, then at war with a power friendly to the United States.

1868, between the United States and the Swan Creek and Black River Chippewas and the Munsee or Christian Indians of the State of Kansas.

Accompanying the treaty is a letter from the Secretary of the Interior, dated the 30th ultimo, together with the papers therein designated.

ANDREW JOHNSON.

WASHINGTON, *July 9, 1868.*

To the Senate of the United States:

I transmit to the Senate, for consideration with a view to ratification, additional articles to the treaty between the United States and His Majesty the Emperor of China of the 18th June, 1858, signed in this city on the 4th instant by the plenipotentiaries of the parties.

ANDREW JOHNSON.

WASHINGTON, *July 10, 1868.*

To the Senate of the United States:

·I transmit to the Senate, for consideration with a view to ratification, a convention between the United States and the Mexican Republic, signed in this city by the plenipotentiaries of the parties on the 4th instant, providing for an adjustment of claims of citizens of the United States on the Mexican Government and of Mexican citizens on the Government of the United States. ANDREW JOHNSON.

WASHINGTON, *July 10, 1868.*

To the Senate of the United States:

Referring to my message to the Senate of the 23d of May last, I herewith transmit a further report from the Secretary of State, with an accompanying document, relative to late occurrences in Japan.

ANDREW JOHNSON.

WASHINGTON, *July 14, 1868.*

To the Senate of the United States:

I transmit to the Senate a report from the Secretary of State, inclosing a list of the States of the Union whose legislatures have ratified the proposed fourteenth article of amendment to the Constitution of the United States, and also a copy of the resolutions of ratification, as called for in the Senate's resolution of the 9th instant, together with a copy of the respective resolutions of the legislatures of Ohio and New Jersey purporting to rescind the resolutions of ratification of said amendment which had previously been adopted by the legislatures of these two States, respectively, or to withdraw their consent to the same.

ANDREW JOHNSON.

WASHINGTON, *July 15, 1868.*

To the Senate and House of Representatives:

I hereby transmit to Congress a report, with the accompanying papers, received from the Secretary of State, in compliance with the requirements of the eighteenth section of the act entitled "An act to regulate the diplomatic and consular systems of the United States," approved August 18, 1856.

ANDREW JOHNSON.

WASHINGTON, *July 15, 1868.*

To the Congress of the United States:

I submit herewith a correspondence between the Secretary of State and Mr. Robert B. Van Valkenburgh, minister resident of the United States in Japan. It seems to show the importance of an amendment of the law of the United States prohibiting the cooly trade.

ANDREW JOHNSON

WASHINGTON, *July 17, 1868.*

To the Senate of the United States:

I transmit to the Senate, in compliance with its resolution of the 9th instant, a report from the Secretary of State, communicating a copy of a paper received by him to-day, purporting to be a resolution ratifying on the part of the State of Louisiana the proposed amendment to the Constitution of the United States known as Article XIV.

ANDREW JOHNSON.

WASHINGTON, *July 18, 1868.*

To the Senate of the United States:

I transmit to the Senate, in compliance with its resolution of the 9th instant, a report from the Secretary of State, communicating a copy of a paper received by me on the 18th instant, purporting to be a resolution of the senate and house of representatives of the State of South Carolina, ratifying the proposed amendment to the Constitution of the United States known as Article XIV.

ANDREW JOHNSON.

WASHINGTON, D. C., *July 18, 1868.*

To the Senate and House of Representatives:

Experience has fully demonstrated the wisdom of the framers of the Federal Constitution. Under all circumstances the result of their labors was as near an approximation to perfection as was compatible with the fallibility of man. Such being the estimation in which the Constitution is and has ever been held by our countrymen, it is not surprising that any proposition for its alteration or amendment should be received with reluctance and distrust. While this sentiment deserves commendation and encouragement as a useful preventive of unnecessary attempt to change its provisions, it must be conceded that time has developed imperfections and omissions in the Constitution, the reformation of which has been demanded by the best interests of the country. Some of these have been remedied in the manner provided in the Constitution itself. There are others which, although heretofore brought to the attention of the people, have never been so presented as to enable the popular judgment to determine whether they should be corrected by means of additional amendments. My object in this communication is to suggest certain defects in the Constitution which seem to me to require correction, and to recommend that the judgment of the people be taken on the amendments proposed.

The first of the defects to which I desire to direct attention is in that clause of the Constitution which provides for the election of President and Vice-President through the intervention of electors, and not by an immediate vote of the people. The importance of so amending this clause as to secure to the people the election of President and Vice-President by their direct votes was urged with great earnestness and ability by President Jackson in his first annual message, and the recommendation was repeated in five of his subsequent communications to Congress, extending through the eight years of his Administration. In his message of 1829 he said:

To the people belongs the right of electing their Chief Magistrate; it was never designed that their choice should in any case be defeated, either by the intervention of electoral colleges or by the agency confided, under certain contingencies, to the House of Representatives.

He then proceeded to state the objections to an election of President by the House of Representatives, the most important of which was that the choice of a clear majority of the people might be easily defeated. He then closed the argument with the following communication:

I would therefore recommend such an amendment of the Constitution as may remove all intermediate agency in the election of the President and Vice-President. The mode may be so regulated as to preserve to each State its present relative weight in the election, and a failure in the first attempt may be provided for by confining the second to a choice between the two highest candidates. In connection with such an amendment it would seem advisable to limit the service of the Chief Magistrate to a single term of either four or six years. If, however, it should not be adopted, it is worthy of consideration whether a provision disqualifying for office the Representatives in Congress on whom such an election may have devolved would not be proper.

Although this recommendation was repeated with undiminished earnestness in several of his succeeding messages, yet the proposed amendment was never adopted and submitted to the people by Congress. The danger of a defeat of the people's choice in an election by the House of

Representatives remains unprovided for in the Constitution, and would be greatly increased if the House of Representatives should assume the power arbitrarily to reject the votes of a State which might not be cast in conformity with the wishes of the majority in that body.

But if President Jackson failed to secure the amendment to the Constitution which he urged so persistently, his arguments contributed largely to the formation of party organizations, which have effectually avoided the contingency of an election by the House of Representatives. These organizations, first by a resort to the caucus system of nominating candidates, and afterwards to State and national conventions, have been successful in so limiting the number of candidates as to escape the danger of an election by the House of Representatives.

It is clear, however, that in thus limiting the number of candidates the true object and spirit of the Constitution have been evaded and defeated. It is an essential feature in our republican system of government that every citizen possessing the constitutional qualifications has a right to become a candidate for the office of President and Vice-President, and that every qualified elector has a right to cast his vote for any citizen whom he may regard as worthy of these offices. But under the party organizations which have prevailed for years these asserted rights of the people have been as effectually cut off and destroyed as if the Constitution itself had inhibited their exercise.

The danger of a defeat of the popular choice in an election by the House of Representatives is no greater than in an election made nominally by the people themselves, when by the laws of party organizations and by the constitutional provisions requiring the people to vote for electors instead of for the President or Vice-President it is made impracticable for any citizen to be a candidate except through the process of a party nomination, and for any voter to cast his suffrage for any other person than one thus brought forward through the manipulations of a nominating convention. It is thus apparent that by means of party organizations that provision of the Constitution which requires the election of President and Vice-President to be made through the electoral colleges has been made instrumental and potential in defeating the great object of conferring the choice of these officers upon the people. It may be conceded that party organizations are inseparable from republican government, and that when formed and managed in subordination to the Constitution they may be valuable safeguards of popular liberty; but when they are perverted to purposes of bad ambition they are liable to become the dangerous instruments of overthrowing the Constitution itself. Strongly impressed with the truth of these views, I feel called upon by an imperative sense of duty to revive substantially the recommendation so often and so earnestly made by President Jackson, and to urge that the amendment to the Constitution herewith presented, or some similar proposition, may be submitted to the people for their ratification or rejection.

Recent events have shown the necessity of an amendment to the Constitution distinctly defining the persons who shall discharge the duties of President of the United States in the event of a vacancy in that office by the death, resignation, or removal of both the President and Vice-President. It is clear that this should be fixed by the Constitution, and not be left to repealable enactments of doubtful constitutionality. It occurs to me that in the event of a vacancy in the office of President by the death, resignation, disability, or removal of both the President and Vice-President the duties of the office should devolve upon an officer of the executive department of the Government, rather than one connected with the legislative or judicial departments. The objections to designating either the President *pro tempore* of the Senate or the Chief Justice of the Supreme Court, especially in the event of a vacancy produced by removal, are so obvious and so unanswerable that they need not be stated in detail. It is enough to state that they are both interested in producing a vacancy, and, according to the provisions of the Constitution, are members of the tribunal by whose decree a vacancy may be produced.

Under such circumstances the impropriety of designating either of these officers to succeed the President so removed is palpable. The framers of the Constitution, when they referred to Congress the settlement of the succession to the office of President in the event of a vacancy in the offices of both President and Vice-President, did not, in my opinion, contemplate the designation of any other than an officer of the executive department, on whom, in such a contingency, the powers and duties of the President should devolve. Until recently the contingency has been remote, and serious attention has not been called to the manifest incongruity between the provisions of the Constitution on this subject and the act of Congress of 1792. Having, however, been brought almost face to face with this important question, it seems an eminently proper time for us to make the legislation conform to the language, intent, and theory of the Constitution, and thus place the executive department beyond the reach of usurpation, and remove from the legislative and judicial departments every temptation to combine for the absorption of all the powers of government.

It has occurred to me that in the event of such a vacancy the duties of President would devolve most appropriately upon some one of the heads of the several Executive Departments, and under this conviction I present for your consideration an amendment to the Constitution on this subject, with the recommendation that it be submitted to the people for their action.

Experience seems to have established the necessity of an amendment of that clause of the Constitution which provides for the election of Senators to Congress by the legislatures of the several States. It would be more consistent with the genius of our form of government if the Senators were chosen directly by the people of the several States. The objections to the election of Senators by the legislatures are so palpable that I deem it unnecessary to do more than submit the proposition for such an amendment, with the recommendation that it be opened to the people for their judgment.

It is strongly impressed on my mind that the tenure of office by the judiciary of the United States during good behavior for life is incompatible with the spirit of republican government, and in this opinion I am fully sustained by the evidence of popular judgment upon this subject in the different States of the Union.

I therefore deem it my duty to recommend an amendment to the Constitution by which the terms of the judicial officers would be limited to a period of years, and I herewith present it in the hope that Congress will submit it to the people for their decision.

The foregoing views have long been entertained by me. In 1845, in the House of Representatives, and afterwards, in 1860, in the Senate of the United States, I submitted substantially the same propositions as those to which the attention of Congress is herein invited. Time, observation, and experience have confirmed these convictions; and, as a matter of public duty and a deep sense of my constitutional obligation "to recommend to the consideration of Congress such measures as I deem necessary and expedient," I submit the accompanying propositions, and urge their adoption and submission to the judgment of the people.

ANDREW JOHNSON.

JOINT RESOLUTION proposing amendments to the Constitution of the United States.

Whereas the fifth article of the Constitution of the United States provides for amendments thereto in the manner following, viz:

"The Congress, whenever two-thirds of both Houses shall deem it necessary, shall propose amendments to this Constitution, or, on the application of the legislatures of two-thirds of the several States, shall call a convention for proposing amendments, which in either case shall be valid to all intents and purposes as part of this Constitution when ratified by the legislatures of three-fourths of the several States or by conventions in three-fourths thereof, as the one or the other mode of ratification may be proposed by the Congress: *Provided*, That no amendment which may be made prior to the year 1808 shall in any manner affect the first and fourth clauses in the ninth section of the first article, and that no State, without its consent, shall be deprived of its equal suffrage in the Senate:"

Therefore,

Be it resolved by the Senate and House of Representatives of the United States of America in Congress assembled (two-thirds of both Houses concurring), That the following amendments to the Constitution of the United States be proposed to the legislatures of the several States, which, when ratified by the legislatures of three-fourths of the States, shall be valid to all intents and purposes as part of the Constitution:

"That hereafter the President and Vice-President of the United States shall be chosen for the term of six years, by the people of the respective States, in the manner following: Each State shall be divided by the legislature thereof in districts, equal in number to the whole number of Senators and Representatives to which such State may be entitled in the Congress of the United States; the said districts to be composed of contiguous territory, and to contain, as nearly as may be, an equal number of persons entitled to be represented under the Constitution, and to be laid off for the first time immediately after the ratification of this amendment; that on the first Thursday in August in the year 18—, and on the same day every sixth year thereafter, the citizens of each State who possess the qualifications requisite for electors of the most numerous branch of the State legislatures shall meet within their respective districts and vote for a President and Vice-President of the United States; and the person receiving the greatest number of votes for President and the one receiving the greatest number of votes for Vice-President in each district shall be holden to have received one vote, which fact shall be immediately certified by the governor of the State to each of the Senators in Congress from such State and to the President of the Senate and the Speaker of the House of Representatives. The Congress of the United States shall be in session on the second Monday in October in the year 18—, and on the same day in every sixth year thereafter; and the President of the Senate, in the presence of the Senate and House of Representatives, shall open all the certificates, and the votes shall then be counted. The person having the greatest number of votes for President shall be President, if such number be equal to a majority of the whole number of votes given; but if no person have such majority, then a second election shall be held on the first Thursday in the month of December then next ensuing between the persons having the two highest numbers for the office of President, which second election shall be conducted, the result certified, and the votes counted in the same manner as in the first, and the person having the greatest number of votes for President shall be President. But if two or more persons shall have received the greatest and an equal number of votes at the second election, then the person who shall have received the greatest number of votes in the greatest number of States shall be President. The person having the greatest number of votes for Vice-President at the first election shall be Vice-President, if such number be equal to a majority of the whole number of votes given; and if no person have such majority, then a second election shall take place between the persons having the two highest numbers on the same day that the second election is held for President, and the person having the highest number of the votes for Vice-President shall be Vice-President. But if there should happen to be an equality of votes between the persons so voted for at the second election, then the person having the greatest number of votes in the greatest number of States shall be Vice-President. But when a second election shall be necessary in the case of Vice-President and not necessary in the case of President, then the Senate shall choose a Vice-President from the persons having the two highest numbers in the first election, as now prescribed in the Constitution: *Provided*, That after the ratification of this amendment to the Constitution the President and Vice-President shall hold their offices, respectively, for the term of six years, and that no President or Vice-President shall be eligible for reelection to a second term."

SEC. 2. *And be it further resolved*, That Article II, section 1, paragraph 6, of the Constitution of the United States shall be amended so as to read as follows:

"In case of the removal of the President from office, or of his death, resignation, or inability to discharge the powers and duties of said office, the same shall devolve on the Vice-President; and in the case of the removal, death, resignation, or inability both of the President and Vice-President, the powers and duties of said office shall devolve on the Secretary of State for the time being, and after this officer, in case of vacancy in that or other Department, and in the order in which they are named, on the Secretary of the Treasury, on the Secretary of War, on the Secretary of the Navy, on the Secretary of the Interior, on the Postmaster-General, and on the Attorney-General; and such officer, on whom the powers and duties of President shall devolve in accordance with the foregoing provisions, shall then act as President until the disability shall be removed or a President shall be elected, as is or may be provided for by law."

SEC. 3. *And be it further resolved*, That Article I, section 3, be amended by striking out the word "legislature," and inserting in lieu thereof the following words, viz: "Persons qualified to vote for members of the most numerous branch of the legislature," so as to make the third section of said article, when ratified by three-fourths of the States, read as follows, to wit:

"The Senate of the United States shall be composed of two Senators from each State, chosen by the persons qualified to vote for the members of the most numerous branch of the legislature thereof, for six years, and each Senator shall have one vote."

SEC. 4. *And be it further resolved,* That Article III, section 1, be amended by striking out the words "good behavior," and inserting the following words, viz: "the term of twelve years." And further, that said article and section be amended by adding the following thereto, viz: "And it shall be the duty of the President of the United States, within twelve months after the ratification of this amendment by three-fourths of all the States, as provided by the Constitution of the United States, to divide the whole number of judges, as near as may be practicable, into three classes. The seats of the judges of the first class shall be vacated at the expiration of the fourth year from such classification, of the second class at the expiration of the eighth year, and of the third class at the expiration of the twelfth year, so that one-third may be chosen every fourth year thereafter."

The article as amended will read as follows:

ARTICLE III.

SEC. 1. The judicial power of the United States shall be vested in one Supreme Court and such inferior courts as the Congress from time to time may ordain and establish. The judges, both of the Supreme and inferior courts, shall hold their offices during the term of twelve years, and shall at stated times receive for their services a compensation which shall not be diminished during their continuance in office; and it shall be the duty of the President of the United States, within twelve months after the ratification of this amendment by three-fourths of all the States, as provided by the Constitution of the United States, to divide the whole number of judges, as near as may be practicable, into three classes. The seats of the judges of the first class shall be vacated at the expiration of the fourth year from such classification; of the second class, at the expiration of the eighth year; and of the third class, at the expiration of the twelfth year, so that one-third may be chosen every fourth year thereafter.

WASHINGTON, D. C., *July 18, 1868.*

To the House of Representatives:

In compliance with the resolution adopted by the House of Representatives on the 13th instant, requesting "copies of all instructions, records, and correspondence connected with the commission authorized to negotiate the late treaty with the Great and Little Osage Indians, and copies of all propositions made to said commission from railroad corporations or by individuals," I transmit the accompanying communications from the Secretary of the Interior, together with the papers to which they have reference.

ANDREW JOHNSON.

WASHINGTON, *July 20, 1868.*

To the Senate of the United States:

I transmit to the Senate, in compliance with its resolution of the 9th instant, a report from the Secretary of State, communicating a copy of a paper received by me this day, purporting to be a resolution of the senate and house of representatives of the State of Alabama ratifying the proposed amendment to the Constitution of the United States known as Article XIV.

ANDREW JOHNSON.

WASHINGTON, *July 24, 1868.*

To the Senate of the United States:

I transmit herewith a letter from the Secretary of the Navy, inclosing a report of a board of naval officers appointed in pursuance of an act of Congress approved May 19, 1868, to select suitable locations for powder magazines.

ANDREW JOHNSON.

WASHINGTON, *July 27, 1868.*

To the House of Representatives:

I transmit to the House of Representatives, in answer to their resolution of the 24th instant, the accompanying report* from the Secretary of State.

ANDREW JOHNSON.

VETO MESSAGES.

WASHINGTON, D. C., *March 25, 1868.*

To the Senate of the United States:

I have considered, with such care as the pressure of other duties has permitted, a bill entitled "An act to amend an act entitled 'An act to amend the judiciary act, passed the 24th of September, 1789.'" Not being able to approve all of its provisions, I herewith return it to the Senate, in which House it originated, with a brief statement of my objections.

The first section of the bill meets my approbation, as, for the purpose of protecting the rights of property from the erroneous decision of inferior judicial tribunals, it provides means for obtaining uniformity, by appeal to the Supreme Court of the United States, in cases which have now become very numerous and of much public interest, and in which such remedy is not now allowed. The second section, however, takes away the right of appeal to that court in cases which involve the life and liberty of the citizen, and leaves them exposed to the judgment of numerous inferior tribunals. It is apparent that the two sections were

---

* Relating to absence from his post of the consul at Panama.

conceived in a very different spirit, and I regret that my objections to one impose upon me the necessity of withholding my sanction from the other.

I can not give my assent to a measure which proposes to deprive any person "restrained of his or her liberty in violation of the Constitution or of any treaty or law of the United States" from the right of appeal to the highest judicial authority known to our Government. To "secure the blessings of liberty to ourselves and our posterity" is one of the declared objects of the Federal Constitution. To assure these, guaranties are provided in the same instrument, as well against "unreasonable searches and seizures" as against the suspensions of "the privilege of the writ of *habeas corpus*, * * * unless when, in cases of rebellion or invasion, the public safety may require it." It was doubtless to afford the people the means of protecting and enforcing these inestimable privileges that the jurisdiction which this bill proposes to take away was conferred upon the Supreme Court of the nation. The act conferring that jurisdiction was approved on the 5th day of February, 1867, with a full knowledge of the motives that prompted its passage, and because it was believed to be necessary and right. Nothing has since occurred to disprove the wisdom and justness of the measures, and to modify it as now proposed would be to lessen the protection of the citizen from the exercise of arbitrary power and to weaken the safeguards of life and liberty, which can never be made too secure against illegal encroachments.

The bill not only prohibits the adjudication by the Supreme Court of cases in which appeals may hereafter be taken, but interdicts its jurisdiction on appeals which have already been made to that high judicial body. If, therefore, it should become a law, it will by its retroactive operation wrest from the citizen a remedy which he enjoyed at the time of his appeal. It will thus operate most harshly upon those who believe that justice has been denied them in the inferior courts.

The legislation proposed in the second section, it seems to me, is not in harmony with the spirit and intention of the Constitution. It can not fail to affect most injuriously the just equipoise of our system of Government, for it establishes a precedent which, if followed, may eventually sweep away every check on arbitrary and unconstitutional legislation. Thus far during the existence of the Government the Supreme Court of the United States has been viewed by the people as the true expounder of their Constitution, and in the most violent party conflicts its judgments and decrees have always been sought and deferred to with confidence and respect. In public estimation it combines judicial wisdom and impartiality in a greater degree than any other authority known to the Constitution, and any act which may be construed into or mistaken for an attempt to prevent or evade its decision on a question which affects the liberty of the citizens and agitates the country can not fail to be attended with unpropitious consequences. It will be justly held by a large portion of the people as an admission of the unconstitutionality of the act on which its judgment may be forbidden or forestalled, and may interfere with that willing acquiescence in its provisions which is necessary for the harmonious and efficient execution of any law.

For these reasons, thus briefly and imperfectly stated, and for others, of which want of time forbids the enumeration, I deem it my duty to withhold my assent from this bill, and to return it for the reconsideration of Congress.

ANDREW JOHNSON.

WASHINGTON, D. C., *June 20, 1868.*

To the House of Representatives:

I return without my signature a bill entitled "An act to admit the State of Arkansas to representation in Congress."

The approval of this bill would be an admission on the part of the Executive that the "Act for the more efficient government of the rebel States," passed March 2, 1867, and the acts supplementary thereto were proper and constitutional. My opinion, however, in reference to those measures has undergone no change, but, on the contrary, has been strengthened by the results which have attended their execution. Even were this not the case, I could not consent to a bill which is based upon the assumption either that by an act of rebellion of a portion of its people the State of Arkansas seceded from the Union, or that Congress may at its pleasure expel or exclude a State from the Union, or interrupt its relations with the Government by arbitrarily depriving it of representation in the Senate and House of Representatives. If Arkansas is a State not in the Union, this bill does not admit it as a State into the Union. If, on the other hand, Arkansas is a State in the Union, no legislation is necessary to declare it entitled "to representation in Congress as one of the States of the Union." The Constitution already declares that "each State shall have at least one Representative;" that the Senate "shall be composed of two Senators from each State," and "that no State, without its consent, shall be deprived of its equal suffrage in the Senate."

That instrument also makes each House "the judge of the elections, returns, and qualifications of its own members," and therefore all that is now necessary to restore Arkansas in all its constitutional relations to the Government is a decision by each House upon the eligibility of those who, presenting their credentials, claim seats in the respective Houses of Congress. This is the plain and simple plan of the Constitution; and believing that had it been pursued when Congress assembled in the month of December, 1865, the restoration of the States would long since have been completed, I once again earnestly recommend that it be adopted by each House in preference to legislation, which I respectfully submit is not only of at least doubtful constitutionality, and therefore unwise and dangerous as a precedent, but is unnecessary, not so effective in its operation as the mode prescribed by the Constitution, involves additional delay, and from its terms may be taken rather as applicable to a Territory about to be admitted as one of the United States than to a State which has occupied a place in the Union for upward of a quarter of a century.

The bill declares the State of Arkansas entitled and admitted to representation in Congress as one of the States of the Union upon the following fundamental condition:

That the constitution of Arkansas shall never be so amended or changed as to deprive any citizen or class of citizens of the United States of the right to vote who are entitled to vote by the constitution herein recognized, except as a punishment for such crimes as are now felonies at common law, whereof they shall have been duly convicted under laws equally applicable to all the inhabitants of said State: *Provided*, That any alteration of said constitution, prospective in its effect, may be made in regard to the time and place of residence of voters.

I have been unable to find in the Constitution of the United States any warrant for the exercise of the authority thus claimed by Congress. In assuming the power to impose a "fundamental condition" upon a State which has been duly "admitted into the Union upon an equal footing with the original States in all respects whatever," Congress asserts a right to enter a State as it may a Territory, and to regulate the highest prerogative of a free people—the elective franchise. This question is reserved by the Constitution to the States themselves, and to concede to Congress the power to regulate the subject would be to reverse the fundamental principle of the Republic and to place in the hands of the Federal Government, which is the creature of the States, the sovereignty which justly belongs to the States or the people—the true source of all political power, by whom our Federal system was created and to whose will it is subordinate.

The bill fails to provide in what manner the State of Arkansas is to signify its acceptance of the "fundamental condition" which Congress endeavors to make unalterable and irrevocable. Nor does it prescribe the penalty to be imposed should the people of the State amend or change the particular portions of the constitution which it is one of the purposes of the bill to perpetuate, but as to the consequences of such action leaves them in uncertainty and doubt. When the circumstances under which this constitution has been brought to the attention of Congress are considered, it is not unreasonable to suppose that efforts will be made to modify its provisions, and especially those in respect to which this measure prohibits any alteration. It is seriously questioned whether the constitution has been ratified by a majority of the persons who, under the act of March 2, 1867, and the acts supplementary thereto, were entitled to registration and to vote upon that issue. Section 10 of the schedule provides that—

No person disqualified from voting or registering under this constitution shall vote for candidates for any office, nor shall be permitted to vote for the ratification or rejection of the constitution at the polls herein authorized.

Assumed to be in force before its adoption, in disregard of the law of Congress, the constitution undertakes to impose upon the elector other and further conditions. The fifth section of the eighth article provides that "all persons, before registering or voting," must take and subscribe an oath which, among others, contains the following clause:

That I accept the civil and political equality of all men, and agree not to attempt to deprive any person or persons, on account of race, color, or previous condition, of any political or civil right, privilege, or immunity enjoyed by any other class of men.

It is well known that a very large portion of the electors in all the States, if not a large majority of all of them, do not believe in or accept the political equality of Indians, Mongolians, or negroes with the race to which they belong. If the voters in many of the States of the North and West were required to take such an oath as a test of their qualification, there is reason to believe that a majority of them would remain from the polls rather than comply with its degrading conditions. How far and to what extent this test oath prevented the registration of those who were qualified under the laws of Congress it is not possible to know, but that such was its effect, at least sufficient to overcome the small and doubtful majority in favor of this constitution, there can be no reasonable doubt. Should the people of Arkansas, therefore, desiring to regulate the elective franchise so as to make it conform to the constitutions of a large proportion of the States of the North and West, modify the provisions referred to in the "fundamental condition," what is to be the consequence? Is it intended that a denial of representation shall follow? And if so, may we not dread, at some future day, a recurrence of the troubles which have so long agitated the country? Would it not be the part of wisdom to take for our guide the Federal Constitution, rather than resort to measures which, looking only to the present, may in a few years renew, in an aggravated form, the strife and bitterness caused by legislation which has proved to be so ill timed and unfortunate?

ANDREW JOHNSON.

WASHINGTON, D. C.,
June 25, 1868.

To the House of Representatives:

In returning to the House of Representatives, in which it originated, a bill entitled "An act to admit the States of North Carolina, South Carolina, Louisiana, Georgia, Alabama, and Florida to representation in Congress," I do not deem it necessary to state at length the reasons which constrain me to withhold my approval. I will not, therefore, undertake at this time to reopen the discussion upon the grave constitutional questions involved in the act of March 2, 1867, and the acts supplementary thereto, in pursuance of which it is claimed, in the preamble to this bill, these States have framed and adopted constitutions of State government

Nor will I repeat the objections contained in my message of the 20th instant, returning without my signature the bill to admit to representation the State of Arkansas, and which are equally applicable to the pending measure.

Like the act recently passed in reference to Arkansas, this bill supersedes the plain and simple mode prescribed by the Constitution for the admission to seats in the respective Houses of Senators and Representatives from the several States. It assumes authority over six States of the Union which has never been delegated to Congress, or is even warranted by previous unconstitutional legislation upon the subject of restoration. It imposes conditions which are in derogation of the equal rights of the States, and is founded upon a theory which is subversive of the fundamental principles of the Government. In the case of Alabama it violates the plighted faith of Congress by forcing upon that State a constitution which was rejected by the people, according to the express terms of an act of Congress requiring that a majority of the registered electors should vote upon the question of its ratification.

For these objections, and many others that might be presented, I can not approve this bill, and therefore return it for the action of Congress required in such cases by the Federal Constitution.

ANDREW JOHNSON.

WASHINGTON, D. C.,
July 20, 1868.

To the Senate of the United States:

I have given to the joint resolution entitled "A resolution excluding from the electoral college the votes of States lately in rebellion which shall not have been reorganized" as careful examination as I have been able to bestow upon the subject during the few days that have intervened since the measure was submitted for my approval.

Feeling constrained to withhold my consent, I herewith return the resolution to the Senate, in which House it originated, with a brief statement of the reasons which have induced my action. This joint resolution is based upon the assumption that some of the States whose inhabitants were lately in rebellion are not now entitled to representation in Congress and participation in the election of President and Vice-President of the United States.

Having heretofore had occasion to give in detail my reasons for dissenting from this view, it is not necessary at this time to repeat them. It is sufficient to state that I continue strong in my conviction that the acts of secession, by which a number of the States sought to dissolve their connection with the other States and to subvert the Union, being unauthorized by the Constitution and in direct violation thereof, were from the beginning absolutely null and void. It follows necessarily that when the rebellion terminated the several States which had attempted to secede continued to be States in the Union, and all that was required to enable them to resume their relations to the Union was that they should adopt the measures necessary to their practical restoration as States. Such measures were adopted, and the legitimate result was that those States, having conformed to all the requirements of the Constitution, resumed their former relations, and became entitled to the exercise of all the rights guaranteed to them by its provisions.

The joint resolution under consideration, however, seems to assume that by the insurrectionary acts of their respective inhabitants those States forfeited their rights as such, and can never again exercise them except upon readmission into the Union on the terms prescribed by Congress. If this position be correct, it follows that they were taken out of the Union by virtue of their acts of secession, and hence that the war waged upon them was illegal and unconstitutional. We would thus be placed in this inconsistent attitude, that while the war was commenced and carried on upon the distinct ground that the Southern States, being component parts of the Union, were in rebellion against the lawful authority of the United States, upon its termination we resort to a policy of reconstruction which assumes that it was not in fact a rebellion, but that the war was waged for the conquest of territories assumed to be outside of the constitutional Union.

The mode and manner of receiving and counting the electoral votes for President and Vice-President of the United States are in plain and simple terms prescribed by the Constitution. That instrument imperatively requires that "the President of the Senate shall, in the presence of the Senate and House of Representatives, open all the certificates, and the votes shall then be counted." Congress has, therefore, no power, under the Constitution, to receive the electoral votes or reject them. The whole power is exhausted when, in the presence of the two Houses, the votes are counted and the result declared. In this respect the power and duty of the President of the Senate are, under the Constitution, purely ministerial. When, therefore, the joint resolution declares that no electoral votes shall be received or counted from States that since the 4th of March, 1867, have not "adopted a constitution of State government under which a State government shall have organized," a power is assumed which is nowhere delegated to Congress, unless upon the assumption that the State governments organized prior to the 4th of March, 1867, were illegal and void.

The joint resolution, by implication at least, concedes that these States were States by virtue of their organization prior to the 4th of March, 1867, but denies to them the right to vote in the election of President and Vice-President of the United States. It follows either that this assumption of power is wholly unauthorized by the Constitution or that the States so excluded from voting were out of the Union by reason of the rebellion, and have never been legitimately restored. Being fully satisfied that they were never out of the Union, and that their relations thereto have been legally and constitutionally restored, I am forced to the conclusion that the joint resolution, which deprives them of the right to have their votes for President and Vice-President received and counted, is in conflict with the Constitution, and that Congress has no more power to reject their votes than those of the States which have been uniformly loyal to the Federal Union.

It is worthy of remark that if the States whose inhabitants were recently in rebellion were legally and constitutionally organized and restored to their rights prior to the 4th of March, 1867, as I am satisfied they were, the only legitimate authority under which the election for President and Vice-President can be held therein must be derived from the governments instituted before that period. It clearly follows that all the State governments organized in those States under act of Congress for that purpose, and under military control, are illegitimate and of no validity whatever; and in that view the votes cast in those States for President and Vice-President, in pursuance of acts passed since the 4th of March, 1867, and in obedience to the so-called reconstruction acts of Congress, can not be legally received and counted, while the only votes in those States that can be legally cast and counted will be those cast in pursuance of the laws in force in the several States prior to the legislation by Congress upon the subject of reconstruction.

I can not refrain from directing your special attention to the declaration contained in the joint resolution, that "none of the States whose inhabitants were lately in rebellion shall be entitled to representation in the electoral college," etc. If it is meant by this declaration that no State is to be allowed to vote for President and Vice-President *all* of whose inhabitants were engaged in the late rebellion, it is apparent that no one of the States will be excluded from voting, since it is well known that in every Southern State there were many inhabitants who not only did not participate in the rebellion, but who actually took part in the suppression, or refrained from giving it any aid or countenance. I therefore conclude that the true meaning of the joint resolution is that no State a *portion* of whose inhabitants were engaged in the rebellion shall be permitted to participate in the Presidential election, except upon the terms and conditions therein prescribed.

Assuming this to be the true construction of the resolution, the inquiry becomes pertinent, May those Northern States a portion of whose inhabitants were actually in the rebellion be prevented, at the discretion of Congress, from having their electoral votes counted? It is well known that a portion of the inhabitants of New York and a portion of the inhabitants of Virginia were alike engaged in the rebellion; yet it is equally well known that Virginia, as well as New York, was at all times during the war recognized by the Federal Government as a State in the Union—so clearly that upon the termination of hostilities it was not even deemed necessary for her restoration that a provisional governor should be appointed; yet, according to this joint resolution, the people of Virginia, unless they comply with the terms it prescribes, are denied the right of voting for President, while the people of New York, a portion of the inhabitants of which State were also in rebellion, are permitted to have their electoral votes counted without undergoing the process of reconstruction prescribed for Virginia. New York is no more a State than Virginia; the one is as much entitled to representation in the electoral college as the other. If Congress has the power to deprive Virginia of this right, it can exercise the same authority with respect to New York or any other of the States. Thus the result of the Presidential election may be controlled and determined by Congress, and the people be deprived of their right under the Constitution to choose a President and Vice-President of the United States.

If Congress were to provide by law that the votes of none of the States should be received and counted if cast for a candidate who differed in political sentiment with a majority of the two Houses, such legislation would at once be condemned by the country as an unconstitutional and revolutionary usurpation of power. It would, however, be exceedingly difficult to find in the Constitution any more authority for the passage of the joint resolution under consideration than for an enactment looking directly to the rejection of all votes not in accordance with the political preferences of a majority of Congress. No power exists in the Constitution authorizing the joint resolution or the supposed law—the only difference being that one would be more palpably unconstitutional and revolutionary than the other. Both would rest upon the radical error that Congress has the power to prescribe terms and conditions to the right of the people of the States to cast their votes for President and Vice-President.

For the reasons thus indicated I am constrained to return the joint resolution to the Senate for such further action thereon as Congress may deem necessary.

ANDREW JOHNSON.

WASHINGTON, *July 25, 1868*

To the Senate of the United States:

Believing that a bill entitled "An act relating to the Freedmen's Bureau, and providing for its discontinuance," interferes with the appointing power conferred by the Constitution upon the Executive, and for other reasons, which at this late period of the session time will not permit me to state, I herewith return it to the Senate, in which House it originated, without my approval.

ANDREW JOHNSON.

PROCLAMATIONS.

By the President of the United States of America.

A PROCLAMATION.

Whereas in the month of July, A. D. 1861, in accepting the condition of civil war which was brought about by insurrection and rebellion in several of the States which constitute the United States, the two Houses of Congress did solemnly declare that that war was not waged on the part of the Government in any spirit of oppression, nor for any purpose of conquest or subjugation, nor for any purpose of overthrowing or interfering with the rights or established institutions of the States, but only to defend and maintain the supremacy of the Constitution of the United States and to preserve the Union, with all the dignity, equality, and rights of the several States unimpaired, and that so soon as those objects should be accomplished the war on the part of the Government should cease; and

Whereas the President of the United States has heretofore, in the spirit of that declaration and with the view of securing for it ultimate and complete effect, set forth several proclamations offering amnesty and pardon to persons who had been or were concerned in the aforenamed rebellion, which proclamations, however, were attended with prudential reservations and exceptions then deemed necessary and proper, and which proclamations were respectively issued on the 8th day of December, 1863, on the 26th day of March, 1864, on the 29th day of May, 1865, and on the 7th day of September, 1867; and

Whereas the said lamentable civil war has long since altogether ceased, with an acknowledgment by all the States of the supremacy of the Federal Constitution and of the Government thereunder, and there no longer exists any reasonable ground to apprehend a renewal of the said civil war, or any foreign interference, or any unlawful resistance by any portion of the people of any of the States to the Constitution and laws of the United States; and

Whereas it is desirable to reduce the standing army and to bring to a speedy termination military occupation, martial law, military tribunals, abridgment of the freedom of speech and of the press, and suspension of the privilege of *habeas corpus* and of the right of trial by jury, such encroachments upon our free institutions in time of peace being dangerous to public liberty, incompatible with the individual rights of the citizen, contrary to the genius and spirit of our republican form of government, and exhaustive of the national resources; and

Whereas it is believed that amnesty and pardon will tend to secure a complete and universal establishment and prevalence of municipal law and order in conformity with the Constitution of the United States, and to remove all appearances or presumptions of a retaliatory or vindictive policy on the part of the Government attended by unnecessary disqualifications, pains, penalties, confiscations, and disfranchisements, and, on the contrary, to promote and procure complete fraternal reconciliation among the whole people, with due submission to the Constitution and laws:

Now, therefore, be it known that I, Andrew Johnson, President of the United States, do, by virtue of the Constitution and in the name of the people of the United States, hereby proclaim and declare, unconditionally and without reservation, to all and to every person who, directly or indirectly, participated in the late insurrection or rebellion, excepting such person or persons as may be under presentment or indictment in any court of the United States having competent jurisdiction upon a charge of treason or other felony, a full pardon and amnesty for the offense of treason against the United States or of adhering to their enemies during the late civil war, with restoration of all rights of property, except as to slaves, and except also as to any property of which any person may have been legally divested under the laws of the United States.

In testimony whereof I have signed these presents with my hand and have caused the seal of the United States to be hereunto affixed.

[SEAL.]   Done at the city of Washington, the 4th day of July, A. D. 1868, and of the Independence of the United States of America the ninety-third.

ANDREW JOHNSON.

By the President:

WILLIAM H. SEWARD, *Secretary of State.*

BY THE PRESIDENT OF THE UNITED STATES OF AMERICA.

A PROCLAMATION.

Whereas by an act of Congress entitled "An act to admit the States of North Carolina, South Carolina, Louisiana, Georgia, Alabama, and Florida to representation in Congress," passed on the 25th day of June, 1868, it is declared that it is made the duty of the President, within ten days after receiving official information of the ratification by the legislature of either of said States of a proposed amendment to the Constitution known as article fourteen, to issue a proclamation announcing that fact; and

Whereas the said act seems to be prospective; and

Whereas a paper purporting to be a resolution of the legislature of Florida adopting the amendment of the thirteenth and fourteenth articles of the Constitution of the United States was received at the Department of State on the 16th of June, 1868, prior to the passage of the act of Congress referred to, which paper is attested by the names of Horatio

Jenkins, jr., as president *pro tempore* of the senate, and W. W. Moore as speaker of the assembly, and of William L. Apthoop, as secretary of the senate, and William Forsyth Bynum, as clerk of the assembly, and which paper was transmitted to the Secretary of State in a letter dated Executive Office, Tallahassee, Fla., June 10, 1868, from Harrison Reed, who therein signs himself governor; and

Whereas on the 6th day of July, 1868, a paper was received by the President, which paper, being addressed to the President, bears date of the 4th day of July, 1868, and was transmitted by and under the name of W. W. Holden, who therein writes himself governor of the State of North Carolina, which paper certifies that the said proposed amendment, known as article fourteen, did pass the senate and house of representatives of the general assembly of North Carolina on the 2d day of July instant, and is attested by the names of John H. Boner, or Bower, as secretary of the house of representatives, and T. A. Byrnes, as secretary of the senate; and its ratification on the 4th of July, 1868, is attested by Tod R. Caldwell, as lieutenant-governor, president of the senate, and Jo. W. Holden, as speaker house of representatives:

Now, therefore, be it known that I, Andrew Johnson, President of the United States of America, in compliance with and execution of the act of Congress aforesaid, do issue this proclamation, announcing the fact of the ratification of the said amendment by the legislature of the State of North Carolina in the manner hereinbefore set forth.

In testimony whereof I have signed these presents with my hand and have caused the seal of the United States to be hereto affixed.

[SEAL.]   Done at the city of Washington, this 11th day of July, A. D. 1868, and of the Independence of the United States of America the ninety-third.

ANDREW JOHNSON

By the President:

WILLIAM H. SEWARD, *Secretary of State.*

BY THE PRESIDENT OF THE UNITED STATES OF AMERICA.

A PROCLAMATION.

Whereas by an act of Congress entitled "An act to admit the States of North Carolina, South Carolina, Louisiana, Georgia, Alabama, and Florida to representation in Congress," passed the 25th day of June, 1868, it is declared that it is made the duty of the President, within ten days after receiving official information of the ratification by the legislature of either of said States of a proposed amendment to the Constitution known as article fourteen, to issue a proclamation announcing that fact; and

Whereas on the 18th day of July, 1868, a letter was received by the President, which letter, being addressed to the President, bears date of July 15, 1868, and was transmitted by and under the name of R. K. Scott, who therein writes himself governor of South Carolina, in which letter was inclosed and received at the same time by the President a paper purporting to be a resolution of the senate and house of representatives of the general assembly of the State of South Carolina ratifying the said proposed amendment, and also purporting to have passed the two said houses, respectively, on the 7th and 9th of July, 1868, and to have been approved by the said R. K. Scott, as governor of said State, on the 15th of July, 1868, which circumstances are attested by the signatures of D. T. Corbin, as president *pro tempore* of the senate, and of F. J. Moses, jr., as speaker of the house of representatives of said State, and of the said R. K. Scott, as governor:

Now, therefore, be it known that I, Andrew Johnson, President of the United States of America, in compliance with and execution of the act of Congress aforesaid, do issue this my proclamation, announcing the fact of the ratification of the said amendment by the legislature of the State of South Carolina in the manner hereinbefore set forth.

In testimony whereof I have signed these presents with my hand and have caused the seal of the United States to be hereto affixed.

[SEAL.]   Done at the city of Washington, this 18th day of July, A. D. 1868, and of the Independence of the United States of America the ninety-third.

ANDREW JOHNSON.

By the President:

WILLIAM H. SEWARD. *Secretary of State.*

BY THE PRESIDENT OF THE UNITED STATES OF AMERICA.

A PROCLAMATION.

Whereas by an act of Congress entitled "An act to admit the States of North Carolina, South Carolina, Louisiana, Georgia, Alabama, and Florida to representation in Congress," passed on the 25th day of June, 1868, it is declared that it is made the duty of the President, within ten days after receiving official information of the ratification by the legislature of either of said States of a proposed amendment to the Constitution known as article fourteen, to issue a proclamation announcing that fact; and

Whereas a paper was received at the Department of State on the 17th day of July, 1868, which paper, bearing date of the 9th day of July, 1868, purports to be a resolution of the senate and house of representatives of the State of Louisiana in general assembly convened ratifying the aforesaid amendment, and is attested by the signature of George E. Bovee, as secretary of state, under a seal purporting to be the seal of the State of Louisiana:

Now, therefore, be it known that I, Andrew Johnson, President of the United States of America, in compliance with and execution of the act of Congress before mentioned, do issue this my proclamation, announcing the fact of the ratification of the said amendment by the legislature of the State of Louisiana in the manner hereinbefore set forth.

In testimony whereof I have signed these presents with my hand and have caused the seal of the United States to be hereto affixed.

[SEAL.] Done at the city of Washington, this 18th day of July, A. D. 1868, and of the Independence of the United States of America the ninety-third.

ANDREW JOHNSON.

By the President:

WILLIAM H. SEWARD, *Secretary of State.*

BY THE PRESIDENT OF THE UNITED STATES OF AMERICA.

A PROCLAMATION.

Whereas by an act of Congress entitled "An act to admit the States of North Carolina, South Carolina, Louisiana, Georgia, Alabama, and Florida to representation in Congress," passed the 25th day of June, 1868, it is declared that it is made the duty of the President, within ten days after receiving official information of the ratification by the legislature of either of said States of a proposed amendment to the Constitution known as article fourteen, to issue a proclamation announcing that fact; and

Whereas a letter was received this day by the President, which letter, being addressed to the President, bears date of July 16, 1868, and was transmitted by and under the name of William H. Smith, who therein writes himself governor of Alabama, in which letter was inclosed and received at the same time by the President a paper purporting to be a resolution of the senate and house of representatives of the general assembly of the State of Alabama ratifying the said proposed amendment, which paper is attested by the signature of Charles A. Miller, as secretary of state, under a seal purporting to be the seal of the State of Alabama, and bears the date of approval of July 13, 1868, by William H. Smith, as governor of said State:

Now, therefore, be it known that I, Andrew Johnson, President of the United States of America, in compliance with and execution of the act of Congress before mentioned, do issue this my proclamation, announcing the fact of the ratification of the said amendment by the legislature of the State of Alabama in the manner hereinbefore set forth.

In testimony whereof I have signed these presents with my hand and have caused the seal of the United States to be hereto affixed.

[SEAL.] Done at the city of Washington, this 20th day of July, A. D. 1868, and of the Independence of the United States of America the ninety-third.

ANDREW JOHNSON.

By the President:

WILLIAM H. SEWARD, *Secretary of State.*

By the President of the United States of America.

A PROCLAMATION.

Whereas by an act of Congress entitled "An act to admit the States of North Carolina, South Carolina, Louisiana, Georgia, Alabama, and Florida to representation in Congress," passed the 25th day of June, 1868, it is declared that it is made the duty of the President, within ten days after receiving official information of the ratification by the legislature of either of said States of a proposed amendment to the Constitution known as article fourteen, to issue a proclamation announcing that fact; and

Whereas a paper was received at the Department of State this 27th day of July, 1868, purporting to be a joint resolution of the senate and house of representatives of the general assembly of the State of Georgia, ratifying the said proposed amendment and also purporting to have passed the two said houses, respectively, on the 21st of July, 1868, and to have been approved by Rufus B. Bullock, who therein signs himself governor of Georgia, which paper is also attested by the signatures of Benjamin Conley, as president of the senate, and R. L. McWhorters, as speaker of the house of representatives, and is further attested by the signatures of A. E. Marshall, as secretary of the senate, and M. A. Hardin, as clerk of the house of representatives:

Now, therefore, be it known that I, Andrew Johnson, President of the United States of America, in compliance with and execution of the act of Congress before mentioned, do issue this my proclamation, announcing the fact of the ratification of the said amendment by the legislature of the State of Georgia in the manner hereinbefore set forth.

In testimony whereof I have signed these presents with my hand and have caused the seal of the United States to be hereto affixed.

[SEAL.] Done at the city of Washington, this 27th day of July, A. D. 1868, and of the Independence of the United States of America the ninety-third.

ANDREW JOHNSON.

By the President:

William H. Seward, *Secretary of State.*

By the President of the United States of America.

A PROCLAMATION.

In the year which is now drawing to its end the art, the skill, and the labor of the people of the United States have been employed with greater diligence and vigor and on broader fields than ever before, and the fruits of the earth have been gathered into the granary and the storehouse in marvelous abundance. Our highways have been lengthened, and new and prolific regions have been occupied. We are permitted to hope that long-protracted political and sectional dissensions are at no distant day to give place to returning harmony and fraternal affection throughout the Republic. Many foreign states have entered into liberal agreements with us, while nations which are far off and which heretofore have been unsocial and exclusive have become our friends.

The annual period of rest, which we have reached in health and tranquillity, and which is crowned with so many blessings, is by universal consent a convenient and suitable one for cultivating personal piety and practicing public devotion.

I therefore recommend that Thursday, the 26th day of November next, be set apart and observed by all the people of the United States as a day for public praise, thanksgiving, and prayer to the Almighty Creator and Divine Ruler of the Universe, by whose ever-watchful, merciful, and gracious providence alone states and nations, no less than families and individual men, do live and move and have their being.

In witness whereof I have hereunto set my hand and caused the seal of the United States to be affixed.

[SEAL.] Done at the city of Washington, this 12th day of October, A. D. 1868, and of the Independence of the United States the ninety-third.

ANDREW JOHNSON.

By the President:
WILLIAM H. SEWARD, *Secretary of State.*

EXECUTIVE ORDERS.

BY THE PRESIDENT OF THE UNITED STATES.

EXECUTIVE ORDER.

WASHINGTON, *December 17, 1867.*

It is desired and advised that all communications in writing intended for the executive department of this Government and relating to public business of whatever kind, including suggestions for legislation, claims, contracts, employment, appointments, and removals from office, and pardons, be transmitted directly in the first instance to the head of the Department to which the care of the subject-matter of the communication properly belongs. This regulation has become necessary for the more convenient, punctual, and regular dispatch of the public business.

By order of the President:

WILLIAM H. SEWARD,
Secretary of State.

GENERAL ORDERS, No. 104.

HEADQUARTERS OF THE ARMY,
ADJUTANT-GENERAL'S OFFICE,
Washington, December 28, 1867.

By direction of the President of the United States, the following orders are made:

I. Brevet Major-General E. O. C. Ord will turn over the command of the Fourth Military District to Brevet Major-General A. C. Gillem, and proceed to San Francisco, Cal., to take command of the Department of California.

II. On being relieved by Brevet Major-General Ord, Brevet Major-General Irvin McDowell will proceed to Vicksburg, Miss., and relieve General Gillem in command of the Fourth Military District.

III. Brevet Major-General John Pope is hereby relieved of the command of the Third Military District, and will report without delay at the Headquarters of the Army for further orders, turning over his command to the next senior officer until the arrival of his successor.

IV. Major-General George G. Meade is assigned to the command of the Third Military District, and will assume it without delay. The Department of the East will be commanded by the senior officer now on duty in it until a commander is named by the President.

V. The officers assigned in the foregoing orders to command of military districts will exercise therein any and all powers conferred by acts of Congress upon district commanders, and also any and all powers pertaining to military-department commanders.

* * * * * * *

By command of General Grant:

E. D. TOWNSEND,
Assistant Adjutant-General.

GENERAL ORDERS, No. 10.

HEADQUARTERS OF THE ARMY,
ADJUTANT-GENERAL'S OFFICE,
Washington, February 12, 1868.

The following orders are published for the information and guidance of all concerned:

EXECUTIVE MANSION,
Washington, D. C., February 12, 1868.

General U. S. GRANT,
Commanding Armies of the United States, Washington, D. C.

GENERAL: You will please issue an order creating a military division, to be called the Military Division of the Atlantic, to be composed of the Department of the Lakes, the Department of the East, and the Department of Washington, and to be commanded by Lieutenant-General William T. Sherman, with his headquarters at Washington.

Until further orders from the President, you will assign no officer to the permanent command of the Military Division of the Missouri.

Respectfully, yours,

ANDREW JOHNSON.

Major-General P. H. Sheridan, the senior officer in the Military Division of the Missouri, will temporarily perform the duties of commander of the Military Division of the Missouri, in addition to his duties of department commander.

By command of General Grant:

E. D. TOWNSEND,
Assistant Adjutant-General.

EXECUTIVE MANSION,
Washington, D. C., February 21, 1868.

Hon. EDWIN M. STANTON,
Washington, D. C.

SIR: By virtue of the power and authority vested in me as President by the Constitution and laws of the United States, you are hereby removed from office as Secretary for the Department of War, and your functions as such will terminate upon the receipt of this communication.

You will transfer to Brevet Major-General Lorenzo Thomas, Adjutant-General of the Army, who has this day been authorized and empowered to act as Secretary of War *ad interim*, all records, books, papers, and other public property now in your custody and charge.

Respectfully, yours,

ANDREW JOHNSON.

EXECUTIVE MANSION,
Washington, D. C., February 21, 1868.

Brevet Major-General LORENZO THOMAS,
Adjutant-General United States Army, Washington, D. C.

SIR: The Hon. Edwin M. Stanton having been this day removed from office as Secretary for the Department of War, you are hereby authorized and empowered to act as Secretary of War *ad interim*, and will immediately enter upon the discharge of the duties pertaining to that office.

Mr. Stanton has been instructed to transfer to you all the records, books, papers, and other public property now in his custody and charge.

Respectfully, yours,

ANDREW JOHNSON.

GENERAL ORDERS, No. 17.

HEADQUARTERS OF THE ARMY,
ADJUTANT-GENERAL'S OFFICE,
Washington, March 28, 1868.

By direction of the President of the United States, Major-General W. S. Hancock is relieved from command of the Fifth Military District and assigned to command of the Military Division of the Atlantic, created by General Orders, No. 10, of February 12, 1868.

By command of General Grant:

E. D. TOWNSEND,
Assistant Adjutant-General.

EXECUTIVE MANSION,
Washington, D. C., May 28, 1868.

The chairman of the committee of arrangements having requested that an opportunity may be given to those employed in the several Executive Departments of the Government to unite with their fellow-citizens in paying a fitting tribute to the memory of the brave men whose remains repose in the national cemeteries, the President directs that as far as may be consistent with law and the public interests persons who desire to participate in the ceremonies be permitted to absent themselves from their duties on Saturday, the 30th instant.

By order of the President:

WM. G. MOORE, *Secretary.*

EXECUTIVE MANSION,
Washington, D. C., June 1, 1868.

Major-General John M. Schofield having been appointed, by and with the advice and consent of the Senate, Secretary for the Department of War, is hereby relieved from the command of the First Military District, created by the act of Congress passed March 2, 1867.

Brevet Major-General George Stoneman is hereby assigned, according to his brevet rank of major-general, to the command of the said First District and of the Military Department of Virginia.

The Secretary of War will please give the necessary instructions to carry this order into effect.

ANDREW JOHNSON.

GENERAL ORDERS, NO. 25.

HEADQUARTERS OF THE ARMY,
ADJUTANT-GENERAL'S OFFICE,
Washington, June 3, 1868.

I. The following order of the President has been received from the War Department:

WASHINGTON, *June 2, 1868.*

The President with deep regret announces to the people of the United States the decease, at Wheatland, Pa., on the 1st instant, of his honored predecessor James Buchanan.

This event will occasion mourning in the nation for the loss of an eminent citizen and honored public servant.

As a mark of respect for his memory, it is ordered that the Executive Departments be immediately placed in mourning and all business be suspended on the day of the funeral.

It is further ordered that the War and Navy Departments cause suitable military and naval honors to be paid on this occasion to the memory of the illustrious dead.

ANDREW JOHNSON.

II. In compliance with the instructions of the President and of the Secretary of War, on the day after the receipt of this order at each military post the troops will be paraded at 10 o'clock a. m. and the order read to them, after which all labor for the day will cease.

The national flag will be displayed at half-staff.

At dawn of day thirteen guns will be fired, and afterwards, at intervals of thirty minutes between the rising and setting sun, a single gun, and at the close of the day a national salute of thirty-seven guns.

The officers of the Army will wear crape on the left arm and on their swords and the colors of the several regiments will be put in mourning for the period of six months.

By command of General Grant:

E. D. TOWNSEND,
Assistant Adjutant-General.

SPECIAL ORDER.

NAVY DEPARTMENT,
Washington, June 3, 1868.

The death of ex-President James Buchanan is announced in the following order of the President of the United States:

[For order see preceding page.]

In pursuance of the foregoing order, it is hereby directed that thirty minute guns be fired at each of the navy-yards and naval stations on Thursday, the 4th instant, the day designated for the funeral of the late ex-President Buchanan, commencing at noon, and on board the flagships in each squadron upon the day after the receipt of this order. The flags at the several navy-yards, naval stations, and marine barracks will be placed at half-mast until after the funeral, and on board all naval vessels in commission upon the day after this order is received.

GIDEON WELLES, *Secretary of the Navy.*

GENERAL ORDERS, No. 33.

HEADQUARTERS OF THE ARMY,
ADJUTANT-GENERAL'S OFFICE,
Washington, June 30, 1868.

By direction of the President of the United States, the following orders are made:

I. Brevet Major-General Irvin McDowell is relieved from the command of the Fourth Military District, and will report in person, without delay, at the War Department.

II. Brevet Major-General Alvan C. Gillem is assigned to the command of the Fourth Military District, and will assume it without delay.

By command of General Grant:

E. D. TOWNSEND,
Assistant Adjutant-General.

GENERAL ORDERS, No. 44.

HEADQUARTERS OF THE ARMY,
ADJUTANT-GENERAL'S OFFICE,
Washington, July 13, 1868.

By direction of the President, Brigadier and Brevet Major-General Irvin McDowell is assigned to the command of the Department of the East.

The headquarters of the department will be transferred from Philadelphia to New York City.

By command of General Grant:

E. D. TOWNSEND,
Assistant Adjutant-General.

GENERAL ORDERS, No. 55.

HEADQUARTERS OF THE ARMY,
ADJUTANT-GENERAL'S OFFICE,
Washington, July 28, 1868.

The following orders from the War Department, which have been approved by the President, are published for the information and government of the Army and of all concerned:

The commanding generals of the Second, Third, Fourth, and Fifth Military Districts having officially reported that the States of Arkansas, North Carolina, South Carolina, Louisiana, Georgia, Alabama, and Florida have fully complied with the acts of Congress known as the reconstruction acts, including the act passed June 22, 1868, entitled "An act to admit the State of Arkansas to representation in Congress," and the act passed June 25, 1868, entitled "An act to admit the States of North Carolina, South Carolina, Louisiana, Georgia, Alabama, and Florida to representation in Congress," and that, consequently, so much of the act of March 2, 1867, and the acts supplementary thereto as provides for the organization of military districts, subject to the military authority of the United States, as therein provided, has become inoperative in said States, and that the commanding generals have ceased to exercise in said States the military powers conferred by said acts of Congress: Therefore the following changes will be made in the organization and command of military districts and geographical departments:

I. The Second and Third Military Districts having ceased to exist, the States of North Carolina, South Carolina, Georgia, Alabama, and Florida will constitute the Department of the South, Major-General George G. Meade to command. Headquarters at Atlanta, Ga.

II. The Fourth Military District will now consist only of the State of Mississippi, and will continue to be commanded by Brevet Major-General A. C. Gillem.

III. The Fifth Military District will now consist of the State of Texas, and will be commanded by Brevet Major-General J. J. Reynolds. Headquarters at Austin, Tex.

IV. The States of Louisiana and Arkansas will constitute the Department of Louisiana. Brevet Major-General L. H. Rousseau is assigned to the command. Headquarters at New Orleans, La. Until the arrival of General Rousseau at New Orleans, Brevet Major-General Buchanan will command the Department.

V. Brevet Major-General George Crook is assigned, according to his brevet of major-general, to command the Department of the Columbia, in place of Rousseau, relieved.

VI. Brevet Major-General E. R. S. Canby is reassigned to command the Department of Washington.

*　　　*　　　*　　　*　　　*　　　*　　　*

By command of General Grant:

E. D. TOWNSEND,
Assistant Adjutant-General.

Under and in pursuance of the authority vested in the President of the United States by the provisions of the second section of the act of Congress approved on the 27th day of July, 1868, entitled "An act to extend the laws of the United States relating to customs, commerce, and navigation over the territory ceded to the United States by Russia, to establish a collection district therein, and for other purposes," the port of Sitka, in said Territory, is hereby constituted and established as the port of entry for the collection district of Alaska provided for by said act; and under and in pursuance of the authority vested in him by the fourth section of said act the importation and use of firearms, ammunition, and distilled spirits into and within the said Territory, or any portion thereof, except as hereinafter provided, is entirely prohibited, under the pains and penalties specified in said last-named section: *Provided, however,* That under such regulations as the Secretary of the Treasury may prescribe, in accordance with law, such articles may, in limited quantities, be shipped coastwise from United States ports on the Pacific coast to said port of Sitka, and to that port only in said Territory, on the shipper giving bonds to the collector of customs at the port of shipment, conditioned that such articles will on their arrival at Sitka be delivered to the collector of customs, or the person there acting as such, to remain in his possession and under his control until sold or disposed of to such persons as the military or other chief authority in said Territory may specially designate in permits for that purpose signed by himself or a subordinate duly authorized by him.

Done at the city of Washington, this 22d day of August, A. D. 1868, and of the Independence of the United States the ninety-third.

ANDREW JOHNSON, *President.*

SPECIAL ORDERS, No. 219.

HEADQUARTERS OF THE ARMY,
ADJUTANT-GENERAL'S OFFICE,
Washington, September 12, 1868.

*   *   *   *   *   *   *

18. By direction of the President, Brevet Major-General L. H. Rousseau, brigadier-general, commanding Department of Louisiana, is hereby assigned to duty according to his brevet rank of major-general. This order to take effect when General Rousseau assumes command.

19. By direction of the President, paragraph 12 of Special Orders, No. 70, May 23, 1868, from this office, assigning Brevet Major-General R. C. Buchanan, colonel First United States Infantry, to duty according to his brevet rank of major-general, is hereby revoked, and he is hereby assigned to duty according to his brevet rank of brigadier-general, in order that he may command the District of Louisiana. This order to take effect when General Rousseau assumes command of the Department of Louisiana.

By command of General Grant:

J. C. KELTON,
Assistant Adjutant-General.

GENERAL ORDERS, No. 82.

HEADQUARTERS OF THE ARMY,
ADJUTANT-GENERAL'S OFFICE,
Washington, October 10, 1868.

The following order has been received from the President, and by his direction is published to the Army:

The following provisions from the Constitution and laws of the United States in relation to the election of a President and Vice-President of the United States, together with an act of Congress prohibiting all persons engaged in the military and naval service from interfering in any general or special election in any State, are published for the information and government of all concerned:

[Extract from Article II, section 1, Constitution of the United States.]

The executive power shall be vested in a President of the United States of America. He shall hold his office during the term of four years, and, together with the Vice-President, chosen for the same term, be elected as follows:

Each State shall appoint, in such manner as the legislature thereof may direct, a number of electors equal to the whole number of Senators and Representatives to which the State may be entitled in the Congress; but no Senator or Representative, or person holding an office of trust or profit under the United States, shall be appointed an elector.

[Extract from Article XII, amendment to the Constitution of the United States.]

The electors shall meet in their respective States and vote by ballot for President and Vice-President, one of whom at least shall not be an inhabitant of the same State with themselves. They shall name in their ballots the person voted for as President, and in distinct ballots the person voted for as Vice-President; and they shall make distinct lists of all persons voted for as President, and of all persons voted for as Vice-President, and of the number of votes for each, which lists they shall sign and certify and transmit sealed to the seat of the Government of the United States, directed to the President of the Senate. The President of the Senate shall, in the presence of the Senate and House of Representatives, open all the certificates, and the votes shall then be counted. The person having the greatest number of votes for President shall be the President, if such number be a majority of the whole number of electors appointed; and if no person have such majority, then from the persons having the highest numbers, not exceeding three, on the list of those voted for as President, the House of Representatives shall choose immediately, by ballot, the President. But in choosing the President the votes shall be taken by States, the representation from each State having one vote. A quorum for this purpose shall consist of a member or members from two-thirds of the States, and a majority of all the States shall be necessary to a choice. And if the House of Representatives shall not choose a President, whenever the right of choice shall devolve upon them, before the 4th day of March next following, then the Vice-President shall act as President, as in the case of the death or other constitutional disability of the President.

[Extract from "An act relative to the election of a President and Vice-President of the United States, and declaring the officer who shall act as President in case of vacancies in the offices both of President and Vice-President," approved March 1, 1792.]

SEC. 1. *Be it enacted by the Senate and House of Representatives of the United States of America in Congress assembled*, That * * * electors shall be appointed in each State for the election of a President and Vice-President of the United States * * * in every fourth year succeeding the last election, which electors shall be equal to the number of Senators and Representatives to which the several States may by law be entitled at the time when the President and Vice-President thus to be chosen should come into office: *Provided always*, That where no apportionment of Representatives shall have been made after any enumeration at the time of choosing electors, then the number of electors shall be according to the existing apportionment of Senators and Representatives.

["An act to establish a uniform time for holding elections for electors of President and Vice-President in all the States of the Union," approved January 23, 1845.]

Be it enacted by the Senate and House of Representatives of the United States of America in Congress assembled, That the electors of President and Vice-President shall be appointed in each State on the Tuesday next after the first Monday in the month of November of the year in which they are to be appointed: *Provided*, That each State may by law provide for the filling of any vacancy or vacancies which may occur in its college of electors when such college meets to give its electoral vote: *And provided also*, When any State shall have held an election for the purpose of choosing electors, and shall fail to make a choice on the day aforesaid, then the electors may be appointed on a subsequent day in such manner as the State shall by law provide.

[Extracts from "An act relative to the election of a President and Vice-President of the United States, and declaring the officer who shall act as President in case of vacancies in the offices both of President and Vice-President," approved March 1, 1792.]

SEC. 2. *And be it further enacted*, That the electors shall meet and give their votes on the said first Wednesday in December, at such place in each State as shall be directed by the legislature thereof; and the electors in each State shall make and sign three certificates of all the votes by them given, and shall seal up the same, certifying on each that a list of the votes of such State for President and Vice-President is contained therein, and shall, by writing under their hands or under the hands of a majority of them, appoint a person to take charge of and deliver to the President of the Senate, at the seat of Government, before the first Wednesday in January then next ensuing, one of the said certificates; and the said electors shall forthwith forward by the post-office to the President of the Senate, at the seat of Government, one other of the said certificates, and shall forthwith cause the other of the said certificates to be delivered to the judge of that district in which the said electors shall assemble.

SEC. 3. *And be it further enacted,* That the executive authority of each State shall cause three lists of the names of the electors of such State to be made and certified, and to be delivered to the electors on or before the said first Wednesday in December, and the said electors shall annex one of the said lists to each of the lists of their votes.

SEC. 4. *And be it further enacted,* That if a list of votes from any State shall not have been received at the seat of Government on the said first Wednesday in January, that then the Secretary of State shall send a special messenger to the district judge in whose custody such list shall have been lodged, who shall forthwith transmit the same to the seat of Government.

SEC. 5. *And be it further enacted,* That Congress shall be in session on the second Wednesday in February, 1793, and on the second Wednesday in February succeeding every meeting of the electors, and the said certificates, or so many of them as shall have been received, shall then be opened, the votes counted, and the persons who shall fill the offices of President and Vice-President ascertained and declared agreeably to the Constitution.

SEC. 6. *And be it further enacted,* That in case there shall be no President of the Senate at the seat of Government on the arrival of the persons intrusted with the list of the votes of the electors, then such persons shall deliver the lists of votes in their custody into the office of the Secretary of State, to be safely kept and delivered over as soon as may be to the President of the Senate.

*   *   *   *   *   *   *

SEC. 8. *And be it further enacted,* That if any person appointed to deliver the votes of the electors to the President of the Senate shall, after accepting of his appointment, neglect to perform the services required of him by this act, he shall forfeit the sum of $1,000.

[Extract from "An act making compensation to the persons appointed by the electors to deliver the votes for President and Vice-President," approved February 11, 1825.]

Be it enacted by the Senate and House of Representatives of the United States of America in Congress assembled, That the person appointed by the electors to deliver to the President of the Senate a list of the votes for President and Vice-President shall be allowed, on delivery of said list, 25 cents for every mile of the estimated distance by the most usual route from the place of meeting of the electors to the seat of Government of the United States, going and returning.

[Extract from "An act relative to the election of a President and Vice-President of the United States, and declaring the officer who shall act as President in case of vacancies in the offices both of President and Vice-President," approved March 1, 1792.]

SEC. 12. *And be it further enacted,* That the term of four years for which a President and Vice-President shall be elected shall in all cases commence on the 4th day of March next succeeding the day on which the votes of the electors shall have been given.

["An act to prevent officers of the Army and Navy, and other persons engaged in the military and naval service of the United States, from interfering in elections in the States," approved February 25, 1865.]

Be it enacted by the Senate and House of Representatives of the United States of America in Congress assembled, That it shall not be lawful for any military or naval officer of the United States, or other person engaged in the civil, military, or naval service of the United States, to order, bring, keep, or have under his authority or control any troops or armed men at the place where any general or special election is held in any State of the United States of America, unless it shall be necessary to repel the armed enemies of the United States or to keep the peace at the polls. And that it shall not be lawful for any officer of the Army or Navy of the United States to prescribe or fix, or attempt to prescribe or fix, by proclamation, order, or otherwise, the qualifications of voters in any State of the United States of America, or in any manner to interfere with the freedom of any election in any State or with the exercise of the free right of suffrage in any State of the United States. Any officer of the Army or Navy of the United States, or other person engaged in the civil, military, or naval service of the United States, who violates this section of this act shall for every such offense be liable to indictment as for a misdemeanor in any court of the United States having jurisdiction to hear, try, and determine cases of misdemeanor, and on conviction thereof shall pay a fine not exceeding $5,000 and suffer imprisonment in the penitentiary not less than three months nor more than five years, at the discretion of the court trying the same; and any person convicted as aforesaid shall, moreover, be disqualified from holding any office of honor, profit, or trust under the Government of the United States: *Provided*, That nothing herein contained shall be so construed as to prevent any officers, soldiers, sailors, or marines from exercising the right of suffrage in any election district to which he may belong, if otherwise qualified according to the laws of the State in which he shall offer to vote.

SEC. 2. *And be it further enacted*, That any officer or person in the military or naval service of the United States who shall order or advise, or who shall, directly or indirectly, by force, threat, menace, intimidation, or otherwise, prevent or attempt to prevent any qualified voter of any State of the United States of America from freely exercising the right of suffrage at any general or special election in any State of the United States, or who shall in like manner compel or attempt to compel any officer of an election in any such State to receive a vote from a person not legally qualified to vote, or who shall impose or attempt to impose any rules or regulations for conducting such election different from those prescribed by law, or interfere in any manner with any officer of said election in the discharge of his duties, shall for any such offense be liable to indictment as for a misdemeanor in any court of the United States having jurisdiction to hear, try, and determine cases of misdemeanor, and on conviction thereof shall pay a fine of not exceeding $5,000 and suffer imprisonment in the penitentiary not exceeding five years, at the discretion of the court trying the same; and any person convicted as aforesaid shall, moreover, be disqualified from holding any office of honor, profit, or trust under the Government of the United States.

By command of General Grant:

E. D. TOWNSEND,
Assistant Adjutant-General.

WAR DEPARTMENT,
Washington City, November 4, 1868.

By direction of the President, Brevet Major-General E. R. S. Canby is hereby assigned to the command of the Fifth Military District, created by the act of Congress of March 2, 1867, and of the Military Department of Texas, consisting of the State of Texas. He will, without unnecessary delay, turn over his present command to the next officer in rank and proceed to the command to which he is hereby assigned, and on assuming the same will, when necessary to a faithful execution of the laws, exercise any and all powers conferred by acts of Congress upon district commanders and any and all authority pertaining to officers in command of military departments.

Brevet Major-General J. J. Reynolds is hereby relieved from the command of the Fifth Military District.

J. M. SCHOFIELD,
Secretary of War.

FOURTH ANNUAL MESSAGE.

WASHINGTON, *December 9, 1868.*

Fellow-Citizens of the Senate and House of Representatives:

Upon the reassembling of Congress it again becomes my duty to call your attention to the state of the Union and to its continued disorganized condition under the various laws which have been passed upon the subject of reconstruction.

It may be safely assumed as an axiom in the government of states that the greatest wrongs inflicted upon a people are caused by unjust and arbitrary legislation, or by the unrelenting decrees of despotic rulers, and that the timely revocation of injurious and oppressive measures is the greatest good that can be conferred upon a nation. The legislator or ruler who has the wisdom and magnanimity to retrace his steps when convinced of error will sooner or later be rewarded with the respect and gratitude of an intelligent and patriotic people.

Our own history, although embracing a period less than a century, affords abundant proof that most, if not all, of our domestic troubles are directly traceable to violations of the organic law and excessive legislation. The most striking illustrations of this fact are furnished by the enactments of the past three years upon the question of reconstruction. After a fair trial they have substantially failed and proved pernicious in their results, and there seems to be no good reason why they should longer remain upon the statute book. States to which the Constitution guarantees a republican form of government have been reduced to military dependencies, in each of which the people have been made subject to the arbitrary will of the commanding general. Although the Constitution requires that each State shall be represented in Congress, Virginia, Mississippi, and Texas are yet excluded from the two Houses, and, contrary to the express provisions of that instrument, were denied participation in the recent election for a President and Vice-President of the United States. The attempt to place the white population under the domination of persons of color in the South has impaired, if not destroyed, the kindly relations that had previously existed between them; and mutual distrust has engendered a feeling of animosity which, leading in some instances to collision and bloodshed, has prevented that cooperation between the two races so essential to the success of industrial enterprise in the Southern States. Nor have the inhabitants of those States alone suffered from the disturbed condition of affairs growing out of these Congressional enactments. The entire Union has been agitated by grave apprehensions of troubles which might again involve the peace of the nation; its interests have been injuriously affected by the derangement of business and labor, and the consequent want of prosperity throughout that portion of the country.

The Federal Constitution—the *magna charta* of American rights, under whose wise and salutary provisions we have successfully conducted all our domestic and foreign affairs, sustained ourselves in peace and in war, and become a great nation among the powers of the earth—must assuredly be now adequate to the settlement of questions growing out of the civil war, waged alone for its vindication. This great fact is made most manifest by the condition of the country when Congress assembled in the month of December, 1865. Civil strife had ceased, the spirit of rebellion had spent its entire force, in the Southern States the people had warmed into national life, and throughout the whole country a healthy reaction in public sentiment had taken place. By the application of the simple yet effective provisions of the Constitution the executive department, with the voluntary aid of the States, had brought the work of restoration as near completion as was within the scope of its authority, and the nation was encouraged by the prospect of an early and satisfactory adjustment of all its difficulties. Congress, however, intervened, and, refusing to perfect the work so nearly consummated, declined to admit members from the unrepresented States, adopted a series of measures which arrested the progress of restoration, frustrated all that had been so successfully accomplished, and, after three years of agitation and strife, has left the country further from the attainment of union and fraternal feeling than at the inception of the Congressional plan of reconstruction. It needs no argument to show that legislation which has produced such baneful consequences should be abrogated, or else made to conform to the genuine principles of republican government.

Under the influence of party passion and sectional prejudice, other acts have been passed not warranted by the Constitution. Congress has already been made familiar with my views respecting the "tenure-of-office bill." Experience has proved that its repeal is demanded by the best interests of the country, and that while it remains in force the President can not enjoin that rigid accountability of public officers so essential to an honest and efficient execution of the laws. Its revocation would enable the executive department to exercise the power of appointment and removal in accordance with the original design of the Federal Constitution.

The act of March 2, 1867, making appropriations for the support of the Army for the year ending June 30, 1868, and for other purposes, contains provisions which interfere with the President's constitutional functions as Commander in Chief of the Army and deny to States of the Union the right to protect themselves by means of their own militia. These provisions should be at once annulled; for while the first might, in times of great emergency, seriously embarrass the Executive in efforts to employ and direct the common strength of the nation for its protection and preservation, the other is contrary to the express declaration of the Constitution that "a well-regulated militia being necessary to the security of a free state, the right of the people to keep and bear arms shall not be infringed."

It is believed that the repeal of all such laws would be accepted by the American people as at least a partial return to the fundamental principles of the Government, and an indication that hereafter the Constitution is to be made the nation's safe and unerring guide. They can be productive of no permanent benefit to the country, and should not be permitted to stand as so many monuments of the deficient wisdom which has characterized our recent legislation.

The condition of our finances demands the early and earnest consideration of Congress. Compared with the growth of our population, the public expenditures have reached an amount unprecedented in our history.

The population of the United States in 1790 was nearly 4,000,000 people. Increasing each decade about 33 per cent, it reached in 1860 31,000,000, an increase of 700 per cent on the population in 1790. In 1869 it is estimated that it will reach 38,000,000, or an increase of 868 per cent in seventy-nine years.

The annual expenditures of the Federal Government in 1791 were $4,200,000; in 1820, $18,200,000; in 1850, forty-one millions; in 1860, sixty-three millions; in 1865, nearly thirteen hundred millions; and in 1869 it is estimated by the Secretary of the Treasury, in his last annual report, that they will be three hundred and seventy-two millions.

By comparing the public disbursements of 1869, as estimated, with those of 1791, it will be seen that the increase of expenditure since the beginning of the Government has been 8,618 per cent, while the increase of the population for the same period was only 868 per cent. Again, the expenses of the Government in 1860, the year of peace immediately preceding the war, were only sixty-three millions, while in 1869, the year of peace three years after the war, it is estimated they will be three hundred and seventy-two millions, an increase of 489 per cent, while the increase of population was only 21 per cent for the same period.

These statistics further show that in 1791 the annual national expenses, compared with the population, were little more than $1 per capita, and in 1860 but $2 per capita; while in 1869 they will reach the extravagant sum of $9.78 per capita.

It will be observed that all these statements refer to and exhibit the disbursements of peace periods. It may, therefore, be of interest to compare the expenditures of the three war periods—the war with Great Britain, the Mexican War, and the War of the Rebellion.

In 1814 the annual expenses incident to the War of 1812 reached their highest amount—about thirty-one millions—while our population slightly exceeded 8,000,000, showing an expenditure of only $3.80 per capita. In 1847 the expenditures growing out of the war with Mexico reached fifty-five millions, and the population about 21,000,000, giving only $2.60 per capita for the war expenses of that year. In 1865 the expenditures called for by the rebellion reached the vast amount of twelve hundred and ninety millions, which, compared with a population of 34,000,000, gives $38.20 per capita.

From the 4th day of March, 1789, to the 30th of June, 1861, the entire expenditures of the Government were $1,700,000,000. During that period we were engaged in wars with Great Britain and Mexico, and were involved in hostilities with powerful Indian tribes; Louisiana was purchased from France at a cost of $15,000,000; Florida was ceded to us by Spain for five millions; California was acquired from Mexico for fifteen millions, and the territory of New Mexico was obtained from Texas for the sum of ten millions. Early in 1861 the War of the Rebellion commenced; and from the 1st of July of that year to the 30th of June, 1865, the public expenditures reached the enormous aggregate of thirty-three hundred millions. Three years of peace have intervened, and during that time the disbursements of the Government have successively been five hundred and twenty millions, three hundred and forty-six millions, and three hundred and ninety-three millions. Adding to these amounts three hundred and seventy-two millions, estimated as necessary for the fiscal year ending the 30th of June, 1869, we obtain a total expenditure of $1,600,000,000 during the four years immediately succeeding the war, or nearly as much as was expended during the seventy-two years that preceded the rebellion and embraced the extraordinary expenditures already named.

These startling facts clearly illustrate the necessity of retrenchment in all branches of the public service. Abuses which were tolerated during the war for the preservation of the nation will not be endured by the people, now that profound peace prevails. The receipts from internal revenues and customs have during the past three years gradually diminished, and the continuance of useless and extravagant expenditures will involve us in national bankruptcy, or else make inevitable an increase of taxes, already too onerous and in many respects obnoxious on account of their inquisitorial character. One hundred millions annually are expended for the military force, a large portion of which is employed in the execution of laws both unnecessary and unconstitutional; one hundred and fifty millions are required each year to pay the interest on the public debt; an army of taxgatherers impoverishes the nation, and public agents, placed by Congress beyond the control of the Executive, divert from their legitimate purposes large sums of money which they collect from the people in the name of the Government. Judicious legislation and prudent economy can alone remedy defects and avert evils which, if suffered to exist, can not fail to diminish confidence in the public councils and weaken the attachment and respect of the people toward their political institutions. Without proper care the small balance which it is estimated will remain in the Treasury at the close of the present fiscal year will not be realized, and additional millions be added to a debt which is now enumerated by billions.

It is shown by the able and comprehensive report of the Secretary of the Treasury that the receipts for the fiscal year ending June 30, 1868, were $405,638,083, and that the expenditures for the same period were $377,340,284, leaving in the Treasury a surplus of $28,297,798. It is estimated that the receipts during the present fiscal year, ending June 30, 1869, will be $341,392,868 and the expenditures $336,152,470, showing a small balance of $5,240,398 in favor of the Government. For the fiscal year ending June 30, 1870, it is estimated that the receipts will amount to $327,000,000 and the expenditures to $303,000,000, leaving an estimated surplus of $24,000,000.

It becomes proper in this connection to make a brief reference to our public indebtedness, which has accumulated with such alarming rapidity and assumed such colossal proportions.

In 1789, when the Government commenced operations under the Federal Constitution, it was burdened with an indebtedness of $75,000,000, created during the War of the Revolution. This amount had been reduced to $45,000,000 when, in 1812, war was declared against Great Britain. The three years' struggle that followed largely increased the national obligations, and in 1816 they had attained the sum of $127,000,000. Wise and economical legislation, however, enabled the Government to pay the entire amount within a period of twenty years, and the extinguishment of the national debt filled the land with rejoicing and was one of the great events of President Jackson's Administration. After its redemption a large fund remained in the Treasury, which was deposited for safe-keeping with the several States, on condition that it should be returned when required by the public wants. In 1849—the year after the termination of an expensive war with Mexico—we found ourselves involved in a debt of $64,000,000; and this was the amount owed by the Government in 1860, just prior to the outbreak of the rebellion. In the spring of 1861 our civil war commenced. Each year of its continuance made an enormous addition to the debt; and when, in the spring of 1865, the nation successfully emerged from the conflict, the obligations of the Government had reached the immense sum of $2,873,992,909. The Secretary of the Treasury shows that on the 1st day of November, 1867, this amount had been reduced to $2,491,504,450; but at the same time his report exhibits an increase during the past year of $35,625,102, for the debt on the 1st day of November last is stated to have been $2,527,129,552. It is estimated by the Secretary that the returns for the past month will add to our liabilities the further sum of $11,000,000, making a total increase during thirteen months of $46,500,000.

In my message to Congress December 4, 1865, it was suggested that a policy should be devised which, without being oppressive to the people, would at once begin to effect a reduction of the debt, and, if persisted in, discharge it fully within a definite number of years. The Secretary of the Treasury forcibly recommends legislation of this character, and justly urges that the longer it is deferred the more difficult must become its accomplishment. We should follow the wise precedents established in 1789 and 1816, and without further delay make provision for the payment of our obligations at as early a period as may be practicable. The fruits of their labors should be enjoyed by our citizens rather than used to build up and sustain moneyed monopolies in our own and other lands. Our foreign debt is already computed by the Secretary of the Treasury at $850,000,000; citizens of foreign countries receive interest upon a large portion of our securities, and American taxpayers are made to contribute large sums for their support. The idea that such a debt is to become permanent should be at all times discarded as involving taxation too heavy to be borne, and payment once in every sixteen years, at the present rate of interest, of an amount equal to the original sum. This vast debt, if permitted to become permanent and increasing, must eventually be gathered into the hands of a few, and enable them to exert a dangerous and controlling power in the affairs of the Government. The borrowers would become servants to the lenders, the lenders the masters of the people. We now pride ourselves upon having given freedom to 4,000,000 of the colored race; it will then be our shame that 40,000,000 of people, by their own toleration of usurpation and profligacy, have suffered themselves to become enslaved, and merely exchanged slave owners for new taskmasters in the shape of bondholders and taxgatherers. Besides, permanent debts pertain to monarchical governments, and, tending to monopolies, perpetuities, and class legislation, are totally irreconcilable with free institutions. Introduced into our republican system, they would gradually but surely sap its foundations, eventually subvert our governmental fabric, and erect upon its ruins a moneyed aristocracy. It is our sacred duty to transmit unimpaired to our posterity the blessings of liberty which were bequeathed to us by the founders of the Republic, and by our example teach those who are to follow us carefully to avoid the dangers which threaten a free and independent people.

Various plans have been proposed for the payment of the public debt. However they may have varied as to the time and mode in which it should be redeemed, there seems to be a general concurrence as to the propriety and justness of a reduction in the present rate of interest. The

Secretary of the Treasury in his report recommends 5 per cent; Congress, in a bill passed prior to adjournment on the 27th of July last, agreed upon 4 and 4½ per cent; while by many 3 per cent has been held to be an amply sufficient return for the investment. The general impression as to the exorbitancy of the existing rate of interest has led to an inquiry in the public mind respecting the consideration which the Government has actually received for its bonds, and the conclusion is becoming prevalent that the amount which it obtained was in real money three or four hundred per cent less than the obligations which it issued in return. It can not be denied that we are paying an extravagant percentage for the use of the money borrowed, which was paper currency, greatly depreciated below the value of coin. This fact is made apparent when we consider that bondholders receive from the Treasury upon each dollar they own in Government securities 6 per cent in gold, which is nearly or quite equal to 9 per cent in currency; that the bonds are then converted into capital for the national banks, upon which those institutions issue their circulation, bearing 6 per cent interest; and that they are exempt from taxation by the Government and the States, and thereby enhanced 2 per cent in the hands of the holders. We thus have an aggregate of 17 per cent which may be received upon each dollar by the owners of Government securities. A system that produces such results is justly regarded as favoring a few at the expense of the many, and has led to the further inquiry whether our bondholders, in view of the large profits which they have enjoyed, would themselves be averse to a settlement of our indebtedness upon a plan which would yield them a fair remuneration and at the same time be just to the taxpayers of the nation. Our national credit should be sacredly observed, but in making provision for our creditors we should not forget what is due to the masses of the people. It may be assumed that the holders of our securities have already received upon their bonds a larger amount than their original investment, measured by a gold standard. Upon this statement of facts it would seem but just and equitable that the 6 per cent interest now paid by the Government should be applied to the reduction of the principal in semiannual installments, which in sixteen years and eight months would liquidate the entire national debt. Six per cent in gold would at present rates be equal to 9 per cent in currency, and equivalent to the payment of the debt one and a half times in a fraction less than seventeen years. This, in connection with all the other advantages derived from their investment, would afford to the public creditors a fair and liberal compensation for the use of their capital, and with this they should be satisfied. The lessons of the past admonish the lender that it is not well to be overanxious in exacting from the borrower rigid compliance with the letter of the bond.

If provision be made for the payment of the indebtedness of the Government in the manner suggested, our nation will rapidly recover its wonted prosperity. Its interests require that some measure should be taken to release the large amount of capital invested in the securities of the Government. It is not now merely unproductive, but in taxation annually consumes $150,000,000, which would otherwise be used by our enterprising people in adding to the wealth of the nation. Our commerce, which at one time successfully rivaled that of the great maritime powers, has rapidly diminished, and our industrial interests are in a depressed and languishing condition. The development of our inexhaustible resources is checked, and the fertile fields of the South are becoming waste for want of means to till them. With the release of capital, new life would be infused into the paralyzed energies of our people and activity and vigor imparted to every branch of industry. Our people need encouragement in their efforts to recover from the effects of the rebellion and of injudicious legislation, and it should be the aim of the Government to stimulate them by the prospect of an early release from the burdens which impede their prosperity. If we can not take the burdens from their shoulders, we should at least manifest a willingness to help to bear them.

In referring to the condition of the circulating medium, I shall merely reiterate substantially that portion of my last annual message which relates to that subject.

The proportion which the currency of any country should bear to the whole value of the annual produce circulated by its means is a question upon which political economists have not agreed. Nor can it be controlled by legislation, but must be left to the irrevocable laws which everywhere regulate commerce and trade. The circulating medium will ever irresistibly flow to those points where it is in greatest demand. The law of demand and supply is as unerring as that which regulates the tides of the ocean; and, indeed, currency, like the tides, has its ebbs and flows throughout the commercial world.

At the beginning of the rebellion the bank-note circulation of the country amounted to not much more than $200,000,000; now the circulation of national-bank notes and those known as "legal-tenders" is nearly seven hundred millions. While it is urged by some that this amount should be increased, others contend that a decided reduction is absolutely essential to the best interests of the country. In view of these diverse opinions, it may be well to ascertain the real value of our paper issues when compared with a metallic or convertible currency. For this purpose let us inquire how much gold and silver could be purchased by the seven hundred millions of paper money now in circulation. Probably not more than half the amount of the latter; showing that when our paper currency is compared with gold and silver its commercial value is compressed into three hundred and fifty millions. This striking fact makes it the obvious duty of the Government, as early as may be consistent with the principles of sound political economy, to take such measures as will enable the holders of its notes and those of the national banks to convert them, without loss, into specie or its equivalent. A reduction of our paper circulating medium need not necessarily follow. This, however, would depend upon the law of demand and supply, though it should be borne in mind that by making legal-tender and bank notes convertible into coin or its equivalent their present specie value in the hands of their holders would be enhanced 100 per cent.

Legislation for the accomplishment of a result so desirable is demanded by the highest public considerations. The Constitution contemplates that the circulating medium of the country shall be uniform in quality and value. At the time of the formation of that instrument the country had just emerged from the War of the Revolution, and was suffering from the effects of a redundant and worthless paper currency. The sages of that period were anxious to protect their posterity from the evils which they themselves had experienced. Hence in providing a circulating medium they conferred upon Congress the power to coin money and regulate the value thereof, at the same time prohibiting the States from making anything but gold and silver a tender in payment of debts.

The anomalous condition of our currency is in striking contrast with that which was originally designed. Our circulation now embraces, first, notes of the national banks, which are made receivable for all dues to the Government, excluding imposts, and by all its creditors, excepting in payment of interest upon its bonds and the securities themselves; second, legal tender, issued by the United States, and which the law requires shall be received as well in payment of all debts between citizens as of all Government dues, excepting imposts; and, third, gold and silver coin. By the operation of our present system of finance, however, the metallic currency, when collected, is reserved only for one class of Government creditors, who, holding its bonds, semiannually receive their interest in coin from the National Treasury. There is no reason which will be accepted as satisfactory by the people why those who defend us on the land and protect us on the sea; the pensioner upon the gratitude of the nation, bearing the scars and wounds received while in its service; the public servants in the various departments of the Government; the farmer who supplies the soldiers of the Army and the sailors of the Navy; the artisan who toils in the nation's workshops, or the mechanics and laborers who build its edifices and construct its forts and vessels of war, should, in payment of their just and hard-earned dues, receive depreciated paper, while another class of their countrymen, no more deserving, are paid in coin of gold and silver. Equal and exact justice requires that all the creditors of the Government should be paid in a currency possessing a uniform value. This can only be accomplished by the restoration of the currency to the standard established by the Constitution, and by this means we would remove a discrimination which may, if it has not already done so, create a prejudice that may become deep-rooted and widespread and imperil the national credit.

The feasibility of making our currency correspond with the constitutional standard may be seen by reference to a few facts derived from our commercial statistics.

The aggregate product of precious metals in the United States from 1849 to 1867 amounted to $1,174,000,000, while for the same period the net exports of specie were $741,000,000. This shows an excess of product over net exports of $433,000,000. There are in the Treasury $103,407,985 in coin; in circulation in the States on the Pacific Coast about $40,000,000, and a few millions in the national and other banks—in all less than $160,000,000. Taking into consideration the specie in the country prior to 1849 and that produced since 1867, and we have more than $300,000,000 not accounted for by exportation or by returns of the Treasury, and therefore most probably remaining in the country.

These are important facts, and show how completely the inferior currency will supersede the better, forcing it from circulation among the masses and causing it to be exported as a mere article of trade, to add to the money capital of foreign lands. They show the necessity of retiring our paper money, that the return of gold and silver to the avenues of trade may be invited and a demand created which will cause the retention at home of at least so much of the productions of our rich and inexhaustible gold-bearing fields as may be sufficient for purposes of circulation. It is unreasonable to expect a return to a sound currency so long as the Government and banks, by continuing to issue irredeemable notes, fill the channels of circulation with depreciated paper. Notwithstanding a coinage by our mints since 1849 of $874,000,000, the people are now strangers to the currency which was designed for their use and benefit, and specimens of the precious metals bearing the national device are seldom seen, except when produced to gratify the interest excited by their novelty. If depreciated paper is to be continued as the permanent currency of the country, and all our coin is to become a mere article of traffic and speculation, to the enhancement in price of all that is indispensable to the comfort of the people, it would be wise economy to abolish our mints, thus saving the nation the care and expense incident to such establishments, and let our precious metals be exported in bullion. The time has come, however, when the Government and national banks should be required to take the most efficient steps and make all necessary arrangements for a resumption of specie payments. Let specie payments once be earnestly inaugurated by the Government and banks, and the value of the paper circulation would directly approximate a specie standard.

Specie payments having been resumed by the Government and banks, all notes or bills of paper issued by either of a less denomination than $20 should by law be excluded from circulation, so that the people may have the benefit and convenience of a gold and silver currency which in all their business transactions will be uniform in value at home and abroad.

Every man of property or industry, every man who desires to preserve what he honestly possesses or to obtain what he can honestly earn, has a direct interest in maintaining a safe circulating medium—such a medium as shall be real and substantial, not liable to vibrate with opinions, not subject to be blown up or blown down by the breath of speculation, but to be made stable and secure. A disordered currency is one of the greatest political evils. It undermines the virtues necessary for the support of the social system and encourages propensities destructive of its happiness; it wars against industry, frugality, and economy, and it fosters the evil spirits of extravagance and speculation.

It has been asserted by one of our profound and most gifted statesmen that—

Of all the contrivances for cheating the laboring classes of mankind, none has been more effectual than that which deludes them with paper money. This is the most effectual of inventions to fertilize the rich man's fields by the sweat of the poor man's brow. Ordinary tyranny, oppression, excessive taxation—these bear lightly on the happiness of the mass of the community compared with a fraudulent currency and the robberies committed by depreciated paper. Our own history has recorded for our instruction enough, and more than enough, of the demoralizing tendency, the injustice, and the intolerable oppression on the virtuous and well-disposed of a degraded paper currency authorized by law or in any way countenanced by government.

It is one of the most successful devices, in times of peace or war, of expansions or revulsions, to accomplish the transfer of all the precious metals from the great mass of the people into the hands of the few, where they are hoarded in secret places or deposited under bolts and bars, while the people are left to endure all the inconvenience, sacrifice, and demoralization resulting from the use of depreciated and worthless paper.

The Secretary of the Interior in his report gives valuable information in reference to the interests confided to the supervision of his Department, and reviews the operations of the Land Office, Pension Office, Patent Office, and Indian Bureau.

During the fiscal year ending June 30, 1868, 6,655,700 acres of public land were disposed of. The entire cash receipts of the General Land Office for the same period were $1,632,745, being greater by $284,883 than the amount realized from the same sources during the previous year. The entries under the homestead law cover 2,328,923 acres, nearly one-fourth of which was taken under the act of June 21, 1866, which applies only to the States of Alabama, Mississippi, Louisiana, Arkansas, and Florida.

On the 30th of June, 1868, 169,643 names were borne on the pension rolls, and during the year ending on that day the total amount paid for pensions, including the expenses of disbursement, was $24,010,982, being $5,391,025 greater than that expended for like purposes during the preceding year.

During the year ending the 30th of September last the expenses of the

Patent Office exceeded the receipts by $171, and, including reissues and designs, 14,153 patents were issued.

Treaties with various Indian tribes have been concluded, and will be submitted to the Senate for its constitutional action. I cordially sanction the stipulations which provide for reserving lands for the various tribes, where they may be encouraged to abandon their nomadic habits and engage in agricultural and industrial pursuits. This policy, inaugurated many years since, has met with signal success whenever it has been pursued in good faith and with becoming liberality by the United States. The necessity for extending it as far as practicable in our relations with the aboriginal population is greater now than at any preceding period. Whilst we furnish subsistence and instruction to the Indians and guarantee the undisturbed enjoyment of their treaty rights, we should habitually insist upon the faithful observance of their agreement to remain within their respective reservations. This is the only mode by which collisions with other tribes and with the whites can be avoided and the safety of our frontier settlements secured.

The companies constructing the railway from Omaha to Sacramento have been most energetically engaged in prosecuting the work, and it is believed that the line will be completed before the expiration of the next fiscal year. The 6 per cent bonds issued to these companies amounted on the 5th instant to $44,337,000, and additional work had been performed to the extent of $3,200,000.

The Secretary of the Interior in August last invited my attention to the report of a Government director of the Union Pacific Railroad Company who had been specially instructed to examine the location, construction, and equipment of their road. I submitted for the opinion of the Attorney-General certain questions in regard to the authority of the Executive which arose upon this report and those which had from time to time been presented by the commissioners appointed to inspect each successive section of the work. After carefully considering the law of the case, he affirmed the right of the Executive to order, if necessary, a thorough revision of the entire road. Commissioners were thereupon appointed to examine this and other lines, and have recently submitted a statement of their investigations, of which the report of the Secretary of the Interior furnishes specific information.

The report of the Secretary of War contains information of interest and importance respecting the several bureaus of the War Department and the operations of the Army. The strength of our military force on the 30th of September last was 48,000 men, and it is computed that by the 1st of January next this number will be decreased to 43,000. It is the opinion of the Secretary of War that within the next year a considerable diminution of the infantry force may be made without detriment to the interests of the country; and in view of the great expense attending the military peace establishment and the absolute necessity of retrenchment wherever it can be applied, it is hoped that Congress will sanction the reduction which his report recommends. While in 1860 sixteen thousand three hundred men cost the nation $16,472,000, the sum of $65,682,000 is estimated as necessary for the support of the Army during the fiscal year ending June 30, 1870. The estimates of the War Department for the last two fiscal years were, for 1867, $33,814,461, and for 1868 $25,205,669. The actual expenditures during the same periods were, respectively, $95,224,415 and $123,246,648. The estimate submitted in December last for the fiscal year ending June 30, 1869, was $77,124,707; the expenditures for the first quarter, ending the 30th of September last, were $27,219,117, and the Secretary of the Treasury gives $66,000,000 as the amount which will probably be required during the remaining three quarters, if there should be no reduction of the Army—making its aggregate cost for the year considerably in excess of ninety-three millions. The difference between the estimates and expenditures for the three fiscal years which have been named is thus shown to be $175,545,343 for this single branch of the public service.

The report of the Secretary of the Navy exhibits the operations of that Department and of the Navy during the year. A considerable reduction of the force has been effected. There are 42 vessels, carrying 411 guns, in the six squadrons which are established in different parts of the world. Three of these vessels are returning to the United States and 4 are used as storeships, leaving the actual cruising force 35 vessels, carrying 356 guns. The total number of vessels in the Navy is 206, mounting 1,743 guns. Eighty-one vessels of every description are in use, armed with 696 guns. The number of enlisted men in the service, including apprentices, has been reduced to 8,500. An increase of navy-yard facilities is recommended as a measure which will in the event of war be promotive of economy and security. A more thorough and systematic survey of the North Pacific Ocean is advised in view of our recent acquisitions, our expanding commerce, and the increasing intercourse between the Pacific States and Asia. The naval pension fund, which consists of a moiety of the avails of prizes captured during the war, amounts to $14,000,000. Exception is taken to the act of 23d July last, which reduces the interest on the fund loaned to the Government by the Secretary, as trustee, to 3 per cent instead of 6 per cent, which was originally stipulated when the investment was made. An amendment of the pension laws is suggested to remedy omissions and defects in existing enactments. The expenditures of the Department during the last fiscal year were $20,120,394, and the estimates for the coming year amount to $20,993,414.

The Postmaster-General's report furnishes a full and clear exhibit of the operations and condition of the postal service. The ordinary postal revenue for the fiscal year ending June 30, 1868, was $16,292,600, and the total expenditures, embracing all the service for which special appropriations have been made by Congress, amounted to $22,730,592, showing an excess of expenditures of $6,437,991. Deducting from the expenditures the sum of $1,896,525, the amount of appropriations for ocean-steamship and other special service, the excess of expenditures was $4,541,466. By using an unexpended balance in the Treasury of $3,800,000 the actual sum for which a special appropriation is required to meet the deficiency is $741,466. The causes which produced this large excess of expenditure over revenue were the restoration of service in the late insurgent States and the putting into operation of new service established by acts of Congress, which amounted within the last two years and a half to about 48,700 miles—equal to more than one-third of the whole amount of the service at the close of the war. New postal conventions with Great Britain, North Germany, Belgium, the Netherlands, Switzerland, and Italy, respectively, have been carried into effect. Under their provisions important improvements have resulted in reduced rates of international postage and enlarged mail facilities with European countries. The cost of the United States transatlantic ocean mail service since January 1, 1868, has been largely lessened under the operation of these new conventions, a reduction of over one-half having been effected under the new arrangements for ocean mail steamship service which went into effect on that date. The attention of Congress is invited to the practical suggestions and recommendations made in his report by the Postmaster-General.

No important question has occurred during the last year in our accustomed cordial and friendly intercourse with Costa Rica, Guatemala, Honduras, San Salvador, France, Austria, Belgium, Switzerland, Portugal, the Netherlands, Denmark, Sweden and Norway, Rome, Greece, Turkey, Persia, Egypt, Liberia, Morocco, Tripoli, Tunis, Muscat, Siam, Borneo, and Madagascar.

Cordial relations have also been maintained with the Argentine and the Oriental Republics. The expressed wish of Congress that our national good offices might be tendered to those Republics, and also to Brazil and Paraguay, for bringing to an end the calamitous war which has so long been raging in the valley of the La Plata, has been assiduously complied with and kindly acknowledged by all the belligerents. That important negotiation, however, has thus far been without result.

Charles A. Washburn, late United States minister to Paraguay, having resigned, and being desirous to return to the United States, the rear-admiral commanding the South Atlantic Squadron was early directed to send a ship of war to Asuncion, the capital of Paraguay, to receive Mr. Washburn and his family and remove them from a situation which was represented to be endangered by faction and foreign war. The Brazilian commander of the allied invading forces refused permission to the *Wasp* to pass through the blockading forces, and that vessel returned to its accustomed anchorage. Remonstrance having been made against this refusal, it was promptly overruled, and the *Wasp* therefore resumed her errand, received Mr. Washburn and his family, and conveyed them to a safe and convenient seaport. In the meantime an excited controversy had arisen between the President of Paraguay and the late United States minister, which, it is understood, grew out of his proceedings in giving asylum in the United States legation to alleged enemies of that Republic. The question of the right to give asylum is one always difficult and often productive of great embarrassment. In states well organized and established, foreign powers refuse either to concede or exercise that right, except as to persons actually belonging to the diplomatic service. On the other hand, all such powers insist upon exercising the right of asylum in states where the law of nations is not fully acknowledged, respected, and obeyed.

The President of Paraguay is understood to have opposed to Mr. Washburn's proceedings the injurious and very improbable charge of personal complicity in insurrection and treason. The correspondence, however, has not yet reached the United States.

Mr. Washburn, in connection with this controversy, represents that two United States citizens attached to the legation were arbitrarily seized at his side, when leaving the capital of Paraguay, committed to prison, and there subjected to torture for the purpose of procuring confessions of their own criminality and testimony to support the President's allegations against the United States minister. Mr. McMahon, the newly appointed minister to Paraguay, having reached the La Plata, has been instructed to proceed without delay to Asuncion, there to investigate the whole subject. The rear-admiral commanding the United States South Atlantic Squadron has been directed to attend the new minister with a proper naval force to sustain such just demands as the occasion may require, and to vindicate the rights of the United States citizens referred to and of any others who may be exposed to danger in the theater of war. With these exceptions, friendly relations have been maintained between the United States and Brazil and Paraguay.

Our relations during the past year with Bolivia, Ecuador, Peru, and Chile have become especially friendly and cordial. Spain and the Republics of Peru, Bolivia, and Ecuador have expressed their willingness to accept the mediation of the United States for terminating the war upon the South Pacific coast. Chile has not finally declared upon the question. In the meantime the conflict has practically exhausted itself, since no belligerent or hostile movement has been made by either party during the last two years, and there are no indications of a present purpose to resume hostilities on either side. Great Britain and France have cordially seconded our proposition of mediation, and I do not forego the hope that it may soon be accepted by all the belligerents and lead to a secure establishment of peace and friendly relations between the Spanish American Republics of the Pacific and Spain—a result which would be attended with common benefits to the belligerents and much advantage to all commercial nations. I communicate, for the consideration of Congress, a correspondence which shows that the Bolivian Republic has established the extremely liberal principle of receiving into its citizenship any citizen of the United States, or of any other of the American Republics, upon the simple condition of voluntary registry.

The correspondence herewith submitted will be found painfully replete with accounts of the ruin and wretchedness produced by recent earthquakes, of unparalleled severity, in the Republics of Peru, Ecuador, and Bolivia. The diplomatic agents and naval officers of the United States who were present in those countries at the time of those disasters furnished all the relief in their power to the sufferers, and were promptly rewarded with grateful and touching acknowledgments by the Congress of Peru. An appeal to the charity of our fellow-citizens has been answered by much liberality. In this connection I submit an appeal which has been made by the Swiss Republic, whose Government and institutions are kindred to our own, in behalf of its inhabitants, who are suffering extreme destitution, produced by recent devastating inundations.

Our relations with Mexico during the year have been marked by an increasing growth of mutual confidence. The Mexican Government has not yet acted upon the three treaties celebrated here last summer for establishing the rights of naturalized citizens upon a liberal and just basis, for regulating consular powers, and for the adjustment of mutual claims.

All commercial nations, as well as all friends of republican institutions, have occasion to regret the frequent local disturbances which occur in some of the constituent States of Colombia. Nothing has occurred, however, to affect the harmony and cordial friendship which have for several years existed between that youthful and vigorous Republic and our own.

Negotiations are pending with a view to the survey and construction of a ship canal across the Isthmus of Darien, under the auspices of the United States. I hope to be able to submit the results of that negotiation to the Senate during its present session.

The very liberal treaty which was entered into last year by the United States and Nicaragua has been ratified by the latter Republic.

Costa Rica, with the earnestness of a sincerely friendly neighbor, solicits a reciprocity of trade, which I commend to the consideration of Congress.

The convention created by treaty between the United States and Venezuela in July, 1865, for the mutual adjustment of claims, has been held, and its decisions have been received at the Department of State. The heretofore-recognized Government of the United States of Venezuela has been subverted. A provisional government having been instituted under circumstances which promise durability, it has been formally recognized.

I have been reluctantly obliged to ask explanation and satisfaction for national injuries committed by the President of Hayti. The political and social condition of the Republics of Hayti and St. Domingo is very unsatisfactory and painful. The abolition of slavery, which has been carried into effect throughout the island of St. Domingo and the entire West Indies, except the Spanish islands of Cuba and Porto Rico, has been followed by a profound popular conviction of the rightfulness of republican institutions and an intense desire to secure them. The attempt, however, to establish republics there encounters many obstacles, most of which may be supposed to result from long-indulged habits of colonial supineness and dependence upon European monarchical powers. While the United States have on all occasions professed a decided unwillingness that any part of this continent or of its adjacent islands shall be made a theater for a new establishment of monarchical power, too little has been done by us, on the other hand, to attach the communities by which we are surrounded to our own country, or to lend even a moral support to the efforts they are so resolutely and so constantly making to secure republican institutions for themselves. It is indeed a question of grave consideration whether our recent and present example is not calculated to check the growth and expansion of free principles, and make those communities distrust, if not dread, a government which at will consigns to military domination States that are integral parts of our Federal Union, and, while ready to resist any attempts by other nations to extend to this hemisphere the monarchical institutions of Europe, assumes to establish over a large portion of its people a rule more absolute, harsh, and tyrannical than any known to civilized powers.

The acquisition of Alaska was made with the view of extending national jurisdiction and republican principles in the American hemisphere. Believing that a further step could be taken in the same direction, I last year entered into a treaty with the King of Denmark for the purchase of the islands of St. Thomas and St. John, on the best terms then attainable, and with the express consent of the people of those islands. This treaty still remains under consideration in the Senate. A new convention has been entered into with Denmark, enlarging the time fixed for final ratification of the original treaty.

Comprehensive national policy would seem to sanction the acquisition and incorporation into our Federal Union of the several adjacent continental and insular communities as speedily as it can be done peacefully, lawfully, and without any violation of national justice, faith, or honor. Foreign possession or control of those communities has hitherto hindered the growth and impaired the influence of the United States. Chronic revolution and anarchy there would be equally injurious. Each one of them, when firmly established as an independent republic, or when incorporated into the United States, would be a new source of strength and power. Conforming my Administration to these principles, I have on no occasion lent support or toleration to unlawful expeditions set on foot upon the plea of republican propagandism or of national extension or aggrandizement. The necessity, however, of repressing such unlawful movements clearly indicates the duty which rests upon us of adapting our legislative action to the new circumstances of a decline of European monarchical power and influence and the increase of American republican ideas, interests, and sympathies.

It can not be long before it will become necessary for this Government to lend some effective aid to the solution of the political and social problems which are continually kept before the world by the two Republics of the island of St. Domingo, and which are now disclosing themselves more distinctly than heretofore in the island of Cuba. The subject is commended to your consideration with all the more earnestness because I am satisfied that the time has arrived when even so direct a proceeding as a proposition for an annexation of the two Republics of the island of St. Domingo would not only receive the consent of the people interested, but would also give satisfaction to all other foreign nations.

I am aware that upon the question of further extending our possessions it is apprehended by some that our political system can not successfully be applied to an area more extended than our continent; but the conviction is rapidly gaining ground in the American mind that with the increased facilities for intercommunication between all portions of the earth the principles of free government, as embraced in our Constitution, if faithfully maintained and carried out, would prove of sufficient strength and breadth to comprehend within their sphere and influence the civilized nations of the world.

The attention of the Senate and of Congress is again respectfully invited to the treaty for the establishment of commercial reciprocity with the Hawaiian Kingdom entered into last year, and already ratified by that Government. The attitude of the United States toward these islands is not very different from that in which they stand toward the West Indies. It is known and felt by the Hawaiian Government and people that their Government and institutions are feeble and precarious; that the United States, being so near a neighbor, would be unwilling to see the islands pass under foreign control. Their prosperity is continually disturbed by expectations and alarms of unfriendly political proceedings, as well from the United States as from other foreign powers. A reciprocity treaty, while it could not materially diminish the revenues of the United States, would be a guaranty of the good will and forbearance of all nations until the people of the islands shall of themselves, at no distant day, voluntarily apply for admission into the Union.

The Emperor of Russia has acceded to the treaty negotiated here in January last for the security of trade-marks in the interest of manufacturers and commerce. I have invited his attention to the importance of establishing, now while it seems easy and practicable, a fair and equal regulation of the vast fisheries belonging to the two nations in the waters of the North Pacific Ocean.

The two treaties between the United States and Italy for the regulation of consular powers and the extradition of criminals, negotiated and ratified here during the last session of Congress, have been accepted and confirmed by the Italian Government. A liberal consular convention which has been negotiated with Belgium will be submitted to the Senate. The very important treaties which were negotiated between the United States and North Germany and Bavaria for the regulation of the rights of naturalized citizens have been duly ratified and exchanged, and similar treaties have been entered into with the Kingdoms of Belgium and Wurtemberg and with the Grand Duchies of Baden and Hesse-Darmstadt. I hope soon to be able to submit equally satisfactory conventions of the same character now in the course of negotiation with the respective Governments of Spain, Italy, and the Ottoman Empire.

Examination of claims against the United States by the Hudsons Bay Company and the Puget Sound Agricultural Company, on account of certain possessory rights in the State of Oregon and Territory of Washington, alleged by those companies in virtue of provisions of the treaty between the United States and Great Britain of June 15, 1846, has been diligently prosecuted, under the direction of the joint international commission to which they were submitted for adjudication by treaty between the two Governments of July 1, 1863, and will, it is expected, be concluded at an early day.

No practical regulation concerning colonial trade and the fisheries can be accomplished by treaty between the United States and Great Britain until Congress shall have expressed their judgment concerning the principles involved. Three other questions, however, between the United States and Great Britain remain open for adjustment. These are the mutual rights of naturalized citizens, the boundary question involving the title to the island of San Juan, on the Pacific coast, and mutual claims arising since the year 1853 of the citizens and subjects of the two countries for injuries and depredations committed under the authority of their respective Governments. Negotiations upon these subjects are pending, and I am not without hope of being able to lay before the Senate, for its consideration during the present session, protocols calculated to bring to an end these justly exciting and long-existing controversies.

We are not advised of the action of the Chinese Government upon the liberal and auspicious treaty which was recently celebrated with its plenipotentiaries at this capital.

Japan remains a theater of civil war, marked by religious incidents and political severities peculiar to that long-isolated Empire. The Executive has hitherto maintained strict neutrality among the belligerents, and acknowledges with pleasure that it has been frankly and fully sustained in that course by the enlightened concurrence and cooperation of the other treaty powers, namely, Great Britain, France, the Netherlands, North Germany, and Italy.

Spain having recently undergone a revolution marked by extraordinary unanimity and preservation of order, the provisional government established at Madrid has been recognized, and the friendly intercourse which has so long happily existed between the two countries remains unchanged.

I renew the recommendation contained in my communication to Congress dated the 18th July last—a copy of which accompanies this message—that the judgment of the people should be taken on the propriety of so amending the Federal Constitution that it shall provide—

First. For an election of President and Vice-President by a direct vote of the people, instead of through the agency of electors, and making them ineligible for reelection to a second term.

Second. For a distinct designation of the person who shall discharge the duties of President in the event of a vacancy in that office by the death, resignation, or removal of both the President and Vice-President.

Third. For the election of Senators of the United States directly by the people of the several States, instead of by the legislatures; and

Fourth. For the limitation to a period of years of the terms of Federal judges.

Profoundly impressed with the propriety of making these important modifications in the Constitution, I respectfully submit them for the early and mature consideration of Congress. We should, as far as possible, remove all pretext for violations of the organic law, by remedying such imperfections as time and experience may develop, ever remembering that "the constitution which at any time exists until changed by an explicit and authentic act of the whole people is sacredly obligatory upon all."

In the performance of a duty imposed upon me by the Constitution, I have thus communicated to Congress information of the state of the Union and recommended for their consideration such measures as have seemed to me necessary and expedient. If carried into effect, they will hasten the accomplishment of the great and beneficent purposes for which the Constitution was ordained, and which it comprehensively states were "to form a more perfect Union, establish justice, insure domestic tranquillity, provide for the common defense, promote the general welfare, and secure the blessings of liberty to ourselves and our posterity." In Congress are vested all legislative powers, and upon them devolves the responsibility as well for framing unwise and excessive laws as for neglecting to devise and adopt measures absolutely demanded by the wants of the country. Let us earnestly hope that before the expiration of our respective terms of service, now rapidly drawing to a close, an all-wise Providence will so guide our counsels as to strengthen and preserve the Federal Union, inspire reverence for the Constitution, restore prosperity and happiness to our whole people, and promote "on earth peace, good will toward men."

ANDREW JOHNSON.

SPECIAL MESSAGES.

WASHINGTON, *December 8, 1868.*

To the Senate and House of Representatives:

I transmit a copy of a note of the 24th of November last addressed to the Secretary of State by the minister of Great Britain, communicating a decree of the district court of the United States for the southern district of New York ordering the payment of certain sums to the defendants in a suit against the English schooner *Sibyl*, libeled as a prize of war. It is requisite for the fulfillment of the decree that an appropriation of the sums specified therein should be made by Congress. The appropriation is recommended accordingly. ANDREW JOHNSON.

WASHINGTON, *December 11, 1868.*

To the House of Representatives of the United States:

In answer to the resolution of the House of Representatives of the 7th instant, relating to the correspondence with the American minister at London concerning the so-called *Alabama* claims, I transmit a report on the subject from the Secretary of State.

ANDREW JOHNSON.

WASHINGTON, *December 16, 1868.*

To the House of Representatives:

In answer to a resolution of the House of Representatives of the 14th December instant, I transmit the accompanying report* of the Secretary of State. ANDREW JOHNSON.

WASHINGTON, *December 16, 1868.*

To the House of Representatives:

In answer to the resolution of the House of Representatives of the 14th instant, requesting the correspondence which has taken place between the United States minister at Brazil and Rear-Admiral Davis touching the disposition of the American squadron at Rio Janeiro and the Paraguay difficulties, I transmit a report of the Secretary of State upon that subject. ANDREW JOHNSON.

WASHINGTON, *December 16, 1868.*

To the Senate of the United States:

In answer to the resolution of the Senate of the 8th instant, concerning recent transactions in the region of the La Plata affecting the political

* Relating to the sending of a commissioner from the United States to Spain.

relations of the United States with Paraguay, the Argentine Republic, Uruguay, and Brazil, I transmit a report of the Secretary of State, which is accompanied by a copy of the papers called for by the resolution.

ANDREW JOHNSON.

WASHINGTON, *December 18, 1868.*

To the House of Representatives:

I herewith communicate a report of the Secretary of the Interior, in answer to a resolution adopted by the House of Representatives on the 16th instant, making inquiries in reference to the Union Pacific Railroad and requesting the transmission of the report of the special commissioners appointed to examine the construction and equipment of the road.

ANDREW JOHNSON.

WASHINGTON, *January 4, 1869.*

To the Senate of the United States:

I transmit to the Senate, in compliance with the request contained in its resolution of the 15th ultimo, a report from the Secretary of State, communicating information in regard to the action of the mixed commission for the adjustment of claims by citizens of the United States against the Government of Venezuela. ANDREW JOHNSON.

WASHINGTON, *January 4, 1869.*

To the House of Representatives:

I transmit to the House of Representatives a report from the Secretary of State, with accompanying papers, in relation to the resolution of Congress approved July 20, 1867, ''declaring sympathy with the suffering people of Crete.'' ANDREW JOHNSON.

[The same message was sent to the Senate.]

WASHINGTON, *January 4, 1869.*

To the Senate of the United States:

I transmit to the Senate, for its consideration with a view to ratification, an additional article to the convention of the 24th of October, 1867, between the United States and His Majesty the King of Denmark.

ANDREW JOHNSON.

WASHINGTON, *January 5, 1869.*

To the Senate of the United States:

I transmit to the Senate, for its consideration with a view to ratification, a convention between the United States and His Hawaiian Majesty, signed in this city on the 28th day of July last, stipulating for an extension of the period for the exchange of the ratifications of the convention between the same parties on the subject of commercial reciprocity.

ANDREW JOHNSON.

WASHINGTON, *January 7, 1869.*

To the House of Representatives:

I transmit herewith, in answer to a resolution of the House of Representatives of the 16th of December last, a report* from the Secretary of State of the 6th instant.

ANDREW JOHNSON.

WASHINGTON, D. C., *January 8, 1869.*

To the Senate and House of Representatives:

In conformity with the requirements of the sixth section of the act of the 22d of June, 1860, to carry into effect provisions of the treaty with China and certain other Oriental nations, I transmit to Congress a copy of eight rules agreed upon between the Chinese Imperial Government and the minister of the United States and those of other foreign powers accredited to that Government, for conducting the proceedings of the joint tribunal in cases of confiscation and fines for breaches of the revenue laws of that Empire. These rules, which are accompanied by correspondence between our minister and Secretary of State on the subject, are commended to the consideration of Congress with a view to their approval.

ANDREW JOHNSON.

WASHINGTON, *January 8, 1869.*

To the Senate of the United States:

I transmit to the Senate, in answer to their resolution of the 17th ultimo, a report† from the Secretary of State, with an accompanying paper.

ANDREW JOHNSON.

WASHINGTON, *January 11, 1869.*

To the Senate of the United States:

I transmit to the Senate, for its consideration with a view to ratification, a convention between the United States and Belgium upon the subject of naturalization, which was signed at Brussels on the 16th of November last.

ANDREW JOHNSON.

---

*Giving reasons why reductions in the number of officers and employees and in the salaries and expenses of the Department of State should not be made.

†Relating to the exercise or claim by United States consuls in Japan of judicial powers in cases arising between American citizens and citizens or subjects of any foreign nation other than Japan, etc.

WASHINGTON, *January 11, 1869.*

To the Senate of the United States:

I transmit to the Senate, for its consideration with a view to ratification, a convention between the United States and Belgium concerning the rights, privileges, and immunities of consuls in the two countries, signed at Brussels on the 5th ultimo.

ANDREW JOHNSON.

WASHINGTON, *January 11, 1869.*

To the Senate of the United States:

I transmit to the Senate, for its consideration with a view to ratification, an additional article of the treaty of commerce and navigation between the United States and Belgium of the 17th of July, 1858, which was signed at Brussels on the 20th ultimo.

ANDREW JOHNSON.

WASHINGTON, *January 12, 1869.*

To the Senate of the United States:

I transmit a copy of a convention between the United States and Peru, signed at Lima on the 4th of last month, stipulating for a mixed commission for the adjustment of claims of citizens of the two countries. An extract from that part of the dispatch of the minister of the United States at Lima which accompanied the copy referred to, and which relates to it, is also transmitted. It will be seen from this extract that it is desirable that the decision of the Senate upon the instrument should be given as early as may be convenient. It is consequently recommended for consideration with a view to ratification.

ANDREW JOHNSON.

WASHINGTON, D. C.,
January 13, 1869.

To the Senate of the United States:

I herewith lay before the Senate, for its constitutional action thereon, a treaty concluded at Washington, D. C., August 13, 1868, between the United States and the Nez Perce tribe of Indians, which treaty is supplemental to and amendatory of the treaty concluded with said tribe June 9, 1863. A communication from the Secretary of the Interior of the 12th instant, inclosing a copy of a report of the Commissioner of Indian Affairs of the 11th instant, is also herewith transmitted.*

ANDREW JOHNSON.

---

* NOTE BY THE EXECUTIVE CLERK OF THE SENATE.—"The communication from the Secretary of the Interior and this report of the Commissioner of Indian Affairs did not accompany the above communication from the President."

WASHINGTON, *January 14, 1869.*

To the Senate of the United States:

I transmit herewith a report from the Secretary of War, together with the original papers accompanying the same, submitted in compliance with the resolution of the Senate of the 5th instant, requesting such information as is furnished by the files of the War Department in relation to the erection of fortifications at Lawrence, Kans., in 1864 and 1865.

ANDREW JOHNSON.

WASHINGTON, *January 15, 1869.*

To the Senate of the United States:

I transmit, for the opinion of the Senate as to the expediency of concluding a convention based thereupon, a protocol, signed at London on the 9th of October last, for regulating the citizenship of citizens of the United States who have emigrated or who may emigrate from the United States to the British dominions, and of British subjects who have emigrated or who may emigrate from the British dominions to the United States of America.

ANDREW JOHNSON.

WASHINGTON, *January 15, 1869.*

To the Senate of the United States:

I transmit to the Senate, for consideration with a view to its ratification, a copy of a treaty between the United States and Great Britain, signed yesterday at London, providing for the reference to an arbiter of the question of difference between the United States and Great Britain concerning the northwest line of water boundary between the United States and the British possessions in North America. It is expected that the original of the convention will be forwarded by the steamer which leaves Liverpool to-morrow. Circumstances, however, to which it is unnecessary to advert, in my judgment make it advisable to communicate to the Senate the copy referred to in advance of the arrival of the original instrument.

ANDREW JOHNSON.

WASHINGTON, *January 15, 1869.*

To the Senate of the United States:

I transmit to the Senate, for consideration with a view of its ratification, a copy of a convention between the United States and Great Britain, signed yesterday at London, providing for the adjustment of all outstanding claims of the citizens and subjects of the parties, respectively. It is expected that the original of the convention will be forwarded by the steamer which leaves Liverpool to-morrow. Circumstances, however, to which it is unnecessary to advert, in my judgment make it advisable to communicate to the Senate the copy referred to in advance of the arrival of the original instrument.

ANDREW JOHNSON.

WASHINGTON, D. C., *January 18, 1869.*

To the Senate of the United States:

The resolution adopted on the 5th instant, requesting the President "to transmit to the Senate a copy of any proclamation of amnesty made by him since the last adjournment of Congress, and also to communicate to the Senate by what authority of law the same was made," has been received.

I accordingly transmit herewith a copy of a proclamation dated the 25th day of December last. The authority of law by which it was made is set forth in the proclamation itself, which expressly affirms that it was issued "by virtue of the power and authority in me vested by the Constitution, and in the name of the sovereign people of the United States," and proclaims and declares "unconditionally and without reservation, to all and to every person who, directly or indirectly, participated in the late insurrection or rebellion, a full pardon and amnesty for the offense of treason against the United States, or of adhering to their enemies during the late civil war, with restoration of all rights, privileges, and immunities under the Constitution and the laws which have been made in pursuance thereof."

The Federal Constitution is understood to be and is regarded by the Executive as the supreme law of the land. The second section of article second of that instrument provides that the President "shall have power to grant reprieves and pardons for offenses against the United States, except in cases of impeachment." The proclamation of the 25th ultimo is in strict accordance with the judicial expositions of the authority thus conferred upon the Executive, and, as will be seen by reference to the accompanying papers, is in conformity with the precedent established by Washington in 1795, and followed by President Adams in 1800, Madison in 1815, and Lincoln in 1863, and by the present Executive in 1865, 1867, and 1868.

ANDREW JOHNSON.

WASHINGTON, *January 20, 1869.*

To the Senate of the United States:

I transmit herewith a report from the Secretary of War, made in compliance with the resolution of the Senate of the 19th ultimo, requesting information in reference to the payment of rent for the use of the building known as the Libby Prison, in the city of Richmond, Va.

ANDREW JOHNSON.

WASHINGTON, *January 22, 1869.*

To the Senate of the United States:

I transmit to the Senate, for its consideration with a view to ratification, an additional article to the convention between the United States and His Majesty the King of Italy for regulating the jurisdiction of consuls.

ANDREW JOHNSON.

WASHINGTON, *January 22, 1869.*

To the Senate of the United States:

I transmit to the Senate, for its consideration with a view to ratification, an additional article to the convention between the United States and His Majesty the King of Italy for the mutual extradition of criminals fugitives from justice.

ANDREW JOHNSON.

EXECUTIVE MANSION, *January 23, 1869.*

To the Senate of the United States:

I herewith lay before the Senate, for the constitutional action of that body, a treaty concluded at the council house on the Cattaraugus Reservation, in Erie County, N. Y., on the 4th day of December, 1868, by Walter R. Irwin, commissioner on the part of the United States, and the duly authorized representatives of the several tribes and bands of Indians residing in the State of New York. A copy of a letter from the Secretary of the Interior, dated the 22d instant, and the papers therein referred to, in relation to the treaty, are also herewith transmitted.

ANDREW JOHNSON.

WASHINGTON, *January 26, 1869.*

To the Senate and House of Representatives:

I transmit for the consideration of Congress, in conformity with the requirements of the sixth section of the act of the 22d of June, 1860, a copy of certain regulations for the consular courts in China, prohibiting steamers sailing under the flag of the United States from using or passing through the Straw Shoe Channel on the river Yangtse, decreed by S. Wells Williams, chargé d'affaires, on the 1st of June, and promulgated by George F. Seward, consul-general at Shanghai, on the 25th of July, 1868, with the assent of five of the United States consuls in China, G. H. Colton Salter dissenting. His objections to the regulations are set forth in the accompanying copy of a communication of the 10th of October last, inclosed in Consul-General Seward's dispatch of the 14th of the same month to the Secretary of State, a copy of which is also transmitted.

ANDREW JOHNSON.

WASHINGTON, D. C., *January 26, 1869.*

To the Senate and House of Representatives:

I transmit to Congress a report from the Secretary of State, with accompanying documents, in relation to the gold medal presented to Mr. George Peabody pursuant to the resolution of Congress of March 16, 1867.

ANDREW JOHNSON.

WASHINGTON, *January 27, 1869.*

To the House of Representatives:

I transmit to the House of Representatives, in answer to their resolution of the 23d instant, the accompanying report * from the Secretary of State.

ANDREW JOHNSON.

WASHINGTON, *January 27, 1869.*

To the Senate of the United States:

I transmit herewith a communication from the Secretary of War, upon the subject of the resolution of the Senate of the 21st instant, requesting a copy of the report of Brevet Major-General William S. Harney upon the Sioux and other Indians congregated under treaties made with them by the special peace commission.

ANDREW JOHNSON.

WASHINGTON, *January 29, 1869.*

To the House of Representatives of the United States:

I transmit to the House of Representatives, in answer to a resolution of the House of Representatives without date, received at the Executive Mansion on the 10th of December, calling for correspondence in relation to the cases of Messrs. Costello and Warren, naturalized citizens of the United States imprisoned in Great Britain, a report from the Secretary of State and the papers to which it refers.

ANDREW JOHNSON.

EXECUTIVE MANSION, *January 29, 1869.*

To the Senate of the United States:

I herewith lay before the Senate, for its consideration in connection with the treaty with the New York Indians concluded November 4, 1868, which is now before that body for its constitutional action, an additional article of said treaty as an amendment.

A communication, dated the 28th instant, from the Secretary of the Interior, and a copy of a report of the Commissioner of Indian Affairs, explaining the object of the amendment, are also herewith transmitted.

ANDREW JOHNSON.

* Relating to buildings occupied in Washington by Departments of the Government.

WASHINGTON, *February 1, 1869.*

To the House of Representatives:

In answer to the resolution of the House of Representatives of the 16th of December last, in relation to the arrest of American citizens in Paraguay, I transmit a report of the Secretary of State.

ANDREW JOHNSON.

WASHINGTON, *February 1, 1869.*

To the Senate of the United States:

In further answer to the resolution of the Senate of the 8th of December last, concerning recent transactions in the region of the La Plata affecting the political relations of the United States with Paraguay, the Argentine Republic, Uruguay, and Brazil, I transmit a report from the Secretary of State.

ANDREW JOHNSON.

EXECUTIVE MANSION, *February 2, 1869.*

To the Senate of the United States:

I herewith lay before the Senate, for its constitutional action thereon, two treaties made by the commissioners appointed under the act of Congress of 20th July, 1867, to establish peace with certain hostile tribes, viz:

A treaty concluded at Fort Laramie, Dakota Territory, on the 29th April, 1868, with various bands of the Sioux or Dakota Nation of Indians.

A treaty concluded at Fort Bridger, Utah Territory, on the 3d day of July, 1868, with the Shoshone (eastern band) and Bannock Indians.

A communication from the Secretary of the Interior, dated the 2d instant, inclosing a copy of a letter to him from the Commissioner of Indian Affairs of the 28th ultimo, together with the correspondence therein referred to, relating to said treaties, are also herewith transmitted.

ANDREW JOHNSON.

WASHINGTON, *February 3, 1869.*

To the Senate and House of Representatives:

I transmit, for the consideration of Congress, a report from the Secretary of State, and the papers which accompany it, in relation to the encroachments of agents of the Hudsons Bay Company upon the trade and territory of Alaska.

ANDREW JOHNSON.

EXECUTIVE MANSION, *February 4, 1869.*

To the Senate of the United States:

I herewith lay before the Senate, for the constitutional action of that body thereon, the following treaties, concluded with various bands and tribes of Indians by William I. Cullen, special agent for Indians in Montana, viz:

Treaty concluded at Fort Hawley on the 13th July, 1868, with the Gros Ventres.

Treaty concluded at Fort Hawley on the 15th July, 1868, with the River Crow Indians.

Treaty concluded at Fort Benton September 1, 1868, with the Blackfeet Nation (composed of the tribe of that name and the Blood and Piegan tribes).

Treaty with the mixed bands of Shoshones, Bannocks, and Sheepeaters, concluded at Virginia City September 24, 1868.

A letter of the Secretary of the Interior, dated the 3d instant, and the report of the Commissioner of Indian Affairs, dated the 2d instant, explaining the provisions of the several treaties and suggesting an amendment of some of them, and submitting maps and papers connected with said treaties, are also herewith transmitted.

ANDREW JOHNSON.

WASHINGTON, *February 4, 1869.*

To the House of Representatives:

In answer to a resolution of the House of Representatives of the 23d January ultimo, I transmit a report* of the Secretary of State, which is accompanied by a copy of the correspondence called for by the resolution.

ANDREW JOHNSON.

WASHINGTON, *February 8, 1869.*

To the Senate of the United States:

Referring to my communications of the 16th of December, 1868, and of the 1st of February instant, addressed to the Senate in answer to the resolution of that body of the 8th of December last, concerning recent transactions in the region of the La Plata, I transmit a report of the Secretary of State and the papers which accompany it.

ANDREW JOHNSON.

WASHINGTON, *February 9, 1869.*

To the House of Representatives:

In answer to a resolution of the House of Representatives of the 13th ultimo, requesting information as to expenditures by the northwestern boundary commission, I transmit a report from the Secretary of State on the subject, and the papers which accompanied it.

ANDREW JOHNSON.

---

* Relating to the claim of William T. Harris, a United States citizen, to property withheld by the Brazilian Government.

EXECUTIVE MANSION, *February 9, 1869.*

To the Senate of the United States:

I herewith lay before the Senate, for the constitutional action of that body thereon, a treaty concluded on the 2d day of September, 1868, between the United States and the Creek Nation of Indians by their duly authorized delegates.

A letter from the Secretary of the Interior, dated the 8th instant, and a report of the Commissioner of Indian Affairs, dated the 6th instant, in relation to said treaty, are also herewith transmitted.

ANDREW JOHNSON.

WASHINGTON, *February 11, 1869.*

To the Senate of the United States:

I transmit to the Senate, in answer to their resolution of the 21st ultimo, a report from the Secretary of State, with accompanying papers, in relation to the establishment of the Robert College at Constantinople.

ANDREW JOHNSON.

WASHINGTON, D. C., *February 13, 1869.*

To the Senate of the United States:

I herewith lay before the Senate, for their action thereon, a mutual relinquishment of the agreement between the Ottawa and Chippewa Indians of Kansas, which agreement is appended to a treaty now before the Senate between the United States and the Swan Creek and Black River Chippewas and the Munsee or Christian Indians, concluded on the 1st of June, 1868.

A letter of the Secretary of the Interior of the 11th instant, together with the papers therein referred to, is also herewith transmitted.

ANDREW JOHNSON.

WASHINGTON, *February 15, 1869.*

To the Senate of the United States:

I transmit, for the consideration of the Senate with a view to ratification, a convention between the United States of America and the United States of Colombia for facilitating and securing the construction of a ship canal between the Atlantic and Pacific oceans through the continental isthmus lying without the jurisdiction of the United States of Colombia, which instrument was signed at Bogota on the 14th instant.

ANDREW JOHNSON.

EXECUTIVE MANSION, *February 17, 1869.*

To the Senate of the United States:

I herewith lay before the Senate, for its constitutional action thereon, a treaty concluded on the 11th instant, in the city of Washington, between the United States and the Sac and Fox Indians of the Missouri and the Iowa tribe of Indians. A letter of the Secretary of the Interior of the 16th instant, together with the letters therein referred to, accompany the treaty. For reasons stated in the accompanying communications, I request to withdraw from the Senate a treaty with the Sac and Fox Indians of the Missouri, concluded February 19, 1867, now pending before that body. ANDREW JOHNSON.

WASHINGTON, *February 17, 1869.*

To the Senate and House of Representatives:

I transmit to Congress a report from the Secretary of State, with accompanying documents, in relation to the gold medal presented to Mr. Cyrus W. Field pursuant to the resolution of Congress of March 2, 1867. ANDREW JOHNSON.

EXECUTIVE MANSION,
February 17, 1869.

To the Senate of the United States:

I herewith present, for the consideration of the Senate in connection with the treaty with the Brulé and other bands of Sioux Indians now pending before that body, a communication from the Secretary of the Interior, dated the 16th instant, and accompanying letters from the Commissioner of Indian Affairs and P. H. Conger, United States Indian agent for the Yankton Sioux, requesting that the benefits of said treaty may be extended to the Yankton Sioux and all the bands and individuals of the Dakota Sioux. ANDREW JOHNSON.

WASHINGTON, *February 17, 1869.*

To the Senate of the United States:

I transmit to the Senate, in answer to their resolution of the 19th ultimo, relating to fisheries, a report from the Secretary of State and the documents which accompanied it.
ANDREW JOHNSON.

WASHINGTON, D. C.,
February 18, 1869.

To the Senate of the United States:

I transmit to the Senate, for its constitutional action, a treaty concluded on the 13th instant between the United States and the Otoe and Missouria tribe of Indians, together with the accompanying papers.
ANDREW JOHNSON.

WASHINGTON. *February 19, 1869.*

To the Senate and House of Representatives:

I transmit to Congress a copy of a correspondence which has taken place between the Secretary of State and the minister of the United States at Paris, in relation to the use of passports by citizens of the United States in France.

ANDREW JOHNSON.

WASHINGTON, *February 20, 1869.*

To the House of Representatives:

I transmit an additional report from the Secretary of State, representing that Messrs. Costello and Warren, citizens of the United States imprisoned in Ireland, have been released.

ANDREW JOHNSON.

WASHINGTON, D. C., *February 23, 1869.*

To the Senate of the United States:

I transmit herewith a report from the Secretary of the Treasury, on the subject of the resolution of the Senate of the 13th January last, requesting "that the President direct the Secretary of the Treasury to detail an officer to select from the public lands such permanent points upon the coast of Oregon, Washington Territory, and Alaska as in his judgment may be necessary for light-house purposes, in view of the future commercial necessity of the Pacific Coast, and to reserve the same for exclusive use of the United States."

ANDREW JOHNSON.

WASHINGTON, *February 23, 1869.*

To the Senate and House of Representatives:

Referring to my communication to Congress of the 26th ultimo, concerning a decree made by the United States chargé d'affaires in China, on 1st of June last, prohibiting steamers sailing under the flag of the United States from using or passing through the Straw Shoe Channel on the Yangtse River, I now transmit a copy of a dispatch of the 22d of August last, No. 25, from S. Wells Williams, esq., and of such of the papers accompanying it as were not contained in my former communication. I also transmit a copy of the reply of the 6th instant made by the Secretary of State to the above-named dispatch.

ANDREW JOHNSON.

WASHINGTON, *February 24, 1869.*

To the Senate and House of Representatives:

I transmit to Congress a copy of a convention between the United States and the Mexican Republic, providing for the adjustment of the claims of citizens of either country against the other, signed on the 4th day of July last, and the ratifications of which were exchanged on the 1st instant.

It is recommended that such legislation as may be necessary to carry this convention into effect shall receive early consideration.

ANDREW JOHNSON.

WASHINGTON, *March 1, 1869.*

To the Senate of the United States:

In compliance with the request of the Senate of the 27th ultimo, I return herewith their resolution of the 26th February, calling for a statement of internal-revenue stamps issued by the Government since the passage of the act approved July 1, 1862.

ANDREW JOHNSON.

VETO MESSAGES.

WASHINGTON, D. C., *February 13, 1869.*

To the Senate of the United States:

The bill entitled ''An act transferring the duties of trustees of colored schools of Washington and Georgetown'' is herewith returned to the Senate, in which House it originated, without my approval.

The accompanying paper exhibits the fact that the legislation which the bill proposes is contrary to the wishes of the colored residents of Washington and Georgetown, and that they prefer that the schools for their children should be under the management of trustees selected by the Secretary of the Interior, whose term of office is for four years, rather than subject to the control of bodies whose tenure of office, depending merely upon political considerations, may be annually affected by the elections which take place in the two cities.

The colored people of Washington and Georgetown are at present not represented by a person of their own race in either of the boards of trustees of public schools appointed by the municipal authorities. Of the three trustees, however, who, under the act of July 11, 1862, compose the board of trustees of the schools for colored children, two are persons of color. The resolutions transmitted herewith show that they have performed their trust in a manner entirely satisfactory to the colored people of the two cities, and no good reason is known to the Executive why the duties which now devolve upon them should be transferred as proposed in the bill.

With these brief suggestions the bill is respectfully returned, and the consideration of Congress invited to the accompanying preamble and resolutions.

ANDREW JOHNSON.

WASHINGTON, D. C., *February 22, 1869.*

To the House of Representatives:

The accompanying bill, entitled ''An act regulating the duties on imported copper and copper ores,'' is, for the following reasons, returned, without my approval, to the House of Representatives, in which branch of Congress it originated.

Its immediate effect will be to diminish the public receipts, for the object of the bill can not be accomplished without seriously affecting the importation of copper and copper ores, from which a considerable revenue is at present derived. While thus impairing the resources of the Government, it imposes an additional tax upon an already overburdened people, who should not be further impoverished that monopolies may be fostered and corporations enriched.

It is represented—and the declaration seems to be sustained by evidence—that the duties for which this bill provides are nearly or quite sufficient to prohibit the importation of certain foreign ores of copper. Its enactment, therefore, will prove detrimental to the shipping interests of the nation, and at the same time destroy the business, for many years successfully established, of smelting home ores in connection with a smaller amount of the imported articles. This business, it is credibly asserted, has heretofore yielded the larger share of the copper production of the country, and thus the industry which this legislation is designed to encourage is actually less than that which will be destroyed by the passage of this bill.

It seems also to be evident that the effect of this measure will be to enhance by 70 per cent the cost of blue vitriol—an article extensively used in dyeing and in the manufacture of printed and colored cloths. To produce such an augmentation in the price of this commodity will be to discriminate against other great branches of domestic industry, and by increasing their cost to expose them most unfairly to the effects of foreign competition Legislation can neither be wise nor just which seeks the welfare of a single interest at the expense and to the injury of many and varied interests at least equally important and equally deserving the consideration of Congress. Indeed, it is difficult to find any reason which will justify the interference of Government with any legitimate industry, except so far as may be rendered necessary by the requirements of the revenue. As has already been stated, however, the legislative intervention proposed in the present instance will diminish, not increase, the public receipts.

The enactment of such a law is urged as necessary for the relief of certain mining interests upon Lake Superior, which, it is alleged, are in a greatly depressed condition, and can only be sustained by an enhancement of the price of copper. If this result should follow the passage of the bill, a tax for the exclusive benefit of a single class would be imposed upon the consumers of copper throughout the entire country, not warranted by any need of the Government, and the avails of which would not in any degree find their way into the Treasury of the nation. If the miners of Lake Superior are in a condition of want, it can not be justly affirmed that the Government should extend charity to them in preference to those of its citizens who in other portions of the country suffer in like manner from destitution. Least of all should the endeavor to aid them be based upon a method so uncertain and indirect as that contemplated by the bill, and which, moreover, proposes to continue the exercise of its benefaction through an indefinite period of years. It is, besides, reasonable to hope that positive suffering from want, if it really exists, will prove but temporary in a region where agricultural labor is so much in demand and so well compensated. A careful examination of the subject appears to show that the present low price of copper, which alone has induced any depression the mining interests of Lake Superior may have recently experienced, is due to causes which it is wholly impolitic, if not impracticable, to contravene by legislation. These causes are, in the main, an increase in the general supply of copper, owing to the discovery and working of remarkably productive mines and to a coincident restriction in the consumption and use of copper by the substitution of other and cheaper metals for industrial purposes. It is now sought to resist by artificial means the action of natural laws; to place the people of the United States, in respect to the enjoyment and use of an essential commodity, upon a different basis from other nations, and especially to compensate certain private and sectional interests for the changes and losses which are always incident to industrial progress.

Although providing for an increase of duties, the proposed law does not even come within the range of protection, in the fair acceptation of the term. It does not look to the fostering of a young and feeble interest with a view to the ultimate attainment of strength and the capacity of self-support. It appears to assume that the present inability for successful production is inherent and permanent, and is more likely to increase than to be gradually overcome; yet in spite of this it proposes, by the exercise of the lawmaking power, to sustain that interest and to impose it in hopeless perpetuity as a tax upon the competent and beneficent industries of the country.

The true method for the mining interests of Lake Superior to obtain relief, if relief is needed, is to endeavor to make their great natural resources fully available by reducing the cost of production. Special or class legislation can not remedy the evils which this bill is designed to meet. They can only be overcome by laws which will effect a wise, honest, and economical administration of the Government, a reestablishment of the specie standard of value, and an early adjustment of our system of State, municipal, and national taxation (especially the latter) upon the fundamental principle that all taxes, whether collected under the internal revenue or under a tariff, shall interfere as little as possible with the productive energies of the people.

The bill is therefore returned, in the belief that the true interests of the Government and of the people require that it should not become a law.

ANDREW JOHNSON.

PROCLAMATION.

By the President of the United States of America.

A PROCLAMATION.

Whereas the President of the United States has heretofore set forth several proclamations offering amnesty and pardon to persons who had been or were concerned in the late rebellion against the lawful authority of the Government of the United States, which proclamations were severally issued on the 8th day of December, 1863, on the 26th day of March, 1864, on the 29th day of May, 1865, on the 7th day of September, 1867, and on the 4th day of July, in the present year; and

Whereas the authority of the Federal Government having been reestablished in all the States and Territories within the jurisdiction of the United States, it is believed that such prudential reservations and exceptions as at the dates of said several proclamations were deemed necessary and proper may now be wisely and justly relinquished, and that an universal amnesty and pardon for participation in said rebellion extended to all who have borne any part therein will tend to secure permanent peace, order, and prosperity throughout the land, and to renew and fully restore confidence and fraternal feeling among the whole people, and their respect for and attachment to the National Government, designed by its patriotic founders for the general good:

Now, therefore, be it known that I, Andrew Johnson, President of the United States, by virtue of the power and authority in me vested by the Constitution and in the name of the sovereign people of the United States, do hereby proclaim and declare, unconditionally and without reservation, to all and to every person who, directly or indirectly, participated in the late insurrection or rebellion a full pardon and amnesty for the offense of treason against the United States or of adhering to their enemies during the late civil war, with restoration of all rights, privileges, and immunities under the Constitution and the laws which have been made in pursuance thereof.

In testimony whereof I have signed these presents with my hand and have caused the seal of the United States to be hereunto affixed.

[SEAL.]   Done at the city of Washington, the 25th day of December, A. D. 1868, and of the Independence of the United States of America the ninety-third.

ANDREW JOHNSON.

By the President:

F. W. Seward,
Acting Secretary of State.

IMPEACHMENT OF ANDREW JOHNSON, PRESIDENT OF THE UNITED STATES.

On the 24th of February, 1868, the House of Representatives of the Congress of the United States resolved to impeach Andrew Johnson, President of the United States, of high crimes and misdemeanors, of which the Senate was apprised, and arrangements were made for the trial. On the 2d and 3d of March articles of impeachment were agreed upon by the House of Representatives, and on the 4th they were presented to the Senate by the managers on the part of the House, Mr. John A. Bingham, Mr. George S. Boutwell, Mr. James F. Wilson, Mr. Benjamin F. Butler, Mr. Thomas Williams, Mr. John A. Logan, and Mr. Thaddeus Stevens, who were accompanied by the House as a Committee of the Whole. The articles are as follows:

IN THE HOUSE OF REPRESENTATIVES, UNITED STATES,
March 2, 1868.

ARTICLES EXHIBITED BY THE HOUSE OF REPRESENTATIVES OF THE UNITED STATES, IN THE NAME OF THEMSELVES AND ALL THE PEOPLE OF THE UNITED STATES, AGAINST ANDREW JOHNSON, PRESIDENT OF THE UNITED STATES, IN MAINTENANCE AND SUPPORT OF THEIR IMPEACHMENT AGAINST HIM FOR HIGH CRIMES AND MISDEMEANORS IN OFFICE.

ARTICLE I. That said Andrew Johnson, President of the United States, on the 21st day of February, A. D. 1868, at Washington, in the District of Columbia, unmindful of the high duties of his office, of his oath of office, and of the requirement of the Constitution that he should take care that the laws be faithfully executed, did unlawfully and in violation of the Constitution and laws of the United States issue an order in writing for the removal of Edwin M. Stanton from the office of Secretary for the Department of War, said Edwin M. Stanton having been theretofore duly appointed and commissioned, by and with the advice and consent of the Senate of the United States, as such Secretary; and said Andrew Johnson, President of the United States, on the 12th day of August, A. D. 1867, and during the recess of said Senate, having suspended by his order Edwin M. Stanton from said office, and within twenty days after the first day of the next meeting of said Senate—that is to say, on the 12th day of December, in the year last aforesaid—having reported to said Senate such suspension, with the evidence and reasons for his action in the case and the name of the person designated to perform the duties of such office temporarily until the next meeting of the Senate; and said Senate thereafterwards, on the 13th day of January, A. D. 1868, having duly considered the evidence and reasons reported by said Andrew Johnson for said suspension, and having refused to concur in said suspension, whereby and by force of the provisions of an act entitled "An act regulating the tenure of certain civil offices," passed March 2, 1867, said Edwin M. Stanton did forthwith resume the functions of his office, whereof the said Andrew Johnson had then and there due notice; and said Edwin M. Stanton, by reason of the premises, on said 21st day of February, being lawfully entitled to hold said office of Secretary for the Department of War; which said order for the removal of said Edwin M. Stanton is in substance as follows; that is to say:

> EXECUTIVE MANSION,
> *Washington, D. C., February 21, 1868.*

Hon. EDWIN M. STANTON,
> *Washington, D. C.*

SIR: By virtue of the power and authority vested in me as President by the Constitution and laws of the United States, you are hereby removed from office as Secretary for the Department of War, and your functions as such will terminate upon the receipt of this communication.

You will transfer to Brevet Major-General Lorenzo Thomas, Adjutant-General of the Army, who has this day been authorized and empowered to act as Secretary of War *ad interim*, all records, books, papers, and other public property now in your custody and charge.

Respectfully, yours,

> ANDREW JOHNSON.

which order was unlawfully issued with intent then and there to violate the act entitled "An act regulating the tenure of certain civil offices," passed March 2, 1867, and with the further intent, contrary to the provisions of said act, in violation thereof, and contrary to the provisions of the Constitution of the United States, and without the advice and consent of the Senate of the United States, the said Senate then and there being in session, to remove said Edwin M. Stanton from the office of Secretary for the Department of War, the said Edwin M. Stanton being then and there Secretary for the Department of War, and being then and there in the due and lawful execution and discharge of the duties of said office; whereby said Andrew Johnson, President of the United States, did then and there commit and was guilty of a high misdemeanor in office.

ART. II. That on said 21st day of February, A. D. 1868, at Washington, in the District of Columbia, said Andrew Johnson, President of the United States, unmindful of the high duties of his office, of his oath of office, and in violation of the Constitution of the United States, and contrary to the provisions of an act entitled "An act regulating the tenure of certain civil offices," passed March 2, 1867, without the advice and consent of the Senate of the United States, said Senate then and there being in session, and without authority of law, did, with intent to violate the

Constitution of the United States and the act aforesaid, issue and deliver to one Lorenzo Thomas a letter of authority in substance as follows; that is to say:

EXECUTIVE MANSION,
Washington, D. C., February 21, 1868.

Brevet Major-General LORENZO THOMAS,
 Adjutant-General United States Army, Washington, D. C.

SIR: The Hon. Edwin M. Stanton having been this day removed from office as Secretary for the Department of War, you are hereby authorized and empowered to act as Secretary of War *ad interim*, and will immediately enter upon the discharge of the duties pertaining to that office.

Mr. Stanton has been instructed to transfer to you all the records, books, papers, and other public property now in his custody and charge.

 Respectfully, yours,   ANDREW JOHNSON.

then and there being no vacancy in said office of Secretary for the Department of War; whereby said Andrew Johnson, President of the United States, did then and there commit and was guilty of a high misdemeanor in office.

ART. III. That said Andrew Johnson, President of the United States, on the 21st day of February, A. D. 1868, at Washington, in the District of Columbia, did commit and was guilty of a high misdemeanor in office in this, that without authority of law, while the Senate of the United States was then and there in session, he did appoint one Lorenzo Thomas to be Secretary for the Department of War *ad interim*, without the advice and consent of the Senate, and with intent to violate the Constitution of the United States, no vacancy having happened in said office of Secretary for the Department of War during the recess of the Senate, and no vacancy existing in said office at the time, and which said appointment, so made by said Andrew Johnson, of said Lorenzo Thomas, is in substance as follows; that is to say:

EXECUTIVE MANSION,
Washington, D. C., February 21, 1868.

Brevet Major-General LORENZO THOMAS,
 Adjutant-General United States Army, Washington, D. C.

SIR: The Hon. Edwin M. Stanton having been this day removed from office as Secretary for the Department of War, you are hereby authorized and empowered to act as Secretary of War *ad interim*, and will immediately enter upon the discharge of the duties pertaining to that office.

Mr. Stanton has been instructed to transfer to you all the records, books, papers, and other public property now in his custody and charge.

 Respectfully, yours,   ANDREW JOHNSON.

ART. IV. That said Andrew Johnson, President of the United States, unmindful of the high duties of his office and his oath of office, in violation of the Constitution and laws of the United States, on the 21st day of February, A. D. 1868, at Washington, in the District of Columbia, did unlawfully conspire with one Lorenzo Thomas, and with other persons to the House of Representatives unknown, with intent, by intimidation and threats, unlawfully to hinder and prevent Edwin M. Stanton, then and there the Secretary for the Department of War, duly appointed under the laws of the United States, from holding said office of Secretary for the Department of War, contrary to and in violation of the Constitution of the United States and of the provisions of an act entitled "An act to define and punish certain conspiracies," approved July 31, 1861; whereby said Andrew Johnson, President of the United States, did then and there commit and was guilty of a high crime in office.

Art. V. That said Andrew Johnson, President of the United States, unmindful of the high duties of his office and of his oath of office, on the 21st day of February, A. D. 1868, and on divers other days and times in said year before the 2d day of March, A. D. 1868, at Washington, in the District of Columbia, did unlawfully conspire with one Lorenzo Thomas, and with other persons to the House of Representatives unknown, to prevent and hinder the execution of an act entitled "An act regulating the tenure of certain civil offices," passed March 2, 1867, and in pursuance of said conspiracy did unlawfully attempt to prevent Edwin M. Stanton, then and there being Secretary for the Department of War, duly appointed and commissioned under the laws of the United States, from holding said office; whereby the said Andrew Johnson, President of the United States, did then and there commit and was guilty of a high misdemeanor in office.

Art. VI. That said Andrew Johnson, President of the United States, unmindful of the high duties of his office and of his oath of office, on the 21st day of February, A. D. 1868, at Washington, in the District of Columbia, did unlawfully conspire with one Lorenzo Thomas by force to seize, take, and possess the property of the United States in the Department of War, and then and there in the custody and charge of Edwin M. Stanton, Secretary for said Department, contrary to the provisions of an act entitled "An act to define and punish certain conspiracies," approved July 31, 1861, and with intent to violate and disregard an act entitled "An act regulating the tenure of certain civil offices," passed March 2, 1867; whereby said Andrew Johnson, President of the United States, did then and there commit a high crime in office.

Art. VII. That said Andrew Johnson, President of the United States, unmindful of the high duties of his office and of his oath of office, on the 21st day of February, A. D. 1868, at Washington, in the District of Columbia, did unlawfully conspire with one Lorenzo Thomas with intent unlawfully to seize, take, and possess the property of the United States in the Department of War, in the custody and charge of Edwin M. Stanton, Secretary for said Department, with intent to violate and disregard the act entitled "An act regulating the tenure of certain civil offices," passed March 2, 1867; whereby said Andrew Johnson, President of the United States, did then and there commit a high misdemeanor in office.

ART. VIII. That said Andrew Johnson, President of the United States, unmindful of the high duties of his office and of his oath of office, with intent unlawfully to control the disbursement of the moneys appropriated for the military service and for the Department of War, on the 21st day of February, A. D. 1868, at Washington, in the District of Columbia, did unlawfully, and contrary to the provisions of an act entitled "An act regulating the tenure of certain civil offices," passed March 2, 1867, and in violation of the Constitution of the United States, and without the advice and consent of the Senate of the United States, and while the Senate was then and there in session, there being no vacancy in the office of Secretary for the Department of War, and with intent to violate and disregard the act aforesaid, then and there issue and deliver to one Lorenzo Thomas a letter of authority, in writing, in substance as follows; that is to say:

EXECUTIVE MANSION,
Washington, D. C., February 21, 1868.
Brevet Major-General LORENZO THOMAS,
Adjutant-General United States Army, Washington, D. C.

SIR: The Hon. Edwin M. Stanton having been this day removed from office as Secretary for the Department of War, you are hereby authorized and empowered to act as Secretary of War *ad interim*, and will immediately enter upon the discharge of the duties pertaining to that office.

Mr. Stanton has been instructed to transfer to you all the records, books, papers, and other public property now in his custody and charge.

Respectfully, yours,   ANDREW JOHNSON.

whereby said Andrew Johnson, President of the United States, did then and there commit and was guilty of a high misdemeanor in office.

ART. IX. That said Andrew Johnson, President of the United States, on the 22d day of February, A. D. 1868, at Washington, in the District of Columbia, in disregard of the Constitution and the laws of the United States duly enacted, as Commander in Chief of the Army of the United States, did bring before himself then and there William H. Emory, a major-general by brevet in the Army of the United States, actually in command of the Department of Washington and the military forces thereof, and did then and there, as such Commander in Chief, declare to and instruct said Emory that part of a law of the United States, passed March 2, 1867, entitled "An act making appropriations for the support of the Army for the year ending June 30, 1868, and for other purposes," especially the second section thereof, which provides, among other things, that "all orders and instructions relating to military operations issued by the President or Secretary of War shall be issued through the General of the Army, and in case of his inability through the next in rank," was unconstitutional and in contravention of the commission of said Emory, and which said provision of law had been theretofore duly and legally promulgated by general order for the government and direction of the Army of the United States, as the said Andrew Johnson then and there well knew, with intent thereby to induce said Emory, in his official

capacity as commander of the Department of Washington, to violate the
provisions of said act and to take and receive, act upon, and obey such
orders as he, the said Andrew Johnson, might make and give, and
which should not be issued through the General of the Army of the
United States, according to the provisions of said act, and with the further intent thereby to enable him, the said Andrew Johnson, to prevent
the execution of the act entitled "An act regulating the tenure of certain
civil offices," passed March 2, 1867, and to unlawfully prevent Edwin M.
Stanton, then being Secretary for the Department of War, from holding
said office and discharging the duties thereof; whereby said Andrew
Johnson, President of the United States, did then and there commit and
was guilty of a high misdemeanor in office.

And the House of Representatives, by protestation, saving to themselves the liberty of exhibiting at any time hereafter any further articles
or other accusation or impeachment against the said Andrew Johnson,
President of the United States, and also of replying to his answers which
he shall make unto the articles herein preferred against him, and of offering proof to the same, and every part thereof, and to all and every other
article, accusation, or impeachment which shall be exhibited by them, as
the case shall require, *do demand* that the said Andrew Johnson may be
put to answer the high crimes and misdemeanors in office herein charged
against him, and that such proceedings, examinations, trials, and judgments may be thereupon had and given as may be agreeable to law and
justice.

SCHUYLER COLFAX,
Speaker of the House of Representatives.

Attest:

EDWARD McPHERSON,
Clerk of the House of Representatives.

In the House of Representatives, United States,
March 3, 1868.

The following additional articles of impeachment were agreed to, viz:
Art. X. That said Andrew Johnson, President of the United States,
unmindful of the high duties of his office and the dignity and proprieties
thereof, and of the harmony and courtesies which ought to exist and be
maintained between the executive and legislative branches of the Government of the United States, designing and intending to set aside the
rightful authority and powers of Congress, did attempt to bring into disgrace, ridicule, hatred, contempt, and reproach the Congress of the United
States and the several branches thereof, to impair and destroy the regard
and respect of all the good people of the United States for the Congress
and legislative power thereof (which all officers of the Government ought
inviolably to preserve and maintain), and to excite the odium and resentment of all the good people of the United States against Congress and
the laws by it duly and constitutionally enacted; and, in pursuance of his

said design and intent, openly and publicly, and before divers assemblages of the citizens of the United States, convened in divers parts thereof to meet and receive said Andrew Johnson as the Chief Magistrate of the United States, did, on the 18th day of August, A. D. 1866, and on divers other days and times, as well before as afterwards, make and deliver with a loud voice certain intemperate, inflammatory, and scandalous harangues, and did therein utter loud threats and bitter menaces, as well against Congress as the laws of the United States, duly enacted thereby, amid the cries, jeers, and laughter of the multitudes then assembled and in hearing, which are set forth in the several specifications hereinafter written in substance and effect; that is to say:

Specification first.—In this, that at Washington, in the District of Columbia, in the Executive Mansion, to a committee of citizens who called upon the President of the United States, speaking of and concerning the Congress of the United States, said Andrew Johnson, President of the United States, heretofore, to wit, on the 18th day of August, A. D. 1866, did in a loud voice declare in substance and effect, among other things; that is to say:

So far as the executive department of the Government is concerned, the effort has been made to restore the Union, to heal the breach, to pour oil into the wounds which were consequent upon the struggle, and (to speak in common phrase) to prepare, as the learned and wise physician would, a plaster healing in character and coextensive with the wound. We thought and we think that we had partially succeeded; but as the work progresses, as reconstruction seemed to be taking place and the country was becoming reunited, we found a disturbing and marring element opposing us. In alluding to that element I shall go no further than your convention and the distinguished gentleman who has delivered to me the report of its proceedings. I shall make no reference to it that I do not believe the time and the occasion justify.

We have witnessed in one department of the Government every endeavor to prevent the restoration of peace, harmony, and union. We have seen hanging upon the verge of the Government, as it were, a body called, or which assumes to be, the Congress of the United States, while in fact it is a Congress of only a part of the States. We have seen this Congress pretend to be for the Union, when its every step and act tended to perpetuate disunion and make a disruption of the States inevitable. * * * We have seen Congress gradually encroach, step by step, upon constitutional rights, and violate, day after day and month after month, fundamental principles of the Government. We have seen a Congress that seemed to forget that there was a limit to the sphere and scope of legislation. We have seen a Congress in a minority assume to exercise power which, allowed to be consummated, would result in despotism or monarchy itself.

Specification second.—In this, that at Cleveland, in the State of Ohio, heretofore, to wit, on the 3d day of September, A. D. 1866, before a public assemblage of citizens and others, said Andrew Johnson, President of the United States, speaking of and concerning the Congress of the United States, did in a loud voice declare in substance and effect, among other things; that is to say:

I will tell you what I did do. I called upon your Congress that is trying to break up the Government.

*   *   *   *   *   *   *

In conclusion, besides that, Congress had taken much pains to poison their constituents against him. But what had Congress done? Have they done anything to restore the Union of these States? No. On the contrary, they have done everything to prevent it. And because he stood now where he did when the rebellion commenced, he had been denounced as a traitor. Who had run greater risks or made greater sacrifices than himself? But Congress, factious and domineering, had undertaken to poison the minds of the American people.

Specification third.—In this, that at St. Louis, in the State of Missouri, heretofore, to wit, on the 8th day of September, A. D. 1866, before a public assemblage of citizens and others, said Andrew Johnson, President of the United States, speaking of and concerning the Congress of the United States, did in a loud voice declare in substance and effect, among other things; that is to say:

Go on. Perhaps if you had a word or two on the subject of New Orleans you might understand more about it than you do. And if you will go back—if you will go back and ascertain the cause of the riot at New Orleans, perhaps you will not be so prompt in calling out "New Orleans." If you will take up the riot at New Orleans and trace it back to its source or its immediate cause, you will find out who was responsible for the blood that was shed there. If you will take up the riot at New Orleans and trace it back to the Radical Congress, you will find that the riot at New Orleans was substantially planned. If you will take up the proceedings in their caucuses, you will understand that they there knew that a convention was to be called which was extinct by its power having expired; that it was said that the intention was that a new government was to be organized, and on the organization of that government the intention was to enfranchise one portion of the population, called the colored population, who had just been emancipated, and at the same time disfranchise white men. When you design to talk about New Orleans, you ought to understand what you are talking about. When you read the speeches that were made and take up the facts on the Friday and Saturday before that convention sat, you will there find that speeches were made, incendiary in their character, exciting that portion of the population—the black population—to arm themselves and prepare for the shedding of blood. You will also find that that convention did assemble, in violation of law, and the intention of that convention was to supersede the reorganized authorities in the State government of Louisiana, which had been recognized by the Government of the United States; and every man engaged in that rebellion in that convention, with the intention of superseding and upturning the civil government which had been recognized by the Government of the United States, I say that he was a traitor to the Constitution of the United States; and hence you find that another rebellion was commenced, *having its origin in the Radical Congress.*

*   *   *   *   *   *   *

So much for the New Orleans riot. And there was the cause and the origin of the blood that was shed; and every drop of blood that was shed is upon their skirts, and they are responsible for it. I could test this thing a little closer, but will not do it here to-night. But when you talk about the causes and consequences that resulted from proceedings of that kind, perhaps, as I have been introduced here, and you have provoked questions of this kind—though it does not provoke me—I will tell you a few wholesome things that have been done by this Radical Congress in connection with New Orleans and the extension of the elective franchise.

I know that I have been traduced and abused. I know it has come in advance of me, here as elsewhere, that I have attempted to exercise an arbitrary power in resisting laws that were intended to be forced upon the Government; that I had exercised that power; that I had abandoned the party that elected me, and that I was a traitor, because I exercised the veto power in attempting and did arrest for a time a bill that was called a "Freedmen's Bureau" bill; yes, that I was a traitor. And I have been traduced, I have been slandered, I have been maligned, I have been called Judas Iscariot and all that. Now, my countrymen, here to-night, it is very easy to indulge in epithets; it is easy to call a man a Judas and cry out "traitor;" but when he is called upon to give arguments and facts he is very often found wanting. Judas Iscariot—Judas. There was a Judas, and he was one of the twelve apostles. Oh, yes; the twelve apostles had a Christ. The twelve apostles had a Christ, and he never could have had a Judas unless he had had twelve apostles. If I have played the Judas, who has been my Christ that I have played the Judas with? Was it Thad. Stevens? Was it Wendell Phillips? Was it Charles Sumner? These are the men that stop and compare themselves with the Savior, and everybody that differs with them in opinion, and to try to stay and arrest their diabolical and nefarious policy, is to be denounced as a Judas.

 *   *   *   *   *   *

Well, let me say to you, if you will stand by me in this action, if you will stand by me in trying to give the people a fair chance—soldiers and citizens—to participate in these offices, God being willing I will kick them out. I will kick them out just as fast as I can.

Let me say to you in concluding that what I have said I intended to say. I was not provoked into this, and I care not for their menaces, the taunts and the jeers. I care not for threats. I do not intend to be bullied by my enemies nor overawed by my friends. But, God willing, with your help I will veto their measures whenever any of them come to me.

which said utterances, declarations, threats, and harangues, highly censurable in any, are peculiarly indecent and unbecoming in the Chief Magistrate of the United States, by means whereof said Andrew Johnson has brought the high office of the President of the United States into contempt, ridicule, and disgrace, to the great scandal of all good citizens; whereby said Andrew Johnson, President of the United States, did commit and was then and there guilty of a high misdemeanor in office.

ART. XI. That said Andrew Johnson, President of the United States, unmindful of the high duties of his office and of his oath of office, and in disregard of the Constitution and laws of the United States, did heretofore, to wit, on the 18th day of August, A. D. 1866, at the city of Washington, in the District of Columbia, by public speech, declare and affirm in substance that the Thirty-ninth Congress of the United States was not a Congress of the United States authorized by the Constitution to exercise legislative power under the same, but, on the contrary, was a Congress of only part of the States; thereby denying and intending to deny that the legislation of said Congress was valid or obligatory upon him, the said Andrew Johnson, except in so far as he saw fit to approve the same, and also thereby denying and intending to deny the power of the said Thirty-ninth Congress to propose amendments to the Constitution of the United States; and in pursuance of said declaration the said Andrew Johnson, President of the United States, afterwards, to wit, on the 21st day of February, A. D. 1868, at the city of Washington, in the District of Columbia, did unlawfully, and in disregard of the requirement of the Constitution that he should take care that the laws be faithfully executed, attempt to prevent the execution of an act entitled "An act regulating the tenure of certain civil offices," passed March 2, 1867, by unlawfully devising and contriving, and attempting to devise and contrive, means by which he should prevent Edwin M. Stanton from forthwith resuming the functions of the office of Secretary for the Department of War, notwithstanding the refusal of the Senate to concur in the suspension theretofore made by said Andrew Johnson of said Edwin M. Stanton from said office of Secretary for the Department of War, and also by further unlawfully devising and contriving, and attempting to devise and contrive, means then and there to prevent the execution of an act entitled "An act making appropriations for the support of the Army for the fiscal year ending June 30, 1868 and for other purposes," approved March 2, 1867, and also to prevent the execution of an act entitled "An act to provide for the more efficient government of the rebel States," passed March 2, 1867, whereby the said Andrew Johnson, President of the United States, did then, to wit, on the 21st day of February, A. D. 1868, at the city of Washington, commit and was guilty of a high misdemeanor in office.

SCHUYLER COLFAX,

Speaker of the House of Representatives.

Attest:

EDWARD McPHERSON,

Clerk of the House of Representatives.

IN THE SENATE, *March 4, 1868.*

The President *pro tempore* laid before the Senate the following letter from the Hon. Salmon P. Chase, Chief Justice of the Supreme Court of the United States:

WASHINGTON, *March 4, 1868.*

To the Senate of the United States:

Inasmuch as the sole power to try impeachments is vested by the Constitution in the Senate, and it is made the duty of the Chief Justice to preside when the President is on trial, I take the liberty of submitting, very respectfully, some observations in respect to the proper mode of proceeding upon the impeachment which has been preferred by the House of Representatives against the President now in office.

That when the Senate sits for the trial of an impeachment it sits as a court seems unquestionable.

That for the trial of an impeachment of the President this court must be constituted of the members of the Senate, with the Chief Justice presiding, seems equally unquestionable.

The Federalist is regarded as the highest contemporary authority on the construction of the Constitution, and in the sixty-fourth number the functions of the Senate "sitting in their judicial capacity as a court for the trial of impeachments" are examined.

In a paragraph explaining the reasons for not uniting ''the Supreme Court with the Senate in the formation of the court of impeachments'' it is observed that—

To a certain extent the benefits of that union will be obtained from making the Chief Justice of the Supreme Court the president of the court of impeachments, as is proposed by the plan of the Convention, while the inconveniences of an entire incorporation of the former into the latter will be substantially avoided. This was, perhaps, the prudent mean.

This authority seems to leave no doubt upon either of the propositions just stated; and the statement of them will serve to introduce the question upon which I think it my duty to state the result of my reflections to the Senate, namely, At what period, in the case of an impeachment of the President, should the court of impeachment be organized under oath, as directed by the Constitution?

It will readily suggest itself to anyone who reflects upon the abilities and the learning in the law which distinguish so many Senators that besides the reason assigned in the Federalist there must have been still another for the provision requiring the Chief Justice to preside in the court of impeachment. Under the Constitution, in case of a vacancy in the office of President, the Vice-President succeeds, and it was doubtless thought prudent and befitting that the next in succession should not preside in a proceeding through which a vacancy might be created.

It is not doubted that the Senate, while sitting in its ordinary capacity, must necessarily receive from the House of Representatives some notice of its intention to impeach the President at its bar, but it does not seem to me an unwarranted opinion, in view of this constitutional provision, that the organization of the Senate as a court of impeachment, under the Constitution, should precede the actual announcement of the impeachment on the part of the House.

And it may perhaps be thought a still less unwarranted opinion that articles of impeachment should only be presented to a court of impeachment; that no summons or other process should issue except from the organized court, and that rules for the government of the proceedings of such a court should be framed only by the court itself.

I have found myself unable to come to any other conclusions than these. I can assign no reason for requiring the Senate to organize as a court under any other than its ordinary presiding officer for the latter proceedings upon an impeachment of the President which does not seem to me to apply equally to the earlier.

I am informed that the Senate has proceeded upon other views, and it is not my purpose to contest what its superior wisdom may have directed.

All good citizens will fervently pray that no occasion may ever arise when the grave proceedings now in progress will be cited as a precedent; but it is not impossible that such an occasion may come.

Inasmuch, therefore, as the Constitution has charged the Chief Justice with an important function in the trial of an impeachment of the President, it has seemed to me fitting and obligatory, where he is unable to concur in the views of the Senate concerning matters essential to the trial, that his respectful dissent should appear.

S. P. CHASE,
Chief Justice of the United States.

PROCEEDINGS OF THE SENATE SITTING FOR THE TRIAL OF THE IMPEACHMENT OF ANDREW JOHNSON, PRESIDENT OF THE UNITED STATES.

THURSDAY, MARCH 5, 1868.

THE UNITED STATES *vs.* ANDREW JOHNSON, PRESIDENT.

The Chief Justice of the United States entered the Senate Chamber and was conducted to the chair by the committee appointed by the Senate for that purpose.

The following oath was administered to the Chief Justice by Associate Justice Nelson, and by the Chief Justice to the members of the Senate:

I do solemnly swear that in all things appertaining to the trial of the impeachment of Andrew Johnson, President of the United States, now pending, I will do impartial justice according to the Constitution and laws. So help me God.

FRIDAY, MARCH 6, 1868.

THE UNITED STATES *vs.* ANDREW JOHNSON, PRESIDENT.

To accord with the conviction of the Chief Justice* that the court should adopt its own rules, those adopted on March 2 by the Senate sitting in its legislative capacity were readopted by the Senate sitting as a court of impeachment. The rules are as follows:

RULES OF PROCEDURE AND PRACTICE IN THE SENATE WHEN SITTING ON THE TRIAL OF IMPEACHMENTS.

I. Whensoever the Senate shall receive notice from the House of Representatives that managers are appointed on their part to conduct an impeachment against any person, and are directed to carry articles of impeachment to the Senate, the Secretary of the Senate shall immediately inform the House of Representatives that the Senate is ready to receive the managers for the purpose of exhibiting such articles of impeachment agreeably to said notice.

II. When the managers of an impeachment shall be introduced at the bar of the Senate and shall signify that they are ready to exhibit articles

---

* See letter from the Chief Justice, pp. 718–720.

of impeachment against any person, the Presiding Officer of the Senate shall direct the Sergeant-at-Arms to make proclamation, who shall, after making proclamation, repeat the following words, viz:

All persons are commanded to keep silence, on pain of imprisonment, while the House of Representatives is exhibiting to the Senate of the United States articles of impeachment against ———— ————.

after which the articles shall be exhibited; and then the Presiding Officer of the Senate shall inform the managers that the Senate will take proper order on the subject of the impeachment, of which due notice shall be given to the House of Representatives.

III. Upon such articles being presented to the Senate, the Senate shall, at 1 o'clock afternoon of the day (Sunday excepted) following such presentation, or sooner if so ordered by the Senate, proceed to the consideration of such articles, and shall continue in session from day to day (Sundays excepted) after the trial shall commence (unless otherwise ordered by the Senate) until final judgment shall be rendered, and so much longer as may in its judgment be needful. Before proceeding to the consideration of the articles of impeachment the Presiding Officer shall administer the oath hereinafter provided to the members of the Senate then present, and to the other members of the Senate as they shall appear, whose duty it shall be to take the same.

IV. When the President of the United States, or the Vice-President of the United States upon whom the powers and duties of the office of President shall have devolved, shall be impeached, the Chief Justice of the Supreme Court of the United States shall preside; and in a case requiring the said Chief Justice to preside notice shall be given to him by the Presiding Officer of the Senate of the time and place fixed for the consideration of the articles of impeachment as aforesaid, with a request to attend; and the said Chief Justice shall preside over the Senate during the consideration of said articles and upon the trial of the person impeached therein.

V. The Presiding Officer shall have power to make and issue, by himself or by the Secretary of the Senate, all orders, mandates, writs, and precepts authorized by these rules or by the Senate, and to make and enforce such other regulations and orders in the premises as the Senate may authorize or provide.

VI. The Senate shall have power to compel the attendance of witnesses, to enforce obedience to its orders, mandates, writs, precepts, and judgments, to preserve order, and to punish in a summary way contempts of and disobedience to its authority, orders, mandates, writs, precepts, or judgments, and to make all lawful orders, rules, and regulations which it may deem essential or conducive to the ends of justice; and the Sergeant-at-Arms, under the direction of the Senate, may employ such aid and assistance as may be necessary to enforce, execute, and carry into effect the lawful orders, mandates, writs, and precepts of the Senate.

VII. The Presiding Officer of the Senate shall direct all necessary preparations in the Senate Chamber, and the presiding officer upon the trial shall direct all the forms of proceeding while the Senate are sitting for the purpose of trying an impeachment and all forms during the trial not otherwise specially provided for. The presiding officer may, in the first instance, submit to the Senate, without a division, all questions of evidence and incidental questions; but the same shall, on the demand of one-fifth of the members present, be decided by yeas and nays.

VIII. Upon the presentation of articles of impeachment and the organization of the Senate as hereinbefore provided, a writ of summons shall issue to the accused, reciting said articles and notifying him to appear before the Senate upon a day and at a place to be fixed by the Senate, and named in such writ, and file his answer to said articles of impeachment, and to stand to and abide the orders and judgments of the Senate thereon, which writ shall be served by such officer or person as shall be named in the precept thereof such number of days prior to the day fixed for such appearance as shall be named in such precept, either by the delivery of an attested copy thereof to the person accused or, if that can not conveniently be done, by leaving such copy at the last known place of abode of such person or at his usual place of business, in some conspicuous place therein; or, if such service shall be, in the judgment of the Senate, impracticable, notice to the accused to appear shall be given in such other manner, by publication or otherwise, as shall be deemed just; and if the writ aforesaid shall fail of service in the manner aforesaid, the proceedings shall not thereby abate, but further service may be made in such manner as the Senate shall direct. If the accused, after service, shall fail to appear, either in person or by attorney, on the day so fixed therefor as aforesaid, or, appearing, shall fail to file his answer to such articles of impeachment, the trial shall proceed, nevertheless, as upon a plea of not guilty. If a plea of guilty shall be entered, judgment may be entered thereon without further proceedings.

IX. At 12 o'clock and 30 minutes afternoon of the day appointed for the return of the summons against the person impeached the legislative and executive business of the Senate shall be suspended and the Secretary of the Senate shall administer an oath to the returning officer in the form following, viz:

I, —— ——, do solemnly swear that the return made by me upon the process issued on the —— day of —— by the Senate of the United States against —— —— is truly made, and that I have performed such service as herein described. So help me God.

which oath shall be entered at large on the records.

X. The person impeached shall then be called to appear and answer the articles of impeachment against him. If he appear, or any person for him, the appearance shall be recorded, stating particularly if by himself or by agent or attorney, naming the person appearing and the capacity in

which he appears If he do not appear, either personally or by agent or attorney, the same shall be recorded.

XI. At 12 o'clock and 30 minutes afternoon of the day appointed for the trial of an impeachment the legislative and executive business of the Senate shall be suspended and the Secretary shall give notice to the House of Representatives that the Senate is ready to proceed upon the impeachment of —— ——, in the Senate Chamber, which chamber is prepared with accommodations for the reception of the House of Representatives.

XII. The hour of the day at which the Senate shall sit upon the trial of an impeachment shall be (unless otherwise ordered) 12 o'clock m., and when the hour for such sitting shall arrive the Presiding Officer of the Senate shall so announce; and thereupon the presiding officer upon such trial shall cause proclamation to be made, and the business of the trial shall proceed. The adjournment of the Senate sitting in said trial shall not operate as an adjournment of the Senate, but on such adjournment the Senate shall resume the consideration of its legislative and executive business.

XIII. The Secretary of the Senate shall record the proceedings in cases of impeachment as in the case of legislative proceedings, and the same shall be reported in the same manner as the legislative proceedings of the Senate.

XIV. Counsel for the parties shall be admitted to appear and be heard upon an impeachment.

XV. All motions made by the parties or their counsel shall be addressed to the presiding officer, and if he or any Senator shall require it they shall be committed to writing and read at the Secretary's table.

XVI. Witnesses shall be examined by one person on behalf of the party producing them and then cross-examined by one person on the other side.

XVII. If a Senator is called as a witness, he shall be sworn and give his testimony standing in his place.

XVIII. If a Senator wishes a question to be put to a witness, or to offer a motion or order (except a motion to adjourn), it shall be reduced to writing and put by the presiding officer.

XIX. At all times while the Senate is sitting upon the trial of an impeachment the doors of the Senate shall be kept open, unless the Senate shall direct the doors to be closed while deliberating upon its decisions.

XX. All preliminary or interlocutory questions and all motions shall be argued for not exceeding one hour on each side, unless the Senate shall by order extend the time.

XXI. The case on each side shall be opened by one person. The final argument on the merits may be made by two persons on each side (unless otherwise ordered by the Senate, upon application for that purpose), and the argument shall be opened and closed on the part of the House of Representatives.

XXII. On the final question whether the impeachment is sustained the yeas and nays shall be taken on each article of impeachment separately, and if the impeachment shall not, upon any of the articles presented, be sustained by the votes of two-thirds of the members present a judgment of acquittal shall be entered; but if the person accused in such articles of impeachment shall be convicted upon any of said articles by the votes of two-thirds of the members present the Senate shall proceed to pronounce judgment, and a certified copy of such judgment shall be deposited in the office of the Secretary of State.

XXIII. All the orders and decisions shall be made and had by yeas and nays, which shall be entered on the record, and without debate, except when the doors shall be closed for deliberation, and in that case no member shall speak more than once on one question, and for not more than ten minutes on an interlocutory question, and for not more than fifteen minutes on the final question, unless by consent of the Senate, to be had without debate; but a motion to adjourn may be decided without the yeas and nays, unless they be demanded by one-fifth of the members present.

XXIV. Witnesses shall be sworn in the following form, viz:

You, ——— ———, do swear (or affirm, as the case may be) that the evidence you shall give in the case now depending between the United States and ——— ——— shall be the truth, the whole truth, and nothing but the truth. So help you God.

which oath shall be administered by the Secretary or any other duly authorized person.

Form of subpœna to be issued on the application of the managers of the impeachment, or of the party impeached, or of his counsel:

To ——— ———, *greeting:*

You and each of you are hereby commanded to appear before the Senate of the United States on the —— day of ———, at the Senate Chamber, in the city of Washington, then and there to testify your knowledge in the cause which is before the Senate in which the House of Representatives have impeached ——— ———.

Fail not.

Witness ——— ———, and Presiding Officer of the Senate, at the city of Washington, this —— day of ———, A. D. ———, and of the Independence of the United States the ———.

Form of direction for the service of said subpœna:

The Senate of the United States to ——— ———, *greeting:*

You are hereby commanded to serve and return the within subpœna according to law.

Dated at Washington, this —— day of ———, A. D. ———, and of the Independence of the United States the ———.

——— ———,
                                                      Secretary of the Senate.

Form of oath to be administered to the members of the Senate sitting in the trial of impeachments:

I solemnly swear (or affirm, as the case may be) that in all things appertaining to the trial of the impeachment of ——— ———, now pending, I will do impartial justice according to the Constitution and laws. So help me God.

Form of summons to be issued and served upon the person impeached:

THE UNITED STATES OF AMERICA, *ss:*
The Senate of the United States to —— ——, *greeting:*
Whereas the House of Representatives of the United States of America did on the
—— day of —— exhibit to the Senate articles of impeachment against you, the said
—— ——, in the words following:

[Here insert the articles.]

And demand that you, the said —— ——, should be put to answer the accusations as set forth in said articles, and that such proceedings, examinations, trials, and judgments might be thereupon had as are agreeable to law and justice:

You, the said —— ——, are therefore hereby summoned to be and appear before the Senate of the United States of America, at their chamber, in the city of Washington, on the —— day of ——, at 12 o'clock and 30 minutes afternoon, then and there to answer to the said articles of impeachment, and then and there to abide by, obey, and perform such orders, directions, and judgments as the Senate of the United States shall make in the premises, according to the Constitution and laws of the United States.

Hereof you are not to fail.

Witness —— ——, and Presiding Officer of the said Senate, at the city of Washington, this —— day of ——, A. D. ——, and of the Independence of the United States the ——.

Form of precept to be indorsed on said writ of summons:

THE UNITED STATES OF AMERICA, *ss:*
The Senate of the United States to —— ——, *greeting:*
You are hereby commanded to deliver to and leave with —— ——, if conveniently to be found, or, if not, to leave at his usual place of abode or at his usual place of business, in some conspicuous place, a true and attested copy of the within writ of summons, together with a like copy of this precept; and in whichsoever way you perform the service, let it be done at 'east —— days before the appearance day mentioned in said writ of summons.

Fail not, and make return of this writ of summons and precept, with your proceedings thereon indorsed, on or before the appearance day mentioned in the said writ of summons.

Witness —— ——, and Presiding Officer of the Senate, at the city of Washington, this —— day of ——, A. D. ——, and of the Independence of the United States the ——.

All process shall be served by the Sergeant-at-Arms of the Senate unless otherwise ordered by the court.

XXV. If the Senate shall at any time fail to sit for the consideration of articles of impeachment on the day or hour fixed therefor, the Senate may by an order, to be adopted without debate, fix a day and hour for resuming such consideration.

On March 31 Rule VII was amended to read as follows:

VII. The Presiding Officer of the Senate shall direct all necessary preparations in the Senate Chamber, and the presiding officer on the trial shall direct all the forms of proceeding while the Senate are sitting for the purpose of trying an impeachment, and all forms during the trial not otherwise specially provided for, and the presiding officer on the trial may rule all questions of evidence and incidental questions, which ruling shall stand as the judgment of the Senate, unless some member of the Senate shall ask that a formal vote be taken thereon, in which case it shall be submitted to the Senate for decision; or he may, at his option, in the first instance submit any such question to a vote of the members of the Senate.

On April 3 Rule VII was further amended by inserting at the end thereof the following:

Upon all such questions the vote shall be without a division, unless the yeas and nays be demanded by one-fifth of the members present, when the same shall be taken.

On March 13 Rule XXIII was amended to read as follows:

XXIII. All the orders and decisions shall be made and had by yeas and nays, which shall be entered on the record, and without debate, subject, however, to the operation of Rule VII, except when the doors shall be closed for deliberation, and in that case no member shall speak more than once on one question, and for not more than ten minutes on an interlocutory question, and for not more than fifteen minutes on the final question, unless by consent of the Senate, to be had without debate; but a motion to adjourn may be decided without the yeas and nays, unless they be demanded by one-fifth of the members present.

On May 7 Rule XXIII was further amended by adding thereto the following:

The fifteen minutes herein allowed shall be for the whole deliberation on the final question, and not to the final question on each article of impeachment.

FRIDAY, MARCH 13, 1868.

THE UNITED STATES *vs.* ANDREW JOHNSON, PRESIDENT.

Mr. Henry Stanbery, in behalf of Andrew Johnson, the respondent, read the following paper:

In the matter of the impeachment of Andrew Johnson, President of the United States.

Mr. CHIEF JUSTICE: I, Andrew Johnson, President of the United States, having been served with a summons to appear before this honorable court, sitting as a court of impeachment, to answer certain articles of impeachment found and presented against me by the honorable the House of Representatives of the United States, do hereby enter my appearance by my counsel, Henry Stanbery, Benjamin R. Curtis, Jeremiah S. Black, William M. Evarts, and Thomas A R. Nelson, who have my warrant and authority therefor, and who are instructed by me to ask of this honorable court a reasonable time for the preparation of my answer to said articles. After a careful examination of the articles of impeachment and consultation with my counsel, I am satisfied that at least forty days will be necessary for the preparation of my answer, and I respectfully ask that it be allowed.

ANDREW JOHNSON.

Mr. Stanbery then submitted the following motion:

In the matter of the impeachment of Andrew Johnson, President of the United States.

Henry Stanbery, Benjamin R. Curtis, Jeremiah S. Black, William M. Evarts, and Thomas A. R. Nelson, of counsel for the respondent, move the court for the allowance of forty days for the preparation of the answer to the articles of impeachment, and in support of the motion make the following professional statement:

The articles are eleven in number, involving many questions of law and fact. We have during the limited time and opportunity afforded us considered as far as possible the field of investigation which must be explored in the preparation of the answer, and the conclusion at which we have arrived is that with the utmost diligence the time we have asked is reasonable and necessary.

The precedents as to time for answer upon impeachments before the Senate to which we have had opportunity to refer are those of Judge Chase and Judge Peck.

In the case of Judge Chase time was allowed from the 3d of January until the 4th of February next succeeding to put in his answer—a period of thirty-two days; but in this case there were only eight articles, and Judge Chase had been for a year cognizant of most of the articles, and had been himself engaged in preparing to meet them.

In the case of Judge Peck there was but a single article. Judge Peck asked for time from the 10th to the 25th of May to put in his answer, and it was granted. It appears that Judge Peck had been long cognizant of the ground laid for his impeachment, and had been present before the committee of the House upon the examination of the witnesses, and had been permitted by the House of Representatives to present to that body an elaborate answer to the charges.

It is apparent that the President is fairly entitled to more time than was allowed in either of the foregoing cases. It is proper to add that the respondents in these cases were lawyers, fully capable of preparing their own answers, and that no pressing official duties interfered with their attention to that business; whereas the President, not being a lawyer, must rely on his counsel. The charges involve his acts, declarations, and intentions, as to all which his counsel must be fully advised upon consultation with him, step by step, in the preparation of his defense. It is seldom that a case requires such constant communication between client and counsel as this, and yet such communication can only be had at such intervals as are allowed to the President from the usual hours that must be devoted to his high official duties.

We further beg leave to suggest for the consideration of this honorable court that, as counsel careful as well of their own reputation as of the interests of their client in a case of such magnitude as this, so out of the ordinary range of professional experience, where so much responsibility is felt, they submit to the candid consideration of the court that they have a right to ask for themselves such opportunity to discharge their duty as seems to them to be absolutely necessary.

HENRY STANBERY,
B. R. CURTIS,
JEREMIAH S. BLACK, ⎫
WILLIAM M. EVARTS, ⎬ Per H. S.
THOMAS A. R. NELSON, ⎭
Of Counsel for the Respondent.

The above motion was denied, and the Senate adopted the following orders:

Ordered, That the respondent file answer to the articles of impeachment on or before Monday, the 23d day of March instant.

Ordered, That unless otherwise ordered by the Senate, for cause shown, the trial of the pending impeachment shall proceed immediately after replication shall be filed.

MONDAY, MARCH 23, 1868.

THE UNITED STATES *vs.* ANDREW JOHNSON, PRESIDENT.

The answer of the respondent to the articles of impeachment was submitted by his counsel, as follows:

Senate of the United States, sitting as a court of impeachment for the trial of Andrew Johnson, President of the United States.

THE ANSWER OF THE SAID ANDREW JOHNSON, PRESIDENT OF THE UNITED STATES, TO THE ARTICLES OF IMPEACHMENT EXHIBITED AGAINST HIM BY THE HOUSE OF REPRESENTATIVES OF THE UNITED STATES.

Answer to Article I.—For answer to the first article he says that Edwin M. Stanton was appointed Secretary for the Department of War on the 15th day of January, A. D. 1862, by Abraham Lincoln, then President of the United States, during the first term of his Presidency, and was commissioned, according to the Constitution and laws of the United States, to hold the said office during the pleasure of the President; that the office of Secretary for the Department of War was created by an act of the First Congress in its first session, passed on the 7th day of August, A. D. 1789, and in and by that act it was provided and enacted that the said Secretary for the Department of War shall perform and execute such duties as shall from time to time be enjoined on and intrusted to him by the President of the United States, agreeably to the Constitution, relative to the subjects within the scope of the said Department; and, furthermore, that the said Secretary shall conduct the business of the said Department in such a manner as the President of the United States shall from time to time order and instruct.

And this respondent, further answering, says that by force of the act aforesaid and by reason of his appointment aforesaid the said Stanton became the principal officer in one of the Executive Departments of the Government within the true intent and meaning of the second section of the second article of the Constitution of the United States and according to the true intent and meaning of that provision of the Constitution of the United States; and, in accordance with the settled and uniform practice of each and every President of the United States, the said Stanton then became, and so long as he should continue to hold the said office of Secretary for the Department of War must continue to be, one of the advisers of the President of the United States, as well as the person intrusted to act for and represent the President in matters enjoined upon him or intrusted to him by the President touching the Department aforesaid, and for whose conduct in such capacity, subordinate to the President, the President is by the Constitution and laws of the United States made responsible.

And this respondent, further answering, says he succeeded to the office of President of the United States upon and by reason of the death of Abraham Lincoln, then President of the United States, on the 15th day of April, 1865, and the said Stanton was then holding the said office of Secretary for the Department of War under and by reason of the appointment and commission aforesaid; and not having been removed from the said office by this respondent, the said Stanton continued to hold the same under the appointment and commission aforesaid, at the pleasure of the President, until the time hereinafter particularly mentioned, and at no time received any appointment or commission save as above detailed.

And this respondent, further answering, says that on and prior to the 5th day of August, A. D. 1867, this respondent, the President of the United States, responsible for the conduct of the Secretary for the Department of War, and having the constitutional right to resort to and rely upon the person holding that office for advice concerning the great and difficult public duties enjoined on the President by the Constitution and laws of the United States, became satisfied that he could not allow the said Stanton to continue to hold the office of Secretary for the Department of War without hazard of the public interest; that the relations between the said Stanton and the President no longer permitted the President to resort to him for advice or to be, in the judgment of the President, safely responsible for his conduct of the affairs of the Department of War, as by law required, in accordance with the orders and instructions of the President; and thereupon, by force of the Constitution and laws of the United

States, which devolve on the President the power and the duty to control the conduct of the business of that Executive Department of the Government, and by reason of the constitutional duty of the President to take care that the laws be faithfully executed, this respondent did necessarily consider and did determine that the said Stanton ought no longer to hold the said office of Secretary for the Department of War. And this respondent, by virtue of the power and authority vested in him as President of the United States by the Constitution and laws of the United States, to give effect to such his decision and determination, did, on the 5th day of August, A. D. 1867, address to the said Stanton a note of which the following is a true copy:

SIR: Public considerations of a high character constrain me to say that your resignation as Secretary of War will be accepted.

To which note the said Stanton made the following reply:

WAR DEPARTMENT,
Washington, August 5, 1867.

SIR: Your note of this day has been received, stating that "public considerations of a high character constrain" you "to say that" my "resignation as Secretary of War will be accepted."

In reply I have the honor to say that public considerations of a high character, which alone have induced me to continue at the head of this Department, constrain me not to resign the office of Secretary of War before the next meeting of Congress.

Very respectfully yours,

EDWIN M. STANTON.

This respondent, as President of the United States, was thereon of opinion that, having regard to the necessary official relations and duties of the Secretary for the Department of War to the President of the United States, according to the Constitution and laws of the United States, and having regard to the responsibility of the President for the conduct of the said Secretary, and having regard to the permanent executive authority of the office which the respondent holds under the Constitution and laws of the United States, it was impossible, consistently with the public interests, to allow the said Stanton to continue to hold the said office of Secretary for the Department of War; and it then became the official duty of the respondent, as President of the United States, to consider and decide what act or acts should and might lawfully be done by him, as President of the United States, to cause the said Stanton to surrender the said office.

This respondent was informed and verily believed that it was practically settled by the First Congress of the United States, and had been so considered and uniformly and in great numbers of instances acted on by each Congress and President of the United States, in succession, from President Washington to and including President Lincoln, and from the First Congress to the Thirty-ninth Congress, that the Constitution of the United States conferred on the President, as part of the executive power and as one of the necessary means and instruments of performing the executive duty expressly imposed on him by the Constitution of taking care that the laws be faithfully executed, the power at any and all times of removing from office all executive officers for cause to be judged of by the President alone. This respondent had, in pursuance of the Constitution, required the opinion of each principal officer of the Executive Departments upon this question of constitutional executive power and duty, and had been advised by each of them, including the said Stanton, Secretary for the Department of War, that under the Constitution of the United States this power was lodged by the Constitution in the President of the United States, and that, consequently, it could be lawfully exercised by him, and the Congress could not deprive him thereof; and this respondent, in his capacity of President of the United States, and because in that capacity he was both enabled and bound to use his best judgment upon this question, did, in good faith and with an earnest desire to arrive at the truth, come to the conclusion and opinion, and did make the same known to the honorable the Senate of the United States by a message dated on the 2d day of March, 1867 (a true copy whereof is hereunto annexed and marked A), that the power last mentioned was conferred and the duty of exercising it in fit cases was imposed on the President by the Constitution of the United States, and that the President could not be deprived of this power or relieved of this duty, nor could the same be vested by law in the President and the Senate jointly, either in part or whole; and this has ever since remained and was the opinion of this respondent at the time when he was forced as aforesaid to consider and decide what act or acts should and might lawfully be done by this respondent, as President of the United States, to cause the said Stanton to surrender the said office.

This respondent was also then aware that by the first section of "An act regulating the tenure of certain civil offices," passed March 2, 1867, by a constitutional majority of both Houses of Congress, it was enacted as follows:

That every person holding any civil office to which he has been appointed by and with the advice and consent of the Senate, and every person who shall hereafter be appointed to any such office and shall become duly qualified to act therein, is and shall be entitled to hold such office until a successor shall have been in like manner appointed and duly qualified, except as herein otherwise provided: *Provided*, That the Secretaries of State, of the Treasury, of War, of the Navy, and of the Interior, the Postmaster-General, and the Attorney-General shall hold their offices, respectively, for and during the term of the President by whom they may have been appointed and one month thereafter, subject to removal by and with the advice and consent of the Senate.

This respondent was also aware that this act was understood and intended to be an expression of the opinion of the Congress by which that act was passed that the power to remove executive officers for cause might by law be taken from the President and vested in him and the Senate jointly; and although this respondent had arrived at and still retained the opinion above expressed, and verily believed, as he still believes, that the said first section of the last-mentioned act was and is wholly inoperative and void by reason of its conflict with the Constitution of the United States, yet, inasmuch as the same had been enacted by the constitutional majority in each of the two Houses of that Congress, this respondent considered it to be proper to examine and decide whether the particular case of the said Stanton, on which it was this respondent's duty to act, was within or without the terms of that first section of the act, or, if within it, whether the President had not the power, according to the terms of the act, to remove the said Stanton from the office of Secretary for the Department of War; and having, in his capacity of President of the United States, so examined and considered, did form the opinion that the case of the said Stanton and his tenure of office were not affected by the first section of the last-named act.

And this respondent, further answering, says that although a case thus existed which, in his judgment, as President of the United States, called for the exercise of the executive power to remove the said Stanton from the office of Secretary for the Department of War; and although this respondent was of opinion, as is above shown, that under the Constitution of the United States the power to remove the said Stanton from the said office was vested in the President of the United States; and although this respondent was also of the opinion, as is above shown, that the case of the said Stanton was not affected by the first section of the last-named act; and although each of the said opinions had been formed by this respondent upon an actual case, requiring him, in his capacity of President of the United States, to come to some judgment and determination thereon, yet this respondent, as President of the United States, desired and determined to avoid, if possible, any question of the construction and effect of the said first section of the last-named act, and also the broader question of the executive power conferred upon the President of the United States by the Constitution of the United States to remove one of the principal officers of one of the Executive Departments for cause seeming to him sufficient; and this respondent also desired and determined that if, from causes over which he could exert no control, it should become absolutely necessary to raise and have in some way determined either or both of the said last-named questions, it was in accordance with the Constitution of the United States, and was required of the President thereby, that questions of so much gravity and importance, upon which the legislative and executive departments of the Government had disagreed, which involved powers considered by all branches of the Government, during its entire history down to the year 1867, to have been confided by the Constitution of the United States to the President, and to be necessary for the complete and proper execution of his constitutional duties, should be in some proper way submitted to that judicial department of the Government intrusted by the Constitution with the power, and subjected by it to the duty, not only of determining finally the construction and effect of all acts of Congress, but of comparing them with the Constitution of the United States and pronouncing them inoperative when found in conflict with that fundamental law which the people have enacted for the government of all their servants. And to these ends, first, that through the action of the Senate of the United States the absolute duty of the President to substitute some fit person in place of Mr. Stanton as one of his advisers, and as a principal subordinate officer whose official conduct he was responsible for and had lawful right to control, might, if possible, be accomplished without the necessity of raising any one of the questions aforesaid; and, second, if this duty could not be so performed, then that these questions, or such of them as might necessarily arise, should be judicially determined in manner aforesaid, and for no other end or purpose, this respondent, as President of the United States, on the 12th day of August, 1867, seven days after the reception of the letter of the said Stanton of the 5th of August, hereinbefore stated, did issue to the said Stanton the order following, namely:

EXECUTIVE MANSION,
Washington, August 12, 1867.

Hon. EDWIN M. STANTON,
Secretary of War.

SIR: By virtue of the power and authority vested in me as President by the Constitution and laws of the United States, you are hereby suspended from office as Secretary of War, and will cease to exercise any and all functions pertaining to the same.

You wi 1 at once tran fer to General Ulysses S. Grant, who has this day been authorized and empowered to act as Secretary of War *ad interim*, all records, books, papers, and other public property now in your custody and charge.

To which said order the said Stanton made the following reply:

WAR DEPARTMENT,
Washington City, August 12, 1867.

The PRESIDENT.

SIR: Your note of this date has been received, informing me that by virtue of the powers vested in you as President by the Constitution and laws of the United States I am suspended from office as Secretary of War, and will cease to exercise any and all functions pertaining to the same; and also directing me at once to transfer to General Ulysses S. Grant, who has this day been authorized and empowered to act as Secretary of War *ad interim*, all records, books, papers, and other public property now in my custody and charge.

Under a sense of public duty, I am compelled to deny your right under the Constitution and laws of the United States, without the advice and consent of the Senate and without legal cause, to suspend me from office as Secretary of War, or the exercise of any or all functions pertaining to the same, or without such advice and consent to compel me to transfer to any person the records, books, papers, and public property in my custody as Secretary.

But inasmuch as the General Commanding the armies of the United States has been appointed *ad interim*, and has notified me that he has accepted the appointment, I have no alternative but to submit, under protest, to superior force.

And this respondent, further answering, says that it is provided in and by the second section of "An act regulating the tenure of certain civil offices" that the President may suspend an officer from the performance of the duties of the office held by him, for certain causes therein designated, until the next meeting of the Senate and until the case shall be acted on by the Senate; that this respondent, as President of the United States, was advised, and he verily believed, and still believes, that the executive power of removal from office confided to him by the Constitution as aforesaid includes the power of suspension from office at the pleasure of the President; and this respondent, by the order aforesaid, did suspend the said Stanton from office, not until the next meeting of the Senate or until the Senate should have acted upon the case, but, by force of the power and authority vested in him by the Constitution and laws of the United States, indefinitely and at the pleasure of the President; and the order, in form aforesaid, was made known to the Senate of the United States on the 12th day of December, A. D. 1867, as will be more fully hereinafter stated.

And this respondent, further answering, says that in and by the act of February 13, 1795, it was, among other things, provided and enacted that in case of vacancy in the office of Secretary for the Department of War it shall be lawful for the President, in case he shall think it necessary, to authorize any person to perform the duties of that office until a successor be appointed or such vacancy filled, but not exceeding the term of six months; and this respondent, being advised and believing that such law was in full force and not repealed, by an order dated August 12, 1867, did authorize and empower Ulysses S. Grant, General of the armies of the United States, to act as Secretary for the Department of War *ad interim*, in the form in which similar authority had theretofore been given, not until the next meeting of the Senate and until the Senate should act on the case, but at the pleasure of the President, subject only to the limitation of six months in the said last-mentioned act contained; and a copy of the last-named order was made known to the Senate of the United States on the 12th day of December, A. D. 1867, as will be hereinafter more fully stated; and in pursuance of the design and intention aforesaid, if it should become necessary, to submit the said questions to a judicial determination, this respondent, at or near the date of the last-mentioned order, did make known such his purpose to obtain a judicial decision of the said questions, or such of them as might be necessary.

And this respondent, further answering, says that in further pursuance of his intention and design, if possible, to perform what he judged to be his imperative duty, to prevent the said Stanton from longer holding the office of Secretary for the Department of War, and at the same time avoiding, if possible, any question respecting the extent of the power of removal from executive office confided to the President by the Constitution of the United States, and any question respecting the construction and effect of the first section of the said "Act regulating the tenure of certain civil offices," while he should not by any act of his abandon and relinquish either a power which he believed the Constitution had con-

ferred on the President of the United States to enable him to perform the duties of his office or a power designedly left to him by the first section of the act of Congress last aforesaid, this respondent did, on the 12th day of December, 1867, transmit to the Senate of the United States a message, a copy whereof is hereunto annexed and marked B, wherein he made known the orders aforesaid and the reasons which had induced the same, so far as this respondent then considered it material and necessary that the same should be set forth, and reiterated his views concerning the constitutional power of removal vested in the President, and also expressed his views concerning the construction of the said first section of the last-mentioned act, as respected the power of the President to remove the said Stanton from the said office of Secretary for the Department of War, well hoping that this respondent could thus perform what he then believed, and still believes, to be his imperative duty in reference to the said Stanton without derogating from the powers which this respondent believed were confided to the President by the Constitution and laws, and without the necessity of raising judicially any questions respecting the same.

And this respondent, further answering, says that this hope not having been realized, the President was compelled either to allow the said Stanton to resume the said office and remain therein contrary to the settled convictions of the President, formed as aforesaid, respecting the powers confided to him and the duties required of him by the Constitution of the United States, and contrary to the opinion formed as aforesaid that the first section of the last-mentioned act did not affect the case of the said Stanton, and contrary to the fixed belief of the President that he could no longer advise with or trust or be responsible for the said Stanton in the said office of Secretary for the Department of War, or else he was compelled to take such steps as might in the judgment of the President be lawful and necessary to raise for a judicial decision the questions affecting the lawful right of the said Stanton to resume the said office or the power of the said Stanton to persist in refusing to quit the said office if he should persist in actually refusing to quit the same; and to this end, and to this end only, this respondent did, on the 21st day of February, 1868, issue the order for the removal of the said Stanton, in the said first article mentioned and set forth, and the order authorizing the said Lorenzo Thomas to act as Secretary of War *ad interim*, in the said second article set forth.

And this respondent, proceeding to answer specifically each substantial allegation in the said first article, says: He denies that the said Stanton, on the 21st day of February, 1868, was lawfully in possession of the said office of Secretary for the Department of War. He denies that the said Stanton, on the day last mentioned, was lawfully entitled to hold the said office against the will of the President of the United States. He denies that the said order for the removal of the said Stanton was unlawfully issued. He denies that the said order was issued with intent to violate the act entitled

"An act regulating the tenure of certain civil offices." He denies that the said order was a violation of the last-mentioned act. He denies that the said order was a violation of the Constitution of the United States, or of any law thereof, or of his oath of office. He denies that the said order was issued with an intent to violate the Constitution of the United States, or any law thereof, or this respondent's oath of office; and he respectfully but earnestly insists that not only was it issued by him in the performance of what he believed to be an imperative official duty, but in the performance of what this honorable court will consider was, in point of fact, an imperative official duty. And he denies that any and all substantive matters in the said first article contained, in manner and form as the same are therein stated and set forth, do by law constitute a high misdemeanor in office within the true intent and meaning of the Constitution of the United States.

Answer to Article II.—And for answer to the second article this respondent says that he admits he did issue and deliver to said Lorenzo Thomas the said writing set forth in said second article, bearing date at Washington, D. C., February 21, 1868, addressed to Brevet Major-General Lorenzo Thomas, Adjutant-General United States Army, Washington, D. C., and he further admits that the same was so issued without the advice and consent of the Senate of the United States, then in session; but he denies that he thereby violated the Constitution of the United States or any law thereof, or that he did thereby intend to violate the Constitution of the United States or the provisions of any act of Congress; and this respondent refers to his answer to said first article for a full statement of the purposes and intentions with which said order was issued, and adopts the same as part of his answer to this article; and he further denies that there was then and there no vacancy in the said office of Secretary for the Department of War, or that he did then and there commit or was guilty of a high misdemeanor in office; and this respondent maintains and will insist—

1. That at the date and delivery of said writing there was a vacancy existing in the office of Secretary for the Department of War.

2. That notwithstanding the Senate of the United States was then in session, it was lawful and according to long and well-established usage to empower and authorize the said Thomas to act as Secretary of War *ad interim*.

3. That if the said act regulating the tenure of civil offices be held to be a valid law, no provision of the same was violated by the issuing of said order or by the designation of said Thomas to act as Secretary of War *ad interim*.

Answer to Article III.—And for answer to said third article this respondent says that he abides by his answer to said first and second articles in so far as the same are responsive to the allegations contained in the said third article, and, without here again repeating the same answer,

prays the same be taken as an answer to this third article as fully as if here again set out at length; and as to the new allegation contained in said third article, that this respondent did appoint the said Thomas to be Secretary for the Department of War *ad interim*, this respondent denies that he gave any other authority to said Thomas than such as appears in said written authority, set out in said article, by which he authorized and empowered said Thomas to act as Secretary for the Department of War *ad interim;* and he denies that the same amounts to an appointment, and insists that it is only a designation of an officer of that Department to act temporarily as Secretary for the Department of War *ad interim* until an appointment should be made. But whether the said written authority amounts to an appointment or to a temporary authority or designation, this respondent denies that in any sense he did thereby intend to violate the Constitution of the United States, or that he thereby intended to give the said order the character or effect of an appointment in the constitutional or legal sense of that term. He further denies that there was no vacancy in said office of Secretary for the Department of War existing at the date of said written authority.

Answer to Article IV.—And for answer to said fourth article this respondent denies that on the said 21st day of February, 1868, at Washington aforesaid, or at any other time or place, he did unlawfully conspire with the said Lorenzo Thomas, or with the said Thomas and any other person or persons, with intent, by intimidations and threats, unlawfully to hinder and prevent the said Stanton from holding said office of Secretary for the Department of War, in violation of the Constitution of the United States or of the provisions of the said act of Congress in said article mentioned, or that he did then and there commit or was guilty of a high crime in office. On the contrary thereof, protesting that the said Stanton was not then and there lawfully the Secretary for the Department of War, this respondent states that his sole purpose in authorizing the said Thomas to act as Secretary for the Department of War *ad interim* was, as is fully stated in his answer to the said first article, to bring the question of the right of the said Stanton to hold said office, notwithstanding his said suspension, and notwithstanding the said order of removal, and notwithstanding the said authority of the said Thomas to act as Secretary of War *ad interim*, to the test of a final decision by the Supreme Court of the United States in the earliest practicable mode by which the question could be brought before that tribunal.

This respondent did not conspire or agree with the said Thomas, or any other person or persons, to use intimidation or threats to hinder or prevent the said Stanton from holding the said office of Secretary for the Department of War, nor did this respondent at any time command or advise the said Thomas, or any other person or persons, to resort to or use either threats or intimidation for that purpose. The only means in the contemplation or purpose of respondent to be used are set forth fully in the said

orders of February 21, the first addressed to Mr. Stanton and the second to the said Thomas. By the first order the respondent notified Mr. Stanton that he was removed from the said office and that his functions as Secretary for the Department of War were to terminate upon the receipt of that order; and he also thereby notified the said Stanton that the said Thomas had been authorized to act as Secretary for the Department of War *ad interim*, and ordered the said Stanton to transfer to him all the records, books, papers, and other public property in his custody and charge; and by the second order this respondent notified the said Thomas of the removal from office of the said Stanton, and authorized him to act as Secretary for the Department of War *ad interim*, and directed him to immediately enter upon the discharge of the duties pertaining to that office and to receive the transfer of all the records, books, papers, and other public property from Mr. Stanton then in his custody and charge.

Respondent gave no instructions to the said Thomas to use intimidation or threats to enforce obedience to these orders. He gave him no authority to call in the aid of the military or any other force to enable him to obtain possession of the office or of the books, papers, records, or property thereof. The only agency resorted to, or intended to be resorted to, was by means of the said Executive orders requiring obedience. But the Secretary for the Department of War refused to obey these orders, and still holds undisturbed possession and custody of that Department and of the records, books, papers, and other public property therein. Respondent further states that in execution of the orders so by this respondent given to the said Thomas he, the said Thomas, proceeded in a peaceful manner to demand of the said Stanton a surrender to him of the public property in the said Department, and to vacate the possession of the same, and to allow him, the said Thomas, peaceably to exercise the duties devolved upon him by authority of the President. That, as this respondent has been informed and believes, the said Stanton peremptorily refused obedience to the orders so issued. Upon such refusal no force or threat of force was used by the said Thomas, by authority of the President or otherwise, to enforce obedience, either then or at any subsequent time.

This respondent doth here except to the sufficiency of the allegations contained in said fourth article, and states for ground of exception that it is not stated that there was any agreement between this respondent and the said Thomas, or any other person or persons, to use intimidation and threats, nor is there any allegation as to the nature of said intimidation and threats, or that there was any agreement to carry them into execution, or that any step was taken or agreed to be taken to carry them into execution; and that the allegation in said article that the intent of said conspiracy was to use intimidation and threats is wholly insufficient, inasmuch as it is not alleged that the said intent formed the basis or

became part of any agreement between the said alleged conspirators; and, furthermore, that there is no allegation of any conspiracy or agreement to use intimidation or threats.

Answer to Article V.—And for answer to the said fifth article this respondent denies that on the said 21st day of February, 1868, or at any other time or times in the same year before the said 2d day of March, 1868, or at any prior or subsequent time, at Washington aforesaid, or at any other place, this respondent did unlawfully conspire with the said Thomas, or with any other person or persons, to prevent or hinder the execution of the said act entitled "An act regulating the tenure of certain civil offices," or that, in pursuance of said alleged conspiracy, he did unlawfully attempt to prevent the said Edwin M. Stanton from holding the said office of Secretary for the Department of War, or that he did thereby commit, or that he was thereby guilty of, a high misdemeanor in office. Respondent, protesting that said Stanton was not then and there Secretary for the Department of War, begs leave to refer to his answer given to the fourth article and to his answer to the first article as to his intent and purpose in issuing the orders for the removal of Mr. Stanton and the authority given to the said Thomas, and prays equal benefit therefrom as if the same were here again repeated and fully set forth.

And this respondent excepts to the sufficiency of the said fifth article, and states his ground for such exception that it is not alleged by what means or by what agreement the said alleged conspiracy was formed or agreed to be carried out, or in what way the same was attempted to be carried out, or what were the acts done in pursuance thereof.

Answer to Article VI.—And for answer to the said sixth article this respondent denies that on the said 21st day of February, 1868, at Washington aforesaid, or at any other time or place, he did unlawfully conspire with the said Thomas by force to seize, take, or possess the property of the United States in the Department of War, contrary to the provisions of the said acts referred to in the said article, or either of them, or with intent to violate either of them. Respondent, protesting that said Stanton was not then and there Secretary for the Department of War, not only denies the said conspiracy as charged, but also denies any unlawful intent in reference to the custody and charge of the property of the United States in the said Department of War, and again refers to his former answers for a full statement of his intent and purpose in the premises.

Answer to Article VII.—And for answer to the said seventh article respondent denies that on the said 21st day of February, 1868, at Washington aforesaid, or at any other time and place, he did unlawfully conspire with the said Thomas with intent unlawfully to seize, take, or possess the property of the United States in the Department of War, with intent to violate or disregard the said act in the said seventh article referred to, or that he did then and there commit a high misdemeanor in office. Respondent, protesting that the said Stanton was not then and there Secretary for the Department of War, again refers to his former answers, in so far as they are applicable, to show the intent with which he proceeded in the premises, and prays equal benefit therefrom as if the same were here again fully repeated. Respondent further takes exception to the sufficiency of the allegations of this article as to the conspiracy alleged upon the same grounds as stated in the exception set forth in his answer to said article fourth.

Answer to Article VIII.—And for answer to the said eighth article this respondent denies that on the 21st day of February, 1868, at Washington aforesaid, or at any other time and place, he did issue and deliver to the said Thomas the said letter of authority set forth in the said eighth article with the intent unlawfully to control the disbursements of the money appropriated for the military service and for the Department of War. This respondent, protesting that there was a vacancy in the office of Secretary of War, admits that he did issue the said letter of authority, and he denies that the same was with any unlawful intent whatever, either to violate the Constitution of the United States or any act of Congress. On the contrary, this respondent again affirms that his sole intent was to vindicate his authority as President of the United States, and by peaceful means to bring the question of the right of the said Stanton to continue to hold the said office of Secretary of War to a final decision before the Supreme Court of the United States, as has been hereinbefore set forth; and he prays the same benefit from his answer in the premises as if the same were here again repeated at length.

Answer to Article IX.—And for answer to the said ninth article the respondent states that on the said 22d day of February, 1868, the following note was addressed to the said Emory by the private secretary of the respondent:

> EXECUTIVE MANSION,
> WASHINGTON, D. C.,
> *February 22, 1868.*

GENERAL: The President directs me to say that he will be pleased to have you call upon him as early as practicable.

Respectfully and truly, yours,

> WILLIAM G. MOORE,
> *United States Army.*

General Emory called at the Executive Mansion according to this request. The object of respondent was to be advised by General Emory, as commander of the Department of Washington, what changes had been made in the military affairs of the department. Respondent had been informed that various changes had been made which in no wise had been brought to his notice or reported to him from the Department of War or from any other quarter, and desired to ascertain the facts. After the said Emory had explained in detail the changes which had taken place, said Emory called the attention of respondent to a general order which he referred to, and which this respondent then sent for, when it was produced. It is as follows:

GENERAL ORDERS, NO. 17.

WAR DEPARTMENT,
ADJUTANT-GENERAL'S OFFICE,
Washington, March 14, 1867.

The following acts of Congress are published for the information and government of all concerned:

*   *   *   *   *   *   *

"II.—PUBLIC—NO. 85.

"AN ACT making appropriations for the support of the Army for the year ending June 30, 1868, and for other purposes.

*   *   *   *   *   *   *

"SEC. 2. *And be it further enacted,* That the headquarters of the General of the Army of the United States shall be at the city of Washington, and all orders and instructions relating to military operations issued by the President or Secretary of War shall be issued through the General of the Army, and in case of his inability through the next in rank. The General of the Army shall not be removed, suspended, or relieved from command, or assigned to duty elsewhere than at said headquarters, except at his own request, without the previous approval of the Senate; and any orders or instructions relating to military operations issued contrary to the requirements of this section shall be null and void; and any officer who shall issue orders or instructions contrary to the provisions of this section shall be deemed guilty of a misdemeanor in office; and any officer of the Army who shall transmit, convey, or obey any orders or instructions so issued contrary to the provisions of this section, knowing that such orders were so issued, shall be liable to imprisonment for not less than two nor more than twenty years upon conviction thereof in any court of competent jurisdiction.

*   *   *   *   *   *   *

"Approved, March 2, 1867."

*   *   *   *   *   *   *

By order of the Secretary of War:

E. D. TOWNSEND,
Assistant Adjutant-General.

Official:

————— —————,
Assistant Adjutant-General.

General Emory not only called the attention of respondent to this order, but to the fact that it was in conformity with a section contained in an appropriation act passed by Congress. Respondent, after reading the order, observed:

This is not in accordance with the Constitution of the United States, which makes me Commander in Chief of the Army and Navy, or of the language of the commission which you hold.

General Emory then stated that this order had met the respondent's approval. Respondent then said in reply, in substance:

Am I to understand that the President of the United States can not give an order but through the General in Chief, or General Grant?

General Emory again reiterated the statement that it had met respondent's approval, and that it was the opinion of some of the leading lawyers of the country that this order was constitutional. With some further conversation, respondent then inquired the names of the lawyers who had given the opinion, and he mentioned the names of two. Respondent then said that the object of the law was very evident, referring to the clause in the appropriation act upon which the order purported to be based. This, according to respondent's recollection, was the substance of the conversation had with General Emory.

Respondent denies that any allegations in the said article of any instructions or declarations given to the said Emory then or at any other time contrary to or in addition to what is hereinbefore set forth are true. Respondent denies that in said conversation with said Emory he had any other intent than to express the opinion then given to the said Emory, nor did he then or at any time request or order the said Emory to disobey any law or any order issued in conformity with any law, or intend to offer any inducement to the said Emory to violate any law. What this respondent then said to General Emory was simply the expression of an opinion which he then fully believed to be sound, and which he yet believes to be so, and that is that by the express provisions of the Constitution this respondent, as President, is made the Commander in Chief of the armies of the United States, and as such he is to be respected, and that his orders, whether issued through the War Department, or through the General in Chief, or by any other channel of communication, are entitled to respect and obedience, and that such constitutional power can not be taken from him by virtue of any act of Congress. Respondent doth therefore deny that by the expression of such opinion he did commit or was guilty of a high misdemeanor in office; and the respondent doth further say that the said Article IX lays no foundation whatever for the conclusion stated in the said article, that the respondent, by reason of the allegations therein contained, was guilty of a high misdemeanor in office.

In reference to the statement made by General Emory that this respondent had approved of said act of Congress containing the section referred to, the respondent admits that his formal approval was given to said act, but accompanied the same by the following message, addressed and sent with the act to the House of Representatives, in which House the said act originated, and from which it came to respondent:

To the House of Representatives: WASHINGTON, D. C., *March 2, 1867.*

The act entitled "An act making appropriations for the support of the Army for the year ending June 30, 1868, and for other purposes," contains provisions to which I must call attention. These provisions are contained in the second section, which in certain cases virtually deprives the President of his constitutional functions as Commander in Chief of the Army, and in the sixth section, which denies to ten States of the Union their constitutional right to protect themselves in any emergency by means of their own militia. These provisions are out of place in an appropriation act, but I am compelled to defeat these necessary appropriations if I withhold my signature from the act. Pressed by these considerations, I feel constrained to return the bill with my signature, but to accompany it with my earnest protest against the sections which I have indicated.

Respondent, therefore, did no more than to express to said Emory the same opinion which he had so expressed to the House of Representatives.

Answer to Article X.—And in answer to the tenth article and specifications thereof the respondent says that on the 14th and 15th days of August, in the year 1866, a political convention of delegates from all or most of the States and Territories of the Union was held in the city of Philadelphia, under the name and style of the National Union Convention, for the purpose of maintaining and advancing certain political views and opinions before the people of the United States, and for their support and adoption in the exercise of the constitutional suffrage in the elections of Representatives and Delegates in Congress which were soon to occur in many of the States and Territories of the Union; which said convention, in the course of its proceedings, and in furtherance of the objects of the same, adopted a "Declaration of principles" and "An address to the people of the United States," and appointed a committee of two of its members from each State and of one from each Territory and one from the District of Columbia to wait upon the President of the United States and present to him a copy of the proceedings of the convention; that on the 18th day of said month of August this committee waited upon the President of the United States at the Executive Mansion, and was received by him in one of the rooms thereof, and by their chairman, Hon. Reverdy Johnson, then and now a Senator of the United States, acting and speaking in their behalf, presented a copy of the proceedings of the convention and addressed the President of the United States in a speech of which a copy (according to a published report of the same, and, as the respondent believes, substantially a correct report) is hereto annexed as a part of this answer, and marked Exhibit C.

That thereupon, and in reply to the address of said committee by their chairman, this respondent addressed the said committee so waiting upon him in one of the rooms of the Executive Mansion; and this respondent believes that this his address to said committee is the occasion referred to in the first specification of the tenth article; but this respondent does not admit that the passages therein set forth, as if extracts from a speech or address of this respondent upon said occasion, correctly or justly present his speech or address upon said occasion, but, on the contrary, this respondent demands and insists that if this honorable court shall deem the said article and the said first specification thereof to contain allegation of matter cognizable by this honorable court as a high misdemeanor in office within the intent and meaning of the Constitution of the United States, and shall receive or allow proof in support of the same, that proof shall be required to be made of the actual speech and address of this respondent on said occasion, which this respondent denies that said article and specification contain or correctly or justly represent.

And this respondent, further answering the tenth article and the specifications thereof, says that at Cleveland, in the State of Ohio, and on the 3d day of September, in the year 1866, he was attended by a large assemblage of his fellow-citizens, and in deference and obedience to their call and demand he addressed them upon matters of public and political consideration; and this respondent believes that said occasion and address are referred to in the second specification of the tenth article; but this respondent does not admit that the passages therein set forth, as if extracts from a speech of this respondent on said occasion, correctly or justly present his speech or address upon said occasion, but, on the contrary, this respondent demands and insists that if this honorable court shall deem the said article and the said second specification thereof to contain allegation of matter cognizable by this honorable court as a high misdemeanor in office within the intent and meaning of the Constitution of the United States, and shall receive or allow proof in support of the same, that proof shall be required to be made of the actual speech and address of this respondent on said occasion, which this respondent denies that said article and specification contain or correctly or justly represent.

And this respondent, further answering the tenth article and the specifications thereof, says that at St. Louis, in the State of Missouri, and on the 8th day of September, in the year 1866, he was attended by a numerous assemblage of his fellow-citizens, and in deference and obedience to their call and demand he addressed them upon matters of public and political consideration; and this respondent believes that said occasion and address are referred to in the third specification of the tenth article; but this respondent does not admit that the passages therein set forth, as if extracts from a speech of this respondent on said occasion, correctly or justly present his speech or address upon said occasion, but, on the contrary, this respondent demands and insists that if this honorable court shall deem the said article and the said third specification thereof to contain allegation of matter cognizable by this honorable court as a high misdemeanor in office within the intent and meaning of the Constitution of the United States, and shall receive or allow proof in support of the same, that proof shall be required to be made of the actual speech and address of this respondent on said occasion, which this respondent denies that the said article and specification contain or correctly or justly represent.

And this respondent, further answering the tenth article, protesting that he has not been unmindful of the high duties of his office or of the harmony or courtesies which ought to exist and be maintained between the executive and legislative branches of the Government of the United States, denies that he has ever intended or designed to set aside the rightful authority or powers of Congress, or attempted to bring into disgrace, ridicule, hatred, contempt, or reproach the Congress of the United States, or either branch thereof, or to impair or destroy the regard or respect of all or any of the good people of the United States for the Congress or the rightful legislative power thereof, or to excite the odium or resentment of all or any of the good people of the United States against Congress and the laws by it duly and constitutionally enacted. This respondent further says that at all times he has, in his official acts as President, recognized the authority of the several Congresses of the United States as constituted and organized during his administration of the office of President of the United States.

And this respondent, further answering, says that he has from time to time, under his constitutional right and duty as President of the United States, communicated to Congress his views and opinions in regard to such acts or resolutions thereof as, being submitted to him as President of the United States in pursuance of the Constitution, seemed to this respondent to require such communications; and he has from time to time, in the exercise of that freedom of speech which belongs to him as a citizen of the United States, and, in his political relations as President of the United States to the people of the United States, is upon fit occasions a duty of the highest obligation, expressed to his fellow-citizens his views and opinions respecting the measures and proceedings of Congress; and that in such addresses to his fellow-citizens and in such his communications to Congress he has expressed his views, opinions, and judgment of and concerning the actual constitution of the two Houses of Congress, without representation therein of certain States of the Union, and of the effect that in wisdom and justice, in the opinion and judgment of this respondent, Congress in its legislation and proceedings should give to this political circumstance; and whatsoever he has thus communicated to Congress or addressed to his fellow-citizens or any assemblage thereof this respondent says was and is within and according to his right and privilege as an American citizen and his right and duty as President of the United States.

And this respondent, not waiving or at all disparaging his right of freedom of opinion and of freedom of speech, as hereinbefore or hereinafter more particularly set forth, but claiming and insisting upon the same, further answering the said tenth article, says that the views and opinions expressed by this respondent in his said addresses to the assemblages of his fellow-citizens, as in said articles or in this answer thereto mentioned, are not and were not intended to be other or different from those expressed by him in his communications to Congress—that the eleven States lately in insurrection never had ceased to be States of the Union, and that they were then entitled to representation in Congress by loyal Representatives and Senators as fully as the other States of the Union, and that consequently the Congress as then constituted was not in fact a Congress of all the States, but a Congress of only a part of the States. This respondent, always protesting against the unauthorized exclusion therefrom of the said eleven States, nevertheless gave his assent to all laws passed by said Congress which did not, in his opinion and judgment, violate the Constitution, exercising his constitutional authority of return-ing bills to said Congress with his objections when they appeared to him to be unconstitutional or inexpedient.

And further, this respondent has also expressed the opinion, both in his communications to Congress and in his addresses to the people, that the policy adopted by Congress in reference to the States lately in insurrec-tion did not tend to peace, harmony, and union, but, on the contrary, did tend to disunion and the permanent disruption of the States, and that in following its said policy laws had been passed by Congress in violation of the fundamental principles of the Government, and which tended to consolidation and despotism; and such being his deliberate opinions, he would have felt himself unmindful of the high duties of his office if he had failed to express them in his communications to Congress or in his addresses to the people when called upon by them to express his opinions on matters of public and political consideration.

And this respondent, further answering the tenth article, says that he has always claimed and insisted, and now claims and insists, that both in the personal and private capacity of a citizen of the United States and in the political relations of the President of the United States to the peo-ple of the United States, whose servant, under the duties and responsibili-ties of the Constitution of the United States, the President of the United States is and should always remain, this respondent had and has the full right, and in his office of President of the United States is held to the high duty, of forming, and on fit occasions expressing, opinions of and concern-ing the legislation of Congress, proposed or completed, in respect of its wisdom, expediency, justice, worthiness, objects, purposes, and public and political motives and tendencies, and within and as a part of such right and duty to form, and on fit occasions to express, opinions of and concern-ing the public character and conduct, views, purposes, objects, motives, and tendencies of all men engaged in the public service, as well in Congress as otherwise, and under no other rules or limits upon this right of freedom of opinion and of freedom of speech, or of responsibility and amenability for the actual exercise of such freedom of opinion and freedom of speech, than attend upon such rights and their exercise on the part of all other citizens of the United States and on the part of all their public servants.

And this respondent, further answering said tenth article, says that the several occasions on which, as is alleged in the several specifications of said article, this respondent addressed his fellow-citizens on subjects of public and political considerations were not, nor was any one of them, sought or planned by this respondent, but, on the contrary, each of said occasions arose upon the exercise of a lawful and accustomed right of the

people of the United States to call upon their public servants and express
to them their opinions, wishes, and feelings upon matters of public and
political consideration, and to invite from such their public servants an
expression of their opinions, views, and feelings on matters of public and
political consideration; and this respondent claims and insists before this
honorable court, and before all the people of the United States, that of or
concerning this his right of freedom of opinion and of freedom of speech,
and this his exercise of such rights on all matters of public and political
consideration, and in respect of all public servants or persons whatsoever
engaged in or connected therewith, this respondent, as a citizen or as
President of the United States, is not subject to question, inquisition,
impeachment, or inculpation in any form or manner whatsoever.

And this respondent says that neither the said tenth article nor any specification thereof nor any allegation therein contained touches or relates to
any official act or doing of this respondent in the office of President of the
United States or in the discharge of any of its constitutional or legal duties
or responsibilities; but said article and the specifications and allegations
thereof, wholly and in every part thereof, question only the discretion or
propriety of freedom of opinion or freedom of speech as exercised by this
respondent as a citizen of the United States in his personal right and
capacity, and without allegation or imputation against this respondent
of the violation of any law of the United States touching or relating to
freedom of speech or its exercise by the citizens of the United States or
by this respondent as one of the said citizens or otherwise; and he denies
that by reason of any matter in said article or its specifications alleged he
has said or done anything indecent or unbecoming in the Chief Magistrate
of the United States, or that he has brought the high office of President of
the United States into contempt, ridicule, or disgrace, or that he has committed or has been guilty of a high misdemeanor in office.

Answer to Article XI.—And in answer to the eleventh article this
respondent denies that on the 18th day of August, in the year 1866, at the
city of Washington, in the District of Columbia, he did, by public speech
or otherwise, declare or affirm, in substance or at all, that the Thirty-
ninth Congress of the United States was not a Congress of the United
States authorized by the Constitution to exercise legislative power under
the same, or that he did then and there declare or affirm that the said
Thirty-ninth Congress was a Congress of only part of the States in any
sense or meaning other than that ten States of the Union were denied
representation therein, or that he made any or either of the declarations
or affirmations in this behalf in the said article alleged as denying or
intending to deny that the legislation of said Thirty-ninth Congress was
valid or obligatory upon this respondent except so far as this respondent
saw fit to approve the same; and as to the allegation in said article that
he did thereby intend or mean to be understood that the said Congress had
not power to propose amendments to the Constitution, this respondent

says that in said address he said nothing in reference to the subject of amendments of the Constitution, nor was the question of the com-petency of the said Congress to propose such amendments, without the participation of said excluded States, at the time of said address in any way mentioned or considered or referred to by this respondent, nor in what he did say had he any intent regarding the same; and he denies the allegations so made to the contrary thereof. But this respondent, in further answer to and in respect of the said allegations of the said eleventh article hereinbefore traversed and denied, claims and insists upon his personal and official right of freedom of opinion and freedom of speech, and his duty in his political relations as President of the United States to the people of the United States in the exercise of such freedom of opinion and freedom of speech, in the same manner, form, and effect as he has in this behalf stated the same in his answer to the said tenth article, and with the same effect as if he here repeated the same; and he further claims and insists, as in said answer to said tenth article he has claimed and insisted, that he is not subject to question, inquisition, im-peachment or inculpation, in any form or manner, of or concerning such rights of freedom of opinion or freedom of speech, or his said alleged exercise thereof.

And this respondent further denies that on the 21st day of February, in the year 1868, or at any other time, at the city of Washington, in the District of Columbia, in pursuance of any such declaration as in that behalf in said eleventh article alleged, or otherwise, he did unlawfully, and in disregard of the requirement of the Constitution that he should take care that the laws should be faithfully executed, attempt to prevent the execution of an act entitled "An act regulating the tenure of certain civil offices," passed March 2, 1867, by unlawfully devising or contriving, or attempting to devise or contrive, means by which he should prevent Edwin M. Stanton from forthwith resuming the functions of Secretary for the Department of War, or by unlawfully devising or contriving, or attempting to devise or contrive, means to prevent the execution of an act entitled "An act making appropriations for the support of the Army for the fiscal year ending June 30, 1868, and for other purposes," approved March 2, 1867, or to prevent the execution of an act entitled "An act to provide for the more efficient government of the rebel States," passed March 2, 1867.

And this respondent, further answering the said eleventh article, says that he has in his answer to the first article set forth in detail the acts, steps, and proceedings done and taken by this respondent to and toward or in the matter of the suspension or removal of the said Edwin M. Stan-ton in or from the office of Secretary for the Department of War, with the times, modes, circumstances, intents, views, purposes, and opinions of official obligations and duty under and with which such acts, steps, and proceedings were done and taken; and he makes answer to this

eleventh article of the matters in his answer to the first article pertaining to the suspension or removal of said Edwin M. Stanton, to the same intent and effect as if they were here repeated and set forth.

And this respondent, further answering the said eleventh article, denies that by means or reason of anything in said article alleged this respondent, as President of the United States, did, on the 21st day of February, 1868, or at any other day or time, commit or that he was guilty of a high misdemeanor in office.

And this respondent, further answering the said eleventh article, says that the same and the matters therein contained do not charge or allege the commission of any act whatever by this respondent in his office of President of the United States, nor the omission by this respondent of any act of official obligation or duty in his office of President of the United States; nor does the said article nor the matters therein contained name, designate, describe, or define any act or mode or form of attempt, device, contrivance, or means, or of attempt at device, contrivance, or means, whereby this respondent can know or understand what act or mode or form of attempt, device, contrivance, or means, or of attempt at device, contrivance, or means, are imputed to or charged against this respondent in his office of President of the United States, or intended so to be, or whereby this respondent can more fully or definitely make answer unto the said article than he hereby does.

And this respondent, in submitting to this honorable court this his answer to the articles of impeachment exhibited against him, respectfully reserves leave to amend and add to the same from time to time, as may become necessary or proper, and when and as such necessity and propriety shall appear.

ANDREW JOHNSON.

HENRY STANBERY,
B. R. CURTIS,
THOMAS A. R. NELSON,
WILLIAM M. EVARTS,
W. S. GROESBECK,
Of Counsel.

[For Exhibits A and B see veto message of March 2, 1867, pp. 492–498, and special message of December 12, 1867, pp. 583–594.]

Exhibit C.

ADDRESS TO THE PRESIDENT BY HON. REVERDY JOHNSON, AUGUST, 18, 1866.

Mr. PRESIDENT: We are before you as a committee of the National Union Convention, which met in Philadelphia on Tuesday, the 14th instant, charged with the duty of presenting you with an authentic copy of its proceedings.

Before placing it in your hands you will permit us to congratulate you that in the object for which the convention was called, in the enthusiasm with which in every State and Territory the call was responded to, in the unbroken harmony of its deliberations, in the unanimity with which the principles it has declared were adopted, and more especially in the patriotic and constitutional character of the principles themselves, we are confident that you and the country will find gratifying and cheering evidence that there exists among the people a public sentiment which renders an early and complete restoration of the Union as established by the Constitution certain and inevitable.   Party faction, seeking the continuance of its misrule, may momentarily delay it, but the principles of political liberty for which our fathers successfully contended, and to secure which they adopted the Constitution, are so glaringly inconsistent with the condition in which the country has been placed by such misrule that it will not be permitted a much longer duration.

We wish, Mr. President, you could have witnessed the spirit of concord and brotherly affection which animated every member of the convention.   Great as your confidence has ever been in the intelligence and patriotism of your fellow-citizens, in their deep devotion to the Union and their present determination to reinstate and maintain it, that confidence would have become a positive conviction could you have seen and heard all that was done and said upon the occasion.   Every heart was evidently full of joy; every eye beamed with patriotic animation; despondency gave place to the assurance that, our late dreadful civil strife ended, the blissful reign of peace, under the protection, not of arms, but of the Constitution and laws, would have sway, and be in every part of our land cheerfully acknowledged and in perfect good faith obeyed.   You would not have doubted that the recurrence of dangerous domestic insurrections in the future is not to be apprehended.

If you could have seen the men of Massachusetts and South Carolina coming into the convention on the first day of its meeting hand in hand, amid the rapturous applause of the whole body, awakened by heartfelt gratification at the event, filling the eyes of thousands with tears of joy, which they neither could nor desired to repress, you would have felt, as every person present felt, that the time had arrived when all sectional or other perilous dissensions had ceased, and that nothing should be heard in the future but the voice of harmony proclaiming devotion to a common country, of pride in being bound together by a common Union, existing and protected by forms of government proved by experience to be eminently fitted for the exigencies of either war or peace.

In the principles announced by the convention and in the feeling there manifested we have every assurance that harmony throughout our entire land will soon prevail.   We know that as in former days, as was eloquently declared by Webster, the nation's most gifted statesman, Massachusetts and South Carolina went ''shoulder to shoulder through the

Revolution'' and stood hand in hand ''around the Administration of Washington and felt his own great arm lean on them for support,'' so will they again, with like magnanimity, devotion, and power, stand round your Administration and cause you to feel that you may also lean on them for support.

In the proceedings, Mr. President, which we are to place in your hands you will find that the convention performed the grateful duty imposed upon them by their knowledge of your ''devotion to the Constitution and laws and interests of your country,'' as illustrated by your entire Presidential career, of declaring that in you they ''recognize a Chief Magistrate worthy of the nation and equal to the great crisis upon which your lot is cast;'' and in this declaration it gives us marked pleasure to add we are confident that the convention has but spoken the intelligent and patriotic sentiment of the country. Ever inaccessible to the low influences which often control the mere partisan, governed alone by an honest opinion of constitutional obligations and rights and of the duty of looking solely to the true interests, safety, and honor of the nation, such a class is incapable of resorting to any bait for popularity at the expense of the public good.

In the measures which you have adopted for the restoration of the Union the convention saw only a continuance of the policy which for the same purpose was inaugurated by your immediate predecessor. In his reelection by the people, after that policy had been fully indicated and had been made one of the issues of the contest, those of his political friends who are now assailing you for sternly pursuing it are forgetful or regardless of the opinions which their support of his reelection necessarily involved. Being upon the same ticket with that much-lamented public servant, whose foul assassination touched the heart of the civilized world with grief and horror, you would have been false to obvious duty if you had not endeavored to carry out the same policy; and, judging now by the opposite one which Congress has pursued, its wisdom and patriotism are indicated by the fact that that of Congress has but continued a broken Union by keeping ten of the States in which at one time the insurrection existed (as far as they could accomplish it) in the condition of subjugated provinces, denying to them the right to be represented, while subjecting their people to every species of legislation, including that of taxation. That such a state of things is at war with the very genius of our Government, inconsistent with every idea of political freedom, and most perilous to the peace and safety of the country no reflecting man can fail to believe.

We hope, sir, that the proceedings of the convention will cause you to adhere, if possible, with even greater firmness to the course which you are pursuing, by satisfying you that the people are with you, and that the wish which lies nearest to their heart is that a perfect restoration of our Union at the earliest moment be attained, and a conviction that the result can only be accomplished by the measures which you are pursuing. And in the discharge of the duties which these impose upon you we, as did every member of the convention, again for ourselves individually tender to you our profound respect and assurance of our cordial and sincere support.

With a reunited Union, with no foot but that of a freeman treading or permitted to tread our soil, with a nation's faith pledged forever to a strict observance of all its obligations, with kindness and fraternal love everywhere prevailing, the desolations of war will soon be removed; its sacrifices of life, sad as they have been, will, with Christian resignation, be referred to a providential purpose of fixing our beloved country on a firm and enduring basis, which will forever place our liberty and happiness beyond the reach of human peril.

Then, too, and forever, will our Government challenge the admiration and receive the respect of the nations of the world, and be in no danger of any efforts to impeach our honor.

And permit me, sir, in conclusion, to add that, great as is your solicitude for the restoration of our domestic peace and your labors to that end, you have also a watchful eye to the rights of the nation, and that any attempt by an assumed or actual foreign power to enforce an illegal blockade against the Government or citizens of the United States, to use your own mild but expressive words, "will be disallowed." In this determination I am sure you will receive the unanimous approval of your fellow-citizens.

Now, sir, as the chairman of this committee, and in behalf of the convention, I have the honor to present you with an authentic copy of its proceedings.

Counsel for the respondent submitted the following motion:

To the Senate of the United States sitting as a court of impeachment:

And now, on this 23d day of March, in the year 1868, the counsel for the President of the United States, upon reading and filing his answer to the articles of impeachment exhibited against him, respectfully represent to the honorable court that after the replication shall have been filed to the said answer the due and proper preparation of and for the trial of the cause will require, in the opinion and judgment of such counsel, that a period of not less than thirty days should be allowed to the President of the United States and his counsel for such preparation, and before the said trial should proceed.

HENRY STANBERY,
B. R. CURTIS,
THOMAS A. R. NELSON,
WM. M. EVARTS,
W. S. GROESBECK,
Of Counsel.

TUESDAY, MARCH 24, 1868.

THE UNITED STATES *vs.* ANDREW JOHNSON, PRESIDENT.

REPLICATION BY THE HOUSE OF REPRESENTATIVES OF THE UNITED STATES TO THE ANSWER OF ANDREW JOHNSON, PRESIDENT OF THE UNITED STATES, TO THE ARTICLES OF IMPEACHMENT EXHIBITED AGAINST HIM BY THE HOUSE OF REPRESENTATIVES.

The House of Representatives of the United States have considered the several answers of Andrew Johnson, President of the United States, to the several articles of impeachment against him, by them exhibited in the name of themselves and of all the people of the United States, and reserving to themselves all advantage of exception to the insufficiency of his answer to each and all of the several articles of impeachment exhibited against said Andrew Johnson, President of the United States, do deny each and every averment in said several answers, or either of them, which denies or traverses the acts, intents, crimes, or misdemeanors charged against said Andrew Johnson in the said articles of impeachment, or either of them, and for replication to the said answer do say that said Andrew Johnson, President of the United States, is guilty of the high crimes and misdemeanors mentioned in said articles, and that the House of Representatives are ready to prove the same.

SCHUYLER COLFAX,
Speaker of the House of Representatives.
EDW'D McPHERSON,
Clerk of the House of Representatives.

The motion of the counsel for the respondent, submitted on March 23, "that a period of not less than thirty days should be allowed to the President of the United States and his counsel for such preparation and before the said trial should proceed," was denied, and it was

Ordered, That the Senate will commence the trial of the President upon the articles of impeachment exhibited against him on Monday, the 30th of March instant, and proceed therein with all convenient dispatch under the rules of the Senate sitting upon the trial of an impeachment.

MONDAY, MAY 11, 1868.

THE UNITED STATES *vs.* ANDREW JOHNSON, PRESIDENT.

The Chief Justice stated that in compliance with the desire of the Senate he had prepared the question to be addressed to Senators upon each article of impeachment, and that he had reduced his views thereon to writing, which he read, as follows:

SENATORS: In conformity with what seemed to be the general wish of the Senate when it adjourned last Thursday, the Chief Justice, in taking the vote on the articles of impeachment, will adopt the mode sanctioned by the practice in the cases of Chase, Peck, and Humphreys.

He will direct the Secretary to read the several articles successively, and after the reading of each article will put the question of guilty or not guilty to each Senator, rising in his place, in the form used in the case of Judge Chase:

Mr. Senator ———, how say you?   Is the respondent, Andrew Johnson, President of the United States, guilty or not guilty of a high misdemeanor, as charged in this article?

In putting the question on Articles IV and VI, each of which charges a crime, the word "crime" will be substituted for the word "misdemeanor."

The Chief Justice has carefully considered the suggestion of the Senator from Indiana (Mr. Hendricks), which appeared to meet the approval of the Senate, that in taking the vote on the eleventh article the question should be put on each clause, and has found himself unable to divide the article as suggested.   The article charges several facts, but they are so connected that they make but one allegation and they are charged as constituting one misdemeanor.

The first fact charged is, in substance, that the President publicly declared in August, 1866, that the Thirty-ninth Congress was a Congress of only part of the States and not a constitutional Congress, intending thereby to deny its constitutional competency to enact laws or propose amendments of the Constitution; and this charge seems to have been made as introductory, and as qualifying that which follows, namely, that the President, in pursuance of this declaration, attempted to prevent the execution of the tenure-of-office act by contriving and attempting to contrive means to prevent Mr. Stanton from resuming the functions of Secretary of War after the refusal of the Senate to concur in his suspension, and also by contriving and attempting to contrive means to prevent the execution of the appropriation act of March 2, 1867, and also to prevent the execution of the rebel States governments act of the same date.

The gravamen of the article seems to be that the President attempted to defeat the execution of the tenure-of-office act, and that he did this in pursuance of a declaration which was intended to deny the constitutional competency of Congress to enact laws or propose constitutional amendments, and by contriving means to prevent Mr. Stanton from resuming his office of Secretary, and also to prevent the execution of the appropriation act and the rebel States governments act.

The single substantive matter charged is the attempt to prevent the execution of the tenure-of-office act, and the other facts are alleged either as introductory and exhibiting this general purpose or as showing the means contrived in furtherance of that attempt.

This single matter, connected with the other matters previously and subsequently alleged, is charged as the high misdemeanor of which the President is alleged to have been guilty.

The general question, guilty or not guilty of a high misdemeanor as charged, seems fully to cover the whole charge, and will be put as to this article as well as to the others, unless the Senate direct some mode of division.

In the tenth article the division suggested by the Senator from New York (Mr. Conkling) may be more easily made. It contains a general allegation to the effect that on the 18th of August and on other days the President, with intent to set aside the rightful authority of Congress and bring it into contempt, delivered certain scandalous harangues, and therein uttered loud threats and bitter menaces against Congress and the laws of the United States enacted by Congress, thereby bringing the office of President into disgrace, to the great scandal of all good citizens, and sets forth in three distinct specifications the harangues, threats, and menaces complained of.

In respect to this article, if the Senate sees fit so to direct, the question of guilty or not guilty of the facts charged may be taken in respect to the several specifications, and then the question of guilty or not guilty of a high misdemeanor, as charged in the article, can also be taken.

The Chief Justice, however, sees no objection to putting the general question on this article in the same manner as on the others; for, whether particular questions be put on the specifications or not, the answer to the final question must be determined by the judgment of the Senate whether or not the facts alleged in the specifications have been sufficiently proved, and whether, if sufficiently proved, they amount to a high misdemeanor within the meaning of the Constitution.

On the whole, therefore, the Chief Justice thinks that the better practice will be to put the general question on each article without attempting to make any subdivision, and will pursue this course if no objection is made. He will, however, be pleased to conform to such directions as the Senate may see fit to give in this respect.

Whereupon it was

Ordered, That the question be put as proposed by the Presiding Officer of the Senate, and each Senator shall rise in his place and answer "guilty" or "not guilty" only.

SATURDAY, MAY 16, 1868.

THE UNITED STATES *vs.* ANDREW JOHNSON, PRESIDENT.

The Chief Justice stated that, in pursuance of the order of the Senate, he would first proceed to take the judgment of the Senate on the eleventh article. The roll of the Senate was called, with the following result:

The Senators who voted "guilty" are Messrs. Anthony, Cameron, Cattell, Chandler, Cole, Conkling, Conness, Corbett, Cragin, Drake, Edmunds,

Ferry, Frelinghuysen, Harlan, Howard, Howe, Morgan, Morrill of Maine, Morrill of Vermont, Morton, Nye, Patterson of New Hampshire, Pomeroy, Ramsey, Sherman, Sprague, Stewart, Sumner, Thayer, Tipton, Wade, Williams, Willey, Wilson, and Yates—35.

The Senators who voted "not guilty" are Messrs. Bayard, Buckalew, Davis, Dixon, Doolittle, Fessenden, Fowler, Grimes, Henderson, Hendricks, Johnson, McCreery, Norton, Patterson of Tennessee, Ross, Saulsbury, Trumbull, Van Winkle, and Vickers—19.

The Chief Justice announced that upon this article thirty-five Senators had voted "guilty" and nineteen Senators "not guilty," and declared that two-thirds of the Senators present not having pronounced him guilty, Andrew Johnson, President of the United States, stood acquitted of the charges contained in the eleventh article of impeachment.

TUESDAY, MAY 26, 1868.

THE UNITED STATES *vs.* ANDREW JOHNSON, PRESIDENT.

The Senate ordered that the vote be taken upon the second article of impeachment. The roll of the Senate was called, with the following result:

The Senators who voted "guilty" are Messrs. Anthony, Cameron, Cattell, Chandler, Cole, Conkling, Conness, Corbett, Cragin, Drake, Edmunds, Ferry, Frelinghuysen, Harlan, Howard, Howe, Morgan, Morrill of Maine, Morrill of Vermont, Morton, Nye, Patterson of New Hampshire, Pomeroy, Ramsey, Sherman, Sprague, Stewart, Sumner, Thayer, Tipton, Wade, Willey, Williams, Wilson, and Yates—35.

The Senators who voted "not guilty" are Messrs. Bayard, Buckalew, Davis, Dixon, Doolittle, Fessenden, Fowler, Grimes, Henderson, Hendricks, Johnson, McCreery, Norton, Patterson of Tennessee, Ross, Saulsbury, Trumbull, Van Winkle, and Vickers—19.

The Chief Justice announced that upon this article thirty-five Senators had voted "guilty" and nineteen Senators had voted "not guilty," and declared that two-thirds of the Senators present not having pronounced him guilty, Andrew Johnson, President of the United States, stood acquitted of the charges contained in the second article of impeachment.

The Senate ordered that the vote be taken upon the third article of impeachment. The roll of the Senate was called, with the following result:

The Senators who voted "guilty" are Messrs. Anthony, Cameron, Cattell, Chandler, Cole, Conkling, Conness, Corbett, Cragin, Drake, Edmunds, Ferry, Frelinghuysen, Harlan, Howard, Howe, Morgan, Morrill of Maine, Morrill of Vermont, Morton, Nye, Patterson of New Hampshire, Pomeroy, Ramsey, Sherman, Sprague, Stewart, Sumner, Thayer, Tipton, Wade, Willey, Williams, Wilson, and Yates—35.

The Senators who voted "not guilty" are Messrs. Bayard, Buckalew, Davis, Dixon, Doolittle, Fessenden, Fowler, Grimes, Henderson, Hendricks, Johnson, McCreery, Norton, Patterson of Tennessee, Ross, Saulsbury, Trumbull, Van Winkle, and Vickers—19.

The Chief Justice announced that upon this article thirty-five Senators had voted "guilty" and nineteen Senators had voted "not guilty," and declared that two-thirds of the Senators present not having pronounced him guilty, Andrew Johnson, President of the United States, stood acquitted of the charges contained in the third article.

No objection being made, the secretary, by direction of the Chief Justice, entered the judgment of the Senate upon the second, third, and eleventh articles, as follows:

The Senate having tried Andrew Johnson, President of the United States, upon articles of impeachment exhibited against him by the House of Representatives, and two-thirds of the Senators present not having found him guilty of the charges contained in the second, third, and eleventh articles of impeachment, it is therefore

Ordered and adjudged, That the said Andrew Johnson, President of the United States, be, and he is, acquitted of the charges in said articles made and set forth.

A motion "that the Senate sitting for the trial of the President upon articles of impeachment do now adjourn without day" was adopted by a vote of 34 yeas to 16 nays.

Those who voted in the affirmative are Messrs. Anthony, Cameron, Cattell, Chandler, Cole, Conkling, Corbett, Cragin, Drake, Edmunds, Ferry, Frelinghuysen, Harlan, Howard, Morgan, Morrill of Maine, Morrill of Vermont, Morton, Nye, Patterson of New Hampshire, Pomeroy, Ramsey, Sherman, Sprague, Stewart, Sumner, Thayer, Tipton, Van Winkle, Wade, Willey, Williams, Wilson, and Yates.

Those who voted in the negative are Messrs. Bayard, Buckalew, Davis, Dixon, Doolittle, Fowler, Henderson, Hendricks, Johnson, McCreery, Norton, Patterson of Tennessee, Ross, Saulsbury, Trumbull, and Vickers.

The Chief Justice declared the Senate sitting as a court of impeachment for the trial of Andrew Johnson, President of the United States, upon articles of impeachment exhibited against him by the House of Representatives, adjourned without day.

ADDENDA.

[An injunction of secrecy having been placed upon the following messages by the Senate, they were not printed in the Executive Journal covering their period, but were found in the unprinted Executive Journal of the Forty-first Congress while searching for copy for Volume VII, and consequently too late for insertion in their proper places in this volume.]

WASHINGTON, *January 29, 1869.*

To the Senate:

Referring to the three Executive communications of the 15th instant, with which were transmitted to the Senate, respectively, a copy of a convention between the United States and Great Britain upon the subject of claims, a copy of a convention between the same parties in relation to the question of boundary, and a protocol of a treaty between the same parties concerning the rights of naturalized citizens and subjects of the respective parties, I now transmit a copy of such correspondence upon those subjects as has not been heretofore communicated to the Senate.

In the progress of the negotiation the three subjects became to such a degree associated with each other that it would be difficult to present separately the correspondence upon each. The papers are therefore transmitted in the order in which they are mentioned in the accompanying list.

ANDREW JOHNSON.

WASHINGTON, *January 30, 1869.*

To the Senate of the United States:

Referring to the Executive communication of the 15th instant, which was accompanied by a copy of a convention between the United States and Great Britain for the settlement of all outstanding claims, I now transmit to the Senate the original of that instrument, and a report of the Secretary of State pointing out the differences between the copy as submitted to the Senate and the original as signed by the plenipotentiaries.

ANDREW JOHNSON.

WASHINGTON, *January 30, 1869.*

To the Senate of the United States:

Referring to the Executive communication of the 15th instant, which was accompanied by a copy of a convention between the United States and Great Britain providing for the reference to an arbiter of the question of difference between the United States and Great Britain concerning the northwest line of water boundary between the United States and the British possessions in North America, I now transmit to the Senate the original of that instrument, and a report of the Secretary of State pointing out the differences between the copy as submitted to the Senate and the original as signed by the plenipotentiaries.

ANDREW JOHNSON.